PASQUOTANK COUNTY, NORTH CAROLINA

Record of Deeds

1700–1751

COMPILED BY

Gwen Boyer Bjorkman

HERITAGE BOOKS
2016

HERITAGE BOOKS
AN IMPRINT OF HERITAGE BOOKS, INC.

Books, CDs, and more—Worldwide

For our listing of thousands of titles see our website
at
www.HeritageBooks.com

Published 2016 by
HERITAGE BOOKS, INC.
Publishing Division
5810 Ruatan Street
Berwyn Heights, Md. 20740

Heritage Books by the author:

Pasquotank County, North Carolina Record of Deeds, 1700–1751

Quaker Marriage Certificates: Concord Monthly Meeting, Delaware County, Pennsylvania, 1679–1808

Quaker Marriage Certificates: New Garden Monthly Meeting, Chester County, Pennsylvania, 1704–1799

Quaker Marriage Certificates: Pasquotank, Perquimans, Piney Woods, and Suttons Creek Monthly Meetings, North Carolina, 1677–1800

The Descendants of John Meridy Turner (1747–1815) of Fauquier County, Virginia

CD: Pasquotank County, North Carolina Record of Deeds, 1700–1751

CD: Quaker Marriage Certificates

International Standard Book Numbers
Paperbound: 978-1-55613-308-4
Clothbound: 978-0-7884-5968-9

CONTENTS

PREFACE

The Pasquotank County deeds were abstracted from North Carolina Archives Microfilm #C.075.40004 Pasquotank County Record of Deeds 1700-1750, Vols. A, B and Microfilm #C.075.40005 Pasquotank County Record of Deeds 1750-1761, Vols. C, D-E, F-G. This book is a complete abstract of Volumes A and B and a part of Volume C.

Beginning in 1700, the original deeds were brought to the courthouse, acknowledged or proved and copied by the Registrar into the deedbook. The original deed was returned to the grantee. There are some Pasquotank original deeds dated 1666-1947 filed in boxes at the North Carolina Archives. They are filed alphabetically by name, so the Archives staff was unable to identify the deeds dated before 1700 for inclusion in this book. It would be interesting to see the original deed dated 1666.

In 1812 the deedbooks had become so worn that they were ordered to be recopied into new books. Now in 1990 the deedbooks are abstracted, being the third copy from the original deed. This allows for errors by three copyists. Errors which have been made by the first two transcribers are marked with [sic] when I can identify an error. When the deeds were recopied, the original order of the deeds by date of registration was mixed-up. Effort has been made to rearrange the deeds into their original date order. See the Table of Contents for the approximate order by year of registration.

The Deedbook and page number are placed in brackets within the text. All numbers when written out in the original were changed to numerals. All surnames are capitalized. In the index, all abbreviated given names are written out if the meaning is clear from another entry. Anyone signing by mark is usually identified by the transcriber, but not always. Notes made by the transcriber are in parentheses. My notes are in brackets.

RECORD OF DEEDS

The Registrars and Transcribers have not been abstracted with each deed. This is an approximate listing by date.

Registrars:
Thomas Abington 1700-1711 [A:1-A:20]
William Norris 1711-1721 1723-1725 [A:21-A:248, A:271-A:328, B:292]
Edmund Gale 1721-1725 [A:249-A:270, A:329]
John Parker 1725 [A:329-A:342]
Thomas Weeks 1726-1727 [A:351-A:369, A:378-A:412, C:378]
Danl. O'Sheal 1726 [A:369-A:371]
Ben O'Sheal 1726 [A:371-A:377]
Richard Everard 1728 [A:345-A:350]
William Minson 1729-1734 [C:222-C:363, C:377]
Joseph [Joshua?] Smith 1735-1739 [C:364-C:391, B:182-B:252, B:260]
J. Palin 1721, 1737 [A:268, B:203, B:290]
Wm. Shugold 1739 [B:253-257, B:262]
James Craven 1739-1751 [B:258-B:259, B:261, B:263-B:550, A:412-A:454, B:1-181]

Transcribers:
Thomas Jordan Sen. 1816-1818 [A:1-A:197]
John C. Ehringhaus 1818-1819 [A:198-A:454, B:1-B:551, C:222-C:391]
J. M. Jackson no date [A:343, C:366]

Gwen Boyer Bjorkman
Bellevue, Washington

INTRODUCTION

Numerous early explorations were carried out in the southern parts of Virginia. There were attempts made at settlement, but the first known settler was an Indian trader, Nathaniel Batts, who lived in a house at the junction of the Roanoke and Chowan Rivers in 1655.[1] Permanent settlement had begun by the time the Council of Virginia appointed Capt. Samuel Stephens as commander of "the southern plantation" and authorized him to appoint a sheriff on October 9, 1662. It is written directly below the appointment in the notes made by Conway Robinson from the original General Court Orders, "Lands of inhabitants secured to them."[2]

A deposition of Richard Watrey made in 1687 stated that he "designed to go into ye Southard about the year 1662 to see how he might like the Place." He also testified that "Sr. William Berkeley was then lately arrived from england & that He resolved the Inhabitants of the south should hold no longer by Indian Titles, But that He would Grant Pattents."[3] In March of 1663 Thomas Woodward was constituted sole surveyor of Carolina, no doubt to secure those titles to land that had been purchased by the settlers in Carolina from the Indians. Robinson made a note that Berkeley now styled himself as governor of Virginia and Carolina.[4]

On March 24, 1663 Charles II granted a charter for Carolina to eight Lords Proprietors. They named the area Albemarle County and sent a letter to Governor Berkeley authorizing him to appoint a governor and six councillors for Carolina. William Berkeley was the only Proprietor that lived in Virginia and he seemed to be in no hurry to set up a separate government for Carolina.[5]

Governor William Berkeley issued 29 patents for land in Carolina, one on April 1, 1663 and the others on September 25, 1663. The patents were issued on the same terms as other land grants in Virginia. 19 of these 29 patents were for land located in what was to become Pasquotank Precinct when Albemarle County was divided into Carteret, Chowan, Pasquotank and Perquimans precincts sometime before 1668 (table 1).[6]

Late in 1664 Berkeley appointed William Drummond of Virginia Governor of Albemarle County. Drummond's commission reached him on February 23, 1664/5. It was about this time that the Proprietors found that the Charter of 1663 had not included the Albemarle region and a second charter was given by the King on June 30, 1665. It is probable that the government that the Proprietors had authorized was functioning by the summer of 1665, since the will of Mary Fortsen was probated on November 15, 1665.[7]

There are two sources for land grants made in Carolina during the proprietary period; Patent Book 1 in the North Carolina Secretary of State's Land Grant Office and Albemarle County Book of Warrants and Surveys 1681-1706 at the North Carolina State Archives.[8] Six of the 1663 Virginia grants were confirmed in Patent Book 1 and there are two additional 1663 grants. Two other 1663 patents were confirmed in 1679. There are three new patents for 1680, 20 for 1681, and 26 for 1684.[9] Of these 49 patents after 1663, eight are for Pasquotank Precinct. In the 1693 to 1696 time period there are 100 patents for Pasquotank Precinct (table 1).

The earliest recorded deed for land in Pasquotank is found in Norfolk County, Virginia when on the 24th of September 1660 Nathaniel Batts purchased from Kiscutanewh Kinge of Yausapin "all ye Land on ye southwest side of Pascotanck River, from ye mouth of ye sd. River to ye head of new Begin Creeke."[10] There is no record that Nathaniel Batts ever settled on his land. The first evidence of someone settling in Pasquotank is found again in Virginia in the Isle of Wight County will of James Tooke written on February 1, 1659/60. He gave to his daughter a bed and bedding and four cows and a heifer that was already in the custody of his Son in Law, John Harvey, "at the Southward."[11]

Two other known early settlers were Samuel Davis and Henry White. In 1698 Henry White testified in court that he knew Samuel Davis when he lived in the Isle of Wight County and that about the year 1660 "he the sd Samuel and Ann his wife removed themselves unto this Government."[12] Both Henry White and Samuel Davis received Virginia land patents in 1663 (table 1). Henry White's 1663 patent is referred to twice in the Pasquotank deeds (A:6 and A:151). Henry White Sr., and Henry White Jr. settled near Symons Creek that flowed into Little River. Note that in 1663 they were named as Corawtucks Creek and Kecoughtanke River.[13] Deed A:392 confirms that John Harvey's 1679 patent was on the "Creek called Currituck (alias) Symon's Creek."

The patents that are dated May 1, 1668 (table 2) in the Pasquotank deeds are not referring to the actual date of patent, but to the "Great Deed of Grant" that was given by the Lords Proprietors on that date that granted land on the terms and conditions allowed in Virginia. In the 1690's, land grants in Albemarle were based on the Great Deed.[14] Most of these Pasquotank deeds can probably be traced to a patent in the 1693 to 1696 time period.

From the available evidence, it appears that deeds were first recorded in Pasquotank Precinct in the year 1700. At that time the precinct of Pasquotank included an area that would become part of Tyrrell County on the South Shore of Albemarle Sound in 1729 and all of Camden County which was formed out of Pasquotank County in 1777 (see map).[15]

In the Pasquotank County Record of Deeds there are three early patents recorded that are not recorded anywhere else. One is to Danl. Roads in 1677 by John Archdale (B:217), but this is probably a mistake of the transcriber since Roads is named as a minor son of Richard Roads in 1695.[16] Also John Archdale served as Governor from 1694 to 1696 and possibly into 1697. The transcriber most likely read 1677 for 1697.[17] The second early patent is to William Travis in 1688 (A:223). There is good evidence for this in the fact that William Travis attended marriages at Symons Creek Monthly Meeting in 1677, 1679 and 1681 and is mentioned frequently in the Higher Court Records.[18] The third early patent (B:37) is also dated 1688 and is to Henry Palin who also received a Virginia patent in 1663.

The question arises that if Pasquotank Precinct was organized in 1670, why was the recording of deeds not begun until 1700? Perquimans Precinct appears to have started registering their deeds in 1683.[19] Albemarle County did not have a book of deeds, at least that has survived. However, some deeds were acknowledged in the Albemarle Court Records.[20] In the Albemarle County Book of Land Warrants it is apparent that headrights for new land were sold to others and called an assignment. But how was land sold that was already patented?

From the Pasquotank deeds we can illustrate one way that land was transferred. William Travis received his patent from the Lords Proprietors in 1688 (A:233). "By his written Deed of Assignment on the Back of sd Patent" in 1691 he sold the patent to Wm. Sexton, and "by his certain deed of Assignment on the back of the same patent" in 1692 it was sold to George Muschamp, and by his "certain Deed of Assignment on the back of the same patent" in 1694 it was sold to Arthur Workeman. Workeman registered the patent in 1696, but nothing is mentioned of the original patent to Travis or the two assignments before Workeman purchased the patent.[21]

The opportunity to own land brought the early settlers to the Albemarle. Thomas Woodward, the surveyor, wrote Sir John Colleton in 1665, "It bein Land only that they come for."[22] Therefore, the care taken in transferring ownership of that land through the deeds makes them a valuable source for the study of a people and their culture.

---

[1]Lindley S. Butler, "The Early Settlement of Carolina: Virginia's Southern Frontier," Virginia Magazine of History and Biography, 79 (January 1971):20-28.
[2]H. R. McIlwaine, (ed.), Minutes of the Council and General Court of Colonial Virginia, 2nd ed. (Richmond, Virginia State Library, 1979):492-493, 507.
[3]Weynette Parks Haun, Perquimans County North Carolina Deed Abstracts 1681 thru 1729, Book I (Durham, NC, Weynette Parks Haun, 1983):71-72 (no. 380).
[4]McIlwaine, Minutes of the Council, 507.
[5]Mattie Erma Edwards Parker, (ed.), North Carolina Higher-Court Records, 1670-1696, [Volume II] of The Colonial Records of North Carolina [Second Series] (Raleigh: State Department of Archives and History, 1968):xv-xvii.
[6]Nell Marion Nugent, Cavaliers and Pioneers: Abstracts of Virginia Land Patents and Grants 1623-1666, Vol. 1 (Richmond, Dietz Printing Co., 1934):

425-428, 501.
[7]Lindley S. Butler, "The Governors of Albemarle County, 1663-1689" The North Carolina Historical Review, XLVI (July 1969):282-283; Parker, Higher Court Records, [Vol. II], xv-xx.
[8]These records are abstracted in Margaret M. Hofmann, Province of North Carolina 1663-1727 Abstracts of Land Patents, (Weldon, NC, The Roanoke News Company, 1979) and transcribed in Weynette Parks Haun, Old Albemarle County North Carolina Book of Land Warrants and Surveys 1681-1706, (Durham, NC, Weynette Parks Haun, 1984).
[9]William Perry Johnson, "North Carolina Land Grants," The North Carolinian, I (June, September 1955):43-48, 77-79.
[10]Elizabeth Gregory McPherson, "Nathaniel Batts, Landholder on Pasquotank River, 1660," The North Carolina Historical Review, XLIII (January 1966):80.
[11]Isle of Wight County Records, Isle of Wight, Virginia, Will and Deed Book I, 590, as quoted in Butler, "Early Settlement," VMHB, 79:26.
[12]J. R. B. Hathaway, "Miscellaneous Items," North Carolina Historical and Genealogical Register, III (January 1903):146.
[13]Nugent, Cavaliers and Pioneers, Vol. 1, 428.
[14]Parker, Higher Court Records, [Vol. II], xxxv.
[15]David Leroy Corbitt, The Formation of the North Carolina Counties 1663-1943, (Raleigh: The Department of Archives and History, North Carolina Department of Cultural Resources, 1969):xxix.
[16]Parker, Higher Court Records, [Vol. II], 176.
[17]Mattie Erma Edwards Parker, (ed.), North Carolina Higher-Court Records, 1697-1701, [Volume III] of The Colonial Records of North Carolina [Second Series] (Raleigh: State Department of Archives and History, 1971):xxiii.
[18]Gwen Boyer Bjorkman, Quaker Marriage Certificates, Pasquotank, Perquimans, Piney Woods, and Suttons Creek Monthly Meetings, North Carolina, 1677-1800, (Bowie, MD, Heritage Books, 1988):1, 6-7; Parker, Higher Court Records, [Vol. II], 525.
[19]Haun, Perquimans County Deed Abstracts, 3 (no. 13).
[20]Parker, Higher Court Records, [Vol. II], 477.
[21]Hofmann, Abstracts of Land Patents, 25 (no. 254).
[22]William L. Saunders (ed.), The Colonial Records of North Carolina (Raleigh: State of North Carolina, 10 vols., 1886-1890)I:100.

RECORD OF DEEDS

TABLE 1
PASQUOTANK LAND GRANTS BEFORE 1700

1660 PURCHASE FROM INDIANS

Nathaniel Batts All land S.W. side of Pascotanck R. from ye mouth to ye head of New Begin Creek.

1663 VIRGINIA LAND PATENTS

NAME	ACRES	LOCATION
John HARVEY	600A	Symons Cr., Little River[a]
William MUNDAY	300A	Symons Cr., Little River[a]
Henry WHITE Jr.	750A	Symons Cr., Little River[a]
Henry WHITE Sr.	250A	N side of Albemarle Sound[b]
Samuel DAVIS	950A	N side of Albemarle Sound[b]
Thomas SHERWOOD	880A	N side of Albemarle Sound[b]
Thomas STAMPE & James NOAKES	300A	N side of Albemarle Sound[b]
Robert LAWRY	300A	Mouth of New Begun Creek[c]
Henry PALIN	450A	Mouth of New Begun Creek[c]
Richard BULLER	1200A	New Begun Cr., Doctors Cr.
Phillip EVANS	300A	New Begun Creek[c]
William JENNINGS	550A	New Begun Creek[c]
Thomas KEELE	800A	Bay of Pasquotank R.[d]
John BATTLE	640A	W side of Pasquotank R.[d]
Mary FORTSON	2000A	W side of Pasquotank R.[d]
Katharine WOODWARD & Philarete WOODWARD	750A	W side of Pasquotank R.[d]
Robert PEELE	350A	S W side of Pasquotank R.[d]
Thomas RELFE	750A	S W side of Pasquotank R.[d]
Thomas WOODWARD Sr & Thomas WOODWARD Jr	2500A	N side of Pasquotank R.,[d] Arenuse Creek

Sources: Elizabeth Gregory McPherson, "Nathaniell Batts, Landholder on Pasquotank River, 1660," The North Carolina Historical Review, XLIII (January 1966):80; Nell Marion Nugent, Cavaliers and Pioneers: Abstracts of Virginia Land Patents and Grants 1623-1666, Vol. 1 (Richmond, Dietz Printing Co., 1934):425-428.

[a] Carratucks Creek, Kecougtancke River.
[b] Carolina River.
[c] New begin Creek.
[d] Paspetanke River.

TABLE 1 -- Continued

1681 NORTH CAROLINA LAND PATENTS

NAME	ACRES	LOCATION
John BOLTON	100A	New Begun Creek
John DYE	100A	New Begun Creek
Stephen SCOTT	50A	New Begun Creek

1684 NORTH CAROLINA LAND PATENTS

NAME	ACRES	LOCATION
William JOHNSON	160A	E side of Little River
Timothy MEADS	388A	E side of Little River
Zachariah NIXON	323A	E side of Little River
Solomon POOLE	200A	E side of Little River
Charles PROWS	270A	E side of Little River

1693-1696 NORTH CAROLINA LAND PATENTS

NAME	ACRES	LOCATION
William JACKSON	234A	E side of Little River
Thomas SYMONS	200A	N E side of Little River
John HUNT	450A	Little River, Harvey's Cr.
Daniel JOHNSON	240A	Little River, Harvey's Cr.
Thomas SYMONS	96A	Little River, Harvey's Cr.
Jeremiah SYMONS	158A	Little River
Matthew KELLY	360A	joining Jeremiah SYMONS
James DAVIS	160A	joining Matthew KELLY
Dennis GRAHAM	230A	Little River
Robert LOWRY	260A	Little River
Anthony MARKAM	560A	Little River
Morgan THOMAS	250A	Little River
John TOMLINSON	534A	Little River
Thomas TWIDDY	300A	Little River
John WEST	600A	Little River
Robert, Thomas & John WEST	200A	Little River
Arthur WORKMAN	375A	Little River
Sarah SHERWOOD	250A	joining James HUNTER, Capt. HUNT, and WORKMAN.
Patrick BAYLEY	329A	Little River
Henry WHITE	100A	joining Richard CRAIG and Patrick BAYLEY
William JACSON Sr.	116A	joining James DAVIS and Richard CRAIG
Richard CRAGGE	500A	Herring Creek
Patrick BAYLEY	221A	Herring Creek Swamp
John DAVIS	150A	Herring Creek Swamp
Samuel DAVIS	95A	Herring Creek Swamp

TABLE 1 -- Continued

Humphrey BOULTON	250A	New Begun Creek
Elizabeth COATES	150A	New Begun Creek
Henry KEATON	200A	New Begun Creek
Thomas MACKIE	150A	New Begun Creek
Henry PENDLETON	300A	New Begun Creek
Thomas STANTON	424A	New Begun Creek
William MOWBERY	200A	New Begun Creek Swamp
Thomas TOWERS	160A	New Begun Creek Swamp
Maj. Samuel SWANN	457A	New Begun Cr, Akehurst Cr.
Caleb BUNDY	175A	Deep Br., Walnut Br.
Samuel BUNDY	110A	Red Log Br., Walnut Br.
William BUNDY	130A	Deep Branch
James GAD	200A	Deep Run Br, Flatty Creek
Stephen SCOTT	300A	Deep Run Br, Flatty Creek
John BELMAN	314A	Flatty Creek
John BURNSBY, Jr.	200A	Flatty Creek
Peter FURREE	194A	Flatty Creek
John LUMBROZIER	400A	Flatty Creek
Richard POPE	314A	joining John LUMBROZIER
Anthony MARKAM	190A	Flatty Creek
Isaac DELAMARE & Francis DELAMARE	125A	joining Anthony MARKAM
Thomas JONES	230A	joining Anthony MARKAM
Thomas PENDLETON	350A	Flatty Creek
Richard STAMP	200A	Flatty Creek
Benjamin WEST	400A	Flatty Creek
Robert, Thomas & John WEST	250A	Flatty Creek
Charles ONEAL	500A	Flatty Creek, Betty's Cr.
Henry PALIN, Jr.	139A	Little Flatty Creek
Henry PALIN, Jr.	334A	
John BELMAN	280A	Albemarle Sound
Isaac ROWDEN	230A	Albemarle Sound
Daniel AKEHURST	250A	S W side Pasquotank River
Thomas BARCOCK	400A	S W side Pasquotank River
Rowland BUCKLEY	350A	S W side Pasquotank River
William WINDBURY	250A	joining Rowland BUCKLEY
Lawrence KEETON	204A	S W side Pasquotank River
Richard MADREN	150A	S W side Pasquotank River
John MASON	176A	S W side Pasquotank River
Stephen SCOTT	274A	S W side Pasquotank River
John SAWYER & Robert SAWYER	400A	S W side Pasquotank River, Gumberry Swamp
George HARRIS	624A	joining Francis HENDRICK

TABLE 1 -- Continued

Francis HENDRICK	206A	S W side, Nobs Crook Cr.
John BELMAN	198A	Beech Ldg., Nobs Crook Cr.
David PRICHARD	640A	Nobs Crook Cr., Second Br.
Thomas CARTWRIGHT	640A	Spelman's Landing
Ralfe GARNET	250A	joining a Swamp
Philip EVINS	127A	Main Swamp
David PRICHARD,Jr.	155A	joining Philip EVINS
Samuel DAVIS	326A	Pasquotank River
Augustine SEAR	327A	Pasquotank River
William TEMPLE	191A	Pasquotank River
Stephen VINCENT	96A	Pasquotank River
Robert WALLIS	400A	Pasquotank River
Thomas BARCOCK	200A	N E side Pasquotank River
William BRAY	350A	N E side Pasquotank River
Thomas FRENCH	85A	N E side Pasquotank River
John HAWKINS	252A	N E side Pasquotank River
William JENNINGS	450A	N E side Pasquotank River
Thomas JAMES	200A	joining William JINNINGS
Cornelius JONES	300A	N E side Pasquotank River
John JONES	318A	N E side Pasquotank River
Henry SAWYER	190A	joining John JONES
Edward MAYO, Assn of Cornal FITSPATRICK	277A	N E side Pasquotank River, joining Mr. MILLER
William RAMON	450A	N E side Pasquotank River
Capt. Thomas RELF	600A	N E side Pasquotank River
Thomas SAWYER	450A	N E side Pasquotank River
Thomas SAWYER	200A	N E side Pasquotank River
Robert TAYLOR	640A	N E side Pasquotank River
John UPTON	191A	N E side Pasquotank River
Uriah CANNON & John BISHOP	350A	Aranuse Creek
William COLLINS	500A	Aranuse Creek
John TRUEBLOOD & Anne TRUEBLOOD	600A	Aranuse Creek
John DANSON	3650A	Aranuse Cr., Portohunk Cr.
John HAWKINS	350A	Portohunk Creek
Thomas MILLER	640A	Portohunk Creek

Sources: Margaret M. Hofmann, Province of North Carolina 1663-1727 Abstracts of Land Patents, (Weldon, NC, The Roanoke News Company, 1979); William Perry Johnson, "North Carolina Land Grants," The North Carolinian, I (June, September 1955, March 1956):43-48, 77-79, 142-145.

TABLE 2
PASQUOTANK DEEDS WITH DATES BEFORE 1700

YEAR	DEED BOOK:PAGE
1663,	A:6 A:151 A:201 A:407 C:237 C:372 C:381 B:235
1664,	C:372
1667,	C:372
1668,	A:282 A:283 A:290 A:311 A:402 C:336 B:295 B:408 B:447 B:453 A:449 B:46 B:71
1677,	B:217
1679,	A:392
1684,	B:72
1688,	A:223 B:37
1693,	A:44 C:223 C:351
1694,	A:9 A:53 A:87 A:120 A:179 A:197 A:215 A:297 A:321 A:322 A:326 A:350 A:370 A:394 A:396 C:243 C:288 C:289 C:304 C:314 C:372 C:381 B:207 B:230 B:251 B:298 B:345 B:467 B:3
1695,	A:224 A:245 C:281 B:181 B:227
1696,	A:3 A:11 A:89 A:118 A:128 A:153 A:158 A:206 A:333 A:329 A:348 A:365 A:409 C:231 C:312 C:317 C:318 C:325 C:338 B:231 B:189 B:191 B:196 B:231 B:385 B:386 B:388 B:57 B:82 B:126
1697,	A:30 C:373 B:245 B:290 B:341
1698,	A:102 C:291 C:358
1699,	C:278 C:309 B:83

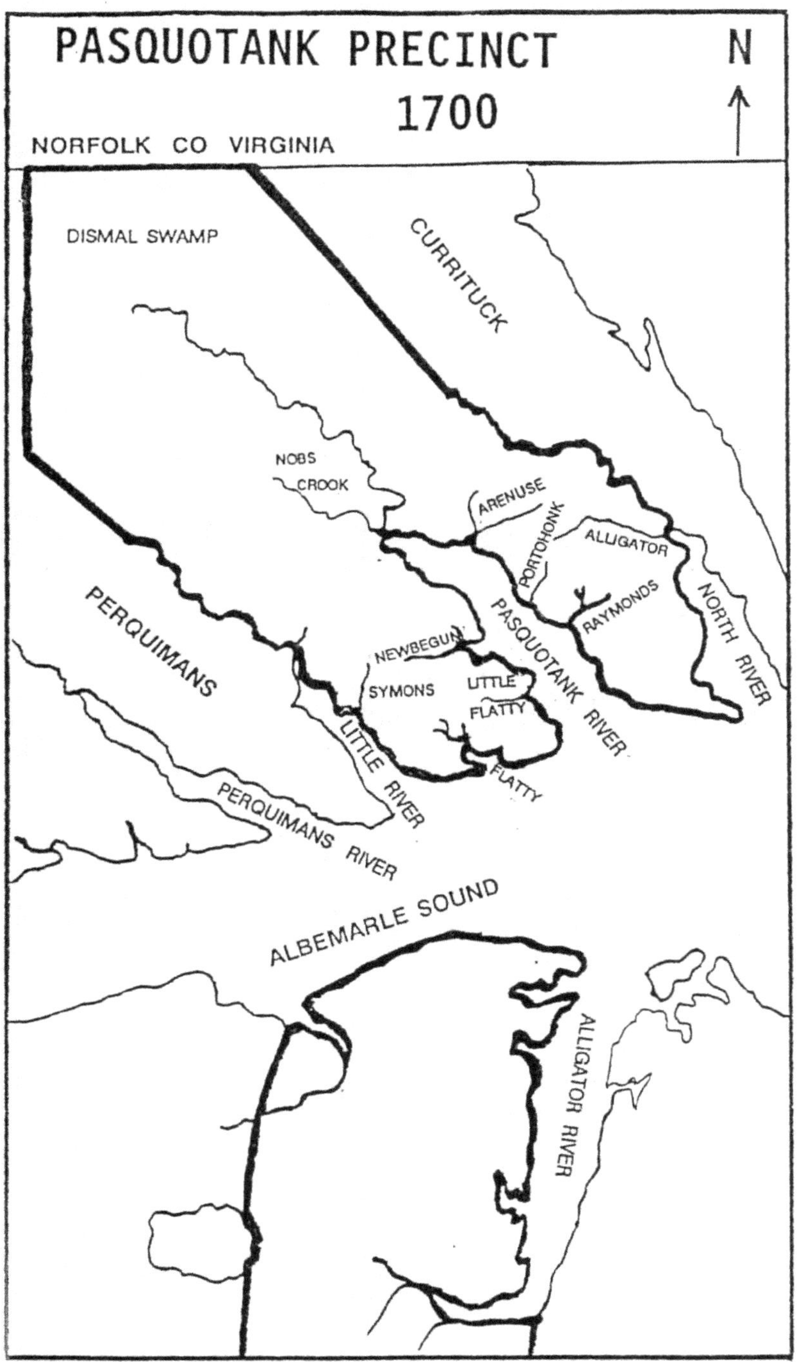

PASQUOTANK PRECINCT
1700
N
NORFOLK CO VIRGINIA
DISMAL SWAMP
CURRITUCK
NOBS
CROOK
ARENUSE
PORTOHONK
ALLIGATOR
RAYMONDS
NORTH RIVER
PERQUIMANS
PASQUOTANK RIVER
NEWBEGUN
SYMONS
LITTLE
FLATTY
LITTLE RIVER
FLATTY
PERQUIMANS RIVER
ALBEMARLE SOUND
ALLIGATOR RIVER

RECORD OF DEEDS VOLUME A 1700-1728

[A:1] An act to Authorize the County Court of Pasquotank to Transcribe such part of the Register's Books of said County as may appear Necessary.

Be it enacted by the General Assembly of the State of North Carolina, and it is hereby Enacted by the authority of the same that the Justices of the County Court of Pasquotank, shall have full power and authority to employ some proper person to Transcribe into a bound book or books such part of the Register's books of said County as may be in a Situation unfit for the preserving the Records of said County, and that the said Records so Transcribed shall be considered to all intents and purposes as Valid as if the Same had been Orginally recorded in said Book or Books. Any law, usage or Custom to the Contrary Notwithstanding. December 1812. Registered April 11th 1816. By Thomas JORDAN P. Regr.

State of North Carolina, Pasquotank County, June Term 1813. In pursuance to an act of the last session of the General Assembly, It is Ordered that Thomas JORDAN Senr. the present Register of this County be appointed to Transcribe into a well bound Books such part of the books in his office as may be considered unfit for preserving the Records and that he furnish Books for that purpose for which together with his Services in Transcribing the Same to be paid out of the County Taxes. It is further Ordered that William T. MUSE, and William T. RELFE be appointed to examine the said Register's Office and to point out to the said Thomas JORDAN such Books, or parts of books, as are in their opinion necessary to be transcribed and further to Contract with him for the Services to be performed by him, and make a Report of their proceedings to this Court. Teste Richard MUSE D.C. Registered April 11th 1816 By Thomas JORDAN P. Regr.

State of North Carolina, Pasquotank County, September Term 1815. William T. MUSE and William T. RELFE who were appointed at June Term 1813 under an Act of the General assembly of 1812 to Examine the Register's office of this County and to point out what Books or parts of books it would be necessary to Transcribe, having yet made no Report. It is

Ordered that Richard MUSE be appointed in the Room of the said William T. RELFE, and that he and the said William T. MUSE perform that Service and make a report of their proceedings to this Court that an Order passed
[A:2] passed at December Term 1813 in regard to the above business be set aside and that this only remains in force. Teste Richard MUSE D. C. Registered April 11th 1816. By Thomas JORDAN.

State of North Carolina, Pasquotank County, September Term 1815. William T. MUSE and Richard MUSE who were appointed to examine the Register's Office in Pursuance to an Act of the General Assembly of 1812 made the following Report "In Pursuance to the Annexed Order of Court we have proceeded to examine the Register's Office of Pasquotank County and find that Books A, B, C, D, E and H contain valuable records & are in a ruinous Situation, they therefore recommend that the whole of the said Books should be transcribed, and that Thomas JORDAN Senr. who was appointed by the Court at June Term 1813 to do the Same shall receive five Shillings, the Sum the Register is now intitled to by Law for each Deed, Bill of sale, or other Instrument of Writing Contained therein to be paid half yearly by the Treasurer of the County if he should make application for the Same, besides furnishing the said Thomas JORDAN Sen with good and Substantial blank books for that purpose: Given under our hands this 6th day of September 1815. Will: T. MUSE, Richard MUSE.

It is ordered that the foregoing report be Confirmed and that the said Thomas JORDAN proceed accordingly. a Copy Teste Richard MUSE D.C. Registered April 11th 1816. By Thomas JORDAN P. Regr.

[A:3] Pasquotank Precinct, October 15 1700. The above assignment was acknowledged in open Court by Rowland BUCKLAND and Elizabeth his wife. Tho: ABINGTON CC. Registered in the Register Book Jun 16th 1700. This the assignment of a Patent dated the 25th day of Ffeby. 1696.

Albemarle County. ... William WINBURY of Pasquotank Precinct ... to Thomas LEWIS of the same place ... for a valuable consideration ... the moyety or one half of a Tract of land by me bought of Rowland BUCKLAND and Elizabeth his wife Situated and being on the South west side of Pasquotank River ... the same to be layed on the opposite part of the said land ... 15th day of October 1700. *Signed*: The Mark of Wm X WINBURY. *Wit*: Henry WHITE, Wm. RELFE. *Ack*: 15 Oct. 1700. *Regt*: 16 Jan 1700.

26 Oct 1700 ... Wm. JENNINGS of the province of North Carolina Cooper ... & Thomas JOHNSON of his own free voluntary will putteth himself apprentice to the abovesaid Wm. JENNINGS to Serve him during the Term and time of [blank] Years from the above date engaging hereby his said master diligently to Serve all his lawful Commands at all times to Obey [A:4] the said Thomas to Obey, as also not to contract matrimony nor commit fornication during the said Term, nor any ways to Waste or [blank] the Goods of his said Master, nor to absent himself from the Service of his said Master during the above Term of Seven years without leave first obtained of his said Master: In consideration of which the above named Wm. JENNINGS doth engage and promise on his part to use his endeavour to teach him the said Thomas JOHNSON the Trade or Occupation of a Cooper, as also during the said Term to find and provide for him Sufficient meat, drink lodging & Cloathing also due Correction and at the expiration of the aforesaid Term to give him what Coopers tools ... day and date above Written. *Signed*: Wm. X JENNINGS his mark, Thomas T JOHNSON his mark. *Wit*: Richd. POPE, Geo. PORDAGE. *Regt*: 21 Feb 1700.

Albemarle County, In the precinct of Pasquotk. ... Robert MORGAN and Elizabeth my Wife for a valuable Consideration in [blank] received hath sold ... unto Matthew WINN all our right ... Deed of Sale from [blank] ... this 12th day of [blank] ... *Signed*: Robert MORGAN, Elizabeth E MORGAN her mark. *Wit*: Phill TORKSEY, Edward X JAMES his mark. *Ack*: [blank] July 1704 by Robert MORGAN to Matthew WINN. *Regt*: 8th. 11th 1804. [sic]

[A:5] July 18th 1704. Francis DELAMARE & Ann my wife for a valuable Consideration to us in hand paid by John MCKEEL ... assign over all our right ... in and to the remaining 100 acres of the within mentioned draught & Tract of land ... being that part that lyes nearest great Flatty Creek bridge. ... *Signed*: Ffrancis DELAMARE, Ann DELAMARE. *Ack*: 18 July 1704 by Mr. Ffrancis DELAMARE & Ann his wife to John MCKEEL. *Regt*: 11 Oct. 1804. [sic]

John JONES and Elizabeth JONES my wife have sold ... to Wm. JAMES of Newbegun Creeke one Entry or Tract of land lying and being at the head of Newbegun Creek containing 120 acres of land, and Joining ... upon the Land formerly Wm. MOWBERY Northward, and upon the land of Wm. CHANCEY Southward. ...the 18th day of the 5th month 1704. *Signed*: The mark of John II JONES, the mark of Eliz. X JONES. *Wit*: [blank] *Ack*: 18 July 1704 by John JONES & Eliz his wife to Wm. JAMES. *Regt*: 11 Oct 1704.

[A:6] Pasquotank Precinct ... William SMISSON and Mary my wife for a Valuable Consideration ... of John DAVIS ... to ... Jno. DAVIS the within draught or plat of land therein contained ... this 19th day of September 1704. *Signed*: Wm. SMISSON, The Mark of Mary M SMISSON. *Ack*: 18 July 1804 [sic] by William SMISSON and Mary his wife to John DAVIS. *Regt*: 7 Oct 1704.

Henry WHITE Senr. of the County of Albemarle in North Carolina for Several reasons that moveth me hereunto but especially for love and affection that I bear to my Son in Law John MORRIS ... make this Deed of Gift ... a parcel of land, the quantity not known out of a Patent in the kings name bearing date the 25th day of September 1663 ... Beginning at a Red Oak on up the side of a little branch, and so nearest a Westerly Course by a Rowe of marked trees to another little branch to a marked Sassifrax marked four ways so up the said branch to the head line Joining upon Robert LOWRY's land so up the said line to the said branch we begun at so down the said branch to the first Station to the Red Oak marked four ways which is the Corner tree. Nevertheless if the said John MORRIS shall see cause to make Sale of the said Land shall proffer the Sale of it to me my heirs Exrs. administrators or assigns and if he or they shall refuse to buy then he the said John MORRIS is left to his freedom to make Sale of it to whom he pleaseth ...
[A:7] this 18th of April 1704. *Signed*: Henry WHITE. *Ack*: Pasquotank Precinct. At a Court held

... 18th day of April 1704 the above Deed of Gift was by Henry WHITE acknowledged in open Court to John MORRIS. *Wit*: [blank] *Regt*: April 27th 1704.

Benjamin GYLES and Mary my wife for ... 13 pounds to us paid or Secured to be paid by William RAWLISON ... sold ... the within plat of land ... 12th day of Feby. 1703/4. *Signed*: The mark of Benja. X GYLES, The mark of Mary X GYLES. *Wit*: Tho: ABINGTON, John CORP. *Ack*: 18 April 1704 by Benjamin GYLES and Mary his wife to Wm. RAWLISON. *Regt*: April 27th 1804. [sic]

William JENNINGS Junr. of Pasquotank Precinct in Albemarle County in North Carolina & Mary my wife send Greeting ... for a valuable consideration to us in hand paid by Robert SAWYER of the Same place ... [A:8] sold ... 92 acres of Land Situate ... on the Northeast side of Pasquotank River, being part of a Patent for 450 acres granted to the said William JENNINGS and layed out by Captain Thomas RELFE deputy Surveyor as to the plot hereunto affixed ... friends Mr. John JENNINGS, Captain Thomas RELFE, Mr. William RELFE & Thomas ABINGTON, or any of them to appear for us at any precinct Court to be held for the precinct of Pasquotank and in open Court ... acknowledge this Deed ... fourth day of Ffeb. 1700. *Signed*: Wm. JENNINGS, The mark of Mary O JENNINGS. *Wit*: The mark of John II JENNINGS. *Ack*: by Thomas ABINGTON attorney to William JENNINGS Junr. and Mary his wife April 15th 1701. *Regt*: April 22nd 1701.

Albemarle County, Pasquotank Precinct, William REED do ... hereby ... sell the within mentioned Land unto Wm. CHANCEY ... 15th day of July 1701. *Signed*: Wm. REED. *Ack*: July 15th 1701 ... by Wm. REED. *Regt*: August 10th 1701.
[A:9] This is an assignment of a Patent granted to Thomas TOWERS dated the first day of Jany. 1694. and by him and his Wife acknowledged in open Court to Wm. REED 17th day of January 1698.

Thomas COOPER of Pasquotank Precinct in Albemarle County in North Carolina planter and Hannah my wife ... 4 pounds 10 shillings ... paid by John JONES of SAWYERS Creek in Pasquotank Precinct ... a Tract of land lying on the Northeast side of Pasquotank River aforesaid ... Thomas SAWYERS Corner Tree, ... to

Nathaniel GRAYS (See Top of page 13.)

Richard POPE of Pasquotank ... for Love and affection I have ... unto my Son Edward POPE for his hereafter better Support, livelihood and maintenance do give ... one Moulatto Boy named Sambo son of my Indian Woman Sarah ... said Mulatto boy to remain in the Custody of me and my wife untill such time as my sd. son shall accomplish the full age of one and twenty years or day of Marriage whichever shall first happen ... Provided that if my said son should depart this Life before he shall happen to attain the age of One and twenty years or day of Marriage then the said Mulatto boy to go to my Exor. or Admr. And I do hereby appoint my trusty and well beloved friend Thomas ABINGTON my attorney to appear at the next Court to be holden for the precinct aforesaid [A:10] and then and there in open Court to acknowledge this present Deed of Gift. *Signed*: Richard POPE this 14th day of April 1701. *Wit*: Richd. PLATER, Hugh CAMPBELL. *Ack*: by Thomas ABINGTON April 15th 1701. *Regt*: April 20th 1701.

Richard POPE of Pasquotank Precinct for Love and affection I have ... unto my daughter Mary POPE for her hereafter better Support, livelihood and maintenance do give ... one Negro Girl named Betty or Bess, I lately bought of one Patrick CREAGH. ... said negro Girl to remain in the Custody of me and Ann my wife and her future increase & proceed to remain to our use untill she shall accomplish the full age of eighteen years or day of Marriage which shall first happen ... and her then future increase said Marys Provided that if my said daughter should happen to depart this Life, before she shall attain her full age of eighteen years or day of Marriage then the said Negro Girl to revert to me or Ann my wife, or the Surviver of us, our Exors. or Administrators and I do hereby appoint my trusty and well beloved friend Thomas ABINGTON my attorney to appear at the next Court to be holden for the precinct aforesaid and then and there in open Court to acknowledge this present Deed of Gift. *Signed*: Richard POPE this 14th day of April 1701. *Wit*: Richd. PLATER, Hugh CAMPBELL. *Ack*: by Thomas ABINGTON April 15th 1701. *Regt*: April 22nd 1701.

[A:11] Pasquotank Precinct. ... Samuel DAVIS

attorney to John HARVEY as by a Letter of attorney now remaining on record on the Registers book of Writings ... Consideration of the redelivery of a bill under the hand and Seal of the said John HARVEY passed as a Consideration for the above assignment, ... sold unto the Said Francis HENRICK ... Interest of the within mentioned Tract of land and premises assigned over to the said John HARVEY by the said Francis HENRICK and Mary his wife. ... 21st day of Ffeby. 1700. *Signed*: Saml. DAVIS. *Wit*: Tho. ABINGTON. *Ack*: by Saml. DAVIS attorney to John HARVEY April 15th 1701. *Regt*: 22 April 1701. This is a Re-assignment of an assignment of a Patent due to Ffra: HENRICK dated the 25th day of Ffeby. 1696.

April 1704. Francis DELAMARE and Ann my wife for a Valuable consideration to us in hand paid by John CORY ... 75 acres of the within mentioned draught or Tract of land ...*Signed*: Ffrancis DELAMARE, Ann DELAMAR. *Wit*: [blank] *Ack*: 18 April 1704 to John COREY by Mr. Francis DELAMAR & Ann his wife. *Regt*: April 27th 1704.

[A:12] April 17th 1704. Richard STAMP and Mary Ann my wife for a Valuable Consideration to us in hand paid do freely assign over all our right title and Interest, of in and to a part of the within Patent of land ... small branch on the Creek between Thomas STAMPS house and ours the Subscribers ... containing by estimation about 80 acres ... unto Thomas STAMP. *Signed*: The mark of Richard R STAMP, The mark of Mary Ann M STAMP. *Wit*: [blank] *Ack*: 18 April 1704 to Thomas STAMP by Richard STAMP and Mary Ann his wife. *Regt*: April 22nd 1704.

The eighth day of the 7th month 1703. ... Edmund CHANCY and Sarah my wife do assign all our right title & Interest ... to Ann PALIN ... of this within mentioned Survey of Land. *Signed*: Edmund CHANCEY, The mark of Sarah CHANCEY. *Wit*: Edward MAYO Junr., Henry H KETEN his mark. *Ack*: July 18th 1704 by Edmund CHANCEY and Sarah his wife. *Regt*: 20the July 1704.

[A:13] (See page 9.) Line for breadth at the road ... along the said GRAYE's line ... 100 acres ... to him the said John JONES ... 14th day of July 1701. *Signed*: The mark of Tho: \ COOPER, The mark of

Hannah H COOPER. *Wit*: Tho: RELFE, Tho: ABINGTON. *Ack*: July 15th 1701 by Thomas COOPER and Hannah his wife. *Regt*: Sept. the first 1701.

... 14 July 1701 Between John TREVEALE and Ann his wife inhabitants of North Carolina and Albemarle County in Pasquotank River of the one party of the aforesaid Government County and River of the other party ... sold ... mansion house or messuage with the appurtenances wherein the sd. John TREVEALE with Ann his wife now dwelleth ... on the North East Side of Pasquotank River ... 640 acres ... as is mentioned in the Patent ... unto the said John BYSHOPP his heirs and assigns during the time as by law shall be required of this our Government or any other Statute Law Established and to this end with a true intent construction ...
[A:14] construction and purpose ... to be delivered by Turf and Twig or any other Law Established by any Statute or Law of our Government ... *Signed*: John I TREVEALE Sign, Ann T TREVEALE her mark. *Ack*: July 15th 1701 by John TREVEALE & Ann his wife. *Regt*: Sept. 1st 1701.

Pasquotank Precinct ... Peter MCGREGORY and Letitia my wife doe for a valuable consideration in hand received ... sell ... unto Daniel PHILLIPPS the within Plantation and lands ... 19 Aug. 1701. *Signed*: The mark of Peter O MCGREGORY, The mark of Latitia C. MCGREGORY. *Wit*: Richard PLATER, Tho: ABINGTON. *Ack*: by Peter MCGREGORY and Letitia his wife 19 Aug. 1701. *Regt*: 1 Sept. 1701.

[A:15] Roxberry 23rd May '2/3
Sr. Your letter bearing date March 11 172/3 I Received, the Contents which I am Surprized with assuring you, that I never Expressed any thing about your debt, before, if it be due (as at present I know nothing to the Contrary) it should have been responded as your self say before this time, but I could not doe it before any knowledge of it. If you will please to send the bond, or a Copy of it I shall endeavour to respond it as soon as possible, I am at present out of a Capacity to send you your money. If you please to Exercise your Patience a Little Longer I shall endeavour to doe what is duly in the matter. I should be very Sorry if any of my dear husbands friends should be damnified for want

of their right. Sr. with tender of Respects to yourself and Madam HENLEY, I [?] your friend and Servant. *Signed*: Mary LAMB.

An Aquittance. Be it known unto all Men by these presents that I Mary TRUEBLOOD have Received of William ROSS the Sum of ffourty pounds of Lawful Money of Carolina in full discharge of all Debts, Reconings, Accounts and Demands whatsoever from the Beginning of the world to this day being October the first one thousand Seven hundred and one. I say recd. by me. *Signed*: Mary TRUEBLOOD. *Wit*: Sarah MEALES, Agnes ROSS, Mary TRUEBLOOD *Regt*: 23 Oct. 1701.

October 21st, 1701. William REED and Christian my wife for a Valuable consideration ... assigned over all my right title and Interest, of in and to the within plot and land ... unto Joseph JORDAN ... *Signed*: Wm. REED. *Ack*: Pasquotank Precinct. by Wm. REED 21 Oct. 1701. *Regt*: 29 Dec. 1701.

[A:16] Ann POPE of Pasquotank Precinct in Albermarle County in North Carolina Widow ... in Consideration of the Natural Love and affection I have and do bear to my son Edward POPE and for and towards his hereafter better Support, livelihood and maintenance, do hereby give assign make over and dispose of to him the said Edward POPE, one large feather bed with good fine Ticking, one Bolster & two Pillows of fine ticking, one pair of fine Sheets, two large fine blankets, one fine large worsted Rugg, one pair of Curtains & valence. Likewise ... one young mare filly branded on the near Shoulder with the Letters RP docked of a bright-bay Colour, and all her increase. ... (Note the remainder of this Deed of Gift not to be found.)

Thomas SYMONS and Rebekah my wife ... for the full sum of 15 pounds ... by John JONES of Pasquotank Precinct as well as for divers other good causes and considerations us hereunto moving ... Sold ... all our right, title and Interest in and to the within mentioned Patent. ... 18th day of [blank] 1703. *Signed*: Thomas SYMONS, The mark of Rebecca RS SYMONS. *Wit*: Wm. RELFE, Ffrancis DELAMARE. *Ack*: Pasquotank Precinct ... 19 Oct. 1703 by Thomas SYMONS & Rebecca his wife ... to John JONES. *Regt*:

Jany. 14th. 173/4.

[A:17] Jacob OVERMAN Junr. ... assign all my right, title and Interest of this within mentioned Patent unto Nathaniel HALL .... 16th day of the 8th month 1703. *Signed*: Jacob OVERMAN, The mark of Rebecca RO OVERMAN. *Wit*: Wm. RELFE, Phill. TORKSEY. *Ack*: 19 Oct. 1703 by Jacob OVERMAN and Rebekah his wife to Nathaniel HALL. *Regt*: 14 Jan. 173/4

Benjamin GYLES of Pasquotank Precinct in North Carolina and Mary my wife ... 10 pounds money of North Carolina ... paid by Thomas PENDLETON of the Same place ... all that Neck or Tract of Land containing 100 acres ... Beginning at a branch runing between a place commonly called ... Dick's folly and the aforesaid Neck so binding on the branch till it comes to the main Road that goes to Caleb BUNDY'S so along the road to the Beaver Dam, ... to Benjamin GYLES ... to Edward MAYO Junr. ... to the main Beaver Dam ... to the bottom of the Neck then along the Swamp Side to Thomas MACKEE'S line, and ... to the branch of the said Dick's Folly ... [A:18] ... *Signed*: The mark of Benja X GYLES, The mark of Mary X GYLES. *Wit*: Ffra: DELAMARE, Tho: ABINGTON. *Ack*: Pasquotank Precinct, 18 July 1703/4 ... Benja. GYLES and Mary his wife to Thomas PENDLETON. *Regt*: 28 Jan. 1703/4.

Thomas PRITCHARD do make over all my right title and Interest of the within mentioned Patent of land to Hugh PRITCHARD ... 18th day of [blank] 1703. *Signed*: Thomas PRITCHARD. *Wit*: Wm. EVERGIN, Benjamin PRITCHARD. *Ack*: Pasquotank Precinct, 1 Jan. 1703 Thomas PRITCHARD to Hugh PRITCHARD. *Regt*: 24 April 1704.

North Carolina, All my right title and Interest in a Tract of Land lying on Flatty Creek Surveyed by Mr. Thomas RELFE which I give my full Interest from me and my heirs to Thomas BOYD Esqr. ... 31 March 1704. [A:19] *Wit*: Saml. HORTON, Wm. COLLINGS. *Ack*: Pasquotank Precinct, 31 March 1704. *Regt*: 24 April 1704.

North Carolina Jany. 27th 1704. William COLLINGS in the Precinct of Pasquotank doth assign all my right and title to the within mentioned unto Robert TEMPLE

Esqr. of the aforesaid Precinct ... And Elizabeth COLLINGS his wife her right of all Dower to the premises. *Signed*: Wm. COLLINGS, Elizabeth COLLINGS. *Wit*: Solomon S DAVIS his mark. *Ack*: Pasquotank Precinct, 18 April 1704 by Capt. William COLLINGS & Elizabeth his wife to Robert TEMPLE. *Regt*: 25 April 1704.

Thomas CARTWRITE Junr. and Mary my wife ... in Consideration of the full Sum of 15 pounds ... paid by William WARREN ... sold ... our plantation and land containing 100 acres ... on the South side of Pasquotank River in a fork between two branches, by my other Tract of Land, and running up the easternmost branch ...
[A:20] Dividing this Tract from our brother Job CARTWRITE'S Land ... (Note the remainder of this Deed missing.)

Albermarle. William Earl of CRAVEN Palatine and the rest of the true and Absolute Lords proprietors of all Carolina ... Thomas STANTON of the County of Albermarle planter in the precinct of North Carolina do hereby give grant enfeoff & confirm unto Mary BROTHERS wife of William BROTHERS Junr. of the County and province aforesaid Plantr. ... about 20 acres of land lying at the head of the sd. Thomas STANTON's line, Joining to Thomas MACKEES' line ... to Thomas PENDLETONS' at the head of Thomas STANTONS' line ... 23 ffebry in the ninth year of the year of our Sovereign Lady Anne ... Anno Dom 1711. *Signed*: Thomas STANTON, Mary STANTON. *Wit*: Jacob SHERWOOD. *Ack*: Pasquotank Precinct, 17 July 1711 Thomas STANTON and Mary his Wife to Mary BROTHERS. *Regt*: 8th 7ber 1711.

John HALL of Baltimore County in the Province of Maryland Gent. have made Ordered & deputed ... my Well beloved friend Edward WILLIAMS of Pasquotank North Carolina Gentleman my true and lawful Attorney ... whatsoever due to me from any person or persons, whatsoever in the Colony of Virginia or Government of North Carolina, ...
[A:21] *Signed*: John HALL. *Wit*: [blank] MATTHEWS Junr., Jos MORRIS Junr. *Ack*: Maryland Baltimore County March 15th 1708/9. Then came the within John HALL before us James PHILLIPS & Aquila PACA two of his Majesties Justices for the aforesaid County of

Baltimore did acknowledge the within Letter of Attorney to be his Act and Deed. *Ack*: Pasquotank Precinct, Edward WILLIAMS came into open Court and proved that the within mentioned Letter of attorney might be admitted to Record which was granted. *Regt*: 8th 7ber 1711.

North Carolina Albermarle County. Eliza. GARNER of the abovesaid Province and County do give ... the one half of my land Beginning at William CARTWRIGHT'S line, to be equally divided from the River to the head of the line between me said Eliza. GARNER & William SIMSON, which said part or parcell of Land ... quit claim ...
[A:22] unto William SIMSON ... being for a valuable Consideration in hand received, and for divers good causes & Considerations ... by Virtue of the delivery of Seven pence half penny in Silver delivered and paid upon Sealing and delivery of the same according to the English Custom & Rule ... 18th September Anno Dom 1710. *Signed*: Eliza. X GARDNER her mark. *Wit*: John BISHOP, Wm. CARTWRIGHT. *Ack*: Pasquotank Precinct, 17 July 1711 Elizabeth GARDNER to Wm. SIMSON. *Regt*: 18th 7ber 1711.

[A:23] Robert WALLIS Esqr. wth. Prudence my wife of the County of Albermarle and the said Precinct of Pasquotank doth ... acknowledge ... unto Mr. Jonathan JACOCKS of the abovesd. Province and County ... a parcel of land, lying and being in the said Robert WALLIS Esqr's his orchard within the Inclosure of his said Plantation containing ten foot Square including the said Place and Continent of land wherein Eliz. JACOCKS lately decd. was lately buried to be within the bounds and liberty of Land so granted, by a Special liberty and priviledge so agreed by the partys above mentioned being for a valuable consideration of 3 pounds in Silver money already recd. ... do quit claim ... to enjoy for a Continual burying place for the said Mr. Jon: JACOCKS or any of his family ... to carry any corpse belonging to the said family to be lawfully buried in a Christian and decent manner ... to be a continual refuge or burying place for any of the said family ... the 17th July Anno Dom 1711. *Signed*: Robert WALLIS, Prudence WALLIS. *Wit*: Wm. REED, W. NORRIS. *Ack*: Pasquotank Precinct October Court 17 July 1711 Mr. Robert WALLIS and his wife to

Mr. JACOCKS. *Regt*: 18 7ber 1711.

[A:24] North Carolina, Albermarle County. John DAVIS and Ruth my wife do assign, ... of this within mentioned Deed of Sale ... unto David BAYLEY ... for a valuable consideration in hand paid ... 21 August 1711. *Signed*: Jno. DAVIS, Ruth R DAVIS her mark. *Wit*: W. NORRIS, J. PALIN. *Ack*: Pasquotank Precinct, At an Orphan Court held ... Augt. 1711 ... by Jno. DAVIS & wife unto David BAYLEY. *Regt*: 19th 7ber 1711.

Henry SWANN of Perquimons Precinct in Albermarle County in North Carolina Merchant have assigned ... friends Mr. Wm. SWANN & Mr. Tho. SWANN both of the County of Albermarle in North Carolina aforesaid to be my lawful attorneys ... to ask Sue for, Levy, require, recover and receive of all and every person or persons Whatsover all and every such Debts ... [A:25] 21 Sept. 1709. *Signed*: Henry SWANN. *Wit*: William ROSS, Robt. R TEMPLE his mark, [blank] X TEMPLE his mark. *Regt*: Pasquotank Precinct, 4 [blank] 1711.

Truman MCBRIDE son and heir of Margt. MCBRIDE decd. do acknowledge all my right title & Interest of & to a Certain Tract of land conveyed and Sold unto the said Margt. MCBRIDE by Thomas COOPER as may appear by his assignment upon the back of his Patent bearing date the 21st January 1706 but now is Conveyed over by me unto John SPENCE ... 21 Aug. 1711. *Signed*: Truman MCBRIDE. *Wit*: W. NORRIS. *Ack*: Pasquotank Precinct, At an Orphans Court 21 Aug. 1711, Truman MCBRIDE to Jno. SPENCE. *Regt*: 19th Sept. 1711.

[A:26] Saml. JACKSON of North Carolina ... 10 pounds ... sold ... unto David BAYLY ... all that part Tract or parcel of land lying and being in the precinct of Pasquotank near the Narrows of Little River ... upon the branch which bounds upon William [blank] ... 30 acres ...Samuel JACKSON do hereby [blank] Presents bind ... myself ... in the Penal Sum of 20 pounds to keep and observe all the articles & agreements
[A:27] 25th Xber 1710. *Signed*: Saml. J JACKSON his mark. *Wit*: W. NORRIS, Jno. I SIMSON his mark. *Ack*: Pasquotank Precinct, At an Orphan Court 21

Aug. 1711 by Saml. JACKSON to David BAYLY. *Regt*: 4 Oct. 1711.

Henry PENDLETON and Eliz. my wife do make over and assign the within mentioned Patent ... to Thomas WOODLEY and his son Jona. WOODLEY that is to say the Moyety or half part to the said Thomas WOODLEY and the other moyety or half part unto his said son Jona. WOODLEY ... 15 Jan. 1711/12. *Signed*: Henry HP PENDLETON his mark. Eliz. E PENDLETON her mark. *Wit*: Ffrancis DELAMARE, John BISHOP. *Ack*: Pasquotank, 15 Jan. 1711/12 to Thomas WOODLEY by Henry PENDLETON & Eliz. his wife. *Regt*: 17 April 1712.

North Carolina Albermarle County. Thos. JAMES with Margaret my wife of Pasquotank Precinct, do ... confirm and surrender from us ... a Certain plantation with an 100 acres of Land more or less lying and being on the Nor East Side of Pasquotank River at the head of SAWYER'S Creek beginning [A:28] at a Corner beech formerly Davis JONES'S ... the said land being part of a tract of land ct. 570 acres formerly in the possession of Jno. JONES Cordwainer which said plantation & land ... Thos. JAMES with Margt. my wife do exonerate quit claim ... unto Robt. MORGAN ... for 12 pounds ... and for Divers other good causes ... 31 March 1711. *Signed*: Thos. T JAMES, Mart. M JAMES. *Wit*: Jas. BOLT, Jas. Z GRANDY. *Ack*: Pasquotank, 15 Jany. 1711/12 by Thos. JAMES & Margt. his wife unto Robt. MORGAN. *Regt*: 17 April 1711.

[A:29] No. Carolina. John BISHOP with Mary my wife ... make over ... unto Mr. Griffith JONES of the abovesd Province ... a certain Tract of land containing 640 acres lying on the Northeast Side of Pasquotank River up on the fork where William JOY lives Joining upon the Orphan land of Richd. ALGRAVE, decd & Richd. OVERTON'S land ... for 24 pounds ... 15 Jany. 1711/12. *Signed*: John BISHOP, Mary BISHOP. *Wit*: Tho. SWANN, Henry HP PENDLETON his mark. *Ack*: Pasquotank, 15 Jany 1711/12 John BISHOP with Mary his wife to Mr. Griffith JONES. *Regt*: 17 April 1712.

No. Carolina. Richard GRAY in right of Hannah my wife & Mary LEWIS do assign over all our right title and Interest of the above Patent with the assignment on the back of the Patent to Mr. Jno. AVERY ... 16 Jany. 1711/12. *Signed*: Richd. R GRAY, Mary M LEWIS. *Wit*: W. NORRIS, Danl. GUTHRY. *Ack*: Pasquotank 15 Jany 1711/12 by R. GRAY & Mary LEWIS to Jno. AVERY. *Regt*: 17 April 1812. [sic]

[A:30] No. Carolina. Ashley EVANS of the province aforesd have made and appointed, and do hereby make confirm and appoint my loving wife Eliz. EVANS my true and Lawful Attorney for me and in my name and Stead to ask demand, recover & receive all sums of moving goods Merchandize, Debts, Legacies ... 30 Oct. 1710. *Signed*: Ashley EVANS. *Wit*: Tho. BOYD, Caleb BUNDY. *Ack*: Pasquotank, 15 Jany. 1711/12 this Letter of Attorney was brought in Court & pray'd to be Registered. *Regt*: 17 April 1712.

Edward BRADSHAW of North Carolina ... for 41 pounds ... to be paid by James TOOKE ... sold ... my land and plantation being Situate in the precinct of Pasquotank upon the head of Great flatty Creek ... 200 acres more or less Surveyed for John CALLEY the 16 9ber 1697.
[A:31] 13 Aug. 1711. *Signed*: Edwd. X BRADSHAW. *Wit*: W. NORRIS, Jno. MEADS. *Ack*: in the Precinct Court 1st 9ber 1711. *Regt*: 28 April 1712.

John WARDNER with the free and Voluntary Consent of Sarah my wife ... in Consideration of 3 pounds ... sell ... unto James TOOKE of the Precinct of Pasquotank in the County of Albermarle Gent ... all that land ... formerly entered and Surveyed by Jno. BELMAN as also ... purchased by the said BELLMAN of Jno. WEST ... all which land lies and is Situate on the Island of Croaton Joining upon a Survey belonging to Col. BOYD ... 600 acres ... commonly called and known by the Name of GODFRYS Hammock
[A:32] 22 Sept. 1711. *Signed*: Jno. J WARDNER, Sarah S WARDNER. *Wit*: W. EVERIGIN, H. PARKIMON, Wm. BOOTH. *Ack*: in the Precinct Court 1st 9ber 1711. *Regt*: 28 April 1712.

No. Carolina. Robert TEMPLE of ye Precinct of Pasquotank as well for the love I bear unto Jno. CREECH of the Same Precinct as for and in Consideration of ye Sum of 20 Shillings ... a Certain Tract of Land ... Containing 40 or 50 acres

[A:33] ... upon Aranuse Creek opposite to William ROSS his land, ... to Griffith JONES during his natural life, provided that the said John CREECH shall not Sell nor let ye said land in any wise, and in Case the said John CREECH should die before his wife Tamar CREECH, then I do hereby give and grant unto her the said land during her widowhood and after the Decease of the said Jno. CREECH and the marriage or decease of his wife Tamar then the said land or plantation with all appurtenances thereunto belonging to return unto me ... 28 June 1712. *Signed*: Robt. R TEMPLE his mark. *Wit*: Saml. BERNARD, Eliz. E LUMLEY. *Ack*: Pasquotank, The above Deed of Gift proved in open Court July 15th 1712.

John HUNT of Pasquotank Precinct Gent. for divers good causes and considerations me hereunto moving do give and bequeath to my Log. Grand daughter Eliz. EVANS a certain Mulatto Woman named Rose and her Child Rose she now hath and her increase that ever she shall have to her my said Grand daughter & her heirs forever, appointing my friend Caleb BUNDY to be her Guardian & to have all the said mulattoe womans Servile work with her increase untill my said Grand daughter shall come to the full age of fourteen years provided that the said Caleb BUNDY do find my said Grand daughter, and her Mulatto woman and her increase Sufficient Clothing and Victuals during the aforesaid Term of years, ... but in Case my Grand daughter shall decease before the expiration of the said time, then the said Caleb BUNDY or his order to deliver the said Mulatto Woman with her increase to my Grandsons equally to be divided between Hunt EVANS, John Hunt EVANS and Bartho' EVANS at the Respective age of Fourteen years and in case either of my Grandsons, decease than the said Caleb BUNDY to deliver the said Mulatto Woman with her increase to the Survivors of them at their ages proportionably, ... 18 March 1706/7. *Signed*: Jno. HUNT. *Wit*: Ben PRITCHARD, Eliz E EVANS, Mary M SEYMURE
[A:34] *Ack*: Pasquotank, 13 July 1712 proved by Ben PRITCHARD and Eliz. EVANS. *Regt*: 12 Aug. 1812. [sic]

Wm. BRAY of Pasquotank Precinct in the province of North Carolina ... in consideration of the sum valuable ... sold ... unto Jno. SCARBRO' Planter of the Precinct of Pasquotank in the Province of North Carolina ... one Neck of Land commonly called by the name Barbecued Neck, Beginning at the mouth of a branch at the beaver dam ... to the line of the said BRAY. ... 29 March 1712 ... *Signed*: Wm. WB BRAY his mark. *Wit*: George X SCARBROUGH his mark, Mothus VAUGHAN. *Ack*: Pasquotank, 22 April 1712, Wm. BRAY to Jno. SCARBRO'. *Regt*: 25 April 1712.

[A:35] Alexr. LEFLEAR with the free voluntary Consent of Anne LEFLEAR my lawful wife ... 10 pounds ... paid by Jona JACOCKS Gent. of the Province of North Carolina ... sell ... by estimation 100 acres lying in the precinct of Pasquotank upon Pasquotank River and part of a greater Tract which Richd. MADREN bought of Mr. Tho. ABINGTON ... I the said Alexr. LEFLEAR purchased of Richd. MADREN out of the aforesd Tract as appears by a bill of Sale date the 16th day of July 1710 ... 4 Oct. 1712. *Signed*: Alexr. X LEFLEAR his mark, Anne H LEFLEAR her mark. *Wit*: Jno. PALIN, W. NORRIS. *Ack*: 4, 8ber 1812 [sic] Alexr. LEFLEAR and Anne his wife to Jno. JACOCKS. *Regt*: 12 Jany. 1712/13.

[A:36] Albermarle. North east side of Pasquotank precinct in the Province of Carolina ... John LAWSON with the consent of Anne LAWSON my true and lawful wife for a Valuable consideration ... sold ... unto Jno. HAWKINS of the aforesaid County all that Tract of land lying and being S E upon the Swamp commonly known by the name of RAYMONDS Swamp and on the North side upon Paul LATHAM Line of that tract of land ye aforesd. Paul LATHAM bought of Jno. PHILPOTT containing 150 acres more or less ... 22 Feby. 1711. Before Sealing tis to be understood that this parcell of land is part of the land Paten'd by Jno. DYE. *Signed*: Jno. I LAWSON his mark, Anne X LAWSON her mark. Signed the 6th August 1712. *Wit*: Garrt. PR PURSELL his mark, Jno. J CARTRIGHT his mark, Sar. S ELLIT her mark. *Ack*: Pasquotank, 21 Oct. 1712 Jno LAWSON and Anne his wife to Mr. Jno. HAWKINS. *Regt*: 12 Jan. 1712/13.

[A:37] Pasquotank, Robt. MORGAN of Pasquotank Precinct ... sell 100 acres of land unto Wm. JENNINGS of the same precinct -- which the said MORGAN bought of Bryan GRACE that formerly belonged to Da:. JONES and 50 acres more or less Joining to the said hundred bounding upon the brod neck Swamp ... a parcel of land containing 150 acres formerly belonging to Jno. JONES and Da: JONES as by Deed of Sale may appear ... 10 Sept. 1712. *Signed*: Robt. MORGAN. *Wit*: Richd. MADREN, Anne X MADREN her mark. *Ack*: Pasquotank, 21 Oct. 1712 Mr. Daniel GUTHRYE attorney of Robt. MORGAN to Wm. JENNINGS. *Regt*: 12 Jan. 1712/13.

Pasquotank, I Symon RICE and Elisher my wife do make over all our right, title and Interest of the Conveyance on the other side from me and my heirs to Wm. RAYMOND and his heirs forever. Witness our hands ye 22nd October 1712. *Signed*: Symon RICE, Elisher 8 RICE her mark. *Wit*: W. NORRIS. *Ack*: 22 Oct. 1812. [sic] Symon RICE and Elisher his wife acknowledged the above assignment in open court. *Regt*: 12 Jan. 1712/13.

[A:38] Pasquotank John SYMONS and Peter SYMONS of the Prct. aforesd. ... for the valuable consideration of 27 pounds ... by Anto. HATCH ... Sold ... our Land and plantation Situate lying and being in the forke of Little River bounding on the land formerly belonging to Jno. DAVIS and by him sold and conveyed to Caleb BUNDY containing by Estimation 351 acres ...
[A:39] 20 Jan. 1712/13. *Signed*: Jno. SYMONS, Peter SYMONS. *Wit*: W. NORRIS, Benja. WEST. *Ack*: Pasquotank, 20 Jan. 1712/13. John SYMONS and Peter SYMONS to Anto. HATCH. *Regt*: 25 Jan. 1712/13.

Wm. RELFE of the precinct of Pasquotank in the Province of North Carolina ... for a valuable consideration in hand paid ... by Jo. REDING of the precinct and Province aforesaid ... sold ... my land lying ... upon Pasquotank River ... and containing by estimation 20 acres more or less ...
[A:40] ... 20 Jan. 1712/13. *Signed*: Wm. RELFE. *Wit*: Jno. PALIN, Edmd. GALE. *Ack*: Pasquotank, 20 Jan. 1712/13 Wm. RELFE unto Jo. REDING. *Regt*: 25 Jan. 1712/13.

Pasquotank, Tho. BOYD of the Precinct of Pasquotank in the Province of North Carolina ... with the free and voluntary Consent of Winnefred BOYD my Lawful wife ... and for the valuable consideration of one Negro Boy Value 30 pounds ... paid by Eliz. EVANS

(attorney of Ashley EVANS) of the Province aforesaid ... sold ... my land and plantation ... in the precinct afsd ... lying between the lands of John FFURRE and Anto. MARKAM lately in possession of Tho. JONES but since Escheated by me Thomas BOYD & containing by estimation [blank] acres ...
[A:41] ... 20 Jan. 1712/13. *Signed*: Tho. BOYD. *Wit*: W. NORRIS, Benja. WEST. *Ack*: Pasquotank, 20 Jan. 1712/13 by Thos. BOYD to Eliz. EVANS attorney of Ashley EVANS. *Regt*: 25 Jan. 1712/13.

Caleb BUNDY of the Province of North Carolina with the Consent of Jane BUNDY my Lawful wife and for a valuable consideration
[A:42] ... by Tho. STANTON ... sold ... my land and Plantation lying upon Little River in the Precinct of Pasquotank and bounded between the lands of Anto. HATCH and John MEADS & lately was in Possession and occupation of Robt. WHITE containing by estimation 50 acres ... 21 Jany. 1712/13. *Signed*: Caleb BUNDY, Jane X BUNDY. *Wit*: W. NORRIS, Benja. WEST.
[A:43] *Ack*: Pasquotank, 21 Jany. 1712/13 by Caleb BUNDY and Jane his wife unto Thos. STANTON. *Regt*: 25 Jan. 1712/13.

Thos. STANTON with the free and Voluntary Consent of Mary STANTON my Lawful wife and for the valuable Consideration of 50 acres a tract of Land to me in hand paid ... sold ... unto Caleb BUNDY ... all that my land and Plantation lying and being on Newbegun Creek in the Precinct of Pasquotank, the said land being it which was Hump BOULTONS, and by him conveyed to me ... as appears by his Endorsement on the back of the Patent, which said Land together with another Tract bounds as follows ... Thos. MACKEY's Corner tree ... down the said Creek to the first station of this said land of Henry BOULTONS, and for the other Tract Joining thereon and being Escheat Land a part of a greater Tract, it bounds as follows, ... Thos. STANTONS line ... all which said land (except 5 acres whereon Wm. BROTHERS now lives) contains 274 acres.
[A:44] the said Land was granted by Patent to the said BOULTON bearing date the 16th of March Anno Dom 1693 ... 20 Jany. 1712/13. *Signed*: Tho: STANTON, Mary STANTON. *Wit*: W. NORRIS, Benja. WEST. Pasquotank County, 20 Jany. 1712/13. Tho. STANTON to Caleb BUNDY. *Regt*: 24 Jan. 1712/13.

Pasquotank, Tho. WEST do acknowledge all my right title & Interest of a Conveyance for Land from Robt. WEST bearing date 22 January 174/5 and acknowledged ye 17 April 1705 unto Jno. MCKEEL ... 20 Jan. 1712/13. *Signed*: Tho. WEST. *Wit*: W. NORRIS. *Ack*: Pasquotank, Jany. 20th 1712/13 by Thos. WEST to John MCKEEL. *Regt*: 24 Jany. 1712/13.

[A:45] I the Subscriber do by these presents assign all my right title and Interest of ye within mentioned bill of Sale which was registered ye 28th day of April 1712 unto Robert KEEL or assigns as witness my hand ye 17th Jany. 1712/13. *Signed*: James TOOKE. *Wit*: Henry PARKINSON, Corns. RATCLIFF. *Ack*: Pasquotank, 20 Jany. 1712/13 James TOOKE unto Robt. KEEL. *Regt*: 24 Jany. 1712/13/

John JENNINGS of Pasquotank Precinct in North Carolina with the Consent of Dorithy my wife ... doth assign over all my right title and Interest of this within mentioned Patent of Land unto my daughter Eliz. REDING ... her heirs forever of her body after our decease. ... 1 Jany. 1707. *Signed*: Jno. I JENNINGS, Dorr: JENNINGS. *Wit*: W. WARREN, Mary CARTWRIGHT, Jo. REDING. *Ack*: Pasquotank, 20 Jany. 1712/13 Mr. Jno. JENNINGS by his wife came into Court and acknowledged the above Assignment to Eliz. REDING & her heirs &c. *Regt*: 25 Jany. 1712/13.

21 April 1713 Between Robt. TEMPLE Senr. of Pasquotank Precinct in the County of Albermarle in the Province of North Carolina planter of the one party & Griffith JONES of the County and Province aforesaid ... for 62 pounds Current money of the Province ...
[A:46] ... 250 acres of land more or less lying and being in the fork of Aranuse Creek, it being part of the Tract or Dividend of land the said Robert TEMPLE lives on ... bounded tree between the sd. Robert TEMPLE & Xtopher WILLIAMS ...
[A:47] *Signed*: Robt. R TEMPLE. *Wit*: Augt. SCARBROUGH, Tho. SWANN. *Ack*: Pasquotank, 21 April 1713 Robt. TEMPLE to Griffith JONES. *Regt*: 22 July 1713.

North Carolina, Jerr. EVERRINGTON of the province

aforesaid ... consideration of 11 pounds ... Sold ... my Tract of land being part of a greater Tract bought of Wm. JOY wth 400 acres the one moyety a half part of which being 200 acres the Westward part ... I have transfered over from me ... unto Griffith JONES gent ... conveyed to me &c. by Wm. JOY by his assignment of the draft of 20 July 1708. ...
[A:48] ... 21 April 1713. *Signed*: Jerr: EVERRINGTON, Han: H EVERRINGTON. *Wit*: W. NORRIS, Ffran. DELAMARE. *Ack*: Pasquotank, 21 April 1713 Jerr: EVERRINGTON & Hannah his wife to Griffith JONES. *Regt*: 22 July 1713.

Pasquotank, Thomas SWANN atturney of Jno. CREECH & Tamer his wife do assign over the within mentioned Sale of land from Henry CREECH and Joyce his wife to ye aforesd Jno. and Tamer formerly acknowledged in April 1709 to Mrs. Jane GOTHARD ... 21 April 1713. *Signed*: Tho: SWANN. *Wit*: W. NORRIS, Jno. X DAYLY. *Ack*: Pasquotank, 21 April 1713 Thomas SWANN to Mrs. Jane GOTHERD. *Regt*: 22 June 1713. (See pg. 55.)

North Carolina, Robt. KEEL of the Precinct of Pasquotank ... with the free voluntary Consent of Tamer KEEL my Lawful wife and for the valuable Consideration of 5 pounds ... paid by Robt. ARMOUR of the precinct and Province afsd. ...
[A:49] my land Containing 100 acres being part of a greater Tract granted unto Wm. RAWLYSON by Patent bearing date the 30 March 1704 and by him the said RAWLISON Coveyed over unto me ... by his assignment on the back of the Patent bearing date the 29 March 1708 ... Benjn. GILES line tree ...
[A:50] 21 April 1713. *Signed*: Robt. KEEL, Tamar KEEL. *Wit*: W. NORRIS, Jno. BELL. *Ack*: Pasquotank, 21 April 1713 Robert KEEL and Tamer his wife to Robert ARMOUR. *Regt*: 21 July 1713.

North Carolina, Tho. EMPSON of the precinct of Pasquotank ... consent of Anne EMPSON my lawful wife ... consideration of 2 pounds ... by Mary CASEY of the precinct and Province aforesd. ... Sold ... 50 acres ... part of a greater Tract of land Surveyed for me the said Thomas EMPSON by Richd. LEARY the 23 March 1709/10 ... George HARRIS'S line ...
[A:51] 21 April 1713. *Signed*: Tho: X EMPSON his mark, Anne EMPSON. *Wit*: W. NORRIS, Saml. BERNARD. *Ack*: 21 April 1713 Thomas EMPSON to Wm. NORRIS

attorney of Mary CASEY. *Regt*: 23 July 1713.

Joseph GLAISTER of Pasquotank in the County of Albermarle North Carolina Shoemaker and Mary my wife for ... 200 pounds good and lawful Sterling money of England ... Sold ... to James TOOKE of Little River Merchant in the Province abovesaid
[A:52] all our plantation ... on Newbegun Creek on the South side of the said Creek ... 300 acres bounded on the West side with the Plantation of Samuel PYKE, and on the east Side with the Plantation of Jno. PALIN, ... all manner of Stock and houshold goods ... 22 day of the Second month commonly called april 1713. *Signed*: Jos: GLAISTER, Mary GLAISTER. *Wit*: Matt: PRITCHARD, Evan JONES, Samll. PIKE. *Ack*: 22 April 1713 Jos: GLAISTER & Mary his wife to Ja TOOKE. *Regt*: 23 July 1713.

[A:53] Wm. SAWYER with Mary my wife ... make over ... 200 acres ... being on the NE side of Pasquotank River, beginning at the SW side ... taken out of a Patent of land Containing 600 acres belonging to Wm. JENNINGS of Aronoes Creek & Tho JOHNSON, and now in the possession of Wm. SAWYER which said Patent bearing date the 1 Jan. & in the 31 year of the Possession of our Province of Carolina 1694 which said land we ... do quit claim ... unto John NORTON ... according to an agreement ... 21 April 1710. *Signed*: Wm. SAWYER, Mary SAWYER. *Wit*: Tho: MILLER, Jno. RELFE. *Ack*: Pasquotank, 21 April 1713 Wm. SAWYER & Mary his wife to Jno. NORTON. *Regt*: 25 June 1713.

[A:54] No. Carolina, Jno. DANN son and heir apparent of the within named ... Consideration of the Sum of 35 pounds ... Set over, unto Robert PALMER ... all my right ... to the within mentioned Patent of Land therein contained. ... the said Patent to my decd. father ... 20 April 1713. *Signed*: Jno. I DANN. *Wit*: John PALIN, Thomas MILLER. *Ack*: Pasquotank, 21 April 1713 Jno. DANN to Robert PALMER. *Regt*: 21 June 1713.

Robt. TEMPLE of the precinct of Pasquotank in North Carolina ... assign over ... 250 acres of land of the within mentioned Patent upon the Eastermost branch of Aranuse Creek ... unto Jno. BLISH Mercht. ... granted By Patent to the within mentioned

Wm. COLLINGS &c. ... 21 April 1713. *Signed*: Robt. R TEMPLE. *Wit*: W. NORRIS.
[A:55] *Ack*: Pasquotank 21 April 1713 Robt. TEMPLE to John BLISH. *Regt*: 26 June 1713.

James COTTON of Albermarle in North Carolina Taylor have assigned ... my trusty and well beloved friend Capn. Benja. WEST of the aforesd. County & Government to be my true and Lawful attorney for me and in my name to do, ... 11 Feby. 1711/12. *Signed*: James COTTON. *Wit*: Evan JONES, Bat HEWIT. *Ack*: Pasquotank, 21 April 1713. The above letter of attorney was proved ... *Regt*: 26 June 1713.

Jno. CREECH late Inhabitant of the precinct of Pasquotank in North Carolina doth make constitute and appoint Mr. Thomas SWANN attorney at Law, my true and lawful attorney ...
[A:56] to sell over and acknowledge in open Court all my Land lying on the head of Aranuse Creek ... It being 50 acres more or less to Mrs. Jane GOTTERD ... Likewise my land lying on the North side of ROSS'S Creek ... during my and my wifes natural Life ... 17 Jany. 1712. *Signed*: Jno. CREECH. *Wit*: Henry SWANN, Griffith JONES. *Ack*: 21 April 1713. *Regt*: 27 June 1713.

Tamar CREECH of Pasquotank do appoint ... my Trusty and well beloved friend Tho SWANN to be my true and lawful attorney ... to make over and acknowledge unto Jane GOTTERD ... all my right ... of one Tract of land lying on the North side of ROSS'S branch according to one Deed indorsed by my husband Jno. CREECH as also all my right of Interest of 40 or 50 acres of Land lying in Robt. TEMPLE's Tract of Land as by Deed under the said TEMPLES hand ... 11 Feby 1712/13. *Signed*: Tamar C CREECH. *Wit*: Tho. PASSINGHAM, Griffith JONES. *Regt*: 27 June 1713.

James TOOKE Mercht. in Little River Albermarle County and Province of North Carolina for divers good cause and Considerations ... 200 pounds of Good and Lawful Sterling money of England ...
[A:57] Sold unto Jo GLAISTER of Pasquotank Shoemaker all that my Plantation lying & being in Newbegun Creek on the South side of the said Creek bounded on the West Side with the plantation of Saml. PIKE, and on the East side with the Plantation

of John PALIN the said Plantation Containing 300 acres ... with all Stocks of Cattle and household goods to me thereunto belonging ... 28 day of 5th mo 1713. *Signed*: James TOOKE. *Wit*: Evan JONES, John DAVIS, Jerr: SYMONS. *Ack*: Pasquotank, 21 July 1713 Mr. James TOOKE to Mr. Jos GLAISTER. *Regt*: 23 July 1713.

No. Carolina, Ffrancis HENDRICKE of the precinct of Pasquotank ... with the free Voluntary Consent of Mary HENDRICKE my lawful Wife and for the valuable Consideration of 20 pounds ... paid by Levi CRESSY of the precinct & province afsd. ...
[A:58] ... Sold ... all that my land ... between the lines of George HARRIS & Jno. LEWIS but now in possession of Jno. AVERY & containing ... 200 acres of land ... 11 July 1713. *Signed*: Ffrancis F HENDRICKE. *Wit*: W. NORRIS, Jno. I SCARFE.
[A:59] *Ack*: Pasquotank, 11 July 1713 Ffrancis HENDRICKE to Levi CRESSY. *Regt*: 23 July 1713.

Robt. KEEL of the precinct of Pasquotank in the Province of North Carolina with the free Voluntary consent of Tamer KEEL my lawful Wife & for the valuable Consideration of 5 pounds ... paid by Steph: MASSAGEE of the precinct and Province aforesaid ... sold ... 60 acres of land lying upon Flatty Creek ... Benja. GILES corner tree ... CALLEY'S corner tree, by a branch of Flatty Creek ..
[A:60] ... 21 July 1713. *Signed*: Robt. KEEL. *Wit*: W. NORRIS, Benja. WEST. *Ack*: 21 July 1713 Robt. KEEL to Stephen MASSAGEE. *Regt*: 23 July 1713.

No. Carolina, Michael MURFEY of Pasquotank Precinct doth oblige myself ... to Mr. Jona. JACOCKS of the above precinct ... 40 pounds Sterlg. money to be paid upon demand hereof in merchantable Commodities of the Country at price Current at some Convt. landing in this precinct ... 15 May 1710. The Condition of this present Obligation is Such that if the above bounden Michael MURFEY with Anne his wife either of them ... Surrender and make over a Certain quantity or parcel of land containing by estimation 100 acres ... lying in the side Neck upon Thos. PENDLETONS line, Wm. ARMOURS line Mr. POPES line & Edwd. MAYO'S line ... unto Mr. Jonathan JACOCKS ...
[A:61] ... then this present Obligation to be void

& of no effect ... *Signed*: Michl. X MURFEY, Anne R MURFEY. *Wit*: Jno. BISHOP, Michl. X MURFEY. *Regt*: Pasquotank, 23 July 1713.

No. Carolina, Albermarle Precinct ... Michl. MURFEY with Anne my wife of Pasquotank Precinct do assign ... a Certain piece or Quantity of land containing ... 100 acres ... unto Mr. Jona. JACOCKS of the above Province County & Precinct being for a valuable consideration of 9 pounds 11 shillings & 6 pence ... parcell of land lying now upon record in the Registering book of Writings for Pasquotank Prect. was Confirmed and made over by a Conveyance bearing date the 17th April 1705 by Benja. GILES & Mary his wife unto Capt. Jno. ROBINSON ... & Since confirmed & made over from Capt. Jno. ROBISON unto Thomas PENDLETON ... sd. Tho' PENDLETON with Mary his wife hath sold and confirmed the abovesd. land ... unto Jno. BISHOP ... & the sd Jno. BISHOP with Mary his wife as upon Record it doth appear ... made over the abovesd. land ... unto Michl. MURFEY ... [A:62] ... 18 April 1710. *Signed*: Michl. X MURFEY, Anne R MURFEY. *Wit*: Jno. BISHOP, Mary M BISHOP. *Regt*: Pasquotank, 23 July 1713.

No. Carolina, Samuel PIKE of the Precinct of Pasquotank ... with the free Voluntary Consent of Jane PIKE my lawful wife for ... Consideration of 140 pounds ... paid by Wm. HAIGE ... Sold ... my land and plantation lying & being Scituate on the South side of Newbegun Creek ... between the plantation of Joseph GLAISTER, and now in the Tenure and possession of Capn. Jno. ROBISON & the plantation of Mr. POPE, but now in the Tenure ... of Anne DELAMARE Widow & relict of Francis DELAMARE Decd. and containing by estimation 300 acres ... [A:63] ... as the said land was granted by Patent to Robt. LOWRY & by him assigned to John NIXON ... 20, 8br, 1713. *Signed*: Saml. PIKE, Jane IP PIKE her mark. *Wit*: W. NORRIS, Jno. BELL. *Ack*: Pasquotank, 8br: 20th. 1713 Samuel PIKE & Jane his wife to Mr. James TOOKE. Atty. Mr. William HAIGE. *Regt*: 23rd 8br: 1713.

Pasquotank, Wm. JENNINGS ... make over all my right title and Interest of and unto the within mentioned Patent
[A:64] except what Wm. SAWYER has Conveyed out of

it to Wm. ROSS. To ... Jno. NORTON ... 20, 8ber, 1713. *Signed*: Wm. X JENNINGS his mark, Mary M JENNINGS her mark. *Wit*: W. NORRIS. *Ack*: Pasquotank, 20 Oct. 1713 Wm. JENNINGS & Mary his wife to Capt. Jno. NORTON. *Regt*: 25 Oct. 1713.

Pasquotank, Jno. NORTON of the precinct aforesd. do assign and make over all my right title & Interest of & unto the within mentioned Patent Except what Wm. SAWYER has conveyed out if it to Wm. ROSS. ... to John BLISH ... 20 Oct. 1713. *Signed*: Jno. NORTON, Marg' M NORTON. *Wit*: W. NORRIS. *Ack*: Pasquotank, 20 8ber 1713 Jno. NORTON & Margt. his wife to Jno. BLISH. *Regt*: 26 8ber 1713.

Sollo. DAVIES with the Consent of Sarah DAVIES my lawful wife do by these Presents, give, grant & assign over all our right title & Interest of in and unto the within mentioned Draft of land unto Wm. ROSS ... 26 Jany. 1713/4. *Signed*: Sollo. DAVIS, Sarah DAVIS. *Wit*: W. NORRIS.
[A:65] *Ack*: Pasquotank, 26 Jany. 1713/4 Sollo. DAVIS & Sarah his wife to Wm. ROSS. *Regt*: 5 Ffeby. 1713/4.

Pasquotank, Geo ELIOAT with the Consent of Elizabeth ELIOAT my lawful wife and for a Valuable consideration in hand received of Richd. STAMP ... made over all our right title & Interest of in and unto the within mentioned land and plantation unto the sd. Richd. STAMP ... 26 Jany. 1713/4. *Signed*: Geo: ELIOAT, Eliz E ELIOAT her mark. *Wit*: W. NORRIS. *Ack*: Pasquotank, 26 Jany. 1713/4 Geo. ELIOT and Elizabeth his wife to Richd. STAMP. *Regt*: 5 Ffeby. 1713/4.

No. Carolina, Tho. BOYD Esqr. of ye prct. of Pasquotank ... consideration of 10 pounds in hand paid by Char. OVERMAN of the prect & Province afsd to David ELDER ... Sold ... unto Charles OVERMAN ... within Mentioned Patent ... was granted unto me.
[A:66] ... 20 Oct. 1713. *Signed*: Tho: BOYD. *Wit*: Theo: HASTINGS, Jos. JENKINS. *Ack*: Pasquotank, 20 Oct. 1713. *Regt*: 23, 8br. 1713.

William WILLIAMS do assign ... within mentioned land to Jno. HUMFREYS ... 26, Jany., 1713/4. *Signed*: W. WILLIAMS. *Wit*: W. NORRIS. *Ack*: 26 Jany. 1713/4 by Wm. WILLIAMS to Dan. COEING to Jno. HUMFREY'S. *Regt*: 5 Ffeby. 1713.

Sollo. DAVIES do assign ... within mentioned plat & Land ... to Jno. SANDERLIN ... 26 Jany. 1713/14. *Signed*: Sollo. DAVIES, Sarah DAVIES. *Wit*: W. NORRIS. *Ack*: Sollo. DAVIES to John SANDERLIN ye 26 Jany. 1713/4. *Regt*: 5 Ffeby. 1713/4.

Patrick QUIDLEY of the prect. afsd. do assign ... above mentioned Tract of land to Martin FRANK ... 20 Oct. 1713. *Signed*: Patrick QUIDLEY. *Wit*: W. NORRIS, Jno. BELL. *Ack*: Pasquotank, 26 Jan. 1713/4 [A:67] ... by Pat: QUIDLEY to Martin FRANK. *Regt*: 5 Ffeby. 1713/4.

No. Carolina, Thomas EMPSON of the precinct of Pasquotank ... with the free Voluntary Consent of Ann EMPSON my lawful wife & for ... 3 pounds ... paid by Hen: NICHOLS of the precinct & Province aforesaid ... sold ... my land and Plantation lying in the fork of Nobbs Crook Creek (except that part of it which is sold to Mary CASEY) by and bounding as follows ... sd CASEYS line ... Geo. HARRIS'S line ... 100 acres ...
[A:68] ... 26 Jany. 1713/4. *Signed*: Tho: EMSON, Anne EMSON. *Wit*: D. GUTHRIE, W. NORRIS. *Ack*: 26 Jany. 1713/4 by Tho: EMSON to Hen: NICHOLLS. *Regt*: 5 Ffeby. 1713/4.

Pasquotank, Richd. GRAY with the voluntary consent of my wife Hannah GRAY ... for a valuable consideration in hand received & paid by John AVERY ... Sold ... 390 acres ... 26 Jany. 1713/4. *Signed*: Richd. GRAY, Han: GRAY. *Wit*: W. NORRIS. *Ack*: 26 Jany. 1713/4 Richd. GRAY & Hannah his wife to Jno. AVERY. *Regt*: 5 Ffeby. 1713/4.

Pasquotank County, John PAINE heir apparent of Tho HARRIS decd. in the precinct aforesd. ... for 10 pounds ... paid by Tho WOODLEY ... sell ...
[A:69] ... all my right title claim or interest which by any manner of Way or means that I the said John PAINE as heir apparent of Thomas HARRIS decd. could pretend to the within mentioned Patent & tract of land therein contained ... 26 Jany. 1713/4. *Signed*: Jno PAINE, Mary PAINE. *Wit*: D GUTHRIE, G HARRIS Junr. *Ack*: the day & year aforesaid to

Tho WOODLY by Jno. PAINE. *Regt*: 5 Ffeby. 1713/4.

No. Carolina, Ffran: HENDRICK with the free & voluntary consent of Mary HENDRICK my lawful wife & for ... 10 pounds in hand paid by Robert CARTWRIGHT in the precinct of Pasquotank & Province aforesaid planter ... Sold ... bounding upon the Main Swamp of Newbegun Creek ... Richd. GRAY'S line ... 100 Acres [A:70] ... 26 Jany. 1713/4. *Signed*: Ffran. F HENDRICK. *Wit*: D GUTHRIE, Tho. ROBISON. *Ack*: Pasquotank, 26 Jany. 1713/4 Francis HENDRICK to Robt CARTWRIGHT. *Regt*: 5 Ffeby. 1713/4.

Jno. HUMFREY'S Junr. do assign & make over all my right title & Interest of in and unto the within mentioned land unto Wm. WILLIAMS ... 26 Jany. 1713/4. *Signed*: Jno. HUMFREYS. *Ack*: 26 Jany. 1713/4 to Wm. WILLIAMS. *Regt*: 5 Ffeby. 1713/4.

[A:71] William RELFE Senr. of Pasquotank doth assign over all my right title & Interest of this within mentioned plat of land unto Wm. CARTWRIGHT ... 27 Dec. 1712. *Signed*: Wm. RELFE. *Wit*: Wm. WARREN, Lidia AVERY. *Ack*: 26 Jany. 1713/4 to Wm. CARTWRIGHT by Wm. RELFE. *Regt*: 5 Ffeby. 1713/4.

Pasquotank, Ffrancis HENDRICK Senr. for ... love I bear to my Son Wm. HENDRICK and in exchange for a Tract of land containing 100 acres formerly given by me to my said son Wm. HENDRICK and now him returned to me, do give and grant unto my sd Son 100 acres of land lying and being upon Jno. MORRIS'S line upon the body of Reeds upwards towards the land which was Matth: REASONS ... 25 9ber 1713. *Signed*: Ffra: F HENDRICK. *Wit*: W. NORRIS, Jno. MARTIN. *Ack*: This Deed of Gift was proved ... by Ffrancis HENDRICK to his Son Wm. HENDRICK ye 26 of Jany. 1713/4. *Regt*: 9 June 1714.

26 Jany. 1713/14. Ffrancis HENDRICK Senr. of the Precinct of Pasquotank do give and make over unto my Son Ffrancis HENDRICK Junr. of the same precinct a Certain piece of land Containing 100 acres, lying and binding on Jno. MORRIS between my line & my son Wm. HENDRICKS land paying the rent that is behind. *Signed*: Ffrancis F HENDRICK. *Wit*: Levi CRESSEY, Richd. R GRAY. *Ack*: 26 Jany. 1713/14 Ffrancis HENDRICK ... deed of gift to his Son Ffra: HENDRICK

Junr. *Regt*: 9 June 1713/14.

[A:72] No. Carolina. George HARRIS Junr. of Albemarle County and Pasquotank do assign ... unto Vall. ROE ... an inhabitant of the abovesd Province County & Precinct a certain parcell or quantity of land by estimation 100 acres more or less taken out of a Patent of 300 acres of land Confirmed & granted to the said Geo. HARRIS bearing date ye 4th day of 8ber 1704 and afterwards confirmed and Sold by the Honoble. Robt. DANIEL Esqr. by virtue of a Commission granted to the said Robert DANIEL Depty. Govr. of No. Carolina by Sr. Nathl. JOHNSON Chf. Govr. of North Carolina & South: which sd land lying & being on the SW side of Pasquotank River & the So. Wt. side of Nobs Crook Creek Beginning ... second branch of Nobs Crook creek ... which sd. Land I the sd. Geo: HARRIS Junr. do ... quit claim ... to Vall ROE ... for the consideration of 5 pounds ... 11 April 1710. *Signed*: Geo. HARRIS Junr. *Wit*: Jno. BISHOP, Anne EMSON. *Ack*: 26 Jany. 1713/14. *Regt*: 10 June 1714.

[A:73] Wm. CARTWRIGHT of Pasquotank in the County of Albemarle & Province of North Carolina ... Sum of £39.17.6 Current money of this Province ... Sold to Jerr MUNDEN of the County and Province aforesaid ... my Plantation whereon I now live containing 200 Acres Situate lying & being in Pasquotank aforesaid excepting only one Neck of land beyond the bee tree branch & runing up to the Cypress Swamp ... by Virtue of a Patent bearing date the 29th day of 9ber 1706. ... 26 Jany. 1713/14. *Signed*: Wm. CARTWRIGHT. *Wit*: Robt. MORGAN, Robt. CARTWRIGHT, Jos. GLAISTER. *Ack*: 26 Jany. 1713/14 to Jerr. MUNDEN. *Regt*: 10 June 1714.

Xtopher WILLIAMS ... all my right ... to the above plat of land and within mentioned Sale to my brother James WILLIAMS ... 26 Jany 1713/14. *Signed*: Chris W WILLIAMS. *Wit*: W. NORRIS. *Ack*: 26 Jany. 1713/14 to James WILLIAMS. *Regt*: 10 June 1714.

[A:74] No. Carolina, Geo HARRIS Senr. of the Precinct of Pasquotank in the Province aforesd. with the free voluntary consent of Eliza. HARRIS my lawful wife and for the valuable consideration of 28 pounds ... paid by Wm. NORRIS of the precinct and province aforesaid ... Sold ... the within mentioned Patent and tract of land ... said land was granted unto me by the within mentioned Patent ... 20 Jany ... 1713/14. *Signed*: Geo: HARRIS Senr., Eliza. X HARRIS. *Ack*: 26 Jany. 1713/14 by Geo HARRIS & Eliza. HARRIS to Wm. NORRIS. *Regt*: 10 June 1714.

Jeremh. MURDEN of Pasquotank in North Carolina doth assign over all my right title and Interest of this within mentioned bill of Sale unto Job CARTWRIGHT ... 6 Jany. 1712/13. *Signed*: Jeremiah MURDEN. *Wit*: Wm. RELFE Senr., Wm. RELFE Junr.
[A:75] *Ack*: Pasquotank, 20 April 1714 Jerr. MURDEN & Mary his wife to Job CARTWRIGHT. *Regt*: 5 May 1714.

I the Subscriber do assign all my Whole right and title of the within mentioned bill of Sale ... unto Samuel NORTHEY ... 9 Jany. 1713/14. *Signed*: Jno. TURNER. *Wit*: Robt. LOWRY, Jera. SYMONS Junr. *Ack*: Pasquotank, 20 April 1714 John TURNER to Saml. NORTHEY. *Regt*: 5 May 1714.

I the Subscriber do assign all my Whole right & title of this within mentioned Patent ... unto Samuel NORTHEY ... 9 Jany. 1713/14. *Signed*: Jno. TURNER. *Wit*: Robt. LOWRY, Jera. SYMONS Junr. *Ack*: Pasquotank, 20 April 1714 John TURNER unto Saml. NORTHEY. *Regt*: 5 May 1714.

North Carolina, Gabriel BURNHAM of the Precinct of Pasquotank in the province aforesd ... the Sum of 10 pounds in hand paid ... by Jno. HOBBS
[A:76] of the precinct and County aforesaid ... Sold ... a Tract of Land containing 416 Acres lying and being upon the fork Creek of Pasquotank ...
[A:77] ... 20 April 1714. *Signed*: Gabl. BURNHAM. *Wit*: W. NORRIS, D. GUTHRIE. *Ack*: Pasquotank, 20 April 1714. *Regt*: 5 May 1714.

Pasquotank, Wm. JOY ... Sum of 6 pounds ... by Corns. FOREHAND ... sell ...
[A:78] ... a parcell of land Containing 100 acres being part of a greater Tract Surveyed by me the said Wm. JOY and by me sold out into parcels the aforesd. 100 acres being adjoining on the Eastward of the Plantation whereon I the said William JOY now lives. 19 April 1714. *Signed*: Wm. WI JOY. *Wit*:

W. NORRIS, Jerr EVERTON. *Ack*: Pasquotank, 20 April 1714 by Wm. JOY to Corns. FOREHAND. *Regt*: 6 May 1714.

Pasquotank, Wm. JOY ... Sum of 4 pounds ... paid by Wm. PHILIPS ...
[A:79] ... sell ... a Tract of land Ct. 100 acres lying in the fork of Pasquotank & Joyning upon the land of Gabl. BURNHAM 19 April 1714. *Signed*: Wm. WI JOY. *Wit*: W. NORRIS, Jerr EVERTON. *Ack*: Pasquotank, 20 April 1714 by Wm. JOY unto Wm. PHILIPS. Regt: 6 May 1714.

Pasquotank, Wm. JOY ... Sum of 9 pounds ... paid by Jos. MONK ... sell ... a Tract of Land Ct. 364 acres, known by the name of the Poplar Tables and lying at the head of Pasquotank River. ...
[A:80] ... 19 April 1714. *Signed:* Wm. WI JOY. *Wit*: W. NORRIS, Jerr EVERTON. *Ack*: Pasquotank, 20 April 1714 Wm. JOY to Joseph MONK. *Regt: 6 May 1714*.

Mary RELFE Widow & Exerx. of the last Will & Testament of Thos. RELFE ... sum of 40 Shillings ... paid by Jos MONK & Jerh. EVERINGTON ... Sell ... an Island of land and Swamp adjoining, and known by the names of Joe's Island lying and being on S.W. side Pasquotank River, above the said Relfe's Plantation.
[A:81] the said Joseph & Jeremiah, ... 20 April 1714. *Signed*: Mary M RELFE. *Wit*: W. NORRIS, Jno. BELL. *Ack*: Pasquotank, 20 April 1714 Mary RELFE to Jos MONK & Jerr EVERINGTON. *Regt*: 6 May 1714.

Griffith JONES do assign over all my right and title of the within Patent to ROBT. TEMPLE ... 15 Ffeby. 1713. *Signed*: Griffith JONES. *Wit*: Hen: SWANN, Jane X GODDARD. *Ack*: 20 July 1714 Griffith JONES to Robt. TEMPLE. *Regt*: Primo Dice Octoberis 1714.

No. Carolina, James TOOK of the Precinct of Pasquotank ... Merchant ... Sum of 15
[A:82] pounds ... paid by Jno. DAVIES of the precinct & Province afsd. Planter ... Sold ... one half of my half quarter or one Sixteeth part of all that Island of Roanoak so called and known, ... which I bought of Benja. EDDY, & he bought of Joshua LAMB of New England Gent. as by a Certain Deed of Sale bearing date ye 30th day of December 1712 ...

20 July 1714. *Signed*: James TOOKE. *Wit*: Jno. BELL, W. NORRIS. *Ack*: Pasquotank, 20 July 1714 Mr. Ja. TOOKE to Mr. Jno. DAVIES. *Regt*: 9th day of 8br 1714.

[A:83] No. Carolina, John & Wm. TOMLIN ... for the love and affection we bear unto Geo. LOWE ... Sold ... parcel of land Containing 130 acres being part of a quarter Tract belonging to the said Jno. & Wm. TOMLIN lying and being Situate in the precinct of Pasquotank at the head of Little River ... 20 July 1714. *Signed*: Jno. TOMLIN, Wm. WT TOMLIN. *Wit*: W. NORRIS, Jo: PEGGS. *Ack*: 20 July 1714 by Jno. & Wm. TOMLIN to Geo: LOWE. *Regt*: 9th 8ber 1714.

No. Carolina, Richd. MARDEN of the precinct of Pasquotank ... with the consent of Anne MADREN my lawful Wife & for the Valuable consideration of 16 pounds paid ... by James GREAVES of the precinct & Province afsd. ... Sold ...
[A:84] ... a certain parcel or tract of land lying & being Situate in the precinct aforesd. & binding between the deep branch that Divides this land from the land which was Alexr. LEFLEARS (but Since conveyed to Jona. JACOCKS,) & the branch that lyes by Wm. MARDENS' the sd. land to contain 200 Acres be the same more or less, it being part of my purchase from Mr. Tho ABINGTON as by his assignment on the back of the Patent bearing date the 7th day of 9br 1704 ... 19 July 1714. *Signed*: Richd. MADREN, Anne X MADREN. *Wit*: W. NORRIS, James PRITCHARD.
[A:85] *Ack*: Pasquotank, 20 July 1714 Richd. MADREN & Anne his wife to James GREAVES. *Regt*: 11 8br 1714.

Benja. EDDY of Boston within the County of Suffolk & province of Massachusetts bay in New England shipwright ... for 18 pounds current money of New England ... by James TOOKE of Roanoak within the County of Albermarle in the province of North Carolina Mercht. ... Sold ... my half quarter or one eighth part, the whole in eight equal parts to be divided of all that certain Island of Roanoke aforesd so called & known, ... which I lately purchased of John LAMB of Roxbery within the County of Suffolk aforesaid Gent. & Susannah his wife, ...
[A:86] 30 Dec. 1712 ... *Signed*: Benja. EDDY. *Wit*: Jos. PROUT, Mary MADHAM. *Ack*: I Mary EDDY wife of

the above named Benja. EDDY freely consent to the Sale of the land within mentioned and release and quit claim all right of Dower or thirds therein. *Signed*: Mary EDDY. *Ack*: Boston in New England Jany. 12th 1712 Benjamin EDDY & Mary his wife Acknowledged this Instrument to be their Act & Deed. *Signed*: Isa. ADDINGTON. *Regt*: 11 Oct. 1714.

Pasquotank, Henry KEATON of the prect. aforesd. ... for the consideration of the Exchange of a Patent from Edward SCOTT heir apparent of Stephen SCOTT decd. for the land and plantation whereon the said SCOTT lived & whereon he died ... made over all my right, title and Interest of in and unto the within Mentioned Patent of Land to the sd. Edward SCOTT ... 19 Oct. 1714. *Signed*: Henry KEATON. *Wit*: W. NORRIS, Benja. WEST.
[A:87] *Ack*: Pasquotank, 19 Oct. 1714 Henry KEATON to Edwd. SCOTT. *Regt*: 5th. 9br. 1714.

Pasquotank, Edwd. SCOTT heir apparent of Steph. SCOTT decd. ... for the Consideration of an Exchange of a Patent from Henry KEATON for the land and plantation whereon the said KEATON now lives, have ... assigned & made over all my right title & Interest of in and unto the within mentioned Pattent of Land unto the said Henry KEATON ... from me the sd. Edward SCOTT, as heir apparent to my father Stephen SCOTT, ... 19 Oct. 1714. *Signed*: Edwd. SCOTT. *Wit*: W. NORRIS, Benja. WEST. *Ack*: Pasquotank, 19 8br. 1714 Edwd. SCOTT to Henry KEATON. *Regt*: 5th. 9ber 1714.

No. Carolina, Thos. WOOLEY with Eliza. my wife of Pasqt. Prect. & province aforesd. do ... make over ... unto Mr. Jona JACOCKS ... a certain plantation with the land thereunto belonging ct. 388 Acres belonging formerly to Mr. Wm. COLLINGS decd. Surveyed by Capt. Thos. RELFE deputy Survr. the 12th day of Sept. as appears by the Plot & A tract of land ct. 96 Acres as appears by a Patent formerly belonging to Step VINCENT which by the said Patent bearing date the first day of Jany. in the thirty first Year of our Possession of our sd. Province of Carolina Ano Dom 1694. which sd. Tract or Dividends of Land we the sd. Thos. WOODLEY with Eliz. my wife do ... quit claim ... unto Mr. Jona. JACOCKS ... which said

[A:88] Tracts of Dividends of land being left unto I the sd Thos. WOODLEY a legacy by my uncle Wm. COLLINGS decd. after the death of my Aunt formerly Eliz COLLINGS now wife of the abovesd. Mr. Jona. JACOCKS. ... which by this present writing we the sd. Thos. WOODLEY with Eliza. my wife do forever exclude ourselves of all our right that now is or ever will be from us and our heirs unto Mr. Jona. JACOCKS & his heirs forever, being for a Valuable Consideration by agreemnt by the sd. Thomas WOODLEY & Mr. Jona. JACOCKS made & concluded ... 12 Aug. 1710. *Signed*: Tho. WOODLEY, Eliza E WOODLEY. *Wit*: Eliza E WALLIS, Eliza. H PEALE. *Regt*: Pasquotank, 24 March 1715.

No. Carolina, Eliza. WOODLEY of Pasquotank Prect. do nominate ... my trusty & Well beloved friend Jno. BISHOP to acknowledge the abovesd Sale of land to Jona. JACOCKS ... 30 July 1711. *Signed*: Eliza. E WOODLEY. *Wit*: Jno. MANN, Wm. GRIFFIN. *Regt*: 24 March 1715.

[A:89] Jno. MASON of the precinct of Pasquotank in the province of No. Carolina ... hath appointed Jno. ARMOUR of the precinct aforesaid my ... Attorney ... to acknowledge at next Court ... one Deed of bargain & Sale of a Certain Tract of Land or plantation therein particularly mentioned & Contained and was made & executed by me the said Jno. MASON to the sd. Thos. PENDLETON ... 30 Nov. 1714. *Signed*: John MASON. *Wit*: Danl. RICHARDSON, Ann X PENDLETON. *Proved*: in open Court Jany. 18th day 1714/15 Per Mr. RICHARDSON. *Regt*: 25 March 1715.

No. Carolina, Jno. MASON of the precinct of Pasquotank in the Province of No. Carolina planter ... in consideration of the Sum of 20 pounds Current money of this Province ... Sold ... unto the sd. Thomas PENDLETON of the same district planter ... all that Tract of land lying & being in Pasquotank aforesaid ct. 200 acres ... according to a Patent thereof legally obtained bearing date the 25th day of Ffeby. 1696 by one James GAD and was afterwards viz the 20th day of March 1697 assigned over to Jno. MASON late father of the aforesaid Jno. MASON the Seller of the sd. Tract of land & plantation & was acknowledged ye 19th day of April 1698 in the precinct Court of Pasquotank

[A:90] ... 30th day of 9br. 1714. *Signed*: John MASON. *Wit*: Danl. RICHARDSON, Jno. ARMURE. 9br. 30th 1714 Recd. of Mr. PENDLETON the above mentioned Sum of £20 in full of all Accounts. *Signed*: John MASON. *Wit*: Danl. RICHARDSON, Robt. KEEL.
[A:91] *Ack*: Pasquotank, 18 Jan. 1714 by Jno. ARMURE atturney of Jno. MASON to Tho. PENDLETON. *Regt*: 25 March 1715.

Robt. KEEL & Tamar my wife of Pasquotank precinct in North Carolina ...for the Sum of 30 pounds Curt. money of this Province ... Sold ... to John ARMURE of Pasquotank aforesd. ... all that plantation whereon we now live lying in Pasquotank afsd. ...
[A:92] ... 2nd Dec. 1714. *Signed*: Robt. KEEL, Tamar KEEL. *Wit*: Danl. RICHARDSON, Tho TP PENDLETON. *Ack*: Pasquotank, 18 Jany. 1714/5 Robt. KEEL. (nothing more entered T. J.)

No. Carolina, Henry PENDLETON of the Precinct of Pasquotank & Province aforesd. ... with the free Voluntary Consent of Eliz PENDLETON my lawful wife ... for 15 pounds paid by Jno. BROTHERS of the precinct & province aforesd. ... Sold ... a parcel of land containing 150 Acres lying & being Situate in the prect. afsd. being part of a greater Tract of 300 Acres of land granted to me by Patent bearing date the 19th day of March 1713/4 ... boundeth as follows beginning upon my own line & so running up the Main Swamp to Zach: KEATONS line binding upon the main Swamp from the beginning to the end of the sd. 150 Acres, ...
[A:93] ... 19th Oct. 1714. *Signed*: Hen: PENDLETON. *Wit*: W. NORRIS, Hen. KEATON. *Ack*: Pasquotank, 18th 8ber 1714 Hen PENDLETON & Eliz his wife to Jno. BROTHERS. *Regt*: 24 March 1715.

Danl. MCKEEL do assign over all my right title & Interest of the Within mentioned land with the Assignmts. to Col. Theophis. HASTINGS ... 19 April 1715. *Signed*: Danl. X MCKEEL. *Wit*: W. NORRIS, Jno. BELL. *Ack*: Pasquotank, April 1715 Danl. MCKEEL to Cola. Theo: HASTINGS. *Regt*: 10 May 1715.

[A:94] Jno. JENNINGS of Pasquotank river in North Carolina, doth by these presents give grant, and bequeath unto my daughter Eliza. REDING & her heirs after me, & my wifes decease, my now dwelling plantation with the land ... this the last day of December in the year of our Lord 1707. *Signed*: Jno. II JENNINGS, Dor. DI JENNINGS. *Wit*: Wm. WARREN, Mary CARTWRIGHT, Robt. CARTWRIGHT. *Ack*: Pasquotank, 19 April 1715. The above Deed was proved in Court by the Oath of Wm. WARREN one of the evidences. *Regt*: 17 May 1715.

Pasquotank, Benja. WEST of the prect. afsd. with the Voluntary Consent of Mary WEST my lawful wife, & for the Valuable Consideration of 8 pounds ... paid by Richd. PHAGAN of the Prect. aforesd. ... within mentioned plat of land ... 19th 8br. 1714. *Signed*: Benja. WEST, Mary M WEST. *Wit*: W. NORRIS. *Ack*: 8br. 19th. 1714. per Benja. WEST & Mary WEST to Richd. PHAGAN. *Regt*: 20th 8br. 1714.

[A:95] Pasquotank, Mary CASSE of the Precinct aforesd & Province of North Carolina ... for £8 ... paid by Jno. COOPER of the Prect. & Province aforesd. ... Sold ... all my right, title & Interest in and unto the within mentioned parcel and tract of land therein Contained ... 16th 8br. 1714. *Signed*: Mary M CASEY. *Wit*: WM. NORRIS, Jerr: EVERTON. *Ack*: 8br. 19th 1714 per Mary CASSE to John COOPER. *Regt*: 20th 8br 1714.

Pasquotank, Wm. SIMSON with the Consent of Mary SIMSON my lawful Wife & for a valuable consideration of 7 pounds & 10 Shillings ... paid by Benja. LOVEWELL ... assign over ... 324 acres of land of within mentioned plat of Land ... 18th Oct. 1714. *Signed*: Wm. SIMSON, Mary M SIMSON. *Wit*: W. NORRIS, Jno X WINBURY. *Ack*: 8br. 19th 1714 per Wm. SIMSON & his wife Mary to Benja. LOVEWELL. *Regt*: 20 8ber 1714.

[A:96] No. Carolina, Jno. NEWBY for ... 2 pounds ... sold ... unto Peter SYMONS ... 15 Acres more or less lying and bounding as follows ... down the branch binding on Jno. NEWBY'S Plantn. ... to the mouth of the sd. branch. ... 19th day of April 1715. *Signed*: Jno. I NEWBY. *Wit*: Jo: PEGGS, Robt. CARTWRIGHT, Jerr: SYMONS Junr. *Ack*: 19 April 1715 per Jno NEWBY to Peter SYMONS. *Regt*: 20 April 1715.

Albermarle, Eliz FITZPATRICK the wife of Corns.

FITZPATRICK ... make Jos. WINSHIP my true & lawful Attorney to Acknowledge in my behalf to Matt. CASEWELL all my right of 150 Acres of Land ... being on the North side of Alligator Creek being taken out of a tract of land being 540 Acres that tract the sd. Corns. FITZPATRICK now lives on ... 18 April 1715. *Signed*: Eliza. FITZPATRICK. *Wit*: Jno. WOODLAND, Jno. LARKINGS, Matt M CARSEWELL. [A:97] *Proved*: in Court April 19th 1715 per Jno. WOODAND.

24 Sept. 1714 between Corns. FITZPATRICK & Frances CASEWELL it being for a piece of land that the sd. Corns. FITZPATRICK sold to the sd. Frances CASEWELL it being 150 Acres more or less ... at the head of a branch between Wm. CASEWELL & the sd. Frances CASEWELL & from thence across the Neck ... down the branch to VOSSES line ... to the Pocoson ... this parcel of land I the said Corns. FITZPATRICK ... do Convey and make over unto Matt. CARSEWELL being Francis CASEWELLS heir ... for a valuable consideration already recd. ... this land taken out of a tract ct. 525 Acres lying over the West side of Alligator Creek of Corns. FITZPATRICK. *Signed*: Corns. FITZPATRICK. *Wit*: Jo: WINSHIP, Jno. WOODLAND. *Ack*: Pasquotank, 19 April 1715, The aforesd. Sale was ackd. to Mat. CASEWELL, heir of Francis CASEWELL by Corns. FITZPATRICK. *Regt*: 12 July 1715.

Matt CASEWELL do assign over all my right title and Interest of this within mentioned Patent. to Jno. WOODLAND ... 19 April 1715. *Signed*: Matt M CASEWELL. *Wit*: Danl. GUTHRYE, Corns. FITZPATRICK. *Ack*: 19 April 1715 by Mat. CASEWELL to Jno. WOODLAND. *Regt*: 12 July 1715.

[A:98] Albemarle. Anne WINSHIP the Widow of Bryant FITZPATRICK decd. do by these presents impower, intrust Matt CASEWELL to be my true & lawful Atty. to acknowledge on my behalf to Corns. FITZPATRICK the Son of Bryant FITZPATRICK all the right of my thirds in Alligator Land being fully satisfied for the Same, of a hundred acres of land for my thirds out of a Tract of land called CANONS being already bounded for more or less before several evidences as follows Robt. COOMBS & John COOMBS, & Jos. WINSHIP ... 18 April 1715. *Signed*: Anne A WINSHIP. *Wit*:

Jos: WINSHIP, Jno. I LARKINGS, Jno. WOODLAND. *Proved*: April 19th 1715 per Jos: WINSHIP & Jno. WOODLAND.

Albemarle Jany. 19th 1714/15. Jos WINSHIP of Pasquotank and County afsd. planter & Anne my wife formerly the relict of Bryan FITZPATRICK for & in Consideration of tract of land ct. 100 Acres part of a Tract of land called CANONS as it is already bounded before Robt. KOOMBS Senr. be it more or less ... quit claim to ... my thirds of any land belonging to me or my Wife Anne formerly the Wife of Bryan FITZPATRICK decd. ... *Signed*: Jos: WINSHIP, Ann A WINSHIP. *Wit*: Robt. COOMBS, Jno. X COOMBS, Jos. WINSHIP. *Ack*: 19 April 1715 by Jos WINSHIP & Anne WINSHIP to Corns. FITZPATRICK. Anne WINSHIP to Corns. FITZPATRICK. *Regt*: 12 July 1715.

[A:99] Albemarle: Eliza. FITZPATRICK the Wife of Bryant FITZPATRICK do by these presents ordain & make Matt CASEWELL my true & lawful Atturney to acknowledge unto Jos: WINSHIP my right of 100 acres of land taken out of a Tract of Land called by the name of CANONS already bounded for more or less, before Robt. COOMBS, Jno. COOMBS, & Jos: WINSHIP ... 18 April 1715. *Signed*: Eliz: FITZPATRICK. *Wit*: Jno WOODLAND, Jno. I LARKINGS, Corns. FITZPATRICK. *Proved*: by Jno WOODLAND 19 April 1715. (P. S. No Certificate of Registration. T. J.)

Albermarle January 19th 1714/15. Corns. FITZPATRICK of the precinct of Pasquotank Gent. doth ... make over to Jos: WINSHIP and his wife ANNE ... part of a Tract of lands called CANONS ... the said land being marked and bounded before Robt. COMBS, Esqr. by estimation 100 acres ... *Signed*: Corns. FITZPATRICK. *Wit*: Robt. COMBS, Jno. I COOMBS, Corns. FITZPATRICK. *Ack*: to Jos: WINSHIP by Corns. & Matt CASEWELL Atturney of Eliza. FITZPATRICK. *Regt*: 13 July 1715.

Pasquotank, Matt CASEWELL heir apparent of the above Ffrancis CASEWELL do ... Sell ... unto Robt. COMBS ... the above mentioned Sale and draft of land therein contained ... 19 April 1715. *Signed*: Matt M CASEWELL. *Wit*: W. NORRIS, Jno. BELL.
[A:100] *Ack*: 19 April 1715 Matt CASEWELL heir of Francis CASEWELL to Robt. COMBS. *Regt*: 13 July 1715.

No. Carolina, Jno. HECKLEFIELD of Perquimons precinct in the County of Albemarle in the Province aforesd. Gent. sends Greeting &c. Whereas Robt. WHITE of the County aforesd. did by his bill of Sale or certain Writing under his hand and Seal bearing date on or about the 20 day of Xbr. 1712 bargain Sell ... unto Wm. HALL of the County afsd. one half part of the time & Service of One Negro man called Guy. Viz three days in every week during the life of the sd. Negro, the propty of the said time & Service & negro to be entirely invested in the sd. Wm. HALL. ... And whereas the sd. Wm. HALL by his assignment or Writing under his hand & Seal bearing date ye 4th day of March 1714/15 did for a Valuable Consideration bargain Sell ... all his right title & Interest in & to the aforesd. Negro and all his sd. Weekly Work then due to him to me the above named Jno. HECKLEFIELD ... for the sum of 40 pounds ... in Current publick bills of this Country with the two years Interest now due thereupon by Mr. James TOOKE of the County aforesd. Mercht. the receipt Whereof I acknowledge ... Sold ... unto the sd. James TOOKE ... all my claim, title right property & Interest in & to the sd. Negro & in and to his sd. weekly work, now due or that shall hereafter be due to me ... [A:101] this my assignment to be good & Valid as well agst. the sd. Wm. HALL ... as agst. all & every other person ... 14 April 1715. *Signed*: Jno. HECKLEFIELD. *Wit*: C. GALE, N. CHEVIN, Ed. GALE. Recd. of the within named James TOOKE by the hands of Mr. Danl. RICHARDSON the within mentioned Sum of 40 pounds in bills with the two years Interest making together the sum of 44 pounds & 16 Shillings being the full Consideration money within mentioned ... 14 April 1714. *Signed*: Jno. HECKLEFIELD. *Wit*: C. GALE, N. CHEVIN, Edmd. GALE. *Regt*: 13 July 1715.

The Deposition of Jane TULLY aged 52 years or thereabouts humbly Sheweth, that being at the house of Mr. Jno. JENNINGS about the last of 8br. or thereabout heard the sd. John JENNINGS say that when his wife went to the Court to acknowledge his land that he sent her to do it with all his heart for he was so lame that he could not go himself to do it, but sent her with free Consent to Acknowlege the land over in Ct. to my daughter Eliza. REDING & her heirs forever, & further ye Deponent Sayeth not. *Signed*: Jane IT TULLY. *Wit*: Ex. & Sworn before me May 2. 1715 Benja. WEST. *Regt*: 22 July 1715.

Pasquotk. Precinct, The Deposition of Eliza. SMITH aged 22 years or thereabout Deposeth & Sayeth that she was at the house of Mr. Jno. JENNINGS when he sent wife Dorr. JENNINGS to Ack. his now dwelling plantation to his daughter Eliza. REDING in his behalf & her own & he sd. was so lame that he could not go himself, & he sd. it should do as well, as if he had gone himself, & further the Deponent Sayeth she went with the said Mrs. JENNINGS to the prect. Court where the said plantation was Acknowledged, accordingly but further sayeth not. *Signed*: Eliza. E SMITH. *Wit*: ... July 16. 1715. Benja. WEST. *Regt*: 22 July 1715.

[A:102] This Indenture made the [blank] day of the Eleventh month called Jany 1698. Between Daniel AKEHURST Secty. of North Carolina & Atty. to Jno. DANSON Draper & Citizen of London of one part, & Robt. MORGAN & [blank] his wife of the other part ... doth Covenant and grant unto ye sd. Robt. MORGAN & [blank] his wife all that plantation or Tract of land on which James WILLIAMS now Dwells known by the name of BURDS folly ct. 200 acres, bounding on the Northeast side of the land now in the Occupation of Jos. SPARNON. I do hereby Set & let out to the sd. ... Robt. MORGAN & [blank] his wife & the Surviver of them: To have hold occupy and peaceable enjoy for & during of their & either of their Natural lives paying yearly & every year at on upon ye 20 Decemr. that shall be in the year 1692 500 lbs of good Merchantable porke, to ye abovesd. Jno. DANSON ... & on default thereof, then & every year after during the time of this Lease, it shall & may be lawful for the sd. Jno. DANSON ... to re-enter & the sd. Robert & [blank] MORGAN to expell & into their own possession again to take the sd Plantation ... And the sd. ROBT. MORGAN & [blank] his wife doth Covenant & promise to build or cause to be built on ye sd. Plantation at their own proper cost & charge a dwelling house of thirty foot long & fifteen foot wide and the same to keep uphold & maintain as also the buildings that are already thereon ... And it is convenanted by & between the partyes abovesd. that ye abovesd. Jno. DANSON shall have free eqress &

regress in and upon ye said plantation to hunt for, kill & remove or bear away what cattle may be found belonging to him on the sd. Plantation: In witness hereunto the sd. Danl. AKEHURST & the sd. Robt. & [blank] MORGAN have hereunto Enterchangeably set their hands & Seals ye [blank] day of the Eleventh month called Jany. 1698. *Signed*: Daniel AKEHURST. *Wit*: Phill. TORKESEY, Mary TORKSEY. (P. S. No Certificate of Probate or Registration T. JORDAN)

[A:103] North Carolina. William SIMSON of the precinct of Pasquotank, & Province afsd. with the free & Voluntary consent of Mary SIMSON my lawful wife, and for the Valuable consideration of 6 pounds, to me in hand paid by John WINBURY of the province aforesd. ... Sold ... a parcel of land containing 200 acres ... being part of a greater Tract Containing 524 acres Surveyed for me the sd. SIMSON by Richard LEARY, the sd. 200 acres lying at the Upper end of the said Survey upon the Main Swamp, of Nobs Crook Creek. ... 18. day of 8br 1714. *Signed*: Wm. SIMSON, Mary M SIMSON her mark. *Wit*: [blank] X LOVEWELL her mark. W. NORRIS. *Regt*: 16 Nov. 1715/6. (P. S. No Certificate of Probate.)

Pasquotank, 15 Sept. 1714 between Samuel DAVIES of the Prect. aforsd. in the Province of North Carolina planter, of the one part, and Jane JONES Widow & Relict of William
[A:104] JONES deceased of the other part ... in Consideration of 20 pounds Current money of the Province aforesaid in hand paid Sett unto Ffarm let unto the said Jane JONES a plantation and parcel of land thereunto belonging containing 120 Acres lying & being in Pasquotank aforesd. on the sd. River side, & Joining on the South side of the plantation on which the abovesd. Samuel DAVIS now liveth ... for & during the full time or term of 18 years, beginning on the Ffeast or Nativity of our Lord next ensuing & so to go on till the full Term aforesd. be fulfilled or expired. ... *Signed*: Saml. DAVIS, Jane II JONES Signum. *Wit*: Danl. GUTHRIE, Jona. JACOCKS. *Regt*: 16 Nov. 1715. P. S. (No Certificate of Probate. T. J.)

North Carolina, Albermarle County, Anne BAILEY of Little River in the precinct of Pasquotank have ...

Constituted my loving Husband David BAILY of the County aforesd. to be my true and lawful attorney for me & in my name place and Stead to Acknowledge in Court two Tracts of land, lying on the North side of Herring Creek up Little River from me unto Nathaniel HALL Junr. ...
[A:105] and Grant unto my said Attorney my ... Authority to Act and do in this Case as if I myself were personally present witness ... 16 Jan. 1715/6. *Signed*: Ann BAYLY. *Wit*: Robert LOWRY. *Proved*: by Robert LOWRY in open Court 17 Jany. 1715/6. *Regt*: 25 Jany. 1715/6.

North Carolina, Albermarle County, David BAILEY with Anne my wife do ... make over ... unto Nathaniel HALL Junr. ... for a valuable consideration ... paid ... 18 May 1715. *Signed*: David BAYLY, Ann BAYLY. *Wit*: Samuel BUNDY, Tamar BUNDY. *Ack*: Pasquotank, 17 Jany. 1715/6 by Davd. BAYLEY &c to Na: HALL. *Regt*: 25 Jany. 1715/6.

1713 ... Thomas SAWYER do by these give unto Henry MCDANIEL a Certain piece of land being part of a Dividend taken up by Thomas SAWYER & Surveyed and Patented in my name for 400 acres ... N E side of Pasquotank River adjoining upon John JOY'S which piece is 100 Acres, being part of the above Tract of land which land I Give from me ... to him the sd. Henry MCDANIEL ...
[A:106] ... his part to be on that side of John JONES his line, and so to be continued by the said line for breadth 200 acres to the place began. ... 9 Dec. 1713. *Signed*: Tho T SAWYER his mark. *Wit*: Timothy READING, Richard R. HASTINGS, Henry HB BUCKLEY. *Ack*: Pasquotank 17 Jany. 1715/6 by Thomas SAWYER to Henry MCDANIEL. *Regt*: 25 Jany. 1715/6.

Thomas SAWYER do assign over all my right and title of the Within mentioned Land between Caleb SAWYER and Richard HASTINGS to be equally to be divided between them. *Signed*: Tho SAWYER his T mark. *Wit*: Timothy READING, Henry HB BUCKLEY, Henry H MCDANIEL. *Ack*: 17 Jany. 1715/6 by Thomas SAWYER to Caleb SAWYER & Richard HASTINGS. *Regt*: 25 Jany. 1715/6.

Thomas SAWYER do assign over all my right and title of this land between Caleb SAWYER and Richard HASTINGS to be equally divided between them.

Signed: Tho T SAWYER his mark. *Wit*: Timothy READING, Henry HB BUCKLEY, Henry H MCDANIEL. *Ack*: Pasquotank 17 Jany. 1715/6 by Thomas SAWYER to Caleb SAWYER & Rich. HASTINGS. *Regt*: 25 Jany. 1715/6.

[A:107] North Carolina. Albemarle 1711, Eliza. EVANS by a lawful power of Atturney from my husband Ashley EVANS ... Sold ... one Negro boy named Samson aged about 3 years of age unto Wm. ARMURE ... for 99 years for the Value of 25 pounds ... 4th day of Feby. *Signed*: Eliza. EE EVANS her mark. *Wit*: Jno. MEEDS, Anne MEADS. *Regt*: 18 Feby. 1715/6. (No Certificate of Probate T. J.)

N Carolina, Tho STANTON & Mary my wife of the precinct of Pasquotank ... in Consideration of 52 Shillings ... paid to us by Wm. JAMES of ye prect. & province abovesd. ... Sold ... 50 acres of Land part of a Patent of 351 Acres of land granted to me the sd. STANTON dated ye 22d 9ber 1714 to be laid out beg: at a poplar Thos. STANTON'S Corner tree in Wm. JAMES line ... along Thos. PENDLETON'S ... 7 May 1715. *Signed*: Thos. TS STANTON his mark, Mary M STANTON her mark. *Wit*: Danll. GUTHRIE, Tho. T PENDLETON. *Ack*: 19 July 1715 by Tho. STANTON & Mary to Wm. JAMES. *Regt*: 25 July 1715.

[A:108] I the Subscriber do by these presents assign all my right title & interest of the within Mentioned bill of Sale unto Thos. STANTON or his assigns forever ... 23 Sept. 1715. *Signed*: Robt. KEEL. *Wit*: Jno. MEADS, Benja. B MILLER his mark. *Ack*: 19th 8ber 1715 by Robt. KEEL to Tho. STANTON. *Regt*: 20th 8br. 1715.

No. Carolina, John AVERY of the precinct of Pasquotank in the County of Albermarle & province aforesd. ... with the Voluntary Consent of Lydia AVERY my lawful wife ... for 6 pounds ... paid by Thos. LEWIS of the precinct County & province afsd. ... Sold ... 100 Acres of land being part of a quarter Tract ct. 390 Acres formerly Surveyed by Richd. GREY and by him sold to the sd. Jno. AVERY which sd. 100 Acres is to be taken out of ye afsd 390 including the clear ground with the land adjoining ...
[A:109] ... 19 July 1715. *Signed*: Jno. I AVERY his mark, Lydia L AVERY. *Wit*: W. NORRIS,

Jno. BELL. *Ack*: 19 July 1715 by Jno. AVERY & Lydia his wife unto Thos. LEWIS. *Regt*: 20 July 1715.

No. Carolina, Jno. AVERY of the precinct of Pasquotank in the County of Albermarle and Province afsd. with the Voluntary Consent of Lydia AVERY my lawful wife ... for the sum of £18 ... paid by Thos. WILLIAMS of the prect. County & province afsd. ... Sold ...
[A:110] ... a parcel of land ct. 290 Acres part of a greater Tract of 390 Acres and Surveyed for Richard GRAY and by him Sold to me the said Jno. AVERY, the sd. 290 Acres lying adjoining to the rod tree ridge in the precinct aforesd. ...
[A:111] ... 19 July 1715. *Signed*: Jno. I AVERY his mark, Lidia L AVERY her mark. *Wit*: W. NORRIS, John BELL. *Ack*: 19 July 1715 by Jno. AVERY & Lydia his wife unto Tho: WILLIAMS. *Regt*: 20 July 1715.

No. Carolina, James SPENCE of the prect. of Pasquotank and province afsd. ... with the voluntary consent of Esther SPENCE my lawful Wife ... for the Valuable consideration of 9 pounds ... to Thos. BETTYS of the prect. & province afsd. ... Sold ... a Tract of land ct. 50 Acres ... being part of a greater Tract of Land ct. 640 Acres, by Patent, granted to Robt. TAYLOR & after his decease by Jno. TEEVEAL & Ann his wife Sold into parcells to Jno. MCDANIEL & Wm. LEEFFMAN and by the sd. LEEFFMAN selling his part of 320 Acres to James SPENCE out of which part as afsd. the sd. James SPENCE doth convey ... Beg: at a gum Capt. RELFE'S Corner tree, & up the sd. Line a mile in length.taking for breadth the quantity of 50 Acres then
[A:112] ... down the run of branch to the river ... 11 June 1715. *Signed*: James SPENCE, Esther E SPENCE her mark. *Wit*: W. NORRIS, Benja. WEST. *Ack*: 17 Aug. 1715 by J. SPENCE and his wife unto Tho: BETTYS. *Regt*: 20 Aug. 1715.

London, 2 Feby. 1712/3. Jno. ARCHDALE of Wickham in the County of Bucks Esqr. have ... delivered a Deed of Gift to Nevil LOW, my Grandson and to his father and mother Emll. & Anne LOWE all of Carolina in America of ... all my plantations or Lands
[A:113] in the North side of Newbegun Creek bounding on the lands of Mr. Jo JORDAN and also COLLETON Island or Little Roanoke as in the Same

Deed of Gift expressed ... appoint my Trusty & Well beloved friend Capt. Jno. ROBINSON of Carolina as my lawful attorney to Acknowledge the same Deed of Gift ... *Signed*: Jo: ARCHDALE. *Wit*: George LIGO, Collingwood WARD, George LUMLEY, Elizabeth WHEELRIGHT. *Proved*: in open Court by Mrs. Eliza. ROBINSON formerly WHEELWRIGHT 8br. 19th. 1715. *Regt*: 20th. 8br. 1715.

10 Feby. in the Eleventh year of the Reign of our Sovereign Lady Ann ... 1712/3 that I Jno. ARCHDALE of Wickham in the County of Bucks in the Kingdom of old England Esqr. in and upon consideration of the true Natural Love & affection I bear to my Loving Grandson Nevil LOW of North Carolina ... this Deed of Gift ... all my plantation ... lying on the North side of Newbegun Creek in Pasquotank River in the Province of North Carolina in America and butting and bounding on the land belonging to Jos. JORDAN of the same ...
[A:114] ... And also I further give and grant ... the one half part or moiety of my Island or tract of land commonly called or known by the name of COLLETON Island or Little Roanoke and upon the Decease of ye afsd. Nevil LOW I do give ... unto my Lo: daughter Ann LOW now wife to Emll. LOW of the aforesd. Province mercht. and the Lawful heirs of her body ... Likewise ... the other half part ... of ye. afsd. Island ... unto my loving Son in law Emll. LOW as foresd. & Anne his present wife ... after ye decease of the sd. Emll. LOW and Anne his wife , then I Give the other half part of the aforesd. Island ... to the lawful heirs of the aforesd. my Lo: Daughter Anne LOWE ...
[A:115] ... 2 Feby. 1712/3. *Signed*: Jo: ARCHDALE. *Wit*: George LIGO, Collingwood WARD, George LUMLEY, Eliz: WHEELRIGHT. *Ack*: 8br. 19th. 1715 by Capt. Jno. ROBINSON Attorney of Jno. ARCHDALE Esqr. to Emll. LOW & Anne LOW. *Regt*: 20th. 8br. 1715.

Pasquotank, Wm. HALL & Hannah my wife of Pasquotank prect. afsd for & in Consideration of the Sum of 36 pounds ... paid by Saml. PIKE of the Same place ... Sold ...
[A:116] ... all the Within Patent & lands ... 27th. 8br. 1714. *Signed*: Wm. HALL, Hannah HALL. *Wit*: Wm. HALL, Peter DENMAN. *Proved*: 19th 8br. 1715 Per Peter DENMAN. *Regt*: 20th 8br. 1715.

North Carolina, Albermarle County, David BAYLEY with Anne my wife ... make over all our whole right of this within mentioned Deed of Sale unto Nathl. HALL Junr. ... for a valuable consideration ... to be paid with sd. Sale of land. ... 18 May 1715. *Signed*: David BALEY, Ann BAYLEY. *Wit*: Samll. BUNDEY, Tamer BUNDEY. *Ack*: 17 Jany. 1715/6 by David BAILEY unto Nathl. HALL Junr. *Regt*: 18 Jany. 1715/6.

[A:117] James MKDANIEL do assign all my right title and Interest of the within mentioned land to Thos. COOPER ... 19 July 1715. *Signed*: James M MKDANIEL mark. *Ack*: 19 July 1715 P. James MKDANIEL unto Thos. COOPER. *Regt*: 20 July 1715.

Pasquotank, Thos. STANTON of the prect. afsd. and for a valuable consideration of 25 pounds in hand paid per Wm. BROTHERS ... unto ye within mentioned Sale of land ... 19th. 8br. 1715. *Signed*: Tho TS STANTON, Mary M STANTON. *Wit*: Wm. NORRIS, Jno. BELL. *Ack*: 19th. 8br. 1715 to Wm. BROTHERS by Tho: STANTON and Mary his wife. *Regt*: 20 8br. 1715.

North Carolina, Jno. MASON of the precinct of Pasquotank in the province afsd. Planter ... consideration of the Sum of £30 Current money of this Province to me in hand paid ... Tho PENDLETON of the Same prect. Planter ... Sold ...
[A:118] ... all that Tract of land lying and being in Pasquotank afsd. ct. 200 Acres ... granted according to a Patt. legally obtained bearing date ye 25th Feby. 1696 to one Ja GAD and was afterwards (to wit) ye 20 day of March 1697 Assigned over to Jno. MASON Decd. late father of ye abovesd. Jno. MASON the now Seller of ye said Tract of land & plantation and was Ack. ye 19th day of April 1698 at the prect. Court of Pasqtk. ...
[A:119] ... 4th April 1716. *Signed*: Jno. MASON. *Wit*: N. CHEVIN, Jno. FOURIE, D. RICHARDSON. *Ack*: 17 April by Jno. MASON to Tho: PENDLETON. *Regt*: 21 April 1716.

No. Carolina, Wm. WALLIS & Ann my wife of Pasquotank prect. in Albemarle County, in the province afsd. ... Sarah BELMAN Widow, Exorx. of ye. last Will & Testament of Jno. BELMAN late of ye. sd. County

decd. having in herself good right & lawful Authority to Sell and dispose of all of the lands whereof ye. sd. Jno. BELMAN died Seized of excepting 100 acres called bushy neck given by the sd. Jno. BELMAN in his last Will and Testament to his Sons John & Robt. did by his Conveyance ... bearing date ye. 19th 7ber 1707 grant bargain Sell & make over unto me the sd. William WALLIS a Certain Tract of land ct. 280 Acres lying at the mouth of Flatty Creek on ye Sound side granted to the sd. Jno. BELMAN by Patent bearing date ye first day of Jany. 1694 ... for sum of £8 ... paid by Robert WAYMOUTH of the Prect. & County afsd. ...
[A:120] ... convey and confirm unto ye. sd. Robt. WAYMOUTH ... 100 acres ... being part of before recited tract of land of 280 acres to me granted ... Beg: ... at ye Sound side runing up into the woods ... a Corner tree of Mr. Richd. STAMPS ...
[A:121] ... 17 April 1716. *Signed*: William WALLIS, [blank]. *Wit*: Jno. MANN, Jno. PALIN. *Ack*: 17 April 1716 per Wm. WALLIS to Robt. WAYMOUTH. *Regt*: 21 April 1716.

No. Carolina, Sarah BRADSHAW wife of Edward BRADSHAW late of Pasquotank prect. in the Province aforesd. hath for a Valuable Consideration of 5 pounds Current money of this province ... Sell ... unto Thos. STANTON of the aforesd. Precinct ... all my right ... unto one plantation or tract of land ct. 200 Acres ... lying & being at the head of Flatty Creek in the prect. afsd. Joining on the lands of Benjamin WEST, Jno. FURRY, Steph. MASSAVE & the sd. Thos. STANTONS & which was heretofore Sold by my sd. Husband unto Mr. James TOOKES Mercht. ... 13 April 1716. *Signed*: Sarah X BRADSHAW. *Wit*: W. NORRIS, Jno. DAVIS. *Ack*: 17 April 1716 pr. Sarah BRADSHAW to Thos. STANTON. *Regt*: 28 April 1716.

[A:122] No. Carolina, Robert LOWRY of ye. prect. of Pasquotank & province afsd. & with ye. Voluntary Consent of Sarah LOWRY my lawful wife ... for a Valuable consideration in hand recd. of Mary JACKSON for her son Tho: JACKSON of ye. prect. & province afsd. ... Sold ... unto the sd. Mary JACKSON for her son Thomas ... a Certain Quantity & parcel of land ct. 311 Acres part of a greater tract of land Surveyed for me and by me Patented, ... being the upper part lying & next adjoining upon David BALEYS

line being the one moiety or half part of ye. sd. Whole tract as afsd. ...
[A:123] ... 19th 8br 1715. *Signed*: Robert LOWRY, Sarah S LOWRY. *Wit*: Jno. BELL, W. NORRIS. *Ack*: 19th. 8br 1715 per Robt. LOWRY &c. *Regt*: 22 8br 1715.

Sol. HORNER & Ell. HORNER his wife & Tho: STAFFORD of North Carolina ... Valuable Consideration of £20 ... to be pd. to the sd. Sol. HORNER & Ell. HORNER his wife ... Sold ... unto Patrick BAYLEY ... a tract of land ct. 200 acres ... in Little River in Pasquotank Precinct Beg: at a White Oak Richd. POOLS Corner tree ... to a pine by the River side
[A:124] then up the River ... 29 Xbr. 1715. *Signed*: Sol HORNER, Ell X HORNER her mark, Tho: STAFFORD. *Wit*: Robert LOWRY, Nathll. HALL, Da: BAYLY. *Ack*: 17th Jan. 1715/6 by Sol. HORNER &c unto Pat BAYLY.
[A:125] Memdum. that We Sol. HORNER & Ell. HORNER do free & discharge ye. within mentioned Tho: STAFFORD from any matter Claim concerning ye. within mentioned Bill of Sale except ye. Ack his right to ye. within Mentioned Land as Witness Our hands ye. 29th. October 1715. *Signed*: Sol HORNER, El HORNER. *Wit*: Robt. LOWRY, Na: HALL, Da BAYLY. *Regt*: 20 Jany 1715/6.

Samuel BUNDY of ye precinct of Pasquotank & Province of North Carolina ... with ye voluntary Consent of Tamer BUNDY my lawful wife ... for Valuable consideration of £14 ... paid by Jno. PARISH of Perquimons ... Sold ... a tract of land of 175 Acres, being ye. one moiety or half part of a greater tract of 351 Acres, Surveyed for Peter SYMONS & by him sold to mr. Ant. HATCH & by ye. sd. HATCH sold to me ye. sd. Saml. BUNDY & now by me ye. sd. BUNDY transfered over unto ye. sd. John PARRISH (Viz.) the one moiety or half part ... lying upon the lines of Caleb BUNDYS Plantation in the forke of Little River ...
[A:126] ... 17 April 1716. *Signed*: Samuel BUNDY, Tamer BUNDY. *Wit*: Robt. LOWRY, W. NORRIS. *Ack*: 17 April 1716 To Jno. PARRISH. *Regt*: 1 June 1716.

Pasquotank, Charles OVERMAN of ye. prect. aforesd. with ye. Voluntary Consent of Anne OVERMAN my lawful wife & for ye valuable Consideration of 10 pounds

... paid by Jacob SHERYEAR ... sell ... the above mentioned assignmt. ... 17 April 1716. *Signed*: Charles OVERMAN, Anne OVERMAN. *Wit*: W. NORRIS, Jno. DAVIS. *Ack*: 17 April 1716 by Cha: OVERMAN to Jacob SHERYEAR. *Regt*: 18 April 1716.

[A:127] No. Carolina April ye 17 1716 At a Court held for ye prect. of Pasquotank ... Then came into Open Court Matt PRITCHARD and Acknowledged that he had Sold all his right title & Interest of the eighth part of Roanoke Island which he recovered by due Course of Law from Joshua LAMB within mentioned as appears more fully uppon the records of the Secretarys Office unto Jno. MAN of this province for Valuable Consideration to ye. sd. Matt. PRITCHARD ... (P. S. No Signing or Probate &c. T. JORDAN)

Jno. DAVIS of the prect. of Pasquotank & Province of North Carolina ... for the Valuable Consideration of £60 ... paid by Charles OVERMAN of ye. prect. & province afsd. ... Sold ... all that Tract of land & plantation Commonly called & known by ye. name of Blonds lying ... upon Herring CREEK otherwise called TWIDDY'S Creek upon Little River being the land of Richard CRAGG & by him patented the which at his decease he bequeathed to Jno. & David BAILEY to be equally divided, the Whole tract ct. 500 Acres the half of which next adjoining to the plantation which was Tho TWEEDY'S to be David BAILEYS & ye. other moyety or half part to be Jno. BAYLY'S ... sold & Conveyed to me ye. sd. Jno. DAVIS ... and now by me the sd. Jno DAVIS sold & conveyed to ye said Charles OVERMAN ... 250 Acres
[A:128] ... 17 April 1716. *Signed*: John DAVIS. *Wit*: W. NORRIS, Jno. SIMSON, Mary MURDEN *Ack*: 17 April 1716 to Charles OVERMAN by Jno. DAVIS. *Regt*: 20 April 1716.

Jno. AVERY with ye Voluntary consent of Lydia AVERY my lawful wife for the Valuable Consideration of 6 pounds Sterl ... paid by Tho: LEWIS of ye prect. & Province afsd. ... sold ... 100 Acres of land ... part of a greater tract of 405 Acres granted by Patt to Fra: HENDRICK ye. 25 Feby 1696. & by him sold to Jno. LEWIS & Same by the sd. LEWIS'S heirs & wife of Richd. GREY widow of the Decd. Jno. LEWIS sold to ye. sd. Jno. AVERY. ye. said land of 100 Acres bounding upon Levi CREECY'S line up to ye. Swamp &

along the Swamp to a marked tree agreed upon by the partys aforesd. ... to the Clear ground belonging to ye. sd. Jno. AVERY where the sd. LEWIS did live ... [A:129] ... 17 April 1716. *Signed*: Jno. I AVERY mark, Lydia L AVERY mark. *Wit*: W. NORRIS. (Memo. No Probate. T. J.)

Pasquotank, Tho. LEWIS of ye. prect. aforesd. with the Voluntary Consent of Sarah LEWIS my lawful wife ... consideration of £12 ... paid by Tho: SMITHSON of ye. prect. aforesd. ... Sell ... all my Estate right ... unto ye. within mentioned Land
[A:130] thereby granted as afsd. ... 17 April 1716. *Signed*: Tho: X LEWIS mark. *Wit*: W. NORRIS, John BELL. *Ack*: 17 April 1716 to Tho. SMITHSON by Tho LEWIS. *Regt*: 7br. 14 1716.

Thos. HOLLOWAY do appoint and make Matthew MIDGET my lawful Atturney to make over two Tracts of land the one to Jno. WITBY, the other to And. WILSON lying on the So. Side of Albemarle Sound in ye. prect of Pasquotank as Witness my hand this 30th. 8br 1712. *Signed*: Tho H HOLLOWAY. *Wit*: Obad: OF FFEUR, Fra: F CASEWELL. Memo. No Certificate of Probate.

Tho. HOLLOWAY of ye. County aforesd do hereby these presents assign all my right ... this within mentioned conveyance unto And. WILSON of the County afsd. ... *Signed*: Tho H HOLLOWAY. *Wit*: Bartho' PHELPS, Danl. D MACKEY. *Ack*: 17 April 1716 to And. WILSON. *Regt*: 18 April 1716..

[A:131] Andrew WILSON do assign over all ye within mentioned Patent from me and my heirs forever unto Matt. MIDGETT ... 29 Oct. 1712 & in ye Eleventh year of the Queen's Reign. *Signed*: And: A WILSON. *Wit*: Corns. FITZPATRICK, Ffra: F CASEWELL, Eben: WHITE. *Ack*: 17 April 1716 to Matt. MIDGET. *Regt*: 18 April 1716.

Anto: HATCH of Pasquotank Prect. do assign my right and title of this Bill of Sale over to Saml. BUNDY for a valuable Consideration of 28 pounds to be paid in Pitch. ... 10th of March 1714. *Signed*: Antho: HATCH. *Ack*: 17 April 1716. *Regt*: 18 April 1716.

No. Carolina, Eml. & Anne LOW of ye. prect. of Pasquotank & Province afsd. ... for ye valuable

Consideration of £40 ... paid by Jno. DAVIS of the precinct & Province afsd. ... sold ... plantation ct. 527 Acres Surveyed for the Honoble. Jno. ARCHDALE Esqr. & by him with other Lands given & granted to us Emll. & Anne LOW as by a Certain Instrument in Writing from under the proper hand and Seal of ye. sd. Jno. ARCHDALE Esquire bearing date in London Ffeby. 2d 1713 now upon record [A:132] in the Registers book of Writings for Pasquotank Precinct ... upon Pasquotank river ... 17 April 1716. *Signed*: Eml. LOW, Anne LOW. *Wit*: [blank] REDING, Na: HALL, Grif. JONES. *Ack*: 17 April 1716. *Regt*: 18 July 1716.

16 April 1716 between Elizabeth JONES of ye. prect. of Pasquotank Widow & relict of Capt. Corns. JONES decd. of ye. one part, & Jon JONES of the same precinct Planter of ye. other part ... [A:133] ... Lords proprietor of Carolina by their Patt & Deed bearing date ye. 9th. day of Jany. 1713/4 did give and grant unto ye. sd. Capt. Corns. JONES a tract of land ct. 536 Acres lying on the NE side of Pasquotank River ... And whereas ye. afsd. Corns. JONES by his last Will and Testament bearing date ye. 8th day of May 1714 hath given devised & bequeathed the aforesd. tract of land ... unto ye. afsd. Eliza. JONES ... in Consideration of the sum of £5 ... paid by Jona. JONES. ... Sold ... parcel of land ct. 150 Acres ... being part of ye. above mentioned 536 Acres & is bounded as sold, on Richards Creek commonly called [blank] being the same tract of land formerly belonging to Saml. MOOR, Junr. & purchased by the same JONES of the sd. MOOR. [A:134] *Signed*: Eliza. JONES. *Wit*: Robt. LOWRY, W. NORRIS. *Ack*: April 17th 1716 to Jona. JONES. *Regt*: 21 April 1716.

16 April 1716 between Eliza. JONES of the prect. of Pasquotank widow and relict of Capt. Corns. JONES decd. of ye one part & Sarah HARRISON of ye. Same precinct Widow ... Lords proprietor of Carolina by their Patent & Deed bearing date ye. 9th. day of Jany. 1713/4 did give and grant unto ye. aforesd. Capt. Corns. JONES a Tract of land of 536 Acres lying on the NE side of Pasquotank River ... And whereas the sd. Corns. JONES by his last Will and Testament bearing date the 8th day of May hath given devised & bequeathed the afsd. tract of land ...

unto the afsd. Eliza. JONES ...
[A:135] ... in Consideration of ye. Sum of 10 pounds Currency ... paid by Sarah HARRISON ... Sold ... parcel of land ct. 100 Acres ... being part or parcell of ye. aforesd 536 Acres. Land Begins on a Swamp Joining to Thos. ELLIOTTS plantation ... to Jos. KINGS (at Seymure) line and along his line to the river ... *Signed*: Eliza. JONES. *Wit*: Danl. RICHARDSON, Eml. LOWE, T. KNIGHT. *Ack*: 16 April 1716 to Sar: HARRISON. *Regt*: April 1716.

Henry CREECH of the Province of North Carolina in the County of Albemarle in ye. precinct of Pasquotank ... in Consideration of the Good Will and Affection I bear unto my lo: bro: Jno. CREECH
[A:136] ... confirm unto ye. said Jno. CREECH ... a Certain tract of land ct. by estimation 50 acres ... on ye. North side of Pasquotank River on the beaver damm Swamp ... Beginning at Mr. Grif JONES line ... to Jno. PAINS line,
[A:137] ... 30 Oct. 1715. *Signed*: Henry H CREECH. *Wit*: Tho: COLLES, Edwd. CARTER. *Ack*: 17 April 1716 to Jno. CREECH. *Regt*: 21 April 1716.

Jno. CREECH of the County of Albermarle in the Province of North Carolina and prect. of Pasquotank plantr. Son of Henry CREECH late of the County Province & prect. aforesd. Decd ... in Consideration of the Sum of 50 pounds Sterling money of Great Britain to me in hand pd. ... by my Bro: Henry CREECH of the County Province & prect. aforesd. planter ... Sold ... all ye Estate right title Interest Share portion ...
[A:138] ... which my sd. father died Seized & possessed of Situate lying and being in the County province & prect. aforesd. ... 29 8ber 1715. *Signed*: Jno. CREECH. *Wit*: Tho: COLLES, Edwd. CARTER. *Ack*: 17 April 1716 to Henry CREECH. *Regt*: 21 April 1716.

North Carolina, Wm. RAWLISON of the precinct of Currituck planter ... Appoint and in my place and Stead put and depute Tobias KNIGHT Esqr. my true and Lawful Atturney for me ... to appear at the next prect. Court to be holden
[A:139] in Pasquotank ... to Acknowledge one Deed of Sale or Conveyance of 120 Acres of land lying at the head of great Flatty Creek ... executed by me to

Jona. JACOCKS Merchant ... 17 Sept. 1716. *Signed*: Wm. WR RAWLISON Signum. *Wit*: Richd. TRANT, Wm. W GRIFFIN. *Proved*: in Open Court 8br. 16 1716 & *Regt*: ye. 18 8br 1716.

William RAWLISON of ye precinct of Currituck in the province of No. Carolina ... Lds. proprirs. of this Province afsd. did by their Deed or Patent bearing date ye. 30th day of March 1704. Give and grant unto me ... tract of Land ct. 120 Acres lying at the head of great flatty Creek in the prect. of Pasquotank Beg: at a Gum by deep run ... Thos. ARMURES Line ... EVINS Line ... Consideration of the Sum of £18 Current money ... pd. by Jona. JACOCKS of ye. Prect. of Pasquotank Mercht. ... Sold ... all that aforesd. plantation or Tract of land ct. 120 Acres ... [A:140] ... 17 Sept. 1716. *Signed*: Wm. WR RAWLISON Signum. *Wit*: T. KNIGHT, Richd. TRANT. *Ack*: 16. 8br 1716 to Jnoa. JACOCKS by Mr. KNIGHT Atty. for Wm. RAWLISON. *Regt*: 18th 8br. 1716.

[A:141] No. Carolina, Thos. STANTON of ye. prect. of Pasquotank & province aforesd. ... Love and affection I have and do bear unto my well beloved Son Elijah STANTON ... do give and grant ... my land & plantation whereon I now live ... after the decease of my Lo: wife Mary STANTON his the sd. Elijah's mother ... the afsd. Deed of Gift from me the said Thomas STANTON to be in force after me and my wifes decease ... 21 Aug. 1716. *Signed*: Thos. TS STANTON. *Wit*: W. NORRIS, John BELL. *Ack*: 21 August 1716. *Regt*: 24 Augt. 1716.

No. Carolina, Honble. Tho: CAREY Esqr. for and in Consideration of the Sum of £100 Crrt. money to me in hand pd. by Na: CHEVIN Esqr. ... Sold ... plantation thereon Situate lying and being on Little River and being that Whereon I now live ... [A:142] 30 Oct. 1707. *Signed*: Thos. CAREY. *Wit*: Edwd. MOSELEY, John HECKLEFIELD, T KNIGHT. *Regt*: 18 April 1716.

Pasquotank, Wm. ARMURE of the prect. aforesd. do Assign and make over all my right title & Interest of in and unto ye. Within mentioned plat of land & land therein Contained unto Danl. GUTHRYE & his heirs & Assigns forever So that a Patent for the Same may Come out in the Name of the sd.

Danl. GUTHRIE ... 26 May 1714. *Signed*: Wm. A ARMURE Signum. *Wit*: Saml. GUTHRIE, Elijah STANTON. *Ack*: 24th. July 1716. *Regt*: 28th. July 1716.

[A:143] Samuel BERNARD of the province of North Carolina in the County of Albemarle ... especially for the Good will and affection I have towards my loving daughters Corderoy BERNARD and Ann BERNARD ... Give ... two young Negroe Girls called Peg. & Sarah (Viz) Corderoy to have Peg & her increase and Ann to have Sarah & her increase ... 16 April 1716. *Signed*: Saml. BERNARD. *Wit*: Jno. BLISH, Jo: SPARNON. *Ack*: 16 April 1716. *Regt*: 18 April.

Pasquotank, Wm. WILSON of the province afsd. do assign and make over all my right title & Interest of the within mentioned Land unto Jno. LOWDEN ... 16 October 1716. *Signed*: Wm. WILSON, Sarah B WILSON. *Wit*: Tho MILLER, Wm. EVERIGIN. *Ack*: 16 8br 1716 to Jno. LOWDEN. *Regt*: 19 8br. 1716.

North Carolina Jany. 13th. 1714/5 I Jos. SPARNON of the prect. of Pasquotank in the County of Abermarle ... do assign over, all my right title & Interest of ye. within mentioned
[A:144] Tract of land unto Wm. BECKETT ... *Signed*: Joseph SPARNON. *Ack*: 17 April 1716 to Wm. BECKETT. *Regt*: 18 April 1716.

No. Carolina, Jno. BELL of ye. prect. of Pasquotank & Province afsd. with the Voluntary Consent of Mary BELL my Lawful wife ... for taking a Patent in my own name for ye. Whole tract of 250 Acres of Land belonging formerly to Hen CREECH and by him Sold out of the Same to me Jno. BELL 40 Acres ye. remainder being 110 Acres of Land lying on the eastermost end of ye. sd. Tract ... Sold ... unto Wm. CREECH & Thos. CREECH ... the aforesd. 110 Acres of Land ... as the Whole was granted to me by Patent bearing date ye. 8th. day of Jany 1715/6 ... 24 July 1716. *Signed*: Jno. BELL, Mary M BELL. *Wit*: W. NORRIS, Wm. W WILLIAMS. *Ack*: 24 July 1716 to Wm. & Thos CREECH. *Regt*: 26 July 1716.

[A:145] William TILLET, Sarah TILLET & John SCARBROUGH Senr. of the County of Albemarle in the Province of North Carolina do ... appoint our Lo: friend Mary SCARBROUGH Senr. our true Lawful and

Undoubted Attorney ... to Acknowledge unto Jno. BLISH Merchant of the County and Province aforesaid ... all Such Deeds of Sale of Lease & Release which we ... have signed unto relating to a Tract of land lying and being on ye North side of Pasquotank River on the head of PRITCHARD Creek of the province & County afsd. ... 9 April 1716. *Signed*: Wm. TILLET, Sarah X TILLET her mark, Jno. SCARBROUGH. *Wit*: Edwd. CARTER, Eliz JONES. *Proved*: in Court April 17. 1716. *Regt*: 18 April 1716.

Wm. TILLET & Jno. SCARBROUGH do assign over all our right title & Interest of in & unto ye within mentioned land to Jno. BLISH ... 17 April 1716. *Signed*: Mary X SCARBROUGH mark Atty. for Wm. & Sarah TILLET. *Wit*: W. NORRIS. *Ack*: 17 April 1716 to Jno. BLISH. *Regt*: 18 April 1716.

[A:146] Jno. BLISH do assign all my right and title of the within mentioned Land to Stephen BURGESS ... 17 April 1716. *Signed*: John BLISH. *Wit*: W. NORRIS. *Ack*: 17 April 1716 to Stephen BURGESS. *Regt*: 18 April 1716.

Wm. JENNINGS of Pasquotank for & in Consideration of Love good Will and Affection that I bear towards my Son in Law Jno. HUMFREYES having & granted ... unto this sd. Jno. HUMFREYES & his wife Elizabeth to them or the Lawful begotten heirs ... and for want of such heirs to return to ye next heirs of the abovesd. Wm. JENNINGS a Certain plantation called Tho: JAMES'S Plantation and all the land thereunto belonging being 80 Acres ... 14 July 1716. *Signed*: Wm. JENNINGS, Mary JENNINGS. *Wit*: James M MKDANIEL mark, Mary X MKDANIEL mark. *Ack*: 24 July 1716 to Jno. HUMFREY'S &c by Tho SAWYER Att. for Wm. JENNINGS. *Regt*: 28 July 1716.

Wm. JENNINGS of Pasquotank for & in Consideration of Love good Will and Affection that I bear towards my daughter Mary RODES & Daniel RODES the Son of Thos. RODES & Mary RODES having given and granted ... unto ye. aforesd. Mary RODES during her life and then [A:147] after her Decease to ye.afsd. Daniel RODES son of Thos. RODES & his heirs forever a Certain Tract of land called by ye. name of hickory neck ... 80 Acres ... but if ye. said Danl. RODES die without issue then ye. sd. land to fall to Charity RODES ...

14 July 1716. *Signed*: Wm. JENNINGS, Mary JENNINGS. *Wit*: James M MKDANIEL, Mary X MKDANIEL. *Ack*: 24 July 1716 per Tho SAWYER Atty. for Wm. JENNINGS to Mary RODES. *Regt*: 28 July 1716.

Wm. GRAY of Pasquotank doth assign over unto Geo GRIFFIN ... 125 Acres of land out of a Patent book in my Name bearing date ye. 8h. of 7ber 1714 it being in Consideration that ye. tract of land was taken up betwixt us ye. sd. George GRIFFIN is to begin at the pine on North River Pecoson ... 6th. of July 1716. *Signed*: Wm. W GRAY. *Wit*: Wm. EVERIGIN, Patrick MCGREGOR. *Ack*: 14th. July 1716 to Geo GRIFFIN. *Regt*: 28th July 1716.

Jno. SYMONS Exr. of the last Will and Testament of Jno. TURNER decd. do Assign over the within mentioned Patent to Edwd. TURNER, by Virtue of a Will made by the sd. Jno. TURNER ... the sd. land being sold by me the sd. Jno. SYMONS to the sd. Jno. TURNER decd. but now is assigned as aforesd. to ye. proper use and behoof of ye. sd. Edward [A:148] TURNER his heirs and Assigns forever ... 24 July 1716. *Signed*: John SYMONS, Damaris SYMONS. *Wit*: W. NORRIS. *Ack*: 24 July 1716 to Amy STAFFORD mother of ye. sd. Edwd. TURNER in behalf of ye. said TURNER. *Regt*: 26 July 1716.

Wm. NORRIS with ye. Consent of Susanna my lawful wife do ... sell ... all our right title & Interest of in and unto ye. within mentioned land, as the Same was granted by Patent and assigned over from the within mentioned Geo: HARRIS unto ye. said Wm. NORRIS unto ye sd Wm SIMSON ... 15 day of Xbr. 1715. *Signed*: W. NORRIS, Susanna NORRIS. *Wit*: Eliz X MAJOR, Tho SMITH. *Ack*: 17th April 1716 to Wm. SIMSON. *Regt*: 25th. April 1715.

Jno. KINSEY of North Carolina and County of Albemarle do Aquit & discharge Thos. STAFFORD of ye. Same County aforesaid agst. any bond that was passed formerly passed to pay ye. sd. Jno KINSEY be it in what form or manner. And I do acquit & discharge ye. sd. STAFFORD of all my fathers Estate that I was to possess from my father Wm. TURNER Senr. or Junr. or any of their Children, that the bill or bond Shall be of no effect or force agst. any of his Children or his heirs as being paid ... 25 Dec.

1714. *Signed*: John CK KINSEY. *Wit*: Richd RATCLIFE, Jos. NEWBY, Jno. KC KINSEY. *Regt*: 26 Aug. 1716. (No Probate)

[A:149] August 28th. 1713. Received of Thomas STAFFORD in full of my proper Estate which was my fathers Estate as witness my hand *Signed*: John TURNER. *Wit*: Robt. LOWRY, James X DAVIS, David JACKSON, John WHITE. *Regt*: 26 Aug. 1716.
John TURNER, Wm. TURNER, Edwd. Turner Orphans. August 28 1816. Received of Tho. STAFFORD in full of all Debts dues & demands of their proper Estate before Mr. Robt. LOWRY, Mr James DAVIS Mr David JACKSON & mr. John WHITE as Witnesses thereunto. *Signed*: Robt LOWRY, James DAVIS, David JACKSON, John WHITE. *Regt*: 26 Aug. 1716.

No. Carolina, Thomas PENDLETON & Margt. my wife of pasquotank prect. & Province aforesd. ... Seized of a Certain Tract of land ct. 309 Acres, lying upon flatty Creek by Patent bearing date ye. 17 day of 7br. 1716 ... in Consideration of ye. Natural Love and Affection we have and do bear unto our well beloved daughter Ann CORPE wife of Wm. CORPE of ye. precinct & province afsd. ... Sold ... all that part of the land mentioned in the sd. Patent that lies in a point or between two branches issuing out of ye. sd. Creek, the one half to be laid out contiguous & adjoining to ye. Plantation being 154½ ... acres ...
[A:150] ... for and during ye. Natural Life of the sd. Ann and after her decease ... unto ye. heirs lawfully begotten between ye. said Wm. and Ann CORPE ... 15 day of April in the 3rd. year of our Sovereign Lord George ... 1717. *Signed*: Thos. TP PENDLETON, Margt. X PENDLETON. *Wit*: Jeremiah SYMONS, George LUMLEY, John CORPE. *Ack*: 16 April 1717 to Wm. CORPE &c. *Regt*: 4 May 1717.

No. Carolina, Robert WHITE of the precinct of Pasquotank and province aforesd. ... for a Valuable Consideration of £100 ... paid by Robt. LOWRY of the prect. & province aforesd. ...
[A:151] ... Sold ... all the land lying and being within the Patent of ye. sd. Robt. LOWRY which belong to me the sd. Robert WHITE as eldest Son of Henry WHITE decd. & which was granted to my father in a Kings Patent bearing date ye. 25 day of 7br 1663 the Corner of which Patent being run did come

within the bounds and limits of the sd. Robert LOWRY'S Patent taking some part thereof which part or parcel as aforesd. with all its rights ... make over unto ye. sd. Robert LOWRY ...
[A:152] ... 16 April 1717. *Signed*: Robert WHITE. *Wit*: W. NORRIS, Jno. DAVIS. *Ack*: 16 April 1717 to Mr. Robt. LOWRY by Robt. WHITE. *Regt*: 4 day [blank] 1717.

Rebekah SYMONS Exrx of the last Will and Testament of Thomas SYMONS Decd. for a Valuable Consideration to me in hand paid do hereby ... Sell unto James TOOKE one Negro man named Antoney. ... 23 9br 1707. *Signed*: Rebecca R SYMONS. *Wit*: Peter SYMONS, Elizabeth SYMONS. *Regt*: 6 May 1717. (Note No probate T. J.)

William SIMSON of the prect. of Pasquotank & Province of North Carolina with the free Voluntary of Mary SIMSON my lawful wife ... for ye. Valuable Consideration of 25 pounds, and a plantation lying upon Pasquotank River between Levi CREECY'S & Daniel RODES' ... Sold ...
[A:153] ct. 125 Acres ... being ye. one moyety or half part of that land which was RELF GARDNERS & by him Patented in the year of our Lord 1696. and at his Death given by Will unto his daughter Elisabeth GARDNER as by Will bearing date ye. 31 day of May 1695 and Since by the sd. Eliz. GARDNER given and granted unto me the sd. Wm. SIMSON ... in a certain Instrument of writing under the proper hand and Seal of ye. said Eliza. GARDNER, from her ... as by ye. sd. Instrument acknowledged in Court of Pasquotk. prect. the 17th day of July 1711 ... also registered in the Registers book of Writings for ye. prect. aforesd. ye. 18th. day of September 1711 which sd. land as aforesd. I the sd. Wm SIMSON do Sell ... unto ye. sd. Wm. NORRIS ... And I the sd. Mary SIMSON for ye. Consideration aforesd. do relinquish ... all my right title and Interest of Dowry or thirds of in and Unto ye. sd. land as also do relinquish all my right & title of Inheritance as being the eldest daughter
[A:154] of the sd, Relfe GARDNER ... 15 Dec. 1715. *Signed*: William SIMSON, Mary M SIMSON. *Wit*: Eliz X MAJOR her mark, Thos. SMITH. *Ack*: 17 April 1716 by Wm. SIMSON and John SIMSON atty. for Mary SIMSON to Wm. NORRIS. *Regt*: 20 April 1716.

Pasquotank, Mary SIMSON wife of Wm. SIMSON and eldest daughter of Ralfe GARDNER decd. do freely & Voluntary of my own Accord make & Constitute my trusty friend John SIMSON to be my true and lawful Attorney ... to Acknowledge unto Wm. NORRIS ... all my right ... either by Dowry or title of Inheritance of in and unto that plantation & land which was lately in possession of my said Husband Given unto him by Eliza. GARDNER & given & bequeathed to her by her father Ralfe GARDNER ... 17 April 1716. *Signed*: Mary M SIMSON. *Wit*: Cha: OVERMAN, Thos. X SMITHSON. *Proved*: 17th April 1716.

Perquimans, Richd. LEARY of the prect. aforesd. do Constitute and appoint my Trusty friend Mr. Robt. KEEL to be my true and lawful Attorney ... to appear at ye. prect. Court of Pasquotank and Acknowledge unto Patrick KELLY & all of ye. Province of Maryland a Deed of Sale of land by me granted unto ye. said Patrick KELLY ... 16 March 1716/17. *Signed*: Richd. LEARY. *Wit*: Thos. RELFE. *Proved*: by Tho. RELFE 16 July and *Regt*: 24 July 1717.

[A:155] Sarah LEARY wife of Richd. LEARY do Constitute and appoint my friend Mr. Robt. KEEL to be my true and lawful Attorney ... to Acknowledge in the prect. Court of Pasquotank a Certain Deed of Sale by my husband granted to Patrick KELLY yt. to say my right of Dower ... 16 March 1716/17. *Signed*: Sarah LEARY. *Wit*: Thos. RELFE. *Proved*: by Tho. RELFE 16 July and *Regt*: 24 July 1717.

Richd. LEARY of the Prect. of Perquimans in the Province of North Carolina planter ... in Consideration of ... 13 pounds Currt. Money of North Carolina to him in hand paid ... by Pat. KELLY late of the province of Maryland ... Sold ... a Certain Tract of land Containing by Estimation 320 Acres ... in the fork of Pasquotank River ... by Land Surveyed in the name of Wm. JOY ... ye. said River Pecoson commonly called ... Wm. JOYS upper Quarter ... [A:156] ... 16 March 1716/17. *Signed*: Rich. LEARY. *Wit*: E. WINGETT, Jno. HOLDSWORTH, Tho: RELFE. *Ack*: by Robt. KEEL Attorney & to Patrick KELLY July 16 1716. *Regt*: 24 July 1717.

Patrick KELLY ... do assign over all my right title

& Interest of ye. Within mentioned to Elizabeth GAMBLING March ye. 30th. 1717. *Signed*: Patrick KELLEY. *Wit*: Gabl. BURNHAM, James GREAVES. *Ack*: 16 July 1717 to Gabl. BURNHAM attorney for Elizabeth GAMBLING. *Regt*: 24 July 1717.

[A:157] North Carolina June 28th 1717. Eliza. GAMBLING in the prect. of Pasquotank and in the Province aforesd. ... appointed my brother in Law Gabriel BURNHAM of the Province & prect. aforesd. to be my true and lawful Attorney ... to get my land from Richard LEARY by way of his Attorney Robert KEEL, and also to Acknowledge a Deed of Gift to my son Joshua GAMBLING bearing date ye. 23d day of May 1717 ... Elizabeth EG GAMBLING her mark. *Wit*: Thomas RELFE, James I JONES his mark. *Proved*: 16 July 1717 by Thos. RELFE and *Regt*: 24 July 1717.

No. Carolina, Eliza. GAMBLING of the prect. of Pasquotank & province aforesd in consideration of the Natural Love & affection which I have & do bear unto my well beloved Son Joshua GAMBLING ... give ... a tract of land lying in the fork of Pasquotank River being the sd. land which I bought of Patrick KELLY and 20 pounds more out of my Estate which was Left me by my father James GAMBLING in his last Will & Testament ... 23 May 1717. *Signed*: Elizab. EG GAMBLING her mark. *Wit*: W. NORRIS, Row. R BUCKLEY. [A:158] *Ack*: July Court in 1717 ye. 16 day by Gabl. BURNHAM Attorney of Eliza. GAMBLING. *Regt*: 24 July 1717.

17 day of June in ye. third Year of our Sovereign Lord George ... King ... 1717. Between Emll. LOW of ye. prect. of Pasquotank and County of Albemarle in the province of North Carolina Merchant and Ann LOW his wife of the one part & John CONNER of ye. Same place Merchant of ye. Other part ... by a Patent bearing date ye. 26 day of Feby. 1696 ... unto Major Samll. SWANN a Tract of Land of 467 Acres ... at the mouth of Newbegun Creek and bounded by the sd. Creek on the South by Pasquotank River on ye. east by a Creek called AKEHURST Creek on ye. West and the land of Mr. Daniel AKEHURST on ye. North: ... And whereas the sd. Major Saml. SWANN by his assignment endorst on ye back of ye. said Grant or Patent bearing date ye. 27 day of Feby 1696 ... Sell unto the Honble. John ARCHDALE Esqr. ... And whereas the sd.

John ARCHDALE by his Deed of
[A:159] Gift bearing date ye. 2d. day of Feby ... did give ... to his Grandson Nevil LOW son of the abovesd. Emll. & Ann LOW and after his decease unto ye. sd. Ann Low ... forasmuch as the sd. Nevil LOW is Since dead ... the sd. Emll. LOW and Ann LOW ... in Consideration of ye Sume of £150 Currt. money of this Province ... paid by ... John CONNER ... Sell ... all ye aforesd. tract of Land ct 467 Acres ... except ye. Several lots part of ye. sd. tract of land as are already Sold ...
[A:160] ...
[A:161] ... *Signed*: Eman. LOW, Anne LOW. *Wit*: Joseph JORDAN, Danll. RICHARDSON, Wm. CARTWRIGHT. *Ack*: 16 July 1717 Emanll. LOW & Ann LOW to Mr. Jno. CONNER. *Regt*: 26 July 1717.

Jno. CONNER ... Allow & Admit that no more or other part ... of ye. within Mentioned tract of land m[?] to Contain 467 Acres is meant and intended by ye. within Written Deed to be bargained for by & Sold to me ... then what doth and shall remain thereout over and above such part ... thereof as was heretofore by the within named Jno. ARCHDALE Esqr. bargained for and Sold to Nicholus NOY Esqr. Jos. JORDAN Gent. & Ffilia Christi JORDAN his now wife being 200 Acres more or less, and then called and known by ye. name of CHANCEY'S Plantation and Whereon the sd. Jos. JORDAN now liveth as by the sd. Deed of bargain and Sale thereof bearing date ye. 7th day of Febry. 1704 ... Jno CONNER ... quit claim to any other part ... of sd. 467 Acres mentioned by the Within Written Deed to be Sold to me ...
[A:162] ... 17 June 1717. *Signed*: Jno. CONNER. *Wit*: Joseph JORDAN, Danll. RICHARDSON, Wm. CARTWRIGHT. *Ack*: 16 July 1717 by Mr. John CONNER to Mr. Emll. LOW & Ann his wife. *Regt*: 27 July 1717.

North Carolina, Emmanuel LOW of the prect. of Pasquotank in the County of Albemarle in the Province afsd. merchant am holden & firmly bound unto John CONNER Merchant in the Sum of 500 pounds Sterling money of great brittain to be paid ... 17 day of June in the third year of ye. reign of our Sovereign Lord George King of great Brittain 1717. The Condition of this Obligation is Such that if ... shall well and truly... keep ... agreements ... in one pair of Indentures of bargain and Sale ... then this Obligation to be Void ... *Signed*: Emanl. LOW. *Wit*: Joseph JORDAN, Danll. RICHARDSON, Wm. CARTWRIGHT. *Regt*: 26 July 1717.

[A:163] North Carolina, Saml. COMMANDER do relinquish all my right ... I had of and to a parcell or part of a tract of land formerly belonging to Mr. John HARVEY my uncle decd. unto Mr. James TOOKE Mercht. now at present possesses yt. Same ... the full Consideration being already pd. And I do impower Nathl. CHEVIN to Acknowledge the Same in any Court of Record. ... 11th of Febry. in the 3rd year of ye. reign of our Sovern. Lord George King of Great Brittain 1716/7. *Signed*: Saml. COMMANDER. *Wit*: N. CHEVIN, Benjn. EDDY. *Ack*: 15 June 1717 by Nathl. CHEVIN attorney ... before me. *Signed*: Christo. GALE Ch: Justice. *Regt*: 24th 7br 1717.

Pasquotank, Jno. DAVIS of ye. prect. aforesd. and Province of North Carolina for ... Consideration of £25 ... paid by James TOOKE Merchant of ye Province and precinct afsd. ... Sold ... the Within mentioned Deed of bargain or Sale of land ... 16 April 1717. *Signed*: John DAVIS, Ruth R DAVIS, her mark. *Wit*: W. NORRIS, Edwd. SCOTT. *Ack*: 16 April 1717 to Mr. J. TOOKE. *Regt*: 24th 7br 1717.

[A:164] No. Carolina, Matthew MIDGET of the precinct of Pasquotank Carpenter ... in Consideration of ye. Sum of £50 ... paid ... by William BARCLIFT of Perquimons Precinct ...Sold ... 540 Acres of land lying upon the South side of Alligator Creek being part of a larger tract of 640 Acres formerly Patented unto me ... bearing date ye. 4 Feby. 1714 the other 100 Acres being by me Sold unto Richd. BURTENSHALL from which it is to be divided by a line ... 27 March 1716. *Signed*: Matthew MIDGET. *Wit*: B. HICKS, Jno. MIXON. *Ack*: 29th March 1716. *Signed*: C. GALE Ch. Just. *Regt*: 12th 9ber 1717.

[A:165] October 17th 1717. Received of Eliza. UPTON Widow and Exorx. of the last Will & Testament of John UPTON decd. one plantation called BUCKINGHAM & one full pewter pot in full of all Legacies ... pursuant to a Will bearing date ye. 30th day of June

1715 ... *Signed*: John U UPTON his mark. *Regt*: 25 January 1717/8.

October 17th 1717. Received of Eliza. UPTON Widow and Exorx. of the last Will and Testament of John UPTON decd. One new feather bed & bolster & pair of holland Sheets and one Worsted Rug 3 New pewter dishes 4 New pewter basins, 4 plates of pewter and one Iron pot in full of all Legacies ... pursuant to a Will bearing date the 30th day of June 1715 ... *Signed*: Peter P BROWN his mark, as marrying Mary the daughter of the said Jno. UPTON decd. *Regt*: 25 Jany. 1717/8.

Jonathan JACOCKS of ye precinct of Pasquotank in ye. Province of North Carolina Gent. ... Whereas the true & absolute Lds. proprietors of Carolina did by their Deed or Patent bearing date ye. 30th day of March 1704 give and grant unto Wm. RAWLINSON of Currituck Precinct ... all yt. plantation or Tract of land ct. 120 Acres lying at the head of great Flatty Creek in the Precinct of Pasquotank ... by deep run ... Tho ARMURES line ... EVANS line ... And whereas the sd. Wm. RAWLINSON by his Deed of Conveyance and bearing date ye. 17th day of 7ber 1716 for a Valuable consideration therein ... Sell ... to me the said
[A:166] Jona. JACOCKS ... the said Patent ... Consideration of the Sum of £12.10 Currt. money of this Province to me in hand pd. by Danl. RICHARDSON of Pasquotank aforesaid Esqr. ... Sold ...
[A:167] ... 30th day of July in the third year of the reign of our Sovereign Lord George King of great Brittain 1717. *Signed*: Jonathan JACOCKS. *Wit*: Tho: BRAY, Tho: HERMAN, Tho: SWANN. *Proved*: 15th 8br. 1717 by Mr. Thomas SWANN. *Regt*: 5th 9br 1717.

Eml. LOWE of the precinct of Pasquotank in the County of Albermarle in the Province of North Carolina merchant ... Whereas Mrs. Anne LOWE my now wife at my special entreaty ... yielded up to John CONNER of Pasquotank aforesaid Merchant ... all her right ... unto a Certain Tract of land lying in Pasquotank aforesaid at the mouth of Newbegun Creek, & is opposite to the land whereon I the said Eml. LOWE now lives yt. ct. 467 Acres, was given and granted to her the said Anne ... after the Decease of her Son Nevel LOWE (Who is Since dead) by her

father the Honourable Jno. ARCHDALE, the then one of the Lds. proprietors
[A:168] of Carolina ... as a recompence & consideration therefore & that my said wife & her children ... may not be Sufferers by such her relinquishing ... Have given ... unto Edwd. MOSELEY of Chowan precinct in the County & Privince afsd. Esqr. & Daniel RICHARDSON of Pasquotank aforesd. Esqr. all the right ... I now have ... in the fouwer following Negroes namely Jupiter, Hany, Bess & Hany, Nero ... to the use & behoof of my self & my said wife during the term of our Joint lives & after my decease if she shall survive me, then to her use and behoof during the term of her natural life, and ... after both our decease, then the absolute property & right in and to the said Negroes themselves or so many of them as shall be then living shall be and Enure to the Child or Children so lawfully begotten on ye body of my said wife ... but in Case no such Child or Children shall be living at the time both our Deceases or at the Decease of the Surviver or longest liver of us then ... to the person or persons ... thereunto appointed by the Surviver of us ... Eml. LOWE doth ... promise ... shall nor may sell ... ye. said Negroes ... without the free Licence and consent of my said Wife & the sd. Edwd. MOSELEY & Danl. RICHARDSON ...
[A:169] 17th day of June in the third year of the Reign of our Sovereign Lord George King of great Britain 1717. *Signed*: Emal. LOW. *Wit*: Wm CARTWRIGHT, Jos. JORDAN, Danl. RICHARDSON. *Ack*: 16the of July 1717 to Mr. MOSELEY & Mr. RICHARDSON. *Regt*: 21 July 1717.

North Carolina, Thomas PALMER and Elizabeth my wife of Pasquotank precinct in Albermarle County ... in Consideration of the Sum of £16.10 Current money of this Province ... paid ... by George ELLIS of the precinct and County aforesd. ... Sell ... all that piece or tract of land lying in the Woods at the head of little flatty Creek or between the branches of little flatty Creek & great flatty Creek being Surveyed for us ... in ... 1709 by Richard LEARY Deputy Surveyor ... ct. 331 Acres ...
[A:170] ... 29th August 1717. *Signed*: Tho: T PALMER The mark of. *Wit*: Jno PALIN, Sarah BULL. *Ack*: 16 Jan. 1717/8 to Geo: ELLIS. *Regt*: 18 Jan. 1717/8.

No. Carolina, Josha. MARKHAM of the precinct of Pasquotank & province aforesd ... consideration of Natural Love and Affection which I have and do bear unto my loving brother Antho: MARKAM of the Same place ... Sold ... my land and plantation lying upon Flatty Creek given and bequeathed unto me in my father Antho. MARKHAMS last Will and Testament ... [A:171] ... 15th October 1717. *Signed*: Josa. MARKHAM. *Wit*: Jno. BELL, W. NORRIS. *Ack*: 15th 8ber 1717. *Regt*: 18th 8ber 1717.

No. Carolina, Anto. MARKHAM of the precinct of Pasquotank & province aforesd ... Consideration of the Natural Love and Affection which I have and do bear unto my Lo. brother Josa. MARKHAM of the Same place ... Sold ...
[A:172] ... all my whole Estate right title ... to the within mentioned land ... 15th October 1717. *Signed*: Anthony MARKHAM. *Wit*: Jno. BELL, W. NORRIS. *Ack*: 15th October 1717. *Regt*: 18th 8ber 1717.

No. Carolina, Joshua MARKHAM of the precinct of Pasquotank & province aforesaid ... in Consideration of the sum of 32 pounds ... paid by James COTTEN of Virginia ... Sold ... all my estate right title ... unto the within Land ... 15th 8ber 1717. *Signed*: Josa. MARKHAM. *Wit*: Jno. BELL, W. NORRIS. *Ack*: 15th 8ber 1717. *Regt*: 18th 8ber 1717.

[A:173] Jno. BILLET of the precinct of Pasquotank in the County of Albermarle ... do make ... my trusty and beloved wife Alice BILLET to be my lawful Attorney to Acknowledge what land I have here given by Deeds of Sale unto my Children that is to Say Saml. WILSON, James BELL, and the wife of James BELL & Nevill BELL ... 24th July 1717. *Signed*: John BILLET. *Wit*: John BELL, John BELL Junr. *Proved*: 8ber 16. 1717. *Regt*: 18. 8ber 1717.

No. Carolina, Whereas the Lords proprietors of Carolina by their great Deed of Grant bearing date the first day of May 1668 did give and grant unto John BILLET of the precinct of Pasquotank and province afsd. a Tract of land of 300 Acres lying in Pasquotank precinct on the South side of the River ... Samuel DAVIS'S Corner tree ... REMPLES Corner

tree ... the said Patent bearing date ye. 30th. day of April 1714 ... John BILLET with the Voluntary consent of Alice BILLET my Lawful wife ... in consideration of the Exchange of another piece of land lying on Poplar Ridge ... Sold ... unto ye. said Saml. WILSON ... 150 Acres of land, it being the land Whereon the Said Samuel WILSON now lives & part of the aforesaid tract of land as by Patent granted ...
[A:174] ... 24th day of July 1717. *Signed*: John BILLET, Alice A BILLET her mark. *Wit*: Jno. BELL Senr, Jno. BELL. *Ack*: 16th 8ber 1717. *Regt*: 18th 8ber 1717.

Henry PENDLETON of the precinct of Pasquotank in North Carolina does by these presents assign Over all my right title & Interest of this Within Patent & plot of land unto Saml. DAVIS of the same place ... 19th Sept. 1716. *Signed*: Henry HP PENDLETON his mark. *Wit*: W. NORRIS.
[A:175] *Ack*: April 16th 1717 to Saml. DAVIS. *Regt*: 18th April 1717.

Charles OVERMAN of ye precinct of Pasquotank and Province of No. Carolina for a Valuable Consideration in hand paid by Danl. JACKSON of the precinct & province aforesd. ... Sold ... 4 Acres & a quarter of the Cypress Swamp lying and being between the Plantations of the said Charles OVERMAN & Danl. JACKSON being the No. East part of the Swamp ... 16th July 1717. *Signed*: Charles OVERMAN. *Wit*: W. NORRIS, John DAVIS. *Ack*: 16 July 1717. *Regt*: 19 July 1717.

[A:176] North Carolina, Saml. BUNDY of ye precinct of Pasquotank & Province aforesd. ... Whereas his Excellency the right Honourable John Lord CARTRET Palatine & the rest of true & Absolute Lds. proprietors according to their great Deed of grant bearing date the first day of May 1668 given to their County of Albermarle under their hands & Seals of their sd. Province did give and grant to me a tract of land ct. 351 Acres lying upon the head of Little River ... which said land was formerly Surveyed for Jno. & Peter SYMONS & by them Sold & assigned over unto Anto. HATCH, and by the sd. Anto. HATCH sold & assigned over to me ye. sd. Saml. BUNDY ... Saml. BUNDY with the Voluntary consent of

Tamer BUNDY my lawful wife and ... for the Valuable consideration of £14 ... paid by Jno. PARRISH of the precinct of Perquimons ... Sold ... the one moiety or half part of the aforesaid tract of Land ct. 351 Acres by Patent granted as aforesd. bearing date ye 13th day of October 1716. the which moiety or half part ct. 175 Acres of land lying and being in the fork of little river upon the lines of Caleb BUNDYS plantation ...
[A:177] ... 16th July 1717. *Signed*: Samuel BUNDY, Tamar BUNDY. *Wit*: W. NORRIS. *Ack*: 16 July 1717. *Regt*: 18 July 1717.

April ye 11th 1717. Jno. HOBBS of the Precinct of Pasquotank in the County of Albermarle have made ... my Loving wife Ffrances HOBBS of ye place aforesaid to be my true and lawful Attorney ... to Acknowledge part of my land to John KITE ... *Signed*: John X HOBBS. *Wit*: Gabl. BURNHAM, John J KITE. *Proved*: & *Regt*: 16 April 1717.

Pasqtk., Jno. HOBBS of precinct aforesaid & Province of North Carolina with the Voluntary consent of Ffrances HOBBS my lawful wife, & for the Valuable consideration of 4 pounds ... paid ... Jno. KITE ... Sold ...
[A:178] ... parcel of Land ct. 80 Acres being part of a greater Tract of [blank] Acres of land by Patent bearing date 27 March 1714 and granted to the said Jno. HOBBS ... lying on the So. Wt. side of the said Jno. HOBBS plantation & to have the breadth of ye. said 80 Acres & for length, to run the full length of the said land according to the Course of the Patent ... 15 April 1717. *Signed*: Jno. HOBBS his X mark, Frances HOBBS her F mark. *Wit*: W. NORRIS. *Ack*: 16 April 1717. *Regt*: 18 April 1717.

Sar. RAYMOND of the province of North Carolina Widow out of the good will & natural affection which I have for and towards my dutiful Children hereafter named do give ... unto my well beloved son Thomas RAYMOND of the Province aforesd. ... one great Iron pot of nine gallons ... two Cows, two Sows and one pewter dish & one pewter plate and as many feathers as will fill a bed tick ...
[A:179] ... as to my handmill I give unto my said son Thomas to be delivered to him after my decease. And further I do give ... unto my dutiful daughter

Mary RAYMOND one feather bed and furniture one Iron pot of Six Gallons, one pewter dish and one pewter plate & one quart pot & one Chest & one Cow & my Linnen Wheel and one mare all which ... to be delivered unto my said daughter Mary RAYMOND ... after my decease only my daughter Sarah RAYMOND to have half the increase of the aforesd. Mare after my decease. And further I Give ... unto my said daughter Sarah RAYMOND one Cow & one ewe and lamb & one pewter dish & one pewter plate, one pewter bason & one pair of fire tongs & one Iron Spit -- one Grid Iron & one looking Glass & one Small table ... after my decease: And further I do give & grant unto my Grand Children Philip TORKSEY Junr. & Sarah TORKSEY to their heirs forever, to each of them one Cow and Calf to be delivered to them after my decease or before as I shall think fit. Further I give unto my daughter Margret TORKSEY One Cow to be delivered after my decease. Further I Give unto my daughter Elizabeth SMITH One Cow to be delivered after my decease, I also give unto my said daughter one Gold ring if my said daughter should decease without a daughter then the said Gold ring to return to my daughter Mary RAYMOND ... 15 Oct. 1717. *Signed*: Sarah S RAYMOND. *Wit*: Saml. BERNARD, Edwd. CARTER. *Ack*: This Deed of Gift 16 Oct. 1717. *Regt*: 18 8br. 1717.

Thomas WOODLEY Cousin & heir apparent to Wm. COLLINS late of Pasquotank precinct in North Carolina decd. and Elizabeth my wife ... Whereas Phil LUDWELL Governor & ye then Council of North Carolina did by Patent bearing date ye. first day of Feby. 1694 give and grant unto William TEMPLE a tract of Land ct. 191 Acres lying on Pasquotank River ...
[A:180] ... [blank] Sold and conveyed to the above named William COLLINS and by the above mentioned Wm. TEMPLE Senr. & Robert & Elizabeth his wife & Elizabeth TEMPLE Widow as in and by a Certain Deed of Sale ... Robert TEMPLE Elizabeth his wife and Elizabeth TEMPLE widow bearing date the 15th day of July 1703 ... and also given by the said Wm. COLLINS in his last Will & Testament to Thos. WOODLEY. Now know ye that We the said Thos. WOODLY & Elizabeth my wife for and in Consideration of 350 Acres of land made and conveyed over to me by Benjamin PRITCHARD & Sarah his wife ... Sold ... all that the above mentioned Tract of land ct. 191 Acres ... 15 April

1718. *Signed*: Thomas WOODLEY, Eliza. WOODLEY. *Ack*: Edwd. SCOTT, Ste SCOTT.
[A:181] *Ack*: 15 April 1718. *Regt*: 3 June 1718.

Ste. RICHARDSON of Pasquotank and Province of North Carolina Planter ... Whereas the true and Absolute Lds. proprietors of Carolina did by their Deed or Patent bearing date ye. 14th day of Jany. 1713/14 Give and grant unto Stephen RICHARDSON a Tract of land ct. 381 Acres lying on ye. So. west side of Pasquotank River ... for a Valuable Consideration to me in hand paid by Jerr. EVERTON of the same place ... Sold ... 40 Acres of the afsd. tract of land ...
[A:182] ... [blank] 1717. *Signed*: Stephen RICHARDSON, Mary M RICHARDSON her mark. *Wit*: W. NORRIS, S. BERNARD. *Ack*: 15th 8ber 1717. *Regt*: 17th 8ber 1717.

Steph RICHARDSON of ye. precinct pasquotank & Province of North Carolina ... for the Valuable consideration of 8 pounds ... paid by Jerr: EVERTON ... Sold ... the within mentioned Pattent of land ... 15th 8ber 1717. *Signed*: Stephen RICHARDSON, Mary M RICHARDSON her mark. *Wit*: W. NORRIS, S. BERNARD. *Ack*: 15th 8ber 1717. *Regt*: 17th 8ber 1717.

Edwd. POPE for a Valuable Consideration ... Sold ... unto Thos. WOODLEY ... the within mentioned Patent of Land
[A:183] ... 15 April 1718. *Signed*: Edward POPE. *Wit*: Edwd. SCOTT, Stephen SCOTT. *Ack*: 15 April 1718. *Regt*: 14 June 1718.

Benja. PRITCHARD with Consent of Sarah Pritchard my lawful Wife & for ye. Valuable consideration of the exchange of another plantation ... Sell ... unto Thos. WOODLEY ... the within mentioned Patent ... 15 April 1718. *Signed*: Benjn. PRITCHARD, Sarah PRITCHARD. *Wit*: Edwd. SCOTT, Ste: SCOTT. *Ack*: 15 April 1718. *Regt*: 14 June 1718.

Jno. RELFE of ye. precinct of Pasquotank and Province of North Carolina with the Voluntary Consent of Elizabeth my wife & for ... the consideration of an Exchange of a Plantation from Jno. MACKDANIEL ... Sold ... tract of Land ct. 300 Acres lying & being on ye. N.W. side of

Pasquotank River ...
[A:184] ... 15 April 1718. *Signed*: John RELFE. *Wit*: [blank] *Ack*: 15 April 1718. *Regt*: 25 June 1718.

Jno. MACDANIELL for divers causes & considerations ... Sold ... unto Jno. RELFE ... the within mentioned ... 15 April 1718. *Signed*: Jno. I MACDANIELL his mark, Eliz E MACDANIELL her mark. *Ack*: 15 April 1718. *Regt*: 25 June 1718.

Jno. NORTON do give and grant unto William JENNINGS and his wife Mary JENNINGS the eastermost room above and below in my house on my plantation in the fork of Aronoose Creek & likewise priviledge of raising of hogs and Cattle and fowls for their own use ... during their Natural lives, and not to let it to any body but to live upon it themselves ... 16 Jany. 1716/1717. *Signed*: John NORTON. *Wit*: Wm. WILSON, Berth B SAXTON. *Proved*: 4th 8ber 1717. *Signed*: Tho: MILLER, John BELL. *Regt*: 25 June 1718.

[A:185] Feby. 20th 1717/8 It is agreed this day between Mrs. Robert PALMER & Mr. Danl. RICE that the lands any ways due to them by Virtue of the Will or otherwise of John DANN lately deceased shall be divided according to the Method following Viz to begin at ye. head of a branch called the bee tree, & so on by a Streight Course to a burnt pine now Standing on the path and from thence continuing the Same course down to the river to be on ye. Same side of the branch Mr. RICE now lives on. This Registered by Petition of Mr. Robert PALMER this 25th of June. *Wit*: W. NORRIS.

Joseph GILFORD of Albermarle ... in consideration of the Sum of 6 pounds Current money of North Carolina to me in hand paid ... by John CARTWRIGHT ... Sold ... a Certain Tract of land ct. by estimation 50 Acres more or less lying and being on the NE side of Pasquotank river beginning at the head of Joseph GILFORDS line & so coming down to the first Cross branch & bounded on the other side by the Pecoson.
[A:186] ... 10 Oct. 1716. *Signed*: Joseph I GILFORD. *Wit*: Phil TORKSEY Senr, Thos. TT TORKSEY. *Ack*: 15 April 1718. *Regt*: 25 June 1718.

North Carolina, Wm. SIMSON of the precinct of

Pasquotank in the province aforesaid with ye. full & Vol. consent of Mary SIMSON my lawful wife, & for the Valuable consideration of 50 pounds in hand paid ... by Jo HACKETT of the precinct aforesaid Ship Carpenter ... Sold ... ye annexed Patent and Tract of land ... I bind myself ... in the Penal Sum of 100 pounds Sterling ... 15 April 1717. *Signed*: Willm. SIMSON, Mary M SIMSON. *Wit*: Tho SWANN, Jno LUMLEY. *Ack*: 15 April 1718. *Regt*: 26 June 1718.

[A:187] Mary WILSON wife of Sam NIXON [*sic*] and daughter of Augt. SCARBRO' decd. of my own accord do make ... my beloved husband Saml. WILSON to be my true and lawful Attorney for me ... to Acknowledge a Deed of bargain & Sale for a tract of land lying and being in Pasquotank River back of Robt. KEELS land, and part of that Tract Surveyed by my father Augustn. SCARBRO' to be Acknowledged to James BELL ... 21 Jany. 1717/8. *Signed*: Mary WILSON. *Wit*: Wm S ARMURE his mark, Danll. D BILLET his mark. *Proved*: by Wm. ARMURE & Danl. BILLET. *Regt*: 23 Jany 1717/8.

Samll. WILSON and Mary my wife heir Apparent of August. SCARBRO' decd. of the precinct of Pasquotank & province of North Carolina ... for the valuable consideration of a Plantation & tract of Land ct. 50 Acres, part of Jno. BILLET'S tract of Land in ye. precinct aforesd. in exchange with James BELL ... Sold ... 100 Acres of land part of a greater Tract of Land Surveyed by our father August. SCARBRO' decd. lying upon Pasquotank River ...
[A:188] ... 18 Nov. 1717. *Signed*: Samuel WILSON, Mary WILSON. *Wit*: Samll. WILSON, Danl. D BILLET, Sarah X BILLET. *Ack*: 21 Jan. 1717/8. *Regt*: 23 Jan. 1717/8.

Wm. RELFE of the Precinct of Pasquotank and Province of North Carolina for ye. valuable consideration of £18 ... paid by Wm. SMITH of the precinct & Province afsd. ... Sold ... a parcel of land ct. 60 Acres ... upon Pasquotank River, beginning at the mouth of broad gut and runing up so far as the head line was Alex. LEFLEARS and so runing down the line Surveyed for me taken
[A:189] out of Danl. RODES'S land being 30 Acres, on that side and 30 Acres out of my Patent ... 15th July 1718. *Signed*: Wm. RELFE. *Wit*: W. NORRIS,

Jno. BELL. *Ack*: 15 July 1718. *Regt*: 16 July 1718.

North Carolina, Benjn. WEST Son and heir apparent of Benjn. WEST of precinct of Pasquotank and Province afsd. do with the Voluntary consent of Eliza. WEST my lawful wife ... for the Valuable consideration of 60 pounds ... paid by Tho: MARKEEL & Province aforesd. ... Sold ... 200 acres of land & plantation ... upon Great Flatty Creek & the plantation whereon ye. said Thos. MCKEEL now lives, Beginning at Flatty Creek bridge ...
[A:190] ... (the remainder of this Deed lost)

Corns. FITZPATRICK of the precinct of Pasquotank & County of Albermarle in his Majesties Province of North Carolina planter for and in Consideration of the Sum of £20 good and lawful Money of great Britain ... Sold ... unto Obadiah FFEAR ... 100 acres ... 4th Ffeby. 1716/7. *Signed*: Corns. FFITZPATRICK. *Wit*: Jno. WOODLAND, Henry COATS. *Ack*: 15th July 1718. *Regt*: 24th 7br 1718.

Corns. FITZPATRICK of Alligator in the County of Albemarle in the Province of North Carolina for and in Consideration ... by George WHITBY Junr. of Alligator in the county and Province aforesaid planter ... Sold ...
[A:191] ... 150 Acres of Land lying on the North side of Alligator Creek, 100 Acres ... Joining on Jos. WINSHIPS line ... 50 Acres ... Joining upon ye. aforesd. 100 it being taken out of that Tract which belongs to the Fort.[?] ... 20 Aug. 1716. *Signed*: Cornelius FITZPATRICK. *Wit*: Jno. WOODLAND, Richd. R WHIDBY. *Ack*: 15 July 1718. *Regt*: 24 7ber 1718.

North Carolina, George WHIDBY Junr. of Alligator in the precinct of Pasquotank & County of Albermarle for & in consideration of the sum of 10 pounds Sterling ... paid by Cornelius FITZPATRICK of Alligator ... Sold ... one half or moiety of a parcel or piece of land ct. 330 Acres lying on ye. north side of Alligator Creek whose Patent bears date ye. 19th day of October 1716 binding on the watry gum branch ... that is to say 105 Acres ...
[A:192] ... 3 April 1718. *Signed*: George WHIDBYE. *Wit*: John WOODLAND, Joseph WINSHIP, Edwd. LININGTON. *Ack*: 15 July 1718. *Regt*: 24 7br 1718.

No. Carolina, Corns. FITZPATRICK of Alligator in ye. precinct of Pasquotank & County of Albermarle for & in Consideration of the sum of 15 pounds current money of North Carolina ... paid by And. OLIVER ... Sold ... one piece of Land called the broad neck on the North side of Alligator Creek near the Houses ... 100 Acres ... binding on Obadiah FEAR Joseph WINSHIPS & HUNTS[?] neck plantn. ... 5 June 1718. *Signed*: Cornelius FITZPATRICK. *Wit*: Edwd. LINNINGTON, Saml. S WEST his mark.
[A:193] Memorandum this above 100 Acres of Land Mr. Corns. FITZPATRICK did lawfully Sell to me, & I paid him for ye. Same but I desire the sd. FITZPATRICK to give Andw. OLIVER this bill of Sale I Selling my right to the said OLIVER and am paid in full for it. ... 5 June 1718. *Signed*: Saml. S WEST his mark. *Wit*: Edwd. LINNINGTON, Andw. X OLIVER. *Ack*: 15 July 1718. *Regt*: 24th 1718.

No. Carolina, Cornelius FITZPATRICK, heir Apparent of Bryan FITZPATRICK Decd. do Assign over all Whole my right and title to Edwd. LINNINGTON from me & my heirs to him and his heirs of ye. within Patent forever ... 15 July 1718. *Signed*: Cornelius FITZPATRICK. *Wit*: W. NORRIS. *Ack*: 15 July 1718. *Regt*: 25 7ber 1718.

Nathl. HALL of Pasqtk. in North Carolina ... consideration of the natural love and affection which I have ... unto my well beloved Son Stephen HALL of the precinct & Province aforesd. ... Sold ... 100 Acres of land part of the tract of land whereon I now live, & lying and being on the So side of a branch to ye. Southward of my plantation ... being the dividing bounds between my sd. Son, Ste: HALL, & my Son Nath. HALL ...
[A:194] ... 15 July 1718. *Signed*: Nathl. NH HALL. *Wit*: W. NORRIS, Jno. BELL. *Ack*: 15 July 1718. *Regt*: 25 Sept. 1718.

Tho SAWYER of the prect. of Pasquotank and Province of North Carolina Planter do make over and Convey to Edward WILLIAMS of the precinct & province aforesaid Canoe builder a certain parcel of Land being taken out of a tract of Land which ye. said SAWYER & WILLIAMS agreed to take up betwixt them equally lying and bounding as followeth ...

Robert MORGAN'S line ... H SAWYER'S line ... Which sd. parcel of land ct. by estimation 376 Acres ... 15 July 1718. *Signed*: Tho T SAWYER his mark. *Wit*: Jno. SAWYER, Antho. HATCH. *Ack*: 15 July 1718. *Regt*: 27th 7ber 1718.

No. Carolina, James MACDANIELL of ye. precinct of Pasquotk. & in the County of Albemarle in the Province of North Carolina ... in Consideration of the Sum of 6 pounds 10 Shillings Current money ... [A:195] ... by Tho: SAWYER Planter of the Precinct & County afsd. ... Set over ... Dividend of land ct. by estimation 50 Acres ... up Pasquotank River and at the head of James MACDANIELLS line and commonly called or known by the name of HARRIS'S ridge ... 15 July 1718. *Signed*: James M MACDANIELL his mark. *Wit*: W NORRIS. *Ack*: 15 July 1718. *Regt*: 27th Sept. 1718.

Jno. RAPIER Son Apparent of Jno. RAPIER deceased late of Pasquotank for ... Valuable consideration of 3 pounds ... paid by Solo. POOLE of ye. prect. afsd. ... Sold ... 67 acres of land & plantation ... upon little river bounded by the land called DENNIS'S on the one side and the plantation whereon ye. said Solo. POOLE now lives, on the other side ... [A:196] ... 15 July 1718. *Signed*: Jno. O RAPIER his mark. *Wit*: W NORRIS, Jno. BELL. *Ack*: 15 July 1718. *Regt*: 27 Sept. 1718.

Amoss TRUEBLOOD of the precinct of Pasquotank and Province of North Carolina ... for the Valuable consideration of 50 pounds ... paid by Jno. TRUEBLOOD of the precinct aforesaid and Province ... Sold ... a certain parcell of land ct. 300 Acres ... upon Oronoes Creek ... Northward to the Mouth of log bridge branch ...
[A:197] ... 15 July 1718. *Signed*: Amoss TRUEBLOOD. *Wit*: W. NORRIS, Jno. FOUREE. *Ack*: 15 July 1718. *Regt*: 27 Sept. 1718.

State of North Carolina, Pasquotank County, March Term 1818. Ordered that John C. EHRINGHAUS Esqr. present Register of this County be appointed to complete the transcribing certain Books in his office, on the same terms & Conditions as was allowed to Thomas JORDAN Sen. late Register; by an Order of September Term 1815.

John TRUEBLOOD of the precinct of Pasquotank & Province of North Carolina ... for the valuable Consideration of £50 ... paid by Amoss TRUEBLOOD of the precinct & province aforesaid ... Sold ... 300 Acres of land part of a greater tract of 600 acres of land granted by late Board dated January 1 1694 ... from the mouth of the Logbridge Branch ... 15 July 1718. *Signed*: John TRUEBLOOD. *Wit*: W. NORRIS, Jno. FOURRE. *Ack*: 15 July 1718. *Regt*: 27 Sept. 1718.

[A:198] Pasquotank, Richd. PHAGAN, for the valuable Consideration of 9 pounds ... paid by Wm. WAYMAN ... sold ... the within mentioned land ... 15 Oct. 1717. *Signed*: Richd. PHAGAN his mark. *Wit*: W NORRIS. *Ack*: 16 Oct. 1717. *Regt*: 1 Oct. 1718.

North Carolina: James JONES of the precinct of Pasquotank & province afores: ... for the valuable Consideration of 3 pounds ... paid by John BRIGHT of the precinct & province aforesaid ... sold ... 50 Acres ... 21 Oct. 1718. *Signed*: James II JONES his mark. *Wit*: W NORRIS. *Ack*: 21 Oct. 1718 to John BRITE. *Regt*: 19 Nov. 1718.

[A:199] North Carolina: James JONES of the prect. of Pasquotank & Province aforesd: ... for the more valuable Consideration of 5 pounds ... paid by Henry BRIGHT of the precinct & province aforesd. ... sold ... 80 Acres ... part of a greater tract by patent granted to Wm. JOY & by him assigned & made over to me ... 21 Oct. 1718. *Signed*: James II JONES his mark. *Wit*: W NORRIS. *Ack*: 21 Oct. 1718 to H. BRIGHT. *Regt*: 10: Debr: 1718.

North Carolina: Wm. JOY of Pasquotank & Province aforesaid; ... for the valuable consideration of 20 pounds ... paid by James JONES of the precinct & province aforesd. ... sold ... the within mentioned patent of land ... 21 Oct. 1718. *Signed*: Wm. WI JOY his mark. *Wit*: W NORRIS. *Ack*: 21 Oct. 1718. *Regt*: 19 Novbr 1718.

[A:200] North Carolina: Wm. JOY of the precinct of Pasquotank & Province aforesaid ... for the valuable consideration of 6 pounds ... paid by Corn: FOREHAND of the precinct & province aforesaid ... sold ...

100 acres; being part of a greater tract, granted to me by Patent bearing date the 16 day of October 1716 ... 21 Oct. 1718. *Signed*: Wm. WI JOY his mark. *Wit*: W NORRIS. *Ack*: to Corn: FOREHAND *Regt*: 25 9br 1718.

North Carolina: Thos. BETTY of the precinct of Pasquotank ... for a valuable consideration in hand already paid; do hereby assign over ... 100 acres ... Mr. Jno. JONES ... 21 Oct. 1718. *Signed*: Thos. BETTY, Mary M BETTY. *Wit*: Jas. BROWN, Corn: FOREHAND. *Ack*: 21 Oct. 1718 to Jno. JONES. *Regt*: 26 Novbr. 1718.

Samuel BERNARD of the province of North Carolina in the County of Albermarle ... for the good will & affection I have towards my loving Sons Samuel BERNARD & Jno. BERNARD, do give ... two young Negroes named or commonly called Tom & Jack viz Samuel to have Tom & John to have Jack ... [A:201] ... 21: day of October 1718. *Signed*: Samuel BERNARD. *Wit*: John BLISH, Thomas COLLES. *Ack*: 21 Oct. 1718. *Regt*: 27th Novbr: 1718.

Wm. BROTHERS ... do assign all my right title & interest, to the above mentioned land, to Jno. MEADS ... 21 Oct. 1718. *Signed*: Wm. W BROTHERS his mark. *Wit*: W NORRIS. *Ack*: 21 Oct. 1718. *Regt*: 27. Novbr: 1718.

North Carolina This Indenture made 21 Oct. 1718; between Robert KEEL of the prect. of Pasquotank & province aforesd & Tamer his wife of the one part & the Honobl. Cott: Wm. REED Esqr. of the other part. Whereas Thomas KEEL late father of the sd Robert KEEL did obtain from the Honobl. Wm. BARTLETT [sic] the late Govr. of Virginia a pattent bearing date the 25. 7br. 1665 [sic] for 800 acres of land, lying in a bay in Pasquotank river ... certified 4 Sept. 1702 under that Colonies Seal, by the Honobl. Francis NICHOLSON Esqr. their Govr. ... Whereas one Will: CRAWFORD Esqr. under some feigned pretence & without any legall power or authority did sell to one Derby SEXTON [blank] the labour of that part of the said 800 Acres whereof the said Robert KEEL now lives, or lately did live, & was lately in the terme[?] & possession of one Augustine SCARBOUROUGH also [?]: & whereto the pretended Title; for the

recovery wharof the said Robert KEEL, did in the month of October 1713 exhibit his Bill in the high Court of Chancery vs the Widow & heirs of the sd. August: SCARBOROUGH & upon a full hearing thereof & of thar answer on the 5 day of November 1714. It was declared ... that the lands & tenements there in question should be & remain to the sd Robert KEEL ... Now this Indenture Witnesseth, that the said Robert KEEL & Tamer his wife for & in Consideration of three Negroes two men & one woman, delivered unto them ... by the said Wm. REED ... sell ... all that part of the 800 Acres of land late in the tennure or occupation of the sd. August. SCARBOROUGH to which he pretended title ...
[A:202] and where the said Robert KEEL now lives, or may lately did live ... *Signed*: Robert KEEL, Tamer X KEEL her mark. *Wit*: John CONNER, John CORP, David Richard John [sic] *Ack*: 21 Oct. 1718 to Cott. Wm. REED by Robert KEEL & Tamer his wife. *Regt*: 21 Nor: 1718.

[A:203] North Carolina: Joab CARTWRIGHT of the prect. of Pasquotank & province aforsd. ... with the free voluntary consent of Lydia CARTWRIGHT my lawful wife ... for the valuable Consideration of 11 pounds ... paid by George HARRIS Junr. of the prect. & province afsd. ... sold ... 100 acres by Will given unto me by my father Thos: CARTWRIGHT dec: & by me sold unto Thos. JOYC[?] & by the sd. Thos. JOIC[?] sold & returned unto me ... known by the name of Jobs old field ... 21 Oct. 1718. *Signed*: Job J CARTWRIGHT his mark, Lidia X CARTWRIGHT her mark. *Wit*: W NORRIS, Levy PURFOY. *Ack*: 21 Oct. 1718 to George HARRIS. *Regt*: 1 Dec. 1718.

[A:204] Henry NICHOLLS of the precinct of Pasquotank & prov. of North Carolina ... free voluntary consent of Mary NICHOLLS my lawful wife ... for the valuable Consideration of 81 pounds ... paid by Edward POPE of the same place ... sold ... 60 acres commonly called blue Buttons; being the land which I bought of Thomas LEWIS, lying upon the southwest side of Pasquotank River above Possam quarter ... 30 Jan. 1717/18. *Signed*: Henry NICHOLLS. *Wit*: W NORRIS, John DAVIS. *Ack*: 15 April 1718 to Ed POPE. *Regt*: 13d xbr 1718.

[A:205] North Carolina. Thomas HENDRICK of the

precinct of Pasquotank & Province afsd. ... for the valuable consideration of 50 pounds ... paid by Captain Benjamin WEST of the prect: & prov: afresd ... sell 635 acres ... the said Land being granted by patent, bearing date the 14 day of December 1715 to my father Francis HENDRICK Doctr. & by him in his life time by will given unto me ... 8 Jun 1717. *Signed*: Thomas H HENDRICK his mark. *Wit*: W NORRIS, Benja. B MILLER his mark. *Ack*: 16 July 1717. *Regt*: 18 July 1717.

[A:206] North Carolina, Thomas HENDRICK of the precinct of Pasquotank & province aforesaid ... make my trusty & well beloved friend William NORRIS, to be my true lawfull Attorney ... to acknowledge unto Capt: Benj: WEST ... a certain tract of Land & plantation, containing 635 acres, commonly called or Known by the name of half way tree ... 8 June 1717. *Signed*: Thomas H HENDRICK his mark. *Wit*: Benja. B MILLER his mark, Benja: WEST. *Proved*: 16 July 1717. *Regt*: 18 July 1717.

Richard MADREN & Ann my wife of Pasquotank precinct in Albermarle County in North Carolina ... whereas the late Honrable Govr. John ARCHIBALD [sic] Esqr. and the Council of North Carolina, aforsd. by pattent; bearing date the 26 day of [blank] 1696, given and granted unto John BELLMAN a tract of land containing 198 Acres, being on the south West side of Pasquotank River ... on Nobs Crook Creek ... John BELLMAN & Sarah his wife, did by their Assignment bearing date the 25th day of October 1700, & then by them acknowledged in the Court of Pasquotank prct. registerd in the Register Book of writing of the precinct of Pasquotank aforesd the 3 day of Decbr 1700 assigned sd patent to the sd Richard MADREN ... in Consideration of the natural love & affection I bear my daughter now wife John RIGGS ... sold ... unto the sd. John RIGGS & Penelope his wife the one half or moiety of the before recited tract of land ... then after their death, to the heirs male of them ... & for want of such issue then to the use of the heirs female of them ... & for want of such issue then to the right heirs of me the sd Richard MADREN ... 15 April 1718. *Signed*: Richard MADREN. *Ack*: 15 April 1718. *Regt*: 18 April 1718.

[A:207] Levy CRESSEY of the Precinct of Pasquotank

& Province of North Carolina with free voluntary Consent of my wife Sarah ... consideration of 20 pounds ... paid by Joseph STOCKLEY of the same place ... sold ... 70 Acres of land, being a part ... of land & Plantation, whereon I now live, the said 70 Acres of land to be taken out proportionably from the whole tract ... beginning upon the Creek adjoining to the land which was Wm. SIMSONS ... 27 Jan. 1717/18. *Signed*: Louis [sic] CRESSEY, Sarah CRESSEY. *Wit*: W NORRIS, Ewd E WHARTON his mark. *Ack*: 15 April 1718. *Regt*: 18 April 1718.

Daniel GUTHRIDGE [sic] ... in consideration of the sum of 60 pounds Current money of this province ... paid by John CONNER of Pasquotank prect. in North Carolina ... sold ... the within mentioned tract of land containing 110 Acres ... & towards a further satisfaction of the Consideration money aforesd I the sd. Daniel GUTHRIE ... sold ...
[A:208] ... eleven head of Cattle Viz four Cows, three two years old Steers, & one two year old heffers, three [?] old [?] with four good Sows thereof the said Cows marked with Caleb BUNDYS mark, one of the Cows being marked with John DAVIS mark & the remainder part both of Cattle & hogs being of my own proper mark. ... 26 Ffeby. 1717/8. *Signed*: Danll. GUTHRIE. *Wit*: Robert JOY, Joseph GORDON. *Ack*: 15 July 1718. *Regt*: 18 July 1718.

4th Jany 1718 & in the 4th year of the reign of our Sovr. Lord George by the Grace of God King of England &c. by & between Trueman MCBRIDE in the precint of Pasquotank in the County of Albermarle & in the Province of North Carolina on the one party & John SOLLEY of the precinct, County & Province abovesd ... in Consideration of the sum of £70 of good & lawful money of Carolina ... sold ...
[A:209] a tract or parcel of land, situate lying & being in the Province of North Carolina on the No. East side of Pasquotank River, commonly known by the name of the Bay Plantation ... *Signed*: Trueman MCBRIDE. *Wit*: Isaac JONES, Wm. REED. Jno. JONES. *Ack*: 20 Jany. 1718/9. *Regt*: 24 Jany 1718/9.

No. Carolina, Trueman MCBRIDE of the Prect. of Pasquotank County of Albermarle & Prect. afsd, for & in consideration of the sum of £70 Current money ... paid by Joh. SOLLEY of the same place ... does assign ... all my right ... to the tract of Land & plantation in the patent within mentioned & by estimation 200 Acres ... 4th Jany 1718/9. *Signed*: *Wit*: Is: JONES, Wm. REED, Jno. J JONES. *Ack*: 20 January 1718/9. *Regt*: 24 Jany. 1718/9.

[A:210] Pasquotank, Jno. NORTON of the Precinct aforesaid ... for the Valuable Consideration of 50 pounds ... paid by Jno. JONES Cordw. ... sold ... the within mentioned Patent of Land ... 22 April 1719. *Signed*: John NORTON. *Wit*: Jno. RELF, Thos. COLLINS. *Ack*: 22 April 1719. *Regt*: 25 April 1719.

North Carolina, Thos: PALMER of the prect: of Pasquotank & Province afrsd., with the free voluntary Consent of [blank] PALMER my lawful wife ... for the valuable Consideration of [blank] pounds ... paid by my brother Robert PALMER of the prect: & prov: afrsd ... sold ... a tract of land ct. 250 Acres, lying on the N E. side of great flatty Creek, beginning at the mouth of Bettys Creek & running all the courses of the Patent, as the same was granted unto me ... 3 Septbr 1715 ...
[A:211] ... 20 Jany 1718/9. Signed: Tho: PALMER. Wit: W NORRIS. Ack: 20 Jany 1718/9. Regt: 21: Jany 1718/9.

8br 8. 1719. received of Eliz. UPTON Widow & Exrx. of Last Will & Testament of Jno. UPTON deceased one plantation called by the name of Abington & one Iron pot, in full for all Legacies bequeath given to me in a Will by my father Jno. UPTON dec: bearing date the 30 day of June 1715, & for the wh. I do hereby acquit & discharge my mother the sd Eliz. UPTON Exrx. as aforesd. Witness my hand this 8 Octbr 1719. *Signed*: Edward UPTON. *Wit*: W NORRIS. *Regt*: 8 Octbr 1719.

No. Carolina, Sollo. SAWYER of the prect: of Pasquotank plantr. for & in Consideration of the sum of 13 pounds, current money of this province ... paid by Jno. SAWYER of the afrsd Prec: Cordw. ... sold ... a parcel of land by estimation 100 acres ... situated in Pasquotank Prct: ... on Thos: SAWYERS Jno. SAWYERS & Robert SAWYERS begining on a Branch on Thos: SAWYERS line ... to Wm. HUMPHRIES line ... to Jno. SAWYERS line ... 22 July 1718.

Signed: Sollo. S SAWYER his mark, Mary M SAWYER her mark. *Wit*: Robert KEEL, Richard R GREGORY his mark. *Ack*: 22 April 1719. *Regt*: 24: April 1719.

Virg: Daniel PHILIPPS of the Colony of Virginia, have sold unto [?] Jn: MARTIN of the Province of North Carolina, 200 Acres of Land according to a p of Deeds of Lease & Release dated the 16 & 17 day of April 1719, the sd Land lying & being in North Carolina on the SW side of Pasquotank River in the sd prect: I do therefore appoint ... Mr. Caleb BUNDY & Jos: JORDAN ... to acknowledge the above ... 19 April 1719. *Signed*: Daniel N PHILIPPS his mark. *Wit*: Geo: NEWTON. Solo: WILSON Jno HIX Nath MARTIN Roger DIBBS.
[A:212] Virg: This day appeared before Samuel BOUSH, one of his Majestys Justices of the peace for the County of Norfolk, John HIX & Roger DIBBS, & made oath ... that they saw Daniel PHILLIPS sign ... the above power of attorney unto Mr. Caleb BUNDY ... 13 July 1719. *Signed*: Sa. BOUSH. *Proved*: Pasquotank Court July 21. 1719. the above Letter of Attorney by Nath: MARTIN. *Regt*: 24 July 1719.

16 April 1719. in the 5th year of the Reign of Our Sovr: Lord George King of Great Brittain &c. between Daniel PHILLIPS of Norfolk County Yeoman of the one part & Jno. MARTIN of the Province of North Carolina Yeoman of the other part ... the sum of 5 shillings sterling money ... paid by the afrsd Jno. MARTIN ... Sold ... one tract or parcel of land ... in a bay on the SW side of Pasquotank River ... ct. 200 Acres, called & known by the name of a bay ... *Signed*: Danl. N PHILLIPS his mark. *Wit*: George NEWTON, John HIX, Nath MARTIN. *Ack*: 21 July 1719 by Caleb BUNDY att of Danl PHILLIPS to Jno. MARTIN. *Regt*: 24 July 1719.

17 April 1719. in the fifth year of the Reign of Our Sovr: Lord George King of Great Brittain &c. Between Daniel PHILLIPS of Norfolk County Yeoman of the one part & Jno. MARTIN of the Province of North Carolina Yeoman on the other part ... the sum of 20 pounds lawful money of Virginia ... to him in hand paid ... Sold ... 200 Acres ... being in a bay the SW side of Pasquotank River ... as by deed ... from Robert KEEL & Tamer his wife ... 17 Aug. 1704 ... in the actual possession of the sd John MARTIN, by virtue of an

Indenture of bargain & sale, to him thereof made, the day before this date hereof, for one whole year made between the sd Daniel PHILLIPS of the one part & the afrsd John MARTIN of the other part ... [A:213] *Signed*: Danl. N PHILLIPS his mark. *Wit*: George NEWTON, John HIX, Nath MARTIN. *Ack*: 21 July 1719 to Jno. MARTIN. *Regt*: 24 July 1719.

... in Consideration of the Love and good affection I bear towards my loveing Sons Viz James FORBUS jun, Bailey FORBUS, Thomas FORBUS & Edward FORBUS having given ... 100 acres of land to each Son, that is for the first three sons & to the youngest 132, as I shall now mention. I give to my Son James 100 acres of Land on which he is now situated, called by the name of the Beaver Dam Neck, & to my son Bailey 100 acres of land, called great neck & little neck, & to my son Thomas 100 Acres land called Poplar Neck & to my Son Edward I give the mannor plantation with 132 acres thereunto belonging after his father & mother decease, & also I give unto my son Bailey a young blk heifer & her future increase when he is situated on his land; but he must bear the loss in the mean time. ... 30 March 1719. *Signed*: James I FORBUS Sign. *Wit*: Thos. DEAL[?], W NORRIS. *Ack*: 21 April 1719. *Regt*: 23 April 1719.

[A:214] Jno. JACOCKS of Pasquotank prct. in the province of North Carolina ... Whereas Thos. STANTON & Mary his wife, by their Conveyance did grant a patent of the remaining part of 215 Acres of land, being about 100 Acres thereof of his in Pasquotank afrsd, the rest being before sold to Thos. MACKEE & Wm. ARMURE, unto one Benja. GILES & Mary his wife ... their Deed or Conveyance, bearing date the 17th April 1705, sell ... all their right ... unto the remaining part of the sd. patent to Captain Jno. ROBINSON Esqr. ... by his deed ... bearing date the 20: Janry 1707, assign ... all his right ... unto Thos: PENDLETON & Margt. his wife ... by their Conveyance bearing date the 3 day of Feby 1707 sell ... unto one Jno BISHOP ... & Mary his wife did by their Deed ... bearing date the 9 day of Jany 1709/10 assign all their right ... unto Michl. MURFEE ... and Anne his wife did by their Deed ... 18 day of April 1710 assign ... all their right ... unto the sd. Jno. JACOCKS as by the several before recited Deeds ... in Consideration of the sum of 10

pounds Current money of this province ... paid by Daniel RICHARDSON Esqr. of Pasquotank ... sold ... 100 acres ...
[A:215] ... 21 Oct. 1718. *Signed*: John JACOCKS. *Wit*: Wm. REED, W NORRIS. *Ack*: 21 Octobr 1718. *Regt*: 24 Octobr 1718.

North Carolina, Samuel DAVIS of the prect. of Pasquotank & Province afrsd, with the free voluntary Consent of Eliz: DAVIS my lawful wife & for the valuable Consideration of 62 pounds ... paid by Capt: Benja. WEST of the prect. & province afsd. ... sold ... a certain quantity or parcel of land ct. 113 acres, being the one moiety or half part of that tract of land, whereon I now live, it being the Southward part thereof, the whole tract ct. 326 acres of land, by patent granted to my father Samuel DAVIS bearing date the first day of Jany 1694 ...
[A:216] ... 5 January 1717/18. *Signed*: Saml. DAVIS, Eliz N DAVIS her mark. *Wit*: Bal. HUIT, Zach: X KEATON. *Ack*: 21: August 1718. *Regt*: 24 9br 1718.

North Carolina, Collo. Wm. REED Esqr. of the prect. of Pasquotank & County of Albermarle, & Province of North Carolina; for ... the sum of 40 pounds Current money ... paid by Mr. Thos. SAWYER of the same prect, County & Prov: abovesd; ... do assign ... all my right ... to the tract of land & plantation in the patent within mentioned ct. by estimation 150 acres ... 19 Jany 1719/20. *Signed*: Wm. REED. *Wit*: Jno. DAVIS Jnr. *Ack*: 19 Jany 1719/20. *Regt*: 12 Feby 1719/20.

N. Carolina, Robert TOFFT, of the Island of Antigua in the West Indies, do hereby acknowledge to have borrowed ... of John PALIN of the Province of North Carolina afsd, the full sum or quantity of thirty & two ounces & six penny. Silver money Spanish coin, the which I promise ... to be paid unto the sd John PALIN ... 31 December 1718. *Signed*: Robert TOFFT. *Wit*: Charles BULL.

No. Carolina Jany 4 1718/9. Received then of John PALIN of the Province afrsd, on board the Schooner, called the Batchelors to say 360 pounds of Tobacco & one Scrutoor[?] to be carried to the Island of Antigua in the West Indies, the which I promise to dispose of to the best advantage & make return thereof according to order, the danger of the Seas only excepted, I say recvd Pr me *Signed*: Robert TOFFT.

North Carolina Jany 3. 1718/9. Recd then of Charles BULL of the prec: afrsd, on Board the Schooner called the Batchlor, that is to say to Oval Tables, to be carried in said Vessel to the Island of Antigua in the West Indies, & the which I promise there to dispose of to the best advantage & make return
[A:217] to him the Dangers of the Seas only excepted. I say received. per *Signed*: Richard [sic] TOFFT.

I the Subscriber do assign all my right, title & interest of in & to the within Writting & tables therein mentioned unto John PALIN or his Assignes. ... 22 March 1719/20. *Signed*: Charles BULL.

Tho: COLLINS of Pasquotank prect in the Prov: of North Carolina, for & in Consideration of the Sum of £60 current money of the sd Prov: ... pd. by Joseph COOPER of the same prect: & province ... sold ... tract of land, situate lying & being on the NE. side of Arrenuse Creek in the prect & prov: afrsd ... the head line which parts Capt: Jno UPTON ... by estimation 100 acres ... Samuel BARNETS line Griff JONES line & Capt: NORTONS line of land as afrsd ... 4 May 1719. *Signed*: Thos: COLLIS. *Wit*: Edw. E FAIRCLODE his mark, Geo: LUMLEY. *Proved*: 21 Jany. 1719. The above Deed was proved by the Evidences to be duely executed in the life time of Thos: COLLIS. *Regt*: 25 Jany 1719.

[A:218] Jno. BLISH of the prect of Pasquotank in the Prov: of North Carolina ... firmly bound unto Wm. WILSON of the prect & prov: afsd in the full sum of 70 pounds sterling money of Great Britain ... dated this 26 day of July 1716. The Condition of this Obligation is such that if the above bounden John BLISH ... acknowledge & make over, a certain piece of Land being part of a larger tract, lying on the North side of Aronuse Creek ... excepting the house & a passage thereunto is owned by agreement & during the time he has trade in this Country, then this obligation to be void ... *Signed*: John BLISH.

Wit: Joseph SPARNON, Thos COTTEN. *Regt*: 9 April 1720.

Mr. Jno. MAKEE & Wm. JENKINS in right of our two wives Eliz: MACKEY & Mary JENKINS, daughters & heiresees app. of Benj: GILES dec: ... for the valuable consideration of [blank] to us in hand paid ... by Thos: PALMER of the prect: of Pasquotank & Province of North Carolina ... sold ... 100 Acres lying & being upon great flatty Creek in the prect: afrsd & the land which Francis DELAMARE sold to John MITCHELL & by the sd Jno. MITCHELL & Mary his wife ... 16 April 1706 acknowledged & sold unto Benjn. GILES ... & now by the sd Jno. MAKEY & Eliz. his wife & Wm. JENKINS & Mary his wife ... sold to ... Thos. PALMER ...
[A:219] 9 Dec. 1718. *Signed*: Jno. X MAKEY his mark, Eliz. X MAKEY her mark, Wm. X JENKINS his mark, Mary X JENKINS her mark. *Wit*: W NORRIS, Robt. R PALMER his mark. *Ack*: 19 April 1719 to Thos PALMER. *Regt*: 25 April 1719.

Account of the Expenses & Disbursements paid & sales Laid by Mrs. Sarah TOMLIN Widow & Admx. of Jno. TOMLIN her late husband dec: out of his Estate since his death. Impr: To a Coffin 12th. a sheet 5t. digging a Grave 5t cyder for the funeral 7t. To 2 ? molasses 6t [?] of Admr. with the Will [?]. To 3 day attendance to [?] [blank] allowd 7t 1 days attend: to [?] To 8 looking after & getting together the hogs 20t 3 days [time?] of a man to go along with me *Total*: £5.13.0 *Signed*: Sarah X PENDLETON her mark. *Ack*: 18 Jany. 1719/20 The above was sworn to before me *Signed*: Jas. PALLIN.

The further Expenses & disbursements out of the said TOMLINS Estate by Mr. Thos: PENDLETON since his intermarriage with the sd Sarah TOMLIN Widow & Admr: Imp. To paymt to St HALL £2.15. ditto to Robert HAOO? £2. Ditto rent to Jas TOOKE £18.16.9. To Mr. NEW HALL 29/4. 2 days attendg Estate 5t to 2 [?] attending one day 5t. To 2 day hire man & horse after the hogs @ 3/6 pday each 14/ taking up mare & Colt 25t. To Taking up the young horse 7/? to time of me & wife 2 days 10t. To 2 app one for two & the other for one day. *Total*: 28.15.1 *Signed*: Thos: TP PENDLETON his mark. *Ack*: The above act was sworn to by Thos: PENDLETON the 18. day of Jany

1719/20 before me J PALIN.

Jerr: MURDEN of the prect. of Pasquotank, County of Albermarle in the Prov: of North Carolina ... assign all my right ... of this Deed & the land therein mentioned from me ... to Coll Wm. REED ... 20 Octbr 1719. *Signed*: Jerr MURDEN, Mary MURDEN. *Wit*: Jno. SOLLEY, Fr: MCBRIDE. *Ack*: 24 day 8br 1719 to Collo Wm. REED by the Vendr. *Regt*: 25 8br 1719.

[A:220] Jerr: MURDEN of the prct. of Pasquotank in the County of Albermarle & in the Prov. of North Carolina, do by these presents assign all my right ... of this Patent to the lands therein mentioned from me ... to Collo Wm. REED ... 20 8br 1719. *Signed*: Jerr: MURDEN, Mary MURDEN. *Wit*: Jno. SOLLEY, Fr: MCBRIDE. *Ack*: 21. 8br 1719 by the Vendr. to the Vendee. *Regt*: 25 Ocbr 1719.

Wm. LEWIS & Elir. my wife ... for a valuable consideration ... by Thos: MACKEEL ... sold ... our Dowry or thirds of in & unto those parts of the lands, which was Benja. WEST, known by the name of the old home plantation ... 20 Jany 1719/20. *Signed*: Wm. X LEWIS his mark, Elir. E LEWIS mark. *Wit*: Jno. FOURREE, Wm. NORRIS. *Ack*: 21 Jany 1719/20 by the Vendr to the Vendee.

Geo: HARRIS Jun[?] of the Prct. of Pasquotank & Prov: of North Carolina ... for the valuable Consideration of 10 pounds ... paid by Jno. HARRIS of the prec & province afrsd ... sold ... a certain quantity of land, being part of a greater tract by patent, bearing date 7' day of Novbr 1701 ... 40 acres ... next adjoining to the plantation which is my fathers Geo: HARRIS in the fork of Nobbs Crook Creek, upon Pasquotank River ... 21 July 1719. *Signed*: Geo: HARRIS, John I HARRIS mark. *Wit*: W NORRIS. *Ack*: 21 July 1719. *Regt*: July 1719.

[A:221] 12 March 1718/9 ... John SCARBOROUGH & Mary SCARBOROUGH his wife & Augustine SCARBOROUGH his son all of the prect. of Pasquotank & Province of North Carolina ... in Consideration of the sum of £20 ... paid by the sd Collo. Wm. REED Esqr. ... sold ... 850 acres of land ... upon Pasquotank River, between the plantation which was Robert WALLOUS & Jno. JENNINGS & formerly in the tenure & possession of

Augt. SCARBOROUGH dec. ... John SCARBORO, Mary M SCARBORO her mark, Augustin X SCARBRO his mark. *Wit*: Christo. I HUDDY, Wm WP PORINGER, W NORRIS. *Ack*: 19 Jay 1719/20 . *Regt*: 20 April 1720.

[A:222] Nich: ALDERSEY of New Kent County in Virginia have named & constituted ... my trusty friend Daniel RICHARDSON Esqr in the County of Albermarle in North Carolina my true & lawful Attorney in sd Government of Carolina, in my name .. to recover & receive of all persons all sums of money tobacco &c to me due ... 1s day of October 1719. *Signed*: Nicho. ALDERSEY. *Wit*: Thos: ARMOUR, Jno. ARMOUR. *Proved*: Pasquotank, this Letter of Atty was proved in Open Court October 20. 1719 by Thos: ARMOUR & Jno. ARMOUR Evidence. *Regt*: 24 Oct. 1719.

Wm. WILSON of the prec: of Pasquotank County of Albamarle and prov: of North Carolina, have constituted ... my well beloved wife Sarah WILSON & Tho MILLER Esqr. to be my true ... Attys, for me ... to ask demand ... all person or persons whatsoever ... all ... Debts ... may be found due ... 19 April 1720. *Signed*: Wm. WILSON. *Wit*: Mak. SCARBROUGH, Sarah SMITHSON. *Proved*: April 19: 1720. *Regt*: 20 April 1720.

[A:223] North Carolina: Anto. HATCH of Perquimans Prect. County of Albermarle Gent: ... Whereas the true & absolute Lords propr. of the Province of North Carolina by Deed of Grant, bearing date the third day of May 1688 in the 20 Year of their possession of the said Province, did give & grant unto Wm. TRAVIS of Albermarle County plantr. a certain tract of land, contg. 200 Acres english measure lying upon the E. side of Little river in the prect. of Pasquotank in the County of Albermarle ... whereas the sd Wm. TRAVIS by his writen Deed of Assignment on the Back of sd Patent, bearing date the 8 day of August 1691 did assign & set over unto Wm. SEXTON & his heirs ... by his certain deed of Assignment on the back of the same patent ... on the 3 day of October 1692 did give ... unto George MUSCHAMP ... by his certain Deed of Assignment on the back of the same patent, bearing date the 15 day of 7br 1694 did assign the same over unto Arthur WORKEMAN ... & his Deed proved in open Court &

registered ... and whereas the true & absolute Lords Propr. of Carolina by Deed of Grant or patent bearing date the 25 Feb 1696 did give & grant unto the sd Arthur WORKEMAN, the afsd tract & parcel of land by a resurvey ct. 375 acres of land ... begining at the mouth of a small Creek issuing out of Little River ... the land of James HUNTER ... FISHERS line ... whereas the sd Arthur WORKEMAN ... by his last will & testament ... bearing date the first day of August 1695 ... did give ... the same to me Anthony HATCH, for & during the term of my life & after my deceased unto Mary the Widow of Jno. CLARK dec: & to her heirs ... in Consideration of the sum of 30 Sterl. Money of Great Brittain, to me paid ... by Mary GLAISTER a Widow formerly called Mary CLARK the Widow of Jno. CLARK dec: ... Confirmed unto the sd Mary GLAISTER ... 7: Dec. 1719. *Signed*: Antho HATCH. *Wit*: Wm. BADHAM, Richd. MUSE, Edm GALE. *Ack*: March 5. 1719/20 Anth HATCH to Mary GLAISTER. *Regt*: 25 April 1720.

[A:224] North Carolina, Mary GLAISTER Widow Spinster formerly called Mary CLARK genl[?] Legatee & Exex of the Last will & testament of Arthur WORKMAN late of Jamaica Mert dec: ... Whereas the sd Arthur WORKMAN being seized ... of a certain tract of land or plantation ct. 375 Acres lying in Pasqt. precinct in Albermarle County, beginning at the mouth of a small branch, issuing out of little River ... lands of James HUNTER ... FISHERS corner tree ... the sd Arthur WORKMAN by his last Will & testament ... 1 Aug. 1695 ... did give ... the same unto Antho. HATCH Son of Mrs. Eles HUNT of Little River, during the term of his natural life, after his natural life ended unto me the sd Mary & my heirs ... And whereas the sd Anthony HATCH, by his certain Deed ... 7 Dec. 1719 ... confirmed unto me ... all his Estate right ... Mary GLAISTER ... in Consideration of the sum of 60 pounds sterling money ... paid by Edmund GALE of Pasqk prect Gent. ... sold ... 375 acres ... N E side of little River ... land that was James HUNTERS now the land of John Meads HUNTER ... Wm. FISHERS corner tree, now the Corner tree of Nathaniel CHEVIN Esqr ...
[A:225] 11 Dec. 1719. *Signed*: Mary GLAISTER. *Wit*: Wm. BADHAM, Anto. HATCH, Richd. MUSE. *Proved*: March 15. 1719/20 by the oath of Anth: HATCH. *Regt*: 1 May 1720.

Jno. RELF of the prect. of Pasquotank County of Albermarle in the Prov: of North Carolina Cooper ... & Samuel WRENCHER of the prect & County of Albermarle & prov of North Carolina Carpenter ... the sum of 10 pounds of good lawful money of North Carolina ... sold ... a tract or parcel of Land, situate lying & being in the province of North Carolina on the N E side of Pasquotank River ct. by estimation 100 Acres, it being out of a greater Dividend 1664 acres bearing date &c [blank] lying between the Creek pocosin & lake wherein the sd Samuel WRENCHER now lives ... 2 July 1719. *Signed*: Jno. RELFE. *Wit*: Robert LOWORY, Lewis CRESSEY. *Ack*: 3 July 1719. *Regt*: 24 July 1719.

[A:226] Wm. TOMLIN of the prect. of Pasquotank & Prov: of North Carolina for ... valuable Consideration of [blank] pounds ... paid by George LOW of the prect & prov aforsd ... sold ... 334 acres part of a greater tract of land ct. 534 acres by Will given to me the sd. Wm. TOMLIN & my brother John TOMLIN by my father Jno. TOMLIN dec: ... 21 Jany. 1718/9. *Signed*: Wm. TOMLIN. *Wit*: W NORRIS. *Ack*: 20 Jany 1718/9. *Regt*: 24 Jany 1718/19.

Wm. CARTWRIGHT of Pasquotank prect: in North Carolina, in Consideration of the love & affection which I bear unto my well beloved son Thomas CARTWRIGHT ... give ... 100 acres ... Henry BUGBIRDS Corner tree ... 21 July 1719. *Signed*: Wm. W CARTWRIGHT his Marke. *Wit*: Gabl. BURNHAM, Fran: MCBRIDE. *Ack*: 21 July 1719. *Regt*: 24 July 1719.

[A:227] North Carolina. John SMITHSON of the prect. of Pasquotank & prov: afrsd ... for the valuable Consideration of 24 pounds ... paid by Jno SCARFE of the prect & prov afrsd ... sold ... parcel of land ct. 100 acres ... on the So West side of Pasquotank River Known by the name of the Deep branch, a part of a greater tract by patent granted to Tho: ABBINGTON & by him sold to Richd. MADRAN & Alex LEFEAR & by him sold to Jonathan JACOCKS & by him sold to Jno. SMITHSON & by him sold to the sd SCARFE ... 9 Ffeby 1718/9. *Signed*: John SMITHSON. *Wit*: Rowland R BUCKLEY mark, Nath. JONES. *Ack*: 21 July 1719. *Regt*: 24 July 1719.

[A:228] Jany 5. 1718/9 Obadiah FEAR of Alligator Creek for ... paid by Fouster YOUNG of the same place ... sold ... tract of land containing 180 Acres ... lying on the north side of Alligator Creek in the County of Albermarle & province of North Carolina ... and I Ann FEAR, the wife of Obediah FEAR doth by these presents freely ... give ... all her right of dower ... *Signed*: Obediah OF FEAR, Ann A. FEAR. *Wit*: John WOODLAND, Eliza X WOODLAND. *Ack*: 21 July 1719. *Regt*: 25 July 1719.

Wm. CREECH & Henry CREECH of Pasquotank prect in North Carolina, for & in Consideration of the sum of 17 pounds Sterling money ... paid by Jno. PERKINS Senr of the prect of Currituck in the afrsd Province ... sold ... tract of land ... in the prect of Pasquotank, being 110 acres & part of a tract sold by Henry CREECH Senr to Jno BELL Senr & since pattend by Jno BELL Senr which sd 110 Acres is since sold by
[A:229] sd Jno BELL to Wm & Thomas CREECH as appears by Deed of Sale. ... 20 Oct. 1719. *Signed*: Wm. X CREECH, Henry HC CREECH mark. *Wit*: Jno. IH HARRISON, Jos: COOPER, Thos SWAN, Saml BERNARD. *Ack*: 21 Oct. 1719. *Regt*: 24 Oct 1719.

Wm. WILSON of Pasquotank Prect: in the Province of North Carolina, Marr-- for & in Consideration of the sum of 110 pounds Currt. Money of the Province ... paid by Wm. BADHAM of the same Prov: Mercht. ... sell ... tract of land, ... on the North Side of Pasquotank River, & at the West side of the mouth of Arenous Creek ... 150 acres ... lines of Wm. ROSS & Richd. FARRELL.
[A:230] ... Sarah the wife of me the sd Wm. WILSON doth by these presents freely willingly give ... her dower ... 23 Sept. 1719. *Signed*: Wm. WILSON, Sarah WILSON. *Wit*: Charles BULL, Geo: LUMLEY. *Ack*: 20 Oct. 1719 to Wm. BADHAM. *Regt*: 7 July 1720.

North Carolina: Jos. MUNCK of the prect of Pasquotank & Province afrsd ... whereas the Lords protr according to their great Deed of Grant bearing date the first day of May 1668 did give & grant unto Jos. MUNK a tract of Land lying in Pasq. prect. ct. 334 acres as by patent bearing date the 10 Feby 1718

... for the Valuable Consideration of 7 pounds to me ... paid by Thos: BETTYS of the prect & prov: afresd ... Sold ... land ct. 174 acres part of the afsd tract patented ... at the mouth of pig Branch ... line of Richd LEARY ... head of the juniper run ... 20 April 1719. *Signed*: Joseph M MUNCK. *Wit*: W NORRIS, Jno. X GREEN mark. *Ack*: 21 April 1719. *Regt*: 23 July 1719.

[A:231] North Carolina: Jos: MONK of the abovesaid Prov: Planter, for & in Consideration of the sum of 8 pounds in good & lawful money of the prov: afsd ... paid by Jno GREEN of the abovesd precinct ... sold ... tract of land situate lying in the fork of Pasquotank river, containing 80 Ares ... being a part of a tract of land, comonly called the Poplar table, binding upon Elisa TOMLINS on the west side & the plantation whereon the sd GREEN now lives ... 11 day of April in the fifth year of the reign of our Sovr. Lord King George ... 1719. *Signed*: Jos: M MONK. *Wit*: Ja: BROWNE, Elisa X GARRAT mark. *Ack*: 21 April 1719. *Regt*: 21 July 1719.

North Carolina: Wm. CARTWRIGHT & Sarah my wife for & in consideration of ... [blank] Pounds ... paid by Henry BUGBIRD of the prect & province aforesaid ... sold ... 100 acres of land ... being part of a greater tract belonging to me the sd Wm. CARTWRIGHT containing 400 acres by Patent granted to me bearing date the 7: day of Jany 1716/7 ... on the South West side of Pasquotank river ... Sandy run branch ... [A:232] ... 21 July 1719. *Signed*: Wm. W CARTWRIGHT mark. *Wit*: Gabll. BURNHAM, Wm. CARTWRIGHT Junr. *Ack*: 21 July 1719. *Regt*: 23 July 1719.

Wm. CARTWRIGHT of the province of North Carolina & in the County of Albermarle & prect of Pasquotank ... make over forever the within written patent & Land to my well beloved Son Wm. CARTWRIGHT jun ... 21 July 1719. *Signed*: Wm. W CARTWRIGHT mark. *Wit*: Nath. JONES, Jno. SMITHSON. *Ack*: 21 July 1719 to Wm. CARTWRIGHT jun. *Regt*: 24 July 1719.

Wm. REED Esqr. of the prect. of Pasquotank in the County of Albermarle & in the Province of North Carolina ... assign all my right ... of this patent & the land therein mentioned, except 107 acres of the sd Land, sold to Thos. SAWYER from me ... to Jeremiah MURDEN ... 20 Oct. 1719. *Signed*: Wm. REED Jane I REED mark. *Wit*: Jno. SOLLEY, Fr: MCBRIDE. *Ack*: 21 Oct. 1719 to Jeremiah MURDEN. *Regt*: 21, Jany 1719/20.

[A:233] Matthew PRITCHARD of Pasquotank Prct. for & in Consideration of the Sum of 20 pounds in Barrel porke ... do hereby assign over all my right ... of the within mentioned patent, to Wm. BROTHERS ... 19 Jany 1719. *Signed*: Matthew PRITCHARD. *Wit*: Jos: JORDAN, Benj: PRITCHARD. *Ack*: 19 Jany 1719/20. *Regt*: 21 Jany 1719/20.

James NEWBY & Elizabeth my wife do ... give & oblige ourselves, to confirm the premises hereafter named, to our Son Robert DAVIS, only we do possess Jno. SYMONS therewith part untill the sd Robert DAVIS becomes to the age of 21 years, he being one Exor to the last Will & Testament of James DAVIS father to the sd Robert DAVIS. And further because our sd son has made choice with the full consent of himself & of his mothers desire, that is to say of Jno. SYMONS to live with & for him to train him the sd DAVIS to weave & do house carpenters work, to write, read & cypher as far as the sd SYMONS can do, provided the sd DAVIS, live with the sd SYMONS till Age & will obey him, also finding the sd DAVIS with necessary food & rainment, as he shall have occasion of during his continuance with sd SYMONS; now followeth what we the said James NEWBY & Elizabeth my wife do give to our Son, first one small bottle Jug, one mug, one good pewter dish, one pewter plate ... one tin Candelstick one pewter bottle, five chairs three Iron pots, one smal table & forms, one [?], one Cow & calf & one young heifer, one Iron bound case with six square bottles, only his mother to have one of the case during her natural life & then to return to sd Robert DAVIS, also we give to our sd Son, one four year old Iron grey horse & one gun with all his fathers Tools except one tennant saw. Now for confirmation & full performance of all these above mentioned Articles, we [?] all parts that are herein concerned, do set our hands & seals this 25 day of the 8 month 1719. *Signed*: Robert DAVIS, Eliz: X NEWBY, Jas IN NEWBY, Jno SYMONS. *Wit*: Robert WHITE, Henry WHITE. *Ack*: 20 8br 1719. *Regt*: 24 Octbr 1719.

Thos: WILLIAMS of the prect of Pasquotank & prov: afrsd ... with the free voluntary Consent of Rebecca WILLIAMS my wife ... for the valuable Consideration of 16 pounds ... paid by James BELL of the prov. afrsd. sold ... parcel of land ct. 290 acres, part of a greater tract, surveyed by Richard GREY & by the sd Richard GREY sold to Jno. AVERY & by the sd John AVERY sold to Thos WILLIAMS ... as by a deed of bargain & sale date the 19th day of July 1715 ... [A:234] ... 22 April 1719. *Signed*: Thos T WILLIAMS mark. *Wit*: Charles BARRON, Jona: JACOBS. *Ack*: 22 April 1719. *Regt*: 23 April 1719.

North Carolina: Thos. RELF of the above sd prov. planter for & in Consideration of the sum of 18 pounds in good & lawful money ... paid by Wm. ROADS of the above sd province ... sold ... tract of land situate lying on the north side of Pasquotank River comonly called Hickory neck, joining to John JONES on the lower side & Jno. RELFS on the north east side, containing 300 acres ... being the lower end of Hickory neck ...
[A:235] 22 April in the fifth Year of the reign of our Sov: Lord George ... 1719. *Signed*: Thos RELF. *Wit*: Nath: JONES, Rob: KEEL. *Ack*: 22 April 1719. *Regt*: 24 April 1719.

Capt. James BROWN of the prct. of Pasquotank & County Albermarle in the Province of North Carolina ... Whereas his Excellency the palatine & the rest of the true & absolute Lords propr. of North Carolina by their grant or patent bearing date the 11 June 1716 for the Consideration therein mentioned ... sell ... unto me a certain tract of land lying in Albermarle County contains 216 acres ... in consideration of 70 pounds sterling money of great Brittain ... paid by Trueman MCBRIDE planter of pasquotank afsd ... sold ... the afsd tract of land ct. 216 acres ... 21 July in the 5 year of the reign of Our Sovr. Lord King George ... 1719. *Signed*: James BROWN. *Wit*: Jno. SOLLEY, James BELL. *Ack*: 21 July 1719. *Regt*: 21 July 1719.

[A:236] N. Carolina: Pasquotank prect: July 21. 1719. James BROWN acknowledged all the land mentioned in the within Patent ... sold ... unto Truman MCBRIDE of the same province ... *Signed*: Jas. BROWN. *Ack*: 21 July 1719 *Regt*: 21 July

1719.

1720 the 22d of the 6th month ... Thomas COMMANDER being heir of James TOOK & John SYMONS being heir of Thomas SYMONS, do for good causes ... set an old Negroe named Tony free from us once having some sort of Claim to him but ... forever do quit & discharge the sd Tony from our Service or our heirs to the ninetieth year of his age we hereby obliging ourselves or our heirs to forfeit the just sum of fore score pounds sterling money of old England if we the sd COMMANDER & SYMONS should pretend to make Servant of the sd Tony ... to the sd Negroe Tony. ... *Signed*: Thos. COMMANDER, John SYMONS. *Wit*: Robert HOSEA, James IN NEWBY his mark, John X BELLMAN his mark. *Regt*: 29 August 1720.

John JONES of the prect of Pasquotank & prov: of North Carolina ... for the Consideration of the love & affection which I have & do bear unto my loving son Abraham JONES of the prect & prov: afsd ... give ... a parcel of land containing 100 acres ... being in the prect. aforesaid ... bounded between the lands of my son Isaac JONES & Wm. RHODES ... but if the sd Abraham JONES die without issue then I give the sd Land to my son Isaac JONES ... 19 April 1720. *Signed*: John JONES, Dorothy JONES. *Wit*: W NORRIS, W LUDFORD. *Ack*: 19 April 1720. *Regt*: 5 May 1720.

[A:237] John JONES of the prect of Pasquotank & prov: of North Carolina ... for the Consideration of the love & affection which I have & do bear unto my loving son Isaac JONES of the prect & prov: afsd ... give ... a parcel of land containing 100 acres ... being between my plantation on the south side of a Branch & my son Abraham JONES land ... 19 April 1720. *Signed*: John JONES, Dorothy JONES. *Wit*: W NORRIS, Wm. LUDFORD. *Ack*: 19 April 1720. *Regt*: 5 May 1720.

John UPTON of Pasquotank prect. in the Province of North Carolina planter for & in Consideration of the sum of 10 pounds in good & lawful money of the prov: afsd ... paid by Charles BOLT of the afsd prect. & Province Plant: ... Sold ... tract of land ... in the prect. of Pasquotank on the north side of Pasquotank river in the prov: of North Carolina ...

near Gumbary[?] Swamp ... line of Edw: UPTONS land ... part of a tract pattend by Jno. UPTON, containing by estimation 60 acres ...
[A:238] 11 April 1720. *Signed*: John B UPTON his mark. *Wit*: George LUMLEY, Isaac JONES, James GREAVES *Ack*: 19 April 1720. *Regt*: 22 April 1720.

Robert SAWYER Snr of Pasquotank river in the County of Albermarle, within his Majesty province of North Carolina yeoman ... in Consideration of the sum of 6 pounds sterling money of Great Brittain ... paid by Jonathan JONES of North Carolina in the County afsd ... sold ... a certain tract of land of 30 acres ... formerly situated by John JONES afsd it being the other side of Pasquotank river afrsd adjacent to the sold land comonly called by the name of the round pen bounded on the sd Robert SAWYER. *Signed*: Robert SAWYER. *Wit*: Wm S STEVEN mark, Jno. JONES. *Ack*: 19 July 1720 to Jonathan JONES. *Regt*: 21 July 1720.

North Carolina: Thos: SAWYER sen of the prect of Pasquotank planter & of the County of Albermarle & of the Province of North Carolina for the sum of 30 pounds Current money ... by Edward WILLIAMS of the same prect & County & province ... sold ... a divident of land, out of a Patent bearing date the 11 Novbr 1719, situate ... North East side of Pasquotank River ct. by Estimation 353 Acres bounding ... on Mr. Robert MORGANS line & Mr. Henry SAWYERS line ...
[A:239] ... 1 Jany 1719/20. *Signed*: Mary M SAWYER mark. *Wit*: Thos SWAN, Jno RELF, John I SAWYER. *Ack*: 19 July 1720 This Deed was acknowledged by Mary SAWYER Exor: of Thos SAWYER to sd WILLIAMS. *Regt*: 21 July 1720.

(See pg. 405) James MKDANIEL & Mary my wife of Pasquotank prect in Albermarle County in North Carolina ... for a valuable Consideration ... paid by Jerr: SEATON of the same place ... sold ... 50 Acres of land more or less, being a part of 430 Acres of land by me the sd James MKDANIEL taken up ... a patent 1 May 1719 ... being on the North East side of Pasq. river ... Thos: SAWYERS Corner tree ... Jno. SCOTTS Corner tree ... *Signed*: James M MKDANIEL mark. *Wit*: Thos: SAWYER, John SAWYER. *Ack*: 19 July 1720. *Regt*: 21 July 1720.

[A:240] July 10th 1720 Wm. JENNINGS of Pasquotank prect. in Albermarle County planter, do bargain & make over, the within mentioned Deed, to Wm. WILLIAMS to him & his heirs forever ... *Signed*: Wm. Y JENNINGS Sigumn. *Wit*: John JONES, John RELF. *Ack*: Jona. JONES Atty of Wm. JENNINGS to Wm. WILLIAMS. *Regt*: 21 July 1720.

12th July 1720 & in the 4th year of the reign of our sovr. Lord King George of Great Brittain &c: between Ja: MKDANIEL & Mary MKDANIEL his wife ... plant. of pasquo: prect in Albermarle County in province of North Carolina & Jno. SPENCE of the same County & prov: ... in Consideration of 10 pounds Current money of this province ... paid ... sold ... one parcel of land ... ct. by estimation 50 Acres ... being part of a tract of land ct. 431 Acres as appears by patent bearing date 3 April 1719 ... formerly granted to Jas: MKDANIEL & bounding as follows ... S.W. to Thos: COOPERS Corner tree ... being known by the name of Toms ridge ... *Signed*: James M MKDANIEL. *Wit*: John I SAWYER, Thos. SAWYER. *Ack*: 19 July 1720. *Regt*: 21 July 1720.

[A:241] James MKDANIEL & Mary my wife in pasqu. prect. in the County of Albermarle in North Carolina ... for a valuable Consideration ... paid by Robert SAWYER sen, of the same place ... sold ... 50 Acres of Land ... being a part of 431 Acres of land ... taken up, which I have received a patent for first of May 1719 ... being on the N E side of Pasquotank River ... to Thos COOPERS Corner tree adjoining Thos: SAWYERS line ... *Signed*: Ja: M MKDANIEL mark. *Wit*: Jerr X SEATON, Thos: SAWYER. *Ack*: 19 July 1720. *Regt*: 21 July 1720.

12 July 1720 in the 4th year of the reign of our sovr. Lord King George &c: between Ja: MKDANIEL & Mary MKDANIEL my wife plant: of pasquotank prect Albermarle County province of North Carolina ... & Thos SAWYER of the same County & prov: ... in Consideration of 6 pounds 10 shillings ... paid ... sold ... one piece of land ... 50 Acres ... being part of a tract of land ct. 431 Acres as appears by patent bearing date 3 April 1719 formerly granted to Jas: MKDANIEL, bounding as follows ... S.W. to the COOPERS Corner tree ... then N W of old Thos SAWYERS

line ... known by the name of HARRISES ridge ... [A:242] *Signed*: James M MKDANIEL. *Wit*: Jno. I SAWYER, Robert R SAWYER. *Ack*: 19 July 1720. *Regt*: 21 July 1720.

Valent. WALLIS son & heir appt of Wm. WALLIS decd: do assign over all my right ... of the within mentioned land (except 100 acres sold by my father to Robert WAYMAN) to my brother Wm. WALLIS ... 19 April 1720. *Signed*: Valentine WALLIS. *Wit*: W NORRIS, Benj: WEST. *Ack*: 19 April 1720. *Regt*: 21 July 1720.

Valentine WALLIS son & heir appt of Wm. WALLIS dec: do assign over all my right ... of the within mentioned patent land therein contained/: excepted 100 acres sold by my father to Robert WAYMAN, to my Brother William WALLIS ... 19 April 1720. *Signed*: Vat WALLIS. *Wit*: W NORRIS, Benj. WEST. *Ack*: 19 April 1720. *Regt*: 21 July 1720.

Wm. MORRIS, with the Consent of Esther MORRIS my wife for a valuable consideration ... assign over all my right ... of the within mentioned deed, to William SIMSON ... 19 April 1720. *Signed*: Wm. X MORRIS mark, Esther 7 MORRIS. *Wit*: Thos STAFFORD, Peter P BROWN. *Ack*: 19 April 1720. *Regt*: 22 July 1720.

George HARRIS for me my heirs & Assigns do assign over all my right ... of the within mentioned land to Job CARTWRIGHT ... 19 Jany 1719/20. *Signed*: George HARRIS Jun:. *Wit*: W NORRIS. *Ack*: 19 July 1720. *Regt*: 22 July 1710.

[A:243] North Carolina: John JONES, in the prect of Pasquotank Blacksmith for & in Consideration of the sum of 6 pounds Curr: money of North Carolina, to me in hand paid ... by Jno WADE of the prect abovesd planter ... sold ... parcel of land situate ... in the prect abovesd ct. by estimation 78 Acres ... on the land of Richd STAMPS & Robert WAYMANS S.W. Albermarle sound, northerly with great flatty Creek ... 26 March 1720. *Signed*: John JONES. *Wit*: Wm. BADHAM, Clement HAMMOND. *Ack*: 19: April 1720. *Regt*: 22 July 1720.

Albermarle in North Carolina ... Arnold WHITE senr:

of the place above sd ... do hereby give ... to my daughter Ann WHITE one Negroe Girl named Doll, that is to say she & her increase to my sd Daughter & the Issue of her body, also to my Son Joshua WHITE, I do give ... one Negroe Girl named Bess & her increase, & I also give ... one Negroe Girl named Jenny unto my daughter Sarah WHITE, & her heirs born of her body, that is to say the sd Negroe Jenny & her increase; further be it known, that I do hereby give ... unto my Son Ishmael WHITE & my daughter Parthenia WHITE to say one Negroe boy named Luke to them the sd Ishmael & Parthenia WHITE the heirs of their body; further be it known, that if any one, or more of them my above named Children shall die before they have issue, then the Negroe or Negroes, that I have hereby to them given, shall be equally divided to & amongst the survivors of those my above named Children, & their heirs lawfully begotten of their body ... *Signed*: Arnold WHITE. *Wit*: Wm. SYMONS, Saml. GUTHRY. *Ack*: This Deed of Gift 19: April 1720. *Regt*: 22 July 1720.

[A:244] Jos: CARTWRIGHT ... for the Consideration of the exchange of a plantation, lying upon Pasquotank River, joining to Levy CRESSEY, wherewith I am fully satisfied ... sold ... unto Douglas ROOD, a piece of land lying upon the [blank] of Jos: REDING & Wm. RELF, given to me by my father Thos: CARTWRIGHT in his last Will & Testament ct. 100 acres ... 19 July 1720. *Signed*: Jo: CARTWRIGHT, Ele X CARTWRIGHT. *Wit*: Levy CRESSEY, Isaac SCARBRO. *Ack*: 19 July 1720. *Regt*: 22 July 1720.

North Carolina: Wm. LUFMAN of the prect of Currituck & province afsd ... for the valuable Consideration of 35 pounds Current money of this prov: ... paid by Thos: WILLIAMS of the prect: of Pasquotank & prov: afsd ... sold ... a tract of land & plantation ct. 150 acres ... in the prect of Pasquotank, between the plantation of Jno. JACOBS & Wm. JONES, being the plantation I formerly lived on [A:245] 19 April 1720. *Signed*: Wm. LUFMAN, Eliz. E LUFMAN. *Wit*: Wm. LUDFORD, Jno. JONES. *Ack*: 19 April 1720. *Regt*: 22 July 1720.

Rolf GARDNER, late of Pasquotank prect decd did by his last Will & Testament bearing date 31 day of May 1695 give & bequeath unto his daughter

Elisa. GARDNER, all his land ... the sd Elisabeth GARDNER, Wm. MORRIS & Ester MORRIS, formerly Esther GARDNER daughter of Rolf GARDNER all of the prect of Pasquotank & Prov: of North Carolina ... for the valuable Consideration of the maintainance of Elisa. GARDNER during her life & the sum of £20 in good specie, of this prov: to be paid to Wm. MORRIS ... sold ... unto the sd Wm. NORRIS ... all that our right ... to any part or parcel of the land, which was formerly our fathers Rolf GARDNER ... 19 July 1720. *Signed*: Elis C GARDNER, Wm. X MORRIS, Esther S MORRIS. *Wit*: Saml. BERNARD, Levi CRESSY. *Ack*: 19 July 1720. *Regt*: 22 July 1720.

[A:246] North Carolina: Benj. LOVEWELL of the prect of pasquotank & prov: afsd ... with the full volut: consent of Ann LOVEWELL my lawfull wife ... for the valu: Consideration of [blank] pounds ... paid by David PARSON of the prect & Province afsd ... give ... parcel of land ct. 100 acres, lying & being situate in the prct afsd, & part of a greater tract surveyed for Wm. SIMSON & by thim sold to Jno. WINBERRY & Benja: LOVEWELL, & now by the sd Benja: LOVEWELL sold out of my part to the sd Da: PARSON it being the land to the westward of my plantation, according to the choice of the Vendee, & bounded by the Gum pond ... 18th 8br 1720. *Signed*: Benj B LOVEWELL his mark, Ann A LOVEWELL her mark. *Wit*: Robert KEEL, Thos: SWAN, James GREAVES. *Ack*: 18th 8br: 1720. *Regt*: 20 8br 1720.

Samuel BUNDY of the prect of Pasquotank & prov: of North Carolina, for divers Causes & Considerations ... for exchange of a tract of land, lying on the fork of Little River, where with I am fully satisfied; by these presents do assign over all my right ... of the within mentioned patent, to Caleb BUNDY ... forever ... 18 day of 8br 1720. *Signed*: Saml. BUNDY. *Wit*: W NORRIS, Wm. SIMSON. *Ack*: 18th 8br 1720. *Regt*: 20 8br 1720.

Samuel BUNDY of the prect of Pasquotank & prov: of North Carolina, do assign over all my right title & interest to the within mentioned Patent & Land therein mentioned to Caleb BUNDY ... 18 day of 8br 1720. *Signed*: Saml. BUNDY. *Wit*: W NORRIS, Wm. SIMSON. *Ack*: 18th 8br 1720. *Regt*: 20 8br 1720.

[A:247] North Carolina: Caleb BUNDY of the prect of Pasquotank & prov: afsd ... for the valuable Consideration of an exchange of land lying on Newbegun Creek, ct. 110 Acres ... sold ... unto the sd Samuel BUNDY ... a tract of Land lying & being upon the head of little River, on the north side, being the land formerly bought of John DAVIS, & also an other parcel which I took up & surveyed ... 18 8br 1720. *Signed*: Caleb BUNDY. *Wit*: W NORRIS, Wm. SIMSON. *Ack*: 18 8br 1720. *Regt*: 20 8br 1720.

North Carolina: James COTTON of Virginia ... for the valuable consideration of 40 pounds ... paid by Robert KEEL of North Carolina. ... Sold ... tract of land lying on south side of great flatty Creek ct. 195 acres, by Joshua MARKHAM sold unto me & ack: the 15th day of October 1717 ...
[A:248] ... 18 October 1720. *Signed*: James J COTTON his mark. *Wit*: Robert KEEL, Richard BRIGHT. *Ack*: 18 Octbr 1720. *Regt*: 20 Octbr 1720.

Virginia: James COTTON of Princess Ann County in the prov. afsd, have made ... well beloved friend Charles MARKHAM of Albermarle in North Carolina, to be my true & lawful attorney, to acknowledge to Robert KEEL of the County afsd ... parcel of land, which I bought of Joshua MARKHAM of the same prect, lying on the South side of flatty Creek ... 11 Octbr 1720. *Signed*: James J COTTON his mark. *Wit*: Robert KEEL, Wm. BRIGHT. *Proved*: 18 8br 1720.

Wm. BRIGHT appeared before me Wm. PAGNER one of his Majesty Justices of the prect of Currituck ... he did see ... James COTTON sign ... the within power of Attorney unto Charles MARKHAM ... 14 October 1720. *Signed*: William PAGNER.

North Carolina: Griffin JONES for the valuable consideration of 10 pounds, to me in hand paid by Alexander SPENCE of the prect of Pasquotank & prov. afsd, do assign over all my right ... unto the within mentioned patent & land ... 18 July 1721. *Signed*: Griff: JONES. *Wit*: Jona. JACOCKS, Jno. RELFE. *Ack*: 18 July 1721. *Regt*: 26 July 1721.

[A:249] Steph: VAUGHAN do assign ... all my right ... of the within mentioned Bill of Sale & platt ... to Jno. CARTWRIGHT ... 14 March 1718/9. *Signed*:

Steph: VAUGHAN. *Wit*: Jno. CONDON, Math. VAUGHAN. *Ack*: 18 July 1721. *Regt*: 26 Sept 1721.

I the subscriber for a valuable Consideration in hand paid, do assign over, unto Captain Richard SANDERSON all my right ... of the within mentioned ... *Signed*: Math MIDGET. *Wit*: Isaac JONES, Jno. GIBSON. *Ack*: 18 July 1721. *Regt*: 26 Sept 1721.

I assign over the said within mentioned unto Jos: HARRISON. *Signed*: John CARTWRIGHT. *Ack*: 18 July 1721 by John CARTWRIGHT to Jos: HARRISON. *Regt*: 26 7br 1721.

Wm. WINBERRY do assign over from me ... my Estate right ... of the within mentioned land unto Albert ALBERTSON ... 18 July 1721. *Signed*: Wm. W WINBERRY. *Wit*: W NORRIS. John SOLLEY. *Ack*: 18 July 1721. *Regt*: 26 7br 1721.

Daniel RICHARDSON for & in Consideration of full payment ... paid by Wm. REED Esqr ... sell ... the within mentioned tract of land ... 30 May 1721. *Signed*: Daniel RICHARDSON. *Wit*: W NORRIS, David BALEY. *Ack*: 18 July 1721. *Regt*: 26 7br 1721.

[A:250] James BELL of the prect: of Pasquotank & province of North Carolina ... with the voluntary Consent of Mary BELL my lawful wife ... for the valuable consideration of 22£ 10s Current money of this province ... paid by Colo. Wm. REED Esqr ... assign over all my right ... of the within mentioned patent ... 16 March 1720/1. *Signed*: James BELL. *Wit*: W NORRIS, Stephen BURGESS. *Ack*: 18 July 1721. *Regt*: 26: 7br 1721.

Nath: HALL of North Carolina ... for the love I bear my Brother Jno. HALL ... give ... 100 acres of land, lying & being on the north side of Little River in the prect. of Pasquotank, binding on the lower side of George LOWS line ... 17 April 1721. *Signed*: Nath: HALL. *Wit*: Robert LOWRY Jur:, Nath: MACKEEL. *Ack*: 18 April 1721. *Regt*: 26 7br 1721.

[A:251] Robert OVERTON, heir apprt. of Richd. OVERTON dec., with the voluntary Consent of Alice OVERTON my lawful wife ... for the valuable consideration of 5 pounds ... paid by Edwd OVERTON

... sold ... the within mentioned patent ... except 100 acres of land sold to Richard BRIGHT ... also 270 acres sold to Francis OVERTON ... 17 Jany. 1720/1. *Signed*: Robert I OVERTON his mark. *Wit*: W NORRIS. *Ack*: 18 July 1721. *Regt*: 26 7br 1721.

Robert OVERTON Son & heir appt. of Richd. OVERTON dec: with the consent of Alice OVERTON my lawful wife ... for the valuable Consideration of 5 pounds ... paid by Francis OVERTON of Pasquotank prct ... Sold ... a parcel of land ct. 275 acres & part of a greater tract ct. 640 acres, granted by Patent to Richard OVERTON, the 10th day of Feby 1719 ... 17 Jany. 1720/1. *Signed*: Robert I OVERTON his mark. *Wit*: W NORRIS, John GIBSON. *Ack*: 18 July 1721. *Regt*: 26 7br 1721.

[A:252] Robert OVERTON Son & heir appt. of Richard OVERTON dec: ... with the Consent of Alice OVERTON my lawful wife ... for the valuable Consideration of 5 pounds ... paid by Richard BRIGHT of the prect of Currituck & prov: of North Carolina ... Sold ... a parcel of land ct. 100 acres, being part of a greater tract ct. 640 acres, granted by Patent to Richard OVERTON bearing date the 10th day of Feby 1719 ... 17 Jany. 1720/1. *Signed*: Robert I OVERTON his mark. *Wit*: W NORRIS, Jno. GIBSON. *Ack*: 18 July 1721. *Regt*: 26 7br 1721.

Nath MKEEL & Jno. MKEEL sons of Jno. MKEEL late of Pasquotank dec: ... for the valuable Consideration of 67 pounds 10 shillings ... paid by Charles WEST of the prect & province afsd ... sold ... a tract of land & plantation ct. 200 acres, lying & being situate on little River, by Patent granted to Robt: WEST. Thos: WEST & Jno. WEST, sold & conveyed to the afsd Jno. MKEEL by deed bearing date 22 Jany 1704/5, acknowledged & recorded in the Registers Book for Pasquotank the 25 April 1705, & by the sd Jno MKEEL by his last Will & Testament, bearing date the 24 Decbr 1706 given & devised to us the afsd Nath: MKEEL & Jno. MKEEL his Sons ...
[A:253] ... 8 July 1721. *Signed*: Nath: MKEEL, Jno. MKEEL. *Wit*: W NORRIS, Sus: NORRIS. *Ack*: 18 July 1721. *Regt*: 27 7br 1721.

N: Carolina: Saml JACKSON of the prect: of Pasquotank & prov: of North Carolina ... for the valuable Consideration of 20 shillings ... paid by Zach: NIXON of the prect of Perquimans in the prov aforsd. sold ... 1 acre of land, lying & being on the N.W. side of hairing Creek upon little River in the prect of Pasquotank & prov: afsd for & towards the use & for the purpose of building a Mill ... with liberty of Egress & Regress in upon & unto the sd acre of land ... 18 July 1721. *Signed*: Saml SJ JACKSON mark. *Wit*: W NORRIS, Alex: Sp[ink blot on paper] *Ack*: 18 July 1721. *Regt*: 27 7br 1721.

[A:254] N: Carolina ... Ja. BELL of the precinct of Pasquotank in the County of Albermarle and in the Province afsd ... bound unto the Honorable Coln: Wm. REED Esqr. in the sum of 500 pounds ster. money of Great Brittain to paid Collo: Wm. REED ... 18the day of July in the 7th year of the Reign of our Sovr. Lord King of Great Brittain & Anno. Dom: 1721 ... if the above bounden Ja. BELL ... truly perform ... a deed of Sale bearing date herewith and this day acknowledged in Court & do or shall within 3 months from the date hereof procure & get out a release patent for the said Wm. REED for 110 Acres of Land formerly belonging to Robert WALLIS and now taken out of the sd. Robert WALLIS rent of relapse Land formerly known & called by the name of Poplar ridge ... then this Obligation to be void ... *Signed*: James BELL. *Wit*: David RICHARDSON, Saml. BERNARD. *Ack*: 18 July 1721. *Regt*: 27 Feby. 1721.

James BELL of the Precinct of Pasquotank in the County of Albermarle in the State of N: Carolina planter ...
[A:255] ... tract of land lying on Pasquotank River called the Poplar Ridge ... 100 acres thereof as CYLIES grant or patent ... in consideration of the sum of 30 pounds sterling money of Great Brittain to me in hand paid ... by the Hona. Coln: Wm. REED of Pasquotank Prect. ... sold ... all the afsd tract of Land ...
[A:256] ... 16 July 1721. *Signed*: James BELL. *Wit*: Danl: RICHARDSON, Saml: BARNARD. *Ack*: 18 July 1721. *Regt*: 27 Feby. 1721.

[A:257] Cornelus FITZPATRICK do hereby ordain ... my friend to be my true & Lawful Deputy & attorney for me & in my name a tract of Land to be acknowledged to Thomas PEARTEE by John FITZPATRICK who is my Lawfull attorney ... July 12th 1721. *Signed*: Cornelius FITZPATRICK. *Wit*: Math. MIDGET, Saml. M MIDGET his mark. *Proved* & *Ack*: 18 July 1721. *Regt*: 27 Feby. 1721.

This Deed made & Indented the 15th day of July 1721 in the seventh year of the Reign of our Sovr. Lord by the Grace of God King of Great Brittain France & Ireland defender of the State between Thos. LEWIS of Pasquotank in the Province of North Carolina of Albermarle County together with the free & willing consent of Ane LEWIS wife of the one part & Benj: COWEING of the other part of Norfolk County ... in Consideration of the sum of 14 pounds Sterling ... Sold ... one certain tract of Land in Pasquotank being part of a tract called & known by the name of Bastable ct. 187 acres being part of a tract of Land ct. 370 Acres patented to Edwd. JONES decd bearing date the 17th May 1717 ... place commonly called the Bear Spring ... joining to Jno. WORRIELL, Henry BRITE & James JONES ...
[A:258] ... *Signed*: Thomas T LEWIS his mark, Ann C. LEWIS. *Wit*: John SOLLEY, John MONK. *Ack*: 18 July 1721. *Regt*: 27 Feby 1721.

North Carolina: Jonathan JACOCKS & Mary my wife of Pasquotank in the County of Albermarle in the province afsd. for & in Consideration of the Sum of 140 pounds in Barrel Pork to his use secured to be paid ... sold ... unto Mathew PRITCHARD ... a certain Plantation whereon
[A:259] we now dwell together with the Land thereunto belonging & containing 388 Acres of Land belonging formerly to William COLLINGS Decd & 96 acres of Land adjoining thereunto formerly owned by Stephen VINCENT all which Land bequeathed by the said COLLINGS in his last will & Testament unto his nephew Thomas WOODLY & since conveyed to Jonathan JACOCKS by a certain Deed ... of the sd Thomas WOODLEY & Elizabeth his wife bearing ye 12th day of Augt. 1710 ... the above said Land lying & being on the south West side of Pasquotank River bounded on the South side by Thomas WILLIAMS'S line and on the North side with Benja. PRITCHARDS line ... 29 July 1721. *Signed*: Jonathan JACOCKS, Mary JACOCKS. *Wit*: Thos. T WILLIAMS his mark. *Ack*: 17 Octr. 1721. *Regt*: 21 Oct. 1721.

[A:260] North Carolina Francis DELAMARE son & heir appears of Francis DELAMARE ... for the valuable consideration of 40 pounds ... paid by Wm. WRIGHT of the precinct of Pasquotank & Province afsd ... sold ... a tract of Land & plantation ct. 240 Acres lying & being on the N.E. of Pasquotank River Jno. FORTRESEYS & Jos. GILFORDS plantations & commonly called Akehurst Ridge ...
[A:261] 20 July 1721. *Signed*: Francis DELAMARE. *Wit*: W NORRIS, Edwd: POPE. *Ack*: 17 Oct. 1721. *Regt*: 21 Oct. 1721.

N. Carolina Amoss TRUEBLOOD of the prect. of Pasquotank & province afsd. ... with the consent of Elizh. TRUEBLOOD my Lawfull wife ... for the valuable consideration of £100 Ster. money of Great Brittain to us paid by Thomas CARTWRIGHT ... sold ... a tract of Land & Plantation ct. 330[?] lying & being upon Pasquotank ... upon George HARRIS'S line to the foot of old horse bridge ... which Land was formerly given by will to the sd. Eliza. TRUEBLOOD formerly Eliza. CARTWRIGHT by her Father Thomas CARTWRIGHT ...
[A:262] ... 17 Octr. 1721. *Signed*: Amoss TRUBLOOD, Eliza. ET TRUBLOOD her mark. *Wit*: W NORRIS, Jo: REDING. *Ack*: 17 Oct. 1721. *Regt*: 24 Oct. 1721.

Thomas CARTWRIGHT for the valuable consideration of £100 Sterling money of Great Brittain ... paid by Amos TRUBLOOD ... do assign over all my right ... unto the within mentioned deed & land therein expressed ... 17 Octr. 1721. *Signed*: Thomas T CARTWRIGHT his mark, Mary X CARTWRIGHT her mark. *Wit*: W NORRIS, Jo: REDING. *Ack*: 17 Oct. 1721. *Regt*: 24 Oct. 1721.

N. Carolina Wm. ROADS of the above sd province planter for & in consideration of the sum of 10 pounds good & Lawfull money of the province afsd. to me ... paid by Jno. JONES of the abovesd. province ... sold ... tract of land situate & lying on the north side of Pasquotank river commonly called Turkey ridge adjoining Thos. PALINS
[A:263] Land on the South East side & Patrick ODANIELLS land on the North East side & John JONES'S own Land on the North west side ct. 130 Acres ... being Turkey Ridge ... 17 Octr. 1721. *Signed*:

William WR RODES his mark. *Wit*: James GRAVES. *Ack*: 17 Oct. 1721. *Regt*: 25 Octr. 1721.

No. Carolina, John RELFE of the above said province cooper ... in Consideration of the sum of 18 pounds in good & Lawful money of the province afsd ... paid by Jno. JONES senr. of the above sd. Province ... [A:264] ... sold ... part of a tract of Land situate & Lying on the North East side of Pasquotank River ct. 200 acres of Land taken out of a Patent ct. 1654 acres commonly called Wolfpit neck ... mouth of the Cypress Branch ... 17 Oct. 1721. *Signed*: Jno. RELFE. *Wit*: Danl: RICHARDSON, Jno. TRUEBLOOD. *Ack*: 17 Oct. 1721. *Regt*: 25 Oct. 1721.

[A:265] Francis DELAMARE of Bath County in Pamplico in the Province of N: Carolina afsd: son & heir of Francis DELAMARE decd. of Pasquotank prct. & province afsd. ... for the Consideration of ... 10 pounds ... assign ... all my right ... to the within mentioned Patent unto John FOURREE of Pasquotank prect. ... 24 July 1721. *Signed*: Francis DELAMARE. *Wit*: Edward SCOTT, Stephen SCOTT. *Ack*: 17 Oct. 1721. *Regt*: 26 Oct. 1721.

Zach: KEATON with the consent of Sarah KEATON my wife & for the valuable consideration of the Exchange of a Plantation with Ephraim OVERMAN ... sold ... all our right ... unto the within mentioned patent & Land ... 17 Jany 1721. *Signed*: Zach: X KEATON his mark, Sarah S KEATON mark. *Wit*: Jno. BROTHERS, Wm. W BROTHERS mark. *Ack*: 17 Jany 1721. *Regt*: 7 Feby 1722.

[A:266] Peter SAWYER Do assign all my right ... of the within mentioned Patent of Land to John RELFE ... 10 Apl. 1721. *Signed*: Peter P SAWYER his mark. *Wit*: W NORRIS, Jos: H MITRANO[?] *Ack*: 18 Apl. 1721 to John RELFE by P. SAWYER. *Wit*: John PALMER Ck P Tem. *Regt*: 24 July 1721.

Thomas MERRIDAY & Elizabeth his wife have bargained & sold unto Edwd. FAIRCLOTH & Francis BROCKETT all our right ... of the within mentioned tract of Land ... 17 Oct. 1721. *Signed*: Thomas MERRIDAY, Eliza. E MERRIDAY her mark. *Wit*: Wm. EVERIDGE, Wm. W BRIGHT his mark. *Ack*: 17 Octr.1721. *Regt*: 19

Octr. 1721.

William JONES Son & heir apparent of William JONES Decd of the precinct of Pasquotank & province afsd. ... with the Voluntary consent of Esther JONES my Lawfull wife ... for the valuable consideration of 25 pounds sterling money of Great Brittain ... paid by John JOHNSON of the precinct & province afsd. ... sold ... quantity of Land ct. 70 acres lying ... between the plantations of Thomas WILLIAMS & the plantation of Joseph JORDAN called Old Jacobs ... [A:267] ... 8 April 1721. *Signed*: Wm. I JONES his mark. *Wit*: W NORRIS, Susa: NORRIS, Danl. WILLIAMS. *Ack*: 18 Apl: 1721. *Wit*: Jno. PALIN ck. P Tem. *Regt*: 20the Augt. 1721.

No. Carolina, William NORRIS & Susan NORRIS of Pasquotank prect. of the Province afsd. ... for the valuable consideration of the sum of 90 pounds ... pd. by Joseph STOKELY of the prect. & Province afsd. [A:268] ... sold ... two tracts of Land Lying & being in the prect. afsd. (viz) 250 Acres of Land & plantation lying between John DAVIS' Land & Wm CARTWRIGHTS Land formerly Relf GARDNERS & 200 acres of Land lying upon the head of Nobs Crook Creek for Wm. SIMPSON & by him sold to John WINBERRY ... assigned over to me ... all the afsd. Land & plantation containing 450 acres ... 17 Jany 1720/21. *Signed*: W NORRIS, Susan NORRIS. *Wit*: John CONNOR, Joseph JORDAN. *Ack*: 18 Apl. 1721. *Wit*: Jn PALIN clk P.T. *Regt*: 20 July 1721.

[A:269] Charles WEST of Pasqk. prect. in the Province of N. Carolina planter ... in Consideration of the sum of 71 pounds & 10 shillings currt. money ... (viz) 1 pound & 10 shillings already paid some months since, as Earnest money & 70 pounds the remainder now to me in hand paid by Lewis Alexander KNIGHT ... sold ... tract of Land containing by estimation 200 acres ... lying & being on the north side of Little river in Pasquotank afsd. & now or late in the tenure & occupation of Tavener? SWELLEY? & which Plantation & Tract of Land I lately purchased of Nathl. Senr Decd. & John MCKEEL his Brother ...
[A:270] ... 16 Feby. 1721/2. *Signed*: Charles WEST. *Wit*: Danl. RICHARDSON, Jno. MCKELL. *Ack*: 20 Feby. 1721/2. *Regt*: 16 Apl. 1722.

N. Carolina ... Wm. LINTON of the prect. of Pasquotank & Province afsd. ... for the valuable consideration of 4 pounds ... paid by Edward BRIGHT of the same place ... sold ... a parcel of Land containing 60 Acres lying & being ... on the N. W. side of Pasquotank River in the fork of the River called Joys Fork ... upon RIDDYS Swamp ... [A:271] ... 16 Apl. 1722. *Signed*: Wm. LINTON. *Wit*: W NORRIS, David BAILY. *Ack*: 16 Apl. 1723. *Regt*: 17 Nov. 1723.

N. Carolina. William JENNINGS senr & heir apparant of Wm. JENNINGS Decd. & grandson also Jno. JENNINGS decd. ... for the valuable consideration of [blank] ... paid by Joseph REDING of the Same place ... Sold ... all my right ... become due to me as heir to my Father or to my Grandfather unto that tract of Land & Plantation which was my Grandfather John JENNINGS & was sold him by Thomas & Mary RELF father of the sd. Thomas RELF & lying & being situate in the prect. of Pasquotank upon Pasquotank River ... [A:272] ... 15 Feb. 1723. *Signed*: William JENNINGS. *Wit*: Mary X HASTINS her mark, John I JENNINGS mark, Elioner E SAWYER mark. *Ack*: 21 Jany. 1723. *Regt*: 9 March 1723/4.

N. Carolina John SAWYER of the prect. of Pasquotank & Province afsd. ... for the valuable consideration of 12 pounds ... paid by John JONES of the same place ... sold ... unto Jonathan JONES ... a parcel of Land containing 50 Acres ... at a branch where the horse road goes over ... to his dwelling House ... to Wm. HUMPHRIES line ... Thomas SAWYERS line .. [A:273] ... 16 Apl. 1723. *Signed*: John I SAWYER his mark. *Wit*: W NORRIS, James PRITCHARD, Wm. W HUMPHRIES his mark. *Ack*: 16 Apl. 1723. *Regt*: 14 Oct. 1723.

N. Carolina Jno. DAILEY of the County of Albermarle in the prect. of Pasquotank for & in consideration of the sum of 2 pounds current money ... paid by John WINN of the afsd Province & County ... do assign ... all my right ... to the said tract of Land or plantation in the patent within mentioned ct. by estimation 296 acres ... 10 July 1723. *Signed*: John X DAILEY his mark. *Wit*: John SOLLEY, Jno. SAWYER. *Ack*: 10 July 1723. *Regt*: 18 Oc. 1723.

[A:274] N. Carolina Wm. STEVENS of the prect. of Pasquotank ... for the valuable consideration of 6 pounds ... have assigned over all my right ... to the within mentioned land & Patent ... to Richard GREGORY Junr. ... 16 July 1723. *Signed*: Will S STEVENS his mark. *Wit*: W NORRIS, James DAILEY. *Ack*: 16 July 1723. *Regt*: 18 Oct. 1723.

N. Carolina Edwd. SCOTT of the prect of Pasquotank & Province afsd. ... with the voluntary consent of Mary SCOTT, my lawfull wife ... for the valuable consideration of 30 Pounds current money ... paid by Caleb SAWYER of ye. Prect. & province aforesaid ... Sold ... a tract of land & Plantation containing 50 acres ... at Henry PENDLETONS line ... the land I now dwell on ...
[A:275] ... 16 July 1723. *Signed*: Edwd. SCOTT, Mary X SCOTT her mark. *Wit*: Stephen DELEMARE, Truman MCBRIDE. *Ack*: 16 July 1723. *Regt*: 2 Octr. 1723.

Pasquotank in No. Carolina, Elijah STANTON of the prect. of Perquimans in the Province aforesd. ... heir Apparent of Thomas STANTON late of Pasquotank Decd. ... with the voluntary consent of Elizabeth STANTON my Lawfull wife ... for the valuable consideration of the Exchange of Plantation lying in Perquimans, belonging to Jno. WINBERRY ... being in the prect. of Pasquotank ... & Bounded upon the Lines of the Plantation of Edmd. GALE Esqr. and the Lines of the Plantation of Jno. MEADS late of Pasquotank decd. it being the Plantation & Land which my father Thomas STANTON last lived on ... & bequeathed the Same to me ... his Son
[A:276] Son & heir apparent ... by estimation 150 acres & part of a greater Tract ct. 250 acres by patent granted to my Father Thomas STANTON ye 1 Feby 1705/6 ... 16th July 1723. *Signed*: Elijah STANTON, Elizabeth X STANTON her mark. *Wit*: W NORRIS, Jona. JONES. *Ack*: 16 July 1723. *Regt*: 9 Oct 1723.

[A:277] North Carolina, Jno JOHNSON of the prect. of Pasquotank Barber for the Consideration of 16 Pounds ... paid by Edmd. GALE Esqr. ... all my right ... to the Lands & Plantation within mentioned ... 1st day of Novr. 1723. *Signed*: Jno JOHNSON. *Wit*: Ad. COCKBURN, J. CLAYTON. *Ack*: 25 Nov. 1723.

Regt: 28 Nov. 1723.

Jno SYMONS of No. Carolina, & prect. of Pasquotank ... do Sign over all my right ... of this within patent from me ... to Edwd. TURNER ... 16 April 1723. *Signed*: John SYMONS. *Wit*: David BAILEY, Jno RELF. *Ack*: 16 April 1723. *Regt*: 28 Nov 1723.

No. Carolina, Jno BROTHERS of the prect. of Pasquotank & Province aforesaid ... for the valuable consideration of 9 pounds ... paid by Richard BROTHERS of the Same Place ... Sold ... a parcel of Land ct. 126 acres being part of a greater tract ct. 620 acres by patent granted to my Father Wm. BROTHERS bearing date the 9th day of Nov. 1714 & by him Willd. to his Children in Severall parcels & which sd parcell of 126 acres afsd (being by my Father devised to me & calld. by the name of the Cow pens & Bounding on the parcell given to my [A:278] Brother Richd. BROTHERS) ... 15 Nov 1723. *Signed*: Jno BROTHERS. *Wit*: W NORRIS, H BELL. *Ack*: 15 Nov 1723. *Regt*: 11 Dec. 1723.

Pasquotank: Thos. BELLOYS of the Prect. afsd. & Province of No. Carolina ... for the valuable consideration of 32. ... paid by Saml. MOORE of the prect & Province afsd ... Sold ... all my right ... unto the within mentioned tract of Land ... [A:279] ... 14 Oct. 1723. *Signed*: Thomas BALLOYS, Mary X BALLOYS her mark. *Wit*: James SPENCE, Truman MCBRIDE. *Ack*: 15 Oct 1723. *Regt*: 12 Nov 1723.

No. Carolina, Thomas LEWIS heir apparent of Thos. LEWIS Decd. ... of ye Prect. of Pasquotank & Province afsd. ... for the valuable consideration of 124 pounds ... sd. Gilbert ALBERTSON ... Sold ... a parcell of Land & plantation ct. 119 acres ... Lying & being between the Lines of Rowland BUCKLEYS & the Land of Geo. HARRIS calld the White Oak Necks, & was the Land & plantation whereon my Father Thos LEWIS lived & whereon he died, & calld & known by the name Possum Quarter ... 15 Oct 1723. *Signed*: Thos LEWIS his mark. *Wit*: W NORRIS, David BAILEY. *Ack*: 15 Oct. 1723. *Regt*: 12 Nov 1723.

[A:280] Jacob SHERWOOD & Eliza. my Wife do constitute our trusty friend Jno. BARNART [blank] of Pasquotank to be our attorney ... to acknd. a Tract of Land to James COLLINS & also to receive such Sum or Sums of money as are due to me from any person ... 27 May 1723. *Signed*: Jacob SHERWOOD, Eliza. X SHERWOOD her mark. *Wit*: W NORRIS, Susa. NORRIS. *Proved*: 15 Octr. 1723. *Regt*: 13 Nov 1723.

No. Carolina, Jacob SHERWOOD of the prct of Pasquotank & Province afsd. ... with the voluntary consent of Elizabeth my Lawful wife ... for the valuable consideration of 25 pounds ... paid by James COLLINS of the prect, & province afsd. Sold ... tract of Land & plantation ... on the Sound side joining to a parcell of Land belonging to Jno WAD in the prect of Pasquotank being the Land which was formerly David ELDERS & by him left to Collo. Thos. BOYD & by the sd BOYD Sold to Charles OVERMAN ... by an assignment upon Record acknowledged in Court of Pasquotank the 20 Oct. 1713 & recorded the 23 Oct 1723 in the Register Book of writings, and by the sd. Charles OVERMAN Sold & assigned to me the sd Jacob SHERWOOD at a Court calld for the prect afsd. the 17 April 1716 & recorded in the Register Book of writings the 18th April 1716, which Sd Land & plantation ct. 80 acres ... is now transfered over from us ...
[A:281] ... 27 May 1723. *Signed*: Jacob SHERWOOD, Eliza X SHERWOOD her mark. *Wit*: W NORRIS, Jno BURYHART, Shinery WOLF. *Ack*: 15 Oct 1723. *Regt*: 13 Nov 1723.

John MCKEEL & Eliza. my wife of pasquotantk & prect of albermarle County in the province of No. Carolina ... in Consideration of the sum of 50 pounds ... paid by Saml. BUNDY Junr. of the Same place ... Sold ... a plantation & tract of Land ct. 110 acres ... in the prect. of Pasquotank near Rich Neck formerly the Lands of Danl. GUTHRYE, & by him Sold ... unto Jno COURTIS ... by deed of assignment bearing date 26 Feby 1717 ...
[A:282] ... 9 Oct. 1723. *Signed*: Jno MCKEEL, Eliza. MCKEELL. *Wit*: Charles BULL, Jno PALIN. *Ack*: 15 Oct 1723. *Regt*: 16 Oct. 1723.

Jas. SPENCE Senr. in the prect.of Pasquotank in the County of Albermarle in the prov. of No. Carolina ... & Truman MCBRIDE of the Same County and prect & prov. afsd planter ... in Consideration of the sum of 40 pounds current money of Carolina ... sold ...

parcel of Land ... in the Fork of Pasquotank river ... ct. 426 acres ... Known by the name of JOYS Forke ... it being a tract out of a patent ct. 640 acres bearing date the first day of may 1668. ... [A:283] ... 15 Oct 1723. *Signed*: Jas SPENCE. *Wit*: Jas PRITCHARD, Saml X PRITCHARD his mark. *Ack*: 15 Oct. 1723. *Regt*: 17 Oct. 1723.

James SPENCE Senr. of the prect. of Pasquotank in the county of albermarle in the province of No. Carolina Sawyer ... & Truman MCBRIDE of the same County and prect & province afsd planter ... in Consideration of the sum of 20 pounds current money of this province ... sold ... a tract & parcel of Land whereon the sd Trueman MCBRIDE now lives ... in the forke of Pasquotank River being a part of a tract of Land ct. by patent 200 acres bearing date the first day of May 1668, which sum of 142 acres of Land has sold & set over to Trum. MCBRIDE ... [A:284] ... 15 Oct 1723. *Signed*: James SPENCE. *Wit*: James PRITCHARD, Saml P PRITCHARD his mark. *Ack*: 15 Oct. 1723. *Regt*: 17 Oct. 1723.

North Carolina June the 7th 1723. Recd. of Mr. Samuel BARNARD a Bond upon Capt Thomas HENRY, the Sum of 59 pounds 8 Shillings, which I am to receive the money for the same or return the Bond again, the danger of the Seas & other casualties Excepted. Pr *Signed*: Nathaniel LATHROP.

Nathl. HALL of North Carolina ... for the Love that I bear to my Brother Ebenezer HALL ... give ... all my right ... to 100 acres of Land, lying & being on the north side of the head of little river in the prect of Pasquotank binding on the Lower side of John HALLS line ... 17 April 1721. *Signed*: Nathl. HALL. *Wit*: Robert LOWRY Jun:, Nathl. MCKEELL. *Ack*: April Court 1721. *Regt*: 14 Feby. 1723/4.

[A:285] North Carolina Pasquotank ... Jas. COLLINS of the prect, & province afsd do nominate ... John MCKEEL to be my true & lawfull attorney to acknowledge a deed of Sale or Bargain for a tract of Land lying upon the branches of Great Flatty Creek unto Thomas PLATER ... 20th Jany 1723/4. *Signed*: Jas. COLLINS, Lucy C COLLINS her mark. *Wit*: Vallantine WALLIS, Joseph OLLIVER. *Proved*: Jany Court 1723/4. *Regt*: 14th Feby 1723/4.

No. Carolina, Jas. COLLINS of the prect of Pasquotank planter, for & in Consideration of the Sum of 20 pounds current money of No. Carolina ... paid by Thos. PLATER of the county & prect aforsd ... sold ... all that tract of Land & plantation which I lately bought of James CARON ... in Pasquotank prect. cont. by estimation 60 acres ... Ben GILES corner tree ... CALLYS Corner tree by a Branch of Flatty Creek ... James COLLINS & Lucy my wife have hereunto Sett our hands & seals this 21st day of September 1723. *Signed*: Jas. COLLINS his mark. *Wit*: Edmd. GALE, Eliza. E MARKHAM her mark. *Ack*: by Jno MCKEEL for James & Lucy COLLINS To Thomas PLATER. *Regt*: 14 Feby 1723/4.

[A:286] James MONK ... for the valuable consideration of 20 pounds ... paid by Truman MCBRIDE of the prect of Pasquotank & prov of No. Carolina ... have assigned over all my right ... of the within mentioned patent of Land ... 21st day of January 1723/4. *Signed*: James X MONK his mark. *Wit*: W NORRIS, David BAILEY. *Ack*: 21 Jany 1723/4. *Regt*: 25 Feby. 1723/4.

Pasquotank, David PRITCHARD Heir apparent of David PRITCHARD Decd of the prect. afsd. & prov. of No. Carolina that for the valuable consideration of 25 to me in hand paid by Jerr MURDEN ... sell ... all my right ... to the within mentioned Patent or tract of Land ... 21 day of Jany 1723/4. *Signed*: the mark of David D PRITCHARD. *Wit*: Benjn. PRITCHARD, John BELMANS X mark. *Ack*: 21 Jany. 1723/4. *Regt*: 23 Feby 1723/4.

Sarah WALLIS do constitute Thomas PLATER to be my true & Lawfull attorney ... to appear at the prect court of Pasquotank the 21st day of Jany 1723/4 & then & there to acknowledge a deed of Bargain & sale for a parcell of Land containing 60 acres unto Alex CROOKSHANKS ... quiting all my right & title of Dowry ... 20 Jany. 1723/4. *Signed*: Sarah X WALLIS hir mark. *Wit*: Jno MCKEEL. *Proved*: 21 Jany. 1723/4. *Regt*: 11 March 1723/4.

[A:287] No. Carolina: Valentine WALLIS of the prect. of Pasquotank Albermarle County in No. Carolina ... with the voluntary consent of

Sarah WALLIS my Lawfull Wife ... for the valuable consideration of 7 pounds ... paid by Alex. CROOKSHANKS of the same prect. County & prov. afsd. ... Sold ... a piece of Land ct. about 60 acres ... upon the W. Side of flatty Creek ... my plantation whereon I now live Bounds ... land whereon Thos. COLLINS now lives ... part of a greater tract by patent granted to Jno BELMAN & by the sd BELMAN Sold to my father Will. WALLIS ... 21 Jany. 1723/4. *Signed*: Vallentine WALLIS, the mark of Sarah X WALLIS. *Wit*: John MCKEEL, David BAILEY. *Ack*: 21 Jany. 1723/4. *Regt*: 13 March 1723/4.

[A:288] No. Carolina, Thomas JESSOP of the prect. of Perquimans in the prov. afsd. ... for the valuable consideration of 100 pounds ... paid by Stephen SCOTT of the prect. of Pasquotank in the prov. afsd ... Sold ... a certain Quantity of Land ct. 157 acres part of a greater tract containing 304 acres formerly belonging to Edwd POPE & by him bequeathed to his wife Sarah POPE who being intermarried with one Thos. WYATT did sell ... to Thos. JESSOP ... by a deed of bargain & sale bearing date the 19th October 1722 & acknowledged in the prect. Court of Pasquotank the 15 of Jany 1722/3 & registered the 9th day April 1723 ... [rest of deed missing]

No. Carolina, Elijah STANTON of the of Pasquotank in the county of Albermarle, planter ... whereas the true & absolute Lords Propts of Carolina by their deed of Grant bearing date the 1 May 1668 in the 36th year of their possession of the sd province did give & grant unto Thomas BOYD of Albermarle ... a certain tract of Land ct. 200 acres English measure lying upon the east side of little River in the prect of Pasquotank in the County of Albermarle ... by his certain deed of assignment on the back of the sd patent bearing date 30 day of September 1708 did assign & sett over unto Thos. STANTON ... all his right ... & whereof the sd Thos. STANTON by his last Will & Testament did give ... unto his wife Mary STANTON ... Mary STANTON ...did by her last Will & Testament give ... to her Son Elijah STANTON ... in Consideration of the sum of 12 pounds ... paid by Edmd GALE of Pasquotank prect
[A:289] ... Sold ... 200 acres ... on the N.E. side of Little River ... 17 April 1722. *Signed*: Elijah

STANTON. *Wit*: Jno BRETT, Thomas WYATT, Richd. SANDERSON. *Ack*: in April Court & *Proved*: by Tho WYATT one of the Evidences. *Regt*: in April 1722.

No. Carolina: Joseph STOKELY for & in Consideration of the Sum of £27 Sterling ... paid by Levi CRESY of Pasquotank ... Sold ... a parcel of Land lying in Pasquotank prect, in Albermarle County as by the within deed will more fully explain, I bought of the sd Levy CRESEY bounded in the sd deed to have & to hold the afsd 70 acres of Land & plantation ... 16 Jany 1721/2. *Signed*: Joseph STOKELY. *Wit*: Edm GALE, W NORRIS. *Proved*: by the oath of Edmd GALE 15 Feby 1721/2. *Regt*: in June 1722.

[A:290] No. Carolina, 6 March 1721/2 ... Albert ALBERTSON, my wife for ... valuable consideration ... give ... unto our Son John ALBERTSON ... a certain tract of land ct. 50 acres ... on the South west side of Pasquotank, commonly calld Beachy Neck ... in case the sd. John ALBERTON without Lawfull Issue then the sd tract of Land to fall unto Jacob ALBERTSON ... & upon his decease without Issue to fall unto his Sisters in Course & that this our deed of Gift be fully approved ... *Signed*: Gilbert [sic] A ALBERTSON his mark, Elisa E ALBERTSON her mark. *Wit*: Henry RAPER, Rowland R BUCKLEY his mark. *Ack*: 17 April 1722.

Will WILSON of Pasquotank prect in the county of Albermarle in the province of North Carolina, Mariner, ... for the Consideration of & Love that I bear towards Robert LOWDEN of the County & province afsd Son of John LOWDEN decd. have given ... 150 acres of Land, Lying on the South Side of Alligator Creek commonly called POPE land ... Provided that the sd. Land be Seated according to the Patent to me granted ... 17 April 1721. *Signed*: Will WILSON. *Wit*: Mac SCARBROUGH, Antho. X COOK his mark. *Ack*: in April Court 1721. *Regt*: in September 1721.

Eliza UPTON Widow & Relict of Jno. UPTON decd in the prect of Pasquotank & the County of Albermarle & in the province of No. Carolina on one part & Griffith GRAY Senr. of the prect. County & prov. afsd of the other part ... in Consideration of the Sum of 2 pounds 10 Shillings of good Lawfull money of Carolina ... Sold ... a certain ... parcell of Land being Sold out of a patent granted to John UPTON bearing date the first day of May 1668 situated ... on the North East Side of Pasquotank River Containing by Estimation 20 Acres ... on a branch to the head of her sd Land & on Griffith GRAYS own line [A:291] ... 15 January 1720. *Signed*: Eliza T UPTON. *Wit*: Will WILSON, Robt R SAYER his mark. *Ack*: in April Court 1721. *Regt*: in Sept. 1721.

Robert COOMS of Alligator in the prect of Pasquotank, County of Albermarle No. Carolina for & in Consideration of the sum of 40 pounds Sterling money of Great Brittain ... paid by Capt. Corn. FITZPATRICK of Alligator ... Sell ... tract of land ... on the North Side of Alligator Creek ... 307 Acres ... Bounding the fort? plantation on the South Side & LUDFORDS Cove on the North & HUNTS plantation on the Neck ...
[A:292] ... Ann COOMS the wife of the sd Robert COOMS ... surrenders all her right of dower ... 14 April 1721. *Signed*: Robt. RC COOMS, Ann A COMS her mark. *Wit*: Edwd. LETHEINGTON, Geo WHIDBEE, Ann MOSES. *Ack*: in April Court 1721 Pr. W LUDFORD Exs Att for Robt COOMS. *Regt*: In Sept.

No. Carolina Truman MCBRIDE did acknowledge all the land mentioned in the within Patent ... Sold ... unto Jas BROWN of the same province & prect. of Currituck ... 17 April 1721. *Signed*: Truman MCBRIDE. *Ack*: 17 July 1722. *Regt*: 26 Oct 1722.

No. Carolina: Andrew GONSALVO of the prect of Currituck in the prov. afsd. with the voluntary consent of Jane GONSALVO my Lawfull wife formerly Jane BRITNELL Sister of Wm BRITNELL & now next kin to the sd Wm BRITNELL Decd for ... consideration of 20 pounds ... paid by Wm GREGORY of the prect of Pasquotank & prov. ... Sold ... plantation lying on the North East side of Pasquotank River formerly Charles GRANDEY & by him Sold & confirmed unto one Joseph SPARNON & by [him] Sold ... to one Wm BRITNELL ... bearing date 5th day of April 1709 ... acknowledged ... in the office of Pasquotank
[A:293] the 27th April 1709 ... containing 50 acres ... 17 [blank] 1722. *Signed*: Andrew A GONSALVO his mark, Jane I GONSALVO her mark. *Wit*: W NORRIS, Wm WRIGHT. *Ack*: 17 July 1722. *Regt*: 26 Oct. 1722.

Levy CRESSY of Pasquotank Prect in the County of Albermarle, the prov. of North Carolina, planter & Sarah my wife ... in consideration of one Negro Girl Calld Anny of the Value & price of 11£ 11S ... paid by Capt Arthur MABBSON ... Sold ... unto Arthur MABSON & Mary his wife ... all that tract of Land containing 80 acres lying in Pasquotank afsd & called or known by the name of CRESSEYS Island for which he obtained a patent from the Lords proprit of Carolina the same bearing date the first day of May 1720 ... sd patent, herewith Surrendred & delivered by us the said Levy CRESSEY & his Wife Mary ... in consideration of the afsd negro Girl, we the sd Levy & my wife Sarah ... Sold ... to the sd Capt Arthur MABSON & Mary his wife, for the value of 7 pounds 10 Shillings & we have also relinquished a debt of 28 pounds 10 Shillings formerly due & owing unto us the sd Arthur MABSON & his wife during her widowhood ... & further I the said
[A:294] Levy CRESSEY have given a writting obligation bearing date the day before the date herof to the sd Arthur MABSON for 13 pounds to be paid ... at such time as are therein ... mentioned ... 29 May 1722. *Signed*: Levi CREESY, Mary CREESY. *Wit*: Danl. RICHARDSON, Margaret M BOWNTY her mark. *Ack*: 17 July 1722. *Regt*: 27 Octr. 1722.

[A:295] Thomas RANKHORN & wife of the County of Albamarle & Province of N.Car. ... for the sum of 4 pounds current money of the sd Colony ... paid by Zacharias NIXON of the same place ... Sold ... a small quantity of Land containing about 5 acres ... above the Mill Dam ... on one of the branches of Little River Eastermost side ... 17 July 1722. *Signed*: Thos. RANKHORN, Hannah H RANKHORN her mark. *Wit*: Jno. SYMONS, Christo. N NICHOLS his mark. *Ack*: 17 July 1722. *Regt*: 27 Octr 1722.

[A:296] 17th day of July 1722 between Thomas BETTY in the Precinct of Pasquotank in the County of Albermarle in the Government of North Carolina, Planter ... and John THACKARY of the Precinct of Chowan in the County and Government aforesaid ... in consideration of the Sum of 4 pounds ... paid by John THACKARAY ... sold ... parcel of Land ... part of a Tract of Land mentioned in a certain Patent bearing date the 10 of Feby 1722 granted to [blank] contg by Estimation 74 acres ... at the head of

Pig Branch ... to the Juniper Run ... *Signed*: Tho: BETTY. *Wit*: [blank] *Ack*: 17 July 1722. *Regt*: 29 Oct. 1722.

[A:297] 1720 ... Christopher WILLIAMS in the Precinct of Pasquotank & the County of Albermarle and in the Province of North Carolina and Ezra ALBERTSON of the Precinct of Perquimans & County & Province abovesaid ... in consideration of the Sum of 60 pounds Sterling Money of England ... Sold ... a parcel of Land ... on the N. E. Side of Pasquotank River containing by Estimation 300 Acres ... being the half-part of 600 acres of Land granted by Patent unto Wm. JENNINGS & Thomas JOHNSON being dated the first day of January 1694 & lies on the S. E. side of the Northern Branch of Arranoos Creek ... and further he the said Christopher WILLIAMS ... to Ezra ALBERTSON ... just sum of 120 pounds Sterling Money of England to be paid on demand on the nonperformance of this present writing ... 18 Oct. 1720. *Signed*: Christo W WILLIAMS his mark. *Wit*: Wm. ROSS, Nich. ROSS, Jno O UPTON his mark. *Ack*: 18 8br 1720. *Regt*: 31 Dec. 1722.

[A:298] Christopher WILLIAMS do assign & set over all my right, title & Interest of the within mentioned Deed of Sale to Ezra ALBERTSON ... 26 July 1720. *Signed*: Chr W WILLIAMS his mark. *Wit*: Jno SOLLERY, Jona. JONES. *Ack*: 18 8br 1720. *Regt*: 21 Xbr 1722.

No. Carolina, Joseph HACKET & Sarah HACKET my lawful wife of the Precinct of Pasquotank and Province afsd ... for the valuable consideration of [blank] pounds ... by Mary GIBBLE of the Prect & Province afsd ... sold ... a Tract of Land ct. 342 Acres ... S.W. Side of Pasquotank River granted by Patent to George HARRIS 1704 ... sold and assigned to Wm. NORRIS 20 Jany 1713/14 ... to Wm. SIMSON 15 of Xbr. 1715 ... to me Joseph HACKETT 15 April 1718 ... 31 Dec. 1720. *Signed*: Joseph HACKETT, Sarah HACKETT. *Wit*: W NORRIS, Jo: O OLIVER his mark. *Ack*: April Court 1721. *Wit*: Jno PALIN, Stephen TOMP. *Regt*: 5 Feby 1723.

[A:299] No. Carolina: Douglas ROOD of the precinct of Pasquotank & Province afsd ... for the valuable consideration of 11 pounds ... paid by Mary GIBBLE widow ... Sold ... 100 acres sold by Joseph CARTWRIGHT to the said Douglas ROOD ... 19 July 1720 ... Recorded 22 July 1720 ... 7 April 1721. *Signed*: Douglas X ROOD. *Wit*: W NORRIS, Susa. NORRIS. *Ack*: in April Court 1721. *Wit*: Jno PALIN clke pr. Temp. *Regt*: 5 Feby 1723.

No. Carolina, To any Orthodox Minister of the Church of England, or in default to any lawful Magistrate. You may Solemnize the Holy Estate of Matrimony (Banns excepted) there appearing to you no-lawful Impediment to the contrary Between William COLLISON of Carteret Precinct & Mary TOWNSEND of Currituck Precinct, and for your [?]dning this shall be your Sufficient Licence: Given under my Hand & Seal of Arms this 20 day of August Ano: Dom: 1722. *Signed*: Tho: POLLOCK. *Regt*: 20 Feby 1722.

[A:300] No. Carolina, Elijah STANTON of Pasquotank Precinct in the County of Albermarle, Planter ... Whereas Edwd. BRADSHAW in his life time was possessed by Survey of a Tract of Land contg. 200 Acres ... upon the head of Flatty Creek ... by his certain Deed bearing date the 13 day of August 1711 did assign ... unto James TOOKE ... deed of assignment on the back side of the said deed, bearing date the 17 day of January 1712/13 did assign the same over unto Robert KEELL ... by his Deed of assignment on the back side of the Said Deed bearing date the 19 October 1715 did assign the same over unto Thomas STANTON ... & whereas Sarah BRADSHAW Widow of the sfsd. Edward BRADSHAW by a certain Deed of Sale bearing date the 13 April 1716, did assign & set over unto Thomas STANTON ... whereas the said Thomas STANTON by his Last will and Testament did give ... unto his wife Mary STANTON ... by her last will & Testament give and bequeath the same to her Son Elijah STANTON ... in consideration of the sum of 20 pounds Sterling ... paid by Jno ARMURE of Pasquotank Precinct Planter, ... Sold ... all that Tract of Land ... contg 200 Acres lying ... on the N. E. Side of Little River ... 18 July 1722. *Signed*: Elijah STANTON. *Wit*: Edmd. GALE, Jos. MARKHAM. *Proved*: Augt. 21. 1722 ... by the Oath of Edmd GALE Esqr. ... Chr. GALE. *Regt*: 20 Feby 1723.

[A:301] Whereas my Father, Richard MADREN having

purchased a Tract of Land of Thomas ABINGTON and dealt out of its same several parcels to several persons and whereas it appears that the said Tract of Land was elapsable for want of [blank] and planting wherefore ... I William MADREN having relapsed the said Tract of Land and to prevent disputes which might arise thereupon by virture thereof and for Confirmation of those sales formerly granted by my Father and especially the within, mentioned do assign over all my Right ... from the said William MADREN ... unto John SCARF ... being for the Consideration within mentioned and already satisfied ... 16 Oct. 1722. *Signed*: Wm. W MADREN his mark, Ann A MADREN her mark. *Wit*: W. NORRIS, Jno. FFOURREE. *Ack*: 16 Oct. 1722. *Regt*: 21 Feby 1723.

David PARSONS for the valuable Consideration of 6 pounds paid by Arthur MABSON ... do assign over all my Right ... of the within mentioned ... 15 Jany 1722/3. *Signed*: David PARSONS. *Wit*: W NORRIS. *Ack*: 15 Jany 1722/3. *Regt*: 21 Feby 1723.

David BALEY of the Precinct of Pasquotank & Province of North Carolina ... for the valuable Consideration of 50 Shillings ... paid by Charles TAYLOR of the Precinct and Province afsd. ... Sold ... the one Moiety, or half part of a patent of 22 Acres of Swamp, granted by Patent to the said David BALEY bearing date the 5th day of April 1722 ... [A:302] ... 15 Jany. 1722/3. *Signed*: David BAYLEY. *Wit*: W NORRIS. *Ack*: 15 Jany 1722/3. *Regt*: 21 Feby 1723.

John PERKINS Senr. in the Precinct of Pasquotank, in the Province of North Carolina Planter, for and in Consideration of the Sum of 12 pounds Sterling ... paid by William STEVENS of the same Precinct & Province ... sold ... unto Wm. STEVENS & Elizabeth his wife ... parcel of Land on Baldridge on the North Side of Pasquotank River ... ct. 40 Acres, being part of a Tract of 250 Acres of Land patented by John BELL Senr, which said 40 Acres was sold by the said John BELL unto Wm. & Thos. CREECH and Since sold ... by Wm. & Henry CREECH unto the afsd. ... lying near or joining upon the Land of William BOCKE decd. now in the possession of Isaac SEABURN ... Westwd. Side of the sd. BOCKETTS Tract of Land ...

[A:303] ... 14 Aug. 1722. *Signed*: John A PERKINS his mark. *Wit*: Mac SCARBOROUGH, Jos. COOPER, Jona JONES? *Ack*: 15 Jany 1722/3. *Regt*: 22 Feby 1723.

Wm. MADREN of the Precinct of Pasquotank, Province of North Carolina ... in consideration of the sum of 16 pounds already paid by James GREAVES of the Precinct and Province afsd. unto my Father Richard MADREN for ... a parcel of Land sold out of a patent granted to Thomas ABINGTON, by my Father Richd. MADREN ... Sold unto the said James GREAVES, which sd. Tract of Land being elapsed for want of [blank] & planting in time, the said Wm. MADREN to Save & Secure the Said Land have obtained a lapse patent bearing date the 1 March 1721. Wherefore to prevent disputes which might arise about the former bargain & Sale which was granted by my Father Richd. MADREN unto the sd James GREAVES ... Sold ... all my right ... parcel of Land ct. 200 acres ... which my father Richd. MADREN did grant unto the sd. James GREAVES in a Deed bearing date the 19th day of July 1714 ...
[A:304] ... 16 Oct. 1722. *Signed*: Willm W MADREN, Ann A MADREN. *Wit*: W NORRIS, Jno. FOURREE? *Ack*: 16 Oct. 1722. *Regt*: 22 Feby 1723.

North Carolina. Pasquotank Prect. October 17th 1721. Mary RELF did acknowledge all the Land mentioned in the within Patent ... sold ... unto Willm RODES of the same Province & Precinct ... *Signed*: Mary M RELF her mark. *Wit*: John SOLLEY, James GREAVES. *Ack*: in Oct. Court 1721. *Regt*: Oct. 1721 Pr. Edmd. GALE.

No. Carolina, Levi CRESSEY of the Precinct of Pasquotank & Province of North Carolina ... with the voluntary consent of Sarah CRESSEY my lawful Wife ... for the valuable consideration of 75 pounds ... paid by Mary GIBBLE of the Prect & Province afsd. ... sold ... a Tract of Land contg. 172 Acres with plantation by patent granted unto the said Levi CRESSEY bearing date the 27 day of 7br 1715 beginning at a Persimon Richd MADREN Corner Tree ... to Geo: HARRIS Line ...
[A:305] ... 19 July 1721. *Signed*: Levi CRESSEY. *Wit*: W NORRIS, Tho: WILLIAMS. *Ack*: in 8br Court 1721. *Regt*: in 8br 1721 Pr Edmd. GALE.

No. Carolina, James BELL for divers good Causes &

Considerations ... by Col Wm. REED Esqr ... Sold ... all the within mentioned Tract of Land contg. 163 Acres & also the within mentioned patent ... 17 April 1722. *Signed*: James BELL. *Wit*: Richd. SANDERSON, Edmd. GALE, Jno. SOLLY. *Ack*: April Court 1722. *Regt*: April 1722.

Jono. JONES of the Prect of Pasquotank do assign over all my Right ... of the within mentioned Land to Jno. HARDING ... 19 July 1720. *Signed*: Jona. JONES. *Wit*: John SOLLEY, John I SAWYER. *Ack*: in April Court 1722. *Regt*: April 1722.

[A:306] James CARON Heir apparent of Stephen MASSAGEE decd. for a valuable Consideration of 7 pounds ... paid by James COLLINS ... assign over all my Right ... of the within mentioned Patents & Lands ... 17 April 1722. *Signed*: James CARON. *Wit*: W NORRIS. *Ack*: in April Court 1722. *Regt*: in April 1722.

David BALEY with the Consent of Ann BALEY my lawful Wife ... for the valuable consideration of 15 pounds ... assign over all our Right ... of the within mentioned patent & Land ... unto Saml. JACKSON ... 17 April 1722. *Signed*: David BALEY, Ann BALEY. *Wit*: W. NORRIS, Jno. FFOURREE. *Ack*: in April Court 1722. *Regt*: in April 1722.

North Carolina: William CARTWRIGHT of Pasquotank Prect. for a valuable Consideration ... give ... unto the Honble Col: Willm. REED Esqr. all my Right ... unto a Tract of Land I have sold unto Jeremh. MURDEN, according to the patent thereof ... 16 April 1723. *Signed*: the marke of William XX CARTWRIGHT. *Wit*: Josa. MARKHAM, Danl. RICHARDSON. *Ack*: 16 April 1723. *Regt*: 19 April 1723.

[A:307] 20 Aug. 1722 Between Thomas WYATT of the Prect. of Pasquotank in the Province of North Carolina Merchant ... and Danl. RICHARDSON of the same place Gentn. ... in Consideration of a Marriage already had & Solemnized between him & Sarah his now Wife and for the tender Love and affection that he beareth toward her and for a competent and sufficient Support ... given ... in trust for the said Sarah ... all the Estate both Real & personal that her late Husband Mr. Edwd. POPE decd. did by his last Will & Testament give ... unto her ... as the Same was at the time of her non marriage ... [A:308] ... *Signed*: Thos. WYATT. *Wit*: W NORRIS, Stephen DELAMARE. *Proved*: by Stephen DELAMARE 14 May 1723. *Regt*: 5th June 1723.

North Carolina. Whereas the within named Thomas WYATT for the consideration within written did give ... all the Estate that Sarah WYATT his now Wife had possessed and enjoyed at the time of the Marriage of which lately belonged to and was left her by Mr. Edward POPE her former Husband decd unto me the said Danl. RICHARDSON ... in Trust, nevertheless for the said Sarah ... as by the within written Deed of Indenture ... Danl. RICHARDSON for divers good causes and considerations ... doth transfer ... unto Mr. Jno. DAVIS, Father of the said Sarah WYATT all my Trust ... unto the aforementioned Estate ... 9th Feby 1722/3. *Signed*: Danl. RICHARDSON. *Wit*: the mark of Margt. M. BOURNS by William SYMONS.

William SYMONS do in the presence of God and under [blank] declare that I did see Danl. RICHARDSON seal and [blank] assignmt. as his act and Deed *Signed*: William SYMONS. Affirmation of William SYMONS taken before me May the 17th 1723. Let the above assignment be registered. *Signed*: Chr. GALE Ch: Just. *Regt*: 5 June 1723.

[A:309] Thomas HOLLOWAY do appoint my loving Friend, Thomas TRUMBALL my true lawful attorney to acknowledge one Tract of Land unto John WHEDBY ... 19 Feby 1722/3. *Signed*: Tho. H HOLLOWAY his mark. *Wit*: Jno. ARNOLD Senr., Jno. ARNOLD Junr.

Be it known unto all to whom these Presents shall come that I John WHEDBY do appoint my loving friend Jno. ARNOLD Senr. my true lawful attorney to acknowledge one Tract of Land called the white oak Land unto John CLARK on his Order ... 19 Feby 1722/3. *Signed*: John WHEDBY. *Wit*: Tho. T TRUMBALL, Jno. ARNOLD Senr.

John WHEDBEY of the Precinct of Currituck in this Province of North Carolina ... whereas the true & absolute Lords Proprietors of Carolina did by their certain Deed or patent bearing date the 24th day of June 1704 give & grant unto John JENNETT of the

County of Albermarle a certain Tract of Land contg. 276 Acres lying on the So side of Albermarle Sound in Perquimans Prect. formerly called the White Oak Land beginning at a Pine, PHELP'S bounded Tree on the Sound Side, thence up the Sound ... [rest of deed missing]

Stephen SAWYER ... agree to and with the sd. Caleb SAWYER ... I am the Heir apparent of the said Thomas SAWYER decd ... sell ... the said some Land & plantation ... 21 April 1724. *Signed*: Stephen S SAWYER his mark. *Wit*: W. NORRIS, William JENNINGS. *Ack*: 21 April 1724. *Regt*: 4 June 1724.

[A:310] North Carolina: Caleb SAWYER of the Prect. of Pasquotank & Province afsd. ... for the valuable Consideration of the Exchange of a plantation & Land with my Brother Stephen SAWYER ... sold ... a parcel of Land which my Father Thos. SAWYER decd., by a Deed passed unto me, and remains upon record in the prect. Office of Pasquotank dated in Jany 1715/6 ... 21 April 1724. *Signed*: Caleb SAWYER. *Wit*: W NORRIS, Robert LOWRY. *Ack*: 21 April 1724. *Regt*: 4 June 1724.

No. Carolina: Joseph COOPER do assign and set over all my Right ... to the within Deed of Sale unto the Honble. William REED Esqr. Presidt. ... 28 August 1723. *Signed*: Joseph COOPER. *Wit*: Abraham TOMAS, Jno. SOLLEY. *Proved*: 20 June 1724 by the Oath of Abraham TOMAS. *Signed*: Christ. GALE. *Regt*: 23 June 1724.

Received of Jeremiah SYMONS Two Barrels of Tobacco weighing four hundred weight Tobacco: which said Barrels of Tobacco I do promise to carry to Bermudas, or to the West Indies & sell at the best advantage I can & make Returns by, the first Opportunity unto him the said SYMONS ... paying freight 10 Shillings Pr each Barrel & Commissions according to customs, only the danger of the Seas excepted unto him ... 24th day of May 1721/2. *Signed*: Daniel SMITH. *Regt*: 30 June 1724.

[A:311] Pasquotank: Amos TRUEBLOOD of the Prect. afsd & Province of No. Carolina, with consent of my wife for the valuable Consideration of 80 pounds ... paid by my Brother John TRUEBLOOD ... sell ... all my Right ... to the within mentioned Patent Tract of Land ... 21 July 1724. *Signed*: Amos TRUEBLOOD. *Wit*: Benj. PRITCHARD, Francs. MCBRIDE. *Ack*: 21 July 1724 by Amos TRUEBLOOD & Elizth. his wife. *Regt*: 1 Sept. 1724.

John TRUEBLOOD of Pasquotank prect. in North Carolina Heir appart. to Elizth. GORMACK Widow & Relict of Patrick GORMACK in the Prect. afsd. decd. ... Whereas John ARCHDALE Govr. [blank] of the then [blank] of No. Carolina did by Patent bearing date the 1 May 1668 give and grant unto Francis HENDRICK a Tract of Land contg 206 Acres lying on the S. W. Side of Pasquotank River in the Prect. afsd. adjoining on Nobs Crook Creek & Richd. MADRENS Corner Tree ... since sold and conveyed unto the abovenamed Patrick GORMACK ... by an assignment on the above said Patent under the hands & seals of Francis HENDRICK & Mary his wife bearing date the 6th day of February 1702 ... & also given by the said Patrick GORMACK in his last Will and Testament to Elisabeth his Wife ... John TRUEBLOOD with consent of my wife for and in Consideration of 30 pounds ... by my Brother Amos TRUEBLOOD ... sold ... all that above mentioned Tract of Land contg 206 Acres ... 21 July 1724. *Signed*: Jno. TRUEBLOOD. *Wit*: Benjn. PRITCHARD, Frans. MCBRIDE. *Ack*: 21 July 1724. *Regt*: 5th 7br 1724.

[A:312] No. Carolina: Edmd. GALE of the Prect. of Pasquotank Gentn. for and in Consideration of the Sum of 45 pounds currt. money of N. C. ... paid by John SCOTT of No. Carolina, ... sold ... all that Tract of Land or Plantation which I lately bought of John JOHNSTON ... on the S. W. Side of Pasquotank River contained by Estimation 70 acres, bounded on N. W. by Thos. WILLIAMS and to the Ed. by Joseph JORDAN'S called old Jacob's: 21 July 1724. *Signed*: Edmd. GALE. *Wit*: Robert LOWRY, W. NORRIS. *Ack*: 21 July 1724. *Regt*: 10 7br. 1724.

No. Carolina, Saml. BUNDY Senr. of the prect. of Pasquotank Planter in Consideration of the Sum of 10 pounds currt. money to me in hand paid ...by Saml. BUNDY Son of Caleb BUNDY of the said prect. planter ... sold ... 150 acres of Land ... on the N. E. Side of Little River being part of a Tract of Land contg. 500 Acres bounded on the River Swamp so joining a

Tract of Land formerly surveyed by David BALEY now Jno. PARISHES ... 21 July 1724. *Signed*: Saml. BUNDY. *Wit*: Edmd. GALE, Josh MKHAM. *Ack*: 21 July 1724. *Regt*: 10 7br. 1724.

[A:313] John M DANIELL of Pasquotank in the Province of No. Carolina, do make over ... all my Right ... unto John RELFE of this within mentioned Conveyance ... 21 July 1724. *Signed*: John I M DANIELL his mark. *Wit*: Robert R SAWYER his mark, Corns. RELF. *Ack*: 21 July 1724. *Regt*: 10th 7br. 1724.

No. Carolina: William PHILLIPS of the prect of Pasquotank & the province afsd. ... for the valuable Consideration of 8 pounds ... paid by Jno. JONES of the same place ... sold ... Tract of Land ... situate in the Fork of Pasquotank adjoining to the Land of mine and being part of the same ... 50 acres [A:314] ... 21 July 1724. *Signed*: Wm. W PHILLIPS, Deborah P PHILLIPS. *Wit*: Frs. MCBRIDE, O. EVANS. *Ack*: 21 July 1724. *Regt*: 11, 7br. 1724.

Henry BUGBIRD do firmly and voluntarily of my own Accord make and constitute my trusty friend Joseph STOKELY to be my true & lawful Attorney for me and in my name to acknowledge unto Jerr MURDEN ... all my Right ... unto that plantation & Land formerly belonging to Willm. CARTWRIGHT Senr, and by him sold to Henry BUGBIRD of Pasquotank ... 21 April 1724. *Signed*: Henry BUGBIRD. *Wit*: Trum. MCBRIDE, Jno. MCDANIELL. *Ack*: 21 July 1724. *Regt*: 29 7br. 1724.

Henry BUGBIRD of Pasquotank Prect. and Province afsd. for the valuable Consideration of a Parcel of Land ... upon the head of Pasquotank as by Deed will appear in Exchange ... sell ... to the said Jere MURDEN ... all my Right ... unto the within mentioned Land ... 15 February 1723. *Signed*: Henry BUGBIRD. *Wit*: Jos: STOKELY, Owen REES. *Ack*: 21 July 1724. *Regt*: 29 7br. 1724.

North Carolina: Jerrh. MURDEN of the Prect. of Pasquotank & Province afsd. with the free voluntary Consent of Mary MURDEN my lawful Wife ... for the valuable Consideration of a Plantation & Tract of Land contg. 100 Acres ... lying between Stephen

RICHARDSON'S & Thomas CARWRIGHTS Junr. ... paid by Henry BUGBIRD of the Prect & Province afsd ... [A:315] ... sold ... a parcel of Land contg. 100 Acres ... at the upper End of the great Island and so running to the upper end of the little Island ... 21 April 1724. *Signed*: Jeremiah MURDEN. *Wit*: Joseph STOKELY, Truman MCBRIDE. *Ack*: 21 July 1724. *Regt*: 29th 7br. 1724.

No. Carolina, Thomas CARTWRIGHT Junr. of the Prect. of Pasquotank & Province afsd., with the free voluntary consent of [blank] CARTWRIGHT my lawful wife, for the valuable Consideration of 2 pounds ... paid by Jereh. MURDEN of the Province afsd. ...sold ... a parcel of Land contg 4 acres ... being part of a Tract of Land belonging to Thos. CARTWRIGHT Junr., the said 4 Acres of Land to be taken out from the largermost End of the said CARTWRIGHT Land ... binding upon a Tract of Land formerly belonging to Henry BUGBIRD and by him sold to Jeremh. MURDEN ... 21 April 1724. *Signed*: Thos. T CARTWRIGHT. *Wit*: Joseph STOKELY, Ann STOKELY. *Ack*: 21 July 1724. *Regt*: 29 7br 1724.

[A:316] No. Carolina, John SANDERLIN of the Prect. of Pasquotank & Province of North Carolina ... for the valuable Consideration of 10 pounds ... paid by Edwd. JAMES of the Prect. & Province afsd. ... sold ... a parcel of Land contg 50 acres ... to Wm. BECKETT'S House ... being part of a greater Tract contg 214 acres by Patent granted to me the said John SANDERLIN ... bearing date the 26 Oct. 1723 ... 21 July 1724. *Signed*: John I SANDERLIN his mark. *Wit*: W NORRIS, David BALEY. *Ack*: 21 July 1724. *Regt*: 3rd day of 8br 1724.

July 21st 1724 in the Prect. of Pasquotank ... James COLLINS of the Prect afsd do assign over all my Right ... of this withinmentioned Deed of Sale unto Richard GRAY of the sd. Prect. ... *Signed*: The mark of James X COLLINS. *Wit*: Thos. T STROMBLEX? his mark, Willm W COLSON mark. *Ack*: 21 July 1724, *Regt*: 6 Oct. 1724.

[A:317] No. Carolina: On a Council held at Edenton the 28th day of March 1723/4.
Prest: The Honble. Willm. REED Esqr. President:
Christo. GALE John LOVICK †

Frs FOSTER Thos. POLLOCK †Esqrs. Deptys.
Richd SANDERSON Maurice MOORE †

Read the petition of John MACKEEL & his wife (late Eliz: SMITH) & Levi MARKHAM Guardian or Curatus to Bartholamew EVANS a Minor in his Behalf herein? that the petitioners are Grandchildren, Heirs & Representatives of John HUNT, late of Little River decd., who by his last Will & Testament, here ready to be produced, did give & bequeath unto the sd Elizth. & Bartho: (now Surviving) the one half of his Estate (that is to say) of the Negroes, Bedding, and the rest of the Moveables, having before given one half thereof to his wife and further the petitioners say that at a Prect. Court 18 July 1721 at Pasqk. forth said Prect. the petitoners obtained an Order that the said Estate given to them should be equally divided between them and taken out of the Custody of Thomas COMMANDER Execr. of James TOOKE, Execr. to the afsd. John HUNT & the same and the Accots. thereof be adjusted & audited by Mr. Edmd. GALE, Mr. Richd. STAMP & Mr. Thos. MCKEELL who were also to divide the same, but so it is, that the said Thos. COMMANDER refused to comply therewith and thought himself aggreived at the said Order & No Time appointed the sd Auditors never asked thereon & through & their defects the sd. Order was rendered insufficient and never complied with, all the Cognizance thereof lying probably before his Honour in Council for Relief, the petitioners pray that pursuant to the said Order that the sd. Estate given as afsd. may be deld. up by the sd. Execrs to the Petrs. & the sd audirs. may be appointed a certain day where the parties concerned may attend to adjust & settle the audts. of the sd Estate and that on this Report thereof deld. to the Provce. Marshall as his Depy. he do seize and deliver the same in kind or value according to law to the Petrs. according to the division thereof to be made by the Auditors afsd. and that the sd. COMMANDER do pay Cost &c. &c.

Ordered That the said Thos COMMANDER do exhibit & adjust the Accots. of the Estate according to the prayer of the petitrs. with Edmd. GALE Esqrs. Thos. MCKEELL, John FOURREAY & Robt. LOWRY or any three of them, sometime betwixt the 20th day of April & the 20th of May next and that he deliver up the petrs. Legacy in the manner prayed for or else the Prov. Marshall is hereby ordered to take Security of the said Thos. COMMANDER in the Sum of 500 pounds for his appearance at the next Council to be held at Edenton & that he stand to & abide such Order as shall be made thereon. Copy. Jno. LOVICK Secy.

In Virtue of the above written Order to us the Dividers of the Estate of M John HUNT decd., We in obedience thereunto met this day at the dwelling House of the above named Mr. Thos. COMMANDER & have divided the sd. Estate & delivered the same according to the sd. Order by the free Will & Consent of the sd. COMMANDER after he had exhibited & adjusted the Accots. of the Said Estate according to the prayer of the petrs. within mentioned also & had paid the balance of the Said Accts. so exhibited & ajusted as afsd. by us this 20th day of May Ano: Dom: 1723. *Signed*: Edmd. GALE, Robt. LOWRY, John FOURREE, Tho: MACKEELL. *Regt*: 6th day of Oct. 1724.

[A:318] No. Carolina, 21 day of July 1724 & in the tenth year of the Reign of our Sovr. Lord George ... between Daniel BILLET Son and Heir of John BILLET late of Pasquotank Precinct decd of the one party & Col. Thos. SWANN of the Precinct of Currituck of the other party ... in the Consideration of the Sum of 100 pounds Stg. money of Gt. Britain ... paid by the said Thos. SWANN ... sold ... Plantation and Tract of Land contg. by Estimation 300 Acres ... on the So. Side of Pasquotank River ... Saml. DAVIS Corner tree ... Robt. TEMPLES Corner Tree ... being the same Land which was granted to my father Jno. BILLET decd by Patent bearing date the 30th day of August 1714 = 200 Acres of which sd Land was given and granted by my said father Jno. BILLET in his lifetime by a Deed ... to one Saml. WILSON decd. the 24th day of July 1717 ... Recorded 16th day of October following and the same 200 Acres after the Death of the Same Saml. WILSON descended to one Joshua WHITE Nephew & Heir of the said Saml. WILSON of whom the said Danl. BILLET hath bought the same as by a Deed from under the hand of the said Joshua WHITE bearing date the 29th day of January 1723 & recorded ... 22 July 1724. *Signed*: Daniel D BILLET. *Wit*: [blank] *Ack*: 22 July 1724. *Regt*: 7 Oct. 1724.

[A:319] No. Carolina, Mary BILLET, wife to the within named Danl. BILLET, do by these presents [blank] & Release all my Right & Title of Dower unto Col: Thos. SWANN ... 22 July 1724. *Signed*: Mary V BILLET. *Wit*: Willm. WILLSON, Peter P BROWNE his mark. *Ack*: 22 July 1723. *Regt*: 7 Oct. 1724.

Daniel BILLET of the Prect. of Pasqk. & Mary my Wife have for and in Consideration of the sum of 200 pounds Truly in hand paid by Col. Thomas SWANN, late of Currituck prect. ... sell ... all our right ... to the within Deed for a Tract of Land contg. by Estimation 200 Acres: ... 22 July 1724. *Signed*: Daniel D BILLET his mark, Mary X BILLET her mark. *Wit*: Wm. WILSON, Peter P BROWNE his mark. This assignmt. was of a Deed passed to Daniel BILLET by Josha. WHITE April 16th 1723 & Reg. 11 7br. 1723. *Ack*: July Court the 22nd 1724. *Regt*: 7 Oct. 1724.

His Excellency the most noble Henry Duke of BEAUFORT Palatin &c. Know ye, that we the said Lds. absolute Proprietors according to our Great Deed of Grant &c., do hereby give & grant unto John BILLET of our said Province a Tract of Land contg 300 Acres lying in Pasquotank Precinct on the So. Side of the River ... Saml. DAVIS Corner Tree ... Robt. TEMPLE Corner tree ... Signed: N. CHEVIN, Chr. GALE, Wm. REED, Chas EDEN, Tho: BOYD, Fras. FOSTER. Recorded in the [blank] Office the 2d 7br. 1714 Pr T KNIGHT Jury.

Daniel BILLET of Pasquotank Prect. Son & Heir of John BILLET the within patentee, have for and in Consideration of the Sum of 200 pounds Sterlg in hand paid by Col. Thomas SWANN ... sell ... the within mentioned Patent & Tract of Land contg. by Estimation 300 Acres ...
[A:320] ... 21 July 1724. *Signed*: Danl. D BILLET. *Wit*: Wm. WILSON, Peter P BROWNE. *Ack*: 22 July 1724. *Regt*: 7th 8br 1724.

North Carolina: Alice BILLET widow late wife of John BILLET of Pasquotank decd ... in my pure widowhood & lawful Authority, have received ... quit claim unto Thomas SWANN ... all my Estate Claim & Right ... by reason of any Dower of and in the third part of one Tenement and plantation & Tract of Land ... on the So. Side of Pasquotank River, contg. by Estimation 300 Acres, the which my decd Husband John BILLET died seized of ... lately in the Tenure & Occupation of my Son Danl. BILLET ... sd

Thomas SWANN lately purchased of my Son Daniel BILLET ... 23rd Jany 1723. *Signed*: Alice A BILLET her mark. *Wit*: Samuel BERNARD, James BELL. *Ack*: 22 July 1724. *Regt*: 7th Oct. 1724.

Henry WHITE & Arnold WHITE with the voluntary Consent of Elisabeth WHITE my lawful Wife and for ... the valuable Consideration of 25 pounds ... paid by David BALEY of the Prect. of Pasqk. Province of No. Carolina ... sold ... Tract of Land contg 308 Acres by Patent granted to us ... bearing date the 30th day of July 1724 ...
[A:321] ... 20 Oct. 1724. *Signed*: Henry WHITE, Arnold WHITE. *Wit*: W. NORRIS, Robt. LOWRY. *Ack*: 20 Oct. 1724. *Regt*: 23 Oct. 1724.

16 Oct. 1724, in the tenth year of the Reign of our Sovn. Lord George ... Amos TRUEBLOOD of the Prect: of Pasquotank & Province of No. Carolina ... for the valuable Consideration of 50 pounds ... paid by Jno. TRUEBLOOD ... Sold ... 300 Acres of Land & Plantation ... on the N. E. Side of Pasquotank River & part of a greater Tract of Land contg. 600 Acres granted by Patent to the afsd. Amos TRUEBLOOD & John TRUEBLOOD bearing date the 1st day of January 1694 & the Moiety or half part thereof beginning at the Mouth of the log bridge branch ...
[A:322] 16 Oct. 1724. *Signed*: Amos TRUEBLOOD. *Wit*: W NORRIS, Robt. LOWRY. *Ack*: 20 Oct. 1724. *Regt*: 8 Jany 1724/5.

John TRUEBLOOD of the Precinct of Pasquotank & Province of North Carolina ... for the valuable Consideration of 50 [blank] ... paid by my Brother Amos TRUEBLOOD ... sold ... 300 Acres of Land & Plantation ... on the N. E. Side of Pasquotank River & part of a greater Tract of Land contg. 600 Acres granted by Patent to me the Said. Jno. TRUEBLOOD & Amos TRUEBLOOD bearing date the first day of January 1694 and the Moiety or half part thereof beginning at the Mouth of the Log bridge branch ... which said 300 Acres of Land my Brother Amos TRUEBLOOD by an assignment of the patent the 21 day of July 1724 and aknowledged ... 21 July 1724 did make over unto me the said John TRUEBLOOD ... and confirmed the same by a Deed bearing equal date with these presents, and I the said John TRUEBLOOD ... do now transfer ... unto the sd Amos TRUEBLOOD ... the sd 300 Acres of land ... 16 Oct. 1724. *Signed*: John TRUEBLOOD. *Wit*: W NORRIS, Robt. LOWRY. *Ack*: 20 Oct. 1724. *Regt*: 8 Jany 1724/5.

[A:323] Amos TRUEBLOOD of the Precinct of Pasquotank & Province of North Carolina ... for the valuable Consideration of 30 pounds ... paid by my Brother John TRUEBLOOD ... Sold ... 206 Acres of land by patent granted to Francis HENDRICK ... sold unto Patrick GORMACK by an assignment on the back of the patent bearing date the 6th day of Feby. 1702 and ... given and demised to his wife Elisabeth GORMACK ... & by my Brother Jno. TRUEBLOOD Heir apparent to the sd. Elisabeth GORMACK granted & sold unto me ... by a Deed having equal date with these presents ... 16 Oct. 1724. *Signed*: Amos TRUEBLOOD. *Wit*: W NORRIS, Robt. LOWRY. *Ack*: 20 Oct. 1724. *Regt*: 8 Jany 1724/5.

John ARMURE of Pasquotank Prect. in No. Carolina, for the valuable Consideration ... all my Right ... of the within mentioned Patent unto Mr Robert LOWRY & Joshua MKHAM ... the lower part of the said Tract of land within mentioned to Robt. LOWRY ... the upper part to Joshua MKHAM ... 20 Oct. 1724. *Signed*: John ARMURE. *Wit*: W NORRIS, Gabl. BURNHAM, Evan. JONES. *Ack*: 20 Oct. 1724. *Regt*: 9 Jany 1724/5.

No. Carolina: William RELFE in the prect. of Pasquotank & Province afsd. Yeoman for and in Consideration of the Sum of 40 pounds current Money ... paid by Jeremh. MURDEN of the same place Planter ... Sold ... parcel of Land ... Line of William RELFE Junr. ... to the River of Pasquotank
[A:324] ... 100 Acres ... 6 May 1724. *Signed*: Wm RELFE. *Wit*: William RELFE Junr., Richd NORCOMBE. *Ack*: 20 Oct. 1724. *Regt*: 11 Jany 1724/5.

Cornelius RYALL of Albermarle County, & the prect. of Pasquotank & Province of North Carolina Planter, for and in Consideration of the Love ... which I have ... towards my dutifull Son Corns. RYALL & my dutiful Daughter Eliza. RYALL of the County & Province afsd. have given ... all ... my Land & Plantation whereon I now dwell contg. 300 Acres to be equally divided betwixt them; my Son Cornelius having the first choice ... after my Decease & the decease of their mother Elisabeth RYALL ... 25 Sept. 1724. *Signed*: Cornelius X RYALL his mark. *Wit*: Wm. WILSON, Danl. M MACKEE his mark. *Ack*: 24 Oct. 1724. *Regt*: 11 Jany 1724/5.

No. Carolina, John DAILLEE of the prect. of Pasquotank in the County of Albermarle and Province afsd. ... in Consideration of the Sum of 40 pounds lawful Money of Gt. Britain ... paid by William REED of the Same place Esqr. ... sold ...
[A:325] ... Tract of Land situate ... N. E. Side of the River Pasquotank ... contg. 50 Acres ... N. E. on the land lately belonging to the Indians, but now the said William REEDS. S. E. on the land of Henry CREECH, S. W. on the Land of the WINNS & N. W. on the said WINNS land which said land is commonly called or known by the name of the Bee Tree Neck being part of a certain Land confirmed by patent to Henry CREECH Senr and by him transferred ... 6 Oct. 1724. *Signed*: John X DAILLEE his mark. *Wit*: Joseph COOPER, Robt. PEYTON, Richd. NORCOMBE. *Ack*: 20 Oct. 1724. *Regt*: 11 Jany. 1724/5.

[A:326] North Carolina: John NORTON of the Prect. of Pasquotank ... for the valuable Consideration of 100 pounds ... paid by James & John CARONE ... sold ... a Tract of land contg. 200 Acres part of a greater Tract granted by Patent to Wm. JENNINGS & Thomas JOHNSON contg. 600 Acres, as by the said patent bearing date the 1 Jany 1694 ... which sd. 200 Acres was sold unto John NORTON ... by William SAWYER ... 21 April 17 [blank] & acknowledged in Court 21 April 1713 & recorded the 25 June 17 [blank] & is now transferred over unto the sd. James & John CARONE ... 20 Oct. 1724. *Signed*: John NORTON. *Wit*: Edwd. FAIRLACK, Gabl. BURNHAM. *Ack*: 20 Oct. 1724. *Regt*: 11 Jany. 1724/5.

Henry SAWYER of the Precinct of Pasquotank, in the County of Albermarle & the Province of North Carolina ... for the natural affections & fatherly love which I have & bear unto my well beloved Son Benja: SAWYER of the Prect & Province afsd ... give ... a Tract of Land contg. 140 Acres lying on the North River Swamp ... on Charles SAWYER'S Line so running to GREGORIES Line it being part of a larger Tract in the whole on Record 510 Acres ...
[A:327] ... 20 Oct. 1724. *Signed*: Henry H SAWYER

his mark. *Wit*: Jer X SEXTON, Caleb SAWYER. *Ack*: 20 Oct. 1724. *Regt*: 12 Jany 1724/5.

Henry SAWYER of the Precinct of Pasquotank, in the County of Albermarle & the Province of North Carolina ... for the natural affections & fatherly love which I have & bear unto my well beloved Son Danl. SAWYER of the Prect & Province afsd ... give ... a Tract of Land contg. 120 Acres lying on the North River Swamp ... on Charles SAWYER'S Line, it being part of a larger Tract contg. in the whole on Record 510 Acres ... 20 Oct. 1724. *Signed*: Henry H SAWYER his mark. *Wit*: Jerre X SEXTON his mark, Caleb SAWYER. *Ack*: 20 Oct. 1724. *Regt*: 12 Jany 1724/5.

Henry SAWYER of the Precinct of Pasquotank, in the County of Albermarle & the Province of North Carolina ... for the natural affections & fatherly love which I have and bear unto my well beloved Son in Law Griffith GRAY ... give ... a Tract of Land contg. 88 Acres lying on the No. River Swamp joining to Thos. SAWYER Senr. ... it being part of a larger Tract contg. in the whole on Record 510 Acres ... [A:328] ... 20 Oct. 1724. *Signed*: Henry H SAWYER his mark. *Wit*: Jerre X SEXTON his mark, Caleb SAWYER. *Ack*: 20 Oct. 1724. *Regt*: 12 Jany 1724/5.

Henry BRIGHT of the Prect of Pasquotank & Province of North Carolina ... for the natural love and affection I have and do bear unto my well beloved Son Charles BRIGHT ... give ... (after mine & my Wife's decease) all my Right ... unto 80 Acres of Land & plantation lying in the forke of Pasquotank & part of a greater Tract called by the name of the Quarter which ... was sold unto me by James JONES as may appear upon Record ... 21 Oct. 1724. *Signed*: Henry X BRIGHT his mark. *Wit*: W NORRIS, Edwd. SCOTT. *Ack*: 21 Oct. 1724. *Regt*: 12 Jany. 1724/5.

No. Carolina. John SCOTT of the prect of Pasquotank & Province afsd Planter, for and in Consideration of the Sum of 45 pounds currt Money ... paid by Joseph HACKETT Shipwright ... Sold ... all that plantation and Tract of land that I bought of Edmund GALE Esqr. lying and being on the S.W. Side of Pasquotank River and bounded with the land of Thos. WILLIAMS decd. on the No. Side and Joseph JORDAN Junr. on the So. Side

... 70 Acres ...
[A:329] ... 21 April 1725. *Signed*: John SCOTT. *Wit*: Edmd. GALE, John CONNER. *Ack*: 21 April 1725. *Regt*: 29 April 1725.

North Carolina: Henry RAPER of the Precinct of Pasquotank & Province afsd: for and in Consideration of the Sum of 6 pounds 5 Shillings to me in hand paid ... sell ... unto Danl. JACKSON Senr. of the Precinct & Province afsd. ... the within Conveyance or Deed of Sale ... 12 Feb. 1724/5. *Signed*: Henry RAPER, Susannah RAPER. *Wit*: Danl. JACKSON Senr., Elizabeth JACKSON, Zachariah JACKSON. *Ack*: 25 April 1725. *Regt*: 13 July 1725.

North Carolina: John DAVIS of the Precinct of Pasquotank & Province afsd. being in Trust for my Daughter Sarah WYATT the wife of Thomas WYATT ... for the valuable Consideration of 80 pounds current Money of North Carolina ... paid by John MCKEEL of the Prect. & Province afsd. ... sold ... one Moiety or half-part of the plantation & Tract of Land ... contg. 314 Acres commonly called Rule Neck as by patent bearing date the 25 Feby 1696 granted to Mr. Richd. POPE ... devised to his Son Edwd. POPE ... in his last Will & Testament devised and bequeathed to his wife Sarah POPE now Sarah WYATT, who intermarrying with Thomas WYATT ... by a Deed of Indenture in Trust made to Danl. RICHARDSON Esqr., in Trust to & for the use, Support & Maintenance of the said Sarah WYATT his Wife did grant unto him the said Danl. RICHARDSON all the Estate Real and Personal which her former Husband Edwd. POPE had by his last Will & Testament bequeathed unto her ... bearing date the 22d Aug. 1722 ... Danl. RICHARDSON ... did Set over and transfer all his Right ... [A:330] ... of the said Deed to Mr. John DAVIS in Trust to and for the sd Sarah as may appear by the said assignment bearing date the 9 Feby 1722/3 ... John DAVIS with the said Sarah WYATT for the Consideration afsd ... sell ... the moity or half part of the afsd. unto the said Jno. MACKEEL ... lying to the Westwd. of the sd. Tract and joining to the land of Samuel BUNDY Junr. ... contg 157 Acres ... sold unto the sd John MACKEEL ... 30 Nov. 1723. *Signed*: John DAVIS, Sarah WYATT. *Wit*: Thos. DAVIS, John I M HARRIS his mark. *Ack*: April Court 1725. *Regt*: 14 July 1725.

North Carolina: Charles TALOR with the voluntary Consent of Rebecca TALOR my lawful wife ... for the valuable Consideration of 20 pounds ... paid by David BAYLEY of the Prect. of Pasquotank and Province of North Carolina ... Sold ... Tract of Land contg. 50 Acres ...
[A:331] ... bounding on the head of Herring Creeke ... 21 June 1725. *Signed*: The Mark of T Charles TALOR, The Mark of T Rebecca TALOR. *Wit*: Henry RAPER, Robt. LOWRY, Junr., Joshua MARKHAM. *Ack*: 20 July 1725. *Regt*: 21 July 1725.

William WILSON of the County of Albermarle and Precinct of Pasquotank and Province of North Carolina Mariner ... in Consideration of the Love and Good Will which I have and do bear towards John JENKINS of the County and Province afsd. have given & granted ... 100 Acres of Land ... lying in Alligator ... near the Bridge that goeth upon Cow Ridge ... to HUNT'S Neck ... to BELL'S Bridge ... 19 July in the 11th year of the Reign of our Sovr. Lord George ... 1725. *Signed*: Wm. WILSON. *Wit*: Joseph WINSHIP, John WOODLAND. *Ack*: 20 July 1725. *Regt*: 22 July 1725.

[A:332] North Carolina: William RELFE in the Precinct of Pasquotank & Province aforesaid Yeoman for and in Consideration of the Sum of 40 pounds current money ... paid by Jeremiah MURDEN of the same place ... Sold ... a certain Tract or parcel of land ... line of Wm. RELF Junr. ... to the River of Pasquotank ... Containing 100 Acres ... 6 May 1724. *Signed*: Willm RELF. *Wit*: Wm RELFE Junr, Robt NEWCOMBE. *Ack*: 20 July 1725. *Regt*: 30 July 1724.[sic]

No. Carolina: Jeremiah MURDEN of the Precinct of Pasquotank doth assign & make over unto Wm RELF of the Prect. aforesd. for the valuable Consideration of the sum of 40 pounds ... sell ... all my Right ... to the within written Premises ... 21 July 1725. *Signed*: Jeremiah MURDEN. *Wit*: Henry RAPER, Saml. BUNDY. *Ack*: 20 July 1725. *Regt*: 30 July 1725.

[A:333] North Carolina: An Inventory and Sale of all the Goods and Chattels of Jeremiah FINCH late of this Province decd. as they were sold at public

Vendue by Mackrara SCARBOROUGH administr. sold at Pasquotank the 14 Dec. 1724 to the several persons here mentioned. Amounting in the whole to the Sum of 54 pounds, 16 Shillings & 6 pence. Viz. To 2 Suits of Drugett Cloth much moth eaten sold to Mac SCARBROUGH. To 2 Muffs & 3 Drawing Knivs sold to Charles BULL. To 2 pair of milled Hoose, 1 Cup & 1 Knife. To 3 Axes, 3 Cap & 3 Sifter Buttons. To 3 yds of wadding, 11 Sticks mohair & 3 hanks of Silk. To 30 dozen of small mohair Buttons. Sold to John PALIN. To 1 Drum & 4 Axes. To 33 Silk Muslin Handkerchiefs. To 6 better Do. To 3yds Drugett a remnant Serge, 6 doz Buttons. Sold Mac SCARBOROUGH. To 3 pair of Milled Hose, 1 Cap, 3 hanks of Silk. to 5 [?] & 2 horn Combs. Sold to Robt. TOLKSEY. To Gands? sold since viz. Feb? To 1 Sword, 2 Pistols & one old Gun. To a parcel of old Clothes. To 1 small Iron Pot with about 3 hundd. nails. To 1 Grindstone, 3 old Tin Measures, 1 do. funnel. Sold Mac. SCARBOROUGH. To a parcel of old papers unsold. To Debts recd. to the Value of ... To Debts not yet recd. amountg to ... Pasquotank July 3rd 1725. Mac: SCARBROUGH Admr. [Calculation of money omitted.]

Pasquotank Court 1725. the above Inventory was brought into Court by Mc SCARBROUGH and Oath made by him that the sd. Inventory & Sale was true and by the Court was ordered to be recorded. *Wit*: John PARKER Clk. Ct. *Regt*: 30 Aug. 1725.

North Carolina: David PRITCHARD, Heir Apparant to David PRITCHARD the Elder late of Pasquotank decd ... Whereas his Excellency the Pallatine and the rest of the true & absolute Lords Proprietors of Carolina according to their great Deed of Grant bearing date the first day of May 1668 did give & grant unto David PRITCHARD a Tract of Land containing 640 Acres lying on the South West Side of Pasquotank River in the County aforesaid Beginning in the fork of Knobs Crook Creek ... bearing date 25 Feb. 1696 ... David PRITCHARD being the next Male heir to the said David PRITCHARD decd. for ... the valuable Consideration of 25 pounds ... paid by [A:334] Saml. PRITCHARD the Elder ... sold ... all my whole Estate, Right & Title ... by virtue of Right of Inheritance descending in a right line from the sd David PRITCHARD the Elder unto the Tract of Land and Plantation commonly called the old Plantation in the sd. Hook of Nobs Crook Creek a part of the afsd. Tract of 640 Acres, being the plantation whereon Henry NICHOLLS lately lived ... 19 Jany. 1724/5. *Signed*: David DP PRITCHARD his mark. *Wit*: W. NORRIS, Jeremiah SYMONS. *Ack*: 29 July 1725. *Regt*: 20 Sept. 1725.

[A:335] No. Carolina: William CARTWRIGHT & Sarah CARTWRIGHT my Wife for ... the valuable Consideration of [blank] pounds ... paid by Henry BUGBIRD of the Precinct & Province afsd. ... sold ... 100 Acres of Land ... being part of a greater Tract belonging to me the sd. Wm. CARTWRIGHT and containing 400 Acres by Patent granted to me bearing date the 7 Jany. 1716/7 ... S. W. side of Pasquotank River ... upon Sandy Run Branch ... 21 July 1719. *Signed*: William W CARTWRIGHT his mark. *Wit*: Gabriel BURNHAM, William CARTWRIGHT Junr. *Ack*: 21 July 1725. *Regt*: 20 Sept. 1725.

Henry BUGBIRD of Pasquotank Precinct & Province afsd. for the valuable Consideration of a parcel of land lying ... upon the head of Pasquotank as by deed will appear I in Exchange ... make over forever from me ... unto the sd. Jeremh. MURDEN ... all my Right ... unto the within mentioned Land ... 15 July 1723. *Signed*: Henry BUGBIRD. *Wit*: Joseph STOKELY, Ann REES. *Ack*: 21 July 1724. *Regt*: 30 Sept. 1725.

[A:336] No. Carolina: Jeremiah MURDEN of the prect. of Pasquotank for the valuable Consideration of the Sum of 20 pounds ... paid by William CARTWRIGHT of the precinct afsd. ... sold ... all my right ... of the within written premises ... by the joint consent of Mary MURDEN my lawful Wife ... 21 July 1725. *Signed*: Jeremiah MURDEN. *Wit*: Henry RAPER, Truman MCBRIDE. *Ack*: 21 July 1725. *Regt*: in folio 146 the 21 Sept. 1725.

David PRITCHARD of Pasquotank Precinct ... for the valuable Consideration of another plantation in Exchange ... sold ... Land & Plantation containing 160 Acres ... upon Nobs Crook Creek formerly the land & plantation of Hugh PRITCHARD my father decd which he bought of Edmund CHANCEY ...
[A:337] ... 19 Jany 1724/5. *Signed*: David DP PRITCHARD his Mark, Pasttence P PRITCHARD her Mark.

Wit: W NORRIS, Jos MARKHAM, Isaac JONES. *Ack*: 21 July 1725. *Regt*: 21 Sept. 1725.

John UPTON of Pasquotank Precinct in the Province of North Carolina Planter, for and in Consideration of the Sum of 10 pounds in good & lawful money of the Province afsd ... paid by Charles BOLT of the afsd Precinct & Province Planter ... Sold ... Tract of Land ... on the North side of Pasquotank River ... near Gumberry Swamp ... line of Edward UPTON'S Land being on the W. Side & part of a Tract patented by John UPTON contg. by Estimation 60 Acres ... 11 April 1720. *Signed*: John X UPTON his mark. *Wit*: George LUMLEY, Isaac JONES, James GRAVES. *Regt*: 21 Sept. 1725.

[A:338] Charles BOLT of the Precinct of Pasquotank of the Province of North Carolina ... for the Sum of 25 pounds ... sold ... all my Right ... of the afsd. Deed to the sd. James JONES ... 21 July 1725. *Signed*: Charles BOLT. *Wit*: James PRITCHARD, Abel ROSS. *Ack*: 21 July 1725. *Regt*: 21 Sept. 1725.

His Excellency the Right Honble. John Lord CARTERETT Palatine and the rest of the true & absolute Lords & Proprietors of Carolina ... according to our Great deed bearing date the 1 May 1668 ... give and grant unto Col. Willm. REED a Tract of Land contg. 640 Acres lying in Pasquotank Precinct ... which land was formerly surveyed for Thomas SAWYER and by him assigned over to the Said Col. Willm. REED, being first due for the Importation of one person for every 50 Acres as appears upon Record underneath this Patent ... [rest of deed missing]

[A:339] Samuel BUNDY of the Prect. of Pasquotank in the Province of North Carolina for and in Consideration of the Love and Good will I have unto my well beloved Son Jeremiah BUNDY doth ... make over all my right ... to the within mentioned premises ... 21 July 1725. *Signed*: Saml. BUNDY. *Wit*: Henry RAPER, Stephen HALL. *Ack*: to Jeremh. BUNDY 21 July 1725. *Regt*: 22 Sept. 1725.

North Carolina: Joshua MARKHAM of the Prect. of Pasquotank, and the Province of North Carolina, Cordwainer, for and in Consideration of the Sum of 15 pounds ... paid by Zachariah NIXON of the Prect.

of Perquimons in the Province afsd. ... Sold ... parcel of Land ... bounding upon a piece of Land formerly belonging to Richd. POOL on one Side, the Fork Swamp on the other contg. 110 Acres ... the day and date above written, in the Tenth year of the Reign of our Sovr. Lord George, King ... 1725. *Signed*: Jos. MARKHAM, Eliza X MARKHAM her mark. *Wit*: Henry RAPER, Saml. BUNDY, Jeremh. BUNDY. *Ack*: 21 July 1725. *Regt*: 23 Sept. 1725.

[A:340] North Carolina: Edward SCOTT with the voluntary Consent of Mary SCOTT, my lawful Wife ... for the valuable Consideration of 81 pounds ... paid by John BROTHERS of the Precinct of Pasquotank in the Province of North Carolina ... sold ... a Tract of Land contg 150 Acres ... bounding upon Newbegun Creek and joining on one side by Henry PENDLETON & on the other Side by the Meeting House land, by patent granted for the Same ... 20 July 1725. *Signed*: Edwd. SCOTT, the mark of Mary X SCOTT. *Wit*: Henry RAPER, Jona. JONES, Truman MCBRIDE. *Ack*: 21 July 1725. *Regt*: 11 [ink blot on paper] 1725.

[A:341] His Excellency the Right Honble. John Lord CARTERETT Palatine and the rest of the true & absolute Lords & Proprietors of Carolina ... according to our Great deed of Grant bearing date the 1 May 1668 ... give and grant unto Richd. MADREN a Tract of Land contg. 430 Acres lying in Pasquotank Prect. on the back of Nobbs Creek Swamp ... FISHER'S Corner tree ... Geo HARRIS'S Corner Tree ... LANES'S Corner Tree ... being first due for the Importation of one person for every 50 Acres as appears upon Record under this Patent ... 1 Oct. 1715. Witness our trusty & well beloved Charles EDEN Esqr. Governor & Commander in Chief and the rest of our trusty and well beloved Counsellors who have hereunto set their Hands. *Signed*: C GALE, T KNIGHTS, C. EDEN, Tho: POLLACK, Frans. FOSTER. *Regt*: in the Secys. Office October 1st 1715 P T KNIGHTS Secy.

William MADREN of the Prect. of Pasquotank & Province of North Carolina have assigned all my Right ... of the within mentioned Patent ... to my Brother Isaac MADREN ... 280 Acres the other part being given to my Sister Ann MADREN by Deed of Gift

... 20 Oct. 1725. *Signed*: William W MADREN his mark. *Wit*: Albert A [ink blot on paper] his mark, Truman [ink blot]. *Ack*: 20 Oct. 1725. *Regt*: 16 Nov. 1725.

[A:342] Willm. MADREN of the Prect. of Pasquotank & Province of North Carolina, Planter ... for the love and Affection which I bear to my well beloved Brother Isaac MADREN of the Prect and Province afsd. ... give ... a certain parcel of Land contg. 280 Acres being part of a Tract of Land which my Sister Ann MADREN has 150 Acres out lying and being on the S.W. Side of Pasquotank River on Nobbs Crook Creek ... 20 Oct. 1725. *Signed*: William W MADREN his mark. *Wit*: Isaac JONES, Truman MCBRIDE. *Ack*: 20 Oct. 1725. *Regt*: 16 Nov. 1725.

William MADREN of the Prect. of Pasquotank & Province of North Carolina, Planter ... for the love and Affection which I have and do bear to my well beloved Sister Ann MADREN of the Prect & Province afsd. ... give ... a certain parcel of Land contg. 150 Acres ... being on the S.W. Side of Pasquotank River binding on Sandy Hill Branch being part of a Tract of Land which I have assigned by Patent to my Brother Isaac MADREN ... 20 Oct. 1725. *Signed*: William W MADREN his mark. *Wit*: Isaac JONES, Truman MCBRIDE. *Ack*: 20 Oct. 1725. *Regt*: 16 Nov. 1725.

[A:343] Isaac JONES of the Prect. of Pasquotank and Province of North Carolina Planter ... for the Sum of 23 pounds good and lawful money of the Province afsd ... paid by Charles BOLL of the same Precinct and Province afsd ... sold ... 100 Acres ... on the No. East Side of Pasquotank River between John JONES my Father's Plantation on a Branch on the So Side of Abraham JONES'S Land included on the S. Side of another Branch Abraham JONES'S Bounds ... (Next 3 pages of Record Book lost here) Retranscribed by J. M. JACKSON.
[A:344] [blank]
[A:345] Robert MORGAN of the Precinct of Pasquotank in the Province of North Carolina ... in Consideration of the natural affection and Fatherly love which I have and do bear unto my well beloved Son Joseph MORGAN of the precinct afsd. ... give ... a parcel of Land lying ... on the N. E. Side of

Pasquotank River contg. 100 Acres ... the Corner tree between myself and William WILLIAMS ... Thomas JONES'S Land It being the 100 Acres of land I bought of Thomas JONES being part of a Tract of land out of a patent bearing date Oct. 22, 1705 Containing by Patent 520 Acres ... 16 July 1728. *Signed*: Robt. MORGAN. *Wit*: Tho: SWANN, John ABBITT, James SPENCE. *Ack*: 16 July 1728. *Regt*: 18 Sept. 1728.

North Carolina: Thomas BETTEYS of the Prect. of Pasquotank and Province afsd. ... with the free and voluntary Consent of Mary BETTEYS my lawful Wife and for the valuable Consideration of 2 pounds ... paid by William WARD in the Prect. and Province afsd. ... Sold ... Tract of land contg. 100 Acres ... West side of Nobb's Crook Creek ...
[A:346] 5 July 1728. *Signed*: Thomas BETTYS. *Wit*: Rob CAHOON?, Jane Mc M.CLELEN? her mark. *Ack*: 16 July 1728. *Regt*: 18 Sept. 1728.

North Carolina: John WORRELL of Pasquotank and in the Province afsd. ... the valuable Consideration of 20 pounds ... paid by Edwd. BRIGHT of North Carolina & in the County of Albemarle and in the prect of Pasquotank ... Sold ... parcel of Land containing 50 Acres ... Bear Spring ... 15 July 1728. *Signed*: John I WORRELL his mark. *Wit*: [blank] ADAMS, Francis N OVERTON his mark, Charles C HUMPHREYS his mark. *Ack*: 16 July 1728. *Regt*: 18 Sept. 1728.

[A:347] Edward BRIGHT of Pasquotank pct. in the Province of North Carolina ... & my lawful Wife Sarah ... for the valuable Consideration of 30 pounds ... paid by Francis OVERTON ... sold ... a parcel of land containing 270 Acres ... part of a greater Tract contg. 640 Acres granted by Patent to Richd. OVERTON ... 15 July 1728. *Signed*: Edward X BRIGHT his mark. *Wit*: ADAMS? Jno. X GREGORY his mark. *Ack*: 16 July 1728. *Regt*: 18 Sept. 1728.

North Carolina: John JENNINGS of Pasquotank Planter for and in Consideration of Value in hand paid by Christopher WILLIAMS of the same Prect. & Province Planter ... Sold ... Tract of Land contg. ... 100 Acres ... commonly known by the name of Schoolhouse Neck lying & being between a Tract of Land called Hickory Neck & a Tract of Land belonging to Robert SAWYER Senr. ...

[A:348] ... 15 July 1728. *Signed*: John [blank] JENNINGS his mark. *Wit*: Joseph MORGAN, Thomas JONES. *Ack*: July 1728. *Regt*: 20 Sept. 1728.

North Carolina: Philip TORKSEY of Pasquotank Precinct in Albemarle County and Province afsd. ... John UPTON by his last will & Testament bearing date the 13 June 1715 did give ... unto Elisabeth UPTON his wife ... Tract of Land, contg. 191 Acres, granted to him ... by Patent bearing date the 25 Feb. 1696 ... being on the North East side of Pasquotank River ... whereas the said Elizabeth UPTON by a Conveyance ... bearing date the 31 Aug. 1721 ... sell ... unto me the sd. Philip TORKSEY the afsd. Tract of Land ... for a valuable Consideration to me in hand paid ... by Valentine GRAY ... did sell ... Deed ... bears date 27 Nov. 1725 ... but through Default and unskilfulness of the Writer of the sd. Assignment the same was found to be imperfect & insufficient to pass the fee simple of the sd. Land ... for the further ... surer and sure making and conveying unto the sd. Valentine GRAY ... (Record Torn) ... 9 Feb. 1727/8. *Signed*: Phill: TORKSEY. *Wit*: Mac SCARBROUGH, Benjn. PRITCHARD, Wm. W WILLIAMS Signum. *Ack*: 16 July 1728. *Regt*: 24 Sept. 1728.

[A:349] North Carolina: Thomas BETTEYS of the prect. of Pasquotank in the Province afsd. ... with the free Consent of Mary BETTEYS my lawful Wife and for the valuable Consideration of 1 pound in hand paid by Rebecca WARD of the Prect. & Province afsd. ... sold ... a Tract of Land ... on the South Side of the Head of Nobb's Crook Creek Swamp ... being part of a Tract of Land held by Patent containing 318 Acres bearing date the 11th day of October 1727 ... cont. 50 Acres ... 15 July 1728. *Signed*: Thomas BETTYS. *Wit*: [blank]ne M MCCLELEN? her mark, Rob: CAHOON?. *Ack*: 16 July 1728. *Regt*: 25 Sept. 1728.

Cornelius RATCLIFT of the Province of Virginia for and in Consideration of the Sum of 15 pounds ... paid by Samuel BUNDY Junr of the Prect. of Pasquotank in North Carolina ... Sold ... a Tract of Land contg. 125 Acres ... joining on the lands of John MACKEEL & John LOMBROSIER & Richd STAMP & Charles WEST ... by a

[A:350] Patent from the true and absolute Lords Proprietors of Carolina, bearing date the 6th day of April 1724 ... 16 April 1728. *Signed*: Cornelius RATCLIFT. *Wit*: Benjn. PRITCHARD, Stephen SCOTT, Danl. GUTHRIE. *Ack*: 15 Oct. 1728. *Regt*: 17 Dec. 1728.

William Earl of CRAVEN Palatine &c. ... do hereby give and grant unto Thomas MILLER of our said County Planter, a Tract of Land containing 640 Acres lying on Pasquotank River in Pasquotank Precinct ... at the mouth of Portahonk Creek ... 1 Jany 1694. Witness our trusty and well beloved Philip LUDWELL Esqr. Governor &c. of our said Province & our trusty & well beloved Counsellors who have hereunto set their hands Philip LUDWELL, Tho: HARVEY, Daniel AKEHURST, Frans. TOMS, Thos. POLLACK. The above written is a true Copy taken from the Records in the Secretary's Office Dec. 20th 1716. T. KNIGHT Secy.

Thomas MILLER of the County of Albemarle and Province of North Carolina and Precinct of Pasquotank do assign all my Right ... of the within mentioned Land unto Philip TORKSEY Junr. ... 11 Nov. 1725. *Signed*: Thomas MILLER. *Wit*: Wm WILSON, Robert R TORKSEY his mark, Sarah WILSON. Except the Grain yards and Twenty yards Square.

[A:351] Thomas MILLER of the County of Albemarle & Province of North Carolina Mariner do make, ... William WILSON Mariner of the County and Province afsd. to be my true ... attorney for me ... to acknowledge ... my Land and Plantation on the north Side of Pasquotank River beginning at the mouth of Portahonk Creek unto Philip TORKSEY Junr. ... 13 Jany. 1725/6. *Signed*: Thomas MILLER. *Wit*: Joseph WINSHIP, John TODD. *Ack*: 18 Jany. 1725/6. *Regt*: 25 Jany. 1725/6.

His Excellency John Lord CARTERET Palatine &c. ... do hereby give and grant unto Joseph WINSHIP of our said County a Tract of Land containing 450 Acres lying on the North Side of Alligator Creek at the head of the sd. Creek called Newfoundland ... end of Ball Ridge ... 2 Aug. 1723 ... Witness our trusty and well beloved William REED Esqr President of our Council & Commander in chief &c. *Signed*: Richard SANDERSON, J. LOVICK, T. POLLOCK, Wm REED, C GALE.

Recorded in the Secretary's Office. J LOVICK Secy.

Joseph WINSHIP and Ann WINSHIP of the County of Albemarle and Province of North Carolina, do assign all our Right ... of the within mentioned Land, unto John TODD, and William WILSON ... 11 Jany. 1725/6. *Signed*: Joseph WINSHIP, Anne WINSHIP. *Wit*: Richard BRITESHALL, John I COMBS his mark. *Ack*: 18 Jany. 1725/6. *Regt*: 25th Jany. 1725/6.

[A:352] His Excellency John Lord GRANVILE Palatine ... give and grant unto William CARTWRIGHT a Tract of Land containing 200 Acres lying in Pasquotank ... 29 Nov. 1706. Witness our trusty and well beloved William GLOVER Esqr. President ... *Signed*: W. GLOVER, Samuel SWANN, John ARDERN. Francis FOSTER, Edwd. MOSELEY. Recorded in the Secretary's Office, 1 Dec. 1707. T KNIGHT Secy.

William REED Esqr. of the Prect. of Pasquotank in the Province of North Carolina ... assign all my Right ... of the within Patent ... to Jeremiah MURDEN ... 22 March 1724/5. *Signed*: Wm. REED, Jane X REED. *Wit*: Danl. GUTHRIE, Willm RELFE. *Ack*: 18 Jany 1725/6. *Regt*: 26 Jany 1725/6.

William CARTWRIGHT of Pasquotank in the County of Albemarle and Province of North Carolina Wheelright ... in Consideration of the ... sum of 39 pounds 17 Shillings and 6 pence current money of this Province ... sold ... to Jeremh. MURDEN of the County & Province afsd. ... all that my Plantation whereon I now live, containing 200 Acres ... being in Pasquotank afsd, excepting only one Neck of Land beyond the Bee Tree Branch & running up to the Cypress Swamp ...
[A:353] ... by virtue of a Patent bearing date the 29 Nov. 1706 ... 26 Jan. 1713. *Signed*: William W CARTWRIGHT his mark. *Wit*: Rob: MORGAN, Robt. CARTWRIGHT, Joseph GLAISTER.

William REED Esqr. do by these presents assign over all my Right ... of the within mentioned Deed of Sale ... to Jeremh. MURDEN ... 22 March 1724/5. *Signed*: Wm REED, Jane X REED. *Wit*: Danl. GUTHRIE, Wm RELFE. *Ack*: 18 Jany 1725/6. *Regt*: 26 Jany. 1725/6.

John BAILY of North Carolina ... for the valuable Consideration of 18 pounds ... sold ... unto Charles TAYLOR ... parcel of land ... upon the Narrows of Little River ... at the mouth of a branch called the Tanner Branch ... to the new Main Road, thence as the Road goes to John RAPER'S line ... 129 Acres ... [A:354] ... 29 Oct. 1725. *Signed*: John I BAILY his mark. *Wit*: Natt. HALL, John J RAPER. *Ack*: 18 Jany. 1725/6. *Regt*: 26 Jany. 1725/6.

North Carolina: 18 Jan. 1725 ... Henry WHITE Son & Heir of Henry WHITE decd. & Arnold WHITE Junr. both of Perquimans Prect. of the one party & Willm. SYMONS of the Prect. of Pasquotank of the other party ... for and in Consideration of one Young Negro Girl & Negro Boy aged between 12 and 25 years of ages to us in hand paid by the sd. William SYMONS ... Sold ... Tract of Land containing 100 Acres ... on the West Side of a Creek called SYMONS Creek bounded on the North Side with a little Branch & small Creek that runs to the Eastern End of the House of Worship commonly called the Quaker Meeting House at Little River ... Tract of Land belonging to Arnold WHITE Senr. ... to the Swamp of the said SYMONS Creek ...
[A:355] ... *Signed*: Henry WHITE, Arnold WHITE. *Wit*: Aaron MORRIS, Thomas OVERMAN. *Ack*: 18 Jany 1725/6. *Regt*: 27 Jany 1725/6.

Henry WHITE and Arnold WHITE Junr. in the County of Albemarle and Province of North Carolina ... whereas our Father Henry WHITE Senr. in the Province afsd. decd. did in his last will and Testament give unto us ... a certain Tract of Land lying on SYMONS Creek ... in Consideration of one Negro Girl aged about 12 years ... sold ... unto Aaron MORRIS ... a parcel of the above mentioned Tract of Land containing 50 Acres ... being on the West Side of the above mentioned SYMONS Creek ... from the Quaker's Meeting House at Little River on Abraham WHITE'S Line N.W. or thereabout to John MORRIS'S Line, about West to Robert WHITE'S Line, ... to Arnold WHITE Seniors's Line ... 18 Jan. 1725. *Signed*: Arnold WHITE, Henry WHITE. *Wit*: William SYMONS, Thomas OVERMAN. 18 Jany 1725/6. *Regt*: 27 Jany 1725/6.

[A:356] John & Elizabeth RELFE of the County of Albemarle living in the Prect. of Pasquotank ... 55

pounds ... paid ... sold ... to Francis MARTIN, a certain Tract of Land containing 300 Acres ... at the South East Side of a Plantation commonly known by the name of HARRIS'S Ridge ... to David PRITCHARD'S Corner Tree ... to the Lake ... 17 Jan. 1725/6. *Signed*: Jno RELF, The mark of Elisabeth E RELF. *Wit*: James CARON, Jno. CARON. *Ack*: 18 Jany 1725/6. *Regt*: 27 Jany 1725/6.

North Carolina: John KING alias SEYMORE of Pasquotank Precinct, Planter ... to Daniel MACKEEY of the same Precinct ... in Consideration of the Sum of 15 pounds of good and lawful Money of the Province afsd. ... sold ... Tract of Land lying near the Mouth of Pasquotank Creek in Pasquotank River containing ... 140 Acres ... surveyed for Henry FOSTER Pr Thomas RELF Deputy Surveyor and transferred by the said FOSTER unto John JENNINGS and by him ... Sold unto Joseph SEYMORE ... acknowledged ... 21 Aug. 1705 by Tho: ABINGTON, attorney for the sd. JENNINGS ...
[A:357] ... 16 Jan. in the 11th year of the Reign of our Sovereign Lord George ... 1725. *Signed*: John KING J alias SEYMORE his mark. *Wit*: M SCARBOROUGH, Wm WILLSON, John SCARBOROUGH. *Ack*: 18 Jany 1725/6. *Regt*: 28 Jany 1725/6.

James WINRIGHT of the Province of North Carolina for and in Consideration of the Sum of 50 pounds money of this Province ... paid by Robert EDNY of the Precinct of Pasquotank ... Tailor ... sell ... Tract of Land called by the name of Newfoundland, containing by patent 640 Acres ... on the Westernmost Fork of Pasquotank River ... 19 Jan. 1725. *Signed*: James WINRIGHT. *Wit*: Gabriel BURNHAM, Tho: LOWTHER. *Ack*: 19 Jan. 1725/6. *Regt*: 28 Jany 1725/6.

[A:358] North Carolina: Philip TORKSEY Senr with Mary, Wife ... for the valuable Consideration of 70 pounds ... paid by Joseph GUILFORD Junr. of the Parish and Province afsd. ... sold ... Tract of Land ... containing 200 Acres of Land ... on the N. E. Side of Pasquotank River between Joseph GUILFORDS Senr and Robert HARRISON'S & George COMP'S? ... 4 Dec. 1725. *Signed*: Philip TORKSEY Senr., Mary TORKSEY. *Wit*: Philip TORKSEY Junr, Robert HARRISON. *Ack*: 19 Jany 1725/6. *Regt*: 28 Jany

1725/6.

His Excellency The Right Honble. John Lord CARTERET Palatine &c. ... Do hereby give and grant unto Philip TOLKSEY of our said County, a Tract of Land containing 80 Acres lying on the No. E. Side of Pasquotank River ... MACBRIDE'S Corner Tree by Cub Swamp ... which sd. Land was formerly surveyed for George GRIFFIN & by him sold and assigned over to the said Philip TOLKSEY ... 10 Dec. 1716. Witness our trusty & well beloved Charles EDEN Esqr. Governor ... *Signed*: Francis FOSTER, T KNIGHT, C EDEN, Tho: POLLOCK, N. CHEVIN. *Regt*: in the Secy's Office 10 Dec. 1716 Pr T KNIGHT Secy.

[A:359] I do assign ... all the Right ... of the within mentioned Patent to John TOLKSEY ... 30 April 1718. *Signed*: Philip TOLKSEY Junr. *Wit*: Joseph I GILFORD sig, Wm. W RIGHT sig, Methusalem VAUGHAN. *Ack*: 19 Jany 1725/6. *Regt*: 29 Jany 1725/6.

William MELTON of the Precinct of Pasquotank and Province of North Carolina ... for the valuable Sum of 40 pounds ... paid by Solomon POOL of the Precinct & Province afsd. ... sold ... Plantation containing 230 Acres ... on the N. E. side of Little River adjoining to the afsd. Solomon POOL'S line as doth appear by a patent and Deeds of Sale of the same ... by the joint Consent of Mary MELTON my Wife ... 26 Oct. 1723. *Signed*: the mark of William XX MELTON. *Wit*: Henry RAPER, Tho: TWEEDY. *Ack*: 7 Feb. 1725. *Regt*: 12 Mar. 1725.

Danl. JACKSON Senr. of North Carolina ... for the love that I bear to my Son Zachariah JACKSON ... all my Right, Title & Interest ... beginning at the Cypress Branch, all my land westerly ... Easternmost Branch of Herring Creek in the Prect. of Pasquotank ... 50 Acres ... by an authentic Deed of Gift ... [A:360] ... 15 Jan. 1725/6. *Signed*: Daniel JACKSON Senr. *Wit*: Tho: TWEDY, Danl. JACKSON Junr, Saml. JACKSON. *Ack*: 19 April 1726. *Regt*: 2 May 1726.

Daniel JACKSON Senr. in North Carolina ... for the love that I bear to my Son Daniel JACKSON ... give ... all my Right, Title ... at the Easternmost Branch of Herring Creek Swamp ... 50 Acres ... in the Precinct of Pasquotank ... by an authentic Deed of Gift ... 15 Jan. 1725/6. *Signed*: Daniel JACKSON Senr. *Wit*: Tho: TWEEDY, Saml. JACKSON, Zachariah JACKSON. *Ack*: 19 April 1725/6. *Regt*: 2 May 1726.

Ebenezer HALL of the Precinct of Pasquotank & Province of North Carolina for the valuable Consideration of 17 pounds ... paid by Daniel JACKSON Senr of the Precinct & Province afsd. ... sold ... all my Right, Title, Claim ... unto Samuel JACKSON Junr. the Son of Danl. JACKSON Senr. of 100 Acres of Land ... upon the North Side of Little River in the Precinct of Pasquotank, binding upon the lower Side of John HALL'S Line
[A:361] 15 April 1726. *Signed*: Ebenezer HALL. *Wit*: William SIMPSON Senr, William W SIMPSON Junr his mark, Abraham A RANKHORN his mark. *Ack*: 19 April 1726. *Regt*: 2 May 1726.

14 Oct. 1725 and in the 11th year of the Reign of our Sovereign Lord George ... William UMPHREYS of the Precinct of Pasquotank & the County of Albemarle and Province of North Carolina ... to Griffith GRAY Senr of the Precinct & County & Province aforesaid ... in Consideration of the Sum of 4 pounds 10 Shillings of good lawful Money of North Carolina ... sold ... parcel of Land containing by Estimation 103 acres out of a Patent granted ... 12 July 1725 ... Solomon DANIEL'S Line ... Willm. UMPHRY'S and Robert SAWYER Junr's their Line ... on the N. E. Side of Pasquotank River ...
[A:362] ... *Signed*: William W UMPHREYS his mark. *Wit*: Jonah. JONES, Robert SAWYER. *Ack*: 19 Apr. 1726. *Regt*: 2 May 1726.

His Excellency John Lord CARTERET Palatine &c. ... give and grant unto John CONDON of our said County a Tract of Land containing 298 acres lying on the North East Side of Pasquotank River ... Thomas GREGORY'S Land ... in the Indian Line ... Gum Creek's line ... SPARNONS Corner ... Land was formerly granted by Patent bearing date 1 March 1719 to Gilbert JAMES and by him elapsed for not seating and planting ... 1 April 1726 Witness my trusty and well beloved Sir Richard EVERARD Baronet Govr. ... *Signed*: Robt. WEST, John BLOUNT, E MOSELEY, Tho: POLLOCK, Richd. EVERARD, Chris GALE, Tho: HARVEY, J LOVICK. *Regt*: in the Secy's Office Pr Robt. FOSTER Depty. Surv.

John CONDON do assign over all my Right to the within mentioned Patent unto Tho: GREGORY Junr. ... 19 April 1726. *Signed*: John I CONDON his mark. *Wit*: Mc. SCARBOROUGH, Gilbert G JAMES his mark. *Ack*: 19 April 1726. *Regt*: 3 May 1726.

His Excellency John Lord CARTERET Palatine &c. ... give and grant unto Richd. OVERTON of Pasquotank Prect. a Tract of Land containing 640 Acres ... [A:363] ... Given under the Seal of the Colony, this 10 Feb. 1719. Witness our trusty and well beloved Charles EDEN Esqr. Governor and the rest of &c. *Signed*: Charles EDEN, Francis FOSTER, Fredk JONES, Richard SANDERSON, Tho: POLLOCK. Recorded in the Secy's office in Book P folio 6? J LOVICK Secy.

Edward OVERTON with free will and Consent of Elizabeth his wife, do sell ... unto Edwd. BRIGHT ... assignment of Patent being 270 Acres; it being already laid out of 640 acres ... 15 April 1726. *Signed*: Edward E OVERTON his mark. *Wit*: Moses LINTON, Catherine C LINTON her mark, Gabr. BURNHAM. *Ack*: 19 April 1726. *Regt*: 5 May 1726.

North Carolina: William LINTON of the Precinct of Pasquotank and Province afsd. ... for the valuable Consideration of 4 pounds ... paid by Edwd. BRIGHT of the same place ... sold ... a parcel of Land contg. 60 Acres ... on the N. W. Side of Pasquotank River, in the Fork of the said River called JOY'S Fork ... KIDDY Swamp ...
[A:364] 16 April 1723. *Signed*: Wm. LINTON. *Wit*: Wm. NORRIS, David BAILEY.

Edwd. BRIGHT with the free will and Consent of Sarah, my wife, ... Do assign all my whole Right ... of this within mentioned Deed ... unto Edwd. OVERTON ... 15 April 1726. *Signed*: Edward X BRIGHT his mark. *Wit*: Moses LINTON, Catharine C LINTON her mark, Gabriel BURNHAM. *Ack*: 19 April 1726. *Regt*: 3 May 1726.

Elisabeth UPTON, Widow and Relict of John UPTON late of Pasquotank decd. ... for the valuable Consideration of 55 pounds ... paid by Philip TORKSEY Junr. ... sold ...
[A:365] ... a Tract of Land and Plantation containing 191 acres granted by Patent to my

aforesaid Husband John UPTON bearing date the 25 Feb. 1696 ... on the North East Side of Pasquotank River and given unto me the said Elisabeth UPTON by my said afsd. Husband John UPTON in his last will and Testament bearing date the 13 June 1715 ... 31 Aug. 1721. *Signed*: Elizabeth E UPTON her mark. *Wit*: W NORRIS, Mac SCARBOROUGH.

Philip TORKSEY Junr do assign over unto Valentine GRAY the within mentioned Deed of Sale as witness my hand this 27 day of November 1725. *Signed*: Philip TORKSEY. *Wit*: Robert Ro TORKSEY his mark, Richd. R GREGORY his mark. *Ack*: 19 April 1726. *Regt*: 4 May 1726.

North Carolina: Edwd. SCOTT of the Precinct of Pasquotank & Province afsd. ... with the voluntary Consent of Mary SCOT my lawful Wife ... for the valuable Consideration of 30 pounds current money ... paid by Caleb SAWYER of the Precinct & Province afsd. ... sold ... a Tract of Land & Plantation contg. 50 Acres ... upon Henry PENDLETON'S line ... down through the sd. Land I now live on ... [A:366] ... 16 July 1723. *Signed*: Edward SCOT, Mary X SCOT her mark. *Wit*: Stephen DELAMARE, Truman MCBRIDE.

Caleb SAWYER for the Consideration of 27 pounds ... paid ... do assign ... all my Right ... of the within mentioned Conveyance ... to John BROTHERS of the Precinct of Pasquotank and Province abovesaid ... 19 April 1726. *Signed*: Caleb SAWYER. *Wit*: Danl. GUTHRIE, Joshua MARKHAM. *Ack*: 19 April 1726. *Regt*: 4 May 1726.

His Excellency the most Noble Henry Duke of BEAUFORT Palatine &c. ... give and grant unto Edward JAMES, a Tract of Land contg. 55 Acres lying in Pasquotank Precinct on the North East Side of the River ... in the Indian's Lines ... Henry CREECH'S Line ... which sd. Land was formerly surveyed for Henry CREECH and by him Sold and assigned over to Edwd. JAMES ... Given under the Seal of the Colony this [blank] day of [blank] 1713/4. Witness our &c. Thomas POLLOCK Esq. President of the Council ... *Signed*: Thos: POLLOCK, Thos. BOYD, N. CHEVIN, Wm. REED.

[A:367] Henry CREECH do assign all my Right, Title,

and Interest of this Patent to William CREECH ... 19 April 1726. *Signed*: Henry HC CREECH his mark. *Wit*: Jona. JONES, James PRITCHARD. *Ack*: 19 April 1726. *Regt*: 4 May 1726.

His Excellency John Ld. CARTERET Palatin &c. ... give and grant unto Henry HAYMAN of our said County a Tract of land containing 100 acres lying on the North River ... which Land was formerly Surveyed for Henry HAYMAN and by his last will and Testament devised to his Son Henry HAYMAN ... Given under the Seal of the Colony this first day of March 1721. Witness our trusty and well beloved Charles EDEN Esqr. Governor &c. *Signed*: C EDEN, Wm. REED, Richd. SANDERSON, Frans. FOSTER, J. LOVICK. Recorded in the Secy's Office J LOVICK Secy.

Henry HAYMAN do assign over all my Right of the within mentioned Patent unto John SANDERLIN & Edward JAMES ... 6 Feb. 1724. *Signed*: Henry H HAYMAN his mark. *Wit*: John SCARBOROUGH. *Ack*: 19 April 1726. *Regt*: 5 May 1726.

Macrora SCARBROUGH & Henry HAYMAN of North Carolina Province and in the Precinct of Pasquotank ... sold ... unto John SANDERLIN & Edward JAMES (of the Prect. and Province afsd) ... Tract of Land commonly called ... HAYMAN'S Island lying on North River ... containing ... 100 acres ...
[A:368] ... [blank] day of Feby. in the 11th year of the Reign of our Sovereign Lord George ... 1724. *Signed*: Mac. SCARBOROUGH, Henry HH HAYMAN his mark. *Wit*: John SCARBROUGH, James H HAYMAN his mark. *Ack*: 19 April 1726. *Regt*: 5 May 1726.

North Carolina: John JONES Weaver of Pasquotank Precinct in Albemarle County and in the Province of North Carolina ... in Consideration of 24 pounds Sterling Money of England ... paid by Robert EDNY Taylor of North Carolina and in Albemarle County and Pasquotank Prect. ... sold ... parcel of Land lying on the N. E. Side of Pasquotank River, containing 200 Acres taken out of a Pattent containing 1654 Acres commonly called Wolfepit Neck ... mouth of the Cypress Branch ...
[A:369] ... 21 April and in the tenth year of the Reign of our Sovereign Lord George ... 1724. *Signed*: John JONES. *Wit*: John CARRON, Truman

MCBRIDE. *Ack*: 21 April 1724. *Regt*: 6 May 1726.

North Carolina: Samuel NORTHY in the Precinct of Pasquotank in the County of Albemarle in the Province afsd. Mariner ... in Consideration of the Sum of 25 pounds ... paid by Susannah NORRIS, widow & Execx. of William NORRIS late of the Prct. afsd. decd., to and for the use and behalf of the Heirs of David NORTHY late of the Province of the Mathatusets? in England decd ... Sold ... parcel of Land purchased by the said David NORTHY in his life time of Henry [blank] ... Newbegun Creek ... Plantations of Thomas PALMER now in the Occupation of the Said Susannah NORRIS ... 50 Acres ... 19 July 1726. *Signed*: Samuel NORTHY. *Wit*: John PALIN, Dan. OSHEAL. *Ack*: 19 July 1726. *Regt*: 8 Aug. 1726.

[A:370] North Carolina: Francis BRACKET of the Prect. of Pasquotank in Albemarle County in the Province afsd. Planter ... whereas John HAWKINS late of the Prect. of Pasquotank afsd. decd. was seized of ... Tract of Land contg. 350 Acres lying at the head of Portahonk Creek in the Precinct afsd. ... by a Patent thereof bearing date the first day of January 1694 ... whereas the said John HAWKINS by his last will and Testament in writing bearing date the [blank] did give ... the sd. Tract of Land ... unto his Cousin Thomas MERRIDAY ... and whereas the said Thomas MERRIDAY and Elisabeth his Wife for a valuable Consideration to them paid by me the said Francis BRACKET and Edward FAIRCLOTH decd. did by their assignment on the back of the Said Patent ... dated the 17th Oct. 1721 assign ... unto us ... all their Right ... and whereas the said Edward FAIRCLOTH is since dead the whole Right and Title of the Said Tract of Land is invested in me ... Francis BRACKET for and in Consideration of the Sum of 40 pounds by the Said Edward FAIRCLOTH in his lifetime paid in part of the Consideration of the said Tract of land to Thomas MERRIDAY ... sold ... unto Sarah FAIRCLOTH Widow ... part of the Said Tract of Land ... to be divided ... near the now Dwelling House of me ... Containing 150 Acres ...
[A:371] ... day of [blank] *Signed*: Francis BRACKET, Mary BRACKET. *Wit*: George BRAY, Willm. BURGES. *Ack*: 19 July 1726. *Regt*: 8 Aug. 1726.

His Excellency John Ld. CARTERET &c. ... give and grant unto Joseph COOPER of Pasquotank Precinct a Tract of Land containing 180 Acres called the Indian Wells lying on the North East Side of Pasquotank River ... on the Sound Side ... which said Land was formerly surveyed for Nathanl GRAY and by him assigned over to John SQUIRES and by the said John SQUIRES assigned ... to Joseph COOPER ... Given under the Seal of the Colony 26 Nov. 1723. William REED Esqr. President. *Signed*: Wm. REED, C GALE, T. POLLOCK, M. MOORE, J. LOVICK. Recorded in the Secy's Office J. LOVICK.

Joseph COOPER of the Prect. of Pasquotank do assign over all my Right ... of the within mentioned Land unto Crora SCARBRO ... 8 Jan. 1725. *Signed*: Joseph COOPER. *Wit*: Wm. BURGES, Jno. SCARBOROUGH. *Ack*: 19 July 1726. *Regt*: 8 Aug. 1726.

North Carolina: George CAROON and Elizabeth his Wife of Pasquotank Prct. in the County of Albemarle in the Province afsd. ... in Consideration of the sum of 34 pounds ... paid by John SCARBOROUGH of the Prect and County afsd. Planter ... sold ... a parcel of land given and bequeathed by the last will & Testament of our decd. Father Cornelius JONES bearing date the 18th day of May 1714 ... on the N. E. Side of Pasquotank River being part of a Tract containing 685 Acres ... assigned to us by the name of Elisabeth JONES ...
[A:372] ... 19 July 1726. *Signed*: George CAROON, Elizth. E CAROON her mark. *Wit*: Chas. BULL, Jno. PALIN. *Ack*: 19 July 1726. *Regt*: 11 Aug. 1726.

16 July 1726 being for a valuable Consideration ... Caleb SAWYER ... Sold ... unto Richd. HASTINGS Junr. ... parcel of Land ... on the N. E. Side of Pasquotank River ... mentioned in Richd. HASTINGS Junrs assignment containing 104 Acres ...
[A:373] ... *Signed*: Caleb SAWYER. *Wit*: Cornelius RELF, Richard SAWYER. *Ack*: 19 July 1726. *Regt*: 11 Aug. 1726.

Caleb SAWYER of the Prect. of Pasquotank Planter and in the County of Albemarle and of the Province of North Carolina for the sum of 30 pounds current Money ... paid by Edward WILLIAMS of the same Precinct and County and Province ... sold ... a

Dividend of Land out of a Pattent bearing date 11 Nov. 1719 ... on the North East Side of Pasquotank River containing ... 365 Acres ... on Robert MORGAN'S line and Henry SAWYER'S line ... this [blank] *Signed*: Caleb SAWYER. *Wit*: Cornelius RELF, Richard SAWYER. *Ack*: 19 July 1726. *Regt*: 11 Aug. 1726.

[A:374] North Carolina 18 July 1726 ... William PHILLIPS late of Pasquotank ... to John HOBBS of the same place ... in Consideration of the Sum of [blank] pounds Sterling money of Gt Britain ... Sold ... Tract of Land containing 300 Acres ... on the Easternmost Fork of Pasquotank River called TOMMALINS Island ... the same Land granted me by Pattent bearing date the 30 March 1721. *Signed*: Wm. W PHILLIPS his Mark. *Wit*: John SYMONS, Esau ALBERTSON. *Ack*: 19 July 1726. *Regt*: 11 Aug. 1726.

[A:375] William BRAY of the Prect. of Pasquotank in North Carolina Planter for and in Consideration of the sum of 15 pounds ... paid by William BURGES of the Prect. & Province afsd. Tailor ... sold ... Tract of Land ... on the North East side of Pasquotank River at the head of RAYMON'S Creek commonly called ... Bushy Neck and lately in possession of one John CONDON containing by Estimation 50 acres ... 28th day of August in the Eleventh year of the Reign of our Sovereign Lord George ... 1725. *Signed*: William WB BRAY his mark. *Wit*: Stephen BURGES, George BRAY.

William BURGES of the Prect. of Pasquotank do assign over all my Right ... of the within mentioned Land to Henry BRAY ... 8 Nov. 1725. *Signed*: Wm. BURGES. *Wit*: Francis BROCKITT, Mary BROCKITT. *Ack*: 19 July 1726. *Regt*: 11 Aug. 1726.

[A:376] North Carolina: William RELF of the Precinct of Pasquotank in the Province of North Carolina aforesaid Planter ... for and in Consideration of the Love, good Will and Affection I have and do bear to my loving Sister Sarah RELF of Pasquotank ... have given ... a certain Neck of Land on Pasquotank River containing 100 Acres ... being a part of that Tract of Land whereon I formerly lived and known by the name of hard? Gut Neck and binding on William SMITHS and Daniel ROADS'S line ... 19

July 1725. *Signed*: William RELF. *Wit*: Benja. PRITCHARD, William SAWYER. *Ack*: 19 July 1726. *Regt*: 11 Aug. 1726.

His Excelly The most noble Henry Duke of BEAUFORT Pallatine &c. ... give and grant unto Bryan FITZPATRICK a Tract of Land containing 350 Acres lying on the East side of Alligator Creek ... 1 April 1713 Witness my &c. Thomas POLLOCK. *Signed*: Thos. POLLOCK, Thos. BOYD, T KNIGHT, N. CHEVIN, C GALE. Recorded in the Secy's Office 29 April 1713. Pr T KNIGHT Secy.

North Carolina) Pasquotank) ... Daniel MACKEE ... for the valuable Consideration of 30 pounds to me in hand paid -- assign and make over all my Right ... of the within Patent unto Captn. Richd. SANDERSON ... 15 July 1726. *Signed*: Daniel M MACKEE his mark. *Wit*: Edmd. GALE, Joseph POTTLE. *Ack*: 19 July 1726. *Regt*: 12 Aug. 1726.

[A:377] North Carolina: 19 July 1726 Between Nathaniel MARTIN of Pasquotank ... and Edmund CHANCY of the same place ... in Consideration of the Sum of 5 pounds to him in hand paid ... Sold ... Two Tracts of Land ... on the Branches of Newbegun Creek being the same land that the said Nathaniel MARTIN Lapst at a Council held in April 1724 out of the Patent granted to the said Edmd. CHANCY the one patent for 449 Acres the other for 482 Acres which patent bears date the 4 Jan. 1714/5 ... *Signed*: Nathaniel MARTIN. *Wit*: Tho: SWANN, John PENDLETON. *Ack*: 19 July 1726. *Regt*: 12 Aug. 1726.

William NORRIS and Susannah NORRIS my Wife do assign over all our Right ... of the within mentioned patent to Robt. LOWRY ... 18 April 1721. *Signed*: W NORRIS, Susannah NORRIS. *Wit*: John SYMONS, Jer SYMONS. *Regt*: 12 Aug. 1726.

[A:378] Anthony ALEXANDER Senr. In the Province of North Carolina and in the County of Albemarle Planter, for the like Value all ready in hand received ... convey ... unto William HARTLE Planter in the Province and County aforesaid a certain Tract of Land containing 200 Acres out of a Patent which I have for that Tract at Alligator, which is called STUMPER Point on the Sound's Side: to be laid out at the north end of the Tract ... 12 Jany 1715/16. *Signed*: Anthony A ALEXANDER his mark. *Wit*: John MIXON, Joseph ALEXANDER. *Ack*: 18 Oct. 1726. *Regt*: 26 Oct. 1726.

North Carolina: 18 Oct. 1726 Between Philip EVANS ... and Thomas SWANN ... in Consideration of the Sum of 60 pounds Sterling ... paid ... sold ... Tract of Land containing by Patent 127 Acres lying on the River of Pasquotank and lower Side of the Swamp called the Swamp of old JOY'S Fork ... Patent bears date the 6 Dec. 1720 and was granted to him as Heir at law to his Father Philip EVANS the Elder by a former Survey ...
[A:379] ... *Signed*: Philip X EVANS his mark. *Wit*: Gabriel BURNHAM, Samuel MORE. *Ack*: 18 Oct. 1726. *Regt*: 26 Oct. 1726.

North Carolina: Thomas SWANN of Pasquotank Prect in the Province aforesaid ... in Consideration of the Good will, natural affection and Love which I have and bear unto my well beloved Cousin William DRUMMOND late of Virginia ... give ... Tract of Land containing by Patent 127 Acres (except one half Acre of the sd. Land next adjoining to the Landing of the said Plantation to build Houses on with full privelege of Egress and Regress to the same Land) Being the same plantation and Tract of Land as was conveyed to me by Philip EVANS by Deed bearing even date with this Presents ... 18 Oct. 1726. *Signed*: Tho: SWANN. *Wit*: Gabriel BURNHAM, Thomas M MOORE? his mark. *Ack*: 18 Oct. 1726. *Regt*: 7 Nov. 1726.

[A:380] North Carolina: Edward TURNER of the Prect. of Perquimans in the county of North Carolina ... in Consideration of the Sum of 20 pounds Sterling money of England ... paid by Nathanl. EVERET of the Prect. of Pasquotank in the County of Albemarle ... sold ... Tract of Land containing 224 Acres lying in Pasquotank Prect. bounded on John DAVIS'S line formerly Richd. GRAY'S ... the Patent being a Relapse in John SYMONS Junr. and assigned to the said TURNER by John SYMONS Senr. ... 18 Oct. 1726 and in the Twelfth year of the Reign of our Sovn. Lord George ... *Signed*: Edward X TURNER his mark. *Wit*: Joseph READING, Lewis Alexr. KNIGHT. *Ack*: 18 Oct. 1726. *Regt*: 7 Nov. 1726.

[A:381] His Excelly John Lord CARTERET Palatine &c. ... give and grant unto William RAYFIELD of our said County, a Tract of Land containing 490 Acres lying in Pasquotank Prect. ... Daniel MACKEY'S line ... which Land was formerly granted by Patent bearing date the 3rd day of August 1719 to Matthew CASWELL and by him elapsed for want of due seating and planting and is now become due to the said William RAYFIELD by virtue of an Order of Council dated April 2d. 1724 ... Witness our trusty and well beloved George BURRINGTON Esqr. Governor. *Signed*: Geo. BURRINGTON, Wm. REED, E MOSELY, Tho: HARVEY, Francis FOSTER, Tho: POLLOCK, C GOFFE, C GALE, J LOVICK. Recorded, J LOVICK Secy.

William RAYFIELD of the County of Albemarle and Province of North Carolina do assign all my Right ... of the within mentioned Land unto Samuel JONES of the County and Province afsd. ... 18 Oct. 1726. *Signed*: William RAYFIELD. *Wit*: Willm WILSON, Danl. GUTHRIE. *Ack*: 18 Oct. 1726. *Regt*: 8 Nov. 1726.

William HARTLY of North Carolina in the County of Albemarle ... for and in Consideration of the Sum of 15 pounds in good and lawful money of the Province ... paid by Seth PHELPS ... sold ... 100 Acres of land ... upon the Sound Side and binding upon the Cattle Branch ...
[A:382] ... 19 April in the Seventh year of the Reign of our Sovereign Lady Ann ... 1710/11. *Signed*: William HARTLEY. *Wit*: Anthony ALEXANDER Junr., John WHEDBEE. *Ack*: 1 Aug. 1718.

I assign all my Right ... of the within mentioned Deed of Sale to Thomas BEST ... *Signed*: Seth PHELPS, Ann S PHELPS her mark. *Wit*: Benjamin ALEXANDER, Richard WHEDBEE. *Ack*: 18 Oct. 1726. *Regt*: 8 Nov. 1726.

18 Oct. 1726 and in the 13th year of the Reign of our Sovereign Lord George ... Between Elijah STANTON of the Prect. of Perquimons in the County of Albemarle in the Province of North Carolina by and with the free Consent of Elisabeth STANTON my wife ... and John ARMOUR of the Prect of Pasquotank and County and Province afsd. ... in Consideration of the Sum of 8 pounds Stg money of Great Britain ...

Sold ... a parcel of land ... on the North East Side of Little River being between John ARMOURS and William WINBURY'S Tracts joining upon Thomas COMMANDER containing 100 Acres ...
[A:383] ... *Signed*: Elijah STANTON, Elisabeth X STANTON her mark. *Wit*: Ben OSHEAL, Isaac JONES. *Ack*: 18 Oct. 1726. *Regt*: 9 Nov. 1726.

William LINTON of Pasquotank in the County of Albemarle and Province of North Carolina Planter ... Sum of 3 pounds by me recvd ... in warranty of [?] in the just Sum of 6 pounds Sterling Money of Gt. Britain to be paid unto William BRITE in the County of Bath in the Province afsd. Planter ... on the nonperformance of the following ... sold ... parcel of Land ... in the Fork of Pasquotank ... Edward BRITE'S Corner Tree ... by the Great Swamp ... containing 50 Acres ... being part of a Tract of Land out of a Patent bearing date July 10th 1722 ... 18 Oct. 1726. *Signed*: William LINTON. *Wit*: Robert KEEL, Isaac JONES. *Ack*: 18 Oct. 1726. *Regt*: 9 Nov. 1726

[A:384] Albemarle County, No. Carolina, His Excelly William Ld. CRAVEN Palatine &c ... gave and grant unto Matthew MIDGET a Tract of land containing 360 Acres lying on the N. W. Side of Alligator Creek in Chowan Prect ... William RAPHELL'S Corner Tree ... for 2 Shillings and 6 pence paid to the honble. the Governor for every 50 Acres ... 16 April 1712. Witness our trusty and well beloved Edwd. HYDE, President of our Council of Carolina &c. *Signed*: Edward HYDE, N. CHEVIN, Tho: BOYD, Tho: PATTERSON. Recorded in the Secy's Office the 16th of April 1712. *Wit*: N. CHEVIN Secy.

Anthony ALEXANDER Senr. hath hereby given ... to my Son Joseph ALEXANDER ... all this within mentioned patent ... 18 Oct. 1723. *Signed*: Anthony A ALEXANDER his mark. *Wit*: Saml. H HOPKINS his mark, Andrew X OLIVER mark. *Ack*: 20 July 1726. *Regt*: 9 Nov. 1726.

No. Carolina, Joseph MUNK of the Precinct of Pasquotank & Province aforesaid ... Whereas the Lords and absolute Proprietors according to their Great Deed of Grant bearing date the 1 May 1668 Did give and grant unto Joseph MUNK a Tract of Land lying in Pasquotank Prect. containing 354 Acres as by patent bearing date the 10 Feby 1718 ... for the valuable Consideration of 7 pounds ... paid by Thomas BETTY'S of the Prect and Province afsd. ... sold ... 174 Acres of Land part of the afsd. Tract ... at the Mouth of Pig Branch ... a line tree of Richd LEARY'S ... a Juniper Run ... [A:385] ... 20 April 1719. *Signed*: Joseph M MUNK his mark. *Wit*: W NORRIS, John X GREEN his mark.

Pasquotank Thomas BETTYS of the Prect afsd. Province of North Carolina ... for the Consideration of 18 pounds ... paid by John THACKRAY of the Precinct afsd. ... sold ... the within mentioned Tract of Land ... 18 Oct. 1726. *Signed*: Tho: BETTYS. *Wit*: An MABSON, Mary MABSON. *Ack*: 18 Oct. 1726. *Regt*: 10 Nov. 1726.

North Carolina: Cornelius FITZPATRICK of Alligator in the Precinct of Pasquotank & County of Albemarle for and in Consideration of the Sum of 15 pounds current Money of North Carolina ... paid by Andrew OLIVER ... sold ... one piece of Land called the broad Neck on the No. Side of Alligator Creek ... 100 Acres of Land ... binding on Obadiah FEARE, Joseph WINSHIP and HUNT'S Neck plantation ... [A:386] ... 5 June 1718. *Signed*: Cornelius FITZPATRICK. *Wit*: Ed. LININGTON, Samuel S WEST? (This above Record torn) desired the sd. FITZPATRICK to give Andrew OLIVER, this Bill of Sale I selling my Right to the said OLIVER and am paid in full ... 5 June 1718. *Signed*: Samuel S WEST? his mark. *Wit*: Edwd. LININGTON, Andrew X OLIVER his mark.

North Carolina: Andrew OLIVER of the Precinct of Chowan and County of Albemarle & Province of North Carolina do assign all my Right ... of the within mentioned Land unto William RAFILL of the County and Province aforesaid Being for a valuable Consideration ... paid ... 29 Sept. 1726. *Signed*: Andrew X OLIVER his mark, Hannah H OLIVER her mark. *Wit*: Wm WILSON, Sarah WILSON, Saml. H HOPKINS his mark. *Ack*: 18 Oct. 1726. *Regt*: 10 Nov. 1726.

His Excelly John Lord CARTERET Palatine &c. ... give and grant unto John CARTERET of our said Province a Tract of Land containing 250 Acres lying on the North East side of Pasquotank River ... North East

End of the Dogwood Ridge ... Beaver Dam Swamp ... which Land was formerly granted by Patent bearing date the 23rd day of March 1713/14 To John and Abigail GUILFORD and by them elapsed for not seating and planting thereon ... [blank] 1726. Witness our trusty and well beloved Sr. Richard EVERARD, Baronet, Governor ... *Signed*: Richd. EVERARD, John BLOUNT, E MOSELEY, C GALE, Rob WEST, J LOVICK. Recorded by Thos. HARVEY, J LOVICK Secy.

[A:387] John CARTWRIGHT do assign over all my Right ... of the within mentioned Land ... unto John GUILFORD ... 16 Jany 1726/7. *Signed*: John CARTWRIGHT. *Wit*: Robert HARRISON, Sarah H HARRISON her mark. *Ack*: 17 Jany 1726/7. *Regt*: 25 Jany 1716/7.

William BROTHERS of Pasquotank Precinct in the County of Albemarle in North Carolina Cooper ... by reason of a Covenant by me made unto and as Bond given to Matthew PRITCHARD to make over and assign to Miriam KEATON Daughter of Henry KEATON decd. ... a certain tract of Land containing 100 Acres ... confirm unto the said Miriam KEATON the afsd Tract of land where formerly the said Henry KEATON hir Father cleared a plantation, planted and Seated, containing as afsd. 100 Acres ... and running from the main (Record Torn) for the said WOODLY and for Wm CHANCY and also for the Said KEATON, then to a great Branch lying and being between the Said BROTHERS and the said KEATON ... it being part of a Tract or Parcel of Land granted to Matthew PRITCHARD from the Palatine and Lords Proprietors by a Patent bearing date the ninth day of January 1713/4, and signed unto me by the said PRITCHARD. The said Land and plantation I do hereby give and grant unto the said Miriam KEATON ... 17 Jan. 1726/7. *Signed*: William W BROTHERS his mark. *Wit*: Robt. LOWRY Junr, John BROTHERS. *Regt*: 25 Jany 1726/7.

James PRITCHARD of the Precinct of Pasquotank and Province of North Carolina ... with the free, voluntary Consent of Mary PRITCHARD my lawful Wife ... for the valuable Consideration of 20 pounds ... by Edward SCOT of the Precinct & Province afsd ... (record torn) ...
[A:388] Sell ... 50 Acres of Land ... being the one Moiety or half part of 100 Acres given and granted unto the Said James PRITCHARD by patent bearing date

9 Sept. 1714 ... at David PRITCHARD'S line ... James PRITCHARD'S Land to the Sandy Branch ... 14 Jan. 1726/7. *Signed*: James PRITCHARD, the mark of Mary M PRITCHARD. *Wit*: Henry RAPER. *Ack*: 14 Jany 1726/7. *Regt*: 26 Jany 1726/7.

His Excelly John Ld. CARTERET Palatine &c. ... give and grant unto Edward SCOT of our Said County a Tract of Land containing 694 Acres, lying at the head of Nobbs Crook Creek in Pasquotank Prect. ... which Land was granted by Patent bearing date the 9th day of Sept. 1714 to James PRITCHARD and by him elapsed for want of seating and planting thereon and is now became due to the said Edwd. SCOT by virtue of an Order of Council dated 27 March 1721. ... Given this 1st day of March 1721. *Signed*: Charles EDEN Esqr. Governor Richd. SANDERSON, C EDEN, Wm. REED, Thos. POLLOCK. (Record torn)

[A:389] Edwd. SCOT of the Prect. of Pasquotank in the Province of North Carolina Planter for and in Consideration of the Love and Good Will I have unto my trusty and well beloved Friend James PRITCHARD of thre Precinct and Province afsd. Planter ... give ... all my Right ... of the within written Premises ... 14 Jany 1726/7. *Signed*: Edward SCOT, the mark of Mary X SCOT. *Wit*: Henry RAPER. *Ack*: 17 Jany 1726/7. *Regt*: 26 Jany 1726/7.

North Carolina: Abraham THOMAS ... in Consideration of the Sum of 36 pounds Sterling ... paid by Griffith JONES ... Sold ... Tract of Land on the North East Side of Pasquotank River and at the head of the Fork of Arranuse Creek and bounded between the Swamp that parts Henry CREECH'S and JOY'S Neck and binding on the Land formerly belonging to Edwd JONES the Elder, Christopher WILLIAM'S Land and John NORTON'S Land: and 50 Acres of Land given by Joseph SPARNON to William BRITNAL, being part of the same Tract: which Tract contains by Estimation 250 Acres: part of which Tract of Land is now in the Tenure and Occupation of Stephen SAULES, which said 250 Acres of Land was given and demised to me the Said Abraham THOMAS by the last Will of Joseph SPARNON decd. ... [A:390] 7 Nov. 1726. *Signed*: Abr THOMAS. *Wit*: (Record Torn) *Ack*: 18 Jany 1726/7 by Mr. Tho. SWANN.

North Carolina: Whereas I Abraham THOMAS have set

our hands & Seals to a writing bearing date with these Presents mentioning that I have granted to Griffith JONES ... Tract of Land lying on the North East side of Pasquotank River and at the head of the Fork of Arranuse Creek containing by Estimation 250 Acres ... I ... made ... in my place ... my well beloved Friend Thomas SWANN my true and lawful attorney ... to acknowledge before the chief Justice ... To the Said Griffith JONES ... 7 Nov. 1726. *Signed*: Abr. THOMAS. *Wit*: M. SCARBOUOUGH, Saml. BERNARD. *Proved*: 18 Jany. 1726/7. *Regt*: 26 Jany. 1726/7.

John RELFE Senr. of the Precinct of Pasquotank in the Province of North Carolina, Planter ... for the just Sum of 20 pounds good and lawful Money ... paid by Isaac JONES of the Prect. and Province afsd. ... sold ... Tract of Land containing 500 Acres ... N. E. Side of Pasquotank Bounding on Francis MARTIN and Robert EDNY Being part of a Tract of land containing by Patent 1654 Acres bearing date 20 Dec. 1726 ... 17 Jany 1726/7. *Signed*: Jno. RELFE. *Wit*: John JONES, Jno. CAROON. *Ack*: 17 Jany 1726/7. *Regt*: 26 Jany 1726/7.

[A:391] William PEPPERRELL of Kittery in the County of York within his Majesty's Province of the Massachusetts Bay in New England Esqr. ... made ... in my stead ... my trusty Friend John SANDERS of Kittery afsd. Mariner to be my true ... and lawful attorney ... to ask, demand, levy, require ... all Sums of Money, Debts, Goods, ... and Things whatsoever ... 12 Oct. 1726 in the 13th year of his Majesty's Reign. *Signed*: Wm. PEPPERRELL. *Wit*: Wm BARTON, Wm M MASON'S mark. *Proved*: 14 Jany 1726/7 before me Jno PALIN. *Regt*: 26 Jany. 1726/7.

North Carolina: Susanna NORRIS of Pasquotank Precinct in Albemarle County in the Province afsd. Widow ... in Consideration of the maternal Love and Affection which I have ... unto my two Sons William NORRIS and John NORRIS & my Daughter Sarah NORRIS have given ... the several Goods, chattels and Monies hereafter mentioned ... unto my said Two Sons William & John my Negro Man called Jack equally between them, also a Cow and Calf to each of them (viz) my brown Cow called Young Dainty to my Son William with her Increase and my Cow called Browney to my Son John with her Increase ... unto my Daughter Sarah my two Cows called Hart & Fillpail ... also a good Feather Bed with Rugg pair of Blankets and a pair of Sheets also one Iron pot that holds about five Gallons ... one Sorrel Mare branded with the figure of Three (3) with all her Increase to be equally divided among my sd Children ... the Sum of Ten pounds of good and lawful money of this Province to the use and Intent of their Schooling and to no other use or advantage whatsoever [A:392] ... also ... two Pewter Plates. 31 Dec. 1726. *Signed*: Susanna NORRIS. *Wit*: John PALIN, Thos. PALIN. *Regt*: 27 Jany 1726/7.

North Carolina: Thomas COMMANDER & Ellen his wife of Pasquotank Prect. in Albemarle County in the Province aforesaid ... in Consideration of the Sum of 500 pounds of good and lawful Money of this Province ... paid by John ARMOUR of the Precinct , County and Province afsd. ... sold ... a certain plantation with 400 acres of Land now in our occupation and whereon we now dwell ... on the Creek called Currituck (alias) SYMON'S Creek ... a patent for the Same bearing date the 27th day of Nov. 1679 Granted to John HARVEY Esqr. ...
[A:393] ... 7 March 1726/7. *Signed*: Tho: COMMANDER, Ellen COMMANDER. *Wit*: for Ellin COMMANDER by Tho: HARVEY, Elisabeth C CALLAWAY her mark. *Wit*: for Thos COMMANDER by Tho: HARVEY, Richd. LEARY. *Ack*: 7 March 1726/7. *Regt*: 3 April 1727.

Robert WALLIS of Core Sound in North Carolina Son and Heir of Robert WALLIS of Pasquotank decd. ... in Consideration of the Sum of 100 pounds paid by Colonel William REED of Pasquotank afsd. ... Sold ... a Tract of Land containing 400 Acres lying in Pasquotank River ... which said Land was patented by my said Father as appears by the patent on
[A:394] Record bearing date the 1 Jan. 1694 and is now in the possession of the said Colonel William REED. ... 18 April 1727. *Signed*: Robert WALLIS. *Wit*: Robert LOWRY, David BAILEY. *Ack*: 18 April 1727. *Regt*: 25 April 1727.

His Excellency John Ld. CARTERET Palatine &c. ... give and grant unto Jane TULLE Widow, a Tract of Land containing, 110 Acres ... Head of Gum Branch

... by a great Swamp coming out of Nobb's Crook Creek ... 1 April 1720. Witness our trusty and well beloved Charles EDEN Esqr. Governor &c. ... *Signed*: C EDEN, Fred: JONES, Tho: POLLOCK, Richd SANDERSON, Wm REED. Recorded in the Secretary's Office J LOVICK Secy.

North Carolina: Jane TULLE of Pasquotank Prect. Widow for and in Consideration of the full and just Sum of 30 pounds Sterlg. ... paid by Thomas CASEY ... Sold ... the within Patent mentioned and confirmed 18 April 1727. *Signed*: Jane IT TULLE her mark. *Wit*: Jonathan HIBBS, Richd. RUDYARD. *Ack*: 18 April 1727. *Regt*: 25 April 1727.

[A:395] John PERKINS Senr. in the Prect. of Pasquotank in the Province of North Carolina Planter ... in Consideration of the Sum of 20 pounds ... paid by William STEVENS of the same Prect and Province ... sold ... unto him the said William STEVENS and Elisabeth his Wife ... Parcel of Land on Bald ridge on the North Side of Pasquotank River ... containing 40 Acres being part of a Tract of 250 Acres patented by John BELL Senr which said 110 Acres was sold by the Said John BELL unto William and Thomas CREECH and since sold and acknowledged by William & Henry CREECH unto the abovesaid John PERKINS Senr. ... 40 Acres ... lying near or joining upon the Land of William BECKET? decd and now in the possession of Isaac SEABURN ... Side of Gum pond, from thence to the Beaver Dam ...
[A:396] ... 14 Aug. 1722. *Signed*: John A PERKINS his mark. *Wit*: Mc SCARBOROUGH, Joseph COOPER, Jona JONES.

North Carolina: William STEVENS and Elizabeth my Wife both of Pasquotank Precinct for and in Consideration of the Sum of 25 pounds Sterling money in hand paid to us by John BELL of the same Precinct ... sell ... all our Estate, Right ... to the within mentioned Deed of Bargain of Sale bearing date the 14 Aug. 1722 Being the same Land bought of John PERKINS Senr. ... acknowledged to us in Pasquotank Court the 15 Jan. 1722/3 containing 40 Acres ... 18 April 1727. *Signed*: William S STEVENS his mark, Elizabeth E STEVENS her mark. *Wit*: [blank] *Ack*: 18 April 1727. *Regt*: 26 April 1727.

North Carolina: Francis BRACKIT of the Prect. of Pasquotank in Albemarle County in the Province afsd Planter ... whereas John HAWKINS late of the Prect. of Pasquotank afsd. decd. was seized and possessed of and in one certain Tract of Land containing 350 Acres lying at the head of Portahonk Creek in the Patent afsd. ... bearing date the 1 Jan. 1694 ... and whereof the said John HAWKINS by his last will and Testament in writing bearing date the [blank] did give ... the sd. Tract of Land ... unto his Cousin Thomas MERRIDAY ... the sd. Thomas MERRYDAY and Elisabeth his wife for a valuable Consideration to them paid by me the said Francis BRACKIT and Edward FAIRCLOTH decd did by their Assignmt. on the back of the said Patent ... dated the 14 Oct. 1725 assign and make over unto us the said Francis BRACKIT
[A:397] and Edward FAIRCLOTH all their Right ... by reason of the Ignorance of the Writer of the said Assignment the said Tract of Land is made and conveyed to us the said Purchasers in Joint Tenancy and whereas the said Edward FAIRCLOTH is since dead the whole Right ... is invested in me the said Francis BRACKIT ... for and in Consideration of the Sum of 40 pounds by the said Edward FAIRCLOTH in his life time paid in part of the Consideration of the said Tract of Land ... Sold ... unto Sarah FAIRCLOTH, widow, Execx of the said Edwd. FAIRCLOTH part of the said Tract of Land according to the first design and Intent of us the said Purchasers to be divided ... near the now Dwelling House of me ... Containing 150 Acres ... 19 July 1726. *Signed*: Francis BRACKIT, Mary BRACKIT. *Wit*: George BRAY, Wm. BURGESS.

[A:398] North Carolina: Sarah FAIRCLOTH of the County of Albemarl and Prect. of Pasquotank & Province of North Carolina. Widow & Execx of the last will and Testament of Edward FAIRCLOTH decd. ... give and grant unto my Son Thomas FAIRCLOTH and my Son John FAIRCLOTH to be equally divided betwixt them and my Son Thomas FAIRCLOTH to have his first choice: all the within mentioned Land unto them ... or the survivor of them ... 19 July 1727. *Signed*: Sarah XX FAIRCLOTH hir mark. *Wit*: Wm WILSON, M. SCARBOROUGH. *Ack*: 19 July 1727. *Regt*: 22 Aug. 1727.

North Carolina: John GUILFORD of Albemarl ... in

Consideration of the Sum of 10,000 pounds current money of North Carolina ... by Thomas FORBUSH ... sold ... a certain Tract of Land by Estimation 125 Acres ... beginning at James FORBUSH Junr's Line & bounding on the Cypress Swamp ... on the N. E. Side of Pasquotank River ... 15 July 1727. *Signed*: John J GUILFORD his mark. *Wit*: Robert HARRISON, Sarah H HARRISON her mark. *Ack*: 18 July 1727. *Regt*: 22 Aug. 1727.

[A:399] Robert MORGAN Senr. of the Prect. of Pasquotank in the Province of North Carolina have for the Love and Good-will & natural affection which I bear to my well beloved Children ... given ... House hold-Goods ... unto my Son Bennet MORGAN ... one large Black Walnut Table and Forms, one large [?] Case with fifteen Pottle-Bottles, one Iron Pot about Ten Gallons, one brass Kettle about Sixteen Gallons, one grinding Stone, one wainscot chest, Three large Pewter Dishes, Two large Pewter Candle Sticks and [?] alls, one Pewter Flaggon, one Pewter Quart Pot, Six Pewter plates, and one pair of Steelyards ... unto my Son Joseph MORGAN one Iron Pot about ten gallons, one Iron Bound Case & Bottles, One pair of Palatine Mill Stones, one chest, one Grinding Stone, Three Pewter Dishes, Six Pewter Plates, one pint Pot, one brass Candlestick, one folding Table, one pewter Bason about five quarts, one pair of Steelyards ... unto my Son Robert MORGAN One Iron pot about Six Gallons, one chest, two Pewter Dishes, one pewter full pot, Two large Basons ... 15 July 1727. *Signed*: Robert MORGAN. *Wit*: [blank] ADAMS, John SAWYER, Thos. T GRANDY his mark, Eliz. E GRANDY her mark. *Ack*: 18 July 1727. *Regt*: 23 Aug. 1727.

North Carolina: Henry PENDLETON of the Prect. of Pasquotank and Province afsd. ... with the voluntary Consent of Elisabeth my Lawful Wife ... for the natural Love and Affection which I have and do bear unto my well beloved Son Thomas PENDLETON ... give ... all the Land lying and being on the North West Side of the Branch called and known by the name of [A:400] "The other Plantation" Containing 100 acres ... being part of the Tract of Land I now dwell on Containing 300 Acres ... 17 July 1727. *Signed*: Henry HP PENDLETON his mark. *Wit*: John BROTHERS, Stephen DELAMARE, Richard RUDYARD. *Ack*: 18 July

1727. *Regt*: 23 Aug. 1727.

Edward WILLIAMS of the Precinct of Pasquotank in the Province of North Carolina, Planter ... for a Tract of Land which my Brother William WILLIAMS has now in his possession and lives on; ... sell ... unto Charles HUMPHREYS of the Prect. and Province afsd. Planter; a certain parcel of Land out of a Patent bearing date the 28th day of Oct. 1725 Lying ... on the N. E. Side of Pasquotank River; the whole Tract by Patent beginning at Gumberry Swamp, The Conveyance hereof beginning at John UPTON'S Corner Tree ... on Edward WILLIAM'S Line to a Branch called the Holly Branch, containing by Estimation 50 acres ... the whole Tract by Patent containing 350 Acres [A:401] ... 18 July 1727. *Signed*: Edward E WILLIAMS his mark. *Wit*: Thomas T GRANDY his mark, Richard SAWYER. *Ack*: 18 July 1727. *Regt*: 23 Aug. 1727.

His Excelly John Lord CARTERET Palatin &c. ... give and grant unto Col. John PALIN of Pasquotank a Tract of Land containing 124 acres lying in Pasquotank Precinct ... John CLARK'S corner tree ... the Mouth of Flatty Creek ... to Mr. DUCKENFIELD'S Line ... 2 June 1727. Witness our trusty and well beloved Sr. Richd. EVERARD, Bart: Govr. *Signed*: Richd. EVERARD, E MOSELEY, Wm. REED, Fran FOSTER, Tho: HARVEY, C GALE, Rd. SANDERSON, Edmd GALE. Recorded in the Secy's Office R. FORSTER Dept. Secy.

North Carolina: John PALIN for and in Consideration of the Sum of 10 pounds of good and lawful and current money of the Province afsd. ... paid by Jacob RIGHTEGU of the Prect of Pasquotank and Province afsd. Joiner ... Sold ... all my Right ... to the within mentioned Patent ... 3 July 1727. *Signed*: Jno. PALIN. *Wit*: Sarah BULL, James J BASSNET his mark. *Ack*: 18 July 1727. *Regt*: 24 Aug. 1727.

[A:402] Thomas FORBUSH with the Consent of Abigail my lawful Wife ... for the valuable Consideration of 30 pounds in hand paid ... by John WHITE of the Prect of Pasquotank and Province of North Carolina ... sold ... a Parcel of Land containing 100 acres ... bounding upon Deep Run ... on John PARISH'S Line ... to George GRIFFIN'S Line ... John GUILFORDS Line

... 19 July 1727. *Signed*: Thomas T FORBUSH his mark. *Wit*: Cornelius RELFE, Samuel SIMMONS. *Ack*: 19 July 1727. *Regt*: 24 Aug. 1727.

North Carolina William WALLIS of the Prect. of Pasquotank and Province afsd. ... for the valuable Consideration of 54 pounds current Money of this Province ... paid by Richard STAMP of the Prect & Province afsd. ... Sold ... one Tract of Land & Plantation containing 180 Acres called ... Sound Tract lying ... upon the Sound Side as by Patent bearing date the 1 May 1668 Granted to John BELMAN and by the Said John BELMAN by his last Will and Testament in Writing bearing date the 5 Nov. 1706 made and constituted his wife Sarah BELMAN his Executrix and by a Clause in the sd. Will, did give her his said Wife full power ... to make Sale of the sd. Lands after his Decease ... and whereas William WALLIS late of this Prect. deceased, did purchase the afsd. Land ... by a Deed of Sale bearing date the 9 Sept. 1707 ... and whereas William WALLIS died seized and possessed of the afsd Lands & Valentine WALLIS Eldest Son apparent and [A:403] lawful Heir to the afsd Lands did give and make over unto his youngest Brother William WALLIS the above mentioned Tract of Land containing 180 acres by an assignment upon the back side of the said Patent ... Therefore Know ye that I the said William WALLIS for the Consideration afsd ... sell to the sd. Richd. STAMP ... the afsd 180 acres of Land lying upon the Sound Side and joining upon the Land of John BOYD ... 30 June 1727. *Signed*: William WALLIS. *Wit*: Jno. MCKEEL, Charles WEST. *Ack*: 18 July 1727. *Regt*: 24 Aug. 1727.

North Carolina 17 July 1727. Robert WHITE of the Prect. of Pasquotank ... do hereby give ... to my Son Joseph WHITE one Negro Woman named Rose ... and her Increase ... also a Mare and Colt and Cow & Calf also to my Son Jonathan WHITE one Negro Boy named Sildin ... also one Cow and Calf and a Mare and Colt ... Also to my Son Zephaniah WHITE one Negro Boy named Robin, also a Mare and Colt and a Cow and Calf ... Also I give unto my Three Sons, Joseph, Jonathan and Zephaniah, one Negro Girl named Hannah and her Increase ... only Jonathan shall have her 15 years first then from year to year, amongst the three above mentioned Also I give ... unto my three youngest children, Anne, Elisabeth and Robert WHITE one Negro Girl named Hager. If in case I have any more Children by my Wife Rebecca WHITE, then the said Hager and her Increase to be equally divided amongst them. Also to my Two Daughters Two mares [A:404] and Colts and their Increase, also to my Son Robert WHITE a young Mare and her Increase ... 17 July 1727. *Signed*: Robert WHITE, Rebecca R WHITE her mark. *Wit*: Arnold WHITE, Joshua WHITE. *Ack*: 18 July 1727. *Regt*: 25 Aug. 1727.

North Carolina John SCARBROUGH Senr of Pasquotank Precinct Planter ... and William BURGESS of the same Precinct ... in Consideration of the Sum of 40 pounds of good and lawful money of the province afsd ... paid by the sd. William BURGESS ... Sold ... Tract of Land lying at the head of RAYMON'S Creek, on Pasquotank River containing ... 300 Acres ... being the Land whereon the Said BURGESS now liveth and part of it being formerly bought of William BRAY ... by a Deed bearing date the 29 March 1712 and the other part being taken up by Entry and Survey ... 10 Jan. in the 11th year of the Reign of our Sovereign Lord George ... 1725. *Signed*: John J SCAROROUGH his mark. *Wit*: M. SCARBOROUGH, Sarah X BRAY her mark, James J HAYMAN. *Ack*: 18 July 1727. *Regt*: 25 Oct. 1727.

[A:405] (See pg. 239) James MCDANIEL of the Precinct of Pasquotank in the Province of North Carolina ... for the Sum of 5 pounds ... paid by William MCDANIEL my Son of the Precinct and Province afsd. ... sold ... 100 acres out of a patent bearing date the 3rd day of April 1719 ... The Tract containing by Patent 431 acres ... the side of the Lake ... to John JONES'S Head Line so binding on John JONES and John SPENCE'S to Thomas SAWYERS ... to the Lake ... 18 July 1727. *Signed*: James ID MCDANIEL his mark. *Wit*: Jos. STOKELY, Jona: JONES. *Ack*: 18 July 1727. *Regt*: 25 Aug. 1727.

North Carolina 17 April 1727 and in the 13th year of the Reign of our Sovgn. Lord George ... Between Griffith JONES ... & William GREGORY ... in Consideration of the Sum of 81 pounds current Money ... paid ... Sold ... Tract of Land containing 100 Acres ... on the North East Side of Pasquotank River and at the head of the Fork of Arranuse Creek and

bounded on the Land the sd. GREGORY now lives on and so on the Line of John NORTON, Edward JAMES'S Line and Christopher WILLIAM'S Line ... including the plantation whereon Stephen SAULS lives on (The Life of the said Stephen SAULS in the sd Land only excepted) ...
[A:406] ... *Signed*: Griff JONES. *Wit*: Tho: SWANN, Tho: WILLIAMS, Saml. WISE. *Ack*: 18 July 1727. *Regt*: 25 Aug. 1727.

Mary JONES Wife of Griffith JONES late of Pasquotank Precinct ... have quit claimed unto William GREGORY being in his posession (by Virtue of the within Deed) ... by Reason of my Dower of and in the third part of one Tenement Containing 100 acres ... the said William GREGORY lately purchased of my Husband Griffith JONES ... 17 July 1727. *Signed*: Mary X JONES her mark. *Wit*: Tho: SWANN, Tho: WILLIAMS, Saml. WISE. *Ack*: 18 July 1727. *Regt*: 25 Aug. 1727.

[A:407] North Carolina 10 March 1726/7 and in the 13th year of the Reign of our Sovereign Lord George ... Between John WALLIS Grandson of Robert WALLIS the Elder of Pasquotank Precinct decd ... and Thomas SWANN of the Prect of Pasquotank and Province afsd. Gent. ... in Consideration of the Sum of 150 pounds Sterling money of Gt. Britain ... Sold ... Tract of Land contained in a Patent granted to my Grandfather Robert WALLIS Deceased, by the right Honble Philip LUDWELL Esqr. ... 25 Sept. 1663 and also by a Deed from Robert KEEL and Thamar his wife, bearing date the 22 Jan. 1706 which lands descended and came to the possession of my eldest Brother, William WALLIS deceased, as Grandson and Heir to Robert WALLIS decd. ... South Side of Pasquotank and joining on a Plantation formerly belonging to Thomas KEEL and sold by Robert KEEL his Son and Heir to Daniel PHILLIPS ...
[A:408] ... *Signed*: John WALLIS. *Wit*: John PENDLETON, Charles DENMAN, Nathaniel MARTIN, Saml. WISE. *Ack*: 18 July 1727. *Regt*: 26 Aug. 1727.

Memorandum: That full and peaceable Possession and seizin was given and delivered by the within named John WALLIS of the messuage, plantation, and Tract of Land within mentioned unto Thomas SWANN for his only use and Estate according to the true Intent and meaning of the said Indenture within mentioned This 13th day of March 1726/7. in the presence of us whose names are subscribed. *Wit*: Charles DENMAN, John PENDLETON, Nathaniel MARTIN, Saml. WISE. *Regt*: 26 Aug. 1727.

North Carolina John SCARBROUGH Senr of Pasquotank Prect. Planter of the one part, and Augustin SCARBROUGH of the same Precinct of the other part ... in Consideration of the Sum of 10 pounds of good and lawful Money of the Province ... paid by Augustin SCARBROUGH ... Sold ... Tract of land lying on the North East Side of Pasquotank River containing 50 acres ... being the Land whereon Augustin now lives which the afsd. John SCARBROUGH bought of George CAROON and have already marked it out of that Tract: but because that the sd. Land is not divided amongst Cornelius JONES'S children according to their Father's Will so the sd Jno SCARBROUGH has not marked the sd 50 Acres all round; but if in case that in laying out the other parts of Cornelius JONES'S children's Land, it should take any of that away then I the said John SCARBROUGH, shall make up the 50 Acres joining convenient to the part whereon Augustin has cleared and settled ... 18 July 1727. *Signed*: John J SCARBROUGH his mark. *Wit*: George BRAY, Francis BRACKET. *Ack*: 18 July 1727. *Regt*: 26 Aug. 1727.

[A:409] Thomas PENDLETON of the Precinct of Pasquotank in the County of Albemarle ... in Consideration of 10 pounds Sterlg ... paid and for the love and affection I bear unto my loving Sister Mary JONES Widow and to Thomas ARMOUR Son of my sd Sister and to the rest of said Sister's Sons do ... sell ... a Parcel of Land lying in the Woods between Flatty Creek and Pasquotank River, containing ... 175 Acres ... being the South East End a part of my Tract of Land containing 350 Acres to be divided and bounded by Flatty Creek old Road as the said Road is now marked on both Sides ... unto the sd Mary JONES for and during her natural life and after her decease unto the sd Thomas ARMOUR and to the Heirs of his Body forever and for want of such Heirs to William ARMOUR Son of the sd Mary JONES and to the Heirs of his Body forever and for want of such Heirs unto Robert ARMOUR, Son of the said Mary JONES and to the Heirs of his Body forever and for want of such Heirs unto John ARMOUR, Son of the said Mary JONES and to the Heirs of his Body forever and for want of such Heirs to the Heirs of the Said Thomas ARMOUR and their Assigns forever ... the afore recited Tract of Land by Patent bearing date 24 Feb. 1696 to me is granted ... 14 May 1697. *Signed*: Thomas TP PENDLETON Signus. *Wit*: Richard PLATER, John MEEDS, W. GLOVER. *Ack*: in the Genl Court 17 May 1697. *Regt*: 4 Nov. 1727.

North Carolina: 16 Oct. 1727 and in the first year of the Reign of our Sovereign Lord George the Second ... Between Thomas SWANN of Pasquotank Precinct of the one party, and John WALLIS of the same Precinct of the other party ... in Consideration of the Sum of 100 pounds ... paid by the Said John WALLIS ... [A:410] ... Sold ... Tract of Land, Containing by Patent 127 Acres (except one half-acre of the sd Land next adjoining to the Landing of the sd Plantation the said Thomas SWANN reserves for himself to build Houses on with full and free Privilege of Egress and Regress to the Same Land) Being the Same Plantation and Tract of Land as was given ... by me the sd Thomas SWANN unto William DRUMMOND deceased, by Deed of Gift bearing date the 18 Oct. 1726 ... *Signed*: Thos. SWANN. *Wit*: Tho: WEEKES, Mc SCARBROUGH. *Ack*: 17 Oct. 1727. *Regt*: 7 Nov. 1727.

North Carolina Thomas PALIN of the County of Albemarl & Precinct of Pasquotank Yeoman with Susannah his Wife ... in Consideration of the Sum of [blank] ... By John PALIN, Edmund GALE, David BAILEY & John CONNOR Gent. (Commissioners appointed for purchasing Land, [blank] ...
[A:411] ... for the purpose of Building and Erecting a Court House ... Sold ... one acre of Land ... on a little Creek that issues or runs out of Newbegun Creek (being part of that Tract of Land which my Wife during her Widowhood purchased of Samuel NORTHY and was by the said Samuel acknowledged to her in the Precinct Court of Pasquotank the [blank] 1726
[A:412] ... 17 Oct. 1727. *Signed*: Tho: PALIN, Susanna PALIN. *Wit*: Tho: WEEKES. *Ack*: 17 Oct. 1727. *Regt*: 18 Nov. 1727.

[C:222] [First part of deed missing] Peter BROWN & his heirs lawfully Begotten of his Body & for default of such issue then to be to the use Benefit & behoof of Thomas BARECOCK ye son of William BARECOCK & Jane his wife his heirs forever -- And the said Margret PEGGS doth hereby ... agree to and with her said Son John PEGGS ... may ... have hold ... of the said Plantation and 100 acres of Land ... (the use and profits thereof during my Natural life only excepted) ... *Signed*: Margret M PEGGS her mark. *Wit*: Wm. MINSON, Thos. PALIN, Lewis JENKINS, Thos X BARECOCK his mark. *Proved*: 31 July 1729 by ye oath of Lewis JENKINS one of ye Evidences. *Signed*: C. J. GALE. *Regt*: 13 Aug. 1729.

North Carolina. John BOYD of ye. prect. of Pasquotank & Province afs'd ... for ye valuable Consideration of 50 pounds Currt money of North Carolina ... paid by Joseph OLIVER of ye Prect of Pasquotank & Province afs'd ... Sold ...
[C:223] ... Known by the name of Isack it being part of a tract ... Joyning to ye Land of Richard STAMP upon the one side & ye Said John BOYDS Land on the other side & ye Sound & upon ye South Side ... Tract of Land Containing 150 acres ... John BOYD & Ann my wife ... [Rest of deed missing]

[First part of deed missing] ... Confirm unto the said John PENDLETON ... a certain tract of Land Containing 235 acres being on the East Side of Little River ... Pattented by William JACKSON in ye year 1693 ...
[C:224] ... 15 Oct. 1729. *Signed*: Joshua MARKHAM, Elizabeth C MARKHAM her mark. *Wit*: Robt? HOOLL?, Richd. RUDYARD. *Ack*: 8. 15. 1729. *Regt*: 10. 12. 1729.

John PENDLETON of the Precinct of Pasquotank & Province of North Carolina ... in Consideration of the Sum 302 pounds Sterling money of Great Brittain ... paid by Joshua MARKHAM ... Sold ... a tract of Land Containing 234 acres .. [Rest of deed missing]

[C:225] [First part of deed missing] ... Him the said Robert TORKSEY ... and the said Philip TORKSEY doth hereby ... agree to & with the said

Robert TORKSEY ... may peaceably enjoy all the said Land ... 14 Oct. 1729. *Signed*: Philip TORKSEY. *Wit*: Francis BRACKITT, Wm. BURGES. *Ack*: Sep: Court ye 15th 1729. *Regt*: Oct: 16 1729.

Edward WHARTON of The Precinct of Pasquotank in the County of Albemarl ... with free voluntary will & consent of Elizabeth my wife which is by Lawful Marriage & for the valuable Consideration of 9 pounds ... paid by Thomas CARTWRIGHT ... sell ... a certain tract of Land begining at a Branch called Tarr Kill Branch ... River Swamp ... 50 acres ... [C:226] ... 15 Oct. 1729. *Signed*: Edward E WHARTON his mark. *Wit*: Thos. TWEEDIE, Esau ALBERSON, [blank] MARTIN. *Ack*: ? 8br Court 1729. *Regt*: 10 ye. 16th 1729.

James NEWBY of the County of Albermarl in the Province of North Carolina ... for the sum of 110 pounds currt money of this Province ... Paid By Benjamin NEWBY of the County afsd & Precinct of Pasquotank ... sold ... 125 acres belonging to the tract I now live on Beginning at John BAYLEYS line on ye N.E. Side of little river ... 13 Oct. 1729. *Signed*: James I NEWBY his mark, Hannah X NEWBY her mark. *Wit*: Zachariah NIXON, Francis MACE? *Ack*: 8. Court ye 15 1729. *Regt*: 10. ye 16. 1729.

[C:227] North Carolina - James NEWBY of the Precinct of Pasquotank & Province of North Carolina ... for the valuable Consideration of 20 Pounds to me in hand paid by my Son Saml. NEWBY of the Precinct afsd & Province afsd ... sold ... parcell of Land containing 150 acres Joining upon Nath. HALL'S ... on the N.E. Side of Little River binding upon a line formerly made between me & James HUFTON ... 13 Oct. 1729. *Signed*: James IN NEWBY his mark. Hannah H NEWBY her mark. *Wit*: Zachariah NIXON, Francis MACE? *Ack*: 8. Ct ye. 15 1729. *Regt*: Ob. 1729.

North Carolina. John PALIN of Pasquotank Precinct in Albermarle County of Province afsd. Esq. Attorney of Deborah FINCH of New England Widdow & Executor & Legatee of Jeremiah FINCH late of this province decd. ... in Consideration of the sum of 35 pounds to me ... paid for the use of ye sd Deborah FINCH by Richard FOTHERGLE of Pasquotank Precinct & Province

afsd Blacksmith ... sold ... parcell of Land ... on the north side of the River & on the West Side of Aranoose Creek ... 150 acres
[C:228] ... bounded by the Lands of Abell ROSS and Richard FERRELL ... 15 8br, 1729. *Signed*: Jno. PALIN. *Wit*: Danl. GUTHRIE, Wm. MINSON. *Ack*: 8br Court ye 15th 1729. *Regt*: 10. ye 16. 1729.

15 Jan. 1728/9 Between Thomas CASEY of Pasquotank Precinct in the Province of North Carolina ... & Thomas SMITHSON of ye afsd Precinct ... in Consideration of the full & Just Sum of 30 pounds ... Sold ... parcell of Land ... Containing 110 acres ... at the head of Gum branch ... by a Great Swamp Coming out of Noobs Crook Creek ... as p. a pattent bearing date May 1, 1720 ...
[C:229] *Signed*: Thomas CASEY. *Wit*: Danl. GUTHRIE, George HARRIS. *Ack*: 8br Court ye 15. 1729. *Regt*: 10. ye 16. 1729.

North Carolina May ye 21 day 1729. William MANDREN & Ann MANDREN his lawful wife and doth make over ... all our right ... of this within mentioned pattent ... unto George HARRIS Junr. of the precinct & prov: afsd. Sold out of this pattent within mentioned 290 acres & the remainder of the sd. pattent ... make over unto the sd. George HARRIS ... *Signed*: William W MADREN his mark. *Wit*: James GREAVES, Henry NICHOLLS. *Ack*: 8br Court ye 15. 1729. *Regt*: 10. ye 16. 1729.

North Carolina The 21 May 1729 Then came into court George HARRIS Junr. & Jone HARRIS his lawful Wife do make over ... all our rights ... of the within mentioned patent ... unto William MADREN of the said County & precinct ... have sold out of this Pattent 150 acres of Land the remainder hereof I do acknowledge unto Wm. MADREN ...
[C:230] ... *Signed*: George HARRIS, Joane HARRIS. *Wit*: James GREAVES, Henry NICHOLLS. *Ack*: 8br Court ye 15. 1729. *Regt*: 10. ye 16. 1729.

His Excelly. John Lord CARTRET Palatin &c. ... Give & grant unto John PENDLETON of our said County a tract of Land containing 120 acres ... deep Run ... ARMOURS Line Tree ... wh said land Danl. RICHARDSON Esqr dyed Seized thereof in fee Having no heirs in this Govt. ye same by Inquisition had taken at ye

Court house for Pasquotank prct. ye 2 day of July 1724 Before John PALIN Esqr. Escheator to Govt & a Jury thereunto Lawfully Sworn was found to Escheat to ye true & absolute Lords Propts & is now become due to ye said Thomas PENDLETON for ye composition money Thereof paid ... 2 Nov. 1727 Witness our trusty & well beloved Sir Richard EVERARD Bart. Govr. &c. *Signed*: Richard EVERARD, Wm. REED, Francis FOSTER, Thos. HARVY, C GALE, Rd. SANDERSON, E. MOSELY, EDMD. GALE. Recorded W. FOSTER Dep. Rec. *Regt*: April ye 6th. 1730.

Willm. Earl of CRAVEN. Give & Grant unto Thomas PENDLETON of our said County a Tract of Land containing 350 acres ... near Flatty Creek ... [C:231] ... 24 July 1696. Witness our trusty & well beloved John ARCHDALE Govr. &c of Carolina & our trusty & well beloved Counsellors who have hereunto set their hands. *Signed*: John ARCHDALE, Daniel AKEHURST, Francis TOMS, Thomas POLLOCK, Samuel SWANN, Henderson WALKER. Recorded in the Secy office. W. GROVER Sec. *Regt*: April 6 1730.

North Carolina. John AVERY of ye Precinct of Hyde Shipwright ... in Consideration of the Sum of 84 Pounds Currt. Money of this Province to me in hand by Thomas CASEY in the County of Albemarle Planter ... Sold ... 340 Acres ... upon the West Side of Pasquotank River ... being between the land of Richard MADREN & the Land of Thomas SMITHSON ... [Rest of deed missing]

[First part of deed missing] Means or procurement and further he the sd. John DAVIS his heirs &c doth covenant & agree to & with him the said Abraham DAVIS ... for the good will & affection I bear to my brother Abraham DAVIS in the non performance of this present writing of Indenture that is to say he the said John DAVIS ...
[C:232] hath and do by these presents Enfeoff Given & make over all his right ... Tract of Land as above Specified ... *Signed*: John DAVIS. *Wit*: William SYMONS, Robt. LOWRY Junr. *Ack*: Jan: Court y. 13. 1729. *Regt*: April the 7th 1730.

11 Jan. 1729/10, and in the third year of the reign of our Sovereign Lord George ye Second ... Between John DAVIS in the precinct of Pasquotank and the

County of Albermarl & in the Province of North Carolina ... and Abraham DAVIS of the Precinct & County & Province abovesd. ... in Consideration of the good will I bear to my Brother Abraham DAVIS ... give ... forever a tract or parcell of Land ... on the South West Side of Pasquotank River it being part Given out of a patent bearing date 1728 ... dividing line between Thos. DAVIS and Abraham DAVIS [C:233] ... to Wm. WINBERRY'S line ... 104 acres ... *Signed*: John DAVIS. *Wit*: Jos. SYMONS, William SYMONS, Robt. LOWRY Junr. *Ack*: Jan: Court ye. 13. 1729. *Regt*: April ye 7th 1730.

North Carolina. John DAVIS of the precinct of Pasquotank & the County of Albermarl & of the Province of North Carolina & out of the Good will & affection I Bear to my Brother David DAVIS of the same Precinct, County, & Province ... give ... my right ... have to the tract of Land ... 127 acres [C:234] ... Jan. 1709/10 *Signed*: John DAVIS. *Wit*: Jos. SYMONS, William SYMONS, Robt. LOWRY Junr. *Ack*: Jan: Court ye. 13. 1729. *Regt*: April ye 7th 1730.

11 Jan. 1729/10 & in the Third year of the reign of our Soverign Lord George the Second ... Between John DAVIS in the precinct of Pasquotank & the County of Albermarl & in the Province of North Carolina ... & Thos. DAVIS of the Prect & County & Province abovesd. ... in Consideration of the good will I Bear to my Brother Thos. DAVIS ... given ... a tract or parcell of Land ... on the South West Side of Pasquotank River it being part given out of a patent bearing date 1728 ... at the River Swamp ... the dividing line between Jno. DAVIS and Thos. DAVIS ... the dividing line Between Thos. DAVIS, David DAVIS, Abraham DAVIS ... containing 200 acres ... [C:235] ... *Signed*: John DAVIS. *Wit*: Jos. SYMONS, William SYMONS, Robt. LOWRY Junr. *Ack*: Jan: Court ye. 13. 1729. *Regt*: April ye 7th 1730.

North Carolina. Thomas CARTWRIGHT Senr. of the prect. of Pasquotank in the County of Albermarle for the good will, Love & natural affectiones I do bear unto my Son Moses CARTWRIGHT I do give & make over unto him & his heirs one parsel of Land Containing 160 acres Beginning at the upper end of the sd Thomas CARTWRIGHT'S line upon the Eastern side of the Waiding Branch & so running down to John HARRIS' line ... 12 Jan. 1729/30. *Signed*: Thos T CARTWRIGHT his mark. *Wit*: Thos. TWEEDIE, Lodwick LG GRAY his mark. *Ack*: Jan: Court ye. 13. 1729. *Regt*: April ye 8th 1730.

[C:236] North Carolina Stephen HALL of the Prect. of Pasquotank & Province of North Carolina ... for the valuable Consideration of 30 pounds in hand pd. by Zachariah JACKSON & Samuel JACKSON Junr. of the prect. & province afsd ... Sell ... Quantity of Land Lying binding Between George LOW'S Line & Saml. JACKSON'S Junr. line the said Land Containing 100 acres ... 30 Dec. 1729. *Signed*: Stephen HALL, Elizabeth HALL. *Wit*: Samuel NEWBY, George X LOW his mark, Eliz E LOW her mark. *Ack*: Jan: Court ye. 13. 1729. *Regt*: April ye 8th 1730.

John MORRIS of the County of Albermarl in North Carolina planter for & in Consideration of the paternal Love & affection that I have and do bear towards my well beloved Son Aaron MORRIS of the County afsd planter Have Given & Granted ... [C:237] ... 50 acres ... out of a Kings patent bearing date the 25 Sept. 1663 ... bounded on the North East Side with Abraham WHITE'S Land ... Joyning on Robert LOWRYS Land ... 14 Jan. 1729. *Signed*: John MORRIS. *Wit*: William SYMONS, John DAVIS. *Ack*: Jan: Court ye. 14. 1729. *Regt*: April ye 8th 1730.

North Carolina Thos. STAMP of the pr.cinct of Pasquotank & province af'd do hereby Give grant Sell make over for ever all my right title interest of the within mentioned patent & tract of Land there unto belonging unto Joseph LOMBROSTER ... 29 March 1729. *Signed*: Thos. STAMP. *Wit*: Jno. MCKEEL, Thos. STAMP. Received of Joseph LOMBROSTER The Sum of 20 pounds Curt: money of this province it being the consideration for the afs'd Land above Expres'd I say recd by me Richard STAMP Brother & heir to Thomas STAMP decd. *Signed*: Richd. STAMP. *Ack*: Jan: Court ye. 13. 1729. *Regt*: April ye 9. 1730.

[C:238] North Carolina Thos. COOK of Edenton in ye Precinct of Chowan in Albermarle County and Province afs'd Bricklayer do hereby assign ... my friend

John PALIN of Pasquotank prect. ... Gent to be my true & Lawful deputy & attorney ... 23 Jan. 1726/7. *Signed*: Thos. COOK. *Wit*: Chas. BULL. W. MINSON.

[C:239] North Carolina Thos. COOK of Edenton in Chowan prect & Province afs'd do hereby as a further power & addition to my sd attorney namely John PALIN of Pasquotank ... to sell & dispose of any of my Land in this Government ... 23 Jan. 1726/7. *Signed*: Thos. COOK. *Wit*: Chas. BULL. Wm. MINSON. *Ack*: Jan: Court ye. 13. 1729. *Regt*: April y: 30. 1730.

North Carolina. 24 Jan. 1728/9. Between John BUNDY of Pasquotank Precinct the elder son & heir of Caleb BUNDY dec. of the one party and Saml. BUNDY of the same prect. of the other party Witnesseth That for as much as natural differences & discords may arise between them and their posterity of & concerning their several rights and titles to Ye. Several tracts of Land Given them by their father's last Will & testament & for preventing any such natural differences the said John BUNDY is very desirous & the more out of his natural Love and affection which he doth bear to his Brother Saml. BUNDY & the better to advance his brother's fortune in ye World hath by these presents Given ... one certain parcell of Land Containing 389 acres ... Except 100 acres of Land ... Being on y. East South East Side of William MORIS Survey made for my father Caleb BUNDY in GRIFFIN Swamp & Joyning on that land as ye Saw John BUNDY Bought of Thomas STANTON ... the Walnut Branch ... to Thomas STANTONS Corner tree ...
[C:240] ... which sd Lands is Taken out of three Surveys & Pattents ... *Signed*: John BUNDY. *Wit*: Thos. SWANN, Zacriah FEILD? *Ack*: April 30. 1730. *Regt*: May 6 1730.

Francis HENDRICK of Craven precinct & Bath County in the Province of North Carolina planter for & in Consideration of ye Sum of 20 pounds ... paid by James COLLINGS of ye. precinct of Pasquotank in Albermarle County & province afs'd planter ...
[C:241] ... sold ... 100 acres lying & being Between Little River & Pasquotank ... Francis HENDRICK Late of Pasquotank in his life time gave by deed of Gift to his Son Francis HENDRICK ... Being part of that Tract of Land which is Commonly Known by ye name of ye half way tree ... 2 April 1728.

Signed: Francis HENDRICK. *Wit*: Thos. T COLLINGS his mark, John HALL. *Ack*: 1729.8. Court y. 14. The foregoing deed was ack. in open Court by Nat HALL Esq atty. for Francis HENDRICK to Ja. COLLINGS. *Regt*: May ye. 11 1730.

Francis HENDRICK of Bath County in the Province of North Carolina planter have constituted ... my good friend Nath HALL Esqr of Pasquotank in Albermarl County & province afs'd to be my true ... attorney ... to acknowledge & make over unto JamesCOLLINGS of Pasquotank planter ... 100 acres of Land ... 2 April 1728. *Signed*: Francis HENDRICK. *Wit*: Thos. T COLLINGS his mark, James X COLLINGS his mark. *Proved*: June 9 The above power of atty was proved by ye oath of Thos. COLLINS before me. *Signed*: J. PALIN. *Regt*: May ye. 11 1730.

[C:242] Thomas JOHNSON for a valuable Consideration to me in hand paid by Wm. JENINGS Senr. & John NORTON ... Sell ... all my right ... to 300 acres of Land being my part of ye w.in mentioned pattent 600 ... 150 acres Being ye one half thereof to ye Said Wm. JENINGS and 150 acres ye remainder Thereof to ye Said John NORTON ... 21 Jan. 1707. *Signed*: Thos. JOHNSON. *Wit*: T. KNIGHTS, John PALIN. *Ack*: 30 Jan. 1707 by John PALIN. *Regt*: 26 May 1730.

North Carolina) Pasquotank County) Wm. JENINGS of Aranoose Creek Cooper do ... make over with Mary my wife all our Right ... unto W. SAWYER ... certain pattent assigned By Philip LUDWELL Govr. & Commander In Chief of North Carolina ... unto ye said William SAWYER ... for a valuable Consideration paid ... 19 July [blank] *Signed*: Wm. W JENINGS his mark, Mary JENINGS. *Wit*: John BISHOP. *Ack*: 19 July 1709 John BISHOP. *Regt*: 26 May 1730.

[C:243] Wm. JENINGS of Arronous Creek Cooper ye wt.in mentioned pattent from us ... unto ye said Wm. JENINGS ... said patent being upon Record in ye gvt office for this Province Signed by the Hon: Philip LUDWELL ... bearing date ye 1 Jan. 1694 as witness our hands & seals this 19th day of July 1709. *Signed*: William SAWYER, Mary M SAWYER her mark. *Wit*: John BISHOP, John NORTON. *Ack*: 19 July 1709 John BISHOP. *Regt*: Copy Transfered out of ye old regr. 26 May 1730.

Peter SAWYER do assign all my right, title and interest of ye. w.in named Pattent of Land to John RELFE ... 11 April 1721. *Signed*: Peter S SAWYER his mark. *Wit*: W. NORRIS, Jos MARKHAM. *Ack*: 18 April 1721. *Wit*: John PATRICK. *Regt*: The foregoing patent w. the four following assignments was registered 26 May 1730.

Charles GRANDY of ye Precinct of Pasquotank in the County of Albermarl & the Province of North Carolina ... for ye just Sum of 34 pounds ... paid ... by Christopher WILLIAMS of ye prect County & province afs'd ... Sold ... ye head of Pasquotank River [C:244] on ye South east Side lying & Being Between John DAVIS Land, David PRITCHARD Being part of ye Same tract wh. David PRITCHARD Lived on Containing ye full quantity of 107 acres of Land ... 14 April 1730. *Signed*: Charles GRANDY. *Wit*: Jona. JONES, Jno. J JENINGS his mark, Benitt MORGAN. *Ack*: 14 April 1730. *Regt*: 12 June 1730.

His Excellency John Lord CARTRET Pall: &c. ... give and grant unto William JAMES a tract of Land containing 351 acres Known by the name of GRIFFON Swamp ... his own Corner tree ... Thomas PENDLETONS [C:245] Robt KEELS corner tree ... Thomas STANTONS corner tree ... wh. land was formerly Granted By patent in ye year 1714 to Thomas STANTON & by him Elapsed for not seating & planting ... 28 Oct. 1726 Witness &c. Sir Richd. EVERRARD Barn: Gentle. &c. *Signed*: Richd. EVERRARD, E MOSELEY, John BLUNT, ROB WEST, J. PALIN, C GALE, Thos. HARVEY, J LOVICK. Recorded By J. LOVICK Secy. *Regt*: 12 June 1730.

His Excelly the right Honble John Lord GRANVILE Palatine &c. ... give & grant to John SYMONS a tract of Land containing 124 acres being on ye South West side of Pasquotank ... Thomas PENDLETONS line ... ye said tract of Land being lapsed for want of seating by Caleb BUNDY ... 17 June 1707. Witness our sd. William GLOVER Esq. president &c. W. GLOVER, Saml. SWANN, Edwd. MOSELY, Francis FOSTER. Recorded in ye Secty office this 18 June 1707. *Regt*: 12 June 1730.

Pasquotank Prct. John SYMONS within named & Damaras my wife For a valuable Consideration already recived do hereby Grant Bargain Sell ... unto William JAMES

... all our Right ... to ye within patent & Land therein Contained ... 15 July 1707. *Signed*: John SYMONS, Damaras SYMONS. *Wit*: Robt. LOWRY, Thos. ABINGTON. *Ack*: 15 July 1707 by John SYMONS & Damaras his wife - Thos. ABINGTON Clk. *Regt*: 12 June 1730.

[C:246] 13 April 1730 Between John BELL of the Precinct of North Carolina of the one part & Joseph GODFREY of ye same prct & province afs'd of the other part ... In Consideration of 50 pounds Currant money ... sold ... a certain Tract of Land containing 40 acres ... between John PERKINS Senr and afsd John BELL ... two log branch ... *Signed*: John BELL. *Wit*: Jonathan JONES. Jno. SCARBROUGH. *Ack*: April Court 1730. *Regt*: 30 June 1730.

[C:247] North Carolina John BELL of ye prect of Pasquotank ... in Consideration of the Sum 50 pounds Curt. money ... sell ... all my estate Right ... to ye wtin mentioned deed of Bargain of Sale Bearing date ye 14 Aug. 1722 being ye same land that John BELL Bought of William STEVENS the same Land was by John PERKINS ack to William STEVENS in Pasquotank dy ye 15 June 1723 containing 40 acres & was by William STEVENS & Eliz. his wife ack to John BELL in Court the 18 day of April 1727 ye same land to have & to hold unto the said Joseph GODFREY ... 13 April 1730. *Signed*: John BELL. *Wit*: Jona. JONES, Jno. SCARBROUGH. *Ack*: April Court 1730. *Regt*: 15 June 1730.

Christp WILLIAMS of ye Precinct of Pasquotank in ye County of Albermarl in North Carolina for a valuable Consideration of 70 pounds ... paid by John SCARBROUGH of the Precinct & Province afs'd I do hereby assign all my right ... of this wtin mentioned deed of sale ... 14 April 1730. *Signed*: Chris: W WILLIAMS his mark. *Wit*: Jona. JONES, Benit MORGAN. *Ack*: April Court 14th day 1730. *Regt*: 15 June 1730.

North Carolina) Pasquotank County) William JENINGS of Pasquotank in the Province afs'd ... assign & make over unto Jeremiah MURDEN of ye prect. afs'd all my right ... unto the within mentioned pattent the remaining part being 182 acres ... 13 April 1730. *Signed*: William JENINGS, Sarah JENINGS.

[C:248] ... *Wit*: William RELFE, Richd. RUDYARD. *Ack*: April Court 1730. *Regt*: 15 June 1730.

Miriam KEETON of the Precinct of Pasquotank & Province of North Carolina ... In Consideration of the sum of 16 pounds ... paid by Thomas SIMONS ... assign over all my right ... to ye within mentioned deed for 100 acres of Land ... as is Contained in ye within deed To Thomas SIMONS ... 14 April 1730. *Signed*: The mark M of Miriam KEETON. *Wit*: Benjn. PRICHARD, John SYMONS. *Ack*: April Court ye 14 day 1730. *Regt*: 15 June 1730.

North Carolina. Jeremiah MURDEN of Pasquotank Precinct in the Province afs'd ... assign ... unto William JENINGS Junr. all my right ... unto the within mentioned pattent containing 160 acres ... 13 April 1730. *Signed*: Jeremiah MURDEN, Mary MURDEN. *Wit*: William RELFE, Rich'd RUDYARD. *Ack*: April Court ye 14 day 1730. *Regt*: 24 June 1730.

John JONES of ye Precinct of Pasquotank in the Province of North Carolina do for a valuable Consideration in hand already received assign ... all my right ...
[C:249] of this within mentioned deed of sale to Charles GRANDY of the Province afs'd ... 14 April 1730. *Signed*: John JONES. *Wit*: Benitt MORGAN, Jnoa. JONES. *Ack*: 14 April 1730. *Regt*: 24 June 1730.

Thomas CASEY of the Precinct of Pasquotank & Province of North Carolina ... for the valuable Consideration of 40 pounds ... paid by Edward SCOTT of ye prect & Province afs'd ... sold ... 240 acres of Land ... on Pasquotank River ... being a part of a tract of Land by pattent bought of John AVERY ... FISHERS Corner Tree ... Thomas SMITHSON'S Line ... Richard MADRENS Line .... 13 April 1730. *Signed*: Edward SCOTT. *Wit*: Thomas X SMITHSON, Benjamin PRITCHARD. *Ack*: April Court ye 14. 1730. *Regt*: 30 June 1730.

North Carolina. 13 April ...
[C:250] 1730. Between Isaac MADREN of the Precinct of Pasquotank of the one part & Thomas SMITHSON of ye. afs'd prect of the other part ... in Consideration of ... 16 pounds 6 Shillings Currt

money of this Province ... Sold ... parll: of Land ... FISHERS Corner tree ... George HARRIS Corner tree ... LEWIS Corner tree ... as By the pattent thereof Bearing date 1715 ... *Signed*: Isaac MADREN. *Wit*: Benjn. PRICHARD, Thos CASEY, Richd RUDYARD. *Ack*: April Court ye 14. 1730. *Regt*: 30 June 1730.

[C:251] North Carolina. James[sic] SCARBROUGH of the Precinct of Pasquotank for and in Consideration of the Sum of 102 pounds Currt. money of this Province ... paid by Peter BROWNE ... Sold ... all my right ... ye within mentioned Land ... reserving 50 acres part thereof Sold unto Austine SCARBROUGH ... 24 Oct. 1729. *Signed*: John J SCARBROUGH his Mark. *Wit*: Thos. PENDLETON, Jno PEGGS, Richd RUDYARD. *Ack*: 14 April 1730. *Regt*: 30 June 1730.

North Carolina Edmond GALE of the County of Albermarl in ye Province afs'd ... in Consideration of the sum of 450 pounds Curt money of said Province ... paid by Oliver SALLTER of ye said Province ... Sold ... parcell of Land ... on ye No East Side of Little River Containing ... 375 acres ... divides this land from the Land that was John HUNTERS now the Land of John PLANTER ... FISHERS Corner tree now the Corner tree of Nathe CHAVIN Esq.
[C:252] ... 26 June 1730. *Signed*: Edmd. GALE. *Wit*: Zeb. CLAYTON, Francis CLAYTON, William I JACKSON his mark. *Ack*: 26 June 1730 C. J. GALE. *Regt*: 2 July 1730.

[C:253] William SAWYER do assign over unto Thomas SAWYER Junr all my right ... of ye within deed ... Excepting 10 acres ... Known by Wm MCDANIELS clearing ... 19 July 1730. *Signed*: Will. SAWYER. *Wit*: Dollinnana RIDY Mark T, Thos. GRAY.

7 July 1730 between Margret GREGORY widow of the Precinct of Pasquotank In the Province of North Carolina and Richard GREGORY her Son of the Place aforesaid of the one part and James GREGORY of the same Precinct & Province of the other Part ... for the love good will and affection wh. she doth bear & hath unto her Son James GREGORY and the said Richard GREGORY ... for the sum of 150 pounds Current money of North Carolina ... Sold ... Parcell of Land ... on the North East side of Pasquotank River whereon the said Margret GREGORY now dwells Except & always

reserved unto the said Margret GREGORY her life time & during her natural life ...
[C:254] ... *Signed*: Margret M GREGORY her mark, Richd. R GREGORY his mark. *Wit*: ADAMS, John BRAY, Thos BRAY. *Ack*: July Court 1730. *Regt*: 8. 12. 1730.

North Carolina. Mary GLOSTER of Pasquotank Precinct widow ... for the good care charge & trouble my friend John BROTHERS has been at wh. my negro Woman Frances & hir child Ruth by these presents after this my natural life is ended
[C:255] Give ... unto the aforesaid John BROTHERS the aforesaid girl named Ruth, he the aforesaid John BROTHERS to Keep & maintain the aforesaid Negro Ruth until she the aforesaid Mary GLOSTER shall take her the said Negro Ruth home which said Negro girl the said Mary GLOSTER is to have the use of & maintain during the Natural Life of her the said Mary GLOSTER & if it should so happen that the said Negro Girl Ruth Should have issue of her Body during the natural life of her the said Mary GLOSTER then such Issue to be & belong unto her the said Mary GLOSTER ... But after the Natural life of her the said Mary GLOSTER is ended then she the said Negro Ruth & what issue shall there after have I the said Mary GLOSTER do by these presents give ... unto him ye said John BROTHERS ... 25 Ober 1726. *Signed*: Mary GLOSTER. *Wit*: Edwd. MAYO, Stephen DELAMAR, Richd. RUDYARD. *Regt*: 23 Sept. 1730.

North Carolina. Edward SCOTT ... wt. the Voluntary consent of Mary SCOTT my Lawful wife ... for the valuable Consideration of 81 pound ... paid by John BROTHERS of the Precinct of Pasquotank in the Province of North Carolina ... Sold ... a tract of Land Containing 150 acres ... Bounding on New Begun Creek & Joining on one side By Henry PENDLETON & on the other side by the meeting house Land by Patent granted for the same Bearing date [blank] ...
[C:256] ... 20 July 1725. *Signed*: Edwd SCOTT, Mary X SCOTT her mark. *Wit*: Henry RAPER, Jona JONES, Truman MCBRIDE. *Ack*: 21 July 1725. Recorded 11 Feb 1725 p. John PARK Reg. *Regt*: 23 Sep 1730.

[C:257] His Excellency John Lord CARTERET Palatine ... give & grant unto John BROTHERS of our said County a tract of Land containing 80 acres being on

Gumb Pole Swamp one of the Branches of New Begun Creek ... 2 Aug. 1726. Witness our Trusty & well beloved Sir Richard EVERARD Bart Governour ... *Signed*: Richd. EVERARD, Wm REED, Fran FOSTER, Thos. HARVEY, E. GALE, C. GALE, Rd SANDERSON, E MOSELEY. Recorded in the Secretaries office Rob FOSTER dep. Secy *Regt*: 10 Oct. 1730.

His Excellency The Most Noble Henry Duke of BEAUFORT Pallatine &c. ...
[C:258] ... give & grant unto John SCOT of our said Province a tract of Land containing 129 acres Lieing in Pasquotank Precinct on Newbegun Creek Beginning at a holly Henry PENDLETONS Corner tree ... 4 Sept. 1714. Witness our &c Charles EDEN Esq. ... *Signed*: C. EDEN, Tho. BOYD, Wm REED, N CHEVIN, Francis FOSTER, C GALE.

N Carolina. John SCOTT of the Precinct of Pasquotank & Province afs'd ... for ye valuable Consideration of 6 pounds 15 Shillings ... paid by John BROTHERS ... sold ... all my estate Right ... [Rest of deed missing]

[First part of deed missing] ...
[C:259] ... in London afs'd ... *Signed*: Daniel DOLLEY, Margt. MOLLESON, Mary DANSON. *Wit*: Jacob GEORGE, Geo BURRINGTON, C. GOFFE. In testimonium Veritaty *Signed*: Richd. WISE Not Pub. 1727. *Regt*: Sept. 30.

Albermarle. William Earle of CRAVEN Palatine ... give & grant unto Henry KEETON of our sd. County Planter a tract of Land Containing 200 acres being on New begun Creek in Pasquotank Precinct Begining ... H. PENDLETONS his Corner tree ...
[C:260] ... 1 Jan. in the 31st year of our possession of our said Province of Carolina 1694. Witness our hands & seals of our trusty beloved Philip LUDWELL Esq. Governor ... *Signed*: Philip LUDWELL, Thos. HARVEY, Daniel AKHURST, Francis TOMS, Thomas POLLOCK. Recorded &c J. GLOVER Clk Sec office.

Pasquotank. Henry KEATON of the Precinct aforesaid ... for the Consideration for the Exchange of a patent from E. SCOTT heir apparent of E. SCOTT decd. for the Land & Plantation whereon the Said S. died

assigned & made over ... all my right ... the within mentioned Patent of Land to the sd. Edwd. SCOTT ... 19 Oct. 1714. *Signed*: Henry KEETON. *Wit*: W. NORRIS, Benj. WEST. ...
[C:261] ... 19 Oct. 1714 Henry KEATON came into court & acknowledged the above assignment to Ed. SCOTT. *Wit*: W. NORRIS Clk. *Regt*: 5 Nov. 1714. The foregoing Pattent & assignment was Registered 3 Oct. 1730.

North Carolina. 26 June 1730 & in the third year of the reign of our Soverign Lord George the Second ... Between Gabriel NEWBY of Perquimins Precinct Gentleman of ye one party & John DEAVES of Pasquotank Prect. Planter of the other Party ... the said Gabriel NEWBY by virtue of a power of Attorney ... from Mrs Mary DANSON of the City of London in the Kingdom of Great Britain Widow ... in Consideration of the Sum of 25 pounds current fine Silver ... paid by the said John DEAVES ... Sold ... Tract of Land Containing 204 Acres ... North Side of Pasquotank River ... Arnoose Creek ... being part of a manor or Larger tract of Land the said Mary DANSON holdeth on the North Side of Pasquotank River ... the said Plantation ... of 254 acres ...
[C:262] ... *Signed*: Gabriel NEWBY atty. to Mary DANSON. *Wit*: Miles GALD, James CHAMBERLAIN. *Regt*: 13 July 1730.

Thomas BETTYS planter of the County of Albermarl in the prect. of Pasquotank planter doth make over all my right ... of this within mentioned pattent unto Ephraim BLANCHARD ... 68 acres of Land ... Joyning on a tract of Land formerly sold unto the widdow Rebecca MUD out of the said Pattent ...
[C:263] ... *Signed*: Thomas BETTYS. *Wit*: William W WARD his mark, George X WARD his mark. *Ack*: July Court 1730. *Regt*: Or. he 10th 1730.

North Carolina. Timothy MEADS of the Precinct of Pasquotank & Province afs'd planter ... for the Love good will & affection ... unto my brother Thomas MEADS of ye prect. & Province afs'd have given ... a tract of Land ... Between the land I formerly held belonging to my father John MEADS Maj. Ed. GALDS & Thomas STANTON as the pattent makes appear ... containing 50 acres ... 2 July 1730. *Signed*: Timothy MEADS. *Wit*: Francis SWEENY, Denis COLLINS.

Ack: July court 1730. *Regt*: ye. 4. 1730.

[C:264] North Carolina. Ann JONES daughter of Cornelius JONES decd. of Pasquotank Prect. in Albermarl County & province aforesd. Spinster am Holden & firmly bound unto Wm. BURGESS of the prect County & province aforesaid Planter in the full & whole sum of 800 pound of good & Lawful money of the province aforesaid to be paid to him ... for the performance whereof I do hereby bind my self ... 14 July 1730. The Condition of this obligation is such whereas the above bound Ann JONES shall by her deed of sale bearing equal date wt. these presents Bargain'd Sold for the Consideration therein mention'd unto the above named Wm BURGESS ... parsell of Land that was given & bequeathed her by the last will & testament of her deceased father Cornelius JONES ... *Signed*: An A JONES her mark. *Wit*: Solomon DAVIS, John CARTWRIGHT. *Ack*: July Court 1730. *Regt*: ye 11. 1730.

Daniel COUYAN [COWAN] of Pasquotank & Tamar my wife both of Albermarl County ... for a valuable Consideration in hand paid ... unto Christoph HUMPHRIES of Pasquotank Precinct
[C:265] one parcell of Land ... between William WILLIAMS his land and John SCOTT'S Land ... 36 acres ... it being a part of a greater tract ... granted to me ... in the year 1721 ... *Signed*: Daniel X COYAN his mark. *Wit*: Jonathan JONES, Robard R CEM[ink blot] *Ack*: April Court 1721. Test J. PALIN Clk pro temp *Regt*: 8 ye 11 1730.

North Carolina. Ann JONES of Pasquotank Prect in Albermarl county & province afs'd Spinster ... the daughter of Cornelius JONES late of ye place afs'd for & in Consideration of the sum of 100 pounds ... paid by Wm. BURGESS of the prect. County & province afs'd Planter ... Sold ...
[C:266] ... parcell of Land ... on the N.E. side of Pasquotank River given & Bequeathed to me in ye Last will & testament of my dec Father ... a piece of Land out of the tract called ROBERTSON all ye Land on ye east Side of the plantation called ye water Million path Walnut tree neck & ye can dance to ye Same Containing more or Less together ... 14 July 1730. *Signed*: Ann A JONES her mark. *Wit*: Solomon DAVIS, John CARTWRIGHT. *Ack*: July court 1730.

Regt: 8. ye 11. 1730.

[C:267] William SAWYER assign over unto Thomas SAWYER Junr. all my right ... with the free consent of Sarah my lawful wife ... the within mentioned deed ... 15 Oct. 1728. *Signed*: W: SAWYER, Sarah X SAWYER her mark. *Wit*: Cornelius RELF, Jeremiah J SAWYER his mark. *Ack*: July Court 1730. *Regt*: Oct. ye 11. 1730.

James ADAMS of the Precinct of Pasquotank in North Carolina mariner am held & firmly bound & obliged unto Jarvas JONES of the Precinct & Province afs'd in the Just sum of 500 pounds currant money of N. Carolina ... 29 June 1730 ... The Condition of the obligation is such that if the above bounden James ADAMS shall & will at the request of the above Jarvas JONES acknowledge according to Law the manor Plantation Given in the last will and testament of John JONES Esq Father of the said Jarvas JONES .... *Signed*: James ADAMS. *Wit*: John SAWYER, James X MACKDANIEL his mark. *Ack*: July Court 1730. *Regt*: 8. ye 11. 1730.

[C:268] William SAWYER of Pasquotank Precinct in the County of Albermarl in the Province of North Carolina Planter For and in Consideration of a valu? in hand paid unto me ... by William M DANIEL of the same Precinct & Province aforesaid ... Sold ... tract of Land containing ... 10 acres ... on the N. Side of Pasquotank ... North River Swamp ... John SCOTS line ... 14 April 1730. *Signed*: William SAWYER. *Wit*: Bennet MORGAN, Jona JONES. *Ack*: July court 1730. *Regt*: Oct ye 11. 1730.

26 May 1730 Between Thomas SAWYER of the Precinct of Pasquotank in the Province of N. Carolina Planter of the one part & Charles SAWYER of the Same Precinct & Province ... For & in Consideration of the sum of 200 pounds current money of North Carolina paid by the said Charles SAWYER ...
[C:269] ... Sold ... Parcell of Land left unto the said Thos SAWYER by his Father John SAWYER last will & testament ... on the north East side of Pasquotank River Joyning on SAWYERS Creek at the plank Bridge containing 100 acres ... John HUMPHRIES corner tree ... formerly the parting bounds between the said John SAWYER & the said Thos. SAWYER now belonging

unto Jonathan JONES ... except always reserv'd to the said Thos. SAWYER 15 feet square for a burying place where John SAWYERS Bones doth lie who was the father of the said Thos SAWYER the said 15 feet square of Ground to be reserved for a burying place & for no other intent use or purpose & one acre of Ground where the chapell doth now stand and is by this deed excepted but not reserved unto the said Thos. SAWYER but the reservation is in & for the Chapell at SAWYERS Creek ...
[C:270] ... *Signed*: Thomas SAWYER, John SAWYER. *Wit*: Wm. O GOYG? his mark, Jarvas JONES. *Ack*: July Court 1730. *Regt*: O. ye 12. 1730.

[C:271] 13 July 1730 Between David PRITCHARD of Pasquotank Cty in the Cty of Albermarl in the Province of North Carolina planter of the one Part and Deliverance RICH of the aforesaid County, & Province Planter of the other Part ... for the value & Consideration of 5 pounds ... sell ... a Parcell of Land ... between Jeremiah SAXTON & Charles GRANDY? ... 100 acres ... part of a tract of Land specified in a grant or pattent Bearing date April 3. 1719 and assigned over to the said David PRITCHARD by Jeremiah MURDEN Jan: 19. 1724 ... *Signed*: David PRITCHARD. *Wit*: Wm. SAWYER. *Ack*: July Court 1730. *Regt*: Oct ye 12. 1730.

[C:272] Thomas GRANDY of the prect of Pasquotank in the County of Albermarl in the Province of North Carolina ... because part of the Land contain'd in my patent Bearing date the 20th day of November 1727 doth properly & solely belong to James WILLIAMS of the Precinct county & Province aforesaid Given unto him by his Brother Xtophrs WILLIAMS ... sold ... unto the said James WILLIAMS One Messuage or certain [Rest of deed missing]

Robert SAWYER Junr. of the Precinct of Pasquotank in the Province of North Carolina ... for the Love good will & affection wh. I have & do bear unto my son in Law Thomas JONES of the Precinct & Province aforesaid have given ... Parcell of Land containing 90 acres ... Thomas COOPERS corner tree ... between the said Thomas JONES & Jacob SAWYER ... on the North East Side of Pasquotank River ...
[C:273] ... as by pattent of the whole tract doth express bearing date May 1. 1719 Granted to James

M DANIEL ... 14 July 1730. *Signed*: Robt. R SAWYER his mark. *Wit*: Gabriell BURNHAM, Natha. HALL. *Ack*: 14 July 1730. *Regt*: 8. the 12. 1730.

Valentine GRAY of the Precinct of Pasquotank In the County of Albermarl in the Province of North Carolina ... for the just sum of 56 pounds ... Sold ... unto my brother John GRAY of the Precinct County & Province aforesaid ... Parcell of Land ... on the North East Side of Pasquotank River ... 51 acres ... Margaret GREGORIES Corner tree ... Thomas GRAY & Stephen GRAYS Corner tree ... through my plantation ... SOLLEYS line tree ... being part of a tract ... wh. formerly belonged to John UPTON ...
[C:274] ... 10 April 1730. *Signed*: Valentine V GRAY his mark. *Wit*: T. ADAMS, Caleb GREGOREY. *Ack*: July Court 1730. *Regt*: 0. ye 12. 1730.

North Carolina. George GREEN of the Precinct of Pasquotank am holden & firmly Bound unto Thomas LEWIS of the same prect ... Sum of 200 pounds in money of North Carolina
[C:275] to ye True performance and payment hereof I Bind my self ... 13 Sept. 1730. The Condition of this Obligation is ... Sold ... unto Thomas LEWIS my ... tract of Land Binding on John THACKRAY land being the manor plantation of the deceasd John GREEN containing 80 acres ... *Signed*: George G GREEN his mark. *Wit*: Jarvas JONES, Solomon S EVERTON.

North Carolina: Pasquotank Pt. John SMITH of ye County of Albermarl in ye Province of North Carolina in ye prect of Chowan ... for ye valuable Consideration of 16 pounds current Money ... paid by Ephraim BLANCHARD of the County & Province aforesaid ... Sold ... parcell of Land Containing 50 Acres ... Being sold from Thomas BEETYS unto Robert WARD Widdow out of a pattent Containing 318 Acres Bearing date 11 Oct. 1727 ... South side of Nobbs Crook Creek Swamp ...
[C:276] ... 26 Nov. 1730. *Signed*: John SMITH. *Wit*: Robt. JEFFRYS, Corns. LULEN? *Ack*: 27 Nov. 1730. *Regt*: March ye 13th 1730.

Pasquotank pt. John MARTIN Weaver in ye prect afs'd and Province of North Carolina for ye valuable Consideration of 10 pounds ... paid by Nathal MARTIN of ye prect ... sell ... ye within mentioned Pattent

& Tract of Land ... 16 Jan. 1721/2. *Signed*: John MARTIN.
[C:277] *Wit*: John PENDLETON, John SMITHSON. *Ack*: Jan. Court 1721/2. *Regt*: Jan. 1721/2. P. W. NORRIS Clk. *Regt*: in March ye 26. 1731.

North Carolina: Edmond GALE of the precinct of chowan and province afs'd Esq. for & in Consideration of ye Sum of 150 pounds Currt. money of said Province to me in hand ... by Thomas PLATER of ye prect of Pasquotank in the said Province Carpenter ... Sold ... parcell of Land ... FISHERS corner tree ... Col. HASTINGS? ... 18 March 1730/1. *Signed*: Edmo. GALE. *Wit*: Rob FOSTER, Eliz CLAYTON. *Ack*: 30 March 1730. *Regt*: March ye 26.

[C:278] [First part of deed missing] Being in ye prect afs'd Containing 330 acres ... line of Mr. PAINES? ... a Survey made for Xt: WAYMOUTH in year 1699 ... To have & to hold ye Same unto ye afs'd Ann STOCKLEY her heirs Ex adms & assigns forever ... *Signed*: George ROW, Jane I ROW. *Wit*: Gabl. BURNHAM, Benj. PRICHARD. *Ack*: July Court 1731. *Regt*: 7 Oct. 1731.

North Carolina. William GASKILLS late of Pasquotank prect. in Albermarl County but now of ye prect. of Carteret & County of Bath ... in Consideration of ye Sum of 100 pounds of good & Lawful money of ye Province afs'd ... paid By Richd. BROTHERS of Pasquotank prect ... planter ... Sold ... my plantation and Land being ... on ye North side of Flatty Creek at ye mouth of ye sd. Creek Containing 260 Acres
[C:279] ... Patent for ye same Land Granted by the Honl. Thomas POLLOCK Esq. president of ye hon Councill unto the said William GASKILL and bearing date the 10the day of July 1772[sic] ... 7 May 1731. *Signed*: William GASKILLS. *Wit*: J. PALIN, W. MINSON. *Ack*: July Court 1731. *Regt*: 8 Oct. 1731.

John MACKEEL of ye prect of Pasquotank & Province of North Carolina Weaver for & in ye Consideration of ye Sum of 100 pounds Curt. Money of this Province to me in hand paid ... by Stephen DELLAMAR of ye prect & Province afs'd ... Sold ...
[C:280] ... tract of land Containing 235 acres ... known by ye name of Rich Neck ... 3 March 1730/1.

Signed: John MACKEEL, Frances F MACKEEL her mark. *Wit*: Zachariah X KEETON Senr. his mark, Ditt: X Jun. his mark. *Ack*: July court 1731. *Regt*: 8r. ye 4. 1731.

North Carolina. Thomas PALMER of Pasquotank prect in Albermarl County & Province afs'd planter ... in Consideration of ye Sum of 44 pounds Curt. money of this Province ... paid by William JAMES of ye prect, County, & Province, afs'd planter ... Sold ... parcel of Land Lieing at ye head of great Flattey Creek Containing 98 acres ... pattent for ye same Granted to me
[C:281] ... by the hon: Sr Richard EVERRARD ... Bearing date ye 7 day of July 1730 ... 19 March 1730/1. *Signed*: Thomas X PALMER his mark. *Wit*: J. PALIN, John ROSS. *Ack*: July court 1731. *Regt*: 8. ye 8. 1731.

North Carolina. Thomas PALING of Pasquotank prect in Albermarl County and Province afs'd ... in Consideration of ye Sum of 25 pounds ... pd by John JURY of Pasquotank prect & Province afs'd ... Sold ... a certain tract of Land lieing on ye N. East side of Pasquotank Containing 300 acres ... line Run by Thomas RELFE ... Patent Granted to Thomas RELFE Bearing date 25 Feb. 1695 Being more or Less unto him ye said John JURY ...
[C:282] ... 13 July 1731. *Signed*: Thomas PALIN. *Wit*: Wm: MINSON, Alexd: SPENCE. *Ack*: July court 1731. *Regt*: O. ye 8. 1731.

North Carolina. Thomas PLATO of Pasquotank County in Albermarl County & Province afs'd ... in Consideration of 77 pounds Currt money of this Province ... paid by Geo WINBURY of ye prect. County & Province afs'd planter ... sold ... plantation Lieing on or near the branch of great Flatty Creek adjoining to ye land of William WINBURY ... 250 acres ... land was Granted by patent Bearing date 30 Aug. 1722 to Edmond GALE & by him ... 13 Jan. 1727 ... conveyed unto me ...
[C:283] .. Elizabeth STANTONS Corner tree in Markt. GATES line ... day of [blank] ... *Signed*: Thomas T PLATO his mark. *Wit*: John MCKEEL, Thomas T JAMES his mark. *Ack*: July 1731. *Regt*: O. ye 8. 1731.

North Carolina. Albert ALBERTSON of ye prect of

perquimons & Province afs'd planter ... in Consideration of the love and good Will & affection wh. I have towards my Loving Brother Jacob ALBERTSON of ye prect afs'd have given ... part of a plantation containing 79 acres of Land ... between the line of Rowland BUCKLEY & ye Land called ye white oak neck & was ye Land & plantation whereon Thomas LEWIS Senr. lived & died & called & Known by ye name of possom quarter ...
[C:283] ... [blank] day of 1731. *Signed*: Albert ALBERTSON. *Wit*: Isaac JONES, Geo G WINBURY his mark. *Ack*: July Court 1731. *Regt*: 8. ye 9. 1731.

North Carolina. Albert ALBERTSON of ye prect of perquimons and County of Albermarl ... in Consideration of ye Love affection & good Will wh. I Bear unto my Loving Sister Mary ALBERTSON of ye prect of Pasquotank Spinster ... give ... tract of Land containing 40 acres ... out of a Larger parcell wh. contains 190 acres of Land & is commonly called & Known by ye posom quarter on ye west side of Pasquotank River ... Beechey Neck Branch ... corner tree of Rowland BUCKLEY'S Land ... poplar Branch ...[blank] day of 1731. *Signed*: Albert ALBERTSON. *Wit*: Isaac JONES, Geo G WINBURY his mark. *Ack*: July Court 1731. *Regt*: O. ye 8. 1731.

[C:284] Bryan FITZPATRICK of ye County of Albermarl & province of North Carolina for the Consideration of ye Sum of 35 pounds to me in hand paid ... Sell unto William WILSON of ye County & Province afs'd ... Tract of Land Containing 212 acres ... called by ye name of HUNTS Neck ... 18 Jan: 1731. *Signed*: Bryan X FITZPATRICK his mark. *Wit*: Matthew CORNELL M his mark, Benjamin ALEXANDER.

I ye Subscriber assign all my right ... of ye wt.in mentioned deed unto Daniell MACKEE ... 24 April 1731. *Signed*: Willm WILLSON. *Wit*: Henry H HARTLEY his mark, John I COMBS. *Ack*: July Court 1731. *Regt*: O. y 9. 1731.

Pasquotank County. David BALEY of ye County of Albermarl & prect of Pasquotank Gent. for & in Consideration of the Sum of 30 pounds ... paid by Zachariah JACKSON of ye same place planter ... Sold ... 50 acres of Land ...
[C:286] ... 1 Dec. 1730 in the fourth year of ye

reign of our Sovereign Lord George ye Second ... *Signed*: David BALEY, Ann BALEY. *Wit*: Saml. JACKSON Junr., David JACKSON Junr. *Ack*: July Court 1731. *Regt*: O. ye 9. 1731.

I Assign all my right ... of this wth.in mentioned pattent to ye said Benjamin ALEXANDER ... 13 July 1731. *Signed*: Bryan X FITZPATRICK his mark. *Wit*: Danl. M MACKEE his mark, Denis U CRONE his mark. *Ack*: July court 1731. *Regt*: O. ye 9. 1731.
The pattent Belonging to ye last assignment was granted by Gov: DANL. to Cornelius FITZPATRICK dated 28th Feb: 1704/5.

Pasquotank prect. Thomas SYMONS Senr. of Pasquotank ... for ye valuable Consideration of ye sum of 55 pounds Current money of this province paid ... do assign all my right ... of ye said deed of assignment ... to William CHANCEY ... 13 July 1731. *Signed*: Thos. SYMONS, Ann SYMONS. *Wit*: Wm. MINSON *Ack*: July court 1731. *Regt*: 8. ye 10. 1731.

12 July 1731 Between Francis MARTIN alias Francis HOBBS Both of ye prect of Pasquotank in ye Province of North Carolina of the one part & William WILLIAMS of ye same prect & province afs'd ... for ye just Sum of 85 pounds Curt money
[C:287] of North Carolina ... Sold ... tracts or parcells of Land as did appertain & belong to John HOBBS decd ... on ye North East Side of Pasquotank River and now belonging to ye said Francis MARTIN being one plantation & ye manor plantation of John HOBS decd near ye fork Bridge Containing 330 acres & one more ... near ye mill Swamp known by ye name of TOMLINS Island pattent by William PHILLIPS ye 30th March 1721 Containing 300 acres ... ye afs'd 630 acres ... *Signed*: Francis F MARTIN his mark, Frances F. MARTIN. *Wit*: Thomas T LOUIS his mark, John I MACKDANIEL his mark, [blank] ADAMS. *Ack*: July court 1731. *Regt*: O. ye. 11. 1731.

N. Carolina) Albermarl Cty) William Earl of CRAVEN Pallt &c ... Give & grant unto William MOBERY [sic] a tract of Land containing 200 acres lieing in Pasquotank prect in ye County afs'd Beginning at an Oak by Newbegun Creek Swamp ... Eliz COATS her corner tree ... by NEWBY Creek Swamp ... ye said Land Being due to the sd NEWBY ...

[C:288] ... To have and to hold ye said land &c unto him ye said William NEWBY his heirs ... Given &c this 11 day of Nov. 1694. Witness our &c Phil: LUDWELL Esq. &c ... *Signed*: Phill LUDWELL, Thomas HARVEY, Daniel AKHURST, Francis TOMES, Thomas POLLOCK. *Regt*: Dec: ye 11. 1731.

Edwd. POPE for a valuable Consideration ... Sold ... unto Thomas WOODLEY ... all my right ... unto ye within mentioned pattent ... 15 April 1718. *Signed*: Edwd. POPE. *Wit*: Edwd. SCOTT, Stephen SCOTT. *Ack*: 15 April 1718. *Wit*: W. NORRIS clk. *Regt*: 14 June 1718 by ye sd. Wm NORRIS & now Reg. ye 11 Dec. 1731.

North Carolina) Albermarl) William Earle of CRAVEN Palt &c ... give & grant unto Elizabeth COATS ... 150 acres Lieing on Newbegun Creek in Pasquotank County begining ... by Newbegun Creek Swamp ...
[C:289] ... this 1 day of Jany 1694. Witness our &c Phil: LUDWELL Esq. &c ... *Signed*: Phill LUDWELL, Thomas HARVEY, Daniel AKHURST, Francis TOMES, Thomas POLLOCK. *Regt*: Dec: ye 11. 1731.

Pasquotank) John POWELL and Eliza My wife formerly Eliz: COATES of Pasquotank prect afs'd for & in Consideration of ... 35 pounds ... paid by Benjamin PRICHARD of the same place ... sold ... all ye within pattent & Land therein mentioned ... 17 Oct 1704. *Signed*: John A POWELL his mark, Eliza. O POWELL hir mark. *Wit*: [blank] *Ack*: O: Court 1704. *Wit*: Thos. ABINGTON Clk. *Regt*: No: 16. 1704 and now registered ye copy from ye original Dec: 11. 1731.

[C:290] North Carolina. William MADREN of ye prect. of Pasquotank & Province afs'd ... in Consideration of the Sum of 20 pounds in Specie country produce and one plantation Lieing up Nobbs Crook Creek containing 294 acres by James PRICHARD of ye prect & province afs'd ... Sold ... a certain tract of Land containing 150 acres Lieing on Pasquotank River ...
[C:291] ... 13 Feb: 1730. *Signed*: Will W MADREN his mark. *Wit*: W. MINSON, John PEGGS. *Ack*: O. court 1731. *Regt*: Decbr. ye 30. 1731.

7 Oct. 1730. Between James GREGORY of the Precinct of Pasquotank & in the County of Albemarle & in the Province of North Carolina of the one Party &

Alexander SPENCE of the Precinct County & Province above of the other Party ... in Consideration of the sum of 15 pounds of good & lawful money of the Province of North Carolina ... sold ... Parcell of Land ... Containing by estimation 20 acres ... on the N. East side of Pasquotank River ... a Corner tree on the said Alex: SPENCE'S line & the Said James GREGORY'S line ... Corner tree on Amos TRUEBLOODS line Excluding the 20 acres ... Sould out of a pattent fomerly granted to Thos. BARCOCK bearing date 1698 ...
[C:292] ... *Signed*: James X GREGORY his mark. *Wit*: John SOLLEY, Ant. WALKINS. *Ack*: O. Court 1731 & *Regt*.

16 May 1731. & in the 3d. year of the Reign of our Sovereign Lord George the 2d. ... between George GREEN in the Precinct of Pasquotank the County of Albemarle & in the Province of North Carolina of the one part & John SOLLEY of the Precinct & County & Province aforesaid of the other Party ... in Consideration of the Sum of 30 Pounds of good & Lawful money of Carolina ... sold ... Parcell of Land ... on the North East Side of Pasquotank River [C:293] in the Fork of the said Run Commonly Known by the name of GREENS Island ... 80 Acres ... Corner tree on John THACKRYS line ... Gabriel BURNHAMS line ... *Signed*: George X GREEN his mark. *Wit*: Joseph SPENCE, Anthony WALKINS. *Proved*: 9 Aug. 1731 By the oath of Joseph SPENCE ... he saw Anthony WILKINS the other Evidence Sign ... *Signed*: Jno PALIN. *Regt*: Jan: 10. 1731.

[C:294] North Carolina: Albert ALBERTSON of the Precinct of Perquimons and County of Albemarle for ... love & affection ... wh. I bear unto my loving sister Mary ALBERTSON of the Precinct of Pasquotank Spinster ... give ... tract of Land containing 40 acres ... out of a Larger parcell wh. contains 190 acres of Land & is commonly called or Known Pocoson Quarter on the west side of Pasquotank River ... Beachy neck Branch ... corner tree of Rowland BUCKLEY'S land ... Poplar Branch ...[blank] day of 1731. *Signed*: Albert ALBERTSON. *Wit*: Isaac JONES, George G WINBURY his mark. *Ack*: July Court 1731. *Regt*: Oct 8th. 1731.

North Carolina: Joseph GUILFORD of Pasquotank &

Province afs'd for & in Consideration of the love & affection & good esteem which I have & do bear unto my two Sons Jacob GUILFORD & John GUILFORD of the Precinct of Pasquotank ... give & grant ... a certain Parcell of Land ... from Phillip TORKSEYS line Robt HARRISON'S line thence to my own Corner tree ... to Joseph HARRISONS line ... to Back Neck [C:295] ... 12 Oct. 1731. *Signed*: Joseph I GUILFORD his mark. *Wit*: W. MINSON, Jos. I GUILFORD. *Ack*: Oct Court 1731. *Regt*: 10 Jan 1731.

North Carolina. Daniel COWAN of the Precinct of Pasquotank & County of Albermarl for & in Consideration of the Love & affection which I have & do bear unto my loving Son Caleb COWAN of the Precinct aforesaid ... give & grant ... tract of Land containing 238 acres granted by Patent to me ... Bearing date the 4 April 1720 & is my manor plantation whereon I now live ... unto him the said Caleb COWAN ... after the decease of me the said Daniel COWAN & Tamar my wife ... 12 Oct. 1731. *Signed*: Danll. X COWAN his mark. *Wit*: Wm. MINSON, Thos. PALIN. *Ack*: O. Court 1731 & *Regt*: 10 Jan 1731.

[First part of deed missing] ... to a dogwood John SCOT'S line ... which land being taken out to a pattent Bearing date ye 1 day of Nov: 1719 Containing 850 acres Granted By pattent to William READ Esq. decd. assigned over by the said William READ Esq. decd to ye Said Thos.
[C:296] SAWYER Senr. decd. ... Thos. SAWYER Junr ... grant to ... Thos. SAWYER Senr. ... 13 Oct. 1730. *Signed*: Thos. SAWYER. *Wit*: Wm. MDANIEL, James SPENCE. *Ack*: O. Court 1731. *Regt*: 10 Jan 1731.

North Carolina. Charles SAWYER of ye Precinct of Pasquotank & County of Albermarl ... in Consideration of 250 pounds Currt money of North Carolina ... paid ... by Hezekiah BUTTERWORTH ... Sold ... all that plantation & land being on SAWYERS Creek on the North Side of Pasquotank River ... formerly called John HUMPHRIES Corner tree ... [C:297] ... 60 acres ... 11 Jany 1731. *Signed*: Charles SAWYER. *Wit*: Wm. MINSON, Jarvis JONES. one acre Excepted whereon ye chapel standeth mention'd before signing. *Ack*: Jan: Court 1731. *Regt*: Feb y 8. 1731.

Thos. JESSOP of Perquimons prect. for & in Consideration of ye Sum of 35 pounds ... paid by Tho SYMONS Senr. of Pasquotank prect ... Sold ... the Tract of Land Lieing & being in Pasquotank Cty being part of a tract of Land Surveyed for the Said Thos. JESSOP Containing 135 acres as by a patent granted to ye sd. JESSOP bearing date ye 1 day of Aug. 1727 ... a line formerly old Caleb BUNDY'S ... to William CHANCEY his line ... to a line Surveyed by Henry WHITE ... to John SYMONS line to a new marked line made by JOY at across ye Land dividing this from ye remaining part of ye above mentioned Tract to ye first Station in BUNDAYS Line Containing 67½ acres [C:298] ... 14 July 1731. *Signed*: Thomas JESSOP. *Wit*: Edwd. MAYO, J. JESSOP. *Ack*: Jan: Court 1731. *Regt*: April 10. 1732.

North Carolina. Joseph REDING of Pasquotank Precinct & Province afs'd ... for the natural Love & affection which I have & do bear unto my Loving Brother Saml. REDING ... give ... tract of Land wh. was bought of William RELF ... 140 acres ... 11 Jan: 1731. *Signed*: Joseph REDING. *Wit*: Wm. MINSON, John PEGGS, David BALY. *Ack*: Jan Court 1731. to Saml. REDING & *Regt*: May 2d. 1732.

[C:299] Jarvis JONES of Albermarl County in Pasquotank in North Carolina Cordwainer ... in Consideration of ye Sum of 80 pounds in good Lawful pork ... paid By John JONES in ye County afs'd ... [Rest of deed missing]

[First part of deed missing] And two hogs unto my Brother Robert Thomas and ever Item I give unto my Brother Thomas forever one young mare they giving unto Eliz: CLARK ye first Colt of ye said mare & I do make & give Jeremiah MURDEN & Stephen DELLMAR my full & Sole Ex: of this my last will & testament ... *Signed*: Will. W CARTWRIGHT his mark. *Wit*: Eliza C CLARK hir mark, Jona. HIBBS, Mary MURDEN. North Carolina Chowan These are to Certify that Stephen DELMAR personally appeared at Edenton in ye prect afs'd & took his Solomn affirmation well & truly to perform ye afore written will of W. CARTWRIGHT dec: ye 16 Feb: 1730. Before me W BADDHAM Justice. Feb. 16. 1730. Proved this will before me Richd. EVERRARD. Recd. June ye. 7. 1732 in ye prect of Pasquotank.

North Carolina. David SCALIN of Princess Ann County in Virginia ... in Consideration of ye sum of 54 pounds this currancy or in default of this Sum 6 Barrls. of good merchantable pork to me paid by Richd. FOTHERGILL of Pasquotank prect. in North Carolina ... quit claim ... one point of Land now being on ye north side of Pasquotank called Indian [C:300] well containing 180 acres ... 11 April 1732. *Signed*: David SCANLAN. *Wit*: W. MINSON. *Ack*: April Co. 1732. *Regt*: July 6. 1732.

North Carolina. Thomas SAWYER Senr. of the Precinct of Pasquotank planter & of the County of Albermarl & of ye Province aforesaid ... for the Sum of 30 pounds Curt money ... paid By Edwd. WILLIAMS of ye same Precinct & County & Province above said ... Sold ... a dividend of Land out of a patent Bearing date ye first day of April 1723 ... on ye north side of Pasquotank Containing ... 375 acres ... Robt MORGANS line ... SAWYERS line tree ... wh. Land was granted by patent Bearing date ye 11 day of Nov: 1719 to ye. hon: Will REED Esq. dec'd & by him Elapsed for want of due Seating & planting and is now become due to James MCDANIEL by Virtue of an ord: of Counsel & is now assigned over to Thos. SAWYER Senr. ...
[C:301] ... 13 July 1731. *Signed*: Thos. SAWYER. *Wit*: Alexander SPENCE, Jarvis JONES. *Ack*: open Court 1732. *Regt*: July ye 6. 1732.

5 Feb. 1731. Jeremiah MURDEN of ye Precinct of Pasquotank in ye Province of North Carolina planter for & in consideration of ye sum of 500 pounds Curt money of North Carolina ... paid by William JENINGS of the same place planter ... Sold ... tract of Land containing 160 acres ...
[C:302] ... *Signed*: Jerh. MURDEN. *Wit*: Geo. ROE, Wm X WAYMAN his mark. *Ack*: April Court 1732.

North Carolina. James MCDANIEL of ye Precinct of Pasquotank & ye County of Albermarl & ye Province of North Carolina & in Consideration of the sum of 2 pounds 10 shillings Currt money ... paid by Thomas SAWYER Senr ... do assign over all my right ... to ye tract of Land & plantation in ye. pattent within Mentioned Containing by estimation
[C:303] 850 acres ... 13 July 1731. *Signed*:

James M MDANIEL his mark. *Wit*: Alexr. SPENCE, Jarvis JONES. *Ack*: April court 1732. *Regt*: July ye 7. 1732.

10 July 1731 Between Thomas GRANDY of ye Precinct of Pasquotank in ye Province afs'd planter of ye one part and John JURY of ye prect: and province afs'd planter of ye other part ... sum of 15 pounds good & Lawful money ... Sold ... tract of Land Containing 100 acres ... being ye whole parcell of Land belonging to John JURY afs'd out of ye Survey of William SIMPSON made over to Mrs Margrett MCBRIDE ack to Thoms. JURY decd. Father of ye said John JURY being now in a pattent granted to Thos. GRANDY afs'd dated Nov: ye 20 1727 ... on ye N. E. side of Pasquotank River ... SAWYERS Creek wh. Land the said John JURY for the Sum afs'd doth acknowledge ... unto ye said Thomas GRANDY ...
[C:304] ... *Signed*: Jno. J JURY his mark. *Wit*: Wm. W DAVIS his mark, Jarvis JONES. *Ack*: April Court 1732. *Regt*: July ye 7 1732.

18 April 1732 Between James CARROON and John CAROON both of ye Precinct of Pasquotank & Province of North Carolina of ye one part ... William GREGORY of ye same Province afs'd of ye other part ... for one Negro man and a plantation ... Sold ... parcell of Land ... on ye N. East side of Pasquotank River in ye fork of Aronouse Creek Containing ... 130 acres ... being part of a tract of Land in a Patent Granted to William JENINGS & Thomas JONSON Baring date 1 Jan. 1694 ... by JURY point ...
[C:305] ... *Signed*: James CARROON, Jno. CARROON. *Wit*: Thos. LOWTHER, Jno. LEEARY. *Ack*: April Ct 1732. *Regt*: July ye 7. 1732.

North Carolina. Joseph WINSHIP of Alligator in ye prect of Terrill & County of Albermarl for & in Consideration of the sum of 105 pounds Currt money of this Province ... paid by Robt CALHOON of ye said County ... Sold ... Tract of Land ... on the N.E. side of Allyator Creek Containing ... 200 acres ... Bounded on ye So. with Will WILSONS ye East wt. Jno. COMES ye North w. Will RAFIELD ye west wt. ye Creek ... formerly patented to CANONS ...
[C:306] ... 18 May 1730. *Signed*: Joseph WINSHIP. *Wit*: Geo LININGTON, John COX. *Proved*: 9 May 1732. J. PALIN. *Regt*: July ye 7. 1732.

James CARROON and John CARROON do assign over a part of this deed Beginning down by the mouth of JUDY? Swamp ... unto George CARROON ... *Signed*: James CARROON, John CARROON. *Wit*: Tho LOUTHER, John LEARY. *Ack*: 11 April 1732. *Regt*: 7 July 1732.

Thomas HARRIS of ye Precinct of Pasquotank in ye Province of North Carolina have granted ... the wt. in mentioned patent from me ... to John HARRIS ... [C:307] ... *Signed*: Thomas T HARRIS his mark, Abagale A HARRIS her mark. *Wit*: Geo ROE, Thos. T CARTWRIGHT his mark. *Ack*: April Court 1732. *Regt*: July 7. 1732.

5 April 1732. William JENINGS, Thos. JENINGS & Joseph JENINGS of ye Precinct of Pasquotank in ye Province of North Carolina planter for and in Consideration of ye Sum of Thousand pounds Currant Money of North Carolina to them in hand paid ... by Jer: MURDEN of ye Same prect. afs'd planter of Pasquotank ... Sold ... 182 acres ... by SAWYER'S Creek ...
[C:308] ... *Signed*: William JENINGS, Thos. JENNINGS, Joseph JENNINGS. *Wit*: Geo ROW, Wm. W WAYMAN his mark. *Ack*: April Court 1732. *Regt*: July ye 7. 1732.

Ann STOCKLEY of Pasquotank Precinct ... do hereby Constitute ... Jno. HIBBS of ye Precinct afs'd my true & Lawful attorney ... to acknowledge & make over to William ACKMAN of ye afs'd prect merchant a tract of land ... sold to ye said William ACKMAN ... 10 April 1732. *Signed*: Ann STOCKLEY. *Wit*: William SANDERS, Aron HILL.

Ann STOCKLEY of Pasquotank Prect in the Province of North Carolina Widdow ...
[C:309] For the valuable Consideration of 120 pounds ... paid by William ACKMAN of ye prect & province afs'd Merchant ... Sold ... parcell of Land ... 330 acres ... land of Will POWERS ... as by a Survey made for Xp: WAYMOUTH in ye year 1699 ... 10 April 1732. *Signed*: Ann STOCKLEY. *Wit*: Jonathan HIBBS, John SCOT. The foregoing letter of Authority & deed was proved in open Court April 17. 1732. *Regt*: July ye. 8. 1732.

21 July 1731 & in the third year of the reign of our Sovereign Lord King George the Second ... between Jno. DAVIS in the Precinct of Pasquotank & in the County of Albermarl In the Province of North Carolina the one part & James SPENCE Junr. of the Precinct & County & Province abovesd. of the other part ... in Consideration of the Sum of 20 pounds of good Lawful money of Carolina ... Sold ... parcell of Land ... on the S.W. Side of Pasquotank River being up ye said river near the head Cont. by estimation 80 acres ...
[C:310] ... *Signed*: John DAVIS. *Wit*: Cha SAWYER, Tho. SAWYER. *Ack*: April 10. 1732 & *Regt*: July 8. 1732.

North Carolina. Thomas FORBUSS of Pasquotank Precinct in Albermarl County & Province afs'd ... in Consideration of the sum of 20 pounds ... paid by John CAROON of Curatuck prect & province afs'd planter ... sold ... a Certain Tract of Land Lying on the N.E. Side of Pasquotank River Containing 132
[C:311] acres ... by ye Lines of John WHITTE, Jno. FORBUS, Denis CRONEY and Baley FORBUS ... 11 April [blank] *Signed*: Thomas X FORBUSS his mark. *Wit*: W MINSON, Tho SAWYER. *Ack*: April Court 1732. *Regt*: July y. 8. 1732.

North Carolina. Thomas PALMER of Pasquotank Precinct in Albermarl County & Province afs'd planter ... in Consideration of the sum of 150 pounds Currt money of this Province ... paid by John PALIN of ye prect & Province afs'd ... Sold ... Tract of Land ... at ye mouth of Little Flatty Creek ... the which I had of Thomas PALIN in Exchange for a plantation situate on Newbegin Creek whereon ye said Thomas PALIN now dwells together with 139 of Land Butted & Bounded as by pattent for ye said land Granted to Henry PALIN
[C:312] decd. bearing date the [blank] day of Feby: 1696 ... 24 Feby. 1731/2. Signed: Thomas X PALMER his mark. Wit: Thomas STEVENS, Oliver ST JOHN. Ack: Ap. Court 1732. Regt: July ye 8. 1732.

John HARRIS ... for ye Consideration of the Sum of 100 pounds curt. money of N. Carolina ... paid by Thomas HARRIS ... sell ... within mentioned Pattent ... 18 July 1731.
[C:313] *Signed*: John IH HARRIS his mark,

Ann X HARRIS her mark. *Wit*: Geo ROW, Jobe JN NICHOLS Signum. *Ack*: April Court 1732. *Regt*: 8 July 1732. *Regt*: 10 July 1732.

His Excellency John Lord CARTWRIGHT Pallat ... give and grant unto Henry WHITE & Arnold WHITE both of Said County a tract of Land containing 308 Acres lying in the County of Pasquotank ... 30 July 1724 Witness our trusty and well beloved George BURRINGTON Esqr. Govr. ... *Signed*: George BURRINGTON, Edward MOSELEY, Thos. HARVEY, Christ GOFFE, Francis FOSTER, Thomas POLLOCK, John BLOUNT. Recorded in the Secy Office John LOVICK Secy. *Regt*: 10 July 1732.

Pasquotank Henry WHITE & Arnold WHITE for the Consideration of 25 Pounds to us paid by David BALEY do hereby assign over all our Rights ... of ye wth.in mentioned Patent and Land ... unto David BALEY & John's heirs ... 20 Dec. 1724. *Signed*: Henry WHITE, Arnold WHITE. *Wit*: W NORRIS, Robt. LOWRY, Albermarl Pct. *Regt*: 10 July 1732.

[C:314] William Earle of CRAVEN Palatine &c. give and grant unto Richd. CRAGG of Our said County Planter a Tract of Land containing 500 Acres lying in Pasquotank prec. ... Herring Creek Mr. Thomas TWEDEY his corner ... Herring Creek Swamp ... 1 Jan. 1694 Witness our trusty and well beloved, Phillip LUDWELL Esq. Governor ... *Signed*: Phill. LUDWELL, Thomas HARVEY, Daniel AKHURST, Fra TOMS, Thomas POLLOCK. Recorded Will GLOVER act. of ye Secr Office. *Regt*: 11 July 1732.

David BALEY of Pasquotank prect North Carolina ... sold ... unto Daniel JACKSON ... 250 Acres of Land being ye half part or moyety of 500 Acres of Land being divided by a North line drawn across ye said Land formerly held by Richd. CRAGG in his Lifetime by Pattent dated 1 Jan. 1694 ... paid unto the said David BALEY ... as much fresh Pork as he ... is able to pay at some convenient Landing in little River & so accordingly every Mast year till the said Sum of 12 pounds Sterling be fully satisfied and paid ... 26th. Day of 7. 1707. *Signed*: David BALEY, Ann BALEY. *Wit*: Scott HOMER, Ann C MURRAN her mark. *Ack*: July 1707 and *Regt*: Nov. 16 1707 by John PALIN Clr. Copyd & *Regt*: 10 July 1732.

[C:315] North Carolina, Daniel JACKSON wth Ann my Wife for a valuable Consideration ... made over all our Right ... of this above said Sale of Land from us ... to David BALEY. 18 Jany. 1708/9. *Signed*: Daniel JACKSON, Ann JACKSON. *Wit*: John BISHOP, Mary BISHOP. *Ack*: Jany Court 1708/9. *Regt*: 22 Jany. 1708/9 John BISHOP Clk. Copd. *Regt*: 10 July 1732.

His Excellency John Lord CARTERET pallt. &c. ... give and grant unto David BALEY of sd. County 22 Acres of Swamp that lies between his Own Land and Charles TAYLORS ... at ye Herring Creek ... 5 April 1722 Witness our trusty & well beloved Thomas POLLOCK Esquire President &c. ... *Signed*: Thomas POLLOCK, C GALE, Richd. SANDERSON, John BLOUNT, J. LOVICK, Thomas POLLOCK Junr. Recording Secretary's Office J. LOVICK. *Regt*: 10 July 1732.

[C:316] North Carolina. Henry WHITE & Arnold WHITE ... Now know ye that we the said Henry WHITE wth the consent of Eliza. WHITE my wife ... for the valuable Consideration ... of 25 pounds ... paid by David BAILEY of the prect. of Pasquotank Province of North Carolina ... Sold ... a tract of Land containing 308 Acres by Patten granted to us ... bearing date the 30th July 1724 ...
[C:317] ... 20 Oct. 1724. *Signed*: Henry WHITE. Arnold WHITE. *Wit*: Will NORRIS, Robt. LOWRY. *Ack*: 20 Oct. 1724. *Regt*: 23 Oct. 1724 Pr. NORRIS Cl. Coppyed and *Regt*: 20 July 1732.

Richard CRAGG bying sick of body but of sound and perfect memory do make this my last will and Testament &c Impr. I bequeath my soul to God &c. 3dly I bequeath all my worldly substance to my well beloved friend Patrick BALEY all my personal estate & Lands and do leave him my sole Executor, only this my now dwelling Plantation I give to John BALEY & David BAILEY his two sons him to take demand & receive all such debts Dues & Demands whatsover is due to me & likewise to pay all Debts Dues & Demands which is justly due by me & to See my body decently buried, as witness my hand and seal this 9th Day of Feby 1695/6. *Signed*: Richd. CRAGG. *Wit*: Samuel DAVIS, Jno. DAVIS. Read Copy Teste T. KNIGHT Cley. *Regt*: 10 July 1732.

Albemarle. Willm. Earle of CRAVEN Palatine ... give and grant unto Denis GRAHAM of our said County a tract of Land containing 230 Acres lying in Pasquotank precinct, in ye County afsd. ... the Pocoson of Little River in John RAPERS line ... Morgan THOMAS his corner Tree ...
[C:318] ... 21 Feby. 1696. Witness our trusty & well beloved John ARCHDALE Esquire Govr. ... *Signed*: John ARCHDALE, DANL. AKHURST, Francis TOMES, Thos. POLLOCK, Saml. SWANN, Henderson WALKER. Recorded Pr. Will GLOVER clk Secr. Office. *Regt*: 10 July 1732.

His Excellency John Ld. CARTRET Palitina &c. ... give and grant unto William MELTON a tract of Land containing 130 Acres lying on the North Side of little River Swamp ... which Land was formerly granted by Patton to Denis GRAHAM ... said Denis GRAHAM dying [blank] thereof the same by a Jury decision had and taken at the Courthouse for Pasquotank prect. ye 20th. of 8. 1719 by Jno PALIN Esqr Excheator General & a Jury Hereunto Sworn found to Excheat ... now be come due to the Said William MELTON for the composition thereof paid according to Law ... 11th. Day of 9m. 1719. witness our trusty & well beloved Charles EDEN Esquire Govr. ... *Signed*: Fred. JONES, C. EDEN, Thomas POLLOCK, Richd. SANDERSON, W REED. Recorded in the Secr. Office J. LOVICK Secr. *Regt*: July the 10

North Carolina His Excellency the Rt. Honbll. John GRANVILLE Esquire Palatine &c. ... give and grant unto John FOURE of our said County a tract of Land containing 194 Acres ... PALEYS Creek in
[C:319] Pasquotank ... Benjamin WEST Corner Tree 13 March 1704. Witness our trusty and well beloved Robert DANIEL Esquire Govr. ... *Signed*: Robert DANIEL, Francis TOMES, Richd. SANDERSON, Will GLOVER. *Regt*: July ye 10th 1732.

North Carolina Robert ROUT late of Pasquotank in ye Province afsd. ... by virtue of a Marriage Solemnized with Holy christian ye widow of the Joseph JORDAN Deceased late of the Precinct & Province aforesaid became entitled to the real & personal Estate & Interest of the late fachachrestia for and during the time & time that the said Marriage lasted and continued or untill the Death of one of us Now know ye that I the said Robert ROUT

for and in Consideration of the sum of 10 pounds to me in hand paid by Joseph JORDAN the son and Heir of the said Feliachristia of the sd. precinct & province and other services and assistance to be done & performed by the said Joseph JORDAN and also to and for the support livelihood & maintanance of the sd. Feliachristia during her natural life ... Sold ... all my right ... to the real or Personal Estate of the sd. Felia Christia which came to me by virtue of sd. marriage ... especially of the land and Plantation wheron the said Joseph JOURDAN now Dwells ...
[C:320] ... 29 May 1732. *Signed*: Robert ROUT. *Wit*: Sarah PALIN, J PALIN. *Ack*: 29 May 1732 before me J PALIN Chief Justice *Regt*: 10 July 1732.

William WAGHMOUTH of Pasquotank Precinct in the Province of North Carolina ... for the valuable Consideration of 10 pounds currant money ... paid by William AIKMAN of the Province afsd. Mercht. ... sold ... parcell of Land ... 330 acres ... mouth of a small Branch which parts of William POWERS ... 20 July 1732. *Signed*: [blank] *Ack*: 20 July 1732 by John PALIN Chf Justice. *Regt*: 24 July 1732.

[C:321] North Carolina. Sarah HARRISON widdow of Pasquotank prect. in Albemarle Co and Province aforesaid ... Whereas Eliza. JONES Widdow Execum & Legette of Corn. JONES late of the precint and County aforsd. Dsd. did by hir Deed and Instrument of Writing bearing 16 of Aprl. 1716 for a valuable Consideration therein mentioned ... Sell unto the sd. Mary HARRISON Widow ... parcel of Land lying on the north Est side of Pasquotank River containing ... 100 ... being part of a tract of Land granted by Pattent unto the said Corl. JONES dated the 9th day of Jny. 1713/4 & by Sd. Coldr. JONES in his last will and Testament dated the 18 May 1714 given divised and bequeathed to the Sd. Eliza. ... Now Know ye that I the said Sarah HARRISON Widow for and in Consideration of the Sum of 60 pounds of good and lawful money of the Province afsd to me ... paid by William HAIGE of the prect County & Province afsd ... sold ... parcel of Land mentioned and conveyed to me by the affsd. Deed from the affsd Elisa. JONES containing ... 100 Acres ...
[C:322] ... 30 June 1732. *Signed*: Sarah HARRISON. *Wit*: Will JOHNS, Mary GLASTIN *Ack*: 30 June 1732

Sarah HARRISON to Will HAIGE by John PALIN Chf Jus. *Regt*: 4 Dec. 1732.

Paul PARMER do hereby promise ... Quit claim to ... a Debt due upon a Bond due to me from Mr. David BAILEY of the Precinct of Pasquk. bearing date Feby 1729 ... Oct. 7 1732. *Signed*: Paul PARMER. *Regt*: The foregoing Instrument of Writing between Mr. David BALEY and Paul PARMER was Registered Decr. 10th. 1732.

North Carolina John BLISH of Pasquotank Precinct this Province of North Carolina Merchant am held and firmly bound unto Thomas COLLIS of the Precinct and Province afsd. Planter in the full and Just Sum of 240 pounds sterling money of Great Brittain ... 26 July 1716. The Condition of this Obigation is such that if the above bounden John BLISH ...
[C:323] ... acknowledged a certain parcel of Land In open Court Lying on the North East of Aronuse Creek formerly belonging to Robert TEMPLE ... Then this obligation to be void otherwise to remain in full force ... *Signed*: John BLISH. *Wit*: Timothy YEATS, Joseph SPARNON. I do assign all my right ... of the within Bond unto Saml. BARNARD ... 2 Decr. 1719. *Signed*: Thomas COLLIS. *Wit*: Ann X BEALS hur mark. Mary M BELL her mark.

Saml. BARNARD do assign over all my right ... of the within mentioned Bond to Timothy YEATS ... 14 April 1720. *Signed*: Saml. BARNARD. *Wit*: T NORRIS, John SOLLEY. By virtue of a power of Attorney from Eliz YEATS to John LOUDON and the sd. LOUDON hath returned the Land unto the sd. BARNARD on paying of the money that was due to the said Thomas YEATS &c. and do assign over the within Bond to Griffith JONES ... 6 Decemr. 1722. *Signed*: Saml. BARNARD. *Wit*: John SOLLY & R F Richd. FARRILL. *Proved*: 14 Feby 1720/21 *Signed*: Thomas MILLER. *Regt*: The above Bond and assignment 2 Jany 1732.

North Carolina John PALIN of Pasquotank Precinct in Albemarle County and Province afsd. ... in consideration of the 200 pounds of good and lawful money of this Province ... paid by Stevin SCOT of the former county & Province Planter ... quit claim ... all such right ... Land & Plantation
[C:324] whereon Mary GLASTER now dwells ... in

Newbegun Creek in Pasquotank afsd. according to a Patton for the Land granted to my decd Grand Farthur Henry PALIN and contains by estimation 450 Acres ... 14 Oct. 1731. *Signed*: John PALIN. *Wit*: Edwd. MAYO. John ETHERIDGE. *Ack*: July Court 1732. *Regt*: 9 Feby 1732.

North Carolina. Will. GRAY of the prect. of Hide in the County of Bath Planter for and in Consideration of the Sum of 5 pounds current money of this Province ... paid by Lathan PURCELL of the prect. of Pasquotank and County of Albemarle Planter ... Sold ... parcel of Land lying and bounding on the North Side of Pasquotank River ... 125 Acres being the half of a Pattan of the denison line ... North River Pocoson ... Including the Plantation to where of the sd. William GRAY formerly did dwell ...
[C:325] ... 14 Feby 1731. *Signed*: Will. W GRAY his mark. *Wit*: Thomas MEREDITH, Thos. SMITH, Rich. Wm. SCLLOETHR? *Ack*: 8 Oct 1732. *Regt*: 10 March 1732/3.

North Carolina, 25th Dec. 1732 between Gabriel NEWBY of Perquimons Prect. Gent. of one party & Sarah BATES of York County in Virginia Widow of the other part ... by virtue of a Power of Atty. and instructions from Mary DANSON of the City of London in the Kingdom of Great Brittain bearing date the 25 Aug. 1727 ... Impowering me the sd. Gabriel NEWBY to sell Lease or to farm let away of hur manor Lands or Tenements within this Province not before sold or Leased ... in Consideration of the sum of 97 pounds 13 Shillings and 2 pence Sterling money of Great Brittain ... paid by Sarah BATES ... Sold ... Tract of Land containing 400 Acres ... on the north Side of Pasquotank River ... mouth of Porrohunk Creek lately called MILLERS Creek ... being part of a manor or larger Tract out of a Pattent bearing Date the 25 Feby 1696. 3,650 Acres ...
[C:326] ... *Signed*: Gabriel NEWBY. *Wit*: Jesse NEWBY. *Ack*: 19 Feby 1732 before W. LITTLE Ct Ju. *Regt*: 26 March 1732.

[C:327] 26th Jany. 1732/3. William MADREN of the Precinct of Pasquotank & Province of North Carolina Planter, for and in Consideration of the love and good Will and affection which I bear ... toward my true and well beloved Brother John RIGGS & Penelope his Wife ... give ... the other half or moyety of the other of the Reggestered Tract of Land containing 99 Acres being the Land and Plantation whereon the said John RIGGS & Penelope his Wife now liveth being the upper most part of the Tract of Land ... Nobs Crook Swamp ... *Signed*: Will. WM MADRIN his mark. *Wit*: George ROW, Richd. PRITCHARD. *Ack*: 12 March 1732 before Wm. LITTLE Ch Jus. *Regt*: 14 Apr. 1733.

23rd Aug. and in the 6th year of the reign of our Sovereign Lord George the Second ... between Margaret JOY & of Pasquotank Precinct & Gabriel BURNHAM of the same prect. ... in Consideration of ... 55 pounds ...
[C:328] ... Sell ... Dividend of Land Cont. 200 Acres ... in the fork of Pasquotank ... part of a Tract containing 640 Pattent to Wm. JOY Decd bearing date the 16. 8br. 1716 ... to James FOREHANDS line ... 23 Aug. 1732. *Signed*: Margery III JOY her mark. *Wit*: John LINTON, Will. ROSS. *Ack*: 8 Oct. 1732. *Regt*: 1 June 1733.

[C:329] Margery JOY Widow of the prect. of Pasquotank ... appoint my Friend John LINTON to be my true & lawful Attorney ... to acknowledge a deed of Sale for Land bearing date the 23 Aug. 1732 to Gabriel BURNHAM & also a Deed of gift bearing Date 5 Sept. 1732 to the said Gabriel BURNHAM ... 9 Oct. 1732. *Signed*: Margery III JOY her mark. *Wit*: Ed. X BRIGHT, Rich. BRIGHT. *Proved*: 8 Oct. 1732. *Regt*: 1 June 1732. [sic]

6th Oct. and in the second [sic] year of the reign of our Sovereign Lord George the Second ... between John LYNTON of the prect. of Pasquotank in North Carolina and Solomon SIKES of Norfolk County of Va. ... in Consideration of the Valuable Sum of 6 pounds Sterling Money of Great Brittain ... paid by the sd. Solo. SIKES ... Sold ... dividend of Land containing 50 Acres ... in the fork of Pasquotank ... being part of the Tract containing 400 Acres Pattent to Thomas LEWIS and Daniel MCPHERSON bearing date the 29 Oct. 1732 ... North to the Dismal Swamp ...
[C:330] *Signed*: John LYNTON. *Wit*: Wm. W ROSS his mark. Edd. X BRIGHT his mark. *Ack*: Oct. Court 1732. *Regt*: 30 July 1733.

8th July 1732 & in the fifth year of the reign of our Sovereign Lord George the second ... between William TAYLOUR of the prect. of Pasquotank in the County of Albemarle & in the Province of North Carolina of the one part and Adam ETHERIDGE of Norfolk County ... in Consideration of the valuable sum of 25 pounds Current money of Virginia ... sold ... Tract of Land ... in the fork of Pasquotank commonly called Learly being part of a Tract where the sd. Will TAYLOUR has obtained a pattent which containeth 500 Acres ... the Mill Swamp ... [C:331] ... binding on the Desart ... sold 250 it being the one half of that Tract ... the South & East part ... and where the said ETHERIDGE has built and cleared as by agreement ... *Signed*: William TAYLOUR. *Wit*: John SOLLEY, Wm. W UPTON, his mark. *Ack*: 8 Oct. 1732. *Regt*: 21 July 1733.

3rd Jan. in the fifth year of the Reign of our Sovereign Lord George the second ... between Thomas LEWIS together with the free and willing concent of Ann his Wife both living in the Precinct of Pasquotank in North Carolina and John LINTON of Norfolk County ... in Consideration of the valuable sum of 14 pounds Sterling money of Great Brittain ... Sold ... dividend of Land containing 125 acres [C:332] ... in the fork of Pasquotank ... being a part of a Tract containing 400 Acres Pattent to Thomas LEWIS & Daniel MCPHERSON bearing date the 23 Nov. 1723 ... by the Bear Spring ... the main Juniper Swamp ... 3 Jan. 1731/2. *Signed*: Thomas L LEWIS his mark, Ann A LEWIS her mark. *Wit*: Daniel S MCPHERSON, James IS SMITH his mark. *Ack*: 8br Court. *Regt*: 22 July 1733.

[C:333] Thomas LEWIS of the Precinct of Pasquotank ... appoint Mr. Gabriel BURNHAM to be my true & lawful Atty. ... to acknowledge a Deed of Sale for Land bearing date the 3 Jan. 1731/2 to the said John LINTON ... 9 Oct. 1732. *Signed*: Thomas L LEWIS his mark. *Wit*: Will. W ROSS his mark, Edwd. x BRITE his mark. *Proved*: Oct. Court. *Regt*: 22 July 1733.

His Excellency the most Noble Henry Duke of BEAUFORT Palatine &c. ... gave and grant unto Anthony ALEXANDER Senr. a Tract of Land containing 640 Acres lying at Stumps Point on the south side of Albemarle Sound and was Surveyed by Will HARLEY and by him assigned over to the said ALEXANDER ... at the mouth of Aligator Bay ... Bartholomew PHELPS Boundary Tree ... 3 Day of Xber 1712 Witness ye Hb. Thomas POLLOCK Esquire President of the Council ... *Signed*: Thomas POLLOCK, Thomas BOYD, C GALE, Nathan CHEVIN, Will. REED, T KNIGHTS. Recorded in the Secy Office Xber. 11th. 1712. Pr. T. KNIGHTS Secr. *Regt*: 15 July 1733.

North Cara. Anthony ALEXANDER Senr. do assign over all my rights ... to the within mentioned Pattent to my Well beloved Son, Anthony ALEXANDER Junr. ... *Signed*: Anthony A ALEXANDER his mark. *Wit*: Benjamin ALEXANDER, Joshua ALEXANDER. Benjamin ALEXANDER of the County and Province
[C:334] within mentioned do assign all my right ... of the within mentioned Land unto Thomas BEST Senr. ... 20 Nov. 1732. *Signed*: Benjn. ALEXANDER. *Wit*: Will. WILLSON, Thomas T BEST Junr. his mark. *Ack*: The above Assignments to Anthony ALEXR. and to Thomas BEST was acknowledged July Court 1733. *Regt*: 15 July 1733.

John PERKINS of Pasquotank Precinct in North Carolina for & in Consideration of the sum of 120 pounds of current money of this Province & 3000 # of Fresh Pork ... paid by John GODFREY of the Precinct of Pasquotank in the aforesaid Province ... Sold ... Tract of Land ... 110 acres and part of a tract sold by Henry CREECH Junr. to Will. BELL Junr. and since pattent to John BELL Senr. with sd. 110 acres since sold by the said John BELL senr. to Will and Thomas CREECH ...
[C:335] ... 10 July 1732. *Signed*: John X PERKINS his mark. *Wit*: Noah BISHOP, Will. TURNER, Jer. SYMONS. *Ack*: 12 July 1732 John PERKINS to John GODFREY before me Jno. PALIN Chf Just. *Regt*: 2 Aug. 1733.

George BRAY of North Caa. and County of Albermarle and prct. of Pasquotank ... and Eliza. My Wife for ... the valuable Consideration of 6 pounds ... paid by John CARTWRIGHT of the Province and prect. afsd. ... Sold ... 66 acres of Land lying Joining to Thomas RAYMANS line & John CARTWRIGHTS line ... 12 8br. 1730. *Signed*: George BRAY, Eliza. X BRAY her mark. *Wit*: Will. BURGES, Thomas SAWYER. *Ack*: 1731. *Regt*: 2 Aug. 1733.

[C:336] 8br. the 10th. 1732 ... Thomas SAWYER Senr. & Thomas SAWYER the Son of Thos. SAWYER of the Precinct of Pasquotank in the Province of North Carolina both Planters for and in Consideration of the sum of 7 pounds current money of North Carolina ... paid by Will. MCDANIEL of the said precincts afsd. Planter ... Sold ... Tract of Land 10 Acres ... on the No. Side of Pasquotank River ... North River Swamp ... John SCOT'S line ... Sold out of a Pattent bearing date 1 May 1668 containing 800 Acres [C:337] ... *Signed*: Thomas SAWYER Sen., Thomas SAWYER. *Wit*: Edward SCOTT, Caleb SAWYER. *Ack*: Oct. Court 1733.[sic] *Regt*: 11 Aug. 1733.

John BELL of Pasquotank prect. in the County of Albemarle in No. Carolina & in Consideration of the sum of 45 pounds currt. Money of this Province ... pd. by George BELL of the said Prect. & Province ... Sold ... my Plantation on the North Side of Pasquotank River commonly called ... SEXTONS Ridge ... on the Beaver Dam Swamp ... (a Division between Wm. BELL and I) it being now in the Possession & occupation of the sd. George BELL containing 80 Acres of Land it being part of a Pattent granted to my Father of 250 Acres & given to me by his last Will and Testament ...
[C:338] ... 10th Day of [?] 1732. *Signed*: John BELL. *Wit*: Eleanor S SIBBON? her mark, Sarah S LUMBLE? her mark. *Ack*: Oct. Ct. 1732. *Regt*: 11 Aug. 1733.

Albemarle . William Earle of CRAVEN Palatina &c. ... give and grant unto Henry PALIN a Tract of Land containing 139 Acres lying in Pasquotank prect. ... Flattys Creek ... Pasquotank River ... to the mouth of Little Flatty Creek ... xxx Day of Feby. 1696. Witness &c. John ARCHDALE Esquire Govenr. ... *Signed*: John ARCHDALE, Danl. AKHURST, Frans. TOMS, Thos. POLLOCK, Saml. SWAN, Henderson WALKER. *Regt*: 11 Aug. 1732.

14 March 1732/3 by and between Cornelius JONES of the Province of North Carolina and Precinct of Pasquok. of the one part and Thomas NEEDHAM of the County of Eliza. City Virginia of the other part ... in Consideration of the Sum of 190 pounds current money of North Carolina ...

[C:339] ... Sold ... parcel of Land ... 336 Acres ... North Side of Pasquotank River commonly called by the name of Cornelius JONES' Old Plantation beginning at the mouth of the Beaver Dam Swamp on the River ... RAYMANS Creek ... to John ARCHERS line ... William JOHNS line ... the remaining part of a Pattent formerly granted to Captn. Corns. JONES bearing date the 9th Jany 1713/14 ... *Signed*: Cornelius X JONES his mark. *Wit*: Will MINSON, George CARAN, Elizabeth MINSON. *Ack*: Or. Court 1733. *Regt*: Or. 31 1733.

[C:340] N Ca. George CARROON of Pasquotank pct. and Province Afsd. ... bound unto Peter BROWN of the sd. prct. and Province afsd. in the full and Just sum of 700 Pounds of good and lawful money of this Province to be paid unto the sd. Peter BROWN ... [blank] Day of [blank] 1730 ... The condition of the Obligation is ... George CARROON hath Sold ... unto John SCARBOROUGH a certain Tract of Land ... on the North side of RAYMONS Creek on the North East side of Pasquotank River ... the sd. Land first left by Will to Eliza. CAROON the now Wife of the abovenamed George CARROON which sd. Tract ... the sd. John SCARBOROUGH hath assigned ... to Peter BROWN ... *Signed*: Geo. CAROON, Eliza. X CAROON her mark. *Wit*: Will JONES, John TORKSEY, Anna LALIFIATION? *Regt*: 7 Jany 1733.

Thomas PALMER of Pasquotank Prect. Planter & Eliza. my Wife ... for the valuable Consideration of 15 pounds payable half in Pork at 45 shillings pr Barrell
[C:341] & half in Corn at 2 shillings pr bushel on or before the 1 March next ... paid by Robert PALMER of the prct. afsd. Planter ... made over ... parcel of Land lying on little flatty Creek binding on the lines of the sd. Robert PALMER containing 62½ Acres ... being part of a larger Tract granted by Pattent to John DANN ... I the sd. Eliza. PALMER formerly Eliza. RICE do make over all manner of Right & title that I have to the abo Premises either by Birthright or Dowery ... 8 March 1732/3. *Signed*: Thos. PALMER T mark, Eliza. PALMER her E mark. *Wit*: Will. AIKMAN, Jacob RITIGA. *Ack*: Oct. Court 1733. Recd. 8 March 1732/3 of the within mentioned Robert PALMER the Sum of 15 pounds in Pork & corn within mentioned ... *Signed*: Thomas T PALMER his mark.

Wit: Wm. AIKMAN, Thos. T GASKILL his mark. The above rept. *Regt*: 26 Dec. 1733.

[C:342] Alexander CROOKSHANKS of Pasquotank prct. in North Carolina Tailor ... for the valuable Consideration of 8 pounds Sterling ... paid by Richd. STAMP Govr. of the Precinct and Province affsd. the wright whereof I hereby acknowledge ... a parcel of Land containing about 60 Acres lying on the South West Side of Flatty Creek ... Plantation on which Valentine WALLIS lives and the line of the Land whereon Thomas COLLINGS did live ... part of a greater Tract by Pattent granted to John BELLMAN and by the said BELLMAN sold to Mth. WALLIS ... 9 Oct. 1733. *Signed*: Alexr. CROOKSHANKS. *Wit*: William AIKMAN, John PEGGS. *Ack*: Oct. Court 1733. *Regt*: 25 Jany 1733.

[C:343] North Carolina Joseph OVERMAN of the prect. of Pasquotank and Province afsd. ... whereas Henry Duke of BEAUFORT Palatine ... did by Pattent bearing date the 4 Oct. 1714 give and grant unto Stephen SCOT a Tract of Land containing 230 Acres ... Thos KIRK'S corner Tree in Stephen SCOTTS line ... Jas. GADS line ... which sd. Land was formerly for William REED and by him assigned over to Joseph JOURDAN & by the sd. JORDAN sold ... unto Patrick QUIDLEY and by the sd. QUIDLEY sold ... to Stephen SCOT and by the sd. SCOT given by Will to his Son Stephen SCOT and by his Son Stephen SCOT Sold ... to Ephraim OVERMAN ... Joseph OVERMAN am being Son and Heir to the said Ephraim OVERMAN ... in Consideration ... of 30 pounds paid ... Sold ... unto my Brother Ephraim OVERMAN ... 200 acres ... 7 July 1733. *Signed*: Joseph I OVERMAN his mark. *Wit*: Daniel CHANCEY, Will. CHANCEY, Ann OVERMAN, Sarah SO OVERMAN her mark. *Ack*: Oct. Court 1733. *Regt*: 8 April 1734.

[C:344] His Excellency the right Honourable John Lord GRANVILLE Palline &c. ... give and grant unto Anthony ALEXANDER a Tract of Land containing 270 acres lying in Aligator ... 20 Nov. 1706. Witness &c. William GLOVER Esqr. President &c. ... *Signed*: Will. GLOVER, Samll. SWAN, John ARDERN, Edwd. MOSELEY, Francis FOSTER. Recorded in the Secys. Office Xr. 1. 1706. Pr. T. KNIGHT.

Anthony ALEXANDER hath here given made over and delivered to my Son Joshua ALEXR. ... all my right and title of the within mentioned Land ... 18 8br. 1733. *Signed*: Antho S ALEXANDER his mark. *Wit*: Saml. H HOPKINS his mark, Andrew X OLIVER his mark. *Ack*: & *Regt*: 15 July 1733.

Valentine WALLACE and also William WALLACE of the Precinct of Pasquotank and Province of No. Cara. ... Jointly nominate ... our trusty friend Levi MARKUM of the Precinct of Pasquotank our Lawful Attorny for us ... to acknd. a certain Deed of Bargain or Sale bearing date with these prts. ... to John BOYD ... 14 Feby 1733. *Signed*: Valentine WALLACE, Wm. WALLACE. *Wit*: John MCKEEL, Richd. GRAY. *Ack*: Jos. ANDERSON.

[C:345] Valentine WALLACE with my Brother Will. WALLACE both of the prect. of Pasquotank and Province of No Ca for ... the valuable Consideration of 360 pounds currt money of this Province as also for 570 acres of Land on Hatterass Banks ... paid by John BOYD of the prct. of Pasquotank affsd. Genl. ... Sold ... Tract of Land wheron I formerly lived containing 290 Acres lying on the South side of Flatty Creek binding on the Land of Richd. STAMP and on the Land of the sd. John BOYD ... 14 Feby 1733. *Signed*: Valentine WALLACE, William WALLACE. *Wit*: John MCKEEL, Richd. GRAY. *Ack*: Apl. Court 1734 by Levi MARKHAM by virtue of a Power of Attoy from Valentine WALLACE & Will. WALLACE unto John BOYD. *Wit*: Joseph ANDERSON Clk. *Regt*: 28 June 1734.

[C:346] No Ca. Henry PENDLETON of the County of Albemarle Planter ... in Consideration of the sum of 100 pounds to me in hand paid by John PENDLETON of Pasquotank prct. Planter ... sold ... parcel of Land ... 150 acres of Land formerly known by Henry PENDLETONS Plantation ... on the South Side of Pasquotank River & bounding on Newbegun Creek Swamp & being half of the Tract of Land contained in a Pattent granted to the sd. John Henry PENDLETON on the 9 May 1713/14 now in the possession of John BROTHERS ... 5 July 1734. *Signed*: Henry HP PENDLETON his mark. *Wit*: Jos. SMITH, Jas. CRAVEN, Jno. BROTHERS. *Ack*: July Court 1734. *Proved*: by the oath of Jos. SMITH & Jas. CRAVEN to John

PENDLETON. *Wit*: James CRAVEN. *Regt*: 6 Sept. 1734.

[C:347] John MARTIN of the County of Albemarle Planter ... in Consideration of the Sum 60 pounds in proclamation money ... paid by John PENDLETON of Pasquotank prect. Planter ... Sold ... parcel of Land ... 150 [acres] of Land formerly known by the name of MING'S Plantation ... on the South Side of Pasquotank River & bounding on the sd. John MARTIN'S old line and likewise on DAVIS'S line & CHANCEY'S Old lines now in the possessn. of Benjamin MILLERS ... 15 Feb. 1733/4. *Signed*: John MARTIN. *Wit*: Win. MAYNARD, W REED, Jas. CRAVEN. *Ack*: Apl. Court 1734 by John MARTIN to John PENDLETON. *Wit*: James CRAVEN D Cl. *Regt*: 6 Sept. 1734.

[C:348] Valentine WALLIS together with my brother Will. WALLIS both of the Prect. of Pasquotank and Province of No Carolina Planters ... for the valuable Consideration of 360 pounds current money of the Province as also 500 Acres of Land on Hatterass Banks ... by John BOYD of the prct. of Pasquotank affsd. Gent. ... sold ... Tract of Land wheron I formerly lived containing 290 Acres lying on the south side of Flatty Creek binding on the Land of Ricd. STAMP and on the Land of the sd. John BOYD ... 14 Feby 1733. *Signed*: Valentine WALLIS, William WALLIS. *Wit*: John MCKEEL, Richd. GRAY. *Ack*: Apl. Court 1734 by Levi MARKHAM by virtue of a Powr of Atty from Val. WALLIS & Wm. WALLIS ... *Wit*: John HENDERSON Clk. *Regt*: O. 29 1734.

[C:349] Joseph OLIVER late of Pasquotank Precinct in the Province of North Caroa. ... for the valuable Consideration of 50 pounds Currt. Money ... paid by John BOYD of the Prect and Province Afsd. Gent. ... Sold ... tract of Land containing 150 Acres ... commonly called by the name of Isaacs adjoining the Land of Richd. STAMP on one side and on the Land of the sd. John BOYD on the other side and on the Sound on the South Side being the Plantation whereon I lived and which I bought of the sd. John BOYD ... 27 Novemr. 1733. *Signed*: Joseph JO OLIVER his mark. *Wit*: John I WHITE his mark, Ann A KINCKAM? hir mark. *Ack*: Apl. court 1734 Joseph OLIVER to John BOYD proved by the oath of John WHITE ... *Wit*: Joseph ANDERSON. *Regt*: 8br. the 29th. 1734.

[C:350] George [WARD] of Pasquotank prct. do Assign & make over all my right and Interest of the within written deed and Tract of Land therein Mentioned to John RICHARDSON of Pasquotank prct. ... 28 Jany 1733. *Signed*: George W WARD his mark. *Wit*: Wm. BRYAN, Ann BRYAN. *Ack*: Aprl. Court George WARD to John RICHARDSON ... *Wit*: Joseph ANDERSON. *Regt*: 8. the 29th. 1734.

Paul PALMER of the Prct. of Perquimons of the County of Albemarle in the Province of North Cara. Surgt. for and in Consideration of the Sum 20 pounds currt. Money of this Province to me in hand paid ... Sold ... 100 Acres unto Joseph SMITH of Pasquotank prct. of the Province Afsd. ... adjoining to the Lands of John CARTWRIGHT Will. GRIFFIN & Will. BURGES ... 10 April 1734. *Signed*: Paul PARMER. *Wit*: Thos. PENDLETON, Constant DAVIDSON. *Ack*: Apl. court 1734 by Paul PARMER to J SMITH ... *Regt*: 8m. 29 1734.

[C:351] No. Ca. Joshua MARKHAM and Elizth. my wife of the Prct. of Pasquotank & Province afsd. ... for the valuable Consideration of 40 pounds in barrell Pork or other commodities ... paid by John DAVIS of the prct. afsd. ... sold ... all the Land ... commonly called by the name of TOMS Field ... Mulbury neck branch ... Robt. LOWERY'S line ... Joseph MARKHAMS Corner Tree ... being part of ye Land granted by Pattent by Will. JACKSON bearing date the 16th day of March 1693 ... 26 Jany 1733. *Signed*: Joshua MARKHAM, Elizth. X MARKHAM her mark. *Wit*: Joseph LOWRY, Isaac L MACKE, Will. BRACKEN. *Ack*: Apl. Court 1733 [sic] Joseph [sic] MARKHAM & Eliza. his Wife unto John DAVIS ... *Wit*: Jos. ANDERSON. *Regt*: 8m. 29th 1734.

[C:352] Charles HUMPHRIES of the prct. of Pasquotank in the Province of North Ca. Planter ... for the valuable Consideration of 40 pounds ... unto Thomas UPTON of the Prct. and Province afsd. Planter a certain parcel of Land ... on the North East Side of Pasquotank River beginning at John UPTON'S Corner Tree ... binding on Edwd. WILLIAMS line ... the Holly Branch ... 50 Acres ... 22 March 1733/4. *Signed*: Chas. C HUMPHRIES his mark. *Wit*: B MORGAN, Ricd. SAWYER. *Ack*: July Court 1734 by Chas. HUMPHRIES to Thos. UPTON ... *Wit*: James CRAVEN Clk. *Regt*: 30 Oct. 1734.

William HAIG of Pasquotank prct. in the County of Albemarle in North Carolina for and in Consideration of the sum of 62 pounds Currt. money of North Cara. ... paid by William WALLACE of the same prect. & Province afsd. ... sold ... my Plantation on the North E. Side of Pasquotank River and the same Plantation which I bought of Sarah HARISON containing ... 100 Acres ... bounded as in ... a Deed ... of Elizth. JONES Ackd. in the Prect. Court [C:353] ... 10 July 1734. *Signed*: Will. HAIG. *Wit*: Will. MINSON, Saml. REDING. *Ack*: July Court 1734 Will. HAIG to Will. WALLACE ... *Regt*: James CRAVEN DC. *Regt*: 8m. the 30th. 1734.

James GREGORY of the prct. of Pasquotank & Province of North Cara. Planter ... for the valuable Consideration of 16 Pounds ... paid .. do sell unto Solomon DAVIS of the Precinct & Province afsd. ... parcel of Land containing ... 10 Acres ... out of a Tract of Land which I bought of my brother Ricd. GREGORY ... on the North East Side of Pasquotank ... 21 Feb. 1733/4. *Signed*: James X GREGORY his mk. *Wit*: Benjn. ROWEN, Ro. MORGAN. *Ack*: July Court 1734 by Jas. GREGORY to Sol DAVIS ... *Wit*: James CRAVEN. *Regt*: 8m. 30th. 1734.

[C:354] 7 March 1731/2 between Christopher WILLIAMS of the Prct. of Pasquotank in the Province of North Cara. Planter of the one part and John SCARBOROUGH of the prct. and Province afsd. ... for the full and Just sum of 70 pounds Lawful money of the Province ... sold ... parcel of Land containing ... 100 Acres ... on the No E side of Pasquotank River commonly known by the name of School house Neck between Hickory and Robt. SAWYER Senr. ... *Signed*: Christopher W WILLIAMS his mark. *Wit*: Robert MORGAN, Joshua X SAWYER his mark. *Ack*: July court 1734 by Chrir. WILLIAMS to SCARBROUGH ... *Wit*: James CRAVEN D Ca. *Regt*: 30 Nov. 1734.

John GODFREY of Pasquotank prct. in the County of Albemarle and Province of No Ca. for and in Consideration of the sum of 100 pounds Current money of No Ca. ... paid by Job GREGORY of the same prct. and Province afsd. ...
[C:355] ... sold ... a Tract of Lying on the No E. Side of Pasquotank River and the Plantation which I

bought of John PERKINS containing 60 Acres ... bounding upon John PERKINS Line & Joseph GODFREYS Line & upon the Beaver Dam Swamp ... 10 July 1734. *Signed*: John IG GODFREY his mark. *Wit*: C PALIN, Will. MINSON. *Ack*: July court 1734 by John GODFREY to Job GREGORY. *Regt*: 31 Oct. 1734.

[C:356] Phillip TORKSEY Senr. of the Prect. of Pasquotank in the Province of North Carolina ... in Consideration of the natural affection and Fatherly Love I have and do bear unto my well beloved children Phillip TORKSEY Robert TORKSEY & Sarah TORKSEY ... given and granted ... unto my three children after my Death as follows first I give unto my eldest son Phillip TORKSEY one half of my plantation and half of the Land thereunto belonging beginning at Porto Hunk Creek and to run to YOKINS? Gutt ... & I give unto my Son Robert TORKSEY the other half of my Plantation from YOKINS? Gutt to my outward bounds ... I give unto my Son Phillip one Feather Bed & Furniture one horse named Tobey and one case of Bottles two cows and calves three Sheep one chest one Iron Pot Two Puter basins one dish and half of my Carpenters & Plantation Tooles & I give to my Son Robert one Negro Man named Jack and one Feather bed and furniture three cows & calves one chest one Iron Pot & one Iron Kettle two Puter dishes one Puter Basin. I give between my Son Robert & daughter Sarah my mare & all her increase. ... 6 Apl. 1733. *Signed*: Phillip X TORKSEY his mark. *Wit*: John SOLLEY, Ewd. UPTON, John FRIHR? *Ack*: July Co 1734 by Phillip TORKSEY senr. to Phillip TORKSEY & the rest of his children ... *Wit*: James CRAVEN Dep Cc. *Regt*: 8br. 31. 1734.

[C:357] No Car. James NEWBEY of New River of North Ca with the consent of my Wife Hannah NEWBEY ... for the Consideration of 3 pounds ... paid & natural affection and Love I have and do bare unto my well beloved Son James NEWBEY Junr. of prct. of Pasquotank & Province of No Ca. ... sold ... 125 acres of Land part of the Tract I bought of John HOFTON lying betwixt my Son Samuel & Benjn. NEWBEY'S Lines ... 2 March 1730. Only I'll have preveledge during my pleasure to raise Hogs. *Signed*: James IN NEWBEY his mark. *Wit*: Charles X TAYLOR his mark, John I BAILEY his mark. *Ack*: July court 1734 by James NEWBEY Senr. to Jas. NEWBEY Junr. ... *Wit*:

James CRAVEN Dept Clk. *Regt*: 31 Oct. 1734.

[C:358] James GREGORY of the Prct. of Pasquotank and County of Albemarle In the Province of North Ca. Planter and Margaret GREGORY his Mother ... and Benjn. KOWING of the same County & prect. and Province afsd. Planter ... in Consideration of the Sum of 100 pounds current money of Carolina ... Sold ... parcel of Land ... on the North E side of Pasquotank River ... containing 100 acres ... John GRAYS line ... John SOLEY'S line ... Alexr. SPENCE' ... on a line agreed by the sd. James GREGORY & Benja. KNAUING ... taken out of a Pattent containing 400 acres of Land bearing date the 5th Feby 1698 19 Feby 1733. *Signed*: James X GREGORY his mark, Margaret M GREGORY mark. *Wit*: B. MORGAN, Hezekiah BUTTERWORTH. *Ack*: July 1734 from James GREGORY to Benjn. KOWING ... James CRAVEN DC. *Regt*: 1 Nov 1734.

[C:359] No Ca Henry CREECH & Benjn. CREECH of Pasquotank river Precict in the Province of North Cara. Planter for & in the Consideration of the sum of 25 pounds Lawful money of the North Carolina ... discharge John TRUBLOOD of the Prect. & Province afsd. Planter ... confirm ... a certain Tract of Land containing ... 100 Acres ... on the North E Side of Pasquotank River ... on the Lands of Griffith JONES John WINN? Henry CREECH John PAINE the father of Benjamin PAINE ... 9 July 1734. *Signed*: Benjn. X CREECH his mark, Henry H CREECH his mark. *Wit*: John SAULS, Jarvis JONES, Jos. MORGAN. *Ack*: July court 1734 by Henry CREECH & Benjn. to John TRUBLOOD. *Regt*: 3 Nov. 1734.

[C:360] No Ca. John PENDLETON of the county of Albemarle Planter ... in Consideration of the sum of 100 pounds currt. money of North Ca. ... paid by John BROTHERS of the Prct. of Pasquotank and Province afsd. ... Sold ... 150 Acres of Land ... on the South Side of Pasquotank River and bounding on Joseph KEATON'S & Ephraim OVERMANS and the remainder part of the sd. tract of Land mentioned in a Pattent bearing date the 19th day of March 1713/4 purchased by the sd. John BROTHERS of Henry PENDLETON the 19th Day of Octor. 1714 ... 12 Sept. 1734. *Signed*: John PENDLETON. *Wit*: John BROOCK, Wm. MIXON, Jas. CRAVEN. *Ack*: 8 Oct. 1734 John PENDLETON to John BROTHERS. *Regt*: 17 Nov. 1734.

[C:361] 8 July 1734 between John LURRY of Pasquotank prct. & Province of No Ca. of the one part & Saml. BARNARD of the Prect. and Province Afsd. ... I the sd. John DAVIS [sic] for and in Consideration of the sum of 50 pounds ... paid by Saml. BARNARD ... Sold ... parcel of Land ... on the North E. Side of Pasquotank River containing ... 100 Acres ... at Pasquotank River side on Saml. BARNARD'S line ... Aranuse Creek ... part of a larger Tract of Land the sd. John DAVIS bought of Gabriel NEWBEY by Deed bearing date June 26th 1730 and by the sd. DAVIS sold to John LURRY ... *Signed*: John LERRY. *Wit*: John CONYER, Cha. SAWYER, Jno. CRAVEN, Benjn. MORGAN. *Ack*: 8 Oct. 1734 John LERRY to Saml. BARNARD. *Wit*: Jos. SMITH DCC. *Regt*: 12 Dec. 1734.

[C:362] 8 July 1734 between John DAVIS of Pasquotank prct. & Province of North Ca. of the one part & John LEARY of the Prect. & Province afsd. of the other part ... Sold ... parcel of Land ... on the North E. Side of Pasquotank River containing ... 100 Acres ... at Pasquotank River side on Saml. BARNARD'S line ... Aranuse Creek ... part of a larger Tract of Land the sd. John DAVIS bought of Gabriel NEWBEY by Deed bearing date June 26th 1730 and by the sd. DAVIS sold to John LEARY ... *Signed*: John X DEANS [sic] his mark. *Wit*: Chas. SAWYER, B. MORGAN. *Ack*: 8 Oct. 1734 John DEANS [sic] to John LEARY. *Wit*: Jos. SMITH DCC. *Regt*: 12 Dec. 1734.

[C:363] His Excellency John Lord CARTERET Pallatin &c. give and grant unto Benjn. LOWELL of our sd. County a Tract of Land containing 524 Acres lying Pasquotank upon Nob's Crook ... which Land was Surveyed for William SIMPSON and by him assigned to the sd. Benjn. LOVELL ... 11 Oct. 1727. Witness our hands &c. Sir Richd. EVERARD Bart Governor &c. ... *Signed*: Richd. EVERARD, Wm. WOOD, C GALE, R. SANDERSON, E. MOSELEY, Edmd. GALE, Francis FOSTER. [?] FORSTER? Dept Secr.

No Ca. Benjn. LOWELL of the prct. of Chowan do assign and make over unto Mr. Thomas SAWYER ... 324 acres of Land being part of the within mentioned Pattent bearing date the 11 Oct. 1727 which lyeth on the South West Side of Pasquotank River & on Nobs Crook Creek the Residue of the sd. Land belonging to

William BRYANT ... 9 Oct. 1734. *Signed*: Benjn. M LOWELL his mark. *Wit*: Will SIMSON, John BOGGS. *Ack*: 8th Day of 8 mo. 1734 Benjn. LOWELL to Thos. SAWYER ... *Wit*: Joseph SMITH. *Regt*: 13 Jany 1734.

[C:364] No Ca. Pasquotank 13 Jan. in the eighth year of the reign of our Sovereign Lord George 2nd ... 1734 between James BELL of the prct. of Cartwright and County of Bath and Province afsd. Planter & Mary his Wife of the one part & John JONES of the prct. of Pasquotank & prov. afsd. Planter of the other part ... in Consideration of the sum of 20 Shillings currt. Money of North Ca. ... sold ... parcel of Land lying ... South west side of Pasquotank River ... 100 Acres ... line of Col. William REED ... the sd. Col. REED decd. ... the Pattent granted to Augustine SCARBROUGH ... *Signed*: James BELL. *Wit*: Will. HERRITAGE, John CONNYERE?, Danl. CHANCEY. *Ack*: James BELL ... Lease to John JONES ... 14 Jany. 1734. *Regt*: 25 Apl. 1735.

[C:365] No Ca. Pasquotank 14 Jan. in the eighth year of the reign of our Sovereign Lord George 2nd ... 1734 between James BELL of the prct. of Cartwright and County of Bath and Province afsd. Planter & Mary his Wife of the one part & John JONES of the Prct. of Pasquotank & Province afsd. Planter of the other part ... in Consideration of the sum of 120 pounds curt. Money of North Carolina ... sold ... parcel of Land lying ... South west side of Pasquotank River ... 100 Acres ... line of Col. William REED ... the sd. Col. REED decd. ... the pattent to Augustine SCARBROUGH Decd. ... [C:366] ... *Signed*: James BELL. *Wit*: John CONNYER, Will. HERRITAGE, Danl. CHANCEY. *Ack*: James BELL ... release to John JONES ... 14 Jany. 1734. *Regt*: 25 Apl. 1735.

North Ca. Elizth. LEE late of the Island of Bermuda but now residing in Pasquotank prct. in North Cara. Widow ... out of the good will Love & natural affection I have & bare to my Two Daughters Jane LEE & Rachael LEE ... give ... one Negro Girl named Liddy and all her increase to be divided equally between them when my Daughter Rachal comes to the age of 21 years, and then my daughter Jane to keep to her own use and Profit the sd. Negro Girl named Liddy she paying unto her Sister Rachael 15 Pounds

Curt. Money Silver also I give ... Jane & Rachael LEE Two Feather beds & bolsters two pair of fine Sheets two pair of curtains & Valins one Pillow & three pair of fine Pillows Burs? & one large Daper Table Cloth, one bed an Bedstead & three Cedar Chests with Locks & Keys & Six new Silver Spoons marked with EL & one Old Silver poringer three old broken Silver Spoons one Silver Salt & nine Peuter Dishes Twenty peuter Plates & one brass Kettle & one Iron Pot & one Large Looking Glass & Sixty pounds in Public Bills of Credit & also all outstanding debts due to me in North Ca. or elsewhere according to a list thereof afsd in the hands of my loving Friend & Brother William LEE ... by equal
[C:367] Portions between them except the Negro Girl named Lydd & her increase ... 19 Apl. 1728. *Signed*: Elizabeth LEE. *Wit*: Thomas SWANN, Will. LEE, Rebecca SWANN. *Ack*: Apl Court 1735 Deed of Gift from Elizabeth LEE to Jane & Rachael LEE ... by William LEE . *Regt*: 26 Aprl. 1735. Elizabeth City, North Carolina.

No Ca. Stephen HALL of the Prct. of Pasquotank with the consent of My Wife Elizabeth HALL ... for the valuable Consideration of 65 pounds ... paid by Saml. NEWBY of the prect. of Pasquotank & Province of North Cara. ... Sold ... 100 Acres of Land Joining on the Northwest side of his Plantation & part of the Tract my Father lived upon being on the South Side of a Branch to the Southward of his Plantation ... dividing bounds between me & my brother Nathaniel's Land ...
[C:368] ... 7 Sept. 1730. *Signed*: Stephen HALL, Elizabeth EH HALL her mark. *Wit*: William I BUNDY his mark, Thos. MOUNTREE. *Ack*: July Court 1732. *Regt*: 11 Apl. 1735.

[A plot of 139 Acres bounding on Swamp is drawn.] I the Subscriber do Assign all my right Title & Interest of this within mentioned Plot unto Jeremiah MURDEN in lieu of 37 Acres of Land which the deceased Jeremh. MURDEN excepted out of a pattent which he formerly sold to me ... 8 Apl. 1735. *Signed*: David PRICHARD. *Wit*: B. MORGAN, Stephen CHANCEY. *Ack*: The within Plot was acknowledged from David PRICHARD to Jeremiah MURDEN at Apl. Court 1735 ... *Regt*: 25 Apl. 1735.

William WARD & Elizabeth my now Wife ... of the Prct. of Pasquotank in the Province of North Cara. ... for a valuable Consideration of 13 Barrels of Pork to us in hand pd. by Ephraim BLANCHARD of the Province above said ... Sold ...
[C:369] ... 100 Acres ... out of a Pattent of 318 Acres taken up by Thomas BETTY in the Year 1728 ... on the west side of Nobs Crook Creek ... between George WARDS? ... BLANCHARDS line ... 8 Apl. 1735. *Signed*: William W WARD his mark, Elizth. E WARD her mark. *Wit*: Robert LOWRY Junr., Edward SCOTT. *Ack*: Apl. Court 1735. *Regt*: 26 Apl. 1735.

North Cara. By virtue of a Commission and Instructions to me directed from the Right Honourable Sr. Nathaniel JOHNSON Govr. of South & North Carolina both upon record in this Govt. hath given power & authority unto me Robert DANIEL Esquire Deputy Govr. of North Cara. with the advice of three or more of the Lords proprietors Deputies to grant & Sell Land ... in Consideration of the Sum of 4 pounds 11 Shillings Sterling ... sell ... unto John & Thomas PALIN a Tract of Land containing 457 Acres ... Governour ARCHDALE'S line Tree ... Edward MAYOE'S corner Tree ... to a great swamp of Flatty Creek
[C:370] ... 2 Sept. 1734 [sic] Witness the sd. Robert DANIEL Esquire & the rest of the Lords proprietors Deputies who have set their hands & Seals *Signed*: Robert DANIEL, Samuel SWANN, Francis TOMES, Will. GLOVER, John ANDREWS. *Regt*: 26 Apl. 1735.

No. Carolina By virtue of a Commission & Instructions to me directed from the Rt. Honourable Sir Nathaniel JOHNSTON Govr. of South & North Carolina both upon record in this Goverment hath given power & authority unto me Robert DANIEL Esquire Deputy Govenour of North Cara. with the advice of three or more of the Lords proprietors Deputies to grant & Sell Land ... in Consideration of the Sum of 50 Shillings Sterling ... sell ... unto John PALIN a Tract of Land containing 250 Acres ... Govr. ARCHDALE'S line ... Mary CLARK'S line ...
[C:371] ... 2 Sept. 1704 Witness I the sd. Robert DANIEL Esquire and the rest of the Lords proprietors Deputies who have hereunto set our hands & Seals *Signed*: Robert DANIEL, Samuel SWANN, Francis TOMES,

Will. GLOVER, John ANDREWS. *Regt*: 26 Apl. 1735.

Will. BERKLEY Kt. & Captain General of Virginia ... Whereas by instructions from the Kings most excellent Majesty directed to me and Councellors of State ... to grant Pattens and to assign such proportions of Lands to all adventurers & Planters as have been heretofore in the like uses wither for Adventurers of Money or for Transportation of People into this Colony according to a Charter of orders from the late Trustees and company & that the same proportion of 50 Acres of Land be granted & Assigned for every person transported hither since Midsummer 1625 and that the same course be continued to all adventurers and Planters untill it shall be otherwise determined by his Majesty.
Now Know Ye that I the sd. Sir William BERKLEY Kt. &c. do with the consent of the Concel of State accordingly give & grant Robert PEELE 350 Acres of Land lying on the South West Side of Pasquotank River between the Land of Doco. RELFE & the Land of John BATTLE containing on the River Side ... due to the said Robt. PEELE by & for the transportation of Seven Persons into the Colony whose names are on the record & mentioned under this Pattent ... as is expressed in a Charter from the Honourable the Trustees and Company dated 18th Novr. 1618 ... [C:372] ... Given at James City under my hand & Seal of the Colony the 25th of Septr. 1663 and in the 15. Year of the Reign of our Sovern. Lord King Charles the Second &c. *Signed*: William BERKLEY. Robert PEELE 350 Acres.

I Robert PEELE do assign over all my right Title & Interest in the within mentioned Pattent unto Thomas RELFE to him his Heirs & assigns forever. Witness my hand & Seal this 14th day Jany 1664. *Signed*: Robert PEELE. *Wit*: John WINNER?, Will. FULLER. *Ack*: 28th 1694. Will. GLOVER.

Thomas RELF do assign all my Right & Title of this within mentioned Pattent of 350 Acres of Land unto James SOWESBEY to him & his Heirs forever Witness my hand this 27th Day of May 1667. *Signed*: Thomas RELFE. *Wit*: John D DYE his mark, Henry H SHIRON?, Mathew X KITTERY, Will W BARSTELLE? his mark. He will not pay for it so I gave him in his Bond again, I took my Pattent again of him. This Pattent for

Thos. HODDEGGEN for John ROWES Widow for her Jane ROWE pd. the Rent 263 Jany 10th 1663.

Thomas RELFE by & with the consent of my Wife Mary do assign over all my right Title of this within mentioned Pattent the one moiety or half part to my Father in law John JENNINGS & the moity or half part to my Brother William RELFE ... 27 Jan. 1693/4. *Signed*: Thomas: RELFE, Mary M RELFE her mark. *Wit*: William JENNINGS, Thomas I SAWYER his mark.

[C:373] John JENNINGS do Assign & make over unto Will. RELF all my Right Title & Interest of the within mentioned Pattent ... 19 July 1697. *Signed*: Record William GLOVER the mark of I John JENNINGS.

His Excellency John Lord CARTERET Palatine ... give and grant unto Will. RALPH of our sd. County a Tract of Land containing 240 acres lying at the head of Pasquotank River at the South West side of the Fork between two Swamps ... 3 Aug. 1728. Witness our trusty & well beloved S Richard EVERARD Bart Governor ... *Signed*: Richd. EVERARD, C. GALE, Thos. POLLOCK, Richd. SANDERSON, Thos. HARVEY, E. MOSELEY, Edmd. GALE. Recorded in the Secy. Office Robert FOSTER Dep Secry.

[C:374] 7 Feby 1734 ... Jeremiah EVERTON of the Prct. of Pasquotank in the Province of North Car. Planter for & in Consideration of the Sum of 120 pounds Curt. money of North Carolina to him in hand by one Will. WARD of the same Prct. aforesd. ... Sell ... Tract of Land containing 60 Acres ... upon the South Side of Pasquotank River ... sd. Jeremh. EVERTONS Tract of Land ... ABINTONS Line ... [C:375] ... *Signed*: Jeremiah EVERTON, Hannah H EVERTON her mark. *Wit*: George ROWE, Samue MANSFIELD. *Ack*: 8 Apl. 1735 from Jeremiah EVERTON with the consent of Hannah his Wife unto Will. WARD. 28 Apl. 173 [blank] .

No Carolina. Jeremiah MURDEN of Albemarle County Planter ... in Consideration of the Sum of 40 pounds to me in hand by Will. RELFE of Pasquotank Prct. Planter ... Sold ... parcel of Land ... ground of Will. RELFE ... Pasq. River ... 100 Acres ... [C:376] ... 8 Apl. 1735. *Signed*: Jeremiah MURDEN. *Wit*: John BROWN, Joseph SMITH. *Ack*: 8 Apl. 1735

Jeremiah MURDEN to Will. RELFE. *Regt*: 29 Apl. 1735.

No Car. John PALIN of Pasquotank Prct. in Albemarle County and Province aforesd. Esqr. Attory. of Deborah FINCH of New England Widow & legate of Jeremiah FINCH late of this Province Decd. ... in Consideration of the Sum of 35 pounds ... paid ... by Ricd. FOTHERGLE of Pasquotank prect. and Province afsd. Blacksmith ... sell ... a parcel of Land ... on the North side of the River on the West side of Aranuse Creek at the mouth of the sd. Creek containing ... 150 Acres ... line of Able ROSS & Ricd. FERRELL.
[C:377] ... 15 Octr. 1729. *Signed*: Jno. PALIN Attoy. *Wit*: Daniel GUTHRIE, Will. MINSON. *Ack*: Octr. Court 1729. *Regt*: 8br. 16th May.[sic]

N Ca. Pasquotank. Ricd. FOTHERGALE ... do assign and make over unto John LURRY ... Title & Interest of the within mentioned Land ... 22 July 1734. *Signed*: Richd. FOTHERGALE. *Wit*: Cornelius RELFE, Ann FOTHERGALE. *Ack*: Apl. Court 1735 Ricd. FOTHERGALE to John LURRY. *Regt*: 30 Apl. 1735.

Mackrora SCARBROUGH & Henry HAYMAN of North Carolina Province & in the Precinct of Pasquotank gent ... sell ... unto John SANDERLIN & Edwd. JAMES of the Precinct & Province afsd. ... Tract of Land commonly called and known by the name of HAYMANS Island lying on North River ... 100 Acres ...
[C:378] ... [blank] day of Feby in the 11th year of the reign of our Sovereign Lord ... 1724. *Signed*: Mac SCARBOROUGH, Henry HH HAYMAN his mark. *Wit*: John SCARBROUGH, James H HAYMAN his mark. *Ack*: . *Regt*: May the 5th 1726 Folio 29th & 30 of my works Pr Thos. WEEKS.

We the Subscribers do assign over all the Right Title & Interests of the within mentioned Deed of Sale to William CREECH ... 8 Aprl. 1735. *Signed*: John HH SANDERLIN his mark, Edwd. X JAMES his mark. *Wit*: Robert SAWYER, Will. SIMPSON. *Ack*: 8 Apl. 1735 John SANDERLIN & Edwd. JAMES to William CREECH. *Regt*: 27 May 1735.

[C:379] No Ca. Oliver SALTER of the Prect. of Perquimons & Province afsd. Cooper for & in Consideration of the Sum of 140 pounds curt. Money of this Province to me in hand pd. by John PEGS of the prct. of Pasqk. & Province afsd. ... Sold ... Moiety of Land ... on the North E. Side of Little River ... on Thos. PLATORS Line at the mouth of Marchy Gutt ... by the now cornfield fence to Perquimans at the head thereof ... 50 Acres of Land [C:380] ... [blank] day of January 1734. *Signed*: Oliver SALTER. *Wit*: W. MINSON, Nathl. MARTIN. *Ack*: Oliver SALTER to John PEGGS 14 Jany 1734. *Regt*: 1 May 1735.

Sir William BERKLEY Knight Governour & Capn. Genl. of Virga. ... give & grant unto Mr. Thos. RELF 750 Acres ... Lying on the South West Side of Pasquotank River ... by Thomas KEEL his Land ... one of Wm. FORSON'S marked Trees ... for the importation of 15 Persons into the Colony ...
[C:381] ... given at James City under my hand & Seal of the Colony this 25 Sepr. 1663 in the fifteenth Year of the Reign of our Sovereign Lord King Charles Second &c. *Signed*: William BERKLEY. Thomas RELFE 750 Acres of Land. *Signed*: Fra. TURKMAN? No Ca. *Regt*: Will. GLOVER CClk.

Thomas RELFE by & with the consent of my Wife Mary do assign over all my Right Title & Interest of the within mentioned Pattent the one moiety or half part to my Father in law John JENNINGS and the other moiety or half part to my Brother Will. RELFE ... 27 Jan. 1693/4. *Signed*: Thomas: RELFE, Mary M RELFE her mark. *Wit*: William JENNINGS, Thomas I SAWYER his mark. *Regt*: Will. GLOVER Clk for Secretaries Office.

John JENNINGS of Pasquotank in North Carolina with the consent of my Wife Dorothy doth by these prts. Assign over all my Right Title & Interest of this within mentioned Patent of Land to my Daughter Elizabeth REDING her & her Heirs of her body forever after our Decd. As
[C:382] Witness my hand this 1 Jan. 1707. *Signed*: John H JENNINGS his mark DI. *Wit*: Will. WARREN, Mary MC CARTWRIGHT her mark, Joseph REDING, Robert CARTWRIGHT. *Ack*: 20 Jany. 1712 Mr. John JENNINGS by Dotherty his Wife to Elizth. REDING. *Wit*: Will. NORRIS Clk. *Regt*: 25 Jan 1712/13 Will. NORRIS Regr. The above Patent was Registered the 6th Day of May 1735.

3 Sept. 1734 & in the 8th year of the Reign of Our Sovereign Lord George the Second ... between Peter SAWYER & his Wife Mary SAWYER in the Prct. of Pasquotank & the County of Albemarle & in the Province of North Carolina of the one part & John SOLLEY of the Prct. County & Province afsd. of the other part ... in Consideration of the Sum of 50 Pounds of Curt. good Lawful Money of North Car. ... paid by the sd. John SOLLY ... Sold ... Tract of Land containing ... 300 Acres ... in his actual Possession ... for one whole Year by Indenture bearing date the day next before the day of the date of these prsts. & by force of the statute for transfering of Use unto possession ... Tenement commonly called or known by the name of SCOTS Old Plantation ... on the North E Side of Pasquotank River up at the Head of SAWYERS Creek being on the South West side ...
[C:383] ...
[C:384] ...
[C:385] ... 3 Sept. 1734. *Signed*: Peter S SAWYER his mark, Mary M SAWYER her mark. *Wit*: William MINSON, William M MCDANIELL. *Ack*: 8 Oct. 1734 Peter SAWYER & Mary SAWYER his Wife ... Deed or Lease to John SOLLY. *Regt*: 5 Aug. 1735.

1 Sept. in the 8th year of the Reign of Our Sovereign Lord George the Second ... 1734 between Peter SAWYER & Mary his Wife of the one part & Major John SOLLEY all of the Prct. of Pasquotank & Province afsd. of the other part ... being Heir at Law for & in Consideration of 5 Pounds of Curt. Money of North Cara. ... paid ...
[C:386] the sd. Major John SOLLY ... Sold ... Tract of Land containing ... 300 Acres ... at the South West Side of SAWYERS Creek ... the whole Pattent was granted by the Honourable [blank] to John SCOTT bearing date the [blank] and is to be delivered to Major John SOLLY at his request ... the sd. Peter SAWYER & Mary SAWYER his Wife being Heir at Law to him the sd. John SOLLY ... *Signed*: Peter S SAWYER his mark, Mary M SAWYER her mark. *Wit*: Will. MINSON, William WM MCDANIELL mark. *Ack*: 8 Oct. 1734 Peter SAWYER & Mary SAWYER his Wife ... Release to John SOLLY. *Regt*: 5 Aug. 1735.

North Carolina. George BRAY of the Prct. of

Pasquotank County of Albemarle and Province of North Cara. of the one part Planter & Will. BURGES of the Prct. & Prov afsd. Tailor of the other part
[C:387] ... in Consideration of the sum of 40 pounds current Bills of the Province afsd. ... Sold ... parcel of Land ... at the fork of RAYMANS Creek ... Poplar Swamp that is the division between George & Henry BRAY ... Thomas BURGESS bounds ... 75 Acres ... 10 Decr. in the reign of our Sovereign Lord George the 2nd. ... 1734. *Signed*: George BRAY. *Wit*: Thomas CARMAN, William JOHNS. *Ack*: 8 July 1734 from George BRAY to Will. BURGES by the oath of Will. JOHNS. *Regt*: Aug Court 1735.

[C:388] No Car. George BRAY of the Prect. of Pasquotank & County of Albemarle & Prov of North Carolina Planter of the one part & Thomas BURGES of Prect. & Province afsd. of the other part ... in Consideration of 18 pounds of Pork according to custom ... paid ... Sold ... parcel ... upon Spring branch ... to Thomas TORKSIES bounds ... 75 Acres ... 16 Decr. in the reign of our Sovereign Lord George ... 1734. *Signed*: George BRAY. *Wit*: Thomas CARMAN, Will. JOHNS. *Ack*: at the court house in Broomfield 8 July deed from George BRAY to Thos. BURGES by the oath of Will. JOHNS. *Regt*: 18 Aug 1735 page (251).

[C:389] Oct. 8th 1734 ... John WINBERRY Senr. in the prct. of Pasquotank in No Ca. for & in Consideration of the Love & good Will that I have & do bare towards my loving Son John WINBURRY Junr. of the same prct. hath given ... Plantation being and lying on the south side of the Original Tract ... at White Oak Point ... 175 Acres ... *Signed*: John X WINBURY his mark. *Wit*: Thos. TAYLOR, George ROWE, William WINBERRY his W mark. *Ack*: 8 Oct. 1734 John WINBERRY to his son John WINBURRY. *Regt*: 24 July 1735.

Oct. 11 1732 ... James MCDONNELL & Will. MCDONNELL his Son ... of the prct. of Pasquotank in the Province of North Carolina Planter ... in Consideration of the sum of 30 pounds
[C:390] Current money of North Carolina ... paid by Caleb SAWYER of the sd. Prct. ... sold ... Tract of Land containing 100 Acres ... on the North Side of Pasquotank River ... part of a greater Tract that

belonged to Thomas SAWYER & was given by him to Henry MCDONNELL it being Joined upon John JONES' line ...
[C:391] ... *Signed*: James M MCDONNELL his mark, William WM MCDONNELL his mark. *Wit*: Edward SCOTT, Peter P BROWN his mark. *Ack*: 8 Oct. 1732. *Regt*: 29 Sept. 1735.

7 Octr. 1733 ... Thomas CARSEY of the Precinct of Pasquotank in the Province of North Carolina Planter for & in Consideration of the Sum of 42 pounds currt. Money of North Carolina to me in hand Paid by Edward SCOTT ... [Rest of deed is missing]

[B:181] North Carolina. Surveyed for Francis HENDRICKS 206 acres grn. Oct. 24th 1695. Thomas RELFE Surveyor. William Earl of CRAVEN Palatine &c. ... give and grant unto Francis HENDRICK a Tract of Land contg. 206 Acres lying on the S.W. Side of Pasquotank River; Beginning at Richard MADREN'S Corner Tree ... Nobs Crook Creek ... the Beach Landing ... Given under the Colony the 25th day of Feb. 1696. Witness. For the Transportation Saml. SWANN, John ARCHDALE, of Francis HENDRICKS. Henderson WALKER, Daniel AKHURST, James MORIS?, Jonathan HUTCHINS, Edwd. WOODLE, Abra WOTTLE, Francis TOMS, Thomas POLLOCK. A True Copy exam'd with the Record Pr James CRAVEN Depy. Sury. *Regt*: [blank] day of Jan. 1701 By James CRAVEN.

[B:182] [First of deed is missing] Delivery of these Presents by Edwd. SCOTT of the same Precinct afsd. the Receipt whereof to full Content & Satisfaction the said Thomas CASEY doth by these presents acknowledge ... Thomas CASEY ... Sold ... unto Edwd. SCOTT ... a certain Tract of Land Contg. 840 acres ... FISHER Corner Tree ... up the Said FISHER Line to ... binding on SCOTT'S SMITHSONS Line ... up Thos. SMITHSON'S Line ... a Branch of Cypress Branch ... Richd. MADREN'S Line ... *Signed*: Thos. CASEY. *Wit*: Thos. TAYLOR, Jonathan HIBBS. *Ack*: Thomas CASEY to Edwd. SCOTT 14 Jany. 1734. *Regt*: 29 Sept. 1735.

[B:183] 10 July 1731 ... Thomas HARRIS of the Precinct of Pasquotank of the Province of North Carolina Planter, for the Consideration of the Love, Good Will and affection which I have & do bear towards my Loving Brother John HARRIS of the same Precinct afsd. Planter have given ... Tract of Land contg 100 Acres ... Moses CARTWRIGHT'S Corner ... the Weeding Branch ... the Great Swamp ... *Signed*: Thos. T H HARRIS his mark, Abigail H HARRIS her mark. *Wit*: L. ROW, Richard PRITCHARD. *Ack*: July Court 1732. *Regt*: 29 Sept. 1735.

William BRAY of the Precinct of Pasquotank in North Carolina Planter for and in Consideration of the Sum of 15 pounds ... paid by William BURGES of the Precinct & Province afsd. Tailor ... Sold ... Tract of Land ... on the N. E. Side of Pasquotank River at the head of RAYMANS Creek commonly called & known by the name of Beachy Neck & lately in possession of one John CONDON Contg. by Estimation 50 Acres ... [B:184] ... 28 Aug. in the Eleventh year of the Reign of our Sovn. Lord George ... 1725. *Signed*: Wm. WB BRAY. *Wit*: Stephen BURGES, George BRAY.

William BURGES of the Precinct of Pasquotank do assign over all my Right ... of the within Land to Henry BRAY ... 8th Nov. 1725. *Signed*: Wm. BURGES. *Wit*: Francis BRACKIT, Mary BRACKIT.

Henry BRAY of the Precinct of Pasquotank do assign ... all my Right ... of the within mentioned Land to Christopher BRAY ... 10 July 1725. *Signed*: Henry HB BRAY his mark. *Wit*: John BROWN?, Jos: SMITH.

13 Dec. 1734 In the 8th Year of the Reign of our Sovn. Lord George the Second ... between Relfe BARKER of the City of Norfolk & John ABBITT of North Carolina ... in Consideration of the valuable Sum of 180 pounds Current Money of North Carolina ... paid by John ABBITT ... sold ... parcel of
[B:185] Land ... Fork of Pasquotank River ... 216 Acres taken out of a Patent bearing date July 21. 1719 ... *Signed*: R. BARKER. *Wit*: Gab: BURNHAM, Benjn. BURNHAM. *Ack*: 2 Aug. 1735 W. SMITH C.J. *Regt*: 3 Sept. 1735.

North Carolina. 23 April and in the year of our Sovn. Lord George the Second ... Between Solomon EVERTON of Pasquotank & Gabl. BURNHAM of the same Precinct ... in Consideration of the valuable Sum of 50 pounds ... paid by the sd. Gabriel BURNHAM ... Sold ... Tract of Land containing 100 acres ... in the fork of Pasquotank ... Land of James FOREHAND and Gabl. BURNHAM ...
[B:186] ... 23 April 1735. *Signed*: Solomon S EVERTON his mark. *Wit*: Geo: ROW, Robt. EDNEY. *Ack*: 14 Oct. 1735 from Solomon EVERTON to Gabl. BURNHAM by the Oath of William WILLIAMS who was present at the time of the Sealing. *Regt*: 7 Nov. 1735.

No. Carolina, Samuel BUNDY Senr. of the County of Albemarle and Precinct of Pasquotank Planter for and in Consideration of the parental Love and affection

I have ... towards my well beloved Son Josiah BUNDY of the place afsd. Planter have given ... plantation Situate lying near the head of Little River upon the N. E. Side of the Said River it being part of the plantation that I the sd. Saml. BUNDY now live on ... 200 acres of Land from the upper Side of the sd. Land ... 2nd day of the 6th Month vulgarly [B:187] called August 1735. *Signed*: Samuel BUNDY. *Wit*: Joseph ROBINSON, Thomas NICHOLSON, John NIXON. *Ack*: from Samuel BUNDY Sr. to his Son Josiah BUNDY 14 Oct. 1735. *Regt*: 7 Nov.

North Carolina: We William MINSON and William UPTON for & in Consideration of the Sum of 20 pounds Sterling Current Money of Gt. Britain ... paid by Samuel ETHERIDGE ... Sold ... parcel of Land ... Contg. 180 acres ... known by the name of PRIMUES? Ridges? ... Thomas ELK'S Land ... William UPTON'S Land ... 4th Jany [blank] *Signed*: W MINSON, Wm. X UPTON his mark. *Wit*: John LURRY, Jno. PEGGS. *Ack*: Jany Court 1735 Wm. MINSON & Wm. UPTON to Saml. ETHERIDGE. *Regt*: 16 Dec. 1735.

Phillip DISON of Virginia Ship Carpenter ... appoint my loving friend Jno. RELFE Senr. my true & lawful attorney ... to sell and convey ... all such Land as I am now possessed of in North Carolina ... 25 Oct. 1735. *Signed*: Phillip DISON. *Wit*: Cornelius RELFE, Charles SAWYER. *Regt*: 26 Jany 1735.

[B:188] John PHILLIPS of the Town and County of Norfolk Mariner ... appointed ... Charles SAWYER of Pasquotank Precinct in the Province of North Carolina personally to appear in the Precinct Court afsd of Pasquotank and in due form of law in my Behalf acknowledge, a certain Deed Poll of Bargain & Sale bearing equal date with these presents made between John RELFE of Carolina afsd. & in me the said John PHILLIPS of the one part and Cornelius RELFE and John RELFE [blank] of the other part, for 418 Acres of Land in the Precinct afsd. ... 25 Oct. 1735. *Signed*: John PHILLIPS. *Wit*: John RELFE Senr, Alexr. MCPHERSON. *Regt*: 26 Jany. 1735.

North Carolina) Pasquotank) John RELFE Senr. Attorney of Philip DISON of Virginia ... for the valuable Consideration of 15 pounds ... paid by Charles SAWYER ... Sold ... Tract of Land lying on the N.W. Side of of the White Oak Branch Contg. 100 Acres, being part of a greater Tract surveyed by Thomas COOPER & now transferred to Charles SAWYER [B:189] 13 Jan. 1735. *Signed*: John RELFE Senr. *Wit*: Jno. CARON, Thos. TAYLOR. *Ack*: 13 Jan. 1735 by John RELFE Senr. Attorney of Philip DISON. *Regt*: 27 Jany 1735.

North Carolina. John RELFE Senr. and John PHILLIPS of the County of Pasquotank ... for the valuable Consideration of 50 pounds current money of North Carolina ... paid by Cornelius RELFE & John RELFE Junr. ... sold ... Tract of Land lying on the N.W. Side of SAWYERS Creek Contg. 418 acres viz 318 acres Surveyed by John JONES Senr. bearing date the 1 Apr. 1696 & 100 purchased by the sd. John JONES by Conveyance of Thomas JONES Junr. which said Lands was given by Will to Jno. JONES Son and Heir of the sd. John JONES Senr. and given by Will by John JONES Jr. to John RELFE Senr. & John PHILLIPS and now transferred to Cornelius and John RELFE Junr. ... [B:190] ... 25 Oct. 1735. *Signed*: John RELFE Senr., John PHILLIPS. Memo: It is agreed between the Parties ... that the within Consideration Money of 50 pounds is to be paid in good merchantable Barrel Pork after the rate of 45 Shillings Carolina Money pr Barrel to be delivered at N. W. Landing in Virginia on or before the 10th Feb. 1736/7. *Wit*: Charles SAWYER, Alexr. MCPHERSON. *Ack*: Jany Court 1735. *Regt*: 26 Jany. 1735.

14 Jan. 1735/6. between Lodwick GRAY of Pasquotank in North Carolina of the one part & John SIMPSON of Perquimons Precinct & Province of North Carolina of the other part ... in Consideration of the Sum of 4,500 pounds fresh Pork ... paid by John SIMPSON ... Sold ... parcel of Land ... on the S.W. Side of Weeding Branch, beginning, at John HARRIS'S Corner Tree ... Bee Tree Branch ... Contg 90 acres ... [B:191] ... *Signed*: Lodwick LG GRAY his mark. *Wit*: Jos. SMITH, William RELFE. *Ack*: 13 Jany. 1735 Lodwick GRAY to John SIMPSON. *Regt*: 26 Jany 1735.

North Carolina Joseph OVERMAN of the Precinct of Pasquotank and Province afsd. ... Whereas William Earl of CRAVEN Pallatine ... by Patent bearing date the 1 Feb. 1696 give and grant unto Lawrence KEATON a Tract of Land Contg. 204 acres lying in Pasquotank Precinct on the S.W. Side of Pasquotank River ... back of Henry PENDLETON ... which Land after the death of the said Lawrence KEATON was possessed by his Brother Zachariah KEATON & by the sd. Zachariah KEATON sold and conveyed to Ephriam OVERMAN, now know ye that I the said Joseph OVERMAN being Son and Heir to the said Ephraim OVERMAN have for and in Consideration of the Sum of 60 pounds of good and lawful money to me in hand paid ... sold ... unto Daniel CHANCEY of the Same place ... all that part of the above mentioned Tract of Land which lies on the S.E. Side of a certain Swamp ... Contg. 104 Acres ... 5 Jany 1735. *Signed*: Joseph I OVERMAN his mark. *Wit*: Willm. DAVIS, Jonathan REDING. *Ack*: 13 Jany 1735 Joseph OVERMAN to Daniel CHANCEY. *Regt*: 14 Feb. 1735.

[B:192] His Excelly. John Lord CARTERET, Palatine ... give and grant unto Ephriam OVERMAN of our Said County a Tract of Land contg. 40 Acres Beginning at a Gum Lawrence KEATON'S Line Tree ... KIRKS Corner Tree ... which Land formerly granted by patent to John PEGGS dated the 20 Nov. 1723 and by him elapsed for not Seating and planting thereon & is now become due to the sd. Ephraim OVERMAN ... 6 Aug. 1728 ... Witness our trusty and well beloved Sr. Richd. EVERARD Bart. Governor ... *Signed*: Richd EVERARD, Richd SAUNDERSON, E MOSELY, Thos POLLOCK, Wm REED, C GALE, J PALIN. Recorded in the Secy's Office Robt. FORSTER, Dept. Secy.

North Carolina: Joseph OVERMAN Son and Heir to the within mentioned Ephraim OVERMAN for the valuable Consideration of 10 pounds to me in hand paid ... Sold ... unto Danl. CHANCEY of the Province afsd. ... the within mentioned patent ...
[B:193] 5 Jany 1735. *Signed*: Joseph I OVERMAN his mark. *Wit*: Wm. DAVIS, Jonathan REDING. *Ack*: 13 Jany 1735. *Regt*: 14 Feby 1735.

North Carolina. Oliver ST. JOHN of the Precinct of Pasquotank Cooper for and in Consideration of the Sum of 100 pounds Current Money of North Carolina ... paid by William TURNER ... sold ... Tract of Land Contg 224 Acres ... on John DAVIS'S Line formerly Richard CRAGG'S ... the Cypress Swamp ... by Patent granted for the same in John SYMONS Junr.

being a Relapse in his name & assigned by the sd. John SYMONS to Edward TURNER of the Precinct afsd & assigned over by the sd. Edwd. TURNER to the sd. Nathaniel EVERITT ... and assigned over to Wm. AIKMAN, to Oliver ST. JOHN ...
[B:194] ... 28 Jan. 1734. *Signed*: Oliver ST. JOHN. *Wit*: Robt. FORSTER, Wm MAXWELL. *Ack*: 28 Jan. 1734 Oliver ST. JOHN to Willm. TURNER. *Regt*: 16 Mar. 1735

North Carolina: 21 Jany in the 9th year of the Reign of our Sovn. Lord George the Second ... 1735 Between I Major Griffith JONES of the Precinct of Pasquotank & Province of North Carolina of the one part ... in Consideration of the Sum of 5 pounds Current money of North Carolina ... paid by William GREGORY ... Sold ... Parcel of Land Contg. 100 acres ... on the N.E. Side of Pasquotank River and commonly called or known by the name of COOPER'S Land ... Ivey Point Landing on George CARON'S Line ... *Signed*: Griffith GJ JONES Pr Signum. *Wit*: John CONNYER, Jacob I GREGORY, Pr Signum.

[B:195] 24 Jan. in the ninth year of the Reign of our Sovereign George the Second ... 1735 Between Major Griffith JONES of the Precinct of Pasquotank & Province of North Carolina of the one part and William GREGORY of the Precinct & Province afsd Planter of the other part ... in Consideration of the Sum of 100 pounds Currt money of North Carolina ... paid ... Sold ... unto the Said William GREGORY in his actual possession now being by virtue of an Indenture ... Bearing date the day before the day of the date of these presents ... Parcel of Land contg. 100 acres ... on the N.E. Side of Pasquotank River and commonly called or known by the name of COOPER'S Land ... Ivey Point bounding on George CARON'S Line ... *Signed*: Griffith G.J. JONES Pr Signum. *Wit*: John CONNYER, Jacob GREGORY, Pr Signum. *Ack*: 13 April 1736 from Major Griffith JONES to Wm. GREGORY proved by the oaths of John CONNYERS & Jacob GREGORY. *Regt*: 17 April 1736.

[B:196] North Carolina. Daniel CHANCEY of the Precinct of Pasquotank and Province afsd. ... Whereas William Earl of CRAVEN Palatine ... by Patent bearing date the 1 Feb. 1696 give and grant unto Lawrence KEATON a Tract of Land Contg. 204 acres lying in Pasquotank Precinct on the S.W. Side

of Pasquotank River ... back of Henry PENDLETON'S ... which Land after the Death of the said Lawrence KEATON was possessed by his Brother Zachariah KEATON and by the sd. Zacha. KEATON sold and conveyed to Ephriam OVERMAN & after the death of the Said Ephraim OVERMAN possessed by his Son Joseph OVERMAN and by the said Joseph OVERMAN Sold and conveyed to Daniel CHANCEY ... and also John Lord CARTERET Palatine ... did by patent bearing date the 6 Aug. 1728 give & grant unto Ephraim OVERMAN a Tract of Land contg 40 acres ... on the S.W. Side of Pasquotank River ... Lawrence KEATON'S line ... KIRK's Corner Tree ... which Land was formerly granted to John PEGGS by Patent bearing date the 20 Nov. 1723 ... and became due to the Said Ephraim OVERMAN ... 6 Aug. 1728 and after the death of the Said Ephraim OVERMAN possessed by his Son Joseph OVERMAN and by the Said Joseph OVERMAN Sold and conveyed to Danl. CHANCEY ... in Consideration of 80 pounds paid ... sold ... unto Jonathan REDING of the Same place ... all that part of the above mentioned Land Containing 104 Acres ... And also all the abovementioned Land contained in the Said Ephraim OVERMAN'S patent ...
[B:197] ... 4 Feby 1735/6. *Signed*: Danl. CHANCEY. *Wit*: Wm. DAVIS, John JONES, John PIKE. *Ack*: 13 Jany 1736 Danl. CHANCEY to Jona. REDING. *Regt*: 17 April 1736.

16 Jany 1735 Job NICHOLS of the Precinct of Pasquotank in the Province of North Carolina Planter for and in Consideration of the Love, Good will & affection that I have towards my well beloved Brother William NICHOLS of the same precinct afsd. planter ... give ... the Manor plantation whereon he now lives and the Woodland Ground belonging to it. *Signed*: Job J NICHOLS his mark. *Wit*: George ROW, Henry H NICHOLS his mark. *Ack*: April Court 1736.

13 April 1736. David PRITCHARD in the Precinct of Pasquotank in the Province of North Carolina Planter for and in Consideration of the Value of an Exchange ... by Jeremiah MURDEN of the same Precinct afsd ...
[B:198] ... Sell ... 2 acres of Land by a patent and plot that was surveyed by William MINSON for David PRITCHARD and 96 acres of Land that is excepted in the Said Patent ... Pasquotank River ... *Signed*: David PRITCHARD, Jeremiah MURDEN. *Wit*:

Geo. ROW, Thos. SAWYER. *Ack*: 13 April 1736 David PRITCHARD to Jeremiah MURDEN. *Regt*: 22 May 1736.

[B:199] William DAVIS of North Carolina of the Precinct of Pasquotank being Son & Heir to Samuel DAVIS decd. of the same place ... in Consideration of the Sum of 200 pounds paid ... have assigned over unto William CHANCEY of the same place ... all my Right ... the within patent ... 13 April 1736. *Signed*: William DAVIS. *Wit*: Jonathan REDING, Charles OVERMAN. *Ack*: 13 April 1736 William DAVIS to William CHANCEY. *Regt*: 24 May 1736.

North Carolina. 3 April in the 9th year of our Lord George the Second ... between John WALLIS of Pasquotank & John JONES of the same Precinct ... in Consideration of the valuable Sum of 110 pounds paid ... Sold ... a certain Tract of Land Contg. by Patent 127 Acres except one half acre of the said Land to the Heirs of Col. Thos. SWANN decd ... on the S. E. Side of JOY'S Creek ... *Signed*: John J.W. WALLIS his mark. *Wit*: Gabl. BURNHAM, John MACKBRIDE. *Ack*: 13 April 1736 from John WALLIS to John JONES. *Regt*: 26 May 1736.

[B:200] North Carolina Zachariah KEATON the Elder, of Pasquotank Precinct in Albemarle County & Province afsd. Planter ... in Consideration of the Sum of 26 pounds ... paid unto the public Treasury of the Precinct afsd. for the clearing of a Mortgage of the Land whereon I now live by my Son Zacha. KEATON of the same place Planter and for the paying and discharging of the Charges & Taxes wherewith the sd Land & plantation is incumbered as also for the natural Love and affection that I have ... unto my said Son Zachariah ... give ... unto him the Sd. Zachariah KEATON the younger all that part or parcel of my Land and plantation hereafter mentioned (that is to say) the Easternmost end of the Land and the plantation already cleared ... Anne ELLIS'S Line to John LOMBROSIER'S Line (which sd. Branch or Branches beforementioned is wellknown to my Children and near neighbors ... Excepting and reserving to myself the use occupation & manuring? of one full half part of all the said Land, cleared or uncleared, for the planting, tilling? and Pasture Land for and during the time of my own natural Life & the natural Life of my wife Sarah KEATON ...

13th April 1736. *Signed*: Zacha. X KEATON his mark. *Wit*: Josu SMITH, John I BASNET his mark, Solomon POOL. *Ack*: April 13th 1736 Zacha KEATON Snr to Zacha KEATON Jr. *Regt*: May 26th 1736.

[B:201] John SOLLEY of the Precinct of Pasquotank, of the County of Albemarle and the Province of North Carolina for and in Consideration of the Sum of 30 pounds of fresh Pork or current Money ... paid by John THACKARY of the same Precinct County and Province abovesaid ... assign ... all my right ... in the Deed within mentioned ... 15 March 1734/5. *Signed*: John SOLLEY. *Wit*: Jno. RELFE Senr., Wm. BRYAN. *Ack*: John SOLLEY to John THACKARY April Court 1736. *Regt*: 14 July 1736.

John SYMONS do for myself and Heirs transfer and make over all my Right ... of the within mentioned Land according to the Bounds mentioned & contained in this Patent unto William SYMONS ... 17 July 1736. *Signed*: John SYMONS. *Wit*: Jer. SYMONS, Zacha. FIELD, Robert DAVIS. *Ack*: July Court 1736 John SYMONS to William SYMONS. *Regt*: 19 July 1736.

[B:202] North Carolina. William TOMLIN of the County of Albemarle & Precinct of Perquimans Planter ... in Consideration of one Negro Man and the Sum of 20 pounds in good merchantable Pork and the Sum of Ten pounds in Cash ... by Thomas WINSLOW of the Precinct afsd. ... Sold ... Thomas WINSLOW planter ... 200 Acres ... upon the N. E. Side of Little River ... the Fork Swamp ... George LOW'S Corner Tree ... 3 July 1736. *Signed*: William W TOMLINS his mark. *Wit*: Thomas NICHOLSON, Elisabeth LOW, Eliza. E WELCH her mark. *Ack*: July Court 1736 Willm. TOMLINS to Thomas WINSLOW. *Regt*: 19 July 1736.

[B:203] North Carolina Joseph HASKET of the Precinct of Pasquotank and Province afsd. Shipwright for and in Consideration of the Sum of 150 pounds Curt Money of the afsd. Province to me in hand paid ... by John JONES of the same Precinct and Province Planter ... Sold ... Tract of Land that I bought of John SCOTT, and by the said SCOTT bought of Edmd. GALE Esqr. as by SCOTT'S Deed to me bearing date the 21st day of April 1725 ... on the S. W. Side of

Pasquotank River and bounded with the Land of Thos. WILLIAMS decd. on the North Side and Joseph JORDAN'S Junr on the South Side ... 70 Acres ... 14 Aug. 1736. *Signed*: Jos: HASKET. *Wit*: W. REED, Eliza. REED. *Ack*: Jany Court 1736 Pr James CRAVEN Clk Ct. *Regt*: 9 April 1737. Pr J PALIN Reg.

North Carolina. Pasquotank Precinct . John JONES for a good and valuable Consideration to me in hand paid, more especially for the Exchange of other Land Pr assignment bearing same date herewith ... assign ... the within mentioned Deed ... unto Jonathan REDING ... 12 Jany 1736. *Signed*: John JONES. *Wit*: Wm DAVIS, Wm JOHN'S?, John CONNYER. *Ack*: Jany Court 1736 John JONES to Jonathan REDING. *Regt*: 9 April 1737.

[B:204] William AIKMAN of Pasquotank Precinct in the Province of North Carolina Merchant for ... the valuable Consideration of 150 pounds Current Money ... paid by John WADE Junr of the Precinct & Province afsd. Planter ... Sold ... all my Right ... parcel of Land ... 330 Acres ... the Land of William POWERS? ... 1 Sept. 1733. *Signed*: [blank] *Wit*: Robt. R ARMOUR, John DAVIS. *Regt*: 19 April 1737.

North Carolina: Griffith JONES Senr of the Precinct of Pasquotank in the County of Albemarle ... in Consideration of 100 pounds Stg. money of Great Britain paid ... by my Son Griffith JONES Junr of the afsd. Precinct ... Sold ... 220 Acres of Land ... the bounded Tree between the Said Robert TEMPLE & Christopher WILLIAMS ... (Excepting the [blank] as far as the Bridge & within the above Bounds) ... [B:205] 20 Dec. 1735. *Signed*: Griffith JONES. *Wit*: Barnard BANGER, Willaby PRICE, Elisa D DUNN her mark. *Ack*: April Court 1737 Griffith JONES Senr. to Griffith JONES Junr. Pr Willm REED Depy Clk. Co. *Regt*: 27 April 1737.

North Carolina) Pasquotank) John RELFE & Thomas SAWYER of the Precinct of Pasquotank & the Province of North Carolina have for ... the valuable Consideration of 40 pounds ... paid down by Caleb KOEN of the Same Precinct & Province afsd. ... I do acknowledge ... Tract of Land lying on the N. E. Side of Pasquotank River which binding on Edwd. WILLIAMS'S Line & Eastward on Richd. SAWYER'S Line

Containing 100 Acres ... to Willm. WILLIAMS Line ... Joseph MORGAN'S Line ... taken out of a Patent Contg 850 acres bearing date 1 April 1723 ...
[B:206] 12 April 1737 and in the ninth year of the Reign of our Sovereign Lord George the Second ... *Signed*: John RELFE Junr., Tho: SAWYER. *Wit*: Cornelius RELFE, Chas: SAWYER. *Ack*: April Court 1737 Willm. REED, Depy Clk Ct. *Regt*: 24 April 1737.

William CREECH of North Carolina Province and in the Precinct of Pasquotank Gentn. ... Sold ... unto Edwd. WILLIAMS of the Precinct & Province afsd. ... Tract of Land commonly called ... MAYNARD'S Island lying on the North River ... 100 acres ... 5 Feby 1735/6. *Signed*: William W CREECH his mark. *Wit*: George GRASON, Phileigh P PAINE her mark, Lodwick WILLIAMS. *Ack*: 12 April 1737. *Regt*: 23 May 1737.

[B:207] North Carolina) Pasquotank Precinct) 23 March in the Eleventh year of the Reign of our Sovereign Lord George the Second ... 1737 Between Joshua MARKHAM of the one part and Benjamin SYMONS all of the Precinct of Pasquotank and Province of North Carolina afsd. of the other part ... in Consideration of the Sum of 5 pounds Current Money of North Carolina ... Sold ... parcel of Land contg. 184 Acres ... E. Side of Little River ... including the whole Patent ... granted by the Honble Philip LUDWELL to William JACKSON bearing date 1693/4 ... *Signed*: Joshua MARKHAM. *Wit*: Thomas HUNTER, Saml. SWANN. *Ack*: 12 April 1737. *Regt*: 23 May 1737.

[B:208] 26 March 1737 and in the Eleventh year of the Reign of our Sovn Lord George the Second ... Between Joshua MARKHAM of the Precinct of Pasquotank and County of Albemarle in the province of North Carolina of the one party and Benjamin SYMONS of the Precinct & County and Province abovesd. of the other party ... in Consideration of the Sum of 222 pounds Current Money of North Carolina ... Sold ... Tract of Land contg. 184 Acres ... E. Side of Little River
[B:209] ...
[B:210] ... 24 March 1737 *Signed*: Joshua MARKHAM. *Wit*: Thomas HUNTER, Saml. SWANN. *Ack*: April Court 1737 Joshua MARKHAM to Benjamin SYMONS. *Regt*: 24 May 1737.

North Carolina) Pasquotank Precinct) 23 March 1737 and in the Eleventh year of the Reign of our Sovn Lord George the Second ... Between Joshua MARKHAM of the one part and Benjamin SYMONS all of the Precinct of Pasquotank & Province of North Carolina afsd. of the other part ... in Consideration of the Sum of 5 pounds Current Money of North Carolina ... Sold ... parcel of Land contg. 311 Acres ... the whole patent on the E. Side of Little River which patent was granted by the Honble. George BURRINGTON Esqr. Governor to John ARMOUR bearing date the 30 March ... *Signed*: Joshua MARKHAM. *Wit*: Thos. HUNTER, Saml. SWANN. *Ack*: April Court 1737 Joshua MARKHAM to Benjamin SYMONS. *Regt*: 24 May 1737.

[B:211] 26 March 1737 and in the 11th year of the Reign of our Sovn Lord George the Second ... between Joshua MARKHAM in the Precinct of Pasquotank & the County of Albemarle and in the province of North Carolina of the one part ... in Consideration of the Sum of 222 pounds good Current lawful Money of North Carolina ... paid by the said Benjamin SYMONS ... Sold ... parcel of Land contg. 311 Acres ... commonly called or Known by the name of John ARMOUR ... on the E. Side of Little River
[B:212] ...
[B:213] ... 24 March 1737 *Signed*: Joshua MARKHAM. *Wit*: Thos. HUNTER, Saml. SWANN. *Ack*: April Court 1737 Joshua MARKHAM to Benjamin SYMONS. *Regt*: 24 May 1737.

North Carolina) Pasquotank Precinct) John GODFREY of Pasquotank Precinct in the County of Albemarle & Province of North Carolina for and in Consideration of 14 pounds proclamation ... paid by Edward JAMES of the Precinct and Province afsd. ... Sold ... parcel of land lying on the N. E. Side of Pasquotank River ... on the Beaver Dam ... on the said Edward JAMES'S and William BECKETT'S Land ... Joseph GODFREY'S Land ... between John GODFREY'S Land & the said Land .... [blank] Acres ...
[B:214] 12 April 1737. *Signed*: John IG GODFREY. *Wit*: Wm. TURNER, John CONNYERS. *Ack*: April Court 1737. *Regt*: 9 June 1737.

North Carolina John WINN of Pasquotank in North Carolina ... in Consideration of the Sum of 60 pounds Sterling money of Gt. Britain paid ... by

Abel ROSS ... of the above sd. Precinct ... sold ... parcel of Land ... on the North Side of Arenuse Creek ... on Capt. ROSS'S line running on Thomas GRANDES Line so to James WILLIAMS Line binding upon Edwd. WILLIAM'S Corner Tree so binding upon Edward UPTON'S and so to John WINN'S, a Beach marked for Thomas GRAY ... 196 acres taken out of a Patent contg. 296 acres ... excepting 100 Acres granted to Thomas GRAY ... 8 Oct. 1734. *Signed*: John J WINN his mark. *Wit*: John TRUEBLOOD, Thos. SAWYER. *Ack*: 8 Oct. 1734 John WINN to Abel ROSS. *Regt*: 9 June 1737.

[B:215] John SMITH of the Precinct of Hide in the County of Bath and Province of North Carolina for and in Consideration of the Sum of 25 pounds ... paid by Jonathan HIBBS of the Precinct of Pasquotank and Province afsd. ... Sold ... Tract of Land ... S. W. Side of Pasquotank River ... William SAWYER'S Line ... Contg. 60 acres ... granted by two Deeds of Sale one from William RELFE and one from Danl. RHODES both bearing date 1734 ... 2 March 1737. *Signed*: John SMITH. *Wit*: Hezechh. CARTWRIGHT, William SAWYER. *Ack*: April Court 1737. *Regt*: 9 June 1737.

Paul PALMER of the Colony of North Carolina & County of Albemarle & Prect. of Perquimans for and in Consideration of the Sum of 50 pounds Current Money of the afsd. Province ... paid by Henry BRAY of the afsd Province Husbandman ... Sold ...
[B:216] ... all that Tract of Land on the North Side of Pasquotank River ... lying between the Lands of John CARTERET William BURGES John TORKSEY John CARON & William GRIFFIN ... except 120 acres adjoining to Willm. GRIFFIN & John CARTWRIGHT 100 belonging to Joseph SMITH & 20 acres to William GRIFFIN ... 11 April 1737. *Signed*: Paul PALMER. *Wit*: Thomas BURGES, Philip TORKSEY, Griffith JONES. *Ack*: April Court 1737. *Regt*: 5 July following.

North Carolina. Daniel ROADS of the Precinct of Pasquotank and Province afsd. ... in Consideration of the Sum of 100 pounds Currt Money ... paid by David BOWLS of the Prect. of Pasquotank & Province afsd. ... Sold ... Tract of Land lying ... on the S.W. Side of Pasquotank River contg. 100 Acres ... being part of a Tract of Land
[B:217] Granted by Patent unto the Said Danl. ROADS

by John ARCHDALE Esqr. bearing date 1677 ... Jonathan HIBBS Line Tree ... William SAWYERS Line ... CARTWRIGHTS Creek ... Pasquotank River ... 23 Feby 1736/7. *Signed*: Danl. D ROADS his mark. *Wit*: Jonathan HIBBS, William SAWYER. *Ack*: April Court 1737. *Regt*: 6 July following.

11 Dec. 1736 & in the ninth year of the Reign of our Sovn Lord George ... Between Jeremiah MURDEN of the County of Albemarle in the Province of North Carolina of the one part and Jeremiah MURDEN his Son of the Same County & Province afsd. of the other party ... in Consideration of the natural Love and affection which I have and bear unto my Son ... give ... Tract of Land ... N. E. Side of Pasquotank River & joining on the Mouth of SAWYER'S Creek commonly known or called by the name of William JENNINGS Plantation Contg. ... 182 Acres ...
[B:218] ... *Signed*: Jeremiah MURDEN. *Wit*: Joseph SPENCE, Robert SPENCE. *Ack*: July Court 1737 Jeremh. MURDEN Senr to Jeremh. MURDEN Junr. *Regt*: July the [blank] 1737.

29th day of January & in the 8th year of the Reign of our Sovn Lord George the Second ... Between John KITE together with his wife Margaret KITE both living in the Precinct of Pasquotank in No. Carolina & Charles KITE of the other party in the Precinct abovesd. ... in Consideration of the Love and affection that he hath for his Son Charles KITE ... give ... 90 acres of Land ... half the Land and plantation whereon I now dwell ...
[B:219] ... 29 Jany 1734/5. *Signed*: John J KITE his mark. *Wit*: Barnard BANGER, Thos. L LANES his mark. *Ack*: July Court 1737. *Regt*: 13 Oct. 1737.

North Carolina. Saml. RENSHER of Pasquotank Precinct and in Albemarle County Carpenter ... in Consideration of the Love, Good will and affection which I have & do bear towards my loving Brother in law James SMITH and my loving Sister Frances SMITH his wife both of the Parish Province and County afsd. ... give ... one Tract of Land being part of the Tract where I now live and the part of the Tract that they now live on called the hollow Poplar ... 50 acres ... 14 Oct. 1724. *Signed*: Samuel RENCH[ink blot] *Wit*: Robert EDNEY, Ann A EDNEY her mark. I assign over all my Right ... of this within mentioned Deed to my Son Saml. SMITH ... 11 Mar. 1737. *Signed*: James JS SMITH his mark. *Wit*: Robert EDNEY.

North Carolina) Pasquotank) William MACKDANIEL of the Precinct of Pasquotank & Province of North Carolina Planter ... for the valuable Consideration of 100 pounds paid ... by James MACKDANIEL ... Tract of Land lying on the N. E. Side of Pasquotank River Contg. 40 acres ... a dividing Line ... between the afsd. James MACKDANIEL & his Brother Michael MACDANIEL ...
[B:220] ... Sold ... 11 July 1737. *Signed*: William MACDANIEL. *Wit*: Michael X MACKDANIEL his mark, Robt. MORGAN. *Ack*: July Court 1737. *Regt*: 13 Oct. 1737.

[B:221] North Carolina Thomas PENDLETON Junr and Joseph PENDLETON of Pasquotank Precinct & County of Albemarle & Province afsd. Planters ... in Consideration of the Sum or quantity of 4 Barrels of good and merchantable Pork ... paid by Charles WEST of the Precinct, County and Province afsd. ... Sold ... Plantation Contg. 120 Acres which was granted to our Father Thomas PENDLETON decd. by Patent bearing date the 2 Nov. 1727 and is registered in the Register Book of Writing for Pasquotank Precinct in Fo. 33 ... Land hath formerly been called or known by the name of ROLLISONS ... 4 March 1736/7. *Signed*: the mark of Thos. P PENDLETON, Jos. X PENDLETON his mark. *Wit*: Thomas STAMS?, Jno PALIN.

[B:222] 25 March 1736/7 ... Thomas HARRIS of the Precinct of Pasquotank in the Province of No. Carolina Planter for and in Consideration of the Sum of 40 pounds Current Money of North Carolina paid ... by John SWINDALL of the same Precinct ... Sold ... parcel of Land Contg. 50 acres ... in the Fork of Nobs Crook Creek ... Job NICHOLS'S Line to TRICKLONS? Branch ... the School lands commonly known by the name of Turkey Ridge ... *Signed*: Thos. TH HARRIS his mark. *Wit*: Edward SCOTT, Elihu ALBERTSON.

[B:223] Alexander SPENCE of the Precinct of Pasquotank and County of Albemarle in the Province of North Carolina planter ... & Ann my Wife for and in Consideration of the Sum of 100 pounds of this

Country Specie to us in hand paid for a part of a Tract of Land lying on the N. E. Side of Pasquotank given and granted by the ... Proprietors unto Thomas COOPER of the place afsd. & by him sold unto the Widow Margt MCBRIDE and by her given unto John SPENCE and since transferred by will to Alexander SPENCE being the half of John SPENCES Manor plantation ... David SPENCES his Corner Tree ... contg. 140 acres ... by Sarah TRUEBLOOD of the Province and Precinct afsd. ... sold ... 140 acres as afsd. ...
[B:224] ... [blank] 1737 & in the Ninth year of the Reign of our Sovn. Lord George the Second ...
Signed: Alexander SPENCE, Ann A SPENCE her mark.
Wit: Jeremh. SYMONS, William W TERRILL his mark.
Ack: July Court 1737 by Alexr. SPENCE & Ann SPENCE.
Regt: October 1737.

North Carolina William BURGES of the Prect. of Pasquotank & County of Albemarle & Province of No. Carolina Tailor of the one part & Thomas TORKSEY of the Prect & Province afsd. Planter ... in Consideration of 50 pounds in Pork at the accustomed price ... Sold ... parcel of Land ... on the S. W. Side of RAYMONS Creek ... & across the Land as it is divided by the afsd. William BURGES & Thos. TORKSEY to the upper Line ... 300 Acres ...
[B:225] ... given by ... the Proprietors to me as will appear upon Record bearing date the 2d day of August 1730 ... 16 Dec. in the Reign of our Sovn. Lord George the 2d. ... 1734. P.S. The sd. William BURGES doth except one half acre of Land lying at the Landing where the House now Standith. *Signed*: Wm. BURGES. *Wit*: Thos. CORMAN, George BRAY. *Ack*: July Court 1737. *Regt*: 13 Oct. 1737.

Sir John THOMPSON Knt. Lord Mayor of the City of London in pursuance of an act of Parliament made and passed in the fifth year of the Reign of our Sovn Lord George (King) the Second entitled an act for the more easy Recovery of Debts in his Majesty's plantations & Colonies in America do hereby certify that on the day of the date hereof personally came and appeared before me Gamaliel GARDNER apprentice to Anne HINDES of Great St. Helens London Packer & Archibald WYNNE of Great St. Helens London Gentleman, being persons well known and worthy of good Credit & by solemn Oath which they then

Severally took before me upon the holy Evangelists of almighty God did Solemnly and Sincerely declare, testify & depose to be true the Several Matters and Things mentioned & contained in the original affidavitt hereto annexed. In Faith and Testimony whereof I the Said Lord Mayor have caused the Seal of the Office of Mayoralty of the Said City of London to be hereunto put and affixed and the Certificate & Letter of attorney, mentioned & referred to in & by the said affidavits to be hereunto also annexed. Dated in London the 11 July 1737. By the Court. Pasquotank. The aforementioned Instrument of Writing was duly registered in the Register Book for the Precinct afsd. the 13 Dec. 1737. *Wit*: James CRAVEN Regr.

[B:226] Archibald WYNNE of Great St. Helens London Gentleman maketh Oath that he ... did on the 27 May last past See George LOW Cityson & Packer of London mentioned in the letter of attorney hereunto annexed for and as his act and Deed to the uses therein mentioned & that the name Archibald WYNNE thereunto Subscribed as a Witness to the due Execution of the said Letter of attorney is of this Deponents own proper Hand Writing *Signed*: Archibald WYNNE. Sworn the 11 July 1737 Before me Jno. THOMPSON Mayor. *Regt*: 23 Dec. 1737.

Gamaliel GARDNER, apprentice to Ann HINDS, widow of Great St. Helens London Packer, maketh Oath that he the Deponent did on the 23 May last past (at the Request of Mr. George LOW) in the Instruments hereunto annexed named, Search the Marrige Register Book of the Parish of St. Andrews by the Wondrake? in the City of London for an Entry of the Marriage of Nevil LOW & Anne WENSLEY (in which) this Deponent did then find an Entry had been made that the said Nevil LOW & Anne WENSLEY was married by License in the Said Parish Church on the 22 Aug. 1713 And this Deponent further maketh Oath, that he desired? a Certificate of the said Marriage, the same was granted this Deponent, and signed by William GRANGER, Rector of the said Parish & is hereunto annexed, which Said Certificate the Deponent carefully examined & compared with the said Register Book and found the same to be and is a true Copy of the Substance of the sd. Entry. *Signed*: Gamaliel GARDNER. Sworn the 11 July 1737, Before me

Jno. THOMPSON, Mayor. *Regt*: 24 Dec. 1737.

These are to satify? whom it may concern, that Nevil LOW & Anne WENSLEY were married by License in the Parish Church of St. Andrew by the Wardrobe? in the City of London, the 22 Aug. 1713. As Witness my hand this 23 May 1737. *Signed*: William GRANGER, Rector of the said Parish. *Regt*: 24 Dec. 1737.

[B:227] Whereas John ARCHDALE Esqr. formerly Governor of South & North Carolina did in and by his Deed poll bearing date on or about the 12 July 1695 for the Considerations therein mentioned give and grant unto Emanuel LOW then Citizen of London and Anne his wife (who was the daughter of the Said John ARCHDALE / all that his plantation a Tract of Land lying at the S. W. Side of Pasquotank River at the Mouth of Newbegun Creek and then in the possession of William COLLINS Contg. ... 1000 Acres ... for during their joint natural Lives and the Life of the longest Liver of them and after their decease to their Son Nevil LOW and his Heirs and assigns forever ... and whereas ... John ARCHDALE of Wickham in the County of Bucks in Great Britain Esqr. did by his Deed poll bearing date on or about the 11 July 1712 for the Considerations therein mentioned give ... unto his Grandson Nevil LOW (in his actual possession then being) all that ... Tract of Land lying and being on the North Side of Newbegun Creek in Pasquotank River in the Province of North Carolina in America butting & bounding on the Land then belonging to Jo: JORDAN ... & ... also ... gave ... the Moiety or halfpart of the Island or Tract of Land commonly called or known by the name of Colleton Island or Little Roanoke & upon the decease of the said Nevil LOW the abovementioned John ARCHDALE gave the above recited premises unto his Daughter Anne LOW mother to the said Nevil LOW & Wife to the said Emanl. LOW then of No. Carolina, Merchant and the Heirs of her Body forever And he likewise thereby gave the other moiety or halfpart of the said Island of Colleton or Little Roanoke to his said Son in law Emanl. LOW & Anne his Wife and the longer Liver of them and after their decease to the Heirs of the Body of Anne LOW and their Heirs forever ... and whereas the said Emanl. LOW & Anne his wife & Nevil their Son are all long since dead leaving George LOW of London Packer the Eldest and

only Son of the said Nevil LOW & the Grandson of the sd. Emanl. LOW & Anne LOW which said George LOW as the Heir at Law of the said Nevil LOW, Emanl. LOW & Ann LOW & as such is entitled to all the above mentioned Premises. Now know all Men By these presents that I the said George LOW Citizen & Packer of London have made constituted & appointed ... Henry WENSLEY of London Gentleman my true & lawful attorney ... to enter into all & every or any part of the herein beforementioned premises ... and in my name ... to expell renounce & put out the Tenants & Occupiers of the Same ... but in case all or any of the Tenants ...
[B:228] ... shall refuse to allow? peaceable and quiet possession ... my said Atty ... to commence, begin Sue implead & prosecute any action ... in any Court ... concerning the Recovery of the premises herein before mentioned ... I hereby further authorize ... my said Atty on recovering ... to dispose of & lett the same by Lease in my name for any term of years not exceeding Seven years receiving an annual valuable Consideration for the Same ... or in case he can find a convenient & advantageous purchaser for the same premises ... to sell & dispose of the Same ... 27 May 1737 & in the Tenth year of the Reign of our George the Second King of Great Britain. *Signed*: George LOW. *Wit*: Archibald WYNNE, R. FORSTER. *Regt*: 13 Nov. 1737.

[B:229] North Carolina. John KIGHT of the Prect of Pasquotank & Province afsd. for the valuable Consideration of 10 pounds ... paid ... William WILLIAMS ... sold ... 90 Acres of Land being part of a greater Tract contg 716 acres of Land by Patent bearing date the 27 March 1714 granted to HOOKS and the Said 90 acres of land lying on the South Side of the said John HOOKS plantation ... 7 Jany 1737/8. *Signed*: John ((KIGHT his mark. *Wit*: Gabl. BURNHAM, Joshua GAMBLING, Obadiah O SEXTON his mark. *Proved*: Jany Court 1737 by the Oaths of Joshua GAMBLING & Obadiah SEXTON. *Regt*: 16 Jany 1737.

North Carolina. 7 May 1737 & in the eleventh year of the Reign of our Sovn Lord George the Second ... Between Griffith JONES of the Prect of Pasquotank & Province afsd. of the one part & Thomas HUNTER of the Prect & Province afsd. Merchant ... Griffith JONES & Elisabeth his wife for and in Consideration

of the Sum of 90 pounds Stg. of Gt Britain ... sold ... Tract of Land being part of a Tract of Land contained in a Patent granted to Wm. COLLINS [B:230] by the right Honble Philip LUDWELL Esqr. ... 1694 beginning at a Bridge which is betwixt Major Griffith JONES his House and the Store Landing ... to the Fork Landing Contg ... 100 acres ... on the N. E. Side of Pasquotank River in the fork of Areneuse Creek ... contg in the said patent & a Deed from Robert TEMPLE to Griffith JONES being dated the 21 April 1713 ... *Signed*: Griffith G JONES his mark, Eliza. G JONES her mark. *Wit*: John LURRY, John BROOKS.
[B:231] *Ack*: at the Court House in Broomfield on Tuesday [blank] 1737. *Regt*: 22 March 1737.

North Carolina Joseph KEATON of the Prect of Pasquotank and Province of North Carolina ... whereas William Earl of CRAVEN Palatine and the rest of the true & absolute Lords Proprietors of Carolina By their Deed of Grant bearing date the 1 May 1668 did give and grant unto Stephen SCOTT a Tract of Land contg 274 acres lying in the Prect afsd whose Bounds are inserted in the patent bearing date the 25 Feby 1696 which patent and Tract of Land hath since been conveyed and assigned over from Edwd SCOTT , Heir apparent to Stephen SCOTT to Henry KEATON also decd as in & by their assigns to the back side of the patent bearing date the 19 Oct. 1714 ... Now Know ye that I the said Joseph KEATON Son and Heir apparent of Henry KEATON for ... the valuable Consideration of 200 pounds lawful Money of the province together with two small parcels of Lands one upon Newbegun Creek and the other joining on Zachariah KEATON ... acknowledged in open Court by Stephen SCOTT & Ruth his wife of the precinct of Pasquotank in the province afsd ... sold ... a plantation contg 274 acres of Land lying in the precinct afsd on Newbegun Creek granted by patent [B:232] ... 10 Jan 1737/8. Signed: Jos. KEATON. Wit: James GEORGE, Zacha KEATON. Ack: Regt: May 24 1738.

Alexander CROOKSHANKS of Pasquotank Precinct in North Carolina Tailor for ... the valuable Consideration of 8 pounds Sterling ... paid by Richard STAMP Gentlemen of the Precinct & Province afsd. ... Sold ... a parcel of Land contg about 60 acres lying and being on the S. W. Side of Flatty Creek ... the plantation on WATS [blank] bounds & the line of the Land wheron Thomas COLLINS did live ... part of a greater Tract by patent granted to John BELMAN & by the Said BELMAN Sold to Willis WALLIS ... 9 Oct. 1733. *Signed*: Alexander CROOKSHANKS. *Wit*: Wm. AIKMAN, Jno PEGGS. *Ack*: Oct. Court 1733. *Regt*: 25 Jany [blank]

[B:233] Richard STAMP of the Precinct of Pasquotank & Province of No. Carolina for the valuable Consideration of 50 pounds lawful Money of this Province afsd. do ... assign over all my Right ... of the within mentioned Deed to the Said Benjn. MASSEGY ... 5 Oct. 1737. *Signed*: Richd. STAMP. *Wit*: Francis MACKEELS X mark. *Ack*: Jany Court 1738. *Regt*: 24 May 1738.

Zachariah KEATON Sarah my wife ... in Pasquotank Precinct in Albemarle County & Province afsd for & in consideration of 97 acres of Land to us well and sufficiently conveyed ... by Stephen SCOTT Hannah his wife ... paid ... sold ... 50 acres of Land Butted & Bounded as in & by a certain Deed or Instrument of writing from Thomas MACKIE & Margery his wife to Ephraim OVERMAN bearing date the 16th day of August 1709? ... being part of the sd Tract of Land whereon the Said Thomas MACKIE dwelt & by him sold & made over to Ephraim OVERMAN by force and virtue of the afsd Deed & by the said Ephraim OVERMAN & Sarah his wife sold ... unto me the said Zacha KEATON as by their Deed bearing date the 16th day of January last may appear ... 21 [blank] 1723/4. *Signed*: Zacha X KEATON his mark, Sarah KEATON C her mark. *Wit*: Sarah BULL, Jno PALIN, Zacha X KEATON his mark.

[B:234] North Carolina. Stephen SCOTT & Ruth my wife ... for the Consideration of a patent assigned me from Edward SCOTT to Henry KEATON of the Land & plantation whereon the Meetinghouse stands and now in the possession of Soll KING have ... made over all our Right ... unto the within mentioned Deed of Sale ... unto Joseph KEATON ... Jany 10th 1737/8. *Signed*: Stephen SCOTT, Ruth SCOTT. *Wit*: James GEORGE, Zacha Z KEATON his mark. *Ack*: Jany Court 1737. *Regt*: in folio 338 8ber 13th 1739.

North Carolina. 6 April 1738 Between Caleb ELLIOT of Perquimons Precinct in the Province afsd. Planter & Mary his Wife & Peter HUNNICUTT, late of the County of Prince George in the Colony of Virginia & Sarah his Wife of the one part and James GEORGE and David GEORGE of the Prect. of Pasquotank in the Province of North Carolina afsd. Merchants of the other part ... in Consideration of the Sum of 600 pounds currt Money of the Said Province to them in hand paid ... Sold ... Tract of Land lying in Pasquotank Prect afsd. on Newbegun Creek ... Edward PAYNES Land ... Joseph GLASTER'S Line ... 300 acres [B:235] ... granted by Sir William BERKELY Governor of Virginia unto one Robert LOWRY in ... 1663 & ... conveyed ... to one Saml. PIKE and by the said PIKE & Jane his wife to one William HAIGE ... by his Deed the 20 Oct. 1713 and patented by the said HAIGE from the late Lords Proprietors of Carolina the 29 March 1715 and now fallen by [blank] to the said Caleb and Peter in right of their Wives under the said William HAIGE ... *Signed*: Caleb E ELLIOT his mark, ELLIOT Mary, Peter HUNNICUT, Sarah Sar: HUNNICUT her mark. *Wit*: Miles GALE, Jos: ANDERSON. *Ack*: April 6th ... Mary ELLIOT & Sarah HUNNICUT having been first privately examined. *Regt*: 24 May 1738.

[B:236] 29 Jan. and in the Eighth year of the Reign of our Sovn Lord George the Second ... Between Charles KITE of the Prect. of Pasquotank & Province of North Carolina & William WILLIAMS of the Prect. abovesaid of the other part ... in Consideration of the Sum of 12 pounds ... paid ... convey and confirm ... a parcel of Land Contg 90 acres ... by the Creek Swamp ... a plantation whereon John KITE dwells ... 11 April 1738. *Signed*: Charles X KITE his mark. *Wit*: Zachariah CHANCEY, Jacob CHANCEY, John BONNER? *Ack*: April Court 1738. *Regt*: 24 May 1738.

12 Feby 1737/8 ... Dennis SAWYER of the Prect of Pasquotank in the Province of North Carolina Planter for and in Consideration of the Sum of 13 pounds Current Money of this Province ... paid by Caleb SAWYER of the Same Precinct afsd. ... Sold ... Tract of Land contg 100 Acres ... on the North Side of Pasquotank afsd. commonly called by the name of [blank] Beginning
[B:237] ... Zacha. SAWYER'S line ... the Creek

Swamp ... to John SCOTTS Corner Tree ... and Soln SAWYER and Caleb SAWYERS Line ... *Signed*: Dennis SAWYER. *Wit*: Jona. HIBBS, Robt. KEEL. *Ack*: 11 April 1738. *Regt*: 24 May 1738.

14 Feby 1734/5 I Daniel JACKSON Senr being Sick & weak in Body but in sound and perfect Senses and Memory First I give and bequeath my Soul to God that first gave it me and Secondly I commit my Body to the Earth from whence it came. After my Body being decently buried & my just Debts paid I bestow my worldly Estate as follows. To my Son Danl. JACKSON I give and bequeath a Silver Spoon & my Druggit Vest & Breeches & what I have disposed myself with for his Share. To my son Zachariah JACKSON I give and bequeath my Case of Bottles & what I have [B:238] disposed myself with for his Share. To my Son Saml. JACKSON I give and bequeath a Silver Spoon and what I have disposed myself with for his Share. The plantation whereon I now live from Branch to Branch as far as round the Nothermost Clearly lade I give & bequeath unto my Son David JACKSON unto him & his Heirs & to be free at his Father's Death and to receive what is his near the Neck of Land over the Branch from Branch to Branch. I do give & bequeath unto my Son William JACKSON unto him and his Heirs the long Glade Tract of Land. I do give and bequeath unto my Son Joab JACKSON unto him and his Heirs -- if Either of the Three should die without Issue his Land shall return unto the Living All the rest of my moveable Estate I give the use of it to my Wife Ann JACKSON and during her Lifetime or Widowhood and after her Decease or Marriage all to return to Ruth JACKSON and Ann JACKSON & David JACKSON & Elisabeth JACKSON & William JACKSON & Joab JACKSON. [Rest of will missing]

North Carolina. Thomas JESOP of the Prect. of Perquimans in the Province afsd. ... for the valuable Consideration of 100 pounds ... paid by Stephen SCOTT of the Prect of Pasquotank in the Province afsd. ... Sold ... 157 Acres part of a greater Tract contg 314 Acres formerly belonging to Edward POPE and by him bequeathed unto his wife Sarah POPE who being intermarried with one Thomas WYATT did Sell and confirm the said 157 Acres of Land to Thomas JESOP ... 19 Oct. 1722 & acknowledged in the Precinct Court of Pasquotank the 15 Jan.

1722/3 & Registered the 9 April 1723 ...
[B:239] ... 26 Aug. 1722. *Signed*: Thomas JESOP. *Wit*: W NORRIS, Edwd. MAYO Jr. *Ack*: 21 April 1724 by Thomas JESOP and his wife to Stephen SCOTT. *Regt*: 11 April 1724. Pr. W. NORRIS Reg.

North Carolina Stephen SCOTT & Ruth my wife ... in Consideration of a patent assigned over from Edward SCOTT to Henry KEATON for the Land & Plantation whereon the meeting House stands & now in the possession of Solomon KING & Have ... made over all our Rights ... unto the remaining part of the Said Land contained in the within mentioned Deed of Sale being by Estimation Sixty acres ... unto Joseph KEATON ... interlined before sealed that Stephen SCOTT hath reserved to himself a privilege to raise Hogs on the lower part of the Land hereby assigned ... 10 Jan. 1737/8. *Signed*: Stephen SCOTT, Ruth SCOTT. *Wit*: James GEORGE, Zacha. Z KEATON'S mark. *Ack*: Jany Court 1738. *Regt*: May 24th By Jos. SMITH.

[B:240] Samuel NEWBY & Ann my Wife of Perquimans in North Carolina for & in Consideration of 165 pounds Current Money of the sd. Province ... paid by Thomas WINSLOW Junr of the place afsd ... Sold ... Two parcels of Land situate lying and being in Pasquotank Prect. on the S. E. Side of Newbegun Creek ... one piece ... to Stephen SCOTTS formerly MACKEY'S Line ... Contg by Estimation 50 Acres ... the other piece ... by a place commonly called and known by the name of Dick's Folly ... the old Road that went to Caleb BUNDY'S to the Beaver Dam ... contg by Estimation 10 acres ... 21 Feb. 1736/7. *Signed*: Saml. NEWBY, Ann A NEWBY her mark. *Wit*: John SMITH, John WINSLOW, Rt. WILSON. *Ack*: July Court 1737. *Regt*: 8 July 1738.

North Carolina. 4 Jan. and in the Eighth year of the Reign of our Sovn Lord &c. Between James JONES of the Prect. of Pasquotank of the one part and Wm. OVERTON of the Said Prect. of the other part ... in Consideration of the valuable Sum of 25 pounds Stg. money of Gt. Britain ... paid ... Sold ...
[B:241] ... Tract of Land lying ... in the Fork of Pasquotank River contg. 50 acres ... by the Mill Run ... old Henry BRIGHT'S Line ... 4 Jan. 1736/7. *Signed*: James JONES. *Wit*: Joseph MACKFARSON,

Charles X BRIGHT his mark, Thomas L LEWIS mark. *Ack*: July Court 1737. *Regt*: 10 July 1738.

March 26th 1735 Recd. of Eliza. BRYANT & David BAILEY Exex. & Exer. of the last will & Testament of John ARMOUR Esqr. decd. the full part and portion, belonging to my wife Anne, which by her Father the said John ARMOUR'S last will & Testament was bequeathed to her. I say recd. in full. *Signed*: Pr me John WAD. *Wit*: Joshua MARKHAM, Joseph BAILEY. *Regt*: 24 July 1738.

[B:242] April 5th 1736 Recd. of Eliza. BRYAN & David BAILEY Exex. & Exer. of the last will & Testament of John ARMOUR Esqr. decd. the full part and portion belonging to my wife Mary ARMOUR, which by her Father the said John ARMOUR'S last will & Testament was bequeathed to her. I say recd. in full. *Signed*: Pr John HASELL. *Regt*: 24 July 1738.

North Carolina 10 July in the year of our Sovn Lord, George the Second ... Between Willm. LEWIS & Sarah his Wife of the one part & Robert PALMER of the other part & all of the Prect. of Pasquotank & Province afsd. ... in Consideration of ... 80 pounds ... paid by Robert PALMER ... Sold ... Parcel of Land ... near Little Flatty Creek being within the said Robert PALMERS Patent, Contg by Estimation 62 acres and a half ... 20 July 1738. *Signed*: William LEWIS, Sarah S LEWIS her mark. *Wit*: Jos. SMITH, Thos. PENDLETON. *Ack*: July Court 1738. *Regt*: 13 Oct. 1739.

No. Carolina 11 July 1738 Between Henry WENSLEY Mariner, Lawful attorney of George LOW of London Citizen & Packer of the one part & Thomas PENDLETON of the Prect. of Pasquotank & Province afsd. Planter of the other part ... in Consideration of the Sum of 2,200 pounds Currt. Money of the Said Province ... paid by Thomas PENDLETON ...
[B:243] ... Sold ... Tract of Land ... on the S. W. Side of Pasquotank River at the Mouth of Newbegun Creek whereon the said PENDLETON now lives, also that parcel ... commonly called Colletons Island or Little Roanoke both which Tracts were given by John ARCHDALE Esqr. to Nevil LOW ... *Signed*: Henry WENSLEY. *Wit*: Mac SCARBOROUGH, Jos: ANDERSON, Jos:

SMITH. *Ack*: July Court 1738. *Regt*: 20 July 1738.

North Carolina. Joseph REDING of the Prect. of Pasquotank in the County of Albemarle in the Province of No. Carolina ... in Consideration of the natural love and affection which I have ... unto my well beloved Daughter Ann JONES the Wife of Henry JONES of the Prect, County & Province afsd. ... give ... one Negro Girl named Moll with her Increase forever, about the age of 12 years ...
[B:244] ... [blank] Jan. 1723/4. *Signed*: Jos: REDING. *Wit*: Wm. RELFE, Wm X LEWIS his mark. *Ack*: 21 July 1724. *Regt*: 10 Oct. 1724. The above Deed was *Regt*: 24 Aug. 1738.

Albemarle. Willm. Earl of CRAVEN Palatine ... give and grant unto Danl. ROADS a Tract of Land contg 220 acres lying on the S. W. Side of Pasquotank River in the County afsd. ... Robert PEELES Corner Tree ...
[B:245] 10 May 1697. Witness our Trusty and well beloved John ARCHDALE Esqr. Governr. &c. of Carolina ... *Signed*: John ARCHDALE, Danl. AKEHURST, Francis TOOMES, Thomas POLLOCK, Samuel SWANN, Henderson WALKER. *Regt*: 24 Aug. 1738.

North Carolina. Courtney ABBITT of the Precinct of Pasquotank and Province of North Carolina Widow, for the Love, Good Will and affection which I have ... towards my loving sons John MERCHANT and Caleb ABBITT of the Prect & Province afsd. Have given ... to John MERCHANT one good Feather Bed & furniture & two peuter Dishes, one large one & a small one, and four large new peuter plates and one year old Mare and all her Increase & two Cow Calves and all their Increase, and one Silver Cup marked TVJ & one Silver Spoon CM & his Father's Gun and to the above Said Caleb ABBITT, one good feather Bed and furniture, two peuter Dishes one large one & one small one, & four new large peuter plates & one Mare Colt and her Increase & two Cow Calves and all thir Increase to be delivered to the said John MERCHANT & Caleb ABBIT when they shall come to the years of 21 or day of Marriage & it is hereby meant and intended, that if either of my Sons should die without Issue, let his part of all to the Survivor & if it happen that they both die without Issue, that the abovementioned premises shall return to the first Donor and her Heirs forever ... *Signed*: Cortney C ABBITT her mark. *Wit*: Gabl. BURNHAM, John JONES, William MATHEWS. *Ack*: July Court 1738. *Regt*: 8ber 13th 1739.

[B:246] North Carolina. 10 July in the Eleventh year of the Reign of our Sovn Lord George the Second ... Between William LEWIS and Sarah his wife of the one part & Robert PALMER of the other part all of the Prect of Pasquotank & Province afsd. ... in Consideration of the ... sum of 80 pounds ... Sold ... parcel of land lying ... near Little Flatty Creek being within the Said Robert PALMER'S Patent containing ... 62 acres and a half ... 10 July 1738. *Signed*: William LEWIS, Sarah [blank] LEWIS her mark. *Wit*: Jos: SMITH, Thos. PENDLETON.

7 Oct. 1738 Between William BROTHERS of Pasquotank Precinct in the Province of North Carolina of the one part and William HIXSON of the said Province & Prect of the other part ... parcel of Land ... known by name of SAWYER'S plantation willed & bequeathed unto the said William BROTHERS by his Father John BROTHERS the 28 Nov. 1733 & conveyed unto the Said John BROTHERS by one Caleb SAWYER who purchased the sd. Land of and from a certain Edwd. SCOTT & Mary his wife the 16 July 1723 ... in Consideration of the Sum of 160 pounds Curcy of the afsd. Province ... paid ... sold ... Parcel of Land ... Henry PENDLETON'S Line ... to the Land the abovesaid SCOTT formerly dwelt on ...
[B:247] ... Contg 50 acres ... *Signed*: Wm. BROTHERS. *Wit*: Solomon KING, C BANFIELD. *Ack*: Jany Court 1738. *Regt*: 14 April 1739.

North Carolina 10 Oct. in the tenth year of the Reign of our Sovn Lord George the Second ... between James SPENCE of Pasquotank & John MACKBRIDE of the same Precinct of the other part ... in Consideration of the valuable Sum of 10 pounds ... paid ... Sold ... parcel of land contg. 130 acres being taken out of a patent contg 200 acres lying in the fork of Pasquotank bearing date in the year 1716 ... on Mr. ABBITTS Line ...
[B:248] ... 9 Oct. 1737. *Signed*: James SPENCE. *Wit*: John KELLEY, Jacob SAWYER. *Ack*: July Court 1738. *Regt*: 8ber. 13th. 1739.

North Carolina. 7 April in the tenth year of the

Reign of our Sovn Lord George the Second ... Between James SPENCE of the Prect. of Pasquotank planter of the one part and Jacob SAWYER of the same Prect. of the other part ... in Consideration of the valuable Sum of 12 pounds ... paid ... Sold ... parcel of land contg. 100 acres .... being taken out of a patent contg 640 being in the fork of Pasquotank bearing date 1719 ... at ABBITS Corner Holley ... John KELLY'S Line down to John MACKBRIDES Line ... 11 April 1738. *Signed*: James SPENCE. *Wit*: John KELLEY, John MACKBRIDE. *Ack*: July Court 1738. *Regt*: 13th. Octr. 1739.

[B:249] April 13th 1736 ... Jeremh. MURDEN of the Prect of Pasquotank in the Province of North Carolina Planter for and in Consideration of the Sum of or value of an Exchange ... by David PRITCHARD of the same Prect. afsd. ... sell ... Tract of Land Contg 200 acres ... *Signed*: Jeremiah MURDEN. *Wit*: George [blank], Thomas SAWYER. *Ack*: 13 Jan. 1736. *Regt*: 13 April 1739 (page 365)

[B:250] North Carolina 3 April in the tenth year of our Sovn Lord George the Second ... Between James SPENCE of the Prect of Pasquotank & John KELLEY of the Same Prect of the other part ... in Consideration of the valuable Sum of 30 pounds ... paid ... parcel of Land Contg 60 acres being taken out of a patent contg. 200 acres lying in the fork of Pasquotank bearing date in the year 1716 ... John MACKBRIDE'S Line ... 11 April 1738. *Signed*: James SPENCE. *Wit*: Jacob SAWYER, Alexander SPENCE. *Ack*: July Court 1738. *Regt*: 13 Oct. 1739.

John MACKBRIDE of the Prect of Pasquotank & County of Albemarle and Province of North Carolina for and in Consideration of the Sum of 70 pounds Currt Money of North Carolina ... paid ... by John DUGAN of the same County and Province ... Sold ... Tract of Land Contg 100 acres ... part of a Tract belonging to a relapsed Patent bearing date April 2d 1724 & granted to Truman MACKBRIDE ... at a Corner Tree of [B:251] John KELLEYS ... joining on James GAULTS? ... 1738/9. *Signed*: John MACKBRIDE. *Wit*: Jos: SMITH, Will: POWELL, William SHUGOLD. *Ack*: Jany Court 1738. *Regt*: Oct. 13th 1739.

North Carolina Samuel JACKSON Senr of the County of

Albemarle & Precinct of Pasquotank for and in Consideration of the Sum of 80 pounds current money of the Province ... paid by Zacha NIXON of the same place Farmer ... sold ... parcel of Land contg 100 acres ... (it being part of his patent) one bearing date 1694 the other 1714 ... JACKSON'S Line ... Beaver Dam Swamp ... mouth of the Cypress Branch ... [B:252] third day of the 8th Month commonly called October Anno Dom 1738 in the Eleventh year of the Reign of our Sovn Lord George the 2d. &c. *Signed*: Samuel SJ JACKSON his mark, Mary M JACKSON her mark. *Wit*: Phinehas NIXON, Joseph J JACKSON his mark. *Ack*: Jany Court 1738. *Regt*:

North Carolina Pasquotank: Major Griffith JONES of Pasquotank & Province afsd for and in Consideration of 62 pounds Current money of said Province paid ... by Capt. John LURRY of the Prect. of Currituck & Province afsd. ... Sold ... on the North East Side of Pasquotank River in the fork of Arenuse Creek & on the North Side of the Main Road ... on COOPER'S Line ... Sd. Land to be an equal Square ... [B:253] ... 10 July 1738. *Signed*: Majr. Griffith G JONES his mark, Elisabeth E JONES her mark. *Wit*: Griffith JONES Junr, John BROOKES? *Ack*: July Court 1738. *Regt*: 14 July 1739.

North Carolina. 10 April in the Eleventh year of our Sovn Lord George the Second ... Between Willm WAYMOUTH of the one part & Thomas SAWYER of the other part all of the Prect of Pasquotank & Province afsd. ... in Consideration of ... 100 pounds ... paid ... Sold ... Parcel of Land ... on the N. E. Side of Knob's Crook Creek known by the name of Paradise ... *Signed*: William W WAMOUTH his mark. *Wit*: William SHUGOLD, Mc SCARBOROUGH. *Ack*: April Court 1739.

[B:254] 6 April in the Eleventh year of the Reign of our Sovn Lord George the Second ... 1739 Between Charles SAWYER of Albemarle County & the Prect. of Pasquotank & Anne his wife pt. & Truman SPENCE of the sd. County & Prect. of the other part ... for the valuable Consideration of 100 pounds Currt Money of No. Carolina ... paid ... sold ... 100 acres of Land ... lying on the N. W. Side of the White Oak Branch being part of a Tract of Land Surveyed for Thomas COOPER, transferred to Charles SAWYER & now to Truman SPENCE ... 6 April 1739. *Signed*: Charles SAWYER. *Wit*: Caleb SAWYER, Alexander SPENCE. *Ack*: April Court 1739.

[B:255] Zacha. SAWYER of the County of Pasquotank in the Province of North Carolina for & in Consideration of the Sum of 25 pounds to me in hand paid by John COOK of the Province afsd. ... Sold ... plantation lying on the N. E. Side of Pasquotank River ... on the Island Swamp ... to Caleb SAWYER'S Line ... to Thomas COOPERS line ... Contg 100 acres ... 10 April 1739. *Signed*: Zachariah SAWYER. *Wit*: Israel LAMBETH, Jno. J SCARBRO his mark. *Ack*: April Court 1739. *Regt*: July 14th.

North Carolina. Deborah STAMP of the County of Pasquotank & Province afsd. Widow ... in Consideration of the natural affection which I have and do bear to my well beloved children Thomas Richard & Mariam STAMP ... give ... to my Son Thomas STAMP I give a young Cow & Calf, 2 Peuter Dishes, 2 peuter Basins, 6 peuter plates. I give to my Daughter Mariam one young Cow & Calf, 2 peuter Basins & 6 Peuter plates. I give my Son Richard STAMP one Negro Wench named Nancy, Two negro Girls named Jenny and Dye, one feather Bed and a pair of Sheets, one Blanket, one Rugg, one Bedstead, [B:256] one Bolster, one Cord & Matt. also Eight head of Sheep, one young Mare, two young Cows & Calves one Iron pot and Hook, and a frying pan ... if my Son Richard should die before he arrives at the age of Twenty one years being now about one year old, or should die without Issue that then ... the afsd. Negro Woman called Nancy shall remit to me the sd. Deborah Increase to wit Jenny & Dye & such as she may hereafter have in the minority of the said Richard to my Son Thomas & my Daughter Mariam to be equally divided between them ... 10 April 1739. *Signed*: Deborah DA STAMP hir mark. *Wit*: Mac SCARBOROUGH, Jos ANDERSON.

North Carolina Zachariah KEATON Senr of Pasquotank County in Province afsd planter ... in Consideration of the Sum of 10 pounds ... & also for the natural Love and affection that I have to my Son Patrick ... have given ... all my Land beyond a small Branch or Gulley that runs near the cleared Land where I now live and so across my land from David GEORGE'S Line

& John LUMBROSIAS Line being the Westernmost part of my land ... reserving the use and profits of said land during the time of my natural Life & the natural life of my wife Sarah KEATON ...
[B:257] ... 7 April 1739. *Signed*: Zachariah X KEATON Senr his mark. *Wit*: James GEORGE, David GEORGE, Joseph ARMOUR. *Ack*: April Court 1739. *Regt*: July the 17th 1739.

17 Dec. 1735 in the 8th year of the Reign of our Sovn Lord George ... Between Jeremiah EVERTON of the Prect. of Pasquotank & County of Albemarle & Province of No. Carolina of the one part & John CHAMBALAIN of the Same Prect of the other part ... for the love and good will I bear towards my Daughter Catharine CHAMBALAIN & her Husband John CHAMBALAIN ... give ... parcel of Land ... on the S. side of Pasquotank River ... joining upon a Deed purchased by Jno. CHAMBALIN from Wm WARD, to her and her Heirs & if she dies without Issue the sd. Land to be made good to John CHAMBERLIN and his Heirs ... it being for 15 acres of Land ... *Signed*: Jeremiah EVERTON. *Wit*: John LINTON, Rachel R EVERTON her mark, Jeremiah EVERTON. *Ack*: April Court 1739. *Regt*: 14 July 1739.

[B:258] No. Carolina) Pasquotank Prect) Peter BROWN of the Prect & Province afsd. ... for the Love Good will & natural affection I have and bear towards my loving Daughters Jane BROWN & Margaret BROWN, have given ... unto my Daughter Jane BROWN One Negro Girl named Doll, one Feather Bed and furniture, One Iron pot about 4 Gallons, two plates, one peuter Dish, Two young Cows & Calves. Likewise I have given ... unto my Daughter Margt. BROWN, one Negro Boy named Sampson, one feather Bed & furniture, one Iron 4 gallon pot, two peuter plates, one peuter Dish, Two young Cowes & Calves ... 10 April 1739. *Signed*: Peter P BROWN his mark. *Wit*: William BURGES, John BROOKES. *Ack*: April Court 1739. *Regt*: 8ber 13th 1739.

[B:259] Thomas SAWYER & Truman SPENCE & Tamer SPENCE his wife of the Prect. of Pasquotank in the province of North Carolina Planter ... for the just Sum of 40 shillings ... paid by Danl. SAWYER of the Prect. & Province afsd. ... sold ... parcel of Land ... on the N. E. Side of Pasquotank River contg 50 acres ... to Edwd. WILLIAMS Line ... on Danl SAWYERS & Griffith GRAY'S Line ... being part of a Tract of Land Thomas SAWYER bought of James MCDANIEL out of a patent bearing date the 1 April 1738 Contg 850 acres granted by Patent to James MCDANIEL, assigned over by the sd. James MCDANIEL to Thomas SAWYER & now sold by Truman & Tamer SPENCE unto Danl SAWYER ... 10 April 1739. *Signed*: Thomas SAWYER, Trueman SPENCE, Tamer X SPENCE her mark. *Wit*: Joseph TAYLOR, Alexander A SAWYER his mark, Dorothy X HASTINS hir mark, Jona. JONES. *Regt*: 8ber 10th 1739.

[B:260] Robert and Anne SPENCE of the Prect. of Pasquotank in the Province of North Carolina Planter for ... the just Sum of 6 pounds ... paid by Caleb SAWYER of the Prect and Province afsd. ... Sold ... parcel of Land ... on the N. E. Side of Pasquotank River ... Caleb KOENS Corner Tree ... Richard SAWYER'S Line ... Edwd. WILLIAM'S Line ... contg 100 acres ... part of a Tract of Land that Thomas SAWYER bought of James MCDANIEL out of a patent bearing date the 1 April 1723 Contg 850 acres granted by Patent to James MCDANIEL, assigned ... to Thomas SAWYER & now sold by Robert & Anne SPENCE his wife unto Caleb SAWYER ... 10 April 1739. *Signed*: Robert SPENCE, Thomas SAWYER. *Wit*: Charles SAWYER, Alexander SPENCE. *Ack*: April Court 1739. *Regt*: Page 680.

[B:261] 6 April in the 11th year of the Reign of our Sovn Lord George ... 1739 Between Daniel SAWYER of Albemarle County and Prect of Pasquotank & Mary SAWYER his wife of the one part, and John SCARBOROUGH of the said County & Precinct of the other part ... for the valuable Consideration of 25 pounds Currt Money of No. Carolina ... paid ... sold ... 130 acres ... called the Light plate ... being part of a patent granted to Henry and Robert SAWYER and bearing date 22 Nov. 1714 ... marked Trees of Captn. SAWYER & Danl CONGS? ... 6 April 1739. *Signed*: Daniel SAWYER. *Wit*: B BANGER, James SPENCE, Isaac LAMBETH. *Ack*: April Court 1739. *Regt*: 13 Oct. 1739.

[B:262] 2 Feb. in the Twelfth year of the Reign of our Sovn Lord George ... 1738 Between Truman SPENCE of Albemarle County Prect of Pasquotank & Tamer his

Wife of the one part & John SOLLY of the sd County and Prect of the other part ... for the valuable Consideration of 60 pounds Currt Money of North Carolina ... paid ... Sold ... 218 Acres of Land ... at a place commonly called & Known by SPENCES and the said Land being part of a patent granted to Alexander SPENCE Senr for 318 Acres of Land being dated the 10 July 1723 ... at a Branch that divides the Land from Captn. SOLLY ... Richd TERILS Line ... 218 acres of Land 100 excepted from the patent which was given to his Son Robert SPENCE ... *Signed*: Truman SPENCE, Tamer X SPENCE her mark. *Wit*: Barnard BANGER, Griffith JONES. *Ack*: April Court 1739. *Regt*: page 382.

[B:263] His Excelly John Lord CARTERET Palatin ... give and grant unto Robert PALMER of our said County a Tract of Land contg 182 acres lying by Flatty Creek on Willm WAYMOUTH'S line called by the name of Sound Neck ... PALMERS Line ... 1 Nov. 1727 ... Witness our trusty and well beloved Sir Richd EVERD. Bart. Governor ... *Signed*: Richd. EVERARD, Richd. SANDERSON, William REED, E. MOSELY, Edward GALE, Thos. FOSTER Depy Survy. *Regt*: Francis FOSTER.

North Carolina) Pasquotank) Robert PALMER Senr Planter in sd. County, have given ... all my Right ... of the within Contents being 182 acres of Land to John BASNET Planter in sd County ... the Consideration for which ... is hereby acknowledged to be fully paid ... 10 April 1739. *Signed*: Robert R PALMER Sr. his mark. *Wit*: James GEORGE, Joseph J KEATON his mark. *Ack*: April Court 1739. *Regt*: 13 Oct. 1739.

[B:264] Pasquotank William JOY for and in Consideration of the Sum of 6 pounds ... paid by Cornelius FOREHAND ... sell ... Parcel of Land contg 100 acres being part of a greater Tract surveyed by me ... and sold out into parcels the afsd 100 acres being adjoining on the Eastward of the plantation whereon I ... now live ... 1714. *Signed*: Wm. W JOY his mark. *Wit*: W. NORRIS, Jeremiah EVERTON. *Ack*: 20 April 1714 Willm. JOY to Corns. FOREHAND. *Regt*: 6 May 1714.

April 10th 1739. James FOREHAND do acknowledge and make over 50 acres of Land out of this Deed that part on which my House stands ... unto Richard FOTHERGALE ... *Signed*: James X FOREHAND his mark. *Wit*: James GROVE?, Jon. GROVE?.

[B:265] 7 Feby 1734 ... Jeremiah EVERTON of the Prect of Pasquotank in the Province of North Carolina Planter for and in Consideration of the Sum of 120 pounds current money of North Carolina ... paid by Willm. WARD of the Same Prect. afsd. ... sell ... Tract of Land contg 60 acres ... upon the South Side of Pasquotank River ... taken out of the lower Side the Jeremh. EVERTON'S Tract of Land ... Little Branch ... ALBERTSON'S Line ...
[B:266] ... *Signed*: Jeremiah EVERTON, Hannah H EVERTON her mark. *Wit*: George ROW, Saml. MANSFIELD. *Ack*: 8th April 1735 from Jeremh. EVERTON with the Consent of Hannah his Wife unto Wm. WARD. *Regt*: 28 April 1735 Test Jos SMITH P.R.

Oct. 13th 1735 I William WARD do ... acknowledge to Catherine CHAMBERLIN ... the within mentioned Deed to John CHAMBERLIN ... *Signed*: William W WARD his mark. *Wit*: Solomon S EVERTON his mark, Rachel R EVERTON, Jeremiah EVERTON.

North Carolina) Pasquotank) July Court 1739. John POINTER? late of the Said County Planter was attached to answer to Thomas HUNTER of a plea of Trespass on the Case and whereupon the said Thomas by Joseph ANDERSON his atty complains that whereas the said John on the 3 May 1738 at the County afsd was indebted to the said Thomas 16 pounds and 9 pence ... in good and merchantable Salt Pork at the rate of 45 Shillings a Barrel for divers good wares and Merchandises ... sold ... the said John ... hath not yet paid ... to the damages of him the Said Thomas 60 pounds Current Money of the said Province and thereof he brings this Suit &c. *Signed*: Jos. ANDERSON for Plt. John DOE, Richd. ROE are pledge of pers.

[B:267] North Carolina) Pasquotank) July Court 1739. John BARCO late of the Sd County Planter was attached to answer to Thomas HUNTER of a plea of Trespass on the Case and whereof the said pltf by Joseph ANDERSON his atty complains that whereas the Deft. on the 4 June 1738 at the County afsd made his certain Note in Writing ... promised to pay to the pltf 116 pounds weight of good fresh Pork and seven Bushels and one peck of Indian Corn, or Seven pounds 10 Shillings ... the said deft. ... hath not paid ... to pltfs damage 15 pounds and thereof he brings this Suit *Signed*: Jos. ANDERSON for Plt. pledge &c.

North Carolina, Pasquotank July Court 1739. Richard GREGORY of the sd County Planter was attached to answer to Thomas HUNTER of a plea of Trespass on the Case & whereupon the sd Thomas by Joseph ANDERSON his atty complains that whereas the Said Richard on the 5 Feby 1732 at the County afsd made his certain bill or Note in Writing ... promised to pay to the said Thomas 33 pounds 16 Shillings Current Money of the said Province for value received ... hath not yet paid ... to the pltfs damage 60 pounds & thereof he brings this Suit *Signed*: Jos. ANDERSON) John DOE, Richd. ROE are pledge of pres.

[B:268] North Carolina, Pasquotank July Court 1739. Thomas LOWTHER? late of the sd County Gentm. was attached to answer to Thomas HUNTER of a plea of Trespass on the Case and whereupon the sd Thomas HUNTER by Joseph ANDERSON his atty complains that whereas the Sd. Defendt. on the 26 March 1734 at the County afsd made his certain Note or Bill in Writing ... promised to pay to the Pltf on order 18 pounds 17 Shillings & 6 pence Currt Money of the sd. Province upon demand for value recd. ... is yet liable to pay ... to the pltfs damage 30 pounds and thereof he brings this Suit *Signed*: Jos. ANDERSON, for Pltf) John DOE, Richd. ROE) pledge of pres.

North Carolina, Pasquotank July Court 1739. Thomas BARCOCK late of the sd County Planter was attached to answer to Thomas HUNTER of a plea of Trespass on the Case, whereof the sd pltf. by Joseph ANDERSON his atty complains. That whereas the Sd. Deft. on the 8 May 1736 at the County afsd made his certain Note in Writing ... promised to pay to the Pltf 1 pound 10 Shillings & & in good & merchantable fresh pork at 12 Shillings & 6 pence per hundred weight at or before the 10 Jany next ensuing ... for value recd. ... is still liable ...
[B:269] to pltfs damage 20 pounds and thereof he brings this Suit *Signed*: Jos. ANDERSON, for Pltf

pledge &c.

North Carolina) Pasquotank) July Court 1739. William WARD late of the Said County Planter was attached to answer to Thomas HUNTER of a plea of Trespass on the Case and whereupon the said Thomas by Joseph ANDERSON his atty complains that whereas the said William on the 23 Dec. 1737 at the Court afsd made a certain Bill ... Three Barrels of good and merchantable Salt Pork & 120 pounds weight of fresh Pork on or before the 25 Dec. 1738 at the Dwelling House of the said Thomas ... still liable to pay ... to the damage of him the Said Thomas 80 pounds Current Money of the said Province and thereof he brings this Suit *Signed*: Jos. ANDERSON for Plt. John DOE, Richd. ROE are pledge of pers.

[B:270] 5 Dec. 1735 ... Thomas SAWYER of the Precinct of Pasquotank in the Province of North Carolina Planter for and in Consideration of the Sum of 100 pounds Current Money of this Province ... paid by William WAMAN of the Province afsd. ... Sold ... parcel of Land Contg 262 acres lying on the North Side of Knobs Crook Creek sold out of a greater patent bearing date the [blank] day of [blank] ... FAGAN'S Branch ... Nathanl. GRAY'S Line ... Thomas SAWYER'S Line to Wm. BRYAN'S Line ... *Signed*: Thomas SAWYER. *Wit*: Geo: ROW, Dennis SAWYER, Edward E ROW his mark.

[B:271] North Carolina Peter SAWYER & Mary SAWYER my wife of the Prect of Pasquotank & Province afsd. ... for the valuable Consideration of 110 pounds ... paid by Jonathan JONES of the same place ... Sold ... a parcel of Land contg 175 acres ... on the N. E. Side of Pasquotank River ... SAWYERS Creek ... Christopher HUMPHREY'S Line ... a larger parcel of Land formerly belonging to John SCOTT father [blank] Wife Mary & by Descent [blank] in my said Wife ... 21 Aug. 1733. *Signed*: Peter P SAWYER his mark, Mary R SAWYER her mark. *Wit*: B. MORGAN, Edward TILLIE, Moses M [blank] his mark.

[B:272] Thomas SAWYER of the Precinct of Pasquotank in the Province of North Carolina Planter ... for the just Sum of 50 pounds ... paid by Richard SAWYER of the Precinct & Province afsd. ... Sold ... parcel of Land ... on the N. E. Side of Pasquotank River contg 100 acres ... binding on my head line where now I live ... William WILLIAMS Line ... part of a Tract of Land out of a patent granted to James MACKDANIEL bearing date 1723 and assigned to Thomas SAWYER Senr a quantity of Land contg 850 acres to the sd. Richard SAWYER ... 11th day of [blank] *Signed*: Thomas SAWYER. *Wit*: Caleb SAWYER, John BURNHAM. *Ack*: July Court 1738

April 10th 1739. I James FOREHAND doth acknowledge and make over 50 Acres of Land out of this Deed that part on which my House stands ... unto Richd FOTHERGALE ... *Signed*: James X FOREHAND his mark. *Wit*: James GRAVES, Jane? GRAVE.

North Carolina) Pasquotank) Nevil BELL of Carteret Prect. & Bath County of North Carolina ... in Consideration of the Sum of 83 pounds Current Money of North Carolina in hand paid by John JONES of Pasquotank Prect. in the County of Albemarle & Province afsd. planter ... Sold ... parcel of Land [B:273] ... DAVIS'S Line ... which land was left to the said Nevil BELL by his [blank] BILLET. Relation of the said Will being had may at large appear. ... contg by Estimation 50 acres ... 7 Sept. 1738. *Signed*: Nevil N BELL Signum. *Wit*: Wm. HANLIN?, Wm BROTHERS, David LEWIS.

North Carolina Bath county, Carteret Prect. Nevill BELL of Carteret Prect. in County of Bath and Province of North Carolina Planter do nominate & appoint my well beloved Friend William DAVIS of Pasquotank Prect. & County of Albemarle & Province afsd. planter to be my true & lawful attorney for to acknowledge a certain parcel of Land lying on the South Side of Pasquotank River by Estimation 50 acres which Land was left unto me by my Grandfather John BILLET by his last Will & Testament ... 7 Sept. 1738. *Signed*: Nevill BELL his N mark. *Wit*: Wm. HANLIN, Wm. BROTHERS, David LEWIS. *Proved*: by the Oath of Wm BROTHERS one of the Evidences thereto 8 Jan. 1738/9.

Pasquotank County. Jonathan REDING of the Precinct of Pasquotank & Province afsd. planter for and in Consideration of the Sum of 150 pounds Current Money of the afsd. Province to me in hand paid ... by John JONES of the said Precinct & Province Planter ...

Sold ... Tract of Land that I bought of said JONES (and by Said JONES bought of Joseph HACKETT) & by said HACKET bought of John SCOTT & by said SCOTT bought of Edmund GALE Esqr. as by the said SCOTT'S Deed to me bearing date the 21
[B:274] day of April 1725 ... on the S. W. Side of Pasquotank River & bounded with the Land of Thos. WILLIAMS decd. on the N. Side of the River & Joseph JORDAN Junr on the South Side ... contg 70 acres ... 11 July 1739. *Signed*: Jonathan REDING. *Wit*: Thos. REDING, Henry PALIN. *Ack*: July Court 1739. *Regt*: 17 July 1739.

11 April and in the 11th year of the Reign of our Sovn Lord George the Second ... between James JONES of the Precinct of Pasquotank of the one part and Moses MACFERSON of the other part ... in Consideration of the valuable Sum of 10 pounds Sterling to me in hand paid ... sold ... Tract of Land contg 50 acres being part of a Tract that the said James JONES now lives on ... on the Mile Swamp David JONES Corner Tree ... Charles BRIGHT'S Line
[B:275] ... 11 April 1738. *Signed*: James JONES. *Wit*: Gab: BURNHAM, John BURNHAM. *Ack*: July Court 1739. *Regt*: 17 July 1739.

3 Sept. in the Sixth year of the Reign of our Sovn Lord George the Second ... Between Robert EDNEY together with the free Consent of Ann his wife both living in the prect. of Pasquotank in North Carolina & Thomas LEWIS of the other part in the County afsd. ... in Consideration of the valuable Sum of 30 pounds Sterling money of Gt Britain ... paid ... Sold ... dividend of Land lying situate on the N. E. Side of Pasquotank River contg 200 acres taken out of a patent contg 1654 acres commonly called Wolfe Pit Neck ... Mouth of the Cypress Branch ...
[B:276] ... 3 Sept. 1733. *Signed*: Robert EDNEY, Ann A EDNEY. *Wit*: John LINTON, William WD DAVIS his mark. *Ack*: July Court 1739. *Regt*: 17 July 1739.

North Carolina Francis MACE of Nansemond County in Virginia ... for the valuable Consideration of 20 pounds Current Money of this Province ... paid by James NEWBY of the Prect of Pasquotank & Province of North Carolina ... Sold ... unto the said James NEWBY Senr ... piece of Land contg 234 acres, including the fork Swamp ... John TOMLINSON'S &

Zachariah NIXONS Corner on the fork Swamp on the head of Little River ... James NEWBY'S Corner ... 26 Nov. 1734. *Signed*: [blank] *Wit*: Benj. BN NEWBY, James IN NEWBY. *Wit*: Francis MACE, Ann X MACE. *Ack*: July Court 1739. *Regt*: 17 July 1739.

[B:277] 14 Jan. 1734/5 and in the Eighth year of the Reign of our Sovereign Lord George ... Jarvis JONES of Pasquotank Prect. in North Carolina Planter of the one part & John DAVIS of the same place of the other part ... in Consideration of the Sum of 200 pounds Current Silver Money ... paid ... Sold ... all the remaining part of a certain ... plantation ... on the North Side of Pasquotank River ... which sd. whole Tract of land was 1717 Surveyed for John JONES and patented by him ... and divided in Several lots amongst his Sons ... 300 acres ... corner of John JONES Land on the Edge of the River Pocoson ... two Islands ...
[B:278] *Signed*: Jarvis JONES. *Wit*: William SHERGOLD, Jona. JONES. *Ack*: July Court 1739. *Regt*: 18 July 1739.

North Carolina. James NEWBY Senr. of the County of Albemarle and Prect. of Pasquotank Planter for and in Consideration of the Sum of 12 pounds in Specie or good rated Commodities of this Government to me in hand paid by James BOSWELL of the Prect and place afsd. Planter ... sell ... parcel of Land lying on the N. E. Side of Little River in the fork of Little River on the head of the fork Swamp it being part of the Tract of Land that the afsd. James NEWBY now dwells on ... head of said Swamp ... 50 acres ...
[B:279] ... 24 Feb. 1739. *Signed*: James IN NEWBY his mark, Hannah HN NEWBY her mark. *Wit*: Charles CT TALOR, Thomas MACKEE Jurat, Ed. WARD. *Ack*: July Court 1739. *Regt*: 18 July 1739.

[B:280] North Carolina) Pasquotank) Major Griffith JONES of the Province afsd. ... in Consideration of the natural affection & Love I have and do bear unto my well beloved Son Griffith JONES of the Province afsd. ... give ... my Goods, Chattels, Leases, Debts, ready Money, plate, Jewels, Rings, Household Stuff, apparel, utensils, Brass, Peuter, Bedding & all other my Substance whatsover moveable & immoveable Quick & Dead ... otherwise than my own Maintenance in a decent handsome manner during life

... 9 July 1738. *Signed*: Griffith Grif JONES his mark. *Wit*: John BROOKES, Willoughby PRICE, St. BERNARD. *Proved*: 2 Nov. 1738 W. SMITH C. J. *Regt*: 22 Sept. 1739.

[B:281] John MARTIN of the County of Albemarle Planter ... in Consideration of the Sum of 60 pounds in proclamation Money to me in hand paid by John PENDLETON of Pasquotank Prect. Planter ... Sold ... 150 Acres of Land formerly known by the name of MINGS Plantation lying and being on the South Side of Pasquotank River ... John MARTINS old Line & likewise on DAVIS & CHANCES old Lines now in the possession of Benjamin MILLER ... 15 Feby 1733/4. *Signed*: John MARTIN. *Wit*: Will. MAYNARD, W. REED, James CRAVEN. *Ack*: April Court 1734 by Jno. MARTIN to Jno. PENDLETON. *Regt*: 6 Sept. 1734.

John PENDLETON Planter of the Prect & Province herein mentioned for and in Consideration of the sum of 70 pounds proclamation money to me in hand paid by William DAVIS Planter of the Province & Precinct afsd. ... assign ... all my Interest and Title of the within mentioned Deed of Sale ... 25 Nov. 1738. *Signed*: John PENDLETON. *Wit*: Thomas HUNTER, Rebecca HUNTER. *Ack*: Jany Court 1738. *Regt*: 22 Sept. 1739.

[B:282] Joseph OVERMAN Son of Ephraim OVERMAN of Pasquotank County departed this Life the 24th day of September Anno Dom 1737.
Benjamin PRITCHARD Senr departed this Life the 21 day of Septmr. A. D. 1739.
Ann GEORGE departed this Life the 17th day of Feby 1737 formerly Ann ELLIS the wife of Mr David GEORGE.
James GEORGE the Son of David GEORGE and Ann his wife Born the 7th day of Feby 1737.
David GEORGE Gentn. & Ann ELLIS was lawfully married the 27th day of December 1736.
James GEORGE Esqr & Sarah HAIG was lawfully married the 15th day of August 1736.
William HAIG Son to William HAIG and Sarah his wife now the wife of the afsd James GEORGE departed this life the 29th day of April 1737.
David GEORGE Gentn. & Elisabeth BARCLIFT Daughter of Thomas BARCLIFT late of the County of Perquimans in the Province afsd. decd. was lawfully married the first day of Jany 1738.

David BALEY Esqr. was married to Esther WALLIS Widow of Robert WALLIS late of Coresound the 21st May 1738.
Simon BALEY Son of David BALEY Esqr. & Esther his wife was born in Pasquotank the 19th day of September 1739.
Regt: 8 Jany 1739 Pr James CRAVEN Regr.

[B:283] 20 Oct. 1736 Between Thomas GRANDY of the Prect of Pasquotank and the Province of North Carolina planter of the one party & Caleb GRANDY of the same place and Province afsd. Planter of the other party ... for the just sum of 100 pounds ... paid ... Sold ... Tract of Land contg 100 acres ... taken out of a patent ... which containeth 385 acres bearing date the 20 Oct. 1727 which Land was patented by Thomas GRANDY Senr. Father to the afsd. Caleb GRANDY & Thos. GRANDY ... on the N. E. Side of Pasquotank River ... Edwd. WILLIAMS Line Tree ... GRANDY'S Swamp ... Robert MORGAN'S Line Tree ... SAWYER'S Creek ... *Signed*: Caleb GRANDY. *Wit*: George GRASON, B. MORGAN. *Ack*: July Court 1738 Caleb GRANDY to Thomas GRANDY. *Regt*: 12 Oct. 1739.

North Carolina Timothy MEADS of the Prect of Pasquotank ... for the valuable Consideration of 20 pounds Current money of this Province ... paid by Thomas MEADS of the Prect. & Province afsd. ... parcel of Land ... on the N. E. Side of Little River ... at the fork of the Creek Mr. Oliver SOLTERS Line [B:284] ... to the main Road then up the said Timothy MEADS Line ... contg 55 acres ... 10 July 1738. *Signed*: Timothy MEADS. *Wit*: Ter. SWEENEY, Francis X LADEN his mark. *Ack*: July Court 1739. *Regt*: 12 Oct. 1739 in folio 412.

20 March 1736/7 & in the tenth year of the Reign of our Sovn Lord George ... Between John DAVIS and his wife Elisabeth DAVIS of Pasquotank Prect. in North Carolina Planter of the one part and Abel ROSS of the same place on the other part ... in Consideration of the Sum of 200 pounds Currt Silver money ... Sold ... plantation ... on the North Side of Pasquotank River ... called purchased Manor Land ... formerly made over ... unto John DAVIS by Gabriel NEWBY attorney
[B:285] to Mrs Mary DANSON Widow in London ... said remaining part ... 154 acres ... Corner Tree of

Saml BARNETT'S Land ... Mouth of Arenuse Creek ... part of a larger Tract of Land which sd. DAVIS bought of Gabriel NEWBY atty in fact to Mary DANSON [B:286] ... John X DAVIS his mark, Elisabeth X DAVIS her mark. *Wit*: Richd. FOTHERGALE, Francis F MACLIN his mark, John WALLIS. *Ack*: Oct. Court 1739. *Regt*: 13 Oct. 1739 in fol. 413.

Richard FOTHERGALE for and in Consideration of the Sum of 18 pounds 10 Shillings ... paid by Benjamin BURNHAM ... Sell ... parcel of land contg 50 acres ... in the fork of Pasquotank being the Land that was formerly James FOREHANDS ...
[B:287] 9 Oct. 1739. *Signed*: Richard FOTHERGALE. *Wit*: John GRILLS?, Joseph MACFARSON. *Ack*: Oct. Court 1739. *Regt*: 13 Oct. 1739 in folio 415.

North Carolina Moses MORGAN of the County of Pasquotank Planter and of the County of Albemarle & of the Province of North Carolina for the Sum of 200 pounds Current ... paid by Robert MORGAN of the same County and Province ... Sold ... 100 acres given to me the said Moses MORGAN in my father's will ... on the N. E. Side of Pasquotank River ... on William WILLIAMS Line Bennet MORGAN'S Line Edwd. WILLIAMS Line & Joseph MORGAN'S Line ...
[B:288] ... 28 Sept. 1739. *Signed*: Moses MORGAN. *Wit*: Lodwick WILLIAMS, John GRAY. *Proved*: Oct. Court 1739 by the oath of Lodwick WILLIAMS. *Regt*: 13 Oct. 1739 in folio 416.

North Carolina Nathaniel GRAY & Ann my Wife of the Precinct of Pasquotank & Province afsd. out of the Good will and Love that I bear unto David PRITCHARD & for the better Support and maintenance of the said David PRITCHARD ... give ... one parcel of Land contg 100 acres ... on the Swamp of Nobb's Crook Creek ... lands of William WAYMAN ... lands of William WARD ... 25 Jan. 1738/9. *Signed*: N. GRAY Senr, Ann GRAY. *Wit*: William WILLIAMS Jun, David CARTWRIGHT, Nathanl. GRAY. *Ack*: Oct. Court 1739. *Regt*: 13 Oct. 1739 in folio 417.

[B:289] 6 Oct. 1738 Between Absalum GRANDY of the Precinct of Pasquotank in the Province of North Carolina Planter of the one part and Caleb GRANDY of the Prect and Province afsd. of the other part ... for the just Sum of 70 pounds good & lawful Money

... sold ... parcel of land contg 70 Acres ... it being part of a Tract of Land which Thomas GRANDY Father to the afsd. Caleb GRANDY purchased of John JOY in the year 1731 ... on the N. E. Side of Pasquotank River ... Robert MORGAN'S Corner Tree ... on North Ridge pond ... *Signed*: Caleb GRANDY. *Wit*: Thos GRANDY, John BUNS?. *Ack*: Oct. Court 1739. *Regt*: 13 Oct. 1739 in folio 418.

[B:290] 8 Oct. 1739 Between Thomas GREGORY Senr of the County of Pasquotank and in the Province of North Carolina of the one party and Nathan GREGORY of the same place and Province afsd of the other party ... for the valuable Consideration of 100 pounds ... Sold ... Tract of land ... on the N. E. Side of Pasquotank River my now dwelling plantation with 160 acres ... and bounded as it is by patent no ways touching of the 100 that is over and above which the patent specifies that I formerly disposed of unto my Son Jacob GREGORY which said patent bearing date the 9 May 1697 ... *Signed*: Thos. T GREGORY his mark. *Wit*: B. MORGAN, Wm. O GREGORY his mark, Jacob I GREGORY mark. *Proved*: Oct. Court 1739 by the Oath of William GREGORY. *Regt*: 13 Oct. 1739 in folio 419.

North Carolina) Pasquotank County) Nathanl. GRAY and Anne my Wife for and in Consideration of 50 pounds Proclamation Money to us in hand paid do assign all our Right ... of the within Deed to William WARD ... 9 Oct. 1739. *Signed*: Nathaniel N GRAY his mark, Anne A GRAY mark. *Wit*: William SHERGOLD, William RELFE. *Ack*: Oct. Court 1739. [B:291] ... *Regt*: 13 Oct. 1739 in folio 420. The Deed whereon the above assignmt is endorsed was registd the 15th July 1728 in folio 13 .

North Carolina: Samuell JACKSON of Pasquotank in the County of Albemarle in North Carolina ... in Consideration of the Sum of 4 pounds 10 Shillings to him paid ... by Thomas TWIDDY of the Prect & County afsd. ... Sold ... parcel of Land contg 50 acres ... Bounded on Zachariah NIXON's Mill Swamp and Abraham RANKHORNS Line ... 17 June 1737. *Signed*: S J Samuel JACKSON. *Wit*: [blank] *Ack*: Oct. Court 1737 Saml JACKSON to Thomas TWIDDY. *Regt*: 13 Oct. 1739 in folio 421.

[B:292] 12 July 1736 ... John MACDANELL of the Prect of Pasquotank in the Province of North Carolina, Planter for & in Consideration of the Sum of 5 pounds 10 Shillings in Specie of this Province ... paid by Deliverance RICH of the Prect. afsd ... Sold ... Tract of Land contg 100 acres ... James JAMES'S Land ... *Signed*: John I MACDANELL his mark. *Wit*: Geo: ROW, Jean I ROW her mark. *Ack*: July Court 1736. *Regt*: 13 Oct. 1739 in folio 422.

[B:293] William WAMAN of the Precinct of Pasquotank in the Province of North Carolina Planter for and in Consideration of the Sum of 100 pounds Current Money of this Province ... paid by Thos. SAWYER of the same Prect. ... sold ... Tract of Land contg 200 acres ... on the North Side of Nobb's Crook Creek called by the name of Paradise sold out of a greater Patent bearing date [blank] ... head of William JENNINGS Branch ... *Signed*: Willm. W WAMAN his mark. *Wit*: Geo ROWE, Dennis SAWYER, Edwd E ROW his mark. *Ack*: April Court 1739. *Regt*: 13 Oct. 1739 in folio 423.

[B:294] 24 Sept. in the Tenth year of the Reign of our Sovn Lord George the Second ... Between Francis MARTIN of the Precinct of Pasquotank & Richd FOTHERGALE of the same Prect of the other part ... in Consideration of the valuable Sum of 65 pounds in Specie & paying the Mortgage Bonds ... Sold ... Tract of Land contg 300 acres ... David PRITCHARDS Corner Tree ... to the Lake ... 24 Sept. 1736. *Signed*: Francis F MARTIN his mark. *Wit*: Gab: BURNHAM, Abel ROSS. *Ack*: July Court 1737. *Regt*: 13 Oct. 1739 in fol 424.

[B:295] North Carolina) Pasquotank Prect) Thomas GREGORY of the Prect and Province afsd. for and in Consideration of the Sum of 15 Barrels of Pork ... paid by Jacob GREGORY of the same place ... Sold ... parcel of land ... on the N. E. Side of Pasquotank River Containing ... 100 acres ... Manor Swamp ... TACKIT[TOOKES?] Branch ... Gumpond line ... Hickory Branch ... out of a Patent granted to the afsd. Thomas GREGORY by the Lords Proprietors of No. Carolina for 267 acres bearing date 1 May 1668 ... 4 Dec. 1738. *Signed*: Thomas T GREGORY his mark. *Wit*: Joseph GODFREY, John BROOKES. *Ack*: April Court 1739. *Regt*: 13 Oct. 1739 in fol 426.

[B:296] North Carolina 3 April in the tenth year of the Reign of our Sovn Lord George the Second ... Between John MACKBRIDE of the Precinct of Pasquotank Planter of the one part, and John KELLEY of the same Precinct of the other part ... the valuable Sum of 20 pounds ... paid ... Sold ... parcel of Land contg 100 acres ... being taken out of a patent contg 640 acres being in the fork of Pasquotank bearing date 1719 ... at Marplepon? ... edge of New Backaroo? ... 11 April 1738. *Signed*: John MACKBRIDE. *Wit*: Alexander SPENCE, William WILLIAMS Junr. *Ack*: July Court 1738. *Regt*: 13 Oct. 1739 in folio 427.

North Carolina) Pasquotank Prect) William MACK [sic] of the Precinct of Pasquotank and the Province of North Carolina planter ... for the valuable Consideration of 100 pounds ... paid down by Michael MACKDANELL ... Tract of Land lying on the N. E. Side of Pasquotank River contg 40 acres ... the dividing Line ... Solomon SAWYER'S Line ...
[B:297] ... Sold ... 11 July 1737 in the 9th year of the Reign of our Sovn Lord George the Second ... *Signed*: William WM MACDANIEL his mark. *Wit*: Charles SAWYER, Jona. JONES. *Ack*: July Court 1737. *Regt*: 13 Oct. 1739 in fol 428.

[B:298] Albemarle Whereas His Excelly William Earl of CRAVEN Palatine ... 17 Oct. 1694 hath given power ... unto me John ARCHDALE Esqr Governor of North & South Carolina ... in Consideration of the Sum of 36 pounds 10 Shillings ... Sell ... unto John DANSON Citizen and Draper of London a Tract of Land contg 3,650 acres ... on the No. Side of Pasquotank River ... at the Mouth of Portahonck Creek ... Arenuse Creek ... 21 Feb. 1696. *Signed*: John ARCHDALE, Daniel AKEHURST, Francis TOMES, Thomas POLLOCK, Samuel SWANN, Henderson WALKER. *Regt*: in the Secy's Office W. GLOVER Clk.

Barbara DANSON of the Parish of St. Andrew Holbourn London Spinster being sick and infirm in Body but of sound mind & memory, thanks be to God for the same do make and ordain this my last Will & Testament in Writing in Manner following (that is to say) I give demise & bequeath unto Margaretta MOLLISON & Daniel DOLLEY the plantations and Settlements that are upon the Neck of Land on the N. E. Side of Pasquotank

River in North Carolina Containing 3,600 acres be the same more or less with all the Settlements movables or immoveables Rents or arrears of Rent, that is due or shall become due unto me and also four Baronys in the Province of North Carolina contg 48,000 acres to be taken up and also 43 pounds in the hands of
[B:299] Daniel OLIVER and William WEST each living in Boston in New England unto them the said Margaretta MOLLISON and Danl. DOLLEY to be equally divided between them share and share alike and if either of them die the part and share of the other of them to go to the Survivor of them the sd. Margaret MOLLISON & Daniel DOLLEY ... 8 April 1726. *Signed*: the mark of Barbara DANSON. *Wit*: William LEADES?, Thomas DOLLEY, Thomas ANDERSON.
[Two documents in Latin relating to the will.]

[B:300] No. 1 This Indenture Tripartite made the 14 day of Jan. in the third year of the Reign of our Sovn Lord George the Second ... 1729 Between Danl. DOLLEY of the Parish of St. Andrews Holbourn London Ironmonger & Margaret MOLLISON of the Parish of St. Bottulph Aldersgate Street London Spinster Devisees in the last will and Testament of Barbara DANSON late of the Parish of St. Andrews Holbourn London Spinster decd, who was only Sister and Heiress of Jothan DANSON decd., who was only Son and Heir of John DANSON Esqr. decd. late one of the Lords Proprietors of the Province of Carolina of the first part, Mary DANSON Widow & Relict of the sd. John DANSON Mother of the sd. Barbara DANSON of the Second part and Michael TREPPASS of the Parish of St. Giles Cripplegate London Joiner of the third part ... in Consideration of the Sum of 5 Shillings of lawful Money of Gt. Britain to them the said Danl. DOLLEY, Margaret MOLLISON, & Mary DANSON ... paid by Michael TREPPASS ... Sold ... all then the plantations and Settlements that are upon the Neck of Land on the N. E. Side of Pasquotank River in North Carolina containing 3,600 Acres ... given and bequeathed to the said Daniel DOLLEY & Margaretta MOLLISON in and by the sd last will and Testament of the said Barbara DANSON ... term of one whole year ... *Signed*: Daniel DOLLY, Margta. MOLLESON, Mary DANSON. *Wit*: W. MASSEY, James HUSSEY.

[B:301] No. 2 This Indenture Tripartite made the

15 day of Jan. in the third year of the Reign of our Sovn Lord George the Second ... 1729 Between Daniel DOLLEY of the Parish of St. Andrews Holbourn London Ironmonger & Margaret MOLLISON of the Parish of St. Buttolphs Aldersgate London Spinster Devisees in the last will & Testament of Barbara DANSON late of the Parish of St. Andrews Holbourn London Spinster deceased ... only Sister and Heiress of Jonathan DANSON decd., who was only Son and Heir of John DANSON Esqr. decd. late one of the Lords Proprietors of the Province of Carolina of the first part, Mary DANSON Widow & Relict of the sd. John DANSON & Mother of the sd. Barbara DANSON of the Second part and Michael TREPPASS of the Parish of St. Giles Cripplegate London Joiner of the third part Whereas the Said Barbara DANSON by her last will & Testament ... 8 April 1726 did give ... unto the said Margaretta MOLLESON & Daniel DOLLEY the plantations and Settlements that are upon that Neck of Land on the N. E. Side of Pasquotank River in North Carolina 3,600 acres ... And also four Barony's ... Containing 48,000 acres to be taken up and if either of them should die the part and Share of the other of them should go to the Survivor ... In Trust for and to the only Benefit of the said Mary DANSON ... And whereas the said Michael TREPPASS hath agreed with the said Danl. DOLLEY Margaretta MOLLESON and Mary DANSON for the absolute purchase of the said plantations Settlements Baronys and Premises in North Carolina afsd. for the Sum of 200 pounds ... in Consideration of the Sum of 200 pounds of lawful Money of Great Britain to the said Mary DANSON ... paid ... And also in Consideration of the Sum of 5 Shillings of like lawful Money to the said Danl. DOLLEY and of the like Sum of 5 Shillings to the Said Margaretta MOLLESON ... Sold ...
[B:302] ...
[B:303] ...
[B:304] ... *Signed*: Daniel DOLLY, Margta. MOLLESON, Mary DANSON. *Wit*: W. MASSEY, James HUSSEY.

No. 3 21 Jan. in the third year of the Reign of our Sovereign Lord George the Second ... 1729 Between Michael TREPPASS of the Parish of St. Giles Cripplegate London Joiner of the one part & Danl. DOLLEY of the Parish of St. Andrews Holbourn London Ironmonger of the other part ... in Consideration of the Sum of 5 Shillings of lawful Money of Gt.

Britain ... paid ... sold ... all those the plantations ... upon the Neck of Land on the N. E. Side of Pasquotank River ... Containing 3,600 acres ... and also all those four Baronys ... contg 48,000 acres ... Term of one whole year ...
[B:305] ... *Signed*: Michael TREPPASS. *Wit*: Jno. DOLLEY, Jams HUSSEY.

No. 4 22 Jan. in the third year of the Reign of our Sovereign Lord George the Second ... 1729 Between Michael TREPPASS of the Parish of St. Giles Cripplegate London Joiner of the one part & Daniel DOLLEY of the Parish of St. Andrews Holbourn London Ironmonger of the other part ... in Consideration of the Sum of 200 pounds of lawful Money of Gt. Britain ... paid ... sold ... all those the plantations ... upon the Neck of Land on the N. E. Side of Pasquotank River ... Containing 3,600 acres ... and also all those four Baronys ... contg 48,000 acres ...
[B:306] ...
[B:307] ... *Signed*: Michael TREPPASS. *Wit*: Jno. DOLLEY, Jams HUSSEY.

No. 5 20 Feb. in the 12th year of the Reign of our Sovereign Lord George the Second ... 1738 Between Robert DOLLEY of Soulden in the County of Oxford Grazier Brother and Heir of Danl. DOLLEY late of the Parish of St. Andrews Holbourn London Ironmonger deceased of the one part and William DOLLEY of the Parish of St. Andrews Holbourn in the County of Middlesex Ironmonger Nephew of the said Robert DOLLEY of the other part ... in Consideration of the Sum of 5 Shillings of lawful Money of Gt. Britain ... paid ... sold ... all those the
[B:308] plantations ... upon the Neck of Land on the N. E. Side of Pasquotank River ... Containing 3,600 acres ... and also all those four Baronys ... contg 48,000 acres ... Term of one whole year ... *Signed*: Robert DOLLEY. *Wit*: Wm. ROUND, Philip ROBERTS.

No. 6 21 Feb. in the 12th year of the Reign of our Sovn Lord George the Second ... 1738 Between Robert DOLLEY of Soulden in the County of Oxford Grazier Brother and Heir of Daniel DOLLEY late of the Parish of St. Andrews Holbourn London Ironmonger deceased of the one part and William DOLLEY of the Parish of St. Andrews Holbourn in the County of Middlesex

Ironmonger Nephew of the said Robert DOLLEY of the other part ... in Consideration of the natural Love and affection which he hath ... to the said William [B:309] DOLLEY and for and in Consideration of the Sum of 5 Shillings of lawful Money of Gt. Britain ... paid ... sold ... all those the plantations ... upon the Neck of Land on the N. E. Side of Pasquotank River ... Containing 3,600 acres ... and also all those four Baronys ... contg 48,000 acres [B:310] ... *Signed*: Robert DOLLEY. *Wit*: Wm. ROUND, Philip ROBERTS.

[B:311] James HUSSEY of Shorter's Court Throgmorton Street London Gentleman John DOLLEY of Aldersgate Street London Coffeeman and Philip ROBERTS of Throgmorton Street London Gentleman severally make oath and first the sd. James HUSSEY for himself severally saith that the two several parchment writings hereunto annexed marked No. 1 and No. 2 purporting to be Indentures of Bargain and Sale for a year and Release thereon bearing date respectively the 14th & 15th days of January 1729 the Bargain & Sale for a year being Tripartite ... names ... appearing to be subscribed to the said Deeds are of the proper handwriting of them the said parties respectively who either signed the same in the presence of this Deponent or acknowledged their Several Handwritings to this Deponent ... [B:312] ... John DOLLEY further maketh Oath that he very well knew Danl. DOLLEY ... he being this Deponents Elder Brother and that he died on or about the 26 June 1735 without Issue and without making any ... Will & that Robert DOLLEY of Soulden County of Oxford Grazier is Eldest Brother and Heir at Law of the said Danl. DOLLEY deceased. ... *Signed*: James HUSSEY, John DOLLEY, Phil: ROBERTS. *Wit*: Sworn this 21 March 1738 before Micajah PERRY Mayor.

Thomas BENNETT of the Parish of St. Sepulchres London Ironmonger being one of the people called Quakers upon his solomn affirmation saith that he very well knew and was personally acquainted with John DANSON late Citizen & Draper of London decd. the person mentioned in the letter of attorney hereunto annexed (he being Brother in law to this affirmant) and this affirmant saith that the said John DANSON departed this Life Intestate at London on or about the 4 Nov. 1722 bearing issue only three

Children viz Jotham DANSON, Barbara DANSON, & Mary DANSON ... Mary DANSON ... departed this Life Intestate and unmarried at Greenwich in the county of Kent ... on or about 6 Aug. 1723 ... Jotham DANSON ... departed this life ... about the middle of Aug. 1724 at Rotterdam in Holland Intestate and without ever having been married ...
[B:313] ... Barbara DANSON ... departed this Life on or about 10 April 1726 without ever having been married but ... made her last Will ... whereby she devised all her real and personal Estate to Margaretta MOLLESON & Daniel DOLLEY ... *Signed*: Tho: BENNETT. Affirmed the 21 March 1738 before Micajah PERRY Mayor.

Whereas John ARCHDALE Esqr. heretofore Governor of North & South Carolina ... for the Consideration therein mentioned sell ... unto John DANSON ... 3,650 Acres of Land ... on the North Side of Pasquotank River ... at the mouth of Portahonk Creek ... Arenuse Creek ... the sd. John DANSON ... departed this life on or about 4 Nov. 1722 Intestate whereby the said Tract of land ... descended to Jotham DANSON his only Son ... departed this life on or about the 15 Aug. 1724 Intestate and unmarried ... Barbara DANSON his only Sister ... departed this life unmarried on or about the 10 April 1726...
[B:314] Will ... 8 April 1726 by which she gave ... all ... unto Margaret MOLLESON & Daniel DOLLEY ... by their letter of attorney dated the 25 Aug 1727 impowered Mr. Gabriel NEWBY of North Carolina ... to sell ... whereas in and by Indentures Tripartite Sold ... unto the sd. Michael TREPPASS ... Sold ... unto Danl. DOLLEY ... departed this life 26 June 1735 Intestate and without Issue ... to his Eldest brother ... Robert DOLLEY ...
[B:315] ... Sold ... unto William DOLLEY ... And whereas it not being known to the said William DOLLEY what has been done by the said Gabriel NEWBY ... and he is since dead ... hereby appoints Henry WENSLEY his attorney to call the Exrs of the sd. Gabl. NEWBY to an account ... to collect rents ... grant leases ... renew all old leases ...
[B:316] ... sell and dispose of the Right I have to take up those four Baronys ... 21 March 1738 ... *Signed*: William DOLLEY. *Wit*: Archibald WYNNE, Richd. BAYFIELD.

[B:317] Richard BAYFIELD Clerk to Archibald WYNNE of Broad Street Buildings London Gentleman maketh Oath that he did on the 21 March 1738 see William DOLLEY of the Parish of St. Andrews Holborn in the County of Middlesex Ironmonger duly execute seal and deliver the letter of attorney ... *Signed*: Richard BAYFIELD. *Wit*: Sworn 21 March 1738 before Micajah PERRY Mayor.

Micajah PERRY Esqr. Lord Mayor of the city of London ... do hereby certify ... Richard BAYFIELD by Solemn Oath ... did depose and the said Thomas BENNETT (being one of the people called Quakers) by Solemn affirmation ... James HUSSEY ... John DOLLEY ... Philip ROBERTS ... by Solemn Oath ... before me ... have caused the Seal of the Office of Mayoralty of London to be hereunto put ...
[B:318] James HUSSEY, John DOLLEY, and Philip ROBERTS to be hereunto also annexed. Dated in London the 21 March 1738. Man. These may certify that the afsd. Writings, Patent, Will, and Deeds, from Folio 430 to 451 were duly registered and examined the 2 Jan. 1739. Pr. James CRAVEN. P. R.

North Carolina. Peter SAWYER & Mary my Wife of the Precinct of Pasquotank and Province afsd. ... for the valuable Consideration of 10 pounds Sterling Money ... paid by Christopher HUMPHREYS of the same place ... Sold ... parcel of Land contg 25 acres ... on the N. E. Side of Pasquotank River ... along the sd. Christopher HUMPHREYS ... William WILLIAMS Line ... Danl. COINS line ... part of a larger piece of land formerly belonging to John SCOTT father of Mary my said Wife and by descent is vested in my said Wife ... 8 Oct. 1733. *Signed*: Peter [blank] SAWYER his mark, Mary [blank] SAWYER her mark. *Wit*: John ROSS, John JONES, Thos. X GRANDY his mark. *Ack*: Oct. Court 1733. *Regt*: 8 Jany 1739.

[B:319] North Carolina. Henry PENDLETON and John PENDLETON both of Pasquotank Precinct & County of Albemarle in the Province afsd. ... for the Love and affection which we have and do bear unto Thomas DAVIS and Ann his Wife the Daughter of the said Henry and Sister of the sd. John ... give ... a Negro Boy now in the immediate possession of the sd. Henry PENDLETON and commonly called or known by the name of Josiah ... 18 May 1732. *Signed*: Henry

H P PENDLETON his mark. *Wit*: W. MINSON, Susanna PALIN. *Ack*: Oct. Court 1737. *Regt*: 29 Oct. 1739.

7 Jan. 1739 and in the 12th year of the Reign of our Sovn Lord George ... between Christian REED of the one Party and William GREGORY of the County of Pasquotank and the Province of North Carolina of the other party ... in Consideration of 1,300 pounds ... paid ... Sold ... Tract of Land ... N. E. Side of Pasquotank River ... known by the name of the Indians Land ... by a Deed expressed to my Father William REED Esqr. which said Deed bearing date 26 April 1722/3 ... containing 640 Acres ... North River to John DALYS Line ... GREGORYS Corner Tree .. [B:320] ... to Jacobs Swamp Bridge on the Cause-way ... the whole Tract of Land that my Father purchased of the Nation of Indians by Consent of Governor and Council ... *Signed*: Christian REED. *Wit*: Btt. MORGAN, Thos. GRANDY. *Ack*: Jany Court 1739. *Regt*: 10 Jan. 1739.

Nechlass SPINKS of the County of Pasquotank in the Province of North Carolina for and in Consideration of the Sum of 40 pounds ... paid by John PUGH of the County of Pasquotank in the Province of North Carolina ... Sold ... Tract of Land ... on the N. E. Side of Pasquotank River Contg ... 80 acres ... William JENNINGS Line ...
[B:321] ... & Dorothy SPINKS the Wife of me the Said Nicholas SPINKS ... surrenders all her Right ... 13 Aug. 1739. *Signed*: Nicholas SPINKS. *Wit*: Jona. JONES, Henry SAWYER, John J SCARBOROUGH his mark. *Ack*: Jan. Court 1739. *Regt*: 10 Jan. 1739.

John BELLMAN of the County of Pasquotank in North Carolina Planter for and in Consideration of the Sum of 145 pounds Current Bills of this Province ... paid by Samuel BUNDY of the afsd. County and Province ... Sold ... Tract of Land ... on the head of Branch proceeding out of the Creek whereon Zachariah NIXON built his Mills and joining on Charles
[B:322] OVERMAN'S Land & Joseph MORRIS'S land contg ... 100 Acres by Patent it being the whole patent purchased by my father named John BELMAN of James DAVIS formerly of Little River ... Mary BELMAN the Wife of me John BELMAN doth by these presents ... surrender all her Right ... 17th day of the 10th

Month called December in the year 1739. *Signed*: John X BELMAN his mark, Mary X BELMAN her mark. *Wit*: John SYMONS, Thomas SYMONS, Elisa M MORRIS her mark. *Ack*: Jan. Court 1739. *Regt*: 10 Jany 1739.

22 Feb. 1738/9 in & between William WILLIAMS of Kampton County in Virginia of the one part & Benjamin PRITCHARD of Pasquotank County of Albemarle & Province of North Carolina Cordwainer of the other part ... with consent of my Mother Rebecca WILLIAMS as also my Wife for and in Consideration of the just and full Sum of 200 pounds Current Bills of the afsd Province ... paid ... sold ...
[B:323] ... Tract of Land ... S. W. Side of Pasquotank River ... Wm COLLINS Corner ... Daniel AKHURST Corner ... Wm JONES Corner ... which Land formerly was surveyed by William LUFMAN and by him assigned ... to my Father Thomas WILLIAMS and by him in his last Will and Testament given ... unto me Containing 155 acres ... by a Patent bearing date the 1 March 1722 ... *Signed*: Wm. WILLIAMS. *Wit*: Thos. PRITCHARD, Eliza PRITCHARD, Elenor MARTIN. *Ack*: Jan. Court 1739. *Regt*: 10 Jan. 1739.

John & Mary RELPH of the Precinct of Pasquotank in the Province of North Carolina Planter ... for the just Sum of 33 pounds to me in hand paid by Caleb KOEN of the Precinct & Province afsd. ... Sold ... parcel of Land ... on the N. E. Side of Pasquotank River ... Joseph MORGAN'S Corner Tree ... William WILLIAMS Line ... Caleb SAWYER'S Line ... Edwd. WILLIAMS Line ... 100 Acres ... being part of a Tract of Land as Thomas SAWYERS bought of James MCDANIEL out of a Patent bearing date 1 April 1723
[B:324] Containing 850 Acres Granted by Patent to James MCDANIEL assigned over ... to Thomas SAWYER and now sold by John & Mary RELPH his wife unto Caleb KOEN ... [blank] day of [blank]. *Signed*: John RELPH, Thomas SAWYER. *Wit*: Robert MORGAN, Joseph MORGAN. *Ack*: Jan. Court 1739. *Regt*: 10 Jan. 1739.

John SANDERLIN Senr. of the North East Parish of the County of Pasquotank Turner for and in Consideration of Love, good will and affection which I have ... towards my loving Son John SANDERLIN Turner of the same Parish and County Planter ... give ... 100 acres of Land being my Manor plantation ... after my

Life and my Wife's Life ... 7 Jan. 1739. *Signed*: John SANDERLIN Senr. *Wit*: John HOURM?, Robert T SANDERLIN his mark. *Ack*: Jan. Court. *Regt*: 10 Jany 1739.

[B:325] John WYNN of the County of Pasquotank Planter for and in Consideration of Love Good will & affection which I have ... towards my loving Son Ezekial WYNN of the County ... give ... my Mulatto Boy named George ... 13 Dec. in the Twelfth year of the Reign of our Sovn Lord George ... 1739. *Signed*: John J WINN his mark. *Wit*: Willoughby PRICE, Abel ROSS. *Ack*: Jany Court 1739. *Regt*: 10 Jan. 1739.

No. Carolina William BUNDY of the County of Perquimans Planter for and in Consideration of the Swap or Exchange of a certain plantation of Thomas NICHOLSON lying in the County of Perquimans on the South West Side of Little River ... Sold ... unto ... Thomas NICHOLSON of the County of Pasquotank Planter ... plantation ... in the fork of Little River on the N. E. Side ... it being the Tract of land ... that the said Thomas NICHOLSON now dwells on containing according to patent bearing date the 20th Nov. 1739 483 acres ... surveyed for the afsd. William BUNDY and Patent in his own name ...
[B:326] ... Mary BUNDY the Wife of me the said William BUNDY doth ... surrender all her Right ... 8 April 1740. *Signed*: William BUNDY, Mary M BUNDY her mark. *Wit*: Thomas OVERMAN, Joseph ROBINSON. *Ack*: April Court 1740. *Regt*: 19 May 1740.

[B:327] North Carolina Thomas NICKELSON of the County of Pasquotank Planter, for and in Consideration of the Sum of 125 pounds Current Money of North Carolina to me in hand paid by Aaron HILL of the County of Chowan Planter ... Sold ... Tract of Land ... fork of Little River containing ... 135 acres ... near the Horse Bridge and Little Run? ... land belonging to the sd NICHOLSON ... Pine Branch ... 8th day of the 2d Month called April 1740. *Signed*: Thomas NICHOLSON. *Wit*: William BUNDY, Thomas OVERMAN, Saml. BUNDY. *Ack*: April Court 1740. *Regt*: 19 May 1740.

[B:328] October 13th 1735 I William WORD do oblige myself to acknowledge to Catherine CHAMBERLAIN, her and the Heirs of her Body and for want of such Heirs then to come to John CHAMBERLIN the within mentioned Deed ... *Signed*: Wm. W WORD his mark. *Wit*: Solomon EVERTON, Rachael RI EVERTON her mark. Jeremiah EVERTON. *Proved*: April Court 1740 assignment from William WORD to Catherine CHAMBERLIN was duly proved by the Oath of Jeremiah EVERTON. *Regt*: 19 April 1740. Memorandum that the above assignment of the Deed is written in folio 223 from Jeremiah & Hannah EVERTON to Wm. WORD.

17 March and in the Twelfth year of the Reign of our Sovn Lord George the Second ... between William OVERTON living in the Precinct of Pasquotank in North Carolina & Thomas HALL of the other party of the County afsd. ... in Consideration of the valuable Sum of 10 pounds Sterling Money of Great Britain ... paid ... Sold ... Tract of Land containing 125 acres ... 29 March 1740. *Signed*: William S OVERTON his mark. *Wit*: Isaac BRIGHT, Charles X BRIGHT his mark, William WATT. *Ack*: April Court 1740. *Regt*: 19 May 1740.

[B:329] North Carolina. Perquimans County. John PARISH and John BARCLIFT for and in Consideration of the Sum of 85 pounds in good merchantable barreled pork ... paid by Saml. BUNDY of the County of Pasquotank & Province afsd. ... discharge the said Samuel BUNDY the younger ... Sold ... one Moiety or half part of a certain Tract of Land containing by Estimation 350 acres ... on the N. E. Side of Little River in the fork of said River binding upon the afsd. Saml. BUNDY the youngers Land & the lower Side and adjacent to Samuel BUNDY the Elder's Land Commonly known by PARISH'S Land ... Ann PARISH the Wife of the said John PARISH & Ann BARCLIFT the Wife of the Said John BARCLIFT do both ... give ... all our Right & Title of Dowry ...
[B:330] ... 26 Jan. 1739/40. *Signed*: John PARISH, John BARCLIFT, Ann X PARISH her mark, Ann X BARCLIFT her mark. *Wit*: Joseph ROBINSON, Thomas NICKELSON, Michael MURPHY. *Ack*: April Court 1740. *Regt*: 20 May.

John BUNDY of the County of Pasquotank & Precinct of North Carolina Planter for & in Consideration of the Sum of 30 pounds Current money of the province afsd. ... paid ... by Saml. BUNDY the younger of the Province & County afsd. planter ... Sold ... Tract of Land ... in GRIFFIN Swamp ... bounded on that

Land which Caleb BUNDY purchased of his Brother Saml. BUNDY & that Land the sd. Saml. BUNDY now lives on & upon a Tract of Land commonly called REASONS'S ...
[B:331] ... 12 March and in the thirteenth year of our Sovn Lord King George the Second ... 1739/40. *Signed*: John BUNDY. *Wit*: Thos. PRITCHARD, Ann READING, Thomas HUNTER. *Ack*: April Court 1740. *Regt*: 20 May 1740 in folio (466).

17 April 1740 in & between Samuel NEWBY & Elisabeth his Wife of Pasquotank County of the one part & Thomas OVERMAN of the County of Perquimans & Province of North Carolina of the other part ... in Consideration of ... 24 Barrels of merchantable Pork ... paid ... Sold ... Land ... which I bought of Stephen HALL which Land was conveyed to the said Stephen by his Father by one deed of Sale bearing date the 15 July 1718 ... to the Southward of old Nathanl HALLS plantation ... to Saml. NEWBY'S Line ... to Little River Swamp containing 100 acres ...
[B:332] ... *Signed*: Saml. NEWBY, Elizabeth E NEWBY her mark. *Wit*: Wm. BUNDY, Richd. MCCLURE. *Ack*: April Court 1740. *Regt*: 20 May 1740.

North Carolina) Pasquotank) William BROTHERS Senr Planter in the County ... in Consideration of the Sum of 100 pounds Currency ... Sold ... unto Jeremiah WILCOX Planter in said County ... my plantation & land lying and being in the North Side of Great Flatty Creek at the Mouth ... contg. about 260 acres ... granted by the Honble Thomas POLLOCK Esqr. President ... unto William GASKINS bearing date the 10 July 1722 ... sold to Richd BROTHERS decd. late of this County and by Descent fallen to the said William BROTHERS ...
[B:333] ... 6 June 1739. *Signed*: Wm. W BROTHERS his mark. *Wit*: James GEORGE, David GEORGE. *Ack*: April Court 1740. *Regt*: 20 May 1740.

North Carolina) Pasquotank) William BROTHERS Planter in the County ... bound to pay ... Jeremiah WILCOX planter in the said County ... 600 pounds Currency ... 6 July 1739. The Condition of the above Obligation is ... defend the Title of the annexed Deed ... then the above Obligation to be void ... *Signed*: Wm. W BROTHERS his mark. *Wit*: James GEORGE, David GEORGE. *Ack*: April Court 1740.

Regt: 20 May 1740.

North Carolina John CAROON of Currituck County & Province afsd. Gentleman ... in Consideration of the Sum of 400 pounds Current Money of the said Province ... paid by William BURGES of Pasquotank County & Province afsd. planter ... Sold ... Tract of Land lying on the N. East Side of Pasquotank River containing 132 acres ... Lines of John WHITE, John FORBUSH, Dennis CRONEY and Baily FORBUSH ...
[B:334] ... 8 April 1740. *Signed*: Jno. CARON. *Wit*: John LURRY, Peter P BROWN his mark, John W BEELS his mark. *Ack*: April Court 1740. *Regt*: 21 May 1740.

North Carolina) John CAROON Gentleman of Currituck County ... bound to pay ... Wm BURGES Planter in Pasquotank ... 200 pounds proclamation Money ... 8 April 1740. The Condition of the above Obigation is ... quietly and peaceably possess ... Tract of Land ... then this Obigation to be void ... *Signed*: Jno. CAROON. *Wit*: James GEORGE, Thomas PRITCHARD, John X BAILS his mark. *Ack*: April Court 1740. *Regt*: 21 May 1740.

Elizabeth GRANDY of the County of Pasquotank and the Province of North Carolina ... for the Love, Good Will, & natural affection which I bear unto my Children ... to be possessed ... to my Son Absalom GRANDY one feather Bed & Bolster, Rug and pair of Sheets and one black Walnut folding Table & one Iron pot of about 10 Gallons, two large peuter Basins & two peuter Dishes and four Cow Chairs and one Chest with two Drawers and one grey Horse called Prince & one old Bay Mare called
[B:335] Jamey and all my Hog kind as I am at this time possessed with and one Cow that useth up the River at Solomon SAWYERS and one Cow & Calf that is at Caleb SAWYERS which said Cow named Nancy and five head of Sheep & to my Granddaughter Elisabeth one Cow & Calf & to my Granddaughter Grace one Cow and Yearling the Cow called Brindy and likewise to my Grandson Thomas WRICHARDS one feather Bed & Bolster and one green Rug and a pair of Sheets, the Bed that I called my own & one Cow and a four year old Heifer that uses at Griffith GRAYS at North River & to my Granddaughter Ann JELICO a yearling Heifer & to my Son Caleb GRANDY one Chest commonly called and known

by the name of his father's chest & to my Grandson Thomas WRICHARDS one Cow and Calf & to my Son Thomas GRANDY one Stone Jug of about Three Gallons & to my Daughter Phillis Two Spinning Wheels and all the rest of my whole Estate as well Obigatory as by account to my Son Absalom GRANDY freely to be possessed of -- and all the rest as aforementioned -- Given under my Hand & Seal this [blank] day of Feb. 1739. *Signed*: Eliz X GRANDY her mark. *Wit*: George GRASOM, Mary M CARPIN her mark, B. MORGAN. *Ack*: April Court 1740. *Regt*: 21 May 1740.

North Carolina William REED of the Precinct of Pasquotank and Province afsd. for and in Consideration of the Sum of 120 pounds ... paid by Zachariah SAWYER of the Precinct afsd. have assigned over all my Right ... to the within mentioned Deed ... 17 Jan. 1736/7. *Signed*: W REED. *Wit*: Joseph REDING, Matthew P REDING his mark. April Court 1740. *Proved*: by the Oath of Jos: REDING. *Regt*: 21 May 1740. The Deed on which the above assignment is written is registered in folio 23 the 16th day of Xber 1729. Pr W. MINSON Regr.

5 Jan. 1730 I assign over the within mentioned Deed to Willm LEE ... *Signed*: William TURNER, Elizabeth X TURNER her mark. *Ack*: April Court 1740. *Regt*: 21 May 1740. Memorandum: The Deed on which the above assignment is written, is regist. in the old Book folio (27) the 11th day of October 1724 by Wm. NORRIS Regr.

[B:336] North Carolina) Pasquotank County) 8 July 1740 between John JONES of the County and Province afsd. of the one part & Col. Thomas HUNTER of the County & Province afsd. of the other part ... in Consideration of the Sum of 70 pounds paid ... Sold ... parcel of Land ... on the S. W. Side of Pasquotank River ... joining to DAVIS'S ... sd. Land was left to sd. Nevell BELL by his Grandfather ... 50 Acres ... in a Deed from Nevell BELL to John JONES bearing date the 7 Sept. 1738 ... *Signed*: John JONES. *Wit*: Charles SAWYER, Thomas WEEKS. *Ack*: July Court 1740. *Regt*: 11 July 1740.

[B:337] I resign all my Right ... of the within Deed over to Col: Thomas HUNTER ... 8 July 1740. *Signed*: John JONES. *Wit*: Charles SAWYER, Tho:

WEEKS. *Ack*: July Court 1740. *Regt*: 11 July 1740. Memorandum The Deed on which the above assignmt is is written in folio (398) By Joseph SMITH. Register.

North Carolina, Pasquotank Precinct William GREGORY of the Prect. & Province afsd. do make over all my Right ... of this within written Deed unto Major Griffith JONES ... 28 Feb. 1737. *Signed*: William O GREGORY his mark. *Wit*: John LURRY, Jacob I GREGORY his mark. July Court 1740. *Proved*: by the Oath of John LURRY & Jacob GREGORY. *Regt*: 11 July 1740. Memorandum The Deed on which the afsd. assignmt is Registd in folio (275) By Joseph SMITH. Regr.

North Carolina) Pasquotank County) Griffith JONES Senr. in Consideration of the Sum of 5 Shillings to me in hand paid by Thomas HUNTER doth make over all my Right ... of the within mentioned Lease ... 7 July 1740. *Signed*: Griffith G JONES his mark. *Wit*: John LURRY, Jno. CARON. July Court 1740. *Proved*: by the Oath of John LURRY. *Regt*: 11 July 1740. The Deed is registd in folio 275.

[B:338] North Carolina) Pasquotank) William GREGORY of the Precinct and Province afsd. do make over all my Right ... of this within written Deed unto Major Griffith JONES ... 28 Feb. 1737. *Signed*: William O GREGORY his mark. *Wit*: John LURRY, Jacob I GREGORY his mark. July Court 1740. *Proved*: by the Oath of John LURRY & Jacob GREGORY. *Regt*: 11 July 1740.

North Carolina) Pasquotank County) Griffith JONES Senr. for a valuable Consideration to me in hand paid doth make over unto Thomas HUNTER all my Right ... of the within Deed and assignment ... 7 July 1740. *Signed*: Griffith G JONES his mark. *Wit*: John LURRY, Jno. CAROON. July Court 1740. *Proved*: by the Oath of John LURRY. *Regt*: 11 July 1740. Memorandum: The Deed of the afsd. assignmt. is registd. in page (276)

North Carolina) Pasquotank County) 8 July 1740 Between Henry PALIN & Thomas PALIN of the County & Province afsd. of the one part & Sarah PALIN of the County and Province afsd. of the other part ... in Consideration of the Sum of 200 pounds ... paid ... sold ... parcel of Land part of the Said 450 acres that is the Southernmost end and that lies highest

up the Branches of Little Flatty Creek adjoining to the Land that David GEORGE & the Land whereon John JENNINGS now lives to be equally divided by Henry PALIN & Thomas PALIN according to the purport of their Father's Will ... 225 acres ...
[B:339] ... *Signed*: Henry PALIN, Thos. PALIN. *Wit*: Thos. HUNTER, John BROOKES. July Court 1740. *Proved*: by the Oath of John BROOKES. *Regt*: 11 July 1740.

North Carolina) Pasquotank County) 8 July 1740 between Thomas NICHOLSON of the County & Province afsd. of the one part & Samuel BUNDY of the County and Province of the other part ... in Consideration of the Sum of 50 pounds ... paid ... sold ... unto Samuel BUNDY the Son of Caleb BUNDY ... parcel of Land ... on the N. E. Side of Little River ... 140 Acres ... part of a Tract of Land containing 500 Acres it being already divided ... to have that part that lyeth upon the Upper Side of the said Line ...
[B:340] ... *Signed*: Thos. NICKELSON. *Wit*: Stephen HALL, Gideon BUNDY, John I LOW his mark. *Ack*: July Court 1740. *Regt*: 11 July 1740.

North Carolina John JONES of the County of Pasquotank & Province afsd. planter for and in Consideration of the Sum of 140 pounds current Money of the Province afsd ... paid ... by Joseph JORDAN of the same place planter ... sold ... Tract of Land that I bought of the said Jonathan REDING and by the said REDING bought of John JONES & by the said JONES bought of Joseph HACKETT & by the Said HACKETT bought of John SCOTT and by the said SCOTT bot of Edmd. GALE Esqr. as by the Said SCOTT Deed bearing date the 21 April 1725 ... on the S. W. Side of Pasquotank River & bounded on the Land of Thomas WILLIAMS decd. on the North Side & Joseph JORDAN on the South Side ... Containing ... 70 acres ...
[B:341] ... 10 April 1740. *Signed*: John JONES. *Wit*: Thomas HUNTER, Joseph PRITCHARD. *Ack*: July Court 1740. *Regt*: 14 July 1740.

9 May 1740 Between Sampson GREGORY of the County of Pasquotank and the Province afsd. of the one party & Jacob GREGORY of the same place & Province afsd. planter of the other party ... Jacob GREGORY ... for the just Sum of 100 pounds ... paid down by the afsd. Sampson GREGORY ... Sold ... parcel of Land

containing 100 Acres ... taken out of a Patent bearing date the 7th day of May 1697 ... on the N. E. Side of Pasquotank River ... Tar Kiln Branch ... the main Road ... Hickory Branch ... *Signed*: Jacob I GREGORY his mark. *Wit*: Joab I GREGORY his mark, B. MORGAN, Wm. O GREGORY Signum. *Ack*: April Court 1740. *Regt*: 14 July 1740.

[B:342] 25 April 1740 between Joab GREGORY of the County of Pasquotank & the Province of North Carolina of the one party & Thomas GREGORY Senr. of the same place and province afsd. planter of the other party ... Thomas GREGORY Senr. ... for the just Sum of 200 pounds good & lawful Money ... paid by the afsd. Joab GREGORY ... Sold ... parcel of Land containing 737 Acres ... the whole Tract ... patent bearing date the 25th November 1714 ... on the North East Side of Pasquotank River ... on the Indians Line my former Corner Tree ... Manor Branch ... Hickory Branch ... *Signed*: Thos. T GREGORY his mark. *Wit*: B. MORGAN, Wm. GREGORY. July Court 1740. *Proved*: by the Oath of William GREGORY. *Regt*: 15 July 1740.

North Carolina) Pasquotank) 14 May in the twelfth year of the Reign of our Sovn Lord George the Second ... Between John SCARBOROUGH of Pasquotank County of the one part & William JONES of the said County of the other part ... for the
[B:343] valuable Consideration of 100 pounds Current Money of North Carolina ... paid ... sell ... 130 acres of Land ... commonly called the Light place ... part of a Patent granted to Henry & Robert SAWYER bearing date the 22 Nov. 1714 ... marked Trees of Captain SAWYERS & Daniell COEN ... 16 May 1740. *Signed*: John J SCARBOROUGH Signum. *Wit*: Gabl. BURNHAM, Caleb SAWYER. *Ack*: July Court 1740. *Regt*: 15 July 1740.

Thomas GREGORY of the County of Pasquotank & the Province of North Carolina have for a valuable Consideration ... sold unto Thomas GRAY of the same place and Province afsd. one Negro Man named Toney ... 7 Jan. 1739. *Signed*: Thomas T GREGORY his mark. *Wit*: Hannah X GREGORY her mark, Thos. SAWYER. July Court 1740. *Proved*: by the Oath of Thomas SAWYER. *Regt*: 15 July 1740.

[B:344] North Carolina Solomon POOL of Pasquotank County and Province abovesaid planter ... the love and good will which I bear unto my Brother Patrick POOL of the County and Province afsd. Planter have given ... plantation & the land thereunto belonging whereon he now lives ... 8 July 1740. *Signed*: Solomon POOL. *Wit*: John POOL, Richard MCCLURE. *Ack*: July Court 1740. *Regt*: 15 July 1740.

North Carolina George ROW of the County of Pasquotank in the Province afsd. Carpenter for and in Consideration of the Sum of 250 pounds current Money of North Carolina ... paid ... by Saml. Saban PLOMER of the County of Pasquotank afsd. Esqr. ... sold ... tract of land ... 100 acres ... fork of Nobs Crook Creek ...
[B:345] John HARRIS'S line ... 3 July 1740. *Signed*: Geor. ROW. *Wit*: Thomas M MAYO his mark, Isa. ARTHAUD. July Court 1740. *Proved*: by the Oath of Isaac ARTHAUD. *Regt*: 15 July 1740.

Whereas John ARCHDALE Esqr. Governor of North and South Carolina in America in pursuance of the Instructions given him ... Lords Proprietors ... 16 Oct. 1694 ... Deed poll bearing date the 21 Feb. 1696 ... for the Considerations therein mentioned Sell ... unto John DANSON late Citzen & Draper of London decd a Tract of Land containing 3,650 Acres ... on the North Side of Pasquotank River ... at the mouth of Portahonk Creek ... Arenuse Creek ...
[B:346] ... And whereas the sd. John DANSON ... departed this Life in or about 4 Nov. 1722 Intestate whereby the said Tract of Land ... descended to Jothan DANSON his only Son and Heir ... departed this Life in or about the 15 Aug. 1724 Intestate and unmarried, whereby the said Premises descended to Barbara DANSON his only Sister and Heiress ... departed this life unmarried on or about the 10th day of April 1726 having first made her last Will and Testament in writing bearing date the 8th day of April 1726 by which she gave and devised all that the Tract of Land ... and also four Baronies in the Province of Carolina Contg. 48,000 acres to be taken up unto Margaretta MOLLESON and Daniel DOLLEY & the Survivor of them ... Whereas in and by Indres Tripartitie of Lease & Release bearing date respectively the Lease the 14th and the Release the 15th Jan. 1729 ... made between the Said

Margaretta MOLLESON & Danl. DOLLEY of the first part, Mary DANSON the Widow and Admr. of the Said John DANSON & Mother of the said Barbara DANSON of the Second part & Michael TRESPASSE of the third part ... Sold ... Tract of Lands ... Contg 48,000 Acres ... by Indentures of Lease & Release bearing date respectively the Lease the 21st & the Release the 22nd Jan. 1729 made ... between Michael TRESPASS of the one part & the said Daniel DOLLEY of the other part ... for the Consideration therein mentioned ... Sold ... unto Danl. DOLLEY ... [B:347] ... And whereas the said Danl. DOLLEY ... departed this life on ... 26 June 1735 Intestate and without Issue whereby the said premises descended to his Eldest Brother ... Robert DOLLEY of Soulden in the County of Oxford Grazier And whereas by Indentures of Lease and Release bearing date respectively the Lease the 20th and the Release the 21st Feb. 1738 ... between the Said Robert DOLLEY of the one part and William DOLLEY of the Parish of St. Andrews Holburn in the County of Middlesex Ironmonger of the other part ... sold ... all that Tract of Land ... before mentioned ... William DOLLEY ... appoint Henry WENSLEY late of London Gentleman, but now of North Carolina in America my true & lawful atty ... to sell ... all or any part of the Premises ... 4 Feb. 1739 & in the 13th year of the Reign of our Sovereign Lord George the Second ... *Signed*: William DOLLEY. *Wit*: Archibald WYNNE, Richard BAYFIELD.

Richard BAYFIELD Clerk to Archibald WYNNE of Broad Street Buildings London Gentleman maketh Oath that he did ... on the 4 Feb. see William DOLLEY of the Parish of St. Andrew Holburn in the County of Middlesex Ironmonger ... sign ... *Signed*: Richard BAYFIELD. Sworn this 5 Feb. 1739 before me John SALTER Mayor.

[B:348] John SALTER Knt. Lord Mayor of the City of London ... Do Hereby certify that on the day & date hereof personally came and appeared before me Richard BAYFIELD Clerk to Archibald WYNNE of Broad Street Buildings London Gentleman ... I the Said Lord Mayor have caused the Seal of the office ... City of London to be hereunto put and affixed & the Letter of Attorney mentioned ... also annexed ... 5 Feb. 1739. *Signed*: Man. *Regt*: from Folio 486 to

490 the 16 July 1740.

North Carolina: William TURNER of the County of Albemarle and Precinct of Pasquotank Planter for and in Consideration of the Sum of 40 pounds Current money of the Province ... paid by Stephen HALL of the same place Planter ... Sold ... Tract of Land ... between Little River and Pasquotank River Containing 100 Acres being that 100 Acres which Francis HENDRICK late of Pasquotank in his Life Time gave to his Son Francis HENDRICK ... being part of that Tract of Land which is commonly known by the name of the half way Tree ...
[B:349] ... 10 July 1732 & in the fifth year of the Reign of our Sovereign Lord George the Second ... *Signed*: William TURNER. *Wit*: Thos. WEEKS, Ann WEEKS. *Ack*: July Court 1732. *Regt*: 16 July 1740.

Thomas TAYLOR & Betty WOODLEY Junr. was Married 22 Jan. 1738. And Mary TAYLOR, Daughter of Thomas TAYLOR & Betty his Wife was born 15 March 1739.

13 April 1740 between John BROWN of Pasquotank County and Province afsd. Planter of the one part and Thomas PENDLETON the younger Son of Henry PENDLETON of the County and Province Planter of the other part ... John BROWN Son of Peter BROWN for and in Consideration of one young Negro ... paid by the said Thomas PENDLETON ... sold ...
[B:350] ... Tract of Land ... on Newbegun Creek ... conveyed by my Father Peter BROWN to the said Thomas PENDLETON ... by a Deed bearing date 1729 ... *Signed*: John BROWN. *Wit*: Wm. BURGES, Peter BROWN Signum P, Sarah BROWN Signum S. *Ack*: Oct. Court 1740. *Regt*: 12 Nov. 1740.

12 April 1740 William WAMAN of the County of North Carolina Planter for and in Consideration of the Sum of 500 pounds Current Money of North Carolina ... paid ... by Elender WAMAN Spinster of the same County afsd. ... sold ... Tract of Land contg 238 acres ... North Side of Nobs Crook Creek formerly sold out of a greater Patent bearing date the [blank] day of [blank] ... SAWYER'S Line ...
[B:351] ... *Signed*: Wm. W WAMAN his mark. *Wit*: George ROW, Valentine R ROW his mark. *Ack*: *Regt*: 12 Nov. 1740.

14 May 1740 Elender WAMAN of North Carolina for and in Consideration of the Sum of 500 pounds Current Money of North Carolina ... paid ... William WAMAN Planter of the same County afsd. ... sold ... parcel of Land Containing 176 acres ... North Side of Nobs Crook Creek ... SIMSONS Corner ... Jno. SIMONS'S & DAVIS Corner ... SAWYER'S Corner ... SAWYER'S Branch [B:352] ... *Signed*: Elender E WAMAN her mark. *Wit*: George ROW, Valentine R ROW his mark. *Ack*: Oct. Court 1740. *Regt*: 12 Nov. 1740.

North Carolina. Ephraim OVERMAN of Pasquotank County in the Province afsd. Weaver ... in Consideration of the Sum of 200 pounds Current Money of the said Province ... paid ... sold unto William HIXON of Pasquotank County in the Province afsd. all my Right ... unto the within mentioned Deed ... 12 Jan. 1740/1. *Signed*: Ephraim E OVERMAN his mark. *Wit*: Saml. HEIGHE, A. DRESER, Jos. ANDERSON. *Ack*: Jan. Court 1740/1 from Ephraim OVERMAN to William HIXON. Test. Thos. TAYLOR. *Regt*: 10 Feby 1740/1.

William WINBURY of the County of Pasquotank Planter in the Province of North Carolina ... in Consideration ... of 100 pounds current Money of this Province ... paid by Nowell WINBURY of the same County afsd. planter ... sold ... Tract of Land ... [B:353] ... contg ... 125 acres ... on the South Side of Pasquotank River ... Edward WHARTON'S Corner Tree ... John WINBURY ... 6 Dec. in the fourteenth year of the Reign of our Sovereign Lord George the Second ... 1740. *Signed*: William W WINBURY his mark. *Wit*: Wm. ABERCROMBIE, William WILLIAMS. *Ack*: Jan. Court 1740/1. *Regt*: 10 Feb. 1740/1.

15 April in the fourteenth year of the Reign of our Sovereign Lord George the Second ... 1741 Between Robert SPENCE of the County of Pasquotank & in the Province of North Carolina & Ann SPENCE his wife of the one part & John SOLLEY of the Said County & Province of North Carolina of the other part ... for the valuable Consideration of 50 pounds Current Money of North Carolina ... paid ... sold ... [B:354] ... 100 acres of Land ... at a place commonly called and known by the name of James SPENCES Clearing ... part of a Patent granted to Alexander SPENCE Senr. for 318 acres of Land being dated 10 July 1723 which said 100 acres lies on the

East Side of the Patent and includes the whole Patent which was given by Will to his Son Robert SPENCE ... *Signed*: Robert SPENCE. *Wit*: James GEORGE, William HIXON, S. PLOMER. *Ack*: April Court 1741. *Regt*: 24 April 1741.

[B:355] John BUNDY of the County of Pasquotank in the Province of North Carolina ... in Consideration of 200 pounds Current Money of North Carolina to me in hand paid ... by Saml. BUNDY of the County & Province afsd. ... sold ... parcel of land containing ... 110 acres ... by Pasquotank Road Caleb BUNDY his Corner Tree ... Walnut Branch ... 15 April 1741. *Signed*: John BUNDY. *Wit*: Wm: SHERGOLD, Thos. HUNTER, William DAVIS, Jos: REDING. *Ack*: April Court 1741. *Regt*: 25 April 1741.

[B:356] North Carolina James PRITCHARD & Samuel PRITCHARD of the County of Pasquotank and Province afsd. ... in Consideration of the Sum of 20 pounds Current Money of North Carolina ... paid ... by James Poolman DUFFEY of the same County & Province ... Sold ... unto the sd. James Poolman DUFFEY & Mary his wife ... parcel of Land containing ... 100 acres ... the Second Branch ... Turkey Branch ... 15 April 1741. *Signed*: James PRITCHARD, Samuel PRITCHARD. *Wit*: William SHERGOOLD, Thomas PRITCHARD, John IVEY. *Ack*: April Court 1741. *Regt*: 15 Apr. 1741.

[B:357] North Carolina John SOLLEY do assign and set over the within Lease to Robert SPENCE ... 15 April 1741. *Signed*: John SOLLEY. *Wit*: James GEORGE, William HIXON. *Ack*: April Court 1741. *Regt*: 15 Apr. 1741. The Lease was registd 15 Aug. 1735 Pr Jos: SMITH Regr.

North Carolina) Pasquotank County) John RIGGS and Penelope RIGGS his wife and Saml. PRITCHARD of the Province & County afsd. for and in Consideration of 86 pounds ... paid by Amos TRUEBLOOD ... sold ... one part of a registered Tract of Land whereon the said John RIGGS & Penelope his Wife now lives containing ... 99 acres ... on the S. W. Side of Pasquotank River ... the uppermost part of the said Tract ... Nobs Crook Swamp ... Pipin Tree Branch ... the old Bridge & the main Swamp ... 14 April 1741. *Signed*: John IR RIGGS his mark, Penelope P RIGGS her mark, Samuel PRITCHARD. *Wit*: Thomas TRUEBLOOD, Joab CHARTWRIGHT, Abel TRUEBLOOD. *Ack*: April Court 1741. *Regt*: 25 April 1741.

[B:358] North Carolina) Pasquotank County) John SOLLEY do assign ... unto Robert SPENCE all my Right to the within Bond ... 15 April 1741. *Signed*: John SOLLEY. *Wit*: James GEORGE, William HIXON. *Ack*: April Court 1741 Col. John SOLLEY to Robert SPENCE. *Regt*: 28 April.

North Carolina John SOLLEY of the County of Pasquotank in the Province of North Carolina for and in Consideration of the Sum of 50 pounds Current Money ... paid ... assign ... Robert SPENCE all my Right ... Plantation in the Deed within mentioned containing ... 300 acres ... 15 April 1741. *Signed*: John SOLLEY. *Wit*: James GEORGE, William HIXON. *Ack*: April Court 1741 . *Regt*: 28 April 1741. The original Deed is Registd in folio 242.

[B:359] North Carolina) Pasquotank County) John ALBERTSON and Jacob ALBERTSON ... bound unto William WARD ... Sum of 100 pounds Sterling for the true performance of payment ... 30 Jan. 1741. The Condition of this Obligation is such that if the above bounden John ALBERTSON & Jacob ALBERTSON ... assure unto the said Wm. WARD ... part of a Tract of Land that is known by the name of Possum Quarter specified in a Deed ... 30 Jan. 1740/1 that then this Obigation to be void ... 31 Jan. 1740/1. *Signed*: John ALBERTSON, Jacob ALBERTSON. *Wit*: Wm. ABERCROMBIE, Tho: TAYLOR. *Ack*: April Court 1741. *Regt*: 7 May 1741.

6 April 1741 ... James PRITCHARD & Samuel PRITCHARD of the Precinct of Pasquotank in the Province of North Carolina Planters for and in Consideration of the Sum of 20 pounds of this Province ... paid by Thomas PRITCHARD of the Precinct afsd. Planters ... sold ... a certain Tract of land
[B:360] Containing 120 acres ... in the fork of Nobs Crook Creek ... Turkey Branch ... *Signed*: James PRITCHARD, Saml. PRITCHARD. *Wit*: Geo: ROW, Richard PRITCHARD. *Ack*: April Court 1741. *Regt*: 7 May 1741.

[B:361] 6 April 1741 ... James PRITCHARD & Samuel

PRITCHARD of the Precinct of Pasquotank in the Province of North Carolina for and in Consideration of the Sum of 20 pounds of this Province ... paid by John IVEY of the same Precinct afsd. Planter ... sold ... a certain Tract of land Containing 100 acres ... fork of Nobs Crook Creek ... Mouth of JOHNSON'S follow branch ... *Signed*: James PRITCHARD, Saml. PRITCHARD. *Wit*: Geo: ROW, Thomas PRITCHARD. *Ack*: April Court 1741. *Regt*: 7 May 1741.

[B:362] North Carolina William WARD of Pasquotank County in the Province afsd. ... in Consideration of the Sum of 100 pounds Current Money of the Province ... paid ... by George WARD of the same County and Province ... sold ... parcel of Land containing ... 50 acres ... Henry NICKELS Line ... with the free Consent of my Wife Elisabeth WARD ... 14 April 1741. *Signed*: William W WARD his mark. *Wit*: Thomas RELFE, Thomas TAYLOR, Saml. HEIGHE. *Ack*: April Court 1741. *Regt*: 8 May 1741.

[B:363] 6 April 1741 ... James PRITCHARD & Saml. PRITCHARD of the Precinct of Pasquotank in the Province of North Carolina for and in Consideration of the Sum of 20 pounds ... paid by Richard PRITCHARD of the same ... sold ... a certain Tract of land Containing 200 acres ... fork of Nobs Crook Creek ... James PRITCHARDS Line ... Turkey Branch ... John JURYS Land ... Sandy Hill Branch ... *Signed*: James PRITCHARD, Saml. PRITCHARD. *Wit*: Geo: ROW, Thos. PRITCHARD. *Ack*: April Court 1741. *Regt*: 8 May 1741.

[B:364] 6 April 1741 ... James PRITCHARD & Saml. PRITCHARD of the Precinct of Pasquotank in the Province of North Carolina for and in Consideration of the Sum of 20 pounds of this province ... paid by James WARD of the same Prect afsd Planter ... sold ... a certain Tract of land Containing 175 acres ... fork of Nobs Crook Creek ... Mouth JOHNSONS Follow Branch ... Turkey Branch ...*Signed*: James PRITCHARD, Saml. PRITCHARD. *Wit*: Geo: ROW, Thos. PRITCHARD. *Ack*: April Court 1741. *Regt*: 8 May 1741.

[B:365] North Carolina. Henry WENSLEY late of London but now of the Province of North Carolina ... Whereas William DOLLEY of St. Andrews Holburn in the County of Middlesex in the Kingdom of Great Britain

Ironmonger ... by his letter of attorney ... in Consideration of the Sum of 200 pounds Sterling Money of Great Britain ... paid by Thomas PENDLETON of the County of Pasquotank in the Province of North Carolina Gent. ... Sold ... parcel of land ... Containing 3,650 acres ... at the Mouth of Portahunk Creek ... Arenuse Creek ... (Except such ... parcels of the said Land as have ... been ... sold by Mr. Gabriel NEWBY by virtue of a power of attorney ...
[B:366] ...
[B:367] ... 18 March 1740. *Signed*: Henry WENSLEY. *Wit*: William SHERGOLD, John ETHERIDGE, Saml. SWANN. *Ack*: 18 March 1740 W. SMITH C.J. *Regt*: 9 May 1741.

John DAVIS in the County of Pasquotank within the Province of North Carolina Planter for and in Consideration of 400 pounds in good lawful Money of the Province ... paid by William WINBURY of the County & Province afsd. Planter ... Sold ... 300 Acres ... on the North Side of the River of Pasquotank ... John JONES Landing ... Isaac JONES Land ...
[B:368] ... 19 Feb. in the fourteenth year of the Reign of our Sovereign Lord King George the Second ... 1740. *Signed*: John DAVIS his X mark, Eliza. X DAVIS her mark. *Wit*: William ABERCROMBIE, Nowell WINBURY, John BURNHAM, Alse A WINBURY her mark. *Ack*: April Court 1741. *Regt*: 11 May 1741.

North Carolina. George WINBURY of the County of Pasquotank in the Province afsd. ... in Consideration of the Sum of 50 pounds Current Money of the said Province ... paid by Robert HOSEA of the said Province ... sold ... a certain piece of land joining to the said Robert HOSEA'S Land lately bought of William WINBURY Containing ... 50 acres ... Corner tree between the said George WINBURY & the said HOSEA ...
[B:369] ... 14 April 1741. *Signed*: George WINBURY. *Wit*: John BARCLIFT, J. SWEENY. *Ack*: April Court 1741. *Regt*: 12 May 1741.

North Carolina. William WINBURY of the County of Pasquotank in the Province afsd. ... in Consideration of the Sum of 180 pounds Current Money of the said Province ... paid by Robert HOSEA of the said Province ... sold ... plantation whereon I now live ... 150 acres ... on the lines of the plantation of

Edmund GALE Esq. & the Lines of the plantation of Thomas MEADES late of Pasquotank decd ...
[B:370] ... 3 April 1741. *Signed*: William W WINBURY his mark, Eliza. X WINBURY Signum.. *Wit*: Dennis DC COLLINS his mark, Timothy MEADES.. *Ack*: April Court 1741. *Regt*: 12 May 1741.

North Carolina. Robert HOSEA & Dennis COLLINS of the County of Pasquotank in the Province afsd. ... in Consideration of the Sum of 120 pounds current money of the said Province ... paid by Thomas ARMOUR Junr of the said Province ... sold ... parcel of land containing 81 acres ... Robert ARMOURS Line COMMANDERS Corner Tree ...
[B:371] ... 15 April 1741. *Signed*: Robert RH HOSEA his mark, Dennis DC COLLINS his mark. *Wit*: John MARTIN Junr, George WINBURY. *Ack*: April Court 1741. *Regt*: 12 May 1741.

John ALBERTSON & Jacob ALBERTSON do assign over ... all our Right ... of the within mentioned Land unto William WARD ... 30 Jan. 1740/1. *Signed*: John ALBERTSON, Jacob ALBERTSON. *Wit*: William ABERCROMBIE, George W WARD his mark. *Ack*: April Court 1741. *Regt*: 18 May 1741. Memorandum The Deed of this assignmt was registd in the old Book in the year of 1702 April Court By Thos. ABINGTON Regr.

Edward SCOOT of the County of Pasquotank & Province of North Carolina ... with the free voluntary Consent of Mary SCOOT my Wife ... for the valuable Consideration of 80 pounds in good pay ... paid by Edmund JACKSON of the County & Province afsd. ... sold ... 50 Acres of Land ... bought of James PRITCHARD ... 17 Jan. 1726/7 ... at David PRITCHARD'S Line ...
[B:372] ... James PRITCHARD'S Land to the Sandy Branch ... 14 April 1741. *Signed*: Edward SCOOT. *Wit*: William SHERGOOLD, Thomas PRITCHARD, John IVEY. *Ack*: April Court 1741. *Regt*: 18 May 1741.

North Carolina) Pasquotank County) Mary LANGLEY of South Carolina have assigned ... my trusty and well beloved Friends William RELFE and Thomas RELFE of the Province & County afsd. ... lawful attys ...
[B:373] ... 9 Aug. 1740. *Signed:* Mary M LANGLEY her mark. *Wit*: Elisabeth BROOKS, Jno. BROOKS. *Proved*: 20 Feb. 1741 by the Oath of Jno. BROOKS ...

Thos. HUNTER J. P. *Regt*: 24 June 1741.

North Carolina. Henry PENDLETON of Pasquotank Precinct the Elder ... bound unto my Son John PENDLETON ... Sum of 300 pounds Sterling Money ... 21 Aug. 1728. Whereas I have given ... unto my ... Son John PENDLETON one Negro Woman, named Doll and her youngest child named Charity ... his Eldest Son ... to the use of the said John PENDLETON within 30 days after the death of the said Henry PENDLETON then this obligation to be void ... *Signed*: Henry HP PENDLETON his mark. *Wit*: Thomas SWANN, John JONES, Rebecca SWANN.

North Carolina. John PENDLETON of the County of Pasquotank in the Province afsd. Planter for and in Consideration of the Sum of 280 pounds Current Money of the afsd. province ... paid by Thomas TAYLOR, Saml HEIGHE, and William HIXON of the same County & Province ... sold ... all my Right ... unto the within mentioned Bond ... 8 April 1741. *Signed*: John PENDLETON. *Wit*: Henry PALIN.
[B:374] ... *Proved*: April Court 1741 ... by the Oath of Henry PALIN ... *Regt*: 24 June 1741.

North Carolina. 16 June in the fifteenth year of the Reign of our Sovereign Lord George the Second ... 1741 Between Henry WENSLEY formerly of London Gentleman but now of Perquimans County in the Province of North Carolina afsd of the one part & Thomas PENDLETON of the County of Pasquotank & Province afsd. Gentleman of the other part. Whereas George LOW Citizen & Packer of London afsd. in Great Britain did by his Deed or Letter of Attorney dated the 27 May 1737 ... reciting that John ARCHDALE did ... by his Deed Poll bearing date 11 Feb. 1712 ... give ... unto his Grandson Nevil LOW Father of the said George LOW ... all that his the said John ARCHDALES plantation ... on the North Side of Newbegun Creek in Pasquotank River ... bounding on the land then belonging to Joseph JORDAN ...
[B:375] ... and whereas the said Henry WENSLEY hath lately by Judgement of the General Court of this Province received against the Occupiers thereof possession of the said Tract of Lands ... in Consideration of the Sum of 100 pounds lawful Money of Great Britain ... paid by Thomas PENDLETON ... Sold ... parcel of land ... Containing 257 acres ...

[B:376] ... *Signed*: Henry WENSLEY. *Wit*: Peter PAYNE, James CRAVEN, Mac SCARBROUGH. *Ack*: July Court 1741. *Regt*: 31 July 1741.

[B:377] North Carolina) Pasquotank County) 23 March 1740 and in the 13th year of the Reign of our Sovereign Lord George the Second ... Between Sarah TRUEBLOOD of the one part and Jos: MORGAN of the other party ... for the valuable Consideration of 120 pounds Good Specie ... paid down ... sold ... Tract of Land ... on the N. E. Side of Pasquotank River ... David SPENCES Corner Tree ... 140 acres ... to me from Alexander SPENCE and Ann his wife which said Deed was registered 13 Oct. 1739 ... *Signed*: Sarah TRUEBLOOD. *Wit*: Btt. MORGAN, Elihuu ALBERTSON, William W FERRILL his mark.
[B:378] *Ack*: July Court 1741. *Regt*: 1 Aug. 1741.

Daniel TEMPLE of the North East Parish in the County of Pasquotank within his Majesty's Province of No. Carolina yeoman for and in Consideration of the Sum of 50 pounds lawful Money of North Carolina ... paid by Richard COLLINS of the Parish and County afsd Farmer ... sold ... Tract of Land ... West Side of Arenuse Creek Swamp formerly belonging to John WINN known by the name of Forty pound Neck Contg ... 120 Acres ... Bounded according to the Will of the said John WINN decd. ... 11 Nov. 1740. *Signed*: Daniel D TEMPLE his mark. *Wit*: Edward X JAMES, Samuel R ROLLINS Signum. *Ack*: July Court 1741. *Regt*: 1 Aug. 1741.

James PRITCHARD in the County of Pasquotank in the Province of North Carolina Planter for and in Consideration of the Sum of 150 pounds of good and lawful Money of the Province ... paid by Richard PRITCHARD in the County & Province afsd. Planter ... [B:379] ... sold ... Tract of Land ... 50 acres ... on Nobbs Crook Creek ... David PRITCHARDS Corner Tree ... 14 July in the fourteenth year of the Reign of our Sovereign Lord George the Second ... 1741. *Signed*: James PRITCHARD. *Wit*: Wm. ABERCROMBIE, John IVEY. *Ack*: July Court 1741. *Regt*: 1 Aug. 1741.

[B:380] North Carolina. Joseph KEETON of the County of Pasquotank & Province of North Carolina ... in Consideration of the Sum of 144 pounds current Bills of said Province ... paid by

John BUNDY of said County ... sold ... parcel of Land ... being part of a Tract of Land formerly belonging to John BUNDY Senr decd that he the said BUNDY purchased from Jacob MACKEY Beginning at a Branch issuing out of MACKEY'S Creek ... Line of marked Trees formerly marked by the Said Thomas MACKEY & Ephraim OVERMAN decd ... 50 Acres ... 12 Aug. 1741. *Signed*: Joseph KEETON. *Wit*: Samuel BUNDY, Oliver SALTER. *Ack*: October Court 1741. *Regt*: 27th day of Oct 1741.

[B:381] 25 Sept. 1741 and in the Reign of our Sovereign Lord George ... between Jeremiah MURDEN of the County of Pasquotank in the Province of North Carolina of the one part and John MURDEN his son of the Same County and Province abovesaid of the other party ... in Consideration of the natural Love and affection which I have and bear unto my Son John MURDEN have given ... Tract of Land ... on the S. W. Side of Pasquotank River ... commonly Known or called by the Great Island or Lodwick GRAY'S Plantation containing ... 100 Acres ... Great Ash Branch ... to SEXTON'S Line ... *Signed*: Jeremiah MURDEN. *Wit*: Thomas RELFE, Jeremiah MURDEN Junr. *Ack*: Oct. Court 1741. *Regt*: 28 Oct. 1741.

[B:382] North Carolina Jeremiah BUNDY of the County of Pasquotank Planter for and in Consideration of the Sum of 60 pounds Current Money of the Province ... paid by Stephen HALL of the same place Planter ... sold ... Tract of Land ... Contg ... 50 acres ... between the said Jeremiah BUNDYS & Gideon BUNDYS ... Pine Branch ... 12 Jan. 1741. *Signed*: Jeremiah BUNDY. *Wit*: Thomas NICHOLSON, Ann BUNDY her A Mark, Abraham A HENDRICKSON his mark. *Ack*: Oct. Court 1741. *Regt*: 28 Oct. 1741.

[B:383] North Carolina) Pasquotank County) William SIMPSON & Edward JACKSON Planters of the County and place afsd. ... in Consideration of 50 pounds Current money of this Province by Thomas TWEEDY of the county and place afsd. ... sold ... Tract of Land containing 100 acres and a half the Swamp ... S. W. Side of Pasquotank River commonly called Nicks folly ... 13 Oct. 1741. *Signed*: William SIMPSON, Edman [sic] JACKSON. *Wit*: John NORRIS, Patrick POOL. *Ack*: Oct. Court 1741. *Regt*: 29 Oct. 1741.

[B:384] North Carolina) Pasquotank County) 8 April 1741 in the Thirteenth year of the Reign of our Sovereign Lord George the Second ... Between David SPENCE and Alexander SPENCE of the one part and Alexander SAWYER of the other party ... in Consideration of the Sum of 30 pounds ... paid down ... sold ... parcel of Land ... part of a Tract of Land containing 431 Acres as appears by a patent bearing date the 3 April 1719 formerly granted to James MCDANIEL & was ... Sold ... to John SPENCE Father to the afsd. David and Alexander ... bearing date 12 July 1720 ... N. E. Side of Pasquotank River commonly called ... James HASTINGS Ridge ... Thomas COOPERS head line ... *Signed*: David SPENCE, Alexander SPENCE. *Wit*: Thos. SAWYER, Jos: HUMPHRIES. *Ack*: Oct. Court 1741. *Regt*: 29 Oct. 1741.

[B:385] North Carolina: 13 Oct. 1741 Between Samuel JORDAN of the County of Nansemond and Colony of Virginia Gentn. of the one part and William BURGES of Pasquotank County & Province afsd. Planter of the other part ... power of atty ... from Sarah BATES of the County of York and Colony of Virginia ... bearing date the 13 Sept. 1740 ... to acknowledge ... 100 acres of Land ... part of 400 Acres which the afsd Sarah BATES purchased from Gabriel NEWBY late of Perquimans County decd. Atty for Mary DANSON of the City of London Widow &c. bearing date the 25 Dec. 1732 being part of the Manor Lands out of a Patent bearing date the 25 Feb. 1696 Containing 3,650 acres ... in Consideration of the valuable Sum of 37 pounds 10 Shillings Current Money of the Colony of Virginia ... paid by William BURGES ... sold ... 100 acres ... on the N. E. Side of Pasquotank River commonly called the Manor Land whereon the said William BURGES dwells ... Saml. WILLIAMS Corner Tree ...
[B:386] ... *Signed*: Saml. JORDAN. *Wit*: Ben: BELL, Abel ROSS, Willobe. PRICE. *Ack*: Oct. Court 1741. *Regt*: 13 Nov. 1741.

North Carolina: 13 Oct. 1741 Between Samuel JORDAN of the County of Nansemond & Colony of Virginia Gentn. of the one part and Samuel WILLIAMS of the County of Pasquotank & Province afsd. Planter of the other part ... power of atty ... from Sarah BATES of the County of York & Colony of Virginia ... bearing date the 13 Sept. 1740 ... to acknowledge ... 200

acres of Land ... part of 400 Acres which the afsd Sarah BATES purchased from Gabriel NEWBY late of Perquimans County decd. Atty to Mary DANSON of the City of London Widow &c. bearing date the 25 Dec. 1732 being part of the Manor Lands out of a Patent bearing date the 25 Feb. 1696 Containing 3,650 acres ... in Consideration of the valuable Sum of 75 pounds Current Money of the Colony of Virginia ... paid by Saml. WILLIAMS ... sold ... 200 acres ... on the N. E. Side of Pasquotank River commonly called the Manor Lands whereon the
[B:387] afsd. Saml. WILLIAMS now dwells ... *Signed*: Saml. JORDAN. *Wit*: Ben BELL, Abel ROSS, Willobe. PRICE. *Ack*: Oct. Court 1741. *Regt*: 13 Nov. 1741.

[B:388] No. Carolina, 13 Oct. 1741 Between Saml JORDAN of the County of Nansemond and Colony of Virginia Gentn. of the one part & John SCARBOROUGH of the County of Pasquotank and Province afsd. of the other part ... power of atty ... from Sarah BATES of the County of York & Colony of Virginia ... bearing date the 13 Sept. 1740 ... to acknowledge ... 100 acres of Land ... part of 400 Acres which the afsd Sarah BATES purchased from Gabriel NEWBY late of Perquimans County decd. Atty to Mary DANSON of the City of London Widow &c. bearing date the 25 Dec. 1732 being part of the Manor Lands out of a Patent bearing date the 25 Feb. 1696 Containing 3,650 acres ... (Record Torn)

North Carolina) Pasquotank County) These may certify that the afsd power of atty and Certificate was exhibited in open Court by the afsd Samuel JORDAN and was ordered to be recorded at Oct. Court 1741.

North Carolina 18 April 1741 and in the fourteenth year of the Reign of our Sovereign Lord George ... Between Truman SPENCE of the one party & Richard SAWYER of the other party ... in Consideration of the Sum of 45 pounds ... paid ... sold ... Tract of Land containing 100 acres ... on the N. E. Side of Pasquotank River and lying on the N. E. Side of White Oak Branch it being part of a greater Tract of Land formerly surveyed by Thomas COOPER and now transferred to Richard SAWYER ... by a Deed of Sale ... by the hand of Captn. Charles SAWYER ...
[B:389] ... *Signed*: Truman SPENCE. *Wit*: Bentt. MORGAN, John SAWYER. *Ack*: Oct. Court 1741. *Regt*:

14 Nov. 1741.

13 March 1739 ... John SIMPSON of the Precinct of Chowan in the Province of North Carolina Planter for and in Consideration of the Sum of 18 pounds 2 Shillings and 6 pence Specie ... paid by William SIMPSON of the Precinct of Pasquotank in the Province afsd. Planter ... sold ...
[B:390] ... Tract of Land containing 90 acres ... on the S. W. Side of Wading Branch Beginning at John HARRIS'S Corner Tree ... Bee Tree Branch ... *Signed*: John SIMPSON. *Wit*: Robert LOWRY Junr., John DAVIS. *Ack*: Oct. Court 1741. *Regt*: 14 Nov. 1741.

[B:391] North Carolina) Pasquotank County) Joseph PRITCHARD of the Province and County afsd ... in Consideration of the natural affection & Brotherly Love which I have and bear unto my well beloved Brother Benjamin PRITCHARD of the County and Province afsd. ... give ... plantation ... on the S. W. side of Pasquotank River ... William COLLINS Corner ... Danl. AKHURST Corner ... Willn. JONES Corner ... 150 acres of Land ... patent bearing date 1 March 1722 ... 16 Feb. 1741. *Signed*: Joseph PRITCHARD. *Wit*: Josiah CARTWRIGHT, Abel DRESSER. *Proved*: Oct. Court 1741 by the Oath of Abel DRESSER. *Regt*: 11 Nov. 1741.

[B:392] North Carolina Charles TAYLOR of the County of Albemarle & County of Pasquotank Planter ... for the valuable Consideration of the Sum of 40 shillings ... paid by Zachariah JACKSON of the Province of North Carolina & County of Albemarle & Precinct of Pasquotank Planter ... sold ... a certain parcel of Swamp or the one Moiety or half part of a patent Containing 22 acres of Swamp granted by patent to David BALEY bearing date the 5 April 1722 and purchased ... by the afsd Charles TAYLOR it being part of the Swamp that lies between David BALEY and me the afsd. Zachariah JACKSON ... 14 July 1737. *Signed*: Charles TAYLOR T Signum. *Wit*: Joseph ROBINSON, Benjamin NEWBY BN his mark. *Ack*: Oct. Court 1741. *Regt*: 14 Nov. 1741.

[B:393] Joshua PERISHO of the County of Pasquotank in the Province of North Carolina Planter for and in Consideration of the Sum of 50 pounds of good and lawful Money of the Province afsd. ... paid by

Robert CARTWRIGHT in the County and Province afsd. Planter ... sold ... Tract of land ... 40 acres ... on Pasquotank River ... above the Great Swamp on the head of the said River part of it on the middle Swamp & the rest of it Owen REESES Swamp ... Betty PERISHO the wife of me the said Joshua PERISHO ... surrenders all her Right of Dowry ... 12 Oct. in the fifteenth year of the Reign of our Sovereign Lord King George the Second ... 1741. *Signed*: Joshua PARISHO, Eliza. PARISHO. *Wit*: Richard PRITCHARD, William SAWYER. *Ack*: Oct. Court 1741. *Regt*: 14 Oct. 1741.

[B:394] North Carolina) Bath County) Carteret Precinct) John JONES of Pasquotank Precinct in the County of Albemarle in the Province afsd, Planter do assign all my Right ... as within mentioned Instrument unto James BELL of Carteret Precinct in the County and Province afsd. ... 7 Sept. 1738. *Signed*: John JONES. *Wit*: William HAMBLIN, William BROTHERS, David LEWIS. *Ack*: Oct. Court 1741 assignment of a Lease from John JONES to James BELL was acknowledged by the said JONES to William DAVIS. *Regt*: 8ber the 17th 1741.

North Carolina) Carteret Precinct) John JONES of Pasquotank Precinct in the County of Albemarle in the Province afsd, Planter do assign all my Right ... of the within mentioned Instrument unto James BELL of Carteret Precinct in the County of Bath and Province afsd. ... 7 Sept. 1738. *Signed*: John JONES. *Wit*: Wm. HAMBLIN, W. BROTHERS, David LEWIS. Memorandum The Lease & Release of the above assignment is recorded in this Book in folio 208, 209, 210, 211. *Ack*: Oct. Court 1741 assignment of a Release is as acknowledged by John JONES to William DAVIS. *Regt*: 17 Oct. 1741.

North Carolina John, Phineus, Zachariah & Barnaby NIXON of the County of Perquimans Planters for and in Consideration of of 100 pounds in hand by Samuel JACKSON the younger of the County of Pasquotank Planter ... sold ... a part of a Tract of Land containing 74 acres it being a Conveyance out of a Patent bearing date 1740 ... on the N. E. Side of Little River up Herring Creek Swamp ...
[B:395] ... 12 Oct. 1741. *Signed*: John NIXON, Phineus NIXON, Zachariah NIXON, Barnaby NIXON. *Wit*:

Michael MURPHY, Dorothy NIXON. *Ack*: Oct. Court 1741. *Regt*: 17 Oct. 1741.

Jacob ALBERTSON in the County of Pasquotank in No. Carolina Planter for and in Consideration of the Sum of 50 pounds in good and lawful Money of the Province afsd ... paid by Thomas SAWYER in the County & Province afsd Planter ... sold ... Tract of Land called Opossum Quarter ... S. W. Side of Pasquotank ... 119 acres ... at the River Swamp ... on Edward WHORTON'S Line ... Beach Neck Branch ... [B:396] ... James CLERK and Mary CLERK Brother and Sister to the said Jacob ALBERTSON ... surrender all their right ... 13 April in the fourteenth year of the Reign of our Sovereign Lord King George ... 1741. *Signed*: Jacob ALBERTSON, James CLERK, Mary M CLERK her mark. *Wit*: Joab CARTWRIGHT, William STAFFORD. *Ack*: Oct. Court 1741. *Regt*: 8ber the 17th 1741.

John KNIGHT of the Precinct of Pasquotank in the County of Albemarle Tailor for and in Consideration of love and good will and affection that I have and do bear towards my loving friend James SMITH of the same Precinct and County afsd. Planter have given ... all ... my lands and Tenements, Goods and Chattles now being in my present dwelling House in the precinct afsd. and my Lands known by the name of Horse Stable Neck lying on the S. W. Side of the deceased John HOBBS Manor plantation ... 26 Aug. in the Tenth year of the Reign of our Sovereign Lord King George ... 1736. *Signed*: John KNIGHT. *Wit*: Robert EDNEY, Jeremiah MURDEN, Saml. SMITH. *Ack*: Oct. Court 1741 the afsd. Deed
[B:397] of Gift was proved in open Court by the Oath of Robert EDNEY. *Regt*: 8ber the 17th 1741.

Thomas WINSLOW Junr. of the County of Perquimans in the Province of Carolina for and in Consideration of the Sum of 300 pounds of Current Money of the said Province ... paid by James MORGAN Esqr. of the County and Province afsd. ... sold ... Tract of Land ... on the fork Swamp of Little River containing ... 200 acres ... on the N. E. Side of Little River ... George LOWS Corner Tree ... 29 Sept. 1741 And in the fourteenth year of the Reign of our Sovereign Lord George the Second ... *Signed*: Thomas WINSLOW. *Wit*: Richard CHEASTON, John HENBE IH his mark. *Ack*:

Oct. Court 1741. *Regt*: 17 Oct. 1741.

[B:398] North Carolina. Pasquotank. Zachariah JACKSON for and in Consideration of 16 pounds in Specie ... paid by Samuel JACKSON of the place afsd. ... sold ... parcel of land containing 55 acres and a half ... in the middle of the Swamp formerly known by the name of TAYLORS Swamp ... Gum Branch ... [B:399] this 6 Oct. 1741. *Signed*: Zachariah JACKSON. *Wit*: Dorothy NIXON, Joseph ROBINSON. *Ack*: Oct. Court 1741. *Regt*: 3 Dec. 1741.

John CARTWRIGHT of the County personally appeared ... that about 20 years ago, he saw and read a patent for a piece or Tract of Land lying on the North Side of Pasquotank and ... joining to a plantation now possessed to Thomas MERRIDAY of this County, which said patent was in the name of Isaac GILFORD late of this County, decd. and Grandfather to Joseph GILFORD who now possesses said piece of Land and Plantation bounding upon the afsd. plantation where the said Thomas MERRIDAY now lives ... the said patent was very much shattered and a great many Holes in it he believed caused by the worms ... the afsd plantation now in possession of the afsd. Joseph GILFORD has been peaceably possessed by the GILFORDS ever since he could remember first by the Uncle and then by the Father of the afsd. Joseph GILFORD and further this Deponent saith that he is about 50 years of age ... 9 April 1741. *Signed*: James GEORGE. [sic] *Ack*: Oct. Court 1741 the afsd. Instrument of Writing was exhibited in open Court by the said Joseph GILFORD & was ordered to be Registered. *Regt*: 3 Dec. 1741.

North Carolina 2 March 1740 and in the 13th year of the Reign of our Sovereign Lord George the Second ... Between John SCARBOROUGH of the one party & Benjamin PHILLIPS of the other party ... in Consideration of the Sum of 75 pounds lawful Money ... paid ... sold ... Tract of Land containing 100 acres ... on the N. E. Side of Pasquotank River commonly called ... School House Neck being between Hickory Neck and Robert SAWYERS Senr. ... [B:400] ... *Signed*: John J SCARBOROUGH his mark. *Wit*: Joseph J SAWYER his mark, John SAWYER. *Proved*: Oct. Court 1741 by the Oath of Joseph SAWYER. *Regt*: 3 Dec. 1741.

North Carolina: 24 April 1741 Between John SOLLEY in the Province afsd. Gentn. and Sarah his present wife formerly the wife of Thomas WYAT and before that the wife of Edward POPE of the one part and James GEORGE & David GEORGE of the Province afsd. Merchants of the other part ... in Consideration of the Sum of 400 pounds Current Money ... sold ... Tract of Land ... on Newbegun Creek and Between the said James GEORGE & David GEORGE their Land & John HENLY ... 210 acres ... Tract of
[B:401] Land was granted by Sir William BERKLY Governor of Virginia unto one JENNINGS as is generally believed and afterwards did belong unto one William BATTLE of Nansemond County as by a Judgment in favour of the said William BATTLE ... sold to Richard POPE late of Pasquotank Planter and by the said Edward POPE given by his last will and Testament Given to the afsd. Sarah the present wife of the said John SOLLEY ... *Signed*: John SOLLEY, Sarah SOLLEY. *Wit*: Jona HIBBS, Edward SCOOT. *Ack*: Jan. Court 1741/2 and the said Sarah SOLLEY was first privately examined concerning her Dowry. *Regt*: 24 Feb. 1741.

North Carolina 12 Jan. 1741/2 between John JONES of the County of Pasquotank & Province afsd. Planter of the one part & William DAVIS of the same County & Province of the other part ... in Consideration of the valuable Sum of 400 pounds Current Money of the Province of North Carolina ... sold ...
[B:402] ... Tract of Land out of a Patent bearing date the 20th day of May 1741 contg ... 196 acres DAVIS'S Line ... *Signed*: John JONES. *Wit*: Hezekiah LINTON, William JONES. *Ack*: Jan. Court 1741/2. *Regt*: 29 Mar. 1742.

Timothy MEADS of the County of Pasquotank & Province of North Carolina Planter for and in Consideration of the Sum of 64 pounds lawful Money of this Province to me in hand by Clement HALL of the County of Perquimans and Province afsd. ... sold ... Tract of Land ...
[B:403] ... at the Mouth of Atsmas? Creek ... to Bartholomew EVANS'S Line ... Tho. SAWYER ... 50 acres ... 12 Jan. 1741/2. *Signed*: Timothy MEADS. *Wit*: William DAVIS, Benja. MEADS. *Ack*: Jan. Court 1741/2. *Regt*: 29 Mar. 1742.

12 Jan. 1741/2 and in the fifteenth year of the Reign of our Sovn Lord George ... between Thomas SAWYER and Cornelius JONES of Pasquotank County in North Carolina Planters of the one part & Thomas GRAY of the same place of the other part ... in Consideration of the Sum of 25 pounds Virginia Currency ... paid ... sold ...
[B:404] ... Plantation ... being on the N. E. Side of Pasquotank River ... 80 acres ... John SAWYERS Land & Capt. Charles SAWYER'S Land ... Horse Road ... Thomas SAWYER'S Land ... John HUMPHRIES Land ... Hezekiah BUTTERWORTHS Corner Tree ... *Signed*: Thomas SAWYER, Cornelius X JONES his mark. *Wit*: Berd. BANGER, Wm. W SAWYER his mark. *Ack*: Jan. Court 1741.
[B:405] *Regt*: 29 Mar. 1742.

North Carolina) Pasquotank County) John DURANT King of the Yeopin Indians and of the County and Province afsd. by and with the Consent of the Governor and Council and the Indian Nation for and in Consideration of the Sum of 40 pounds Virginia Money paid ... by Captn. John CARON of the County of Currituck & Province afsd. ... sold ... parcel of land containing 200 Acres ... being part of a patent bearing date the 2 Oct. 1704 [blank] on North River the S. W. Side ... Capt. RELFE'S Line ... Jacob Swamp ... River Swamp ...
[B:406] 3 Dec. 1741. *Signed*: John D DURANT his mark. *Wit*: Cornelius RELF, Jacob CARON, Thomas CAPRON? *Proved*: Jan. Court 1741/2 by the oaths of Cornelius RELFE and Jacob CARON. *Regt*: 29 Mar. 1742.

North Carolina) Currituck County) John DURANT King of the Yeopin Indians do assign this Patent and Land contained therein unto Captn. John CARON ... 3 Dec. 1741. *Signed*: John D DURANT his mark. *Wit*: Cornelius RELF, Thomas CAPRON?, Jacob CARON. *Proved*: Jan. Court 1741/2 by the oaths of Cornelius RELFE and Jacob CAROON. *Regt*: 29 Mar. 1742.

Philip TORKSEY of the County of Pasquotank in the Province of North Carolina ... in Consideration of the natural affection & Brotherly Love which I have ... unto my well beloved Sister Sarah TORKSEY ... given ... a piece of land beginning at YEOKERS? Gut

... if my sd Sister should die without any Issue then to return to him the sd Philip TORKSEY the Giver, which sd. Land belongeth to Robert TORKSEY decd ... 12 Jan. 1741. *Signed*: Philip TORKSEY. *Wit*: John SOLLEY, Berd. BANGER. *Ack*: Jan. Court 1741/2. *Regt*: 29 Mar. 1742.

[B:407] Thomas LEWIS in the County of Pasquotank in the Province of North Carolina planter for and in Consideration of the Sum of 100 pounds in good and lawful Money of the Province ... paid by Henry NICKELS of the County & Province afsd. Planter ... sold ... Tract of Land ... on the South Side of Pasquotank River ... contg ... 60 acres ... called by the name of the White Oak Neck ... long Branch ... 24 Oct. in the 15th year of the Reign of our Sovereign Lord King George the Second ... 1741/2. *Signed*: Thomas L LEWIS his mark. *Wit*: Wm ABERCROMBIE, James SCARF I Signum. *Ack*: Jan. Court 1741/2. *Regt*: 29 Jan. 1742.

[B:408] North Carolina) Pasquotank County) 15 May 1741 & in the 14th year of the Reign of our Sovereign Lord George ... Between Bennitt MORGAN of the one party & Evan LURRY of the other party ... in Consideration of the Sum of 15 pounds ... sold ... Tract of Land Contg 30 acres ... on the N. E. Side of Pasquotank River and lying on the N. E. Side of SAWYER'S Creek it being part of a Tract of Land which Robert MORGAN willed to his Son Bennett MORGAN ... patent bearing date the [blank] 1668 ... Mouth of broad Neck Branch ... School House Branch ... Creek Swamp ... *Signed*: Bett. MORGAN. *Wit*: Richard SAWYER, John BRAY. *Ack*: Jany Court 1741/2. *Regt*: 29 Mar. 1742.

[B:409] Thomas SAWYER do assign unto Jacob ALBERTSON the within mentioned Deed ... 29 Sept. 1740. *Signed*: Thomas SAWYER. *Wit*: Wm. ABERCROMBIE, John DAVIS. *Ack*: Jan. Court 1741/2. *Regt*: 29 Mar. 1742.

Augustine WRIGHT of Pasquotank Precinct in North Carolina ... for the natural Love and affection which I have unto my Brother John DOE [sic] give unto the said John WRIGHT 120 acres of land ... now in his possession joining on the Lands of John TORKSEYS Line from the Great Pocoson at the lower

End of my land ... the which Land fell to me by my father's Death being Heir at Law ... 11 July 1732 and in the 5th year of the Reign of our Sovn Lord George the Second ... *Signed*: Augustine O WRIGHT his mark. *Wit*: Stephen DELEAR, William JOHNS. *Ack*: July Court 1732. *Regt*: 29 Mar. 1742.

4 March & in the 15th year of the Reign of our Sovn Lord George the Second ... Between Thomas HALL living in the County of Pasquotank & in North Carolina and William OVERTON of the other part in the County afsd. ... in Consideration of the valuable Sum of 10 pounds Sterling Money of Great Britain ... paid by the sd. William OVERTON ... sold ... Tract of land contg 125 acres ...
[B:410] ... 8 March 1741/2. *Signed*: Thomas T HALL his mark. *Wit*: Joseph MAKEFARSON, Moses X MACKEFARSON. *Ack*: April Court 1742. *Regt*: 17 April 1742.

North Carolina 13 April 1742 Between Richd. COLLINS of the County of Pasquotank and in the Province afsd. of the one part & Saml. WILLIAMS of the other part ... in Consideration of the valuable Sum of 56 pounds Current Money of the Said Province ... paid ... sold ... Tract of Land ... known by the name of forty pound Neck on Arenuse Creek Containing ... 120 acres ... Beginning at John [blank] Line and butted on the Mill dam ...
[B:411] ... *Signed*: Richard R COLLINS his mark. *Wit*: Thos. CALLOWAY, Griffith JONES. *Ack*: April Court 1742. *Regt*: 17 April 1742.

North Carolina) Pasquotank County) William STAFFORD and Elinor my wife both of North Carolina and County afsd. Planter and Spinster for & in Consideration of the Sum of 100 pounds ... paid by Leml. COOK of the County and Province afsd. practitioner of Physick ... sold ... Tract of Land ... No. Side of Nobs Crook Creek ... 180 Acres ... William BRYANS Land and to the Land of Thomas SAWYER ... William WARD ... George [blank] ... Land of Thomas JENNINGS ...
[B:412] ... 14 April in the fourteenth year of the Reign of our Sovn Lord George the Second ... 1742. *Signed*: William STAFFORD, Elinor E STAFFORD her mark. *Wit*: John JONES, Tho. TAYLOR. *Ack*: April Court 1742. *Regt*: 19 April 1742.

North Carolina. Joseph KEATON Planter & Margaret my Wife of Pasquotank County in the Province afsd ... in Consideration of 150 pounds lawful Money of this Province ... paid by Stephen SCOTT of the County afsd planter ... quit claim ... all such Right ... have of
[B:413] in and to all or any part or parcel of that Land that the said Joseph KEATON bought of the said Stephen SCOTT binding upon Zachariah KEATON'S Land, it being the remainder part of that Land that the said SCOTT bought of Thomas JESOP lying and being in Pasquotank afsd and containing by Estimation 60 acres ... 14th day of April 1742. *Signed*: Joseph KEATON, Margt. X KEATON her mark. *Wit*: David GEORGE, Zachariah JONES, Jno. STEVENSON. *Ack*: April Court 1742. *Regt*: 20 April.

North Carolina Jeremiah WILCOX and Elisabeth my wife ... in Consideration of 300 pounds current Money of this Province in hand paid ... made over all our Right ... unto the within mentioned Deed & Bond unto Patrick KEATON ... 15th day of March 1741/2. *Signed*: Jeremiah J WILCOX his mark, Elisabeth X WILCOX her mark. *Wit*: Stephen SCOTT, Joseph SCOTT, Joseph KEATON. *Ack*: April Court 1742. *Regt*: 20 Apr. 1742. Memorandum The Deed of the within assignmt is Registd. in Book B folio 469.

[B:414] North Carolina) Pasquotank County) Solomon POOL & Sarah POOL my wife of the County and Province abovesaid planter ... Love and Good Will we have to my Brother John POOL of the County and Province abovesaid Planter, have given ... all that plantation ... on the S. Side near the Mouth of Great Flatty Creek known by the name of William WAMAN'S decd. plantation ... 100 acres ... 18 April 1742. *Signed*: Solomon POOL, Sarah POOL. *Wit*: Patrick POOL, Robert LOWRY Junr. *Ack*: April Court 1742. *Regt*: 21 April 1742.

[B:415] North Carolina. Patrick KEATON of the County of Pasquotank in the Province afsd ... Planter for & in Consideration of the valuable Sum of 60 pounds Current Bills of the Province ... paid by Joseph KEATON of the same County and Province ... sold ... Tract of Land Containing by Estimation 60 acres ... it being part of a larger parcel of Lands which he the said Patrick KEATON purchased from

Jeremiah WILCOX of the same County and Province ... Margaret's Swamp ... 12 April 1742. *Signed*: Patrick KEATON. *Wit*: Tho: TAYLOR, Charles WEST. *Ack*: April Court 1742. *Regt*: 20 April 1742.

12 April 1742 and in the year of the Reign of our Sovn Lord George ... Between Alexander LEFTYEAR and his wife Abigail LEFTYEAR of [blank] County in North Carolina Planters of the one part and Jarvis JONES of Norfolk in Virginia on the other part ... in Consideration of the Sum of 40 pounds Sterling Money of Great Britain ... paid ...
[B:416] ... sold ... Tract of Land ... the fork of Pasquotank River ... called the Quarter Land which said Tract of Land was given by Will to the said Abigail LEFTYEAR and her Sister Ann JONES by their Father Edwd. JONES decd. ... 200 and a half acres of Land ... Bear Spring ... Juniper Swamp ... Slate Swamp ... Mile Swamp ... part of a larger Tract of Land which said Land fell to the said Abigail LEFTYEAR by the Death of her Father Edward JONES ...
[B:417] ... *Signed*: Alexr. LEFTEAR, Abigail X LEFTEAR her mark. *Wit*: Thos. L LEWIS his mark, Persilla P SPENCE her mark, John X MARTIN his mark. *Ack*: April Court 1742 by Abigail LEFTEAR. *Proved*: by the Oath of Thos. LEWIS. *Regt*: 21 April 1742.

This Indenture of Lease ... 18 March 1742 and in the fourteenth year of the Reign of our Sovereign Lord George ... Between Benjamin SAWYER and Israel LAMBERT of the County of Pasquotank of the one part & Joseph HUMPHRIES of the same place and Province afsd. of the other party ... for the valuable Consideration of 25 pounds Current Money ... paid down ... sold ... Tract of Land containing ... 130 acres ... on the N. E. Side of Pasquotank River commonly called ... High Ground being part of a patent granted to Henry & Robert SAWYER for 674 acres which said Patent bearing date 1714 ... SAWYER'S Creek ...
[B:418] ... *Signed*: Benjamin SAWYER, Israel LAMBERT. *Wit*: William WILLIAMS Junr., John COOK. *Proved*: April Court 1742 by the Oaths of William WILLIAMS Junr & John COOK. *Regt*: 22 April 1742.

William HIXON of the County of Pasquotank & Province of North Carolina ... Whereas Henry Duke of BEAUFORT

Palatine ... did by Patent bearing date 4 Sept. 1714 give and grant unto Stephen SCOTT a Tract of Land containing 230 acres ... Thomas HICKS Corner Tree in Stephen SCOTTS Line ... James GADS Line ... BROWNS? & SCOTTS Line ... was formerly surveyed for William REED? and by him sold ... to Joseph JORDAN ... sold to Patrick QUEADLY ... sold to Stephen SCOTT ... given by will to his Son Stephen SCOTT ... sold to Ephraim OVERMAN and at the decease of the said Ephraim OVERMAN it legally descended to his Son ... Joseph OVERMAN ... Sold unto his Brother Ephraim OVERMAN ... Sold to William HIXON ... in Consideration of the Sum of 200 pounds lawful Money of North Carolina ... paid by Clement HALL of the County of Perquimans and Province afsd. ... sold ... [B:419] ... all that the abovementioned Tract of Land containing 230 acres ... 6 Feb. 1741/2. *Signed*: William HIXON. *Wit*: Thos. WOOLEY, Elisa E WOODLEY Signum. These may certify ... that I Elisabeth HIXON wife of the abovesaid William HIXON do freely ... resign all my Right ... of Dower ... *Signed*: Eliza. E HIXON her mark. *Ack*: April Court 1742. *Regt*: 22 April 1742.

[B:420] North Carolina) Pasquotank County) Caleb KOEN and Miriam his wife of the Province and County afsd for and in Consideration of the Sum of 30 Pounds ... paid by Amos TRUEBLOOD ... sold ... Tract of Land Contg ... 30 acres ... on the S. W. Side of Pasquotank River ... at the Mouth of Tray Tree Branch ... 23 Jan. 1741/2. *Signed*: Caleb COEN, Meriam COEN. *Wit*: [blank] *Ack*: July Court 1742. *Regt*: 12 Aug. 1742.

[B:421] North Carolina) Pasquotank County) Samuel JACKSON the younger ... in Consideration of 250 pounds lawful Money of North Carolina ... paid by John MORGAN Senr of the County of Perquimans ... sold ... Tract of Land containing ... 100 acres ... on the N. E. Side of Little River ... binding on the Land that was formerly Nathanl. HALLSONS ... land that Zachariah JACKSON sold lately to Thomas PARKER ... 25 Feby 1741/2. *Signed*: Samuel JACKSON the Younger. *Wit*: Jos. ROBINSON, Mary ROBINSON, Jos. NEWBY. *Ack*: July Court 1742. *Regt*: 16 Aug. 1742.

[B:422] 13 Feb. in the 14th year of the Reign of our Sovn Lord George ... 1741/2 between

John O DANIEL of Albemarle County in the Precinct of Pasquotank of the one party & Thomas FENTON of the said County & Precinct of the other party ... for the valuable Consideration of 30 pounds in Specie ... paid ... sold ... plantation whereon I now live contg 40 acres ... which Tract is part of a Tract of Land which was surveyed for Patrick O DANIEL ... on the North Side of Pasquotank River ... 20 Feby 1741/2. *Signed*: John O O DANL his mark. *Wit*: Richard SAWYER, Jos MORGAN, Dennis SAWYER. *Ack*: July Court 1742. *Regt*: 16 Aug. 1742.

[B:423] North Carolina) Pasquotank County) Edward SCOTT of the County and place afsd. ... in Consideration of 55 pounds Current Money of this province by Zachariah JACKSON of the County and place afsd. ... sold ... Tract of Land containing ... 50 Acres ... on the South Side of Pasquotank River ... Turkey Ridge ... 13 July 1752. *Signed*: Edward SCOTT. *Wit*: Samuel JACKSON, Wm. TURNER. *Ack*: July Court 1742. *Regt*: 12 Aug. 1742.

[B:424] North Carolina. Patrick KEETON of Pasquotank County in the Province afsd planter for and in Consideration of the valuable Sum of 80 pounds Currt. Bills of North Carolina to me in hand paid by Zachariah KEETON Junr of the Same County ... sold ... all my Right ... of the afsd. bargained Premises ... 13 July 1742. Signed: Patrick KEETON. Wit: Abel DRESSER, S. PLOMER. Ack: July Court 1742. Regt: 16 August 1742.

North Carolina: 13 July 1742 Between John MORGAN of the County of Perquimans in the Province of North Carolina Executor of the last will & Testament of John MARTIN of the County of Pasquotank & Province afsd. decd. of the one part and Thomas HUNTER Esqr. of Pasquotank County afsd. in the Province afsd. of the other part ... sold at public Vendue for and in Consideration of the valuable Sum of 305 pounds Currt. Bills of the sd. Province ... Tract of land ... S. W. Side of Pasquotank River in the County afsd. Contg ... 200 acres ... which sd. Land formerly belonged to Thomas KEEL ... & descended to his Son Robert KEEL and by the sd. Robert KEEL & Tamer his Wife ... Sold to Danl. PHILLIPS ... sold to the afsd. John MARTIN decd. ...
[B:425] ... *Signed*: John M MORGAN his mark. *Wit*:

S. PLOMER, T. PENDLETON. *Ack*: July Court 1742. *Regt*: 12 Aug. 1742.

North Carolina) Pasquotank County) John MORGAN Executor of the last will & Testament of John MARTIN decd. ... at public vendue, sold and delivered quiet possession, all of the within mentioned Premises unto Thomas HUNTER Esqr. ... 16 April 1742. *Signed*: John M MORGAN his mark. *Wit*: Thos. PENDLETON, Jos. JORDAN, William DAVIS. *Ack*: July Court 1742. *Regt*: 12 Aug. 1742.

[B:426] North Carolina) Pasquotank County) John MORGAN Exr. of the last will & Testament of John MARTIN decd. ... made over all Right ... of the within Premises unto Thomas HUNTER Esqr. ... 16 April 1742. *Signed*: John M MORGAN his mark. *Wit*: Thos. PENDLETON, Jos. JORDAN, William DAVIS. *Ack*: July Court 1742. *Regt*: 12 Aug. 1742.

North Carolina. Oliver SALTER of the County of Pasquotank in the Province afsd. ... in Consideration of the Sum of 1,200 pounds Currt Money of the said Province ... paid by Mr. Joseph READ of the same Province ... sold ... plantation ... on the N. E. Side of Little River containing ... 375 acres ... land that was James HUNTERS Now the land of Thomas MEADS Planter ... FISHERS Corner tree now the Corner Tree of Thomas PLATO decd. ... excepted 50 acres before sold out of the said Tract to John PEGGS at the South Corner of the sd. Land ... [B:427] ... 12 Oct. 1742. *Signed*: Oliver SALTER. *Wit*: William ABERCROMBIE, William SHERGOLD, Tho: TAYLOR. *Ack*: Oct. Court 1742. *Regt*: 15 Nov. 1742.

12 Oct. in the 16th year of the Reign of our Sovereign Lord George ... 1742 Between William ROSS of Pasquotank County in North Carolina Planter of the one part & Jarvis JONES of the County of Norfolk in Virginia Merchant of the other part ... in Consideration of 30 pounds Proclamation Money ... sell ... 74 acres of Land ... known by the name of Cornwall being part of a patent granted to William NORRIS and transferred to Edwd. JONES and willed to the said William ROSS ... the Mile Swamp ... the Mile Pocoson ... 12 Oct. 1742. *Signed*: William W ROSS his mark. *Wit*: J. PENDLETON, Richard SAWYER,

Tho: TAYLOR. *Ack*: Oct. Court 1742. *Regt*: 15 Nov. 1742.

[B:428] 12 Oct. in the 16th year of the Reign of our Sovereign Lord George the Second ... 1742 Between Alexander SPENCE and his wife Persilla of Pasquotank County of the one part & Jarvis JONES of Norfolk County in Virginia Merchant of the other part ... in Consideration of the Sum of 40 pounds Virginia Currency ... sold ... parcel of Land contg ... 66 Acres and a half ... by the Mile Swamp ... by the flat Swamp ... to the Mouth of the Gum Branch ... *Signed*: Alexander SPENCE, Persilla P SPENCE her mark. *Wit*: Tho: TAYLOR, J. PENDLETON, George W WARD his mark. *Ack*: Oct. Court 1742. *Regt*: 15 Nov. 1742.

[B:429] 12 Oct. in the 16th year of the Reign of our Lord George ... 1742 Between Alexander SPENCE and Persilla his wife of Pasquotank in North Carolina Planter of the one part & Jarvis JONES in Norfolk County in Virginia Merchant of the other part ... for the Consideration of the 20 pounds proclamation Money ... sold ... 33 Acres of Land ... known by the name of Cornwall ... being part of a Patent granted to William NORRIS and transferred to William JONES & willed to Persilla JONES his Daughter ... at the Mile Swamp ... on the Great Swamp and flat Swamp ... 12 Oct. 1742. *Signed*: Alexr. SPENCE, Persilla P SPENCE her mark. *Wit*: Tho: TAYLOR, J. PENDLETON, George W WARD his mark. *Ack*: Oct. Court 1742. *Regt*: 15 Nov. 1742.

[B:430] North Carolina 12 Jan. 1741/2 between James WARD of the County of Pasquotank & Province afsd. of the one part and Joshua PERISHO of the same County and Province of the other part ... in Consideration of the Sum of 60 Pounds in good pay /that is to say/ in Pork & Coin ... sold ... parcel of Land being part of a greater parcel Containing 120 Acres which James WARD purchased from James PRITCHARD & Samuel PRITCHARD ... which sd. parcel or half part containing 60 ... John IVEY Corner Tree ... to Turkey Branch ... *Signed*: James W WARD his mark. *Wit*: Rebecca R SMITH her mark, Wm. SAFFORD Jurat. *Proved*: Oct. Court 1742 by the Oath of William STAFFORD. *Regt*: 15 Nov. 1742.

[B:431] North Carolina) Pasquotank) Capt. John LURRY of Currituck & Province afsd. for and in Consideration of 2,000 weight of fresh pork ... paid by William GREGORY of the Precinct of Pasquotank and Province afsd. ... sold ... parcel of Land contg 20 acres ... on the N. E. Side of Pasquotank River in the fork of Arenuse Creek & on the North Side of the main Road ... on COOPERS Line ... to be an equal Square ... 13 July 1742. *Signed*: John LURRY. *Wit*: William HIXON, Robert MORGAN. *Proved*: Oct. Court 1742 by the oath of William. *Regt*: 15 Nov. 1742.

[B:432] North Carolina 4 Aug. 1742 and in the 15th year of the Reign of our Sovereign Lord George the Second ... between William WARD of Pasquotank County Planter of the one part and Thomas SHARBO of Perquimans County in said Province Planter of the other part ... in Consideration of Sum of 225 pounds Currt Money ... sold ... Tract of Land ... on the S. W. Side of Pasquotank River containing ... 50 acres ... South Side of Beach Neck Branch & binding on Edwd. WHARTONS Line ... to Henry NICHOLS Line ... being the same Land I formerly purchased of John and Jacob ALBERTSON and called and known by the name of Bushy? Neck joining on Opossum Quarter ...
[B:433] ... *Signed*: William W WARD his mark. *Wit*: Jos. HENBY? Junr., Saml. PARKER?. *Ack*: Oct. Court 1742. *Regt*: 16 Nov. 1742.

3 March in the 14th year of the Reign of our Sovereign Lord George ... 1741/2 between Michael MCDANIEL of Albemarle County in the Precinct of Pasquotank of the one part & John SAWYER Junr of the sd. County & Precinct of the other part ... in Consideration of 5 pounds in Specie ... sell ... parcel of Land containing 10 acres ... part of a Tract of Land which was surveyed and patented for James MCDANIEL & the sd patent contg 430 acres ... bearing date the 1 May 1719 ... John SAWYER Junr Corner Tree ... John SCOOTS Line ...
[B:434] ... 27 March 1742. *Signed*: Michael X MCDANIEL his mark. *Wit*: Richard SAWYER Jurat, Robert SPENCE, Jacob X HUMPHREYS his mark. *Proved*: Oct. Court 1742 by the Oath of Richd. SAWYER. *Regt*: 16 Nov. 1742.

8 May 1739 ... John SWINDALL of the Precinct of Pasquotank in the Province of North Carolina Planter

for and in Consideration of the Sum of 40 pounds Currt Money of North Carolina ... paid by Thomas HARRIS of the same precinct ... Sold ... Tract of Land containing 50 acres ... in the fork of Nobbs Crook Creek ... at the Main Swamp & binding on Joab NICHOLS Line to Trickelows? Branch ... the School Land commonly known by the name of Turkey Regg ...
[B:435] ... *Signed*: John SWINDALL. *Wit*: Jos: SMITH, James I CLARK his mark. *Proved*: Oct. Court 1742 by the Oath of James CLARK. *Regt*: 16 Nov. 1742.

North Carolina 13 July 1742 Between Henry PALIN & Thomas PALIN both of Pasquotank County in the Province afsd. Planters and Sarah PALIN Widow and Relict of John PALIN lately decd. of the said County and Province of the one part & John JENNINGS of the County and Province afsd. of the other part ... in Consideration of the Sum of 200 pounds currt Bills ... sold ... parcel of Land ... being highest up the Branches of Little Flatty Creek adjoining to the Lands of David GEORGE & the Lands of the sd. John JENNINGS Containing ... 225 acres out of a larger quantity belonging to John PALIN Esqr decd. and given by him by his last will and Testament to the afsd. Henry PALIN and Thomas PALIN and by them bargained & sold to the afsd. Sarah PALIN & now to John JENNINGS ...
[B:436] ... *Signed*: Henry PALIN, Thomas PALIN, Sarah PALIN. *Wit*: Henry WENSLEY, Miriam PALIN. *Ack*: Oct. Court 1742 ... Thomas PALIN came into Court & acknowledged the afsd. Deed to John JENNINGS, then appeared Henry WINSLOW [sic] and made Oath he saw Henry PALIN & Sarah PALIN sign ... *Regt*: 16 Nov. 1742.

North Carolina) Pasquotank) Zachariah JACKSON & Saml. JACKSON the younger for and in Consideration of the Sum of 140 pounds lawful Money of North Carolina to us in hand paid by Thomas PARKER Shipwright of the County & place afsd. ... Sold ... Tract of Land containing 100 acres ... John MORGANS Land that he lately bought of the abovesaid Saml. JACKSON ... George LOWS Land that he gave by his will to his son Edwd. LOW ...
[B:437] ... 11 Oct. 1742. *Signed*: Zachariah JACKSON, Samuel JACKSON. *Wit*: Jona. REDING, Saml. OVERMAN. *Ack*: Oct. Court 1742. *Regt*: 16 Nov. 1742.

28 May 1742 and in the 15th year of the Reign of our Sovereign Lord George ... between Richard FOTHERGALE of the County of Pasquotank in the Province of North Carolina Blacksmith of the one part & John JONES of the same County Pltr. on the other part ... in Consideration of the valuable Sum of 70 pounds in Specie ... sold ... Tract of Land containing 300 acres ... on the N. E. Side of Pasquotank River ... [B:438] being part of a Tract containing 1654 acres patented by John RELFE ... near a Mile below the fork Chappel ... HARRIS'S Ridge ... David PRITCHARD'S Corner Tree ... to the Lake ... *Signed*: Richd. FOTHERGALE. *Wit*: Francis R MARTIN his mark, John O DANIEL his mark, John RICHARDSON. *Ack*: Oct. Court 1742. *Regt*: 16 Nov. 1742.

North Carolina) Pasquotank County) William WAYMOUTH of the County afsd. Planter for and in Consideration of the Sum of 60 pounds Currt Money of this Province ... paid by Ephraim BLANCHARD of the County of Chowan Planter ... sold ... Tract of Land ... [B:439] Containing according to a Patent bearing date the 9th Jany 1713/14 300 acres ... by the side of the Sound DUKENFIELDS Corner Tree ... 15 Sept. 1742. *Signed*: William W WAYMOUTH his mark. *Wit*: Joshua PARISHO, William STAFFORD. *Ack*: Oct. Court 1742. *Regt*: 16 Nov. 1742.

10 Feb. 1741 Between Dorothy SPINKS of the County of Pasquotank in the Province of North Carolina Sole Daughter and Heiress of John HUMPHRIES of the said County of Pasquotank decd. of the one part & Theophilus PUGH of the County of Nansemond in the Colony and Dominion of Virginia Merchant of the other part ... in Consideration of the Sum of 25 pounds Currt Money of Virginia ... [B:440] ... sold ... parcel of Land ... William JENNINGS Line ... containing 80 Acres ... *Signed*: Dorothy X SPINKS her mark. *Wit*: W. BRYAN, Thomas SAWYER, Caleb KOEN, Zackh. SAWYER. *Ack*: Oct. Court 1742. *Regt*: 16 Nov. 1742.

[B:441] North Carolina. 8 Jan. 1733 & in the Sixth year of the Reign of our Sovereign Lord George the Second ... Between John WINN of the Precinct of Pasquotank in the Province of North Carolina, planter of the one part & Thomas GRAY of the Precinct & Province afsd. of the other part ... in

Consideration of the Sum of 10 pounds of good and lawful Money of North Carolina ... sold ... parcel of Land contg. ... 100 acres ... on the N. E. Side of Pasquotank River and being part ... Patent from John Lord CARTERET unto John WINN afsd. and bearing date the 1 April 1723 ... Indian Line ... Capt. Abel ROSS'S Line ... *Signed*: John J WINN Signum. *Wit*: John SOLLEY, John CONNYER. *Ack*: 8 Oct. 1734 John WINN to Thomas GRAY in Bood C Fo. 71. *Regt*: 16 Nov. 1742.

[B:442] North Carolina. Thomas TWEEDY of the County of Albemarle & County of Pasquotank Planter ... for the valuable Consideration of the Sum of 6 pounds in fresh Pork by me Samuel JACKSON Junr. of the Province of North Carolina & County of Albemarle and County of Pasquotank Planter ... sold ... parcel of land ... on Saml. JACKSON Junr Line containing 50 acres ... granted by a patent to Samuel JACKSON Junr. bearing date the 27 March 1741 ... the Easternmost of the Swamp ... 27 March 1741. *Signed*: Thos. TWEEDY. *Wit*: Ann A JACKSON her mark, Wm. W JACKSON his mark. *Ack*: Oct. Court 1742. *Regt*: 17 Nov. 1742.

[B:443] North Carolina Richard MARDREN of the County of Pasquotank and Province afsd. ... in Consideration of the Sum of 20 pounds Current Money of North Carolina ... paid by Abraham MARDREN of the same County ... sold ... Tract of Land ... 100 acres ... the Creek Swamp to the Mouth of the Western Branch ... John HARRIS'S Senr Line ... Valentine ROW'S Line ... 20 Aug. 1742. *Signed*: Richd. MARDREN. *Wit*: Daniel JACKSON Senr., Abraham A RANKHORN his mark. Jas Poolman DUFFEY. *Proved*: Oct. Court 1742 by the Oaths of Jas Poolman DUFFEY & Danl. JACKSON Senr. *Regt*: 17 Nov. 1742.

North Carolina. Thomas HARRIS of the County and place afsd. ... in Consideration of 120 pounds Currt Money of this Province by Zachariah JACKSON of the County and place afsd. ... sold ...
[B:444] ... Tract of Land containing 50 acres ... South Side of Pasquotank River being in the fork of Nobs Crook Creek ... the Main Swamp ... Job NICHOLS Line to Trinkelous? Branch ... commonly known by the name of Turkey Ridge ... 13 Oct. 1742. *Signed*: Tho: T HARRIS his mark. *Wit*: Samuel JACKSON Junr.,

Thos. TWEEDY. *Ack*: Oct. Court 1742 to Zachariah JACKSON. *Regt*: 17 Nov. 1742.

[B:445] North Carolina. 12 Oct. 1742 Between William STAFFORD and Eliner his Wife of the County of Pasquotank in the Province of No. Carolina Planters of the one part and George WARD of the Same County & Province of the other part ... in Consideration of the valuable Sum of 200 pounds Currt Bills of the Province afsd. ... sold ... parcel of land ... on Nobs Crook Creek joining on Thomas JENNINGS ... containing ... 58 acres ... *Signed*: William STAFFORD, Elener E STAFFORD. *Wit*: J PENDLETON, William ABERCROMBIE, Thomas CALLAWAY. *Ack*: Oct. Court 1742. *Regt*: 17 Nov. 1742.

[B:446] North Carolina 10 Sept. 1742 Between James WARD of the County of Pasquotank & Province afsd. of the one part & William STAFFORD of the same County and Province of the other part ... in Consideration of the Sum of 60 pounds in good pay (that is to say) in pork and Coin ... sold ... a parcel of land being part of a greater parcel containing 120 acres which James WARD purchased from James PRITCHARD & Samuel PRITCHARD both of Pasquotank County which sd parcel a half part contg 60 acres ... binding upon Richd. PRITCHARD ... *Signed*: James W WARD his mark, Tamar X WARD her mark. *Wit*: J PENDLETON, George WARD W Signum. *Proved*: Oct. Court 1742 by the Oath of George WARD. *Regt*: 17 Nov. 1742.

[B:447] This Indenture of Lease made this 5 Jan. 1742 and in the fifteenth year of the Reign of our Sovereign Lord George ... Between John HUMPHRIES of the County of Pasquotank of the one party & John GRAY of the same place and province afsd. of the other party ... for the valuable Consideration of 120 pounds ... sold ... Tract of Land ... on the N. E. Side of Pasquotank River Containing 30 acres ... *Signed*: John HUMPHREYS. *Wit*: John O DANIEL his mark, Bennet MORGAN. *Ack*: Jany Court 1742. *Regt*: [blank] Feby 1742.

North Carolina. Willm. BROTHERS Junr. of Pasquotank County in the Province afsd. ... in Consideration of the valuable Sum of 250 pounds Current Bills of North Carolina ... paid by Jeremiah WILCOCKS of the County of Pasquotank in the Province afsd. ... sold

... Tract of Land containing ... 150 acres out of a patent bearing date 1 May 1668 it
[B:448] It being 300 acres granted to Henry PENDLETON late of the County afsd. decd. ... it being the Manor part of the Said 300 acres ... 20 Dec. 1742. *Signed*: William BROTHERS Junr. *Wit*: Jer CHANCY, Tho: TAYLOR. *Ack*: Jany Court 1742. *Regt*: 20 Feby 1742.

North Carolina) Pasquotank County) 18 Oct. 1742 Between John BUNDY of the one part & Samuel BUNDY of the other part ... in Consideration of the need that the afsd. Saml. BUNDY may Stand in of one acre of Land for the use of his water Mill have given ... one acre of Land joining unto the afsd. Saml BUNDY'S Mill Dam upon the East End ...
[B:449] ... *Signed*: John BUNDY. *Wit*: Thomas SYMONS, William BUNDY, Thos. NICHOLSON. *Ack*: Jany Court 1742. *Regt*: 20 Feby 1742.

North Carolina) Pasquotank County) 18 Oct. 1742 John BUNDY of the Province afsd. planter for & in Consideration of the Love and Good Will that I bear towards my loving Brother William BUNDY of the same place planter ... given ... part of a Tract of Land ... 70 Acres ... that my Father John BUNDY purchased of Jacob MACKEY & the said William BUNDY ... to have the head of said tract Bounded by the Branch that runs through the Land just below a plantation Known by the name of Ephraim OVERMAN ... 18th day of the Eighth Month commonly called Oct. 1742. *Signed*: John BUNDY. *Wit*: Thomas SYMONS, Samuel BUNDY, Thomas NICHOLSON.
[B:450] *Ack*: Jany Court 1742 from John BUNDY to William BUNDY. *Regt*: 23 Feby 1743.

Job NICHOLS of the County of Pasquotank in the province of North Carolina for and in Consideration of the Sum of 15 pounds ... paid by George TAYLOR of the County and Province afsd. ... sold ... Tract of Land being on the N. W. End of the said NICHOLS'S Land ... Thomas PRITCHARDS Line ... Edwd. SCOTTS Land ... Job NICHOLS Line ... 50 acres ... 5 Oct. 1742. *Signed*: Job J NICHOLS his mark. *Wit*: Richard PRITCHARD, Thomas PRITCHARD. *Ack*: Jany Court 1742 from Job NICHOLS to George TAYLOR. *Regt*: 23 Feby 1742.

[B:451] North Carolina, 12 Jan. 1743 Between Thomas PENDLETON of the County of Pasquotank and Province of North Carolina Planter of the one part and Saml BARNARD of the same County and Province of the other part ... in Consideration of the Sum of 40 pounds lawful Money of the Province afsd. ... sold ... parcel of Land ... 20 acres ... being on the N. E. Side of Pasquotank River ... Saml BARNARDS Line ... *Signed*: Thomas PENDLETON. *Wit*: Cornelius RELFE, William DAVIS, Jno RODES. *Ack*: Jany Court 1742 from Thomas PENDLETON to Saml. BARNARD. *Regt*: 23 Feby 1742.

[B:452] North Carolina Clement HALL of the County of Perquimans & Province of North Carolina Gent. for & in Consideration of the Love Good will and affection which I have & do bear towards my loving Brother Robert HALL of the County of Pasquotank & Province afsd have given ... part of a Tract of Land ... 100 acres being that part of a Tract of Land containing 230 acres which I lately bought of William HIXSON next joining to Jonathan REDING'S Line whereon the House now stands ... 12 Jan. in the fifteenth year of the Reign of our Sovereign Lord George the Second ... 1742/3.
[B:453] *Signed*: Clement HALL. *Wit*: Thomas WOODLY, Saml. HIGHE, Wm. ABERCROMBIE. *Ack*: Jany Court 1742 Deed of Gift from Clement HALL to Robert HALL. *Regt*: 23 Feby 1742.

(First part of the following Deed torn off) ... sell ... unto the said John NORRIS ... parcel of Land contg ... 150 acres ... on the South Side of Pasquotank River being a Tract ... granted by Patent from William Earl of Craven Palantine &c. and Bearing date the 1 May 1668 ... *Signed*: James PRITCHARD. *Wit*: Ephraim OVERMAN, William BROTHERS, Jonathan REDING. *Ack*: Jany Court 1742 James PRITCHARD to John NORRIS. *Regt*: 23 Feby 1742.

[B:454] North Carolina. 11 Jan. 1742 Between Henry WENSLEY of the County of Perquimans in the Province of North Carolina Gentleman of the one party & John DAVIS of the County of Pasquotank & Province of North Carolina Planter of the other part ... by virtue of a power of Atty & Instructions from George LOW of the City of London Gentleman which Said power and Instructions was proved at Edenton ... in

Consideration of the valuable of two Cows & Calves ... sold ... Tract of Land ... recovered at common Law ... of the afsd. John DAVIS ... on the S. W. Side of Pasquotank River Contg ... 527 acres whereon the afsd. John DAVIS now dwells ... Binding on William WINBURYS and Relf GARNETTS Lands ... *Signed*: Henry WENSLEY. *Wit*: Abel ROSS, Francis LEAK. *Ack*: Jany Court 1742 ...
[B:455] ... from Henry WENSLEY to John DAVIS. *Regt*: 23 Feby 1742.

10 Jan. and in the fifteenth year of the Reign of our Sovereign Lord George the Second ... 1742 Between Thomas LEWIS in North Carolina, Pasquotank County of the one party planter and Jarvis JONES of the Same County of the other part Merchant ... in Consideration of the valuable Sum of 33 pounds 10 Shillings proclamation Money ... sold ... Tract of Land ... on the N. E. Side of Pasquotank River Contg 200 Acres taken out of a patent containing 1,654 acres commonly called ... Wolf Pitt Neck ... *Signed*: Thomas L LEWIS his mark. *Wit*: Henry H NICHOLS his mark, John HARRIS, John SQUIRES. *Ack*: Jany Court 1742. *Regt*: 23 Feby 1742.

[B:456] North Carolina) Pasquotank County) Jehoshaphat SYMONS of the County and Province afsd. Planter, and Lydia my Wife ... bound unto John BUNDY of sd. County & Province Planter in the penal Sum of 500 pounds proclamation ... 18 Aug. 1741. The Condition of this Obigation is ... whereas there has been some dispute ... concerning the Bounds or Division of their Land, hath now agreed upon a Line, ... along a Branch issuing out of the Millpond above a Ridge, built by Caleb BUNDY ... to an old Field known by the name of RAZENERS? old Field ... *Signed*: Jehoshaphat SYMONS, Lydia X SYMONS her mark. *Wit*: Samuel BUNDY, Jean BUNDY. *Proved*: Jany Court 1742 by the affirmation of Saml. BUNDY. *Regt*: 23 Feby 1742.

John HARRIS in the County of Pasquotank in the Province of North Carolina Planter for and in Consideration of the Sum of 100 pounds in good and lawful money of the Province afsd ... paid by Henry NICHOLS of the County & Province afsd. Planter ... sold ... Tract of Land ... on the So. Side of Pasquotank River ... 90 acres ... River Swamp ...
[B:457] ... Ash Branch ... 24 Oct. in the 15th year

of the Reign of our Sovn Lord George the Second ... 1742. *Signed*: John HARRIS. *Wit*: William ABERCROMBIE, James I SCARF his mark, Thomas TAYLOR, Josh. GAMBLING. *Ack*: Jany Court 1742. *Regt*: 23 Feby 1742.

North Carolina. 24 Jan. 1742 ... Thomas HARRIS Senr of the County of Pasquotank and Province of North Carolina planter of the one part & James WARD of the County and Province of the other part ... in Consideration of the Sum of 5 pounds lawful Money of the Province ... sold ...
[B:458] parcel of Land containing ... 50 acres ... on the S. W. Side of Pasquotank River ... at the Mouth of Rum Quarter Branch ... Pessimon Branch ... main Swamp ... *Signed*: Thomas TH HARRIS his Seal. *Wit*: Tho: TAYLOR, John ALBERTSON. *Proved*: April Court 1743 from Thomas HARRIS to James WARD by the Oath of Thomas TAYLOR. *Regt*: 16 May 1743.

[B:459] North Carolina ... George WINBURY of the County of Pasquotank in the Province afsd. ... in Consideration of the Sum of 50 pounds ... paid by Robert HOSEA of the said Province ... sold ... piece of Land joining to the said Robert HOSEAS Land and to my own where I now live containing ... 50 acres ... upon the S. E. Side of my Land Standing by Isaac Clearing commonly called ... 13 April 1743. *Signed*: George WINBURY. *Wit*: Joseph REED, Elizabeth REED. *Ack*: April Court 1743. *Regt*: 16 May 1743.

[B:460] 12 April in the 16th year of the Reign of our Sovereign Lord George ... Between William RODES of Pasquotank County of the one part and Solomon TAYLOR of the said County of the other part ... for the valuable Consideration of 90 pounds Current Money of Carolina ... sold ... 200 acres of Land ... part of a Tract of Land belonging to Wm. RODES and willed to the present William RODES his Son binding on the River Pocoson taking in there four Islands and the Swamp that surrounds the same 200 acres of Land ... 12 April 1743. *Signed*: William RODES. *Wit*: Berd. BANGER, Hez: LINTON. *Ack*: April Court 1743 from William RODES to Solomon TAYLOR. *Regt*: 16 May 1743.

[B:461] North Carolina Samuel Saban PLOMER of Pasquotank County in the Province afsd. Gentn. for and in Consideration of 240 pounds Currt Money of North Carolina ... paid by John DIAL of the County and Province afsd. ... sold ... Tract of land containing ... 140 acres ... on Pasquotank River ... Thomas MILLERS Line ... 4 March 1742. *Signed*: S PLOMER. *Wit*: Daniel WHITE, Jeremiah STEVENS. *Ack*: July Court 1743. *Regt*: 20 July 1743.

North Carolina: John WALLIS of the Province afsd. and County of Pasquotank ... in Consideration of the Sum of 10 pounds in Specie ... paid by John H. TAYLOR of Norfolk County in Virginia ... discharge the sd. John HEALEY ... sold ...
[462] ... 300 acres ... North Side of Pasquotank River ... Bounded by Isaac JONES'S, William RODES, Francis MARTINS Lines & commonly called Dogwood Ridge & binding on the Lake ... being the S. E. Side of a Tract of Land containing 1,604 acres given ... by Patent bearing date the 20 Dec. 1716 unto the said RELPH which said land was formerly surveyed for Robert HARRISON and by him Sold ... unto the said John RELPH ... 12 July 1743. *Signed*: John J WALLIS his mark. *Wit*: Gabriel BURNHAM, J PENDLETON, Jarvis JONES. *Ack*: July Court 1743. ...
[B:463] *Regt*: 20 July 1743.

7 April in the Sixteenth year of the Reign of our Sovereign Lord George the Second ... Between James JONES of the County of Pasquotank of the one part and David JONES of the other part ... in Consideration of the valuable Sum of 20 pounds Sterling paid ... Sold ... Tract of Land containing 100 acres being part of the Tract that the Said James JONES now lives on being bounded ... Mile Swamp ... William OVERTON'S Line ... the Mill Run ... 7 April 1743. *Signed*: James JONES. *Wit*: Moses M MAKFOSEN his mark, Saml. SMITH. *Ack*: July Court 1743 ...
[B:464] *Regt*: 20 July 1743.

North Carolina) Pasquotank County) Jarvis JONES ... in Consideration of the valuable Sum of 32 pounds in Specie ... paid ... by Capt. Gabl. BURNHAM ... made over all my Right ... 200 acres of Land ... 12 July 1743. *Signed*: Jarvis JONES. *Wit*: Zach. CHANCEY, Tho: TAYLOR. *Ack*: July Court 1743. *Regt*: 20 July 1743. Memorandum The Deed of the afsd. assignmt. is registd. in this Book called (C) in folio 94.

Abel ROSS of the County of Pasquotank in the Province of North Carolina ... for the valuable Consideration of 40 pounds ... paid down by Jeremiah SAWYER ... sold ... a certain parcel of woodland Ground containing 10 acres ... on the N. E. Side of Pasquotank River ...
[B:465] ... Patent bearing date 4 April 1721 ... 9 March 1742. *Signed*: Abel ROSS. *Wit*: Willoughby PRICE, Betsy C ISNARD her mark. *Ack*: July Court 1743. *Regt*: 20 July 1743.

Thomas SAWYERS of the Precinct of Pasquotank in the Province of North Carolina ... for the just Sum of 15 pounds ... paid by William WAMOUTH of the Precinct and Province afsd. ... sold ... parcel of Land ... on the S. W. Side of Pasquotank River containing 176 acres ... lying upon Jacob ALBERTSON & each Side of the Cypress Swamp ...
[B:466] ... 12 July 1743. *Signed*: Thomas SAWYER. *Wit*: Job J NICHOLS his mark, William JENNINGS. *Ack*: July Court 1743. *Regt*: 20 July 1743.

11 April in the 16th year of the Reign of our Sovn Lord George ... 1743 Between John COOK of the County and Province of North Carolina of the one party and Caleb SAWYER of the said County and Province afsd. of the other party ... in Consideration of the Sum of 49 Barrels of good merchantable Tar ... sold ... plantation lying on the N. E. Side of Pasquotank River ... Island Swamp ... Caleb SAWYERS Line ... 50 acres ...
[B:467] ... *Signed*: John COOK. *Wit*: Jacob ALBERTSON, Thomas SAWYER. *Ack*: July Court 1743. *Regt*: 20 July 1743.

North Carolina) Pasquotank County) John RELFE of the Province and County afsd. ... in Consideration of the sum of 100 pounds Sterling Money of Great Britain ... paid by Cornelius RELF of the County afsd. ... sold ... parcel of Land ... on the North Side of the River on the Easternmost Branch of Arenuse Creek Containing ... 100 acres ... part of a greater Tract of Land granted by Patent to William JENNINGS & Thomas JOHNSON by the Honble abel Philip LUDWELL bearing date 1 Jan. 1694 ... transferred to William SAWYER ... by William JENNINGS & Mary his wife on the 19 July 1709 and then Sold ... to John

RELF Senr by Peter SAWYER the 18 April 1721 ... [B:468] ... 15 Jan. 1742. *Signed*: John J RELF his mark. *Wit*: Pattison WILSON, Cornelius S JONES his mark. *Proved*: July Court 1743 by the oath of Pattison WILSON. *Regt*: 20 July 1743.

North Carolina) Pasquotank County) 21 April 1743 By & Between Arthur MABSON and Mary MABSON of Beaufort County in the Province afsd. Gentn. &c. of the one part and Joshua SCOOT of the County of Pasquotank in the said Province Planter ... in Consideration of the valuable Sum of 100 pounds in good pay or Specie (that is to say) in good merchantable barreled Pork at the rate of 45 Shillings Pr Barrel ... sold ... parcel of Land ... on the S. W. Side of Pasquotank River ... 150 acres ... William RELFS Corner ... Daniel RODES Line ... REEDS Line ... [B:469] ... *Signed*: Arthur MABSON, Mary MABSON. *Wit*: Abel DRESSER, Thos. RELFE, Tho: TAYLOR. *Proved*: July Court 1743. *Regt*: 25 July 1743.

North Carolina) Pasquotank County) 21 April 1743 By & Between Arthur MABSON of Beaufort County in the Province afsd. Gentn. &c. of the one part and Joshua SCOOT of the County of Pasquotank in the Province afsd. Planter ... in Consideration of the valuable Sum of 100 pounds in good pay or Specie to witt in good Merchantable Barreled Pork at the rate of 45 Shillings Pr Barrel ... sold ... Parcel of Land ... 150 acres ... REEDS Line ... to the N. W. [B:470] part of Job CARTWRIGHTS Field on Flatty ... MABSON'S back Line, so to REEDS Corner ... patent bearing date the 26th day of March 1727 ... *Signed*: Art. MABSON, Mary MABSON. *Wit*: Abel DRESSER, Thos. RELFE, Tho: TAYLOR. *Proved*: July Court 1743. *Regt*: 25 July 1743.

[B:471] North Carolina) Pasquotank County) James WARD ... in Consideration of 32 pounds 5 Shillings in Specie to be paid by William JACKSON of the place afsd. ... sold ... parcel of Land containing 50 acres purchased Land ... at the Mouth of Rum Quarter Branch ... Persimon Branch ... 5 July 1743. *Signed*: James W WARD his mark. *Wit*: Samuel JACKSON, David D JACKSON his mark. *Ack*: July Court 1743. [B:472] ... *Regt*: 20 July 1743.

North Carolina. 13 July 1743 Between

Thomas PENDLETON of the County of Pasquotank in the Province of No. Carolina Gentn. of the one part & Pattison WILSON of the same County & Province of the other part ... whereas William DOLLEY of the Parish of Holburn in the County of Middlesex Ironmonger by virtue of a power of atty and Instructions directed to Henry WENSLEY of North Carolina Gentn. bearing date the 21 March 1738 ... to Sell ... Manor Lands unto the afsd. Thomas PENDLETON ... on the N. E. Side of Pasquotank River ... in Consideration of the valuable Sum ... 39 Barrels of good merchantable Pork ... sold ... parcel of Land being part of the afsd. Manor Lands ... on the N. E. Side of Pasquotank River Contg ... 200 acres ... at the Middle of the Mouth of the Cypress Swamp ... John DAVIS Line ...
[B:473] ... *Signed*: Thomas PENDLETON. *Wit*: Thomas RELFE, Griffith JONES. *Ack*: July Court 1743. *Regt*: 25 July 1743.

George the Second ... in Consideration of the Rents & Duties herein reserved have given and granted ... unto Thomas MACKEY a Tract of Land containing 200 Acres ... on Little River Swamp ... John BAILEY'S Corner ... yearly Rent of 4 Shillings Proclamation Money for every 100 acres hereby granted ...
[B:474] ... Witness our trusty & well beloved Gabriel JOHNSTON Esqr our Captn. General & Governor in Chief at Edenton the 26th July in the 17th year of our Reign 1743. *Signed*: Gabl. JOHNSTON. By his Excelly Command John RICE pro See.

Thomas MACKEY of the Province of North Carolina in the County afsd. planter for and in Consideration of the Sum of 5 pounds current Bills ... paid by John RAPER of the County and Province afsd. do assign over ... all my Right ... of the within patent ... 11 Oct. 1743. *Signed*: Thomas MACKEY. *Wit*: Thomas OVERMAN, Saml. JACKSON Junr. *Ack*: Oct. Court 1743. *Regt*: 22 Nov. 1743.

[B:475] North Carolina) Pasquotank County) John RAPER ... in Consideration of 3 pounds Specie paid by my father John RAPER of the place afsd. in Specie by Solomon POOL Senr of the place afsd. ... sold ... unto Jacob Pool one of the Heirs of the afsd. Solomon POOL ... plantation Containing ... 67 acres ... on the North East Side of Little [blank] ...

John RAPERS Land ... River Swamp ... Solomon POOLS Land known by the name of DENNIS'S Land ... 11 Oct. 1743. *Signed*: John RAPER. *Wit*: Joseph BAILY, Charles TAYLOR. *Ack*: Oct. Court 1743 from John RAPER to Jacob POOL a Minor. *Regt*: 22 Nov. 1743.

[B:476] 4 Oct. 1740 Between James GREGORY of the County of Pasquotank of the one part and William GREGORY of the same place and Province afsd. of the other part ... for the valuable Consideration of 520 pounds ... sell ... parcel of land ... 300 acres ... N. E. Side of Pasquotank River ... North River Swamp ... Indians Line ... Line of him the afsd James GREGORY ... *Signed*: William O GREGORY his mark. *Wit*: John I GREGORY his mark, Bett MORGAN. *Ack*: Oct. Court 1743. *Regt*: 22 Nov. 1743.

[B:477] 15 Feb. 1742/3 Between John GREGORY of the County of Pasquotank of the one party and Caleb GREGORY of the same place and Province afsd. of the other ... for the valuable Consideration of 45 pounds in good Specie ... sold ... Woodland Ground ... N. E. Side of Pasquotank River ... 50 acres of land ... Benjn. SAWYER'S Corner Tree ... North River Swamp ... John GREGORY'S Corner Tree ... part of a larger Tract taken out of a patent bearing date the 1 Feb. 1715 ... 185 acres granted ... Richard GREGORY Father to the afsd. John GREGORY and Caleb GREGORY ... *Signed*: John X GREGORY his mark. *Wit*: Bennett MORGAN, Absalum GRANDY. *Proved*: Oct. Court 1743 the Oath of Absalum GRANDY. *Regt*: 22 Nov. 1743.

[B:478] 19 Aug. 1743 & in the 16th year of the Reign of our Lord George ... Betwixt Lodwick GRAY of the County of Pasquotank in the Province of North Carolina of the one part and Owen REESE of the said County on the other part ... in Consideration of the valuable Sum of 20 pounds in Specie ... paid by Lodwick GRAY ... sell ... Tract of Land containing 83 acres ... on the S. W. Side of Pasquotank River being part of a Tract of 503 Acres called the New Land ... Mouth of Cypress Branch Binding upon James MCDANIELS Land ... *Signed*: Owen REESE. *Wit*: John JONES, Thos. FOREHAND. *Ack*: Oct. Court 1743. *Regt*: 22 Nov. 1743.

[B:479] 19 Aug. 1743 & in the 16th year of the Reign of our Sovereign Lord ... betwixt

Thomas FOREHAND of the County of Pasquotank in the Province of No. Carolina Planter of the one part and Owen REESE of the said County on the other part ... in Consideration of the valuable Sum of 10 pounds in fresh pork ... paid by Thomas FOREHAND ... sold ... parcel of Land containing 52 and a half acres ... on the S. W. Side of Pasquotank River ... part of a Tract of 503 acres commonly called the New Land ... Granine? Branch ... John JONES Land ... *Signed*: Owen REESE. *Wit*: John JONES, Lodwick GRAY. *Ack*: Oct. Court 1743. *Regt*: 22 Nov. 1743.

[B:480] 19 Aug. 1743 & in the Sixteenth year of the Reign of our Lord George ... Betwixt James MCDANIEL of the County of Pasquotank in the Province of No. Carolina Planter of the one part and Owen REESE of the same County on the other part ... in Consideration of the valuable Sum of Two and Thirty in Specie ... paid by James MCDANIEL ... sold ... parcel of Land containing 150 acres ... on the S. W. Side of Pasquotank River being part of a Tract of 503 acres called the New Land ... Granine Branch ... Cypress Branch ... Thomas FOREHANDS Land ... *Signed*: Owen REESE. *Wit*: John JONES, Thomas FOREHAND. *Ack*: Oct. Court 1743. *Regt*: 22 Nov. 1743.

[B:481] 19 Aug. 1743 & in the 16th year of the Reign of our Lord George ... Betwixt Joseph SAWYER of the County of Pasquotank in the Province of No. Carolina planter of the one part & Owen REESE of the said County on the other part ... in Consideration of the valuable Sum of 18 pounds in Specie ... paid by Joseph SAWYER ... sold ... parcel of Land Contg 60 acres ... on the S. W. Side of Pasquotank & being part of a Tract of 503 acres called the New Land ... Lodwick GRAY'S Land ... Cypress Branch ... *Signed*: Owen REESE. *Wit*: John JONES, Lodwick LG GRAY his mark. *Ack*: Oct. Court 1743. *Regt*: 22 Nov. 1743.

[B:482] 2 July 1743 Between Owen REESE of the County of Pasquotank and Province of North Carolina of the one part and Richard BRIGHT of the County & Province afsd. of the other part ... in Consideration of the valuable Sum of 10 pounds in Specie ... sold ... Tract of Land containing 52 and a half acres being part of a patent granted to the said Owen REESE bearing date 1 April 1743 ... on the S. W. Side of Pasquotank River ... in the Dismal ...

[B:483] *Signed*: Owen REESE. *Wit*: Lodwick IG GRAY his mark, James MCDONALD his mark X. *Ack*: Oct. Court 1743. *Regt*: 22 Nov. 1743.

[B:484] 1743 in the Sixteenth year of the Reign of our Sovereign Lord George ... Betwixt John JONES of the County of Pasquotank in the Province of North Carolina Planter of the one part and Owen REESE of the said County on the other part ... in Consideration of the valuable Sum of 13 pounds in Specie ... paid by John JONES ... Sold ... Tract of Land containing 105 acres ... S. W. Side of Pasquotank River being part of a Tract of 503 acres called the New Lands ... Richard BRIGHTS Land ... *Signed*: Owen REESE. *Wit*: Lodwick IG GRAY his mark, Thomas FOREHAND. *Ack*: Oct. Court 1743. *Regt*: 22 Nov. 1743.

[B:485] 22 July in the 16th year of the Reign of our Sovereign Lord King George the Second ... 1743 Between Stephen HALL of Pasquotank County in the Province of North Carolina Planter of the one part & Michael MURPHY of Perquimans County & Province afsd. ... in Consideration of the Sum of 30 pounds 10 Shillings Current Money of the said Province ... sold ... Tract of Land ... head of Little River containing 108 acres ... Samuel BUNDY'S Line ... Desart ... patent bearing date the 1 April 1733 ... now in the Secretarys Office at Edenton ...
[B:486] ... *Signed*: Stephen HALL. *Wit*: Josiah BUNDY, William HASKIT, Thomas NICHOLSON. *Ack*: Oct. Court 1743. *Regt*: 22 Nov. 1743.

11 Oct. 1743 and in the 16th year of the Reign of our Lord George the King Betwixt Thomas RODES of the County of Pasquotank in the Province of North Carolina Planter of the one part And John JONES of the said County planter of the other part ... in Consideration of the Sum of 20 pounds in Specie and 110 pounds in bills ... sold ... Quantity of Lands ... on the N. E. Side of Pasquotank River which said Land Isaac JONES formerly sold to Wm RODES and being part of a Tract contg 155 acres out of a patent bearing date 30 July 1724 ... PRITCHARDS Line to the Creek Swamp ... 77 acres ...
[B:487] ... *Signed*: Thomas RODES . *Wit*: John BURNHAM, Israel LAMBETH. *Ack*: Oct. Court 1743. *Regt*: 22 Nov. 1743.

11 Oct. 1743 & in the Sixteenth year of the Reign of our Lord George ... Between John JONES of the County of Pasquotank in the Province of No. Carolina Planter of the one part & his Brother Evan JONES of the said County of the other part ... for the Love that I bear to my Brother, but more especially that he may settle and live near me, have given ... parcel of Land, but if my said Brother Evan should die without an Heir ... then the said land shall return to the said John JONES ... 120 acres ... on the N. E. Side of Pasquotank River being part of a Tract patented by John RELFE ... Crooked Run Branch ... HAILIES Land ... *Signed*: John JONES. *Wit*: John BURNHAM, Israel LAMBETH. *Ack*: Oct. Court 1743. *Regt*: 22 Nov. 1743.

[B:488] 5 Feb. 1742/3 and in the 16th year of the Reign of our Lord George ... Betwixt John BURNHAM & Elisabeth BURNHAM of the County of Pasquotank & in the Province of No. Carolina planter of the one part & John JONES of the said County on the other part ... in Consideration of the Sum of 10 pounds in Bills ... sold ... quantity of Land ... on the N. E. Side of Pasquotank River being part of a parcel of land Isaac JONES formerly sold to William RODES containing all the Land that lies betwixt the said Isaac JONES Line & the Alderwood RIDGE ... *Signed*: John BURNHAM, Eliza. BURNHAM her X mark. *Wit*: Mary M DAVIS her mark, John J DAVIS his mark. *Ack*: Oct. Court 1743 by John BURNHAM. *Regt*: 22 Nov. 1743.

11 July 1743 Between Benjamin EVANS and Effiah his wife of the one party of the County of Pasquotank & the Province of North Carolina and Richard GREGORY of the same place and province afsd. planter ... sell ... parcel of Land fallen to us by the death of Benjamin PAIN Brother to my wife Effiah afsd. ... N. E. Side of Pasquotank River commonly
[B:489] called ... Janikin Town? ... it being the 50 acres that Henry CREECH decd, Father in law to John PAIN [?] bestowed on the said John PAIN ... for the valuable Consideration of 35 pounds ... *Signed*: Benjamin EVANS, Effiah E EVANS her mark. *Wit*: William DAVIS, B. MORGAN, Thomas GRAY. *Proved*: Oct. Court 1743 by the Oath of Thomas GRAY. *Regt*: 22 Nov. 1743.

North Carolina Caleb GREGORY of Pasquotank County

... in Consideration of the sum of 150 pounds Current Money of Great Britain ... paid by Charles GRANDY of the afsd. Precinct ... Sold ... Tract of Land ... 100 acres ... Charles GRANDY & Thomas SAWYER ... John SAWYER'S Line, so to John UPTON'S Line so to John WINNS Line & so to Amos TRUEBLOODS Line binding upon Solomon DAVIS Line ... [B:490] ... 29 Oct. 1735. *Signed*: Caleb GREGORY. *Wit*: Thomas SAWYER, Richard R GREGORY his mark, John BELL. *Ack*: Oct. Court 1743. *Regt*: 22 Nov. 1743.

6 June 1743 and in the 16th year of the Reign of our Sovereign Lord George ... Between John HOSEA of the County of Pasquotank in the Province of North Carolina by and with the free Consent of Mary my wife of the one part and Robert HOSEA of the County of Pasquotank and Province afsd. of the other part ... in Consideration of the Sum of 100 pounds lawful Bills of this Province ... quit claim ... parcel of land lying ... on the N. E. Side of Little River being between John ARMOURS and the place where Robert HOSEA now lives formerly William WINBURYS joining upon Joseph COMMANDERS Containing 100 acres [B:491] ... *Signed*: John HOSEA, Mary M HOSEA her mark. *Wit*: Robert LOWRY, Richard COLLINS. *Ack*: Oct. Court 1743. *Regt*: 22 Nov. 1743.

North Carolina. Caleb GREGORY of Pasquotank ... in Consideration of the Sum of 150 pounds Currt Money of Gt. Britain ... paid by Thomas SAWYER of the afsd. Precinct ... sold ... 50 acres of land ... Charles GRANDY and Thomas SAWYER so running down upon John SAWYERS Line ... Solomon DAVIS line ... [B:492] ... 29 Oct. 1735. *Signed*: Caleb GREGORY. *Wit*: Charles S GRANDY his mark, Richard R GREGORY mark, John BELL. *Ack*: Oct. Court 1743. *Regt*: 22 Nov. 1743.

Elisabeth BRIGHT of Pasquotank County and Province of North Carolina ... in Consideration of the Love Good will and affection which I have ... towards my loving Son & Daughter Adam BRIGHT & Lavinah UPTON of the same County and Province afsd. have given ... all the Goods and Chattles that I have of my own since the death of my Husband Henry BRIGHT ... equally to be divided between them after my Death ... 4 Aug. 1743. *Signed*: Eliza. X BRIGHT her mark.

Wit: Henry BRIGHT, Henry B BRIGHT his mark, James ROBERTSON. *Proved*: Oct. Court 1743 by the Oaths of Henry BRIGHT Senr & Junr. *Regt*: 22 Nov. 1743.

[B:493] His Excelly John Lord CARTERET Palatine ... give and grant unto John DAVIS of our said County a Tract of Land containing 507 acres lying on the head of Pasquotank River ... David PRITCHARD'S Line ... 31 March 1727 Witness our trusty and well beloved Sr. Richard EVERARD Bart. Governor ... *Signed*: Richard EVERARD, E MOSELY, Thos. HARVEY, Fran: FOSTER, Edmd GALE, C GALE, J WORLEY, Robt. FORSTER Depy Secy.

North Carolina) Pasquotank County) John DAVIS do bargain sell and confirm unto Abraham DAVIS the within patent ... 11 Oct. 1743. *Signed*: John DAVIS. *Wit*: John NORRIS, Robert MURDEN. *Ack*: Oct. Court 1743. *Regt*: 22 Nov. 1743 in Book C. fo. 150.

[B:494] Relf BARKER of the City of New York ... appoint ... well beloved Friend Gabriel BURNHAM of Pasquotank in North Carolina my true and lawful Atty ... to acknowledge in Court a certain deed bearing date from me to John ABBIT ... 30 Dec. 1734. *Signed*: R BARKER. *Wit*: Isaac JONES, Bernd. BANGER. *Proved*: Oct. Court 1743 by the Oath of Bernard BANGER. *Regt*: 22 Nov. 1743.

11 Oct. in the 16th year of the Reign of our Sovereign Lord George ... 1743 Between John DAVIS of the County of Pasquotank of the one part and David DAVIS of the said County of the other part ... for the valuable Consideration of 30 pounds Sterling Money of Great Britain ... sold ... 100 acres of land ... on the head of Pasquotank River ... River Swamp ... James SPENCES Line ...
[B:495] ... *Signed*: John DAVIS. *Wit*: John NORRIS, Robert MURDEN. *Ack*: Oct. Court 1743. *Regt*: 22 Nov. 1743.

John DAVIS of the County of Pasquotank in the Province afsd. ... in Consideration of the Sum of 5 pounds in good pay ... by Thomas DAVIS of the same County and Province afsd. ... sold ... parcel of land ... 100 acres ... on the head of Pasquotank River on the S. W. Side ... James SPENCES and commonly called ... Back ridge ... 9 Oct. 1743.

Signed: John DAVIS. *Wit*: James BYLIELD, Edward E WHORTON his mark. *Proved*: Oct. Court 1743 by the oath of Edwd. WHORTON. *Regt*: 22 Nov. 1743.

[B:496] North Carolina. Caleb COEN & Miriam COEN my wife of the County of Pasquotank in the Province of North Carolina ... in Consideration of the valuable Sum of 220 pounds Current Money of the Province afsd. ... paid by Thomas TAYLOR of the County and Province afsd. ... sold ... parcel of Land ... on the S. W. Side of Pasquotank River at the Narrows commonly called ... MCCLENNANS ... formerly belonged to Patrick GORMACK & Given by his last will to his wife Elisabeth GORMACK and by her decease it fell to her Brother John TRUEBLOOD Heir at law and by the decease of the said John TRUEBLOOD it fell to his Son John TRUEBLOOD and by his decease fell to the afsd. Miriam COEN the only Sister of the last mentioned John TRUEBLOOD ... 270 acres ... 12 Oct. 1743. *Signed*: Caleb COEN, Miriam COEN. *Wit*: Griffith JONES, Cornelius RELF. *Ack*: Oct. Court 1743 Caleb COEN & Miriam COEN his wife to Thomas TAYLOR. *Regt*: 22 Nov. 1743.

[B:497] North Carolina) Pasquotank County) Edward WARDSWORTH for and in Consideration of the Sum of 40 pounds lawful Money of North Carolina ... paid by Thomas PARKER Shipwright of the County and place afsd. ... sold ... Tract of Land containing 50 acres ... James NEWBY Line ... Hairpin Branch ... [B:498] 27 Dec. 1743. *Signed*: Edward WARDWORTH. *Wit*: David BALIE, Joseph BALIE. *Ack*: Jan. Court 1743 Edward WARDWORTH to Thomas PARKER. *Regt*: 17 Jan. 1743.

9 Jan. and in the 16th year of the Reign of our Sovereign Lord George the Second ... Between Gabriel BURNHAM of North Carolina in Pasquotank County of the one part & Joshua GAMBLING of the same County Planter of the other part ... in Consideration of the valuable Sum of 20 pounds Specie ... Sold ... Tract of Land Containing 88 acres ... part of a patent Contg 175 acres granted to Gabl. BURNHAM bearing date 1725 ... Joseph MONKES Corner Tree ... Newfoundland Swamp ... High Bridge Branch ... [B:499] ... *Signed*: Gabl. BURNHAM. *Wit*: James BURNHAM, Jarvis JONES, William TAYLOR. *Proved*: Jan. Court 1743 Gabl BURNHAM Esqr to Joshua GAMBLING

was proved by the Oaths of William TAYLOR & Jarvis JONES. *Regt*: 17 Jan. 1743.

North Carolina. Gabriel BURNHAM of the County of Pasquotank and Province afsd. Esqr. for the Love, Good will, and affection which I have ... towards my loving Grandson Gabriel TAYLOR of the County and Province afsd. Planter have given ... Tract of Land containing 87 acres being part of a patent containing 175 acres bearing date 1725 only Excepting and giving my Son in law William TAYLOR and Mary TAYLOR his wife the use of the said Land during their Lives and then to Gabl. TAYLOR my Grandson ... at the Mouth of the high Ridge Branch ... main Swamp ...
[B:500] ... 9 Jan. 1743/4. *Signed*: Gabl. BURNHAM. *Wit*: James BURNHAM, Jos. GAMBLING, Jarvis JONES. *Proved*: Jan. Court 1743 Gabriel BURNHAM Esqr to Gabriel TAYLOR by the Oath of Jarvis JONES & Joshua GAMBLING. *Regt*: 17 Jan. 1743.

North Carolina) Pasquotank County) Thomas HUNTER Esqr. Treasurer of Pasquotank County ... Whereas John SCOTT late of the said County of Pasquotank did by his Deedpoll dated 25 July 1738 for and in Consideration of the Sum of 70 pounds and 15 Shillings Bill Money by him recd. by me the Said Treasurer of the County afsd. mortgage unto me the said Treasurer for the use of the publick a certain Tract of Land Containing ... 100 acres lying in the said County of Pasquotank (then called Pasquotank Precinct) and on the S. W. Side of Pasquotank River Joining to Job and Thomas CARTWRIGHTS Lines being the plantation the said John SCOTT bought of one Joseph REDING for payment of the said 70 pounds 15 Shillings Bill Money with Interest according to the Directions and purport of an act of assembly of this Province made in the year of our Lord 1735 ... and whereas the said John SCOTT having failed in the payment ... Land was seized by me for Nonpayment ... and advertised for Sale ... by the Space of 30 Days in the Month of June and July last past and on the 14th day of the said Month of July sold at public Vendue to Stephen SCOTT of Pasquotank County afsd. as highest Bidder for the Sum of 160 Pounds lawful Money of the said Province as by the certificate of Samuel HIGHE Vendue Master ... Thomas HUNTER Treasurer of the County afsd. for and in Consideration of the said Sum of 160 pounds ... paid for the use of the publick by the said Stephen SCOTT ... [B:501] ... sell ... Tract of Land in the Said Recited Deed of Mortgage ... 11 Jan. 1743. *Signed*: Thos. HUNTER Treasurer. *Wit*: Thomas NICHOLSON, Joseph ROBINSON. *Ack*: Jan. Court 1743 Thomas HUNTER Treasurer to Stephen SCOTT. *Regt*: 17 Jan. 1743.

North Carolina. 11 Jan. in the Seventeenth year of the Reign of our Lord George ... 1743 Between Mary LOWRY of Pasquotank County in the said Province Widow & Relict of Robert LOWRY of the said County decd. of the one part & Robert LOWRY of the Said County Son of the Said Robert LOWRY decd & also one of the Devisees of his last Will of the other part Whereas Robert LOWRY afsd. decd. by his last Will ... 16 Dec. 1742 devised to the said Robert Party to these presents in fact all that his Manor Plantation whereon he lived ... and whereas the Said Robert LOWRY ... and Mary LOWRY have agreed about the purchasing of the said Mary, not only all the Right she can claim by Virtue of the said Will of her Said Husband decd. but also all her Right of Dower ... in Consideration of the Sum of 400 pounds lawful Money of the Province of North Carolina ... paid ... [B:502] ... Sold ... Manor Plantation ... also it is hereby mutually agreed between the parties ... that the said Mary shall have the Liberty and privilege of the use of the Houses and Gardens & also the Liberty of Cutting firewood and of pasturing her Cattle & other Creatures on the plantation till 1 April next ensuing the date hereof at which time the said Mary LOWRY to leave the Said House and carry off the said plantation all her Cattle & other Creatures ... Robert LOWRY ... to enter upon the said plantation in the meantime and to cultivate, till & work the Same in manner as he shall think proper ... *Signed*: Mary LOWRY. *Wit*: John JONES, David PRITCHARD. *Ack*: Jan. Court 1743 Mary LOWRY to Robert LOWRY. *Regt*: 17 Jan. 1743.

[B:503] North Carolina) Pasquotank County) Samuel COOK of North Carolina & County afsd. for and in Consideration of the Sum of 50 pounds ... paid by Joshua PARISHO of the County and Province afsd Planter ... sold ... Tract of Land ... on the North Side of Nobs Crook Creek ... Containing 180 acres

... Oak Branch unto Nobs Crook Creek Swamp ... to William BRYANS Land ... Land of Thomas SAWYER ... Wm. WARD ... George WARD ... Thomas JENNINGS ... 5 Jan. in the 17th year of the Reign of our Sovereign Lord George the Second ... 1744. *Signed*: Saml. COOK. *Wit*: William STAFFORD, John I SIMSON his mark. *Ack*: Jan. Court 1743 Saml. COOK to Joshua PARISHO. *Regt*: 17 Jan. 1743.

[B:503] North Carolina) Pasquotank County) Thomas CARTWRIGHT of the County and place afsd. Planter for & in Consideration of the Love, Good will, and affection which I have and do bear towards my loving Brother Job CARTWRIGHT of the County abovesaid planter have given ... one part of a registered Tract of Land whereon I the said Thomas CARTWRIGHT & Lidy CARTWRIGHT now dwells ... 75 Acres ... on the S. W. Side of Pasquotank River ... being the uppermost of the said Tract of Land ... old House Branch ... 9 April 1743. *Signed*: Thomas CARTWRIGHT. *Wit*: Thomas TRUEBLOOD, Abel TRUEBLOOD, Josiah TRUEBLOOD. *Proved*: Jan. Court 1743 Thomas CARTWRIGHT to Job CARTWRIGHT by the affirmation of Thomas TRUEBLOOD and Abel TRUEBLOOD. *Regt*: 17 Jan. 1743.

[B:504] 3 Jan. and in the Sixteenth year of the Reign of our Sovereign Lord George the Second ... 1743/4. Between William RODES of North Carolina in Pasquotank County planter of the one part and Robert CHAMBERLIN of the same County on the other part ... in Consideration of the valuable Sum of 28 pounds Specie ... sold ... Tract of Land ... 170 acres ... part of a patent granted to Thomas RELF Containing 475 acres Bearing date 1717 and assigned to William RODES ... at the Mouth of Sandy Run ... Philip EVANS Corner tree ... Main Swamp ... John JONES Ridge ... *Signed*: William RODES. *Wit*: Gab: BURNHAM, James BURNHAM. *Ack*: Jan. Court 1743 William RODES to Robert CHAMBERLIN. *Regt*: 17 Jan. 1743.

[B:505] North Carolina. 10 Jan. 1743 Between Joshua PARISHO of the County of Pasquotank and Province of North Carolina of the one part Planter and William STAFFORD of the same County and Province afsd. ... in Consideration of the valuable Sum of 130 pounds Currt Money of the Province afsd. ... sold ... parcel of Land ... 60 acres ... fork of

Nobs Crook Creek ... John IVEY and Richard PRITCHARDS Corner Tree ... Turkey Branch ... Crab Swamp ... Creek Swamp ...
[B:506] ... *Signed*: Joshua PARISHO. *Wit*: John NORRIS, Hez: CARTWRIGHT. *Ack*: Jan. Court 1743 Joshua PARISHO to Wm. STAFFORD. *Regt*: 17 Jan. 1743.

William WILLIAMS of the Precinct of Pasquotank in the Province of North Carolina Planter ... for the just Sum of 52 pounds to me in hand paid by Caleb COEN of the Precinct and Province afsd. ... sold ... parcel of Land ... N. E. Side of Pasquotank River ... on the E. Side of the Loosing Swamp ... Richard SAWYERS ... 25 acres ... 13 July 1742. *Signed*: William W WILLIAMS his mark. *Wit*: John JONES, Hezekh. BUTTERWORTH. *Ack*: Jan. Court 1743 Willm WILLIAMS Senr. to Caleb COEN. *Regt*: 17 Jan. 1743.

[B:507] No. Carolina: Thomas RELF of Pasquotank County in the Province afsd. ... in Consideration of the Love, Good will, and affection that I have and do bear towards my truely beloved Friend Francis LEAK ... make over ... parcel of Land ... 120 acres ... on the S. W. Side of Pasquotank River out of a Patent bearing date the 3 Aug. 1728 ... 11 Jany 1743. *Signed*: Tho: RELF. *Wit*: William SAWYER, Joshua X SAWYER his mark. *Ack*: Jan. Court 1743 Thomas RELF to Francis LEAK. *Regt*: 17 Jan. 1743.

[B:508] North Carolina) Pasquotank County) Wm. BURGES of Pasquotank County and Province of North Carolina Planter for and in Consideration of the Sum of 100 pounds Bills of North Carolina ... paid by Josiah HART of Pasquotank afsd. ... sold ... Tract of Land ... head of RAYMONDS Creek on the N. E. Side of Pasquotank River & between the Land of Cornelius JONES and the Land of Thomas TORKSEY being of a Patent for 402 acres bearing date the 2 Aug. 1730 ... 11 April 1743. *Signed*: Wm. BURGES. *Wit*: Jno. SCARBROUGH, John HARDING, Mary X BURGES.

13 Feb. in the Sixteenth year of the Reign of our Sovereign Lord George ... 1744 Between John MCDANIEL Albemarle Cty and the Prect of Pasquotank of the one part & Willm. JONES of the said County and Precinct of the other part ... for the valuable Consideration of 250 pounds Bills ... Sold ...
[B:509] ... Tract of Land ... on the N. E. side of

Pasquotank River ... Possum Branch ... River Swamp ... 13 Feb. 1744. *Signed*: John I MACKDANIEL his mark. *Wit*: Richard SAWYER, James PHILLIPS.

North Carolina) Pasquotank County) It is this day agreed between Elizabeth WRIGHT Execx to her Son Augustin WRIGHT Will, and John WRIGHT that they have divided the Land according to the said Will & a Deed bearing date 11 July 1732 Given by Augustin WRIGHT to the said John WRIGHT, it being 120 acres of Land ... on the N. E. Side of Pasquotank River ... the one half of the said Land and by his Will ... he gave to his Brother Wm. WRIGHT the other half ... 3 March 1744. *Signed*: Elisabeth W WRIGHT mark, John A WRIGHT mark. *Wit*: Saml. WILLIAMS, John TORKSEY.

[B:510] North Carolina) Pasquotank County) John DURANT King of the Yeopim Indians, and James BARBER the Consent of the rest of the nation ... with the Consent of the Governor and Counsel ... in Consideration of 180 pounds Currt Money of North Carolina ... paid by Captn. Cornelius RELF ... sold ... parcel of Land contained in a patent bearing date the 2 Oct. 1704 Contg 450 acres ... Jacob Swamp ... Capt. John CARONES Corner Tree ... Bored? Tree Branch ... Sandy Hook ... 20 Feby 1743/4. *Signed*: John I DURANT his mark. *Wit*: John LURRY, Cornelius S JONES his mark.

[B:511] North Carolina. Timothy MEEDS of the County of Pasquotank and Province afsd. Planter ... in Consideration of the Sum of 600 pounds Currt Money of this Province ... paid by John PEGGS of the County afsd. ... sold ... Moiety of Land ... joining to Thomas MUDS Land ... Timothy MEEDS line, containing 100 acres ... 10 April 1744. *Signed*: Timothy MEEDS. *Wit*: Jer SWEENY, Tho: TAYLOR.

[B:512] William BURGES and Thomas BURGES of the County of Pasquotank and Province of North Carolina Planters of the one part and Charles SCARBROUGH of the County & Province afsd. Weaver of the other part ... in Consideration of 200 pounds lawful Money of the Province ... sold ... parcel of Land ... fork of RAYMOND'S Creek ... Main Swamp ... Poplar Swamp that is the Division agreed upon between George and Henry BRAY ... Thomas TORKSEY'S Line ... 150 acres ... Excepting one half acres of high Ground convenient to the Landing ... [blank] Oct. 1744. *Signed*: Wm. BURGES, Thomas BURGES. *Wit*: John SIKES, Benjamin TORKSEY, Peter P BROWN his mark.

Charles SCARBROUGH of Pasquotank County in the Province of North Carolina Planter for & in Consideration of the Sum of Money ... paid by Christopher BRAY of the County and Province afsd. Planter ... sold ...
[B:513] ... Tract of Land ... 50 acres ... Thomas TORKSEY ... Henry BRAY'S Line ... main Swamp ... *Signed*: Charles C SCARBROUGH. *Wit*: Tho: TAYLOR, Saml. WILLIAMS.

North Carolina) Pasquotank County) Samuel BUNDY of the place afsd. Farmer for and in Consideration of the Sum of 300 pounds Currt Money of the said Province to me in hand paid by Thomas NICHOLSON of the place afsd. Farmer ... sold ... all my Right
[B:514] ... unto that Tract of Land that the said Thomas NICHOLSON now dwells on ... in the fork of Little River viz all that part of said land that is below a Line of marked Trees and agreed unto by the said Thomas NICHOLSON & Saml BUNDY ... by a Deed of Sale ... bearing date the 8 July 1740 ... Eleventh day of the Second Month commonly called April 1744. *Signed*: Saml. BUNDY. *Wit*: Joseph ROBINSON, John BUNDY, John J LOW his mark.

North Carolina) Pasquotank County) Thomas NICHOLSON of the County afsd. Farmer ... in Consideration of ... 80 pounds Currt Money of the said Province to me in hand paid by Samuel BUNDY of the place aforesaid. farmer .. sold ... Tract of Land head of Little River contg ... 80 acres ... William BUNDYS Upper Corner Tree ... above the plantation that the said Thomas NICHOLSON now dwells on ... which Land was patented in William BUNDY'S Name ... Corner Line of that Land formerly pattented by John and
[B:515] Peter SYMONS now in the possession of the said Saml BUNDY ... 13th day of the first Month commonly called March 1744. *Signed*: Thomas NICHOLSON. *Wit*: Josiah BUNDY, Wm. HACKETT, Joseph MUNDEN.

Jacob ALBERTSON of the County of Pasquotank in the Province of North Carolina Planter for and in Consideration of the Sum of 50 pounds in good and

lawful Money of the Province afsd. ... paid by James CLERK of the same County and province afsd. Planter ... sold ... Tract of Land ... 100 acres ... on the No. Side of Nobs Crook Creek
[B:516] Called by the name of Paradise, this Deed being for one half of the Tract the whole being 200 Acres ... from Nobs Crook Creek at the Branch called the Middle Branch ... joining upon Willm JENNINGS ... 9 July in the fourteenth year of the Reign of our Sovereign Lord King George the Second ... 1741. *Signed*: Jacob ALBERTSON. *Wit*: Job CARTWRIGHT, Thomas SAWYER.

George the Second ... in Consideration of the Rents and Duties herein Reserved have given granted ... unto Thomas PENDLETON a Tract of Land containing 395 acres ... on No. River Swamp ...
[B:517] ... Witness our trusty and well beloved Gabriel JOHNSTON Esqr and Captain General and Governor in chief at Edenton this 26 July in the Seventeenth year of our Reign 1743. *Signed*: Gab. JOHNSTON. By His Excellys' Command Jas CRAVEN Depy Secy Enroled in the Audrs. Genl. Office the 22d. day of Nov. 1743 by Edwd. GRIFFITH Pro Audr. ...

[B:518] North Carolina. Thomas PENDLETON of Pasquotank County in the Province afsd. Gentn. for and in Consideration of the Sum of 5 Shillings Currt Bills ... paid by Thomas BARCOCK and Wm BRAY have sold and made over to them ... all my Right ... to the within mentioned Patent ... 11 April 1744. *Signed*: Thomas PENDLETON. *Wit*: Cornelius RELF, Thos. TAYLOR. *Ack*: April Court 1744.

North Carolina. William WARD of Pasquotank County in the Province afsd. Planter ... in Consideration of the Sum of 5 Shillings Currt Bills ... paid by Alexander JACK have Sold ... all my Right ... 72 acres of Land ... 11 April 1744. *Signed*: Wm. W WARD his mark. *Wit*: Job CARTWRIGHT, William HIXON. *Ack*: April Court 1744. *Regt*: 1 May 1744.

North Carolina. 11 April 1744 Between Thomas PENDLETON of Pasquotank County in the Province afsd. of the one part Gentn. & Thomas BARCOCK of the County and Province of the other part Planter ... in Consideration of the valuable Sum of 5 Shillings lawful ... sold ... parcel of Land ... out of a

Patent bearing date the 6 Jan. 1742 ...
[B:519] ... Commonly Called ... BARCOCKS Island, the West--North West End of the Island ... *Signed*: Thos. PENDLETON. *Wit*: Cornelius RELF, Tho: TAYLOR.

North Carolina. 11 April 1744 Between Thomas PENDLETON Esqr. of Pasquotank County in the Province afsd. of the one part and William BRAY of the County & Province afsd. of the other part Planter ... in Consideration of the valuable Sum of 5 Shillings currt Bills ... Sold ... parcel of land ... 197 and a half ... Beginning at a Pine it being a division between Wm. BRAY & Thomas BARCOCK out of a patent bearing date the 6 Jan. 1743 ... commonly known by the name of BARCOCKS Island the E. S.E. of the said Island ...
[B:520] ... *Signed*: Thos. PENDLETON. *Wit*: Cornelius RELF, Tho: TAYLOR.

North Carolina. 20 Feb. 1743 Between George TAYLOR of the County of Pasquotank & Province of No. Carolina Planter of the one part & Edwd. SCOTT of the County and Province afsd. of the other part ... George TAYLOR & Elisabeth TAYLOR for and in Consideration of the valuable Sum of 15 pounds ... sold ... parcel of Land ... 50 acres ... along Thomas PRITCHARDS Line ... Richard MURDENS to Edward SCOTTS Corner Tree ... Job NICHOLS line ...
[B:521] ... *Signed*: George i TAYLOR his mark, Elizabeth X TAYLOR her mark. *Wit*: Richard PRITCHARD, Thomas PRITCHARD August 15th.

North Carolina) Pasquotank County) Samuel NORTHY of Calvert County in the Province of Maryland Mariner for and in Consideration of 300 pounds Curry 200 of which to me in hand paid ... by Alexander LANE of Pasquotank County Planter ... the other 100 to be paid on or before the 10 of April next ... sold ... parcel of Land ... 12 June being the Seventeenth year of the Reign of our Sovn Lord George the Second
[B:522] ... 1744. *Signed*: Samuel NORTHY. *Wit*: Benjamin SYMONS, Simon BRYAN, John DAVIS, Wm. TURNER

North Carolina: Clement HALL of Perquimans County & Province afsd. ... in Consideration of ... 150 pounds ... sold unto my loving Brother Robert HALL of Pasquotank and Province afsd. all my Right ... to the within mentioned Deed of Sale ... 8 Sept. 1743.

Signed: Clemt. HALL. *Wit*: Thomas PRITCHARD, Richard CORBETT, The Mark M of Matthew ALBERTSON.

John NEEDHAM, Gideon NEEDHAM & Thomas NEEDHAM according to the last Will & Testament of our decd. Father, have divided the Land between us which was left to us in said Will ... viz John NEEDHAMS Land lying on the Easternmost part of the Tract ... near the Mouth of RAYMOND'S Creek ... Gideon NEEDHAM'S Land adjoining on the westward part of the same ... Thomas NEEDHAM'S Land adjoining westward of the Same being the Remainder of the afsd. Tract ... *Signed*: John NEEDHAM, Gideon NEEDHAM, Thomas NEEDHAM. *Wit*: William BURGES, Josiah HART.

[B:523] Jonathan HIBBS of the County of Pasquotank in the Province of North Carolina House Joiner for and in Consideration of the Sum of 400 pounds Bills ... paid by Thomas CARTWRIGHT of the afsd. County Son to the deceased Job CARTWRIGHT ... sold ... Tract of Land ... S. W. Side of Pasquotank River ... RODES Line ... Wm. SAWYERS Line ... Mouth of broad Gut at the River ... Contg 60 acres ... being a Tract of Land granted by two Deeds of Sale one from Wm. RELFE and the other from Daniel RODES both bearing date 1737 ... 21 June 1744. *Signed*: Jonathan HIBBS. *Wit*: Danl. RODES, Al. JACK. *Proved*: July Court 1746 [sic] by the oath of Alex JACK. *Regt*: 1 Aug. 1744.

The Deposition of George POWERS aged about 40 taken up is the said Land that Will. TAYLOR now lives on sayeth that he began at a White Oak ... the above Bounds was his true Intent ... William UPTON one of the Chain Carriers declares on the Holy Evangelist that the above Deposition was the whole Truth ... George POWERS & William UPTON come personally before me and made Oath on the Holy Evangelist
[B:524] that the above Deposition was the whole Truth ... 16 March 1731/2. *Signed*: Gabl. BURNHAM. *Ack*: North Carolina) Pasquotank County) Jan. Court 1744. *Regt*: 4 Sept. 1744.

North Carolina) Pasquotank County) Robert ARMOUR together with my Son Joseph ARMOUR both of the County and Province afsd. Farmers ... for the valuable Consideration of 200 pounds lawful Money of this Province to us in hand paid ... by

Thomas PENDLETON of the Province and County afsd. Farmer ... sold ... Tract of Land lying and binding on the said Thomas PENDLETON Containing 170 acres ... formerly belong to Thomas PENDLETON decd. Father to the said Thomas PENDLETON purchaser and by the said Thomas PENDLETON decd. sold by a Deed to Mary JONES Sister to the decd. Thomas PENDLETON being the Eastermost part of the premises ... 6 Oct. 1744. *Signed*: The mark of R Robert ARMOUR, Joseph ARMOUR. *Wit*: Thos. PENDLETON, George X PENDLETON his mark, Jno. MCKEEL. *Ack*: Oct. Court 1744 Robert ARMOUR & Joseph ARMOUR. *Regt*: 22 Nov. 1744.

[B:525] Richard MADREN and Abraham MADREN in the County of Pasquotank and Province afsd. in Consideration of the Sum of 30 pounds ... paid by Gabriel BURNHAM Junr ... sold ... parcel of Land containing ... 100 acres ... the Creek Swamp to the Mouth of the Western Branch ... John HARRIS'S Corner Tree ... Valentine ROWES Line ... 28 March 1744. *Signed*: Richard MARDREN, Abraham A MARDREN his mark. *Wit*: Richard PRICHARD, Thomas PRICHARD, Thomas S SMITH his mark. *Proved*: Oct. Court 1744 by the Oath of Thomas PRICHARD. *Regt*: 22 Nov. 1744.

[B:526] 10 Sept. 1744 between Thomas SAWYER of the County of Pasquotank and Province of North Carolina of the one part and Willoughby SAWYER of the same place and Province afsd. of the other part ... for the valuable Consideration of 50 pounds ... sold ... parcel of Land ... on the N. E. Side of Pasquotank contg ... 50 acres ... Charles GRANDY'S Line ... John SAWYER'S Line ... Jonathan JONES Line ... *Signed*: Thomas SAWYER. *Wit*: Bennett MORGAN, Joseph MORGAN, William X PARKER his mark. *Proved*: Oct. Court 1744 by the Oath of Bennett MORGAN. *Regt*: 22 Dec. 1744.

[B:527] Richard SAWYER of the County of Pasquotank in the Province of North Carolina Planter ... for the just Sum of 200 pounds to me in hand paid by Benjamin SAWYER of the County and Province afsd. ... sold ... parcel of Land ... N. E. Side of Pasquotank River Containing 100 acres ... binding on Thomas SAWYER'S Line ... William WILLIAMS'S Line ... part of a Tract of Land out of a Patent granted to James MCDANIEL which said patent bearing date 1723 and assigned to Thomas SAWYER Senr. ... 850 acres ...

1 Feb. 1743/4. *Signed*: Richard SAWYER. *Wit*: Bennett MORGAN, Alexander SAWYER. *Ack*: Oct. Court 1744 from Richard SAWYER to Benjamin SAWYER. *Regt*: 22 Dec. 1744.

[B:528] North Carolina. 10th day of the 8th Month commonly called Oct. 1744 Between Stephen SCOTT of Pasquotank County and Province afsd. ... whereas Joseph GLASTER by his last will and Testament ... 27 Jan. 1718 gave ... Ruth wife of the said Stephen SCOTT and one of the Daughters of the said Joseph GLASTER and also to one Sarah GLASTER another of the Daughters all his lands as well in Carolina as Virginia ... to be equally divided ... whereas the said Ruth ... in virtue of ... a division made between the said Ruth and the said Sarah her Sister is entitled to a plantation ... 150 acres ... adjoining to Lands belonging to David GEORGE ... Now this Indenture ... for the conveying ... of the above recited Tract of Land ... by the Intent that the said Thomas NICHOLSON shall and will reconvey the said Tract of Land ... unto the said Stephen SCOTT ... & to the said Ruth ... in such manner ... so that an absolute ... Estate in fee simple ... in the premises may be fully and absolutely vested in the Survior of the said Stephen & Ruth his Wife ... in Consideration of the Sum of 5 pounds lawful Money of Great Britain ... paid ... Thomas NICHOLSON ... sold ... all that the above recited Tract of Land .. [B:529] ... after the death of the said Stephen SCOTT or of Ruth his wife ... the said Thomas NICHOLSON ... shall immediately on request made to him ... Reconvey the said hereby granted premises ... to the longest Liver or Survivor ... *Signed*: Stephen SCOTT, Ruth SCOTT. *Wit*: Zachariah KEETON, Gideon BUNDY, Abraham BUNDY. *Ack*: Oct. Court 1744 from Stephen SCOTT and Ruth his wife ... to Thomas NICHOLSON. *Regt*: 23 Dec. 1744.

North Carolina) William BURGES OF Pasquotank County in the Province of North Carolina Planter for and in Consideration of affection, Love and Goodwill that I have to my well beloved Daughter Elizabeth and to her Husband Benjamin TORKSEY of Pasquotank afsd. do give ... Tenement ... on the N. E. Side of Pasquotank River ... Line of John WHITE, John FORBESS, William CRONY and Baley FORBESS ... Tract of Land formerly belonged to James FORBESS being

part of a Tract of land which I bought of John CARON ... 26 Dec. 1744. Signed: Wm. BURGES. Wit: Baly B FORBUSH his mark, Clerke? SCARBOROUGH, John BURGES. Ack: Jan. Court 1744.
[B:530] Gift of Land from to Elizabeth and William [sic] TORKSEY ... Regt: 23 Feb. 1744/5.

No. Carolina) Pasquotank County) John NEEDHAM of the County of Pasquotank in the Province afsd ... in Consideration of the valuable Sum of 500 pounds Current Bills ... paid by Jeremiah WILCOCKS ... sold ... 100 acres of Land ... on the N. E. Side of Pasquotank River called RAYMONS Creek ... John HARDINS Land ... 26 Nov. 1744. *Signed*: John NEEDHAM. *Wit*: Shad TAYLOR, Tho: TAYLOR. *Ack*: Jany Court 1744 from John NEEDHAM to Jeremiah WILCOCKS. *Regt*: 23 Feb. 1744/5.

[B:531] North Carolina) Pasquotank County) Aaron HILL of the said County Farmer for and in Consideration of the Sum of 20 pounds current Money of the said Province ... paid by Thomas NICHOLSON Farmer of the same County ... sold ... Tract of Land ... in the fork of Little River containing ... 150 acres ... Land that the said Thomas NICHOLSON and Aaron took up and Surveyed upon the head of their Lands that they so dwell upon ... divided by agreement between them ... in the Desart back of a place that is known by the name of the Jagged Oaks ... 5th day of the 11th Month commonly called Jan. [B:532] 1744/5. *Signed*: Aaron HILL. *Wit*: Joseph MORRIS, John MORRIS, Zachariah MORRIS. *Ack*: Jany Court 1744 from Aaron HILL to Thomas NICHOLSON. *Regt*: 23 Feb. 1744/5.

North Carolina) Pasquotank County) Jeremiah WILCOCKS of the County and Province afsd planter for and in Consideration of the valuable sum of 500 pounds Current Bills ... paid by John NEEDHAM ... made over all my Right ... of the within Deed ... 26 Nov. 1744. *Signed*: Jeremiah J WILCOCKS his mark. *Wit*: Shad: TAYLOR, Tho: TAYLOR. *Ack*: Jany Court 1744 from Jeremiah WILCOCKS to John NEEDHAM. *Regt*: 23 Feb. 1744/5.

John PIKE of Frederick County in the Colony of Virginia ... whereas by Birthright at the decease of my Father I fell Heir ... Tract of Land called

half-way Tree ... Contg 325 acres ... Line that was Matthew RAISINS ... in Consideration of 10 pounds Currt Money of Virginia ... paid ... sold ... unto Saml. PIKE ... parcel of land of the afsd. Tract contg 162½ Acres ...
[B:533] ... lying on the N. E. Side of the aforementd. Tract ... a line run out ... agreement of the sd. Saml. PIKE and Benjamin PIKE Purchaser of the remaining part of the afsd. Tract ... 19 Oct. 1744. *Signed*: John PIKE. *Wit*: John REED, Aaron MORRIS, Peter SYMONS. *Proved*: Jany Court 1744/5 from John PIKE to Samuel PIKE by the affirmation of Aaron MORRIS. *Regt*: 23 Feb. 1744/5.

John PIKE of Frederick County in the Colony of Virginia ... whereas by Birthright at the decease of my Father I fell Heir ... Tract of Land called half-way Tree ... 325 acres ... Line that was Matthew REASONS ... in Consideration of 10 pounds Currt Money of Virginia ... paid ... sold ... unto Benjamin PIKE ... parcel of land of the afsd. Tract contg 162½ Acres ... lying on the N. E. Side of the aforementioned Tract ... a Line run out ... agreement of the said Benjamin PIKE & Saml. PIKE
[B:534] Purchaser of the remaining part of the afsd. Tract ... 19 Oct. 1744. *Signed*: John PIKE. *Wit*: John REED, Aaron MORRIS, Peter SYMONS. *Proved*: Jany Court 1744/5 from John PIKE to Benjamin PIKE by the affirmation of Aaron MORRIS. *Regt*: 23 Feb. 1744/5.

John RELF Son and Heir of the within named John RELF for and in Consideration of ... the Sum of 20 pounds lawfull Bills Money of North Carolina ... paid ... by Willm HIXON ... sold ... all my Right ... of the within mentioned land ... patent unto my Father John RELF decd. ... 9 Jan. 1744. *Signed*: John J RELF his mark. *Wit*: John PENDLETON, Danl. GRANDIN. *Ack*: Jany Court 1744/5
[B:535] Patent of Land from John RELF to William HIXON. *Regt*: 23 Feb. 1744/5.

No. Carolina. 9 April 1745 Between Capt. Gabriel BURNHAM of Pasquotank County in the Province of North Carolina of the one part & Drew HALSTED of the Colony of Virginia Gentn. of the other part ... by virtue of a power of atty and Instructions from Relf BARKER of the City of New York Gentn. bearing date

the 30 Dec. 1744 ... to sell ... parcel of lands ... 500 acres ... on the head of Pasquotank River ... formerly taken up by one James BROWN decd. and recovered of one William TAYLOR by the afsd. Relf BARKER as Heir at law to the afsd. James BROWN ... in Consideration of the valuable Sum of 60 pounds Currt money of Virginia ... paid ... by Drew HALSTEAD ... sold ... [afsd. land] ...
[B:536] ... *Signed*: Gabl. BURNHAM. *Wit*: Robt. HUTCHESON, Thos. TAYLOR, Saml. HEIGHE. *Ack*: April Court 1745 from Gabl. BURNHAM to Drew HALSTEAD. *Regt*: 26 April 1745.

North Carolina) Pasquotank County) Solomon TAYLOR of North Carolina in Pasquotank County in the Province afsd. Planter for and in Consideration of 35 pounds Current Money of Virgina ... paid by Caleb WILSON of Currituck County ... sell ... parcel of Land ... 200 Acres ... lying on Pasquotank on the West Side of the River ... belonging to Wm. ROADS decd. granted by patent to Thomas RELF & transferred to the said Wm. ROADS and willed to the present Wm. ROADS his son binding on the River Pocoson taking in there four Islands namely Terrapin Shell Island, flat Island, HARRIS Island & Butterwood Island & the Swamp surrounds the same four Islands ...
[B:537] ... 9 April 1745. *Signed*: Solomon TAYLOR. *Wit*: James BUTT, John TAYLOR, Shad TAYLOR. *Ack*: April Court 1745 from Solomon TAYLOR to Caleb WILSON. *Regt*: 26 April 1745.

5 Jan. in the 14th year of the Reign of our Sovereign Lord George the Second ... Between John LINTON living in Currituck County & David DUNKIN in Pasquotank County in North Carolina ... in Consideration of the valuable Sum of 25 pounds Sterling Money of Gt Britain ... sold ... piece of land ... situate to Joseph MACFARSON Containing 70 acres taken out of a patent containing 400 Acres ...
[B:538] ... 5 July 1744. *Signed*: John LINTON. *Wit*: William W SIKES his mark, Thomas MILLET, Joseph MACKFARSON. *Proved*: April Court 1745 from John LINTON to David DUNKIN by the Oath of William SIKES. *Regt*: 7 May 1745.

Solomon SIKES of Norfolk County of Virginia and William SIKES of Pasquotank County in the Province of North Carolina and in Consideration of ... 20

pounds Sterling money of Great Britain ... sold ... Tract of Land ... 50 acres ... part of a Tract containing 400 acres pattented to Thomas LEWIS and Daniel MACKFARSON bearing date the 23 Nov. 1723 ... to the Dismal Swamp ...
[B:539] ... *Signed*: Solomon S SIKES his mark. *Wit*: John TAYLOR, James JONES, John X MARTIN his mark. In the nineteen year of the Reign of our Sovereign Lord King George the Second ... 1745. *Proved*: April Court 1745 from Solomon SIKES to William SIKES by the Oath of John TAYLOR & James JONES. *Regt*: 7 May 1745.

Jarvis JONES of Albemarle County in Pasquotank in No. Carolina Cordwainer ... in Consideration of the Sum of 8 pounds in good lawful Pork ... paid by John JONES in the County afsd. ... sold ... Tract of Land containing 70 Acres ... on the
[B:540] North West Side of Pasquotank River ... main Swamp ... to Patrick ODANIELS Land ... 10 Jan. 1731/2. *Signed*: Jarvis JONES. *Wit*: Wm MINSON, Abel ROSS. *Ack*: Jany court 1731/2 & *Regt*: 6 July 1732.

North Carolina) Pasquotank County) John JONES of the County and Province afsd. Junr for and in Consideration of the Sum of 25 pounds in Specie to me in hand paid by Francis MARTIN of the same County ... made over ... all my Right ... of the within mentioned Deed ... 9 April 1745. *Signed*: John JONES. *Wit*: Tho: TAYLOR, Robert HALL. *Ack*: April Court 1745. *Regt*: 2 May 1745.

[B:541] North Carolina. Robert KEEL of the Precinct of Pasquotank ... for the valuable Consideration of a plantation now belonging to Thomas MEADS of the same Precinct & situate on the North East Side of Little River & Butting on the plantation now of Joseph REED together with 180 pounds Current Money of this Province ... made over ... parcel of land ... on the S. W. Side of Great Flatty Creek ... to WESTS Line ... 190 acres ... 14 Feb. 1744/5. *Signed*: Robert KEEL. *Wit*: Jas MOIR, William ARMOUR. *Ack*: April Court 1745 from Robert KEEL to Thomas MEADS. *Regt*: 6 May 1745.

[B:542] North Carolina Thomas MEADS do assign over my Right ... of the within Deed to Robert KEEL ...

Signed: Thos. MEADS. *Wit*: Jas. MOIR, William ARMOUR. *Ack*: April Court 1745 from Thomas MEADS to Robert KEEL. *Regt*: 6 May 1745.

North Carolina) Pasquotank County) Job CARTWRIGHT of the Province and County afsd. for and in Consideration of the sum of 44 pounds 7 shillings and 6 pence Virginia Currency ... paid by Abel TRUEBLOOD ... sold ... one part of a Registered Tract of Land whereon Job CARTWRIGHT Senr formerly lived ... 75 acres ... on the S. W. Side of Pasquotank River ... being the uppermost part of the said Tract ... 5 Jan. 1744/5. *Signed*: Job CARTWRIGHT, Martha M REDING her mark.
[B:543] *Wit*: Thos. TRUEBLOOD, Benja. PRITCHARD, Josiah TRUEBLOOD. *Ack*: April Court 1745 from Job CARTWRIGHT & Martha his wife to Abel TRUEBLOOD. *Regt*: 7 May 1745.

North Carolina) Pasquotank County) Valentine ROWE in the County of Pasquotank and Province afsd. ... in Consideration of the sum of 60 pounds current Money of North Carolina ... paid by James Poolman DUFFEY of the same County and province afsd. ... sold ... Tract of Land ... 50 acres ... Seccon Branch ... to Little Valley ... John HARRIS'S Line ... Samuel Saban PLUMERS Line ... 2 March 1744/5. *Signed*: Valentine R ROWE his mark. *Wit*: Thomas PRITCHARD, William STAFFORD, Joshua PARISHO. *Ack*: April Court 1745 from Valentine ROWE to Jas: Poolman DUFFEY. *Regt*: 7 May 1745.

[B:544] Griffith GRAY of Pasquotank County in the province of North Carolina ... in Consideration of the Sum of 5 pounds Current Money of Virginia ... paid by my Brother John GRAY ... sold ... all my Right ... to a certain Tract of Land ... which my Brother Valentine GRAY formerly bought ... of Philip TORKSEY formerly John UPTONS and is adjoining to ... my afsd. Brother John GRAY now lives ... deed ... bearing date 10 April 1730 ... 9 May 1745. *Signed*: Griffith G GRAY his mark. *Wit*: William X PARKER his mark, Danl. GRANDING. *Proved*: July Court 1745 Griffith GRAY to John GRAY by Daniel GRANDIN. *Regt*: 28 Sept 1745.

[B:545] North Carolina) Pasquotank County) 8 July 1745 Between Thomas LINTON of the Said County of the one part and Hezekiah LINTON of the said County of the other part ... in Consideration of ... 60 pounds ... sold ... plantation ... at a place commonly called the Quarter back of the fork of Pasquotank River ... Edwd. BRIGHTS Corner ... Widow BROWNS Line to the Great Swamp ... to William BRIGHTS Corner Tree ... 90 acres ... *Signed*: Thomas Thom LINTON his mark. *Wit*: Samuel SMITH, Anthony ETHERIDGE, Henry EVANS. *Ack*: July Court 1745 from Thomas LINTON to Hezekiah LINTON. *Regt*: 28 Sept 1745.

[B:546] North Carolina) Pasquotank County) 9 July 1745 Between Hezekiah LINTON of the said County of the one part and Henry EVANS of the said County of the other part ... in Consideration of ... 12 pounds Currt Money of Virginia ... sold ... parcel of land ... a place commonly called the Quarter back of the fork of Pasquotank River it being part of a patent granted to my father William LINTON bearing date the 10 July 1723 ... BARKERS Line ... 50 acres ... *Signed*: Hez: LINTON. *Wit*: Samuel SMITH, Richard OVERTON. *Ack*: July Court 1745 from Hezekiah LINTON to Henry EVANS. *Regt*: 28 Sept 1745.

[B:547] North Carolina) Pasquotank County) 30 Jan. 1745 ... John COOK of the County and Province afsd. Weaver ... in Consideration of ... 60 pounds of good and lawful Bills of the Province afsd. ... paid by Mr. Caleb SAWYER of the afsd. province and County of Pasquotank ... sold ... parcel of land ... on the N. E. Side of Pasquotank River ... Island Swamp ... Caleb SAWYER'S Line to Thomas COOPERS Line ... 100 acres ... *Signed*: John COOK. *Wit*: Josiah NASH, Charles PORTLACK. *Proved*: July Court 1745 from John COOK to Caleb SAWYER by the Oath of Josiah NASH. *Regt*: 28 Sept 1745.

[B:548] North Carolina. 9 July 1744 Between William WARD of the County of Pasquotank in the Province of North Carolina Planter of the one part & Isaac STOKELY of the same County and Province of the other part ... in Consideration of ... 50 pounds current Bills ... sold ... parcel of land ... 50 Acres ... a Branch that comes out of Nobs Crook Creek ... Crab Swamp ... Known by the name of Broad Neck ... *Signed*: Isaac STOKELY. *Wit*: Richard CORBETT, Jas Poolman DUFFY, Josiah CARTWRIGHT. *Ack*: July Court 1745 from Isaac STOKELY to William WARD.

Regt: 28 Sept 1745.

[B:549] No. Carolina: 6 July 1745 and in the 18th year of the Reign of our Sovereign Lord George the Second ... Between Obadiah SEXTON of the County of Pasquotank in the Province of North Carolina of the one party and William SEXTON his Brother of the same County and province abovesaid of the other party ... in Consideration of the natural Love and affection ... give ... Tract of Land ... on the South West Side of Pasquotank River and joining on the River Pocoson commonly called ... Jeremiah SEXTONS plantation contg ... 50 acres ... *Signed*: Obadiah SEXTON. *Wit*: John MACKBRIDE, Abel DRESSER. *Ack*: July Court 1745. *Regt*: 30 Sept 1745.

[B:550] North Carolina) Pasquotank County) Edward LOW of the place afsd. Farmer for and in Consideration of the Sum of 100 pounds Current Money of said province ... paid by George LOW Farmer ... sold ... Tract of Land ... in the County of Pasquotank afsd. contg 50 acres ... Branch issuing out of Little River Pocoson upon the lower Side of my land that I now dwell upon known by the name of OVERMAN'S Nam? Branch ... 8th day of 5th Month commonly called July 1745. *Signed*: Edward X LOW his mark. *Wit*: Thomas NICHOLSON, Gideon BUNDY, Charles OVERMAN. *Ack*: July Court 1745 from Edward LOW to George LOW. *Regt*: 1 Oct. 1745.

[B:551] North Carolina) Pasquotank County) 3 April 1745 and in the rein of Royale Sovreign Lord George the II King ... Between John MACKBRIDE of the Province of North Carolina and the Precinct of Pasquotank Planter of the one party and Jacob SAWYER of the Precinct afsd. Cooper witnesseth that MACKBRIDE in Specie to be paid ... discharge him the said Jacob SAWYER ... given Granted Bargained [Rest of deed missing]

RECORD OF DEEDS VOLUME A 1746-1747

[A:412] North Carolina Francis OVERTON of the County of Pasquotank and Province afsd Planter for the Love and Good Will and Affection which I have and bear towards my loving Son Richard OVERTON of the County and Province afsd. Planter Have given ... a certain Tract of Land containing 170 Acres ... being part of a Tract containing 640 Acres bearing date 1713 only excepting Francis OVERTON & Mary his Wife the Use of the Said Land during their lives. and then to Richard OVERTON my Son ... 7 Oct. 1745. *Signed*: Francis X OVERTON his mark. *Wit*: John MACKBRIDE, Alexander SPENCE, John IVEY. *Ack*: Oct. Court 1745 Deed of Gift from Francis OVERTON to Richard OVERTON. *Regt*: 7 April 1746.

[A:413] North Carolina 3 Sept. 1745 Between William JENNINGS of the County of Pasquotank and Province afsd. of the one part and William NICHOLS of the same County and Province of the other part ... in Consideration of the Sum of 100 pounds in good lawful Money of the Province afsd. ... Sold ... Parcel of Land containing 80 Acres ... at the mouth of the Old House Branch ... *Signed*: William JENNINGS. *Wit*: William ABERCROMBIE, Hannah H ABERCROMBIE her mark. *Ack*: Oct. Court 1745 William JENNINGS to William NICHOLS. *Regt*: 7 April 1746.

[A:414] North Carolina) Pasquotank County) 10 May 1745 Between William NICHOLS of the County and Province afsd. of the one part and Benjamin JENNINGS of the same County & Province of the other part ... in Consideration of the Sum of 100 pounds in good and lawful Money of the Province ... Sold ... a parcel of Land containing 60 Acres ... being on the S.W. Side of Pasquotank River ... Beginning at a Branch called the Log Branch ... binding on Thomas NICHOLS ... *Signed*: William W NICHOLS his Mark. *Wit*: William ABERCROMBIE, [blank] ABERCROMBIE. *Ack*: Oct. Court 1745 Wm. NICHOLS to Benjn. JENNINGS. *Regt*: 7 April 1746.

[A:415] North Carolina) Pasquotank County) George WARD in the County of Pasquotank and Province afsd ... in Consideration of the Sum of 20 pounds Current money of North Carolina ... paid ... by James WARD of the same County and Province ... sold ... parcel of Land containing ... 8 Acres ... at the Mouth of the Great Branch ... to the Great Swamp ... 4 March 1744/5. *Signed*: George M WARD his Mark. *Wit*: Joshua PARISHO, Elisabeth X PARISHO her mark. *Proved*: Oct. Court 1745 by the Oath of Joshua PARISHO from George WARD to James WARD. *Regt*: 7 April 1746.

North Carolina) Pasquotank County) James WARD of the County and Province afsd. ... in Consideration of the Sum of 60 pounds Current money of North Carolina ... paid ... by James PRITCHARD of the same County ... sell ... Parcel of Land containing ... 8 Acres ... at the Mouth of the
[A:416] Great Branch ... to the Great Swamp ... 29 Aug. 1745. *Signed*: James W WARD his mark. *Wit*: Joshua PARISHO, Elizabeth X PARISHO her mark. *Ack*: Oct. Court 1745 from James WARD to James PRITCHARD. *Regt*: 7 April 1746.

John PERKINS and Aimey my Wife of Pasquotank County in the Province of North Carolina Planter for and in Consideration of the Sum of 20 pounds ... paid by Abasanna PERKINS of the County and Province afsd Planter ... sold ... Tract of Land ... on the North East Side of Pasquotank River and the South East End of the Tract ... 100 Acres ... Side of Gum Pond ... to SANDERLIN'S Line commonly called the Forest ...
[A:417] ... (Remainder of Deed missing)

North Carolina Henry PENDLETON of the County of Pasquotank Planter ... in Consideration of the Sum of 80 pounds current Money of the Province ... paid ... by William BROTHERS Junr. of the County & Province afsd ... Sold ... all that half Tract or parcel of Land ... containing by Estimation 150 Acres of Land ... on the South Side of Pasquotank River and bounding on Joseph KEATON'S and Ephraim OVERMAN'S and the remaining part of the said Tract mentioned in a patent bearing date 19 March 1713/4 purchased by the afsd. John BROTHERS of Henry PENDLETON Grandfather to the afsd. Henry PENDLETON the 19 Oct. 1714 ...
[A:418] ... 21 Jan. 1744/5. *Signed*: Henry PENDLETON. *Wit*: Tho: TAYLOR, Job. CARTWRIGHT. *Ack*: Oct. Court 1745 Henry PENDLETON to Wm. BROTHERS. *Regt*: 7 April 1746.

North Carolina William BROTHERS Junr. of Pasquotank County and Province afsd. Planter ... in Consideration of the valuable Sum of 62 pounds, 10 Shillings Current Money of the Colony of Virginia ... paid ... by Thomas PALIN of the County and Province afsd. ... sold ... Half Tract or parcel of Land ... by Estimation 150 Acres of Land ... on the South Side of Pasquotank River & Bounding on Joseph KEATON'S, Ephraim OVERMAN'S and the remaining part of the said Tract mentioned in a patent bearing date the 19 March 1713/14 purchased by John BROTHERS Father to the Said William BROTHERS of Henry PENDLETON Senr. the 19th Oct. 1714 ... 24 Jan. 1744/5. *Signed*: William BROTHERS. *Wit*: Henry PENDLETON, Jno. CRADUX? *Ack*: Oct. Court 1745 Wm. BROTHERS to Thomas PALIN. *Regt*: 7 April 1746.

[A:419] North Carolina Thomas PALIN of Pasquotank and Province afsd. Planter ... in Consideration of the valuable Sum of 60 pounds Current money of the Colony of Virginia ... paid ... by John NEEDHAM of the County and Province afsd. ... sold ... all that half Tract or Parcel of Land ... 150 Acres of Land ... on the South Side of Pasquotank River and Bounding on Joseph KEATON'S, Ephraim OVERMAN'S and the remaining of the sd Tract mentioned in a Patent bearing date the 19 March 1713/14 purchased by John BROTHERS of Henry PENDLETON Sr. the 19th Oct. 1714 ... 28 Sept. 1745. *Signed*: Thos. PALIN. *Wit*: Henry PALIN, John DIALL. *Ack*: Oct. Court 1745 Thomas PALIN to John NEEDHAM. *Regt*: 7 April 1746.

[A:420] North Carolina, Pasquotank County ... 14 Jan. 1745 ... between Robert PALMER of Pasquotank & Province afsd. Planter with Sarah his Wife of the one part and John HOSEA Senr. of County and Province afsd. Planter ... in Consideration of the Sum of 50 pounds Virginia Currency ... sold ... Tract of Land ... being in Flatty Creek ... that was given and granted to the said Robert PALMER'S Mother by her deceased Father containing ... 75 Acres ... at the head of thick Neck Branch ... the first Bridge Branch ... *Signed*: Robert PALMER, Sarah PALMER. *Wit*: George WHEDBEE, William DAVIS Junr. *Ack*: Jan. Court 1745 Robert PALMER & Sarah his Wife to John HOSEA Senr. *Regt*: 7 April 1746.

[A:421] North Carolina. John HOSEA [sic] of the

County of Pasquotank and Province afsd. ... in Consideration of the Sum of 20 pounds current Money of said Province ... paid ... by John HOSEA ... sold ... 175 Acres of Land joining upon the sd. Lands whereof Robert PALMER is now living and joining upon Cornelius RYALLS Line and from thence binding upon the Great Swamp and upon Benjamin PALMER'S Line ... [blank] day of [blank] 1745. *Signed*: Robert PALMER. *Wit*: William DAVIS Junr, George WHEDBEE. *Ack*: Jan. Court 1745 Robert PALMER to John HOSEA. *Regt*: 4 April 1746.

North Carolina) Pasquotank County) John HOSEA of Pasquotank County for and in Consideration of the valuable Sum of 280 pounds Current Bills of this Province ... paid by Joseph KEATON of said County have bargained and sold ... all my Right ... of the within 104 Acres of Land ... this Nineteenth day of [A:422] December 1745. *Signed*: John HOSEA. *Wit*: Richard COLLINS, Theophilus X ARMOUR his mark. *Ack*: Jan. Court 1745 John HOSEA to Joseph KEATON. *Regt*: 7 April 1746.

North Carolina) Pasquotank County) Joseph KEATON of the County and Province afsd. ... for the Consideration of 200 pounds lawful money of this Province ... paid by Benjamin MEADS of the Same place ... Sold ... Two parcels of Land viz. 60 Acres that I purchased of Patrick KEATON as by Deed may appear, and 62 acres as came by my wife as by patent bearing date June the 2d 1727 Granted to Col. John PALIN the which patent was assigned over to Jacob RIGHTAGUY ... 29 Nov. 1745. *Signed*: Mary X KEATON her mark, Joseph KEATON. *Wit*: Thomas MEADS. *Ack*: Jan. Court 1745 Mary KEATON & Joseph KEATON her Husband to Benjn. MEADS. *Regt*: 7 April 1746.

[A:423] North Carolina) Pasquotank County) Cornelius JONES of the County and Province aforesaid for and in Consideration of 20 pounds in Pork & Cows to me in hand paid by Bailey FORBISH ... sell ... 20 Acres of Land ... Beginning on John FORBISH line ... Corner Tree in Bailey FORBISH Survey ... 30 Jan. 1744/5. *Signed*: Cornelius X JONES his Mark. *Wit*: Joseph GODFREY, Mary X BELL her Mark. *Ack*: Cornelius JONES to Baley FORBISH was acknowledged in open Court in due form of law. *Regt*: 7 April 1746.

[A:424] North Carolina) Pasquotank County) Daniel DANN ... for the valuable Consideration of 250 pounds in current Bills of this Province in hand paid by Robert PALMER of the Province afsd. Planter ... sold Tract of land ... 125 acres ... 15 Jan. 1745. *Signed*: Danl. X DANN his mark. *Wit*: Josiah CARTWRIGHT, Josa. MARTIN, John WADE. *Ack*: Jan. Court 1745 Danl. DANN to Robert PALMER. *Regt*: 7 April 1746.

[A:425] 24 July 1745 Between Jacob ALBERTSON of Pasquotank and Province of North Carolina ... and James CLARK of the same County and Province ... in Consideration of the Sum of 300 pounds in good and lawful money of the Province ... Sold ... a parcel of Land, being part of a greater parcel containing 100 acres ... North Side of Knobb's Crook and called by the name of Paradise ... at the Mouth of the Cypress Swamp ... head of William JENNINGS Branch ... Being the half part thereof of 200 acres ... *Signed*: Jacob ALBERTSON. *Wit*: Jas. Poolman DUFFEY, William STAFFORD, William X DELANY his mark. *Ack*: Jan. Court 1745. *Regt*: 7 April 1746 in Book D. Fo. 18.

[A:426] North Carolina) Pasquotank County) Thomas DAVIS of the County of Pasquotank in the Province afsd. ... in Consideration of the sum of 200 pounds current Money of the Province afsd. ... paid by David DAVIS of the same County and Province ... sold ... parcel of Land ... 10 acres ... on the Head of Pasquotank River on the S. W. Side of the River ... joining on the Lands of James SPENCE, commonly called ... Beech Ridge ... 15 Jan. 1745/6. *Signed*: Thomas DAVIS. *Wit*: Josiah CARTWRIGHT, James PRITCHARD *Ack*: Jan. Court 1745. *Regt*: 7 April 1746.

12 Nov. 1745 Between Benjamin JENNINGS of the County of Pasquotank & Province of North Carolina of the one part, and James CLARK of the same place and Province afsd. of the other part ... for the valuable Consideration of 400 pounds Current Bills of this Province ... sold ... Parcel of Land ... on the S. W. Side of Pasquotank River ... 60 acres ... formerly belonging to Wm. NICHOLS decd. ... head of Long Branch ... on Henry NICHOLS Land to the River Swamp ... to the Mouth of Long Branch ...
[A:427] ... *Signed*: Benjamin JENNINGS. *Wit*:

Joseph JONES, Jacob ALBERTSON. *Ack*: Jan. Court 1745. *Regt*: 7 April 1746.

North Carolina) Pasquotank County) 10 Nov. 1745 Between James CLARK of the County and Province afsd. of the one part, and Benjamin JENNINGS of the same County and Province of the other part ... in Consideration of the Sum of 500 pounds in good and lawful Money of the Province ... sold ... Parcel of Land, which was formerly William WAYMANS, which he swapt with Thomas SAWYER, being called Paradise, lying upon Knobs Crook Creek Containing 200 acres ... the Mouth of the Cypress Swamp ... binding upon Wm. NICHOLS ... Willm JENNINGS ... Creek Swamp ... [A:428] ... *Signed*: James I CLARK his mark. *Wit*: Joseph JONES, Jacob ALBERTSON. *Ack*: Jan. Court 1745. *Regt*: 7 April 1746.

North Carolina) Pasquotank County) David DAVIS of the County of Pasquotank in the Province afsd. ... in Consideration of the Sum of 200 pounds current Money of the Province afsd. ... paid by Nathaniel GRAY of the same County & Province ... Sold ... parcel of Land ... 127 Acres ... on the S. W. Side of the head of Pasquotank River ... joining on a place called the Crooked Run ... 15 Jan. 1745/6. *Signed*: David D DAVIS his mark. *Wit*: Josiah CARTWRIGHT, James PRITCHARD. *Ack*: Jan. Court 1745. *Regt*: 17 Jan. 1745.

[A:429] North Carolina) Pasquotank County) John HALELEE of the County and Province aforesaid Taylor ... in Consideration of ... 100 pounds current money of the Colony of Virginia ... paid by Ann BOUT of the County and Province afsd. Spinster ... sell ... the following Articles ... 20 Head of Newt Cattle, 30 head of Hogs with all their Pigs, 3 Feather Beds and Furniture, 2 chests, 1 Trunk, 3 Tables, 1 dozen of Chairs, 4 pots, 5 peuter Dishes, 7 Basins, a dozen and a half of plates, 1 Mill, 1 Box Iron and Frying Pan, a Linen Wheel, 1 Woollen Wheel, 3 pint Bottles, a Scimining Ladle, & flesh forks with Hoes and axes, and all other Moveables belonging to me or as deemed to be mine ... 7 Jan. 1745/6. *Signed*: John HALELEE. *Wit*: Henry REYNOLDS, Tho. TAYLOR, William MOSELY. *Ack*: Jan. Court 1745 Bill of Sale for Goods from John HALELEE to Ann BOUT. *Regt*: 7 April 1746.

North Carolina. Arthur MABSON & Mary my Wife of Carteret County in the Province afsd. ... in Consideration of the natural Love and affection which I bear unto my beloved Daughter Susannah MABSON ... give ... Tract of Land ... 342 Acres ... on the S. W. Side of Pasquotank River granted by Patent to George HARRIS, in the year 1704 & by the said George HARRIS sold to William NORRIS by Deed bearing date 20 Jan. 1715 and by the said William NORRIS to William SIMPSON by Deed bearing date the 15 Dec. & by the said William SIMPSON to Joseph HACKETT by Deed bearing date the 15 April 1718, and by the Said
[A:430] Joseph HACKETT unto the afsd. Mary Wife of the said Arthur [blank] sold by Deed bearing date the 31 Dec. 1732 and now by these Presents by the afsd. Arthur & Mary conveyed unto the sd. Susannah MABSON ... 9 March 1744/5. *Signed*: Ar. MABSON, Mary MABSON. *Wit*: Rd. LOVITT, John NORRIS. *Ack*: 10 May 1745 the sd. Mary being by me examined ... *Signed*: E MOSELEY C Jurt. *Regt*: 10 June 1746.

22 Sept. 1744 and the 16th year of the Reign of our Sovereign Lord George ... Between Robert OVERTON of the County of Currituck in North Carolina Planter of the one part, and Thomas OVERTON of the other County of Pasquotank in North Carolina Planter of the other part ... in Consideration of the Sum of 50 pounds in Coin paid ... sold ... Tract of Land
[A:431] ... in the Fork of Pasquotank River commonly ... called by the name of MECOYE and JOYE, formerly surveyed for MECOYE and JOYE ... main Swamp ... Danl. MECOYES Line ... Great Branch ... 150 acres ... *Signed*: Robert H OVERTON his mark. *Wit*: Alexander SPENCE, Henry EVANS, Persilla P SPENCE her mark. *Proved*: 2 July 1745 Upon the Oath of Alexander SPENCE ... E. HALL CJ. *Regt*: 22 July 1746.

North Carolina) Pasquotank County) Joseph SMITHSON of the Province and County aforesaid ... in Consideration of the Sum of 200 pounds Province Bills ... paid by Abel TRUEBLOOD ... parcel of Land that Jane TULLY formerly was possessed with ... 110 acres ... on the S. W. Side of Pasquotank River ...
[A:432] ... Being on the N. E. Side of Knobs Crook Swamp ... Gum Branch ... 28 Feb. 1745/6. *Signed*: Joseph SMITHSON. *Wit*: Amos TRUEBLOOD, Charles C GRANDY his mark. *Ack*: April Court 1746

Joseph SMITHSON to Abel TRUEBLOOD. *Regt*: 12 Aug. 1746.

North Carolina) Pasquotank County) Amos TRUEBLOOD of the County and Province abovesaid Planter of the one part for and in Consideration of the Sum of 200 pounds Current money of this Province ... paid by Joseph SMITHSON of the County and Province afsd. Planter of the other part ... sold ... 100 acres ... on the N. E. Side of Pasquotank River ... Jamaica Branch on Lower Side of Jamaica Ridge ...
[A:433] ... Solomon DAVIS his Line ... 28 Feb. 1745/6. *Signed*: Amos TRUEBLOOD. *Wit*: Abel TRUEBLOOD, Charles C GRANDY his mark. *Ack*: April Court 1746. *Regt*: 12 Aug. 1746.

North Carolina) Pasquotank County) 25 Feb. 1745/6 Between Daniel RHODES of the County and place aforesaid Planter of the one part & Edward SCOTT of the Same place Planter ... in Consideration of the Sum of 500 pounds Current Money of North Carolina ... sold ... Tract of Land formerly belonging to Daniel RODES decd. ... 85 acres ... on the S. W. Side of Pasquotank River ... David BOLES? Corner Tree, then binding on Thomas RELF'S Line ... Mill Branch ... Mill Dam to the Mouth of a
[A:434] Cypress Branch, binding on David BOULS Line ... *Signed*: Daniel RODES. *Wit*: Richard PRITCHARD, John ALBERTSON, Joseph JONES. *Ack*: April Court 1746. *Regt*: 12 Aug. 1746.

North Carolina) Pasquotank County) 16 Aug. 1745 Between Richd. MADREN of the County and Province afsd. Planter of the one part and James PRITCHARD of the County & Place afsd. of the other part ... in Consideration of Sum of 260 pounds Current Money of this Province ... sold ... part of ... Tract of Land ... 234 Acres lying at the head of Nobs Crook Creek
[A:435] ... containing 140 acres ... Western Branch ... *Signed*: Richd. MADREN. *Wit*: John NORRIS, Ezekiel CARTWRIGHT, Daniel RODES. *Ack*: April Court 1746. *Regt*: 12 Aug. 1746 in Book D Fo. 31.

North Carolina) Pasquotank County) Benjamin BURNHAM of the County of Pasquotank and Province afsd. Planter for the Love, Good will, and affection which I have towards my loving Brother James BURNHAM of the County, and Province afsd. Planter, have given

... Tract of Land containing 200 acres, taken out of a Patent containing 1,654 acres commonly called ... Wolf Pitt Ridge ... Cypress Branch ... 20 May 1746. *Signed*: Benjn. BURNHAM. *Wit*: John BURNHAM, Jacob BURNHAM. *Ack*: July Court 1746. *Regt*: 1 Sept. 1746.

[A:436] 4 Jan. 1745/6 and in the Seventeenth year of the Reign of our Sovereign Lord George the Second ... between William RODES of Pasquotank in the Province of North Carolina of the one part and John BURNHAM of the County and Province afsd. of the other part ... in Consideration of ... 25 pounds Specie ... sold ... parcel of Land ... Mouth of round hill Island ... Mouth of Sandy Run ... John HALELEE'S Line ... Evan JONES'S Corner Tree ... to the River Swamp for 50 acres ... *Signed*: William RODES. *Wit*: Thomas T TRENTON his mark, John JUIE. *Proved*: July Court 1746 by the Oath of John JUIE. *Regt*: 1 Sept. 1746.

No. Carolina, Benjamin BURNHAM of the County of Pasquotank & Province afsd. Planter for the Love Good will and affection which I have and bear towards my loving Brother Jacob BURNHAM of the County and Province afsd. Planter have given ... Tract of Land containing 140 acres binding upon Joshua GAMBLING'S Line ... by the Swamp Side ... [A:437] ... 8 July 1746. *Signed*: Benj. BURNHAM. *Wit*: John BURNHAM, James BURNHAM. *Ack*: July Court 1746. *Regt*: 1 Sept. 1746.

North Carolina) Pasquotank County) James MCBRIDE of the County and Province afsd. ... in Consideration as well as a competent Sum of Money as of sundry [?] and Services unto me in hand already paid down and performed as also for the Maintenance & Provision made for me by my Brother John MCBRIDE of the same place ... sold ... Tract of Land ... James SPENCES Corner Tree ... Pig Branch ... River Pocoson ... 107 Acres ... patented by the proprietors to Benjamin COEN by Patent bearing date the 2 July 1728 and by him bequeathed to me by his last Will & Testament ... 18 March 1745. *Signed*: James MCBRIDE. *Wit*: John KELLY, Randall KELLY. *Ack*: July Court 1746 Release from James MCBRIDE to Jno MCBRIDE. *Regt*: 1 Sept. 1746.

[A:438] North Carolina) Pasquotank County) John COOK Weaver for and in Consideration of the Sum of 150 pounds lawful Money of the said Province ... paid by Macrora SCARBOROUGH of the County of Perquimons and Province afsd. Gentn. ... sold ... Plantation, containing 100 acres of Land ... on the N. E. Side of Pasquotank River ... Deed for the same from Joseph SAWYER bearing date the 12 Jan. 1741 ... together with 11 head of Sheep and 7 head of Cattle, 20 head of Hogs, 2 Feather Beds and Furniture, and 3 Iron pots all now being and remaining on the said plantation ... true Intent ... if ... John COOK ... pay ... to Mac SCARBOROUGH ... 150 pounds ... at or upon the 25 March next ensuing ... together with the lawful Interest thereon, then this ... to be void ... otherwise to remain in full force ... 6 May 1745. *Signed*: John COOK. *Wit*: Elizh. E WILLIAMS her mark, Lam HATCH. *Proved*: July Court 1746 John COOK to Col. Mc SCARBOROUGH by the Oath of Lam HATCH. *Regt*: 1 Sept. 1746.

[A:439] North Carolina) Pasquotank County) Robert PALMER of the County and Province afsd. for & in Consideration of the Sum of 25 pounds current Money of the Province ... paid by John HOSEA ... sell ... part of a Tract of Land situate ... on Flatty Creek Swamp ... upon John WADES Line, then upon the Great Swamp ... upon Benjamin PALMER'S Line ... 170 acres of Land ... 8 July 1746. *Signed*: Robert PALMER. *Wit*: Hen PENDLETON, John REDING. *Ack*: July Court 1746. *Regt*: 1 Sept. 1746 in Book D. folio 35.

North Carolina) Pasquotank County) Jeremiah WILCOX of the County and Province, do for the Consideration of 20 Barrels of Pork and 400 Bushels of Indian Corn ... paid by Abazannah PERKINS of the County & Province afsd. ... do assign over all my Right ... of the within mentioned Deed ...
[A:440] ... 7 June 1746. *Signed*: Jeremiah WILCOCKS. *Wit*: Wm: TEAGUE, Mary TEAGUE. *Ack*: July Court 1746. *Regt*: 1 Sept. 1746.

Benjamin MASSAGY planter in Pasquotank County & Province of North Carolina ... for the Consideration of 55 pounds ... sold ... unto John COMY? Planter ... Tract of Land ... 60 acres ... on the West Side of Great Flatty Creek and lying betwixt a little Creek that runs Westerly out of Flatty Creek And on which the plantation that Valentine WALLIS formerly lived bounds and the line of the Land whereon Thomas COLLINS did live ... part of a Greater Tract by Patent granted to John BELLMAN & by the said BELLMAN sold to William WALLIS ... to him the said John COMEY ... 5 May 1746. *Signed*: Benja. X MASSAGY his mark. *Wit*: James GEORGE, David GEORGE. *Ack*: July Court 1746. *Regt*: 1 Sept. 1746.

North Carolina) Pasquotank County) 8 April 1745/6 Between Edwd. SCOTT of the County and Province afsd. Planter of the one part and Edward JACKSON Planter of the other part ... in Consideration of ... 100 pounds Current Money of the Province ... sold ... [A:441] Parcel of Land ... on the S. W. Side of Pasquotank River and containing ... 50 acres ... Thomas PRITCHARDS Line ... Richd. MADRENS to Edwd SCOTTS Corner Tree ... Job NICHOLS Line ... and Mary SCOTT the Wife of me the said Edwd. SCOTT doth ... yield ... Right of Dower ... *Signed*: Edwd. SCOTT, Mary M SCOTT her mark. *Wit*: John NORRIS, John MEYRIDGE? *Ack*: July Court 1746 Mary SCOTT ... examined. *Regt*: 1 Sept. 1746.

Edmond JACKSON of the County of Pasquotank within his Majesty's Province of North Carolina Farmer for and in Consideration of the Sum of 500 pounds current Money of North Carolina ... paid by Richard PRITCHARD of the County and Province afsd. ... sold ... Tract of Land ... on the S. W. Side of the River ... 50 acres ... said PRITCHARD'S Line, running across James PRITCHARD'S Land, it being the one half granted by Patent to the said PRITCHARD, and conveyed ... to Edwd. SCOTT to the Sandy Branch ... to the Main Swamp ...
[A:442] ... Elisabeth JACKSON the Wife of me ... surrender ... Right of Dowry ... 8 April 1746. *Signed*: Edmond JACKSON, Elisabeth I JACKSON her mark. *Wit*: Edward SCOTT, Danl. RODES, George G ROW his mark. *Ack*: July Court 1746 Elisabeth JACKSON ... examined. *Regt*: 2 Sept. 1746.

North Carolina) Pasquotank County) 10 Oct. 1746 By and Between Saml. MCCOY of the one part, and John MCCOY and Danl. MCCOY of the other part all of the County of Norfolk, in the Colony of Virginia ... in Consideration of the natural Love, Good Will, and affection which I have ... to my two Brothers ...

and further by the Desire and Advice of my Father John MCCOY at his death ... give ... Tract of Land ... on the N. E. Side of Pasquotank in the Fork ... 347 acres, it being part of 634 acres out of a patent bearing date the 1 April
[A:443] 17 [blank] The [blank] of the said plantation for my Brother Danl MCCOY and the other half to my Brother John MCCOY ... *Signed*: Samuel MCCOY. *Wit*: John HAKLEE, Jarvis JONES. *Ack*: Oct. Court 1746. *Regt*: 28 Oct. 1746.

Richard MADREN of North Carolina and County of Pasquotank Planter for and in Consideration of the Love and Goodwill I bear to my loving Brother John MADREN of the County and Province afsd. Planter ... give ... 150 acres of Land at the head of Nobs Crook Creek in the County afsd. ... Western Branch ... James PRITCHARD Junr ... Patent formerly taken up by James PRITCHARD relapsed for want of due Seating and planting thereon by Edward SCOTT which Land Will MADREN purchased 394 acres which is by patent ... 5 Aug. 1746. *Signed*: Richd. MADREN. *Wit*: William ABERCROMBIE, Hannah H ABERCROMBIE her mark, [blank] E EVERTON his mark. *Ack*: Oct. Court 1746. *Regt*: 28 Oct. 1746.

[A:444] 14 Oct. in the twentieth year of the Reign of our Sovereign Lord George the Second ... 1746, Between Isabella BURNHAM of North Carolina Pasquok. County of the one part and Jarvis JONES of the same place Planter ... in Consideration of 5 pounds Sterling money ... acknowledge all the Right of Dower she hath to the Land that did belong to Capt. Gabriel BURNHAM at his Death ... *Signed*: Isabella BURNHAM. *Wit*: James BURNHAM, Thomas GRANDY. *Ack*: Oct. Court 1746. *Regt*: 28 Oct. 1746.

13 Oct. in the twentieth year of the Reign of our Lord George the Second ... 1746 Between Hezekiah LINTON and Lucy LINTON his wife of the County of Pasquotank of the Province of North Carolina planters of the one part and Jarvis JONES of the same place, planter of the other part ... in Consideration of 20 pounds proclamation Money ... sold ... Right of Dower they have to that plantation ... that did belong to William UPTON former Husband to the said Lucy now Wife to the said Hezekiah LINTON ... in the quarter at the head of

Pasquotank River and joining to Thomas and Joseph UPTON'S Land ... *Signed*: Hez. LINTON, Lucy LINTON. *Wit*: Samuel SMITH, John DALY.
[A:445] *Proved*: Oct. Court 1746 Hezekiah LINTON & Lucy LINTON his wife to Jarvis JONES by the Oath of John DALEY. *Regt*: 28 Oct. 1746.

18 Sept. in the twentieth year of the Reign of our Sovereign Lord George the Second ... 1746 Between Joshua GAMBLIN of the County of Pasquotank and Province of North Carolina, Planter of the one part and James BRIGHT and Hezekiah BRIGHT of the County and Province afsd., Planters of the other part ...in Consideration of the Sum of 25 pounds, current money of the Colony of Virginia ... sold ... parcel of Land ... 88 acres ... part of a Tract of Land granted to Gabriel BURNHAM containing 175 acres as by patent bearing date 1725 ... Joseph MUNKS Corner Tree ... on Newfoundland Swamp ... mouth of the High Ridge, then up the High Ridge Branch ...
[A:446] ...
[A:447] ... *Signed*: Joshua GAMBLING. *Wit*: Jarvis JONES, James burnham, Robert TAYLOR. *Ack*: Oct. Court 1746. *Regt*: 28 Oct. 1746.

Evan LURRY and Barbry my Wife of the County of Pasquotank and Province of North Carolina for and in Consideration of the Sum of 50 pounds proclamation money ... paid by Joseph WILLIAMS of the County and Province afsd. ... sold ... parcel of Land ... 130 acres ... being a part of a Tract of Land bought by Edward WILLIAMS of Thomas SAWYER Senr. as by Deed bearing date the 13 July 1730 and since given by Will ... to Evan LURRY being the N. E. Side of the said Tract ... on Robert MORGAN'S Line ... Henry SAWYER'S Line ...
[A:448] ... 15 Oct. 1746. *Signed*: Evan L LURRY his mark, Barbry L LURRY her mark. *Wit*: Cornelius RELF, Isaac ALBERTSON. *Ack*: Oct. Court 1746 Evan LURRY & Barbara LURRY his Wife to Joseph WILLIAMS. *Regt*: 28 Oct. 1746.

Evan LURRY of Pasquotank County in the Province of North Carolina for and in Consideration of the Sum of 50 pounds proclamation money ... paid by Joseph WILLIAMS of the same County and Province afsd. ... sold ... 30 acres of Land ... on North River Side of SAWYER'S Creek, being part of a Tract of Land which

Robert MORGAN decd. willed to his Son Bennet MORGAN ... to Evan LURRY By Deed of Sale bearing date the 30 May 1741 ... Mouth of Broad Neck Branch ... Mouth of the School House Branch ... Creek Swamp ... [A:449] ... [blank] 1746. *Signed*: Evan L LURRY his mark. *Wit*: John COATS, William NORTON. *Ack*: Oct. Court 1746. *Regt*: 28 Oct. 1746.

Joseph WILLIAMS of Pasquotank County and in the Province of North Carolina for and in Consideration of the Sum of 100 pounds proclamation Money ... paid by Evan LURRY of the same County and Province afsd. ... sold ... Tract of Land being part of a Patent bearing date 1668, granted to Edward WILLIAMS known by the name of HARRIS Island containing 486 acres .. [A:450] ... [blank] 1746. *Signed*: Joseph WILLIAMS. *Wit*: William NORTON, John COATS. *Ack*: Oct. Court 1746. *Regt*: 28 Oct. 1746.

Jeremiah MURDEN of North Carolina in Pasquotank County Gentn. for the love, good Will and affection which I do bear towards my loving Grandson Jeremiah SPENCE do ... give ... Tract of Land called by the name of MABSON'S Ridge ... 80 acres ... Middle Swamp ... Joseph SPENCE my Son in Law and his wife Sarah SPENCE to have their Life Time in it as long as Joseph SPENCE lives and his wife during her Widowhood ... 4 March and in the Eighteenth year of the Reign of our Sovereign Lord King George the Second ... 1745. *Signed*: Jeremiah MURDEN. *Wit*: Robert MURDEN, Samuel EDNEY. *Ack*: Oct. Court 1747 [sic]. *Regt*: 28 Oct. 1746.

John MORGAN of the County of Pasquotank within the province of North Carolina for and in Consideration of the quantity of 13 Barrels of good Merchantable Pork ... paid by Patrick KEATON of the County and Province afsd. Planter ... sold ...
[A:451] ... part of a parcel of Land ... 75 acres ... it being half of the plantation left to me by my decd. Grandfather John MORGAN and the other part to my Brother George MORGAN the whole being 150 acres ... on the N. E. Side of Flatty Creek ... Branch coming out of Great Flatty Creek Charles WESTS Corner Tree ... 15 Oct. 1746. *Signed*: John MORGAN. *Wit*: Benjamin PALMER, John X COORK his mark. *Ack*: Oct. Court 1746. *Regt*: 28 Oct. 1746.

Robert SPENCE of the County of Pasquotank and Province of North Carolina Farmer, for and in Consideration of the Sum of 10 pounds Sterling money of Great Britain ... paid by Henry BROWN of the County and Province afsd. ... sold ... Tract of Land ... on the N. E. Side of Pasquotank River ... 100 acres ... Mill Dam Swamp ... Miles MCDANIEL'S Land and Solomon SAWYERS ... to the Lake ... It being part of the plantation whereon Robert SPENCE now liveth and purchased of John SOLLY ...
[A:452] ... & Ann SPENCE the Wife of me ... surrenders all her Right of Dowry ... 26 May 1746. *Signed*: Robert SPENCE, Ann E SPENCE her mark. *Wit*: Thomas O SAWYER his mark, Thomas X HASTINGS his mark. *Ack*: Oct. Court 1746. *Regt*: 28 Oct. 1746.

North Carolina) Pasquotank County) John HALELEE of Pasquotank County in the Province afsd. ... in Consideration of the natural Love and affection which I have and do bear unto my Godson James ROUT of the said County and Province afsd ... give ... 150 acres of Land, being the One half of 300 acres ... which I bought of John WALLIS, being the Manor part thereof, binding on by Isaac JONES, the Lake ... divides the said 300 acres of Land, betwixt my said Godson James ROUT and my Godson John ROUT his Brother ...
[A:453] ... 14 Oct. 1746. *Signed*: John HALELEE. *Wit*: Sam. HEIGHE, Tho: TAYLOR. *Ack*: Oct. Court 1746. *Regt*: 28 Oct. 1746.

North Carolina) Pasquotank County) Edward SCOTT of the County and Province afsd. for and in Consideration of the Sum of 50 pounds Sterling money of Great Britain ... paid by Edmond JACKSON of the County and Province aforesaid ... sold ... Tract of Land granted by Patent from Lord John CARTERET and bearing date the 30 July 1730 ... 209 acres ... George HARRIS Line ... COPPERS Line ...
[A:454] ... Mary SCOTT the Wife of me the said Edward SCOTT ... surrender all her Right of Dowry ... 8 April 1746. *Signed*: Edward SCOTT, Mary M SCOTT her mark. *Wit*: John NORRIS, John MAGRIDGE. *Ack*: July Court 1746. *Regt*: 10 April 1747.

RECORD OF DEEDS VOLUME B 1747-1751

[B:1] North Carolina 13 Jan. 1746/7 by and between Samuel PIKE of said Province and County of Pasquotank Farmer of the one part and Joseph PRITCHARD of the same place Farmer of the other party ... in Consideration of the Sum of 208 pounds Bills of said Province ... sold ... one Moiety or half part of a Tract of Land containing 325 acres according to Patent ... commonly known by the name of half way Tree Land, it being the Land that John PIKE of Frede County in Virginia sold unto me ... 19 Oct. 1744 and registered in the County afsd. ... boundeth as followeth ... Matthew REASONS ... to be equally divided between Joseph PRITCHARD and Benjamin PIKE, as it was to have been divided between the said Samuel PIKE & Benjamin his Brother but hitherto hath not been done ... half part contains ... 162½ acres ... whereon I the said Samuel PIKE now dwell ... on the N. E. Side of the aforementioned Tract of Land ...
[B:2] Sarah PIKE the Wife of the said Samuel PIKE ... give ... Right & Title of Dowry ... *Signed*: Samuel PIKE, Sarah X PIKE her mark. *Wit*: Benjn. PRITCHARD, Sarah PRITCHARD. *Ack*: Jan. Court 1746. *Regt*: [blank] Jan. 1746/7.

North Carolina William BROTHERS Junr of Pasquotank County ... in Consideration of the Sum of 1,100 pounds late lawful Bill Money of North Carolina ... paid ... by Samuel HEIGHT of the same place ... sold ... 150 acres ... bounding upon Newbegun Creek and joining on the one Side by Henry PENDLETON and on the other Side by the Meeting House Land whereon I the said William BROTHERS now live
[B:3] and is part of that 200 acres of Land granted by Patent bearing date the 1 Jan. 1694 by the Proprietors to Henry KEATON and by said Henry KEATON assigned to Edwd. SCOTT ... 19 Oct. 1714 and by Said SCOTT and Mary his Wife conveyed ... 20 July 1725 to John BROTHERS my Father ... if any time hereafter Thomas BROTHERS, Brother to the said William shall appear so as to lay Claim to the above ... released to him ... Samuel HEIGHT ... repaid ... but if a Claim as afsd be made ... after the Expiration of a Lease by Macrora SCARBOROUGH to said Samuel HEIGHT by virtue of that Lease now to be occupied and manured by me till the Expiration of the Same as

part of the Consideration Money, then I the Said William BROTHERS instead of the 1,100 shall ... return to the said Samuel HEIGHT ... only 800 pounds Money ... in Virginia Currency ... 17 Dec. in the Twentieth year of his Majesty's Reign George the Second ... 1746. *Signed*: William BROTHERS Junr. *Wit*: John MCDANIELL, Daniel GRANDIN. *Ack*: Jan. Court 1746. *Regt*: 10 April 1747.

[B:4] North Carolina: 14 Jan. 1746 by and between Robert PALMER of the County of Pasquotank in the Province afsd. Planter of the one part and Benjamin PALMER of the same County and Province of the other part ... in Consideration of the Sum of 250 pounds good and lawful money of North Carolina ... sold ... 50 acres ... by the River Side ... head of Crooked well Swamp ... whereon the said Benjamin PALMER now dwells ... *Signed*: Robert PALMER. *Wit*: Tho TAYLOR, Henry PENDLETON. *Ack*: Jan. Court 1746. *Regt*: 10 April 1747.

[B:5] North Carolina) Pasquotank County) 10 Sept. 1746 between Zachariah JACKSON of the County and Province afsd. of the one part, and Gabl BURNHAM Senr of the other part ... in Consideration of 55 pounds current Money of the Province ... sold ... 50 acres ... South Side of Pasquotank River ... *Signed*: Zachariah JACKSON. *Wit*: Wm ABERCROMBIE, James PRITCHARD. *Proved*: Jan. Court 1746 by the Oath of James PRITCHARD. *Regt*: 10 April 1747.

[B:6] North Carolina) Pasquotank County) John HALELEE of Pasquotank County ... in Consideration of the natural Love and affection which I have and do bear unto my Godson John ROUT ... give ... after the decease of me ... 150 acres of Land ... part of 300 Acres ... bought of John WALLIS lying on the N. E. Side of Pasquotank River ... Sandy Run Binding on John BURNHAM'S Line formerly called RODES Line ... binding on John JONES which was formerly called Francis MARTINS ... PRITCHARDS Corner Tree ... CHAMBALINS to Sandy Run ... one half of the afsd 300 Acres ... 14 Oct. 1746. *Signed*: John HALELEE. *Wit*: Samuel HIGHE, Thomas TAYLOR. *Ack*: in open court ... *Regt*: 27 April 1747 (in Book D. Fo. 70)

[B:7] North Carolina) Pasquotank County) John BASNET ... assign all my Right ... of the within

Patent to John DIALL ... 13 Jan. 1746. *Signed*: John I BASNET his mark, Mary X BASNET her mark. *Wit*: Joshua MARTIN, John REDING. *Ack*: Jan. Court 1746. *Regt*: 27 April 1747.

2 Aug. 1746 and in the Seventeeth year of the Reign of our Sovn Lord George the Second ... between Joshua GAMBLING of the one part and William TAYLOR of the other part ... in Consideration of the valuable Sum of 20 pounds Specie ... sell ... 87 Acres being part of a patent containing 175 Acres bearing date 1725 Beginning at the Mouth of the High Ridge Branch ... Main Swamp ... *Signed*: Joshua GAMBLING. *Wit*: Jacob BURNHAM. *Ack*: April Court 1747. *Regt*: 27 April 1747.

[B:8] North Carolina) Pasquotank County) James CRECH of the County and Province afsd. ... Consideration of 40 pounds Bill ... paid down by Cornelius RELFE ... sold ... part of a Tract of Land lying on the North East Side of the Easternmost Branch of Accomack Creek containing 100 acres together with the plantation that my Grandmother Joyce CRECH lived on, it being a part of a greater Tract of Land [blank] by my Grandfather Henry CRECH and given by will to my Father Henry CRECH ... 7 Aug. 1709 and transferred to Cornelius RELFE ... 4 June 1746 and in the Nineteenth year of our Sovereign Lord King George the Second. *Signed*: James I CRECH his mark. *Wit*: John BEELS his mark, Joseph IH HAMTON mark. *Proved*: July Court 1746 by the Oath of John BEELS. *Regt*: 1 May 1747.

[B:9] Ralph BARKER of the City of New York in the Province of New York in America Gent and Johannah my Wife reposing great Trust and Confidence in Andrew MEAD of Nansemond in Virginia Merchant and Gabriel BURNHAM of the Fork of Pasquotank in North Carolina Esqr. have made ... attornies jointly ... to sell ... Lands ... entitled to within the province of North Carolina ... 28 Sept. in the Eighth year of the Reign of our Sovereign Lord George the Second ... 1734. *Signed*: Ra: BARKER, Joanna BARKER. *Wit*: Ann BROM, Elizth. PARMYTON. Exhibited April Court 1747 ... by Benjamin BURNHAM. *Regt*: 20 May 1747.

[B:10] North Carolina) Pasquotank County) 16 Sept. 1746 Between Gabriel BURNHAM Senr of the County and

Province afsd. Planter of the one part and James PRITCHARD Junr of the same County and Province afsd. Planter of the other part ... 100 pounds current Bills of the Province ... sold ... Parcel of Land ... S. W. Side of Pasquotank River ... 100 Acres ... Creek Swamp binding on John HARRIS'S Line ... Valentine ROW'S Line ... *Signed*: Gabl. X BURNHAM his mark. *Wit*: Joshua PARISHO, James W WARD his mark. *Ack*: Jan. Court 1746. *Regt*: 20 May 1747.

[B:11] North Carolina Henry PENDLETON of the County of Pasquotank & Province afsd. Planter ... love and Goodwill which I bear unto my Cousin William WOODLEY Son of Thomas WOODLEY of the Province and County afsd. ... give ... one Negro Boy named Jack, aged about 8 or 9 years the Son of my Negro Wench Sarah ... Twentieth year of the Reign of our Sovereign Lord George the Second, 17 March 1746/7. *Signed*: Henry PENDLETON. *Wit*: John PEGGS, Laml L KEEL his mark, John GRAY I his mark. *Ack*: April Court 1747. *Regt*: 20 May 1747.

18 Dec. in the Twentieth year of the Reign of our Sovereign Lord George the Second ... 1746 between James and Hezekiah BRIGHT his Son, the said Hezekiah BRIGHT now being of the age of 23 years of the County of Pasquotank, and Province of North Carolina planters of the one part and James GARRETT of the County of Currituck and Province afsd. of the other part ... for 25 pounds Current Silver Money of the Colony of Virginia ... sold ...
[B:12] 88 acres of Land ... part of a Tract of Land granted to Gabl. BURNHAM containing 175 acres as by patent bearing date 1725 ... conveyed to Joshua GAMBLING as by Deed bearing date the 9 Jan. 1743/4 and registered in ... Book C. fo. 159 the 17th day of the same month Jan. last beforementioned ... 18 Sept. 1746 conveyed to James BRIGHT for Life with Remainder to Hezekiah BRIGHT ... unto the said James GARRETT ... during the term of 999 years ... parcel of land ... in the County of Currituck ... 150 acres ... which the said James GARRET had purchased from ... James BRIGHT and Hezekiah BRIGHT his Son ... bearing equal date with these Presents ...
[B:13] ... *Signed*: James I BRIGHT his mark, Hezekiah C BRIGHT his mark. *Wit*: Jarvis JONES, Joseph MCPHERSON, Henry BRIGHT. *Ack*: April Court 1747. *Regt*: 20 May 1747.

13 April 1747 and in the nineteenth year of the Reign of our Sovn Lord George ... between Robert HOSEA of the County of Pasquotank and Province of North Carolina yeoman of the one part and Joseph COMMANDER of the County and Province afsd. of the other part ... 146 pounds lawful Bills of this province ... sold ... 50 acres ... on the N. E. Side of Little River ... Corner Tree of Timothy MEAD'S Land ... Swamp Beach on Joseph COMMANDER'S Line ... [B:14] ... *Signed*: Robert HOSEA. *Wit*: John CONNER, Jno REED. *Ack*: April Court 1747. *Regt*: 20 May 1747.

North Carolina) Pasquotank County) 12 March 1746/7 between Richard PRITCHARD of the County and Province afsd. Planter of the one part and John MADREN of the County &c. afsd. planter of the other part ... 50 pounds Sterling money of Great Britain ... sold ... [B:15] 90 acres ... Danl. RODES Line and then binding on Thomas PRITCHARD'S Line ... *Signed*: Richard PRITCHARD. *Wit*: James Poolman DUFFEY, James PRITCHARD. *Ack*: April Court 1747. *Regt*: 20 May 1747.

Thomas FARCLAY in the County of Pasquotank in the Province of North Carolina ... natural affection and Brotherly Love which I have ... unto my well beloved Brother Edward FARCLAY ... give ... Land being the East Side of the plantation I now live on ... 50 acres ... but if my sd. Brother should die without issue then to return to him the said Thomas FARCLAY ... 1 Dec. 1746. *Signed*: Thomas T FARCLAY his mark. *Wit*: John BELL, W BURGES, Mary M BELL her mark. *Ack*: April Court 1747. *Regt*: 20 May 1747.

[B:16] 10 Oct. 1746 and in the Twentieth year of the Reign of our Sovereign Lord the Second ... between John RELFE of the County of Pasquotank and Province of North Carolina of the one part and Deliverance RICH of the County and Province afsd. ... for 10 pounds Specie ... sold ... 100 acres ... James SPENCES'S Land ... *Signed*: John J RELFE his mark. *Wit*: Charles SAWYER, John BURNHAM. *Ack*: April Court 1747. *Regt*: 20 May 1747.

[B:17] 9 March 1746 between John COOK of the County of Pasquotank and the Province of North Carolina

Weaver of the one party and Benjamin PHILLIPS of the same place and Province afsd. Planter ... for 21 pounds in good [blank] ... sold ... parcel of Woodland Ground ... on the N. E. Side of Pasquotank River containing 50 Acres of Land ... Benjamin PHILLIPS Line ... William JAMES Line Tree ... Capt. RELFS Corner Tree ... on the White Oak Neck Bind on the Said RELFES ... to John PUGH'S head line ... to Christopher WILLIAMS Back Line ... *Signed*: John COOK. *Wit*: Benj. MORGAN, Joseph BRUNT, Zachariah SAWYER. *Proved*: April Court 1747 by the Oath of Joseph BRUNT. *Regt*: 20 May 1747.

North Carolina) Pasquotank County) 13 April 1746 between Benjamin PHILLIPS of the one part, Farmer and Samuel JACKSON the younger of the other part Farmer, both of the County and Province afsd. ... 350 pounds lawful Bill money of the said Province [B:18] ... sold ... 100 acres ... on the N. E. Side of Pasquotank River, known by the name of the Schoolhouse Neck, 50 acres whereof being part of that Land I ... bought of John SCARBOROUGH and the other 50 acres I ... had by Exchange of John COOK Weaver ... deed from John SCARBOROUGH bearing date the 2 March 1740 and the Deed from John COOK ... 9 March 1746 ... marked Line between me the Said Benjamin PHILLIPS and the said John COOK Weaver ... William JONES Line Tree from thence to Capt. Cornelius RELFE Corner Tree standing on White Oak ... John PUGH'S head line ... to Christopher WILLIAMS Back line ...
[B:19] ... *Signed*: Benja. PHILLIPS. *Wit*: Jesse HANLEY, Benja. MUNDEN, John TAYLOR. *Ack*: April Court 1747. *Regt*: 20 May 1747.

Abasanna PERKINS of Pasquotank County in the Province of North Carolina Planter ... for 80 pounds lawful Money ... paid by ... Solomon TEMPLE of the County and Province afsd. Planter ... sold ... 100 Acres ... to SANDERLINS Line commonly called the Forest ... 8 July 1746. *Signed*: Abasanna PERKINS. *Wit*: Jas FORBES, Cornelius SAWYER. *Ack*: April Court 1747. *Regt*: 20 May 1747.

[B:20] Abel ROSS of the County of Pasquotank and the Province of North Carolina have for ... 50 pounds Sterling Money ... paid by James WILLIAMS of the same place, County & Province afsd ... sold ...

Tract of Land ... N. E. Side of Pasquotank River on Arranuse Creek ... Capt. ROSSES line, then binding on Thomas GRANDY'S Line, then Binding on James WILLIAMS line & then binding Edward WILLIAMS line ... Edward UPTON'S Line ... 196 acres taken out of a Patent containing 296 acres ... all that the Patent specifies except 100 Acres granted to Thomas GRAY to the said James WILLIAMS ... 10 Nov. 1737. *Signed*: Abel ROSS. *Wit*: Saml. LOWMAN, Thos. SAWYER, Robert X WILLIAMS his mark. *Proved*: Oct. Court 1746 by the Oath of Saml LOWMAN. *Regt*: 21 July 1747.

North Carolina) Pasquotank County) John GUTHRIE of the Province and County afsd. Planter ... for 250 pounds lawful money of this Province ... paid by Jeremiah WILCOX of the Province and County afsd. ... sold ... 300 acres as by patent may appear granted to Saml. GUTHRIE decd. bearing date April 20, 1724 [B:21] ... 24 April 1747 and in the 20th year of the Reign of our Sovn Lord King Second. *Signed*: John I GUTHRIE his mark. *Wit*: John COREY , Jno MCKEEL. *Proved*: July Court 1747 by the Oath of John COREY. *Regt*: 21 July 1747.

John SANDERLIN Senr. and John SANDERLIN Junr. both of the County of Pasquotank and in the Province of North Carolina Planter for ... 50 pounds lawful Money of the said Province ... paid by Robert SANDERLIN of the Same County and Province afsd. Planter ... sold ... 55 acres ... a Corner Tree, between the afsd. Robert SANDERLIN and the afsd. John SANDERLIN Senr and John SANDERLIN Junr ... Edward JAMES Line ...
[B:22] ... 12 July 1747. *Signed*: John SANDERLIN Senr. his X Mark, John SANDERLIN Junr His W Mark. *Wit*: Edward X JAMES his mark, John LURRY. *Proved*: July Court 1747 by the Oath of Edwd. JAMES. *Regt*: 21 July 1747.

North Carolina Thomas BARKER of Pasquotank County in the Province of North Carolina Planter for ... 25 pounds proclamation Money paid by John COATS ... sold ... one certain Farm ... on the N. E. Side of the sd. River ... 65 Acres ... part of a Tract of Land which I entered and Surveyed contg. 200 acres and lying on the Western Side of the said Tract called the Island beginning at the mouth of a Branch called Tantrough Branch ... to William BRAY'S Line

... 65 Acres ... 24 Jany 1745/6. *Signed*: Thomas BARKER. *Wit*: James FORBES, Eliza FORBES, Absolum GRIMES. *Ack*: July Court 1747. *Regt*: 21 July 1747.

[B:23] North Carolina. Isaac FORBES of Pasquotank County in the Province afsd. Planter ... for 60 pounds lawful Money of the Province afsd. ... paid by William BRAY ... sold ... 62 acres ... Cypress Swamp ... binding on a Line made between the said BRAY and Thomas BURGES ... Dogwood Ridge ... on the N. E. Side of Pasquotank River ... 10 Feby 1746/7. *Signed*: Isaac FORBES. *Wit*: James FORBES, Danl. BRAY, Elisabeth FORBES. *Ack*: July Court 1747. *Regt*: 21 July 1747.

North Carolina. 13 Jan. 1743 Between Thomas SAWYER of the County of Pasquotank and in the Province of North Carolina of the one part and William WARD of the County of Pasquotank and Province afsd. of the other part ... for 70 pounds lawful money of the Province ... sold ... 72 acres ... on the North Side of Knobbs Crook Creek joining to the said William WARDS Land ... called the Long Ridge ...
[B:24] ... *Signed*: Thomas SAWYER. *Wit*: James Poolman DUFFEY, Jacob ALBERTSON. *Ack*: Jan. Court 1743. *Regt*: 21 July 1747.

North Carolina. William WARD of Pasquotank County in the Province afsd. Planter for ... 5 Shillings Current Bills ... paid by Alexander JACK ... sold ... all my Right ... 72 acres of Land ... 11 April 1744. *Signed*: William WARD his W Mark. *Wit*: Job CHARTWRIGHT, William HIXON. *Ack*: April Court 1744. *Regt*: 1 May 1744.

North Carolina. Alexander JACK of Pasquotank County in the Province afsd. Merchant for ... a Swap of Plantations made betwixt Alexander JACK and Jonathan HIBBS, have sold ... all my Right ... to 72 Acres of Land above assigned me from William WARD ... 2 June 1744. *Signed*: Al: JACK. *Wit*: Abel DRESSER, Mark PRIME. *Proved*: July court 1747 by the Oath of Abel DRESSER. *Regt*: 21 July 1747.

[B:25] North Carolina) Pasquotank County) John DAVIS of Pasquotank County and Province afsd. ... with the advice, Consent ... of Dorothy my Wife ... for 100 pounds lawful Money of Great Britain ...

paid by Sarah TRUEBLOOD of the County and Province afsd. Widow ... sold ... Tract of Land ... on the S. W. Side of Pasquotank River ... contg 195 Acres ... Isaac STOKELY'S ... River Swamp ... part of the Land conveyed by Emanuel and Ann LOW to me by their Deed of Sale dated in April 1716 and by Henry WENSELY by his Indenture dated 11 Jan. 1742 By virtue of a power of attorney from George LOW Reconveyed ... unto me the Said John DAVIS ...
[B:26] ... 15 April in the 20th year of his Majesty's Reign George the Second ... 1747. *Signed*: John DAVIS, Dorothy DAVIS. *Wit*: Thomas DAVIS, Isaac ALBERTSON. *Proved*: July Court 1747 by the affirmation of Isaac ALBERTSON and at Oct. Court 1747 following the said Dorothy DAVIS appeared ... *Ack*: her Right of Dower. *Regt*: 14 July 1747.

North Carolina: 14 July 1747 By and Between Benjamin PHILLIPS of the County of Pasquotank in the Province of North Carolina of the one part and William BARNS late of the Province of Pennsylvania but now of the County of Pasquotank in the Province of North Carolina Gentn of the other part ... Benjamin PHILLIPS and Betty PHILLIPS his Wife Daughter of Benjamin KOEN late of the County afsd. decd. for ... 15 pounds Current Money of the Colony of Virginia ... paid by William BARNS ... sold ... Tract of Land ... on the N. E. Side of Pasquotank River contg by Patent 118 acres granted by the said Patent to John JONES Cordwainer and by the sd. Henry SAWYER and Elisabeth his Wife assigned over to Daniel COEN ... by Daniel COEN and Dorothy his Wife assigned over unto the afsd Benjn PHILLIPS ... Henry SAWYERS Corner Tree ...
[B:27] ... *Signed*: Benjamin PHILLIPS, Betty E PHILLIPS. *Wit*: Jno BARNS, Tho. TAYLOR. *Ack*: July Court 1747. *Regt*: 14 July 1747.

North Carolina. Arthur MABSON of Carteret County in the Province afsd. Merchant and Mary my Wife ... for the natural love and affection which we bear to our beloved Daughter Elisabeth MABSON do by these presents give ... 172 acres ... Richd. MADREN'S Corner Tree ... George HARRIS'S Line ... which Land was granted by Patent bearing date the 27th Sept. 1715 unto Levi CREASY and by the sd Levy CREASY conveyed by Deed bearing date the 19th day of July 1721 unto the abovesaid Mary Wife of the afsd Arthur

while Sole ... being the plantation whereon Edwd SCOTT now dwells ...
[B:28] ... 9 March 1744/5. *Signed*: Ar. MABSON, Mary MABSON. *Wit*: Rd. LOVETT, John NORRIS. *Ack*: 10 May 1745 by E MOSELY C Jurt. *Regt*: 14 Aug. 1747.

1 May 1747 Between Richard GREGORY of the County of Pasquotank and the Province of North Carolina of the one party and William GREGORY of the Same place and Province afsd. of the other party ... for 50 pounds ... sold ... Tract of Land ... on the N. E. Side of Pasquotank River & on the head of Arenuse Creek ... 50 acres and commonly called ... Jonacin? Town which said Land and plantation I bought of Benjamin EVANS and Affiah his Wife ...
[B:29] ... *Signed*: Richard R GREGORY his mark. *Wit*: Griffith JONES, Ben. MORGAN. *Proved*: July Court 1747 by the Oath of Griffith JONES. *Regt*: 14 Aug. 1747.

John MADREN of the County of Pasquotank and Province of North Carolina of the one part planter for ... 50 pounds Sterling Money of Great Britain ... paid by James PRITCHARD of the County and Province afsd ... sold ... Tract of Land ... on the S. W. Side of Pasquotank River contg ... 154 acres ... Western Branch ... which James PRITCHARD purchased of Richd MADREN ... 12 March 1746/7. *Signed*: John I M MADREN his mark. *Wit*: James Poolman DUFFEY, Richard PRITCHARD. *Proved*: July Court 1747 by the Oath of James Poolman DUFFEY. *Regt*: 14 Aug. 1747.

[B:30] North Carolina) Pasquotank County) James PRITCHARD of the County and Province afsd for ... the Sum of 6 pounds lawful Money of Great Britain ... paid by James WARD ... sold ... 8 acres ... on the S. W. Side of Pasquotank River ... at the Mouth of the great Branch ... to the Great Swamp ... 15 July 1747. *Signed*: James PRITCHARD. *Wit*: John NORRIS. *Ack*: July Court 1747. *Regt*: 14 Aug. 1747.

13 Oct. 1747 By and Between Thomas TAYLOR Clerk? of the said County of the one part and Francis WOODWARD of the County of Norfolk in the Colony of Virginia of the other part ... Sum of 1 Shilling good and lawful Money of Great Britain ... sold ... parcel of land ... on the N. E. Side of Pasquotank River contg 300 acres commonly called the Horsepond Neck ...

Thomas TAYLOR had surveyed by Richd MCCLURE Surveyor [B:31] ... *Signed*: Tho: TAYLOR. *Wit*: Shad TAYLOR, Thomas MCKEEL. *Ack*: Oct. Court 1747. *Regt*: 19 Oct. 1747.

28 May 1747 & the 19th year of the Reign of our Sovn Lord George the Second ... between William SIKES of the County of Pasquotank in North Carolina of the one part and Joseph MACKFARSIN of the same place ... for 12 pounds Virginia Currency ... sold ... 50 acres ... part of a large Tract of Land of 400 acres and part out of a patent that was taken by Thomas LEWIS and Daniel MACFARSON bearing date March 26 1742/3 ... North to the Dismal Swamp ... [B:32] ... *Signed*: William W SIKES his mark. *Wit*: Henry THOROGOOD, Moses M MACFARSIN his mark, David R JONES his mark. *Ack*: Oct. Court 1747. *Regt*: 19 Oct. 1747.

31 Aug. 1747 and the 20th year of the Reign of our Sovn Lord George the Second ... between Thomas LEWIS of Pasquotank County in North Carolina and Daniel MACFARSON of the County of Norfolk in Virginia of the one part and Joseph MACFARSON of the County of Pasquotank in North Carolina of the other part ... for 19 pounds proclamation money ... sold ... on the N E Side of the River and being part of a larger Tract of Land of 400 Acres patented in the name of the said Thomas LEWIS and Daniel MACFARSON ... contg 325 Acres ... Bear Pond JONES'S Corner Tree ... Jarvis JONES'S Land taken out of the said Patent ... near the Great Swamp Bridge ... Juniper Swamp ... [B:33] ... *Signed*: Thomas L LEWIS his mark, Daniel D MACFARSON his mark. *Wit*: Jarvis JONES, Moses MACFARSON, Alexander SPENCE. *Ack*: Oct. Court 1747 by the said Danl. MACFARSON to Joseph MACFARSON and was proved as to Thomas LEWIS'S signing by the Oath of Captn Jarvis JONES. *Regt*: 19 Oct. 1747.

12 July in the 20th year of the Reign of our Sovn Lord George the Second ... Between Jarvis JONES of the County of Pasquotank and Province of North Carolina Gentn of the one part and David DUNKIN Planter of the same place ... for 13 pounds proclamation Money ... sold ... on the N. E. Side of Pasquotank River being known by the name of the Middle Island and Landing Island being patented by Thomas BETTOS? and said Patent assigned to

John JONES and left by the last Will & Testament of John JONES to Jarvis JONES Son of the said John JONES ... John BISHOPS Corner Tree ... 200 acres of Land ... *Signed*: Jarvis JONES. *Wit*: Joseph MACKFARSON, Saml. SMITH, James GARRETT. *Ack*: Oct. Court 1747. *Regt*: 19 Oct. 1747.

[B:34] North Carolina) Pasquotank County) George WHEDBEE and Ann my Wife ... for and in Consideration of that parental Love and affection that we do bear towards our loving children viz William BOYD, Elisabeth BOYD Winefred BOYD and Thomas BOYD have given ... 240 pounds current Money of Virginia to be paid ... at their Arrival at the age of 21 years or day of Marriage also we give to our Son William BOYD one pair of Shoe Buckles that was his Father's John BOYD ... also we give unto our Daughter Elisabeth BOYD one gold Ring, that was her father John BOYDS, also we give unto our Daughter Winifred BOYD one gold Ring , that was her father John BOYD'S, also we give unto our Son Thomas BOYD one Silver Seal that was his Grandfather Thomas BOYD'S ... 14 Aug. 1746. *Signed*: George WHEDBEE, Ann WHEDBEE. *Wit*: Mary ROBINSON, Mary EVANS, Joseph ROBINSON. *Proved*: Oct. Court 1747 by the affirmation of Joseph ROBINSON. *Regt*: 24 Oct. 1747.

Then paid in part of the within Bond to William BOYD one pari of Silver Shoe Buckles that was his Father's, also paid Elisabeth BOYD one gold Ring that was her father John BOYDS in part of the within Bond, also paid Winifred BOYD one gold Ring, that was her father John BOYD'S in part of the within Bond, delivered to Anthony MARKHAM one Silver Seal in keeping for our Son Thomas BOYD, at his arrival at the age of 20 years or day of Marriage, it being part of the within Bond By Cash paid to Willm BOYD in part of the within Deed, 3 pounds 2 Shillings & 6 pense By Do paid Thos BOYD 3 pounds 2 Shillings & 6 pense in part of the within Bond. These may certify that the afsd Receipts was ordered by Anthony MARKHAM to be registered and is accordingly registd. the 24 Oct. 1747.

[B:35] 31 Aug. 1747 and in the 20th year of the Reign of our Sovn Lord George the Second ... Between Thomas LEWIS of the County of Pasquotank in North Carolina Planter & Daniel MACKFARSON of the County of Norfolk in Virginia of the one part and Jarvis JONES of the County of Pasquotank in North Carolina of the other part ... for 30 pounds Va. Curry. ... sold ... on the N E Side of Pasquotank River ... and contg 75 acres ... being part of a larger Tract contg 400 Acres patented in the name of the said Thos LEWIS and Danl MACKFARSON and known by the name of Bustable, ... Bear Pond JONES'S Corner Tree ... Willm SIKES'S and David DUNKINS former plantation ... *Signed*: Thos. L LEWIS his mark, Danl. X MARKHAM [sic] his mark. *Wit*: Joseph MACKFARSON, Moses M MACKFARSON his mark, Alexander SPENCE. *Ack*: Oct. Court 1747. *Regt*: 24 Oct. 1747.

[B:36] 13 Oct. 1747 & in the 19th year of the Reign of our Sovn Lord George the Second ... Between Jarvis JONES of Pasquotank in North Carolina & Saml. SMITH of the County & Province afsd. of the other part ... 10 pounds Stg Money of Gt Britain ... sold ... Tract of Land ... between Thomas LEWIS and James SMITH, contg 50 acres ... taken out of a patent contg 1654 acres ... *Signed*: Jarvis JONES. *Wit*: Danl. GRANDIN, Joseph MACKFARSON, Isaac STOKELY. *Ack*: Oct. Court 1747. *Regt*: 24 Oct. 1747.

3 Oct. 1747 in the 20th year of the Reign of our Sovn Lord George the Second ... between Zachariah SAWYER of the County of Pasquotank and Province of North Carolina planter of the one part & John DAILY of the same place Planter of the other part... 24 pounds Virginia Curry ... sold ...
[B:37] ... the plantation the above said Zachariah SAWYER now lives on contg ... 50 acres ... the Indian Line, then S. W. to Mathew WIN'S Line ... *Signed*: Zachariah SAWYER. *Wit*: Samuel LOWMAN, Abel ROSS, Jarvis JONES, James I CREECH his mark. *Proved*: Oct. Court 1747 by the Oath of Jarvis JONES. *Regt*: 24 Oct. 1747.

North Carolina) Pasquotank County) 12th day of the Eighth Month called October 1747 Between Wyke HUNNICUTT of the Colony of Virginia Farmer and Sarah his Wife of the one part and Stephen SCOTT of the County of Pasquotank and Province of North Carolina of the other part ... whereas Joseph GLASTER by his last Will and Testament in writing bearing date the 27 Jany 1718 gave and bequeathed to the sd. Sarah Wife of the said HUNNICUTT and one of the Daughters

of the sd. Joseph GLASTER & also to Ruth GLASTER another of the said Joseph GLASTER'S Daughters all his Lands as well in Carolina as Virginia ... to be equally divided between them ... and whereas the said Sarah ... in virtue of ... division made between ... entitled to a plantation ... 150 acres ... adjoining to a Creek, that is between the Houses of the said Stephen SCOTT and John PALIN which Creek makes out of Newbegun Creek & is the lower Bounds of the sd. Land, as also the Beginning Bounds in the Patent of said Lands patented in the name of Henry PALIN bearing date the 4 Nov. 1688 ... 80 pounds Current Money of Virginia ...
[B:38] ... sold ... *Signed*: Wyke HUNNICUTT, Sarah HUNNICUTT. *Wit*: Thomas NICHOLSON, Aaron MORRIS, Joseph ROBINSON. *Ack*: Oct. Court 1747. *Regt*: 24 Oct. 1747.

[B:39] North Carolina) Pasquotank County) Stephen SCOTT of the Province and County afsd. for ... 40 pounds Virginia Curry ... paid by Abel TRUEBLOOD ... sold ... one part of a registered Tract of Land whereon Joseph REDING Senr formerly lived Contg ... 100 acres ... on the S. W. Side of Pasquotank River ... Beginning at the Mouth of the Easternmost Branch of CHARTRIGHTS Creek ... between Thomas and Joseph CHARTWRIGHT ... main Creek Swamp ... 12 Aug. 1747. *Signed*: Stephen SCOTT. *Wit*: Joseph PRITCHARD, Job. WINSLOW, Jos: JORDAN Jr. *Ack*: Oct. Court 1747. *Regt*: 24 Oct. 1747.

North Carolina) Pasquotank County) Joshua PARISHO of the County and Province afsd. ... for 100 pounds Current Bills of this Province ... paid by Joseph SANDERLIN of the same County and Province ... sold ... part of a parcel of Land ... on the S. W. Side of Pasquotank River being the Manor part of the plantation that I the said Joshua PARISHO ...
[B:40] Contg 100 acres ... head of the Oak Branch ... head of Thomas JENNINGS Branch ... 6 March 1746/7. *Signed*: Joshua PARISHO. *Wit*: William BARNS, Tho: TAYLOR. *Proved*: Oct. Court 1747 by the Oath of Thomas TAYLOR. *Regt*: 24 Dec. 1747.

12 Oct. 1747 and in the 21st year of the Reign of our Sovn Lord George the Second ... Between John DAVIS of Pasquotank in North Carolina & Thomas RODES of the County & Province afsd of the other part ...

for 10 pounds current money of Virginia ... sold ... parcel of land ... on Christopher WILLIAMS'S Line & 100 acres of land holding by David DAVIS lying and joining upon James SPENCE'S line & upon the River Swamp containing 50 acres ...
[B:41] ... *Signed*: John DAVIS his J mark. *Wit*: Isaac STOKELY, Joshua X SAWYER his mark. *Proved*: Oct. Court 1747 by the Oath of Isaac STOKELY. *Regt*: 24 Dec. 1747.

N. C) P. C) Benjamin JENNINGS of the County of Pasquotank & Province of North Carolina Planter of the one part ... for 100 pounds Stg Money of Gt Britain ... paid by William JENNINGS my Father ... sold ... on the S. W. Side of Pasquotank River and contg ... 150 acres ... on Nobs Crook Creek ... at the Mouth of Cypress Swamp ... to the Main Swamp ...
[B:42] ... 31 Oct. 1746. *Signed*: Benjamin JENNINGS. *Wit*: William W WAMAN his mark, John HARRIS. *Ack*: Oct. Court 1747. *Regt*: 24 Dec. 1747.

North Carolina) Pasquotank County) 4 July 1745 Between Henry NICHOLS of the County and Province afsd. of the one part and John HARRIS of the same County and Province of the other part ... 100 pounds in good and lawful Money of the Province ... sold ... 60 acres ... head of the long Branch ... to the River Swamp ...
[B:43] ... *Signed*: Henry H N NICHOLS his mark. *Wit*: Wm. ABERCROMBIE, James GRAVES? *Ack*: Oct. Court 1747. *Regt*: 24 Dec. 1747.

No. Carolina) Pasquotank Cy) 3 Sept. 1747 Between Lodwick GRAY of the County and Province afsd. Farmer of the one part and William NICHOLS of the Province afsd of the other part ... for 50 pounds Current money of the Colony of Virginia ... sold ... 83 Acres ... on the S. W. Side of Pasquotank River, being part of a Tract of 508 acres called by the name of the new Land Beginning at the mouth of Cypress Branch Binding on James MCDANIELS Land ... *Signed*: Lodwick L G GRAY his mark. *Wit*: Gabl. W BURNHAM his mark, John I MADREN his mark. *Ack*: Oct. Court 1747. *Regt*: 24 Dec. 1747.

[B:44] 19 Aug. 1747 and in the 21st year of the Reign of our Sovn Lord George the Second ... Between Thomas DAVIS in the Precinct of Pasquotank in the

County of Albemarle and the Province of North Carolina, the one party, & Arthur DAVIS of the Precinct and County & Province afsd. of the other party ... for the good/will I bear to my Son Arthur DAVIS ... give ... 100 acres ... on the S. W. Side of Pasquotank River it being part out of a Patent bearing date 1728 beginning at the River Swamp on a Red Oak upon John DAVIS'S Line ... *Signed*: Thos. T DAVIS. *Wit*: Isaac STOKELY, John J DAVIS his mark. *Proved*: Oct. Court 1747 by the Oath of Isaac STOKELY. *Regt*: 24 Dec. 1747.

[B:45] North Carolina 12 Oct. 1747 and in the 20th year of our Sovn Lord George the Second ... between Edwd. WORDSWORTH of the sd. Province and County of Pasquotank Farmer and Thomas PARKER of the same place Shipwright of the other party ... for paying the Costs of Rights & Warrants and Costs of Surveying after the Entry was made of all that Land that James NEWBY Senr gave to the sd. Edwd. WORDSWORTH by his last Will and Testament ... sold ... all that Land that James NEWBY Senr. ... gave unto me the said Edwd. WARDSWORTH Excepting one Neck lying in the fork of Little River, the next excepting lying over the Horse pond Branch joining to Aaron HILLS Land ... pine Branch ... 50 or 60 acres by Guess ... by reason it hath not as yet been laid off by any Surveyor ... beginning on the other Side ... Horse pen Branch ...
[B:46] ... *Signed*: Edward WORDSWORTH. *Wit*: Joseph ROBINSON, John ROBINSON. *Proved*: Oct. Court 1747 by the Affirmation of Joseph ROBINSON. *Regt*: 24 Dec. 1747.

North Carolina. 17 July 1747 and in the 20th year of the Reign of our Sovn Lord George the Second ... Between Joseph WILLIAMS of the Prect of Pasquotank in the Province of North Carolina, Planter of the one part and I William HUMPHRYS of the Prect and Province afsd Planter of the other part ... for 200 pounds good and lawful Money of North Carolina ... sold ... 30 Acres ... on the N. E. Side of Pasquotank River being a part or parcel of a Tract of land which Robert MORGAN willed to his Son Bennet MORGAN, which was transferred from Bennet MORGAN to Evan LURRY and from Evan LURRY to Joseph WILLIAMS ... Patent bearing date 1668 ... at the Mouth of the broad Neck Branch ... to the Mouth of the

School House Branch ... on the Creek Swamp ... [B:47] ... *Signed*: Joseph WILLIAMS. *Wit*: B. MORGAN, Josiah WILLIAMS. *Proved*: Oct. Court 1747 by the Oath of Bennet MORGAN. *Regt*: 24 Dec. 1747.

North Carolina) Pasquotank County) John DIALL for and in Consideration of the Sum of 30 pounds Virginia to me in hands paid by John BASNET have assigned over all my Right ... 3 Oct. 1747. *Signed*: John DIALL. *Wit*: Wm. BARNS, Tho: TAYLOR. *Proved*: Oct. Court 1747 by the Oath of Thomas TAYLOR. *Wit*: Charles SAWYER. *Regt*: 24 Dec. 1747.

North Carolina. 20 July 1747 and in the 20th year of the Reign of our Sovn Lord George the Second ... Between John HUMPHREYS of the Precinct of Pasquotank in the Province of North Carolina Planter of the one part & Thomas GRAY of the Precinct & Province afsd. of the other part ... for the sum of 10 pounds of good and lawful Money of Virginia ... sold ... 10 Acres ... on the N. E. Side of Pasquotank River and being a part ... granted by patent to William HUMPHRIES Bearing date the 12 July 1725 ... Robert SAWYERS Line ... at the main Road ...
[B:48] ... *Signed*: John HUMPHRIES. *Wit*: William HUMPHRIES, Joseph MORGAN. *Proved*: Oct. Court 1747 by the Oath of William HUMPHRIES. *Regt*: 24 Dec. 1747.

North Carolina) Pasquotank County) Charles WEST of the County and Province afsd Farmer together with my Wife Dinah ... for the natural affection as Parents ought to have to their Children do by these presents give to our three Sons viz Lemuel, Jonathan and Hezekiah WEST our Manor plantation whereon we now dwell ... containing 520 Acres after our decease ... To my son Lemuel that part where he now dwells called Hog Point, together with Wallowing Point and Mulberry Point, to my Son Jonathan that plantation called the New Field and to my Son Hezekiah WEST, the plantation whereon we now dwell, the Said Lands to be divided by Lines run in our life time ...
8 Aug. 1747. *Signed*: Charles WEST, Dinah WEST. *Wit*: John I GUTHRIE his mark, Jno. MCKEEL. *Ack*: Oct. Court 1747. *Regt*: 24 Dec. 1747.

[B:49] Benjamin PALMER of the County of Pasquotank within the Province of North Carolina ... for 125 pounds Current money of the Colony of Virginia ... paid by John HOSEA of the County and Province afsd ... sold ... part of a Tract of Land ... on the head of Thomas ARMOURS line on the S. W. Side of Pasquotank River ... 300 Acres, a Plantation that Benjamin PALMER formerly rented commonly called by the name of PALMER'S Quarter ... to Thomas GASKINS Line ... 12 Jan. 1747. *Signed*: Benjamin PALMER. *Wit*: Benja. BAPTIST, Joseph REED, Simon BRYAN. *Ack*: Jan. Court 1747. *Regt*: 15 Jan. 1747.

[B:50] 11 Dec. 1747 I the Subscriber make over all my Right ... unto Benjamin PALMER ... *Signed*: John HOSEA. *Wit*: David GEORGE, John EVERIGIN. *Ack*: Jan. Court 1747. *Regt*: 15 Jan. 1747. Memr. that the Deed of the afsd Assignmt is recorded in this Book in page (35)

11 Dec. 1747 I the Subscriber make over all my Right ... unto Benjamin PALMER ... *Signed*: John HOSEA. *Wit*: David GEORGE, John EVERIGIN. *Ack*: Jan. Court 1747. *Regt*: 15 Jan. 1747. Memr. that the Deed of the afsd Assignmt is recorded in Book C. April 7. 1746.

Henry BRIGHT Senr. of the County of Currituck and Province of North Carolina ... voluntary Consent of me and Mary my Wife ... for love, good will and natural affection I bear unto my Son in law James ROBERTSON have given ... on the No. Side of Pasquotank River near the great Swamp ... on the Juniper Swamp ... Contg. 162 Acres ...
[B:51] ... 23 Nov. 1747. *Signed*: Henry B BRIGHT his mark. *Wit*: Joseph MACFARSON, Isaac BRIGHT, Charles BRIGHT. *Ack*: Jan. Court 1747. *Regt*: 15 Jan. 1747.

North Carolina) Pasquotank County) Richard PRITCHARD of the County & Province afsd. ... for 200 pounds Province Bills ... paid by Amos TRUEBLOOD ... sold ... one part of a registd Tract of Land whereon Danl. RODES formerly lived, contg ... 100 acres ... on the S. W. Side of Pasquotank River ... Sandhill Swamp ... Thomas PRITCHARD'S Line ... Turkey Branch ... John JURY'S Land upon the main Swamp ...
[B:52] ... 12 Jan. 1747/8. *Signed*: Richard PRITCHARD. *Wit*: Tho: TRUEBLOOD, Abel TRUEBLOOD, Thos. T CARTWRIGHTS mark. *Ack*: Jan. Court 1747.

Regt: 16 Jan. 1747.

Thomas MEADS of the County of Pasquotank within the Province of North Carolina for ... 50 pounds Current Money of the Colony of Virginia ... sold ... to Leml. KEEL ... N. E. Side of Little River ... 50 Acres of Land ... to the main Road, then up the said Timothy MEAD'S Line to the head ...
[B:53] ... 12 Jan. 1747. *Signed*: Thomas MEADS. *Wit*: Tho: TAYLOR, Joseph BAILEY. *Ack*: Jan. Court 1747. *Regt*: 16 Jan. 1747.

Lemuel KEEL and Charles KEEL of the County of Pasquotank within the Province of North Carolina for ... 81 pounds 5 shillings Current Money of the Colony of Virginia ... sold ... unto Joseph REED ... N. E. Side of Little River ... 50 acres of Land ... Oliver SALTER'S line ... to the main Road ... Timothy MEADS Line ...
[B:54] ... 12 Jan. 1747. *Signed*: Leml. L KEEL his mark, Charles C KEEL mark. *Wit*: Tho: TAYLOR, Thos MEADS. *Ack*: Jan. Court 1747. *Regt*: 16 Jan. 1747.

Pasquotank County -- A. Division of the back Plantation of Richard STAMP deceased Between his Widow now Wife to John WILKINS and his Son Thomas STAMP ... the said Widow ... take her third part of the plantation ... and also the division of the plantation on Great Flatty Creek of Richard STAMPS deceased between his Widow Deborah now Wife to John WILKINS and his daughter Miriam STAMP ... to the Barn ... and the Widow ... takes her third part of the plantation ... This is a true and perfect Division of the plantations between the Widow now Wife to John WILKINS and the Children made by us the Subscribers on Oath in the Month of November 1747 of the lands of Richard STAMP decd. *Signed*: Charles WEST, Jno. MCKEEL, Robert LOWRY. Exhibited Jan. Court 1747 by Robert LOWRY Esqr. one of the Dividers and was ordered to be recorded. *Regt*: 16 Jan. 1747.

[B:55] North Carolina) Pasquotank County) James WARD of the Province and County afsd. for ... 100 pounds Province Bills ... paid by Joseph PRITCHARD ... sold ... 8 acres ... on the S. W. Side of Pasquotank River ... Beginning at the Mouth of the Great Branch ... head of Rok? Branch ... a part of Nobs Crook Creek Swamp then binding on the said

Great Swamp ... 26 Sept. 1747. *Signed*: James W WARD his mark. *Wit*: Abel DRESSER, John HARRIS, Jacob ALBERTSON. *Proved*: April Court 1748 by the Oath of Abel DRESSER. *Regt*: 2 July 1748.

12 Oct. 1747 & in the 20th year of the Reign of King George the Second ... Between Abel ROSS of the County of Pasquotank & Province of North Carolina Planter of the one part and Saml. LOWMAN and his Wife Dorothy LOWMAN Daughter of the Said Abel ROSS both of the abovesaid Province as afsd. of the other part ... for the natural Love and
[B:56] Affection which he hath ... give ... 35 acres ... on the Branch Side, that parts Abel ROSS'S Land and Thomas PENDLETON'S Land ... crossing the main Road that's called the down River Road ... part of a larger Tract of 150 acres being Manor Lands ... 12 Oct. 1747. *Signed*: Abel ROSS. *Wit*: Charles SAWYER, Joseph X FERRILL his mark. *Proved*: April Court 1748 by the Oath of Charles SAWYER Esqr. *Regt*: 2 July 1748.

[B:57] 29 July 1747 and in the twenty first year of the Reign of our Sovereign Lord George the Second ... Between John NORRIS of the County of Pasquotank and Province afsd. Farmer of the one part and William BARNS of the County and Province afsd. Gentn. of the other part ... for 100 pounds current money of the Colony of Virginia ... sold ... all that tract or parcel of land granted by Patent from William Earl of Craven Palatine &c. to Richard MADREN & which patent bears date the 25 Feb. 1696 ... *Signed*: Jno. NORRIS, Tamer T NORRIS her mark. *Wit*: James LETORTT?, Motion & CALLBREATH?, Wm NICHOLS, Joseph PRITCHARD. 30 July 1747 Recd. of M. Willm BARNS the just Sum of 50 pounds ... *Signed*: Jno. NORRIS. *Wit*: Jno. BARNS, Nathan MASSY. *Ack*: April Court 1748. *Regt*: 2 July 1748.

[B:58] North Carolina) Pasquotank County) Thomas NICHOLSON of the County of Perquimons Farmer for ... 112 pounds current money of the said Province ... paid by James MORGAN of the County of Pasquotank ... sold ... in the fork of Little River contg ... 150 acres ... it being Land the said Thomas NICHOLSON and Aaron HILL took up & surveyed upon the head of their Lands they then lived on in Partnership and divided by agreement between them by a straight line

... in the Desart back of a place that is known by the name of the Jagged Oaks ... agreeable to a Deed of Sale from the said Aaron to the said Thomas bearing date the 5th day of Jany 1744/5 ... 12 day of [B:59] the Second Month commonly called April 1746. *Signed*: Thos. NICHOLSON. *Wit*: John PERRY, William BUNDY. *Ack*: April Court 1748. *Regt*: 2 July 1748.

North Carolina: 9 April 1748 Between Joseph LOWRY of Pasquotank County in the Province of North Carolina and Ann his Wife of the one part & Robert LOWRY of the County and Province afsd. of the other part ... whereas one Robert LOWRY late of Pasquotank County afsd. decd. did by his last Will and Testament in Writing bearing date the 14 Dec. 1742 give and bequeath unto his Son Joseph LOWRY 100 Acres of Land being part of his Back lands upon Pasquotank Road ... for 50 pounds lawful Money of Gt. Britain ... sold ... 100 Acres ... part of a Tract granted by letters patent bearing date the 30 March 1724 unto John ARMOUR ...
[B:60] ... *Signed*: Joseph LOWRY, Ann X LOWRY her mark. *Wit*: Joseph BAILY, James MORGAN, Joseph ROBINSON. *Ack*: April Court 1748. *Regt*: 2 July 1748.

[B:61] North Carolina) Pasquotank County) Martha CHARTRIGHT Widow ... for the love, good will, and affection which I have and bear towards my three loving children after named, viz Hezekiah CHARTRIGHT, John CHARTRIGHT and Sarah PALMER (Spouse to Robert PALMER) my Daughter and to the three Grand Children of these my two Sons and Daughter afsd. have given ... viz I give to my Son Hezekiah CHARTRIGHT the first foal that is brought of the mare called Jenny, which Mare so called is given to Sarah PALMER my Daughter, also I give unto my sd Son Hezekiah CHARTRIGHT a large Iron pot and Pothooks, also I give unto my Grand Child Claudius CHARTRIGHT Son of the afsd. Hezekiah CHARTRIGHT a small Iron pot and a large peuter Basin. I give unto my son John CHARTRIGHT my own Bed with the whole furniture thereof and those unto belonging with two peuter Basons a peuter Dish, my own Chest a middle Sized Iron pot and pothooks, one Cow and a two year old Bull, Eight old Hogs and Sixteen pigs, fifteen Barrels of Corn & nine [blank] thereof in the hands of Josiah CHARTRIGHT and all other things whatsoever

I have not mentioned is given to said John. Also I give unto my Daughter Sarah PALMER my own riding Mare called Jenny excepting the first foal she brings to my Son Hezekiah as afsd. I give unto the sd. Sarah PALMER two barrels of Corn Also I give unto my Grand Child called Betty PALMER Daughter of the said Sarah a two year old Heifer. Also I give unto my said Daughter Sarah PALMER a peuter Dish I give unto my Grand Child the eldest Son of John CHARTRIGHT not yet named one Cow ... 17 March 1747/8. *Signed*: Martha CHARTRIGHT. *Wit*: Thomas CHARTRIGHT Junr, Anne, Anna CHARTRIGHT her mark. *Proved*: April Court 1748 by the Oath of Thomas CHARTRIGHT Junr. *Regt*: 2 July 1748.

[B:62] North Carolina) Pasquotank County) 1 March 1747 Between William WARD of the County and Province afsd. Planter of the one part and John HIBBS of the afsd County and Province of the other part ... for 500 pounds Current Money of the Province afsd ... sold ... 350 acres ... on the North Side of Nobs Crook Creek being the land whereof the said William WARD formerly lived ... Isaac STOKELYS Corner ... David PRITCHARDS Corner ... *Signed*: William W WARD. *Wit*: S PLOMER, Tho: TAYLOR. *Proved*: April Court 1748 by the Oath of Thomas TAYLOR. *Wit*: Chas SAWYER Chairman. *Regt*: 2 July 1748 in Book D folio 125.

[B:63] North Carolina) Pasquotank County) 5 Feb. 1747 Between Thomas PRITCHARD of the County and Province afsd. Farmer of the one part and John NORRIS of the County and Province afsd of the other part ... for 400 pounds current Money of Carolina ... sold ... Tract of Land, it being conveyed out of a patent contg 646 Acres and was patented by David PRITCHARD, it being situated on the S. W. Side of Pasquotank River ... 120 acres ... Turkey Branch ... Nobs Crook Creek ... *Signed*: Thomas PRITCHARD. *Wit*: Thomas S SMITH his mark, Abram. A MADREN his mark. *Ack*: April Court 1748. *Regt*: 2 July 1748.

North Carolina) Pasquotank County) 3 March 1747 Between Willm NICKELS and Benjamin JENNINGS Farmers of the County & Province afsd. of the one part and Thomas PRITCHARD of the County and Province afsd. of the other part ... for 400 pounds lawful money of North Carolina ... sold ... 80 acres, being the western end of a Tract relapsed by Jeremiah MURDEN and 20 Acres being part of a Tract patented by William WAYMAN it being situate on the S. W. Side of Pasquotank River & on Nobs Crook Creek Swamp ... up the Old House Branch ... head of the Great Branch [B:64] ... Creek Swamp ... *Signed*: Wm. W NICKELS his mark, Benja. JENNINGS. *Wit*: Jno NORRIS, Thomas T JENNINGS his mark. *Ack*: April Court 1748. *Regt*: 2 July 1748.

North Carolina) Pasquotank County) Patrick KEETON of the County and Province afsd for ... [blank] Barrels of good sound merchantable Barreled Pork ... paid by Robert ARMOUR Junr of the County & Province afsd. ... sold ... North Side of Flatty Creek at the Mouth of the said Creek ... 200 acres ... granted by the Honble [blank] POLLOCK Esqr. President and the then Council unto William GASKILLS and bearing date the 10 July 1722 ...
[B:65] ... 29 Jany 1747/8. *Signed*: Patrick KEETON. *Wit*: John PEGGS, Tho: MCKEEL, John LISTER J his mark. *Proved*: April Court 1748 by the Oath of Thomas MCKEEL. *Regt*: 2 July 1748.

North Carolina. Simon BRYAN of the County of Pasquotank in the Province of North Carolina Gentn. ... for the love and affection I ... bear to my Son in law John ARMOUR have given ... three Negro Boys named Ben Isaac and Samey? and a Negro Woman Hannah and her Increase, to be delivered ... to John ARMOUR when he shall arrive to the age of 21 years and in case the said John ARMOUR should die without heirs ... then to my Son Simon BRYAN ...
[B:66] ... 9 April 1748. *Signed*: Simon BRYAN. *Wit*: Joseph BAILY, Isaac STOKELY. *Ack*: April Court 1748. *Regt*: 2 July 1748.

North Carolina) Pasquotank County) John CAROON of Currituck County & Province afsd. for ... 22 pounds current Money of Virginia ... paid by Lodwick GRAY of the County of Pasquotank & Province afsd. ... sold ... 440 acres of Land being part of a patent given ... unto the Yaupim Indians Contg 640 Acres bearing date the 4 April 1724, Except 200 acres sold out of the said patent unto Edward WILLIAMS ... 1 Aug. 1727 ...
[B:67] ... 17 Oct. 1747. *Signed*: John CARON. *Wit*: Jacob CARON, Levi STEWART. *Ack*: April Court 1748. *Regt*: 2 July 1748.

North Carolina Pasquotank County 16 Oct. 1747 Between James PRITCHARD Junr. of the County and Province afsd. Planter of the one part and Richard PRITCHARD of the same County and Province afsd. Planter of the other part ... for 100 pounds current Bills of North Carolina ... sold ... S. W. Side of Pasquotank River and contg ... 100 acres ... Creek Swamp binding on John HARRIS'S Line ... Valentine ROW'S Line ... *Signed*: James PRITCHARD. *Wit*: Thomas PRITCHARD, Thos. S SMITH his mark. *Ack*: April Court 1748. *Regt*: 2 July 1748.

[B:68] 3 March 1747/8 Between Joseph JONES in the County of Pasquotank in the Province of North Carolina Cordwainer of the one part and John MARTIN of the sd County of the other part ... for 25 pounds Virginia currency ... sold ... 70 acres ... North East Side of Pasquotank River ... Main Swamp ... Patrick O'DANIELS Land ... to the Back Line in the Lake ... *Signed*: John I MARTIN his mark. *Wit*: John JONES, Evan JONES. *Ack*: April Court 1748. *Regt*: 2 July 1748.

[B:69] North Carolina) Pasquotank County) Evan LURRY of the County and Province afsd. ... for 22 pounds current money of Virginia ... paid by Lodwick GRAY ... sold ... S. W. Side of North River known by the name of HARRIS'S Island contg ... 240 acres ... Sam's Creek ... part of a greater Tract of Land surveyed and patented by Edward WILLIAMS the 21 Sept. 1723 ... 12 Jany 1747 & in the 21st year of the Reign of King George the Second. *Signed*: Evan E LURRY his mark. *Wit*: Isaac JENNINGS, Bennet MORGAN. *Ack*: Jany Court 1747. *Regt*: 2 July 1748.

North Carolina) Pasquotank County) Ephraim BLANCHARD of Chowan County in the Province afsd. do assign over all my Right ... unto John DIALL of the County and Province afsd. ... 2 June 1747. *Signed*: Ephraim BLANCHARD. *Wit*: Henry PENDLETON, Mary X PENDLETON her mark. *Ack*: Jany Court 1747. *Regt*: 2 July 1748. Memn. The Deed of the afsd. Assignmt is recorded in Book C fo. 77 in the year 1742.

[B:70] 30 Jan. 1747/8 and in the 22nd year of the Reign of our Sovereign Lord George the Second ... Between Thomas DAVIS in the Precinct of Pasquotank & County of Albemarle & the Province of North Carolina of the one party and John DAVIS of the Precinct & County and Province abovesaid of the other party ... for the Good Will I bear to my Son ... give ... 100 acres of Land ... on the S. W. side of Pasquotank River, it being part given out a Patent bearing date 1728 ... Mouth of a Branch between Sarah TRUEBLOODS Land & the Land that the afsd. Thomas DAVIS give to his Son Arthur DAVIS ... to the River Swamp ... *Signed*: Thomas DAVIS. *Wit*: Isaac STOKELY, Jeremh. MURDEN. *Proved*: July Court 1748 by the Oath of Isaac STOKELY. *Regt*: 21 July 1748.

[B:71] North Carolina) Pasquotank County) Benjamin PALMER for ... 50 pounds Currency of the Province afsd. ... paid by Jeremiah WILCOCKS of the County and Province afsd. ... sold ... at a Tar Kiln Branch ... 50 Acres ... Benjamin WESTS Line ... a Conveyance out of a Patent bearing date 1668 ... 12 July 1748. *Signed*: Benjamin PALMER. *Wit*: John SOLLEY, David DAVIS, John BROOKS. *Ack*: July Court 1748. *Regt*: 21 July 1748.

[B:72] North Carolina) Pasquotank County) 14 July 1747 Between Benjamin PALMER of the one part Planter & Richard COLLINS of the other part Planter ... for 50 pounds current Money of the Province ... sold ... part of a greater parcel which was patented by Robert PALMER ... conveyed to Benjn. PALMER ... which part contains 50 acres ... *Signed*: Benjn. PALMER. *Wit*: Aaron MORRIS, Peter SYMONS. *Ack*: July Court 1748. *Regt*: 21 July 1748.

North Carolina Whereas Zachariah NIXON of the County of Pasquotank & Province afsd. in the year of our Lord 1684 having taken up, surveyed and patented in his own name ... N. E. Side of Little River contg ... 323 acres bounded on the lower Side on the land that William TURNER now dwells on and on the upper Side on the land that Solomon POOL now dwells on ... the said Zachariah NIXON dying intestate his Son Zachariah being his Surviving Heir inherited all the abovesaid Land and cultivated the same several years and then at his Death by last Will and Testament ... bequeathed it between his two Sons Zachariah and Barnabee NIXON, Zachariah to have that Moiety or half part joining the afsd. William TURNERS land ... to the old School House near the Main Road ... [B:73] Sum of 1,000 pounds Current Bills of said

Province ... sold at public vendue all my Right ... of all that Moiety or half part of the abovesaid Land, after having first laid out part thereof in half acre Lots for a Town Ship, and the rest for a common to the several purchasers of the afsd. Township only excepting to me the said Zachariah NIXON the two Lots that number 5 and 6, in the plan of the said Town ... the Lot that numbers 72 in said plan which I ... promised to be the highest Bidder upon [blank] discount the price of out of the afsd. Sum of 1,000 pounds I also except my equal share in the Commons in preportion to my Lots with other purchasers And further ... in Consideration of the above Sum of 1,000 pounds Current Bills of the said Province ... paid by the several purchasers of the afsd. Township Known by the name of Nixonton ... sold ... Tract of Land Known formerly by the name of Wind mill point Land but now Known by the name of Nixonton, the Purchasers Names being inserted in the plan of the said Town ... 161½ Acres bounded as abovesaid ...
[B:74] ... 9th day of the fifth Month 1748. *Signed*: Zachariah NIXON. *Wit*: John SYMONS, Joshua DAVIS, Zachariah MORRIS. *Proved*: July Court 1748 by the Oath of John SIMONS. *Regt*: 21 July 1748.

North Carolina: 9 July 1748 Between Zachariah NIXON of the County of Perquimons and Province afsd. Farmer of the one part and Aaron MORRIS of the County of Pasquotank & Province afsd. Farmer of the other part ... for 38 pounds lawful Current Bills of this Province ... sold .. two half acre Lots laid out in Nixonton, one of which is the Lot that numbers 12 in the plan of the said Town butted upon the Water Street on the S. W. Side & on the N. W. Side of that Lot that Joseph NEWBY Junr bought & on the N. E. Side of the main Street & on the S. E. Side on that Lot that William SYMONS bought and the other Lot that numbers 88 in the plan of said
[B:75] Town, bounded on the N. W. Side on the River and on the N. E. Side on the Lot that Grace POOL bought and on the S. E. Side on the Lot that Captn Joseph BAILY bought and on the S. W. Side on the Windmill point or Shipyard ... with his equal share in Common & also his equal Share or Dividend in all such Lots as shall be forfeited to the Township ... by any purchasers refusing or neglecting to comply with the Terms or Conditions of the said Township

... provided he ... observe & comply with the Terms that are or hereafter shall be constituted by our Delegates or Deputies or a Majority of them by building a good reputable House not less than 20 feet long and 15 feet wide within five years from the date of the Sale of said Lots ... *Signed*: Zachh. NIXON. *Wit*: John SYMONS, Joshua DAVIS, Zachariah MORRIS. *Proved*: July Court 1748 by the Oath of John SYMONS. *Regt*: 21 July 1748.

North Carolina. George WINBERRY of Pasquotank Precinct in Albemarle County & Province afsd. ... for 300 pounds Current Money of this Province ... paid by John LISTER of the Precinct County and Province afsd. Planter ... sold ... Tract of Land lying on or near the land or plantation of Thomas ARMOUR & Joseph REED ... the sd. Tract of Land being as yet unsurveyed contg by Estimation 50 Acres ... [B:76] ... 24 Feb. 1748. *Signed*: George WINBERRY. *Wit*: Ebenezer VINE, Robert HOSEA, Mary M ALBERTSON her mark. *Ack*: July Court 1748. *Regt*: 21 July 1748.

North Carolina) Pasquotank County) John DAVIS Senr. of the County afsd. ... for 160 pounds of the late Current Bill Money of this Province ... paid by Joseph SANDERLIN of the County and Province afsd. ... sold ... S. W. Side of Pasquotank River ... 100 acres ... Thomas DAVISS Line upon the River Swamp ... Joshua DAVIS'S ... to a place called MCCLENNANS ... John WINBERRY'S Corner Tree upon the River Swamp ... known by the name of Broad Neck ...
[B:77] ... 11 July 1748. *Signed*: John DAVIS. *Wit*: Isaac STOKELY, Thomas SAWYER. *Proved*: July Court 1748 by the Oath of Isaac STOKELY. *Regt*: 21 July 1748.

North Carolina) Pasquotank County) 18 March 1747 Between John NORRIS of the County of Pasquotank & Province of North Carolina Planter of the one part & Jarvis JONES of the County & Province afsd. of the other part Planter ... for 20 pounds Stg Money of Gt Britain ... sold ... N. E. Side of Pasquotank River and in old JOY'S fork quarter & Known by the name of Cornwall ... Bear Spring ... Juniper Swamp ... Land formerly patented by Willm NORRIS, Father to the said John NORRIS in the year 1715, which patent contains 574 acres ...
[B:78] ... *Signed*: Jno. NORRIS. *Wit*:

Jos: MACKFARSON, Alexa. SPENCE, George G BROWN his mark. *Proved*: July Court 1748 by the Oath of Joseph MACKFARSON. *Regt*: 21 July 1748.

Lathan PURSELL of the County of Pasquotank and Province of North Carolina for ... 30 pounds Proclamation Money ... paid by Robert HARRISON Senr. of the same place ... sold ... tract of Land ... adjoining to the said Robert HARRISON'S Plantation & commonly known by the name of Sandy Ridge ... Land of George KEMP ... John HAWKINS'S Land ... by the School House ... 70 Acres ... 22 Sept. 1747. *Signed*: Lathan PURSELL his mark P. *Wit*: Mc. SCARBOROUGH, Tho: TAYLOR. *Ack*: July Court 1748. *Regt*: 21 July 1748.

[B:79] St. Mary's County in Maryland These may certify whom it may concern that about the year of our Lord 1737 John DIALL & Sarah SHIRLY was duly married by me and that he lived with his said wife about three years and then left here, Given my hand this 26th day of July 1748. *Signed*: Lawrence DEBUTT. Rector of William & Mary Parish in St. Mary's County. *Wit*: George CLARKE.
St. Mary's County in Maryland: July 26. 1748 Then came before me one of his Lordship's Justices of the peace for this County Lawrence DEBUTT Rector of William & Mary Parish in the County & made Oath on the Holy Evangelists that the within mentioned Marriage between John DIALL & Sarah his wife was solemnized by him. Sworn before me. *Signed*: George CLARKE. These may certify that the afsd. Certificate & Proof was recorded the 21 Oct. 1748.

St. Mary's County in Maryland Abraham BRADEN aged 25 years or thereabouts being sworn on the Holy Evangelist, deposeth and sayeth that he was personally acquainted with Sarah DIALL, both in her former Husband SHIRLY'S time and likewise in John DIALL'S Time and that he Saw her alive and well about the Second day of last August. Sworn before one of his Lordship's Justices of the peace for St. Mary's County, this 26th day of July 1748. *Signed*: George CLARKE. *Regt*: 21 Oct. 1748.

St. Mary's County in Maryland Likewise William HILTON aged 19 years or thereabouts being Sworn on the Holy Evangelist deposeth & sayeth, that he in company with Abraham BRADEN saw Sarah DIALL the wife of John DIALL alive & well about the Second day of August last. Sworn before me one of his Lordship's Justices of the peace for St. Mary's County this 26th day of July 1748. *Signed*: George CLARKE. *Regt*: 21 July 1748.

North Carolina Perquimons County William MAGOWN of sd. Parish & Province Planter aged about 40 years being Sworn on the Holy Evangelist, deposeth & saith that he knew Law: DEBUTT, rector of William & Mary Parish in St. Mary's County in Maryland was Rector there when he left Maryland & had been so for many years before & also that he knew George CLARKE to be one of the Eldest Justices in that County & further saith that he verily believes the sd. John DIALL now here in this County of Perquimans & mentioned in a Certificate from Maryland under the hand of the abovesaid DEBUTT dated the 26th day of July 1748 to be the very same John DIALL that married Sarah SHIRLY mentioned in the said Certificate -- Taken on Oath before me one of his Majesty's Justices of the Peace for the said County this 2 Aug. 1748. *Signed*: William MAGOWNE. *Wit*: Tho: WEEKS. *Regt*: 21 July 1748 at the Request of Thos. MEADS.

[B:80] North Carolina) Pasquotank County) John REED of John's Parish County & Province afsd. aged 39 years being sworn on the Holy Evangelist of Almighty God deposeth and Saith, that he the said John REED after his Arrival in Maryland which was in the year 1739 personally knew and was conversant with the Revd. Lawrence DEBUTT being hired by sd. M DEBUTT to teach his then only Son now decd., doth declare the Certificate now in the possession of Thomas MEADS & shown to me before Robert LOWRY, Esqr. to be the handwriting of the said Revd. DEBUTT & that the said John DIALL mentioned in the said Certificate & John DIALL now dwelling in North Carolina, is the Self same persons & further the sd. REED doth declare that to the best of his Knowledge the said Certificate is Witnessed by the hand writing of Col. George CLARKE of St. Mary's County Maryland August the 6th 1748. Then personally appeared before me the within mentioned John REED & made Oath to the above Declaration August the 6th. 1748. *Signed*: Robert LOWRY. October Court 1748. These may certify that Thomas MEADS came into open

Court & prayed to have the afsd. Certificate of Lawrence DEBUTT with the Depositions afsd. recorded. *Regt*: 21 Oct. 1748.

Jacob GILFORT & Mary GILFORT of Pasquotank County in the Province of North Carolina and in Consideration of the Sum of 37 pounds 10 Shillings in Indian Corn paid ... by John SQUIRES of the same County & Province afsd. ... sold ... N. E. Side of Pasquotank River, the same plantation that William HAIG made over to William WALLARD & fell to the said Jacob GILFORT & Mary GILFORT the Wife of the said Gilfort ... by heirship. Contg ... 100 acres ... [B:81] ... 11 Oct. 1748. *Signed*: Jacob I GILFORT his mark, Mary X GILFORT her mark. *Wit*: Gideon NEEDHAM, Eliza. X NEEDHAM her mark. *Ack*: Oct. Court 1748. *Regt*: 21 Oct. 1748.

North Carolina) Pasquotank County) Benjamin PALMER of the County of Pasquotank & Province afsd. for ... 60 pounds Current Money of the Province ... paid by Thomas LISTER of the same place ... sold ... 50 acres ... on the N. E. Side of BETTY'S Creek ... part of a Tract of Land belonging to the afsd. Benjamin PALMER ... 12 April 1748. *Signed*: Benja. PALMER. *Wit*: John ALBERTSON, Saml POYNTER. *Proved*: Oct. Court 1748 by the Oath of John ALBERTSON. *Regt*: 21 Oct. 1748.

[B:82] 12 Oct 1748 and in the 21st year of the Reign of our Sovn Lord George the Second ... Between John DAILY of the County of Pasquotank in North Carolina Planter of the one part and Thomas UPTON of the same place Planter of the other part ... for 24 pounds 8 Shillings Virginia Currency ... sold ... part of a larger Tract of Land that Henry CREECH Grandfather to the sd. John DAILY formerly lived on ... 50 acres ... which the said Henry CREECH ... gave in his last Will & Testament to the Father of the sd. John DAILY and his Mother Frances DAILY and to the Heirs of the said Frances DAILY ... (Remainder of Record torn off)

[blank] day of [blank] in the twenty first year of the Reign of our Sovn Lord George the Second ... Between Henry PALIN and Thomas PALIN of the County of Pasquotank in North Carolina of the one part and William HIXON of the same place ... Sum of [blank]

hundred pounds Stg. money of Gt. Britain ... sold ... N. E. Side of Pasquotank River & containing 300 acres ... being part of a larger Tract of Land containing 600 acres patented by Thomas [blank] Grandfather to the said Henry & Thomas PALIN bearing date the 21st day of [blank] 1696 ... Cypress Branch ... John JURY'S Line ...
[B:83] ... (Remainder of Deed torn off)

(First part of the following Deed torn off) To Have and To Hold the said granted and bargained Premises ... unto him the said Josiah NASH ... the sd. Samuel Sabin PLOMER and Sarah Catherine my Wife ... having in ourselves full power good Right ... 28 Oct. 1747. *Signed*: S PLOMER, Sarah PLOMER. *Wit*: Robt. MURDEN, Joseph HARRON?, Abner BLACKALL. *Ack*: 16 April 1748 E. HALL C. J. *Regt*: 21 Oct. 1748.

North Carolina) Pasquotank County) Rebecca WHITE Relict of Robert WHITE of the County afsd. decd. Spinster ... for the love Good Will and affection which I bear towards my well beloved Grandson John OVERMAN Son of my Son John OVERMAN of the County afsd. decd. have given ... Tract of Land that my Father in law Matthew KALLEY by his last Will and Testament gave and bequeathed to me the sd. Rebecca NEWBY (now WHITE) as may appear by the said Will bearing date the 16th day of April 1699 ... 100 acres ... it being Joseph DAVIS now dwells on and lying on one of the Branches of SYMONS Creek ... Land that Abraham WHITE formerly dwelt on and on the head on the Land that John WHITE dwells on and on the other Side on the land that James NEWBY now dwells on ...
[B:84] 31st day of the first month commonly called March 1750. *Signed*: Rebecca R W WHITE her mark. *Wit*: Thos. OVERMAN, Nehemiah WHITE, Joseph ROBINSON. *Proved*: April Court 1750 by the affirmation of Thomas OVERMAN, Nehemh. WHITE & Joseph ROBINSON. *Regt*: 25 April 1750.

North Carolina Simon BRYAN of Pasquotank County in the Province of North Carolina Gentn for ... the parental Love I have and do bear unto my Children David BRYAN, Winnefred BRYAN, and Joseph BRYAN, have given ... three Negro Girls named Jenny, Die and Phoebe ... Jenny to my Son David, Die to my Daughter Winnifred & Phoebe to my Son Joseph, them and their

Increase to be deld. ... when they shall arrive to the age of 21 years or the day of Marriage ... 10 March 1748/9. *Signed*: Simon BRYAN. *Wit*: Joseph BAILY, Saml. SNOWDEN, John ARMOUR. *Proved*: April Court 1750 by the Oath of John ARMOUR. *Regt*: 25 April 1750.

[B:85] North Carolina) Pasquotank County) Zephaniah WHITE of the place afsd. Farmer for ... the Swap or Exchange of a certain plantation of Robert BAILY'S lying on the Ivey Thicket called David BAILY'S Glades in the County afsd. ... sold ... unto Robert BAILY of the County afsd. Farmer ... N. E. Side of Little River ... 30½ acres ... Beginning at the mouth of a little Creek running out of the River betwixt the Dwelling House that I the said Zephaniah WHITE dwelt in and Nehemiah WHITE ... Land that my Brother Jonathan WHITE dwelt on and thence to Robert LOWRY'S Line ... bounded according to the Will of my Father Robert WHITE ... 13 Dec. 1749. *Signed*: Zephaniah X WHITE his mark. *Wit*: Joseph ROBINSON, John OVERMAN. *Proved*: April Court 1750 by the Affirmation of Joseph ROBINSON. *Regt*: 25 April 1750 in Book D. Fo. 153.

[B:86] North Carolina) Pasquotank County) John LISTER for ... 80 pounds current Money of this Province ... paid by William DAVIS of the County & Province afsd. ... sold ... Tract of Land lying on or near the Land or plantation of Thomas ARMOUR & Joseph REED ... binding on the plantation of George WINBERRY'S ... being yet unsurveyed Contg by Estimation 50 Acres ... 16 March 1749/50. *Signed*: John J LISTER his mark. *Wit*: Jonathan HOWELL, George WINBERRY. *Ack*: April Court 1750. *Regt*: 25 April 1750.

[B:87] 13 Jan. 1749 and in the 22d year of the Reign of our Sovn Lord George ... Between John HASTINGS of the County of Pasquotank in the Province of North Carolina of the one party and Joseph MORGAN of the same place and Province afsd. ... for 60 pounds proclamation money ... sold ... 130 acres of Land ... N. E. side of Pasquotank River, it being the Remainder part of the plantation and Tract of Land which I sold part of to Joseph WILLIAMS ... MORGANS'S Corner Tree ... River Swamp ... Joseph WILLIAMS Bounds ... the main road ... Brine Branch

... Possum Branch ... binding on Thomas SAWYER'S Senr. Land by the Lake ... Corner Tree of Joseph SAWYER'S ... MORGAN'S Land whereon he now lives ... *Signed*: John X HASTINGS his mark. *Wit*: Saml. SMITH, Jona. HUMPHRIES, Solo: TAYLOR. *Ack*: April Court 1750. *Regt*: 25 April 1750.

[B:88] Thomas MEADS of the Province of North Carolina and County of Pasquotank for ... Two plantations and Two Tracts of land containing 350 acres now belonging to Thomas WOODLY at the head of Newbegun Creek situate, together with 5 pounds Proclamation Money ... sold ... S. W. Side of Great Flatty Creek ... WEST'S Line ... Pocoson of Flatty Creek ... 190 acres ... 17 Jan. 1749/50. *Signed*: Thomas MEADS. *Wit*: Emanl. X KNIGHTS his mark, Anne N KNIGHTS her mark, John MCKEEL. *Ack*: April Court 1750. *Regt*: 25 April 1750.

[B:89] North Carolina) Pasquotank County) Thomas WOODLEY of the Province and County afsd. ... for a plantation and Tract of Land contg 190 acres belonging to Thomas MEADS together with 5 pounds proclamation Money ... sold ... two Tracts of Land ... 350 acres ... S. W. Side of Newbegun Creek ... the foremost plantation ... by Newbegun Creek Swamp ... The Overmost plantation ... at Elisabeth COATS'S her Corner Tree ... Newbegun Creek Swamp ... [B:90] 17 Jan. 1749/50. *Signed*: Thomas WOODLEY. *Wit*: Emanl. X KNIGHTS his mark, Anne N KNIGHTS her mark, John MCKEEL. *Ack*: April Court 1750. *Regt*: 25 April 1750.

Elisabeth POINTER, together with my Sister Martha MARKHAM both of the County of Pasquotank and Province of North Carolina for ... the love and good will and affection which I have and do bear unto our loving Niece Mary FOURRE of the same County and Province a certain tract ... bounding with the Lands of MCKEELS, DAVIS'S & KORRUHS Contg 194 acres ... in case she should die without Heir then the sd Land to return back to the afsd. POINTER & Martha MARKHAM or their Heirs equally divided ... 10 April in the 23rd year of the Reign of our Sovn Lord George the Second ... 1749. *Signed*: Elizabeth POINTER, Martha MARKHAM. *Wit*: Thos. MCKEEL, Jonathan HOWELL. *Proved*: April Court 1750 by the Oath of Thos MCKEEL & Jonathan HOWELL. *Regt*: 25 April 1750.

[B:91] 13 Jan. 1749 and in the 32nd [sic] year of the Reign of our Sovereign Lord George ... Between Joseph MORGAN of the County of Pasquotank in the Province of North Carolina of the one party and John HASTINGS of the same place and for ... 60 pounds Proclamation Money ... sold ... N. E. Side of Pasquotank River Contg 100 acres ... Corner tree between myself and William WILLIAMS ... Thomas JAMES'S Line, it being the same 100 acres of Land I bought of Thomas JAMES'S being part of a Tract of Land out of a patent bearing date 22 Oct. 1725 Contg by Patent 520 acres ... 16 Jan. 1749/50. *Signed*: Joseph MORGAN. *Wit*: Saml. SMITH, Jona. HUMPHRIS, Solomon TAYLOR. *Ack*: April Court 1750. *Regt*: 25 April 1750.

[B:92] North Carolina: John HASTINGS of Pasquotank County Planter ... for 200 pounds ... paid by Saml. SCOTTE of Bertie County Merchant ... sold ... 75 acres ... 4 April 1750. *Signed*: John X HASTINGS his mark. *Wit*: Jos: MORGAN, Thos: RELFE. *Ack*: April Court 1750. *Regt*: 25 April 1750.

North Carolina) Pasquotank County) Josiah NASH & Mary NASH my wife ... for 60 pounds Current Money of Virginia ... paid by John LOYD of the Colony of Virginia Gentn. ... sold ... North Side of the River on the West Side of Arenuse Creek at the Mouth of the sd. Creek Contg ... 150 Acres ... on the Lines of Abel ROSS & Richard FERRIL ... patent granted to Samuel Sabin PLOMER & Sarah Catherine his Wife bearing date 22 Nov. 1738
[B:93] ... 2 May 1750. *Signed*: Josiah NASH, Mary NASH. *Wit*: Henry PALIN, Elisha SAWYER. *Ack*: July Court 1750. *Regt*:. 14 July 1750.

John HOSEA of the County of Pasquotank within the Province of North Carolina for ... 125 pounds current Money of the Colony of Virginia ... paid by Abraham HOSEA of the County of Perquimons & Province afsd ... sold ... on the head of Thomas ARMOURS Line on the S. W. Side of Pasquotank River Contg ... 300 acres a plantation commonly called PALMERS Quarter ... Thomas ARMOUR'S Line to Thomas GASKINS'S Line
[B:94] ... 10 July 1750. *Signed*: John HOSEA. *Wit*: Henry DELON, Jesse HENLEY, Job. WINSLOW. *Ack*: July Court 1750. *Regt*: 25 Sept. 1750.

North Carolina: 12 Sept. 1748 between Thomas PENDLETON of the County of Pasquotank and Colony of North Carolina Gentn. of the one part and Saml. WILLIAMS of the County and Province afsd. Planter of the other part ... for 100 pounds Stg. ... sold ... N. E. Side of Pasquotank River being part of the Manor Land that was sold to the sd. Thomas PENDLETON by Henry WINSLOW [sic] the whole Manor Land contg 3650 Acres of Land ... head of the Land whereon Saml. WILLIAMS now lives being his North Corner ... [B:95] ... 500 acres ... commonly called by the name of BAITMAN'S Ridge ... *Signed*: Thos. PENDLETON. *Wit*: Wm. BURGES, Wm. X BURGES his mark, John PENDLETON his P mark. *Proved*: July Court 1750 by the Oath of William BURGES. *Regt*: 25 Sept. 1750.

North Carolina 12 Dec. 1748 Between Samuel WILLIAMS of the County of Pasquotank and Colony of North Carolina Planter of the one part and William BURGES of the County and Province afsd. Planter of the other Part ... for 100 pounds Stg ... sold ... N. E. Side of Pasquotank River being part of the Manor Land that was sold to the sd. Samuel WILLIAMS by Thomas PENDLETON bought of Henry WINSLOW [sic] the whole Tract Contg 3650 Acres of land ... [B:96] ... John SCARBOROUGHS Corner Tree ... William BURGES Line ... John BELLS Path ... part of a Tract of Land called BATEMAN'S Ridge ... 250 acres ... *Signed*: Saml. WILLIAMS. *Wit*: Jno. SCARBOROUGH, Wm. X BURGES Junr his mark, David [blank] BURGES his mark. *Ack*: July Court 1750. *Regt*: 25 Sept. 1750.

[B:97] North Carolina: Isaac HARRISON of Pasquotank County in the Province of North Carolina Planter for ... affection, Love and Good will that I bear to my well beloved Brother Benjamin HARRISON of Pasquotank afsd. do give ... N. E. of Pasquotank River being part of a Tract of Land granted by patent to Robert HARRISON bearing date 1716 and fell to the said Isaac HARRISON by Heirship ... Leml. CURLING now lives ... 18 Feb. 1748/9. *Signed*: Isaac HARRISON. *Wit*: John SQUIRES, Gideon NEEDHAM, Sarah X SQUIRES her mark. *Ack*: July Court 1750. *Regt*: 25 Sept. 1750.

North Carolina 7 Jan. 1746/7 Between Michael MURPHY of Pasquotank County Farmer of the one part and

William LOW of the same place Planter of the other part ... for 100 pounds in Bills ... sold ... head of Little River ... 108 Acres Surveyed and patented by Stephen HALL and sold by him to the said Michael MURPHY ... 22 July 1743 ... Samuel BUNDY'S Line ... [B:98] ... Desert ... *Signed*: Michael MURPHY. *Wit*: Thomas NICHOLSON, Phinihas NIXON, Wm. BUNDY. *Ack*: July Court 1750. *Regt*: 25 Sept. 1750.

[B:99] 13 May in the 22d year of the Reign of our Sovn Lord George the Second ... between [blank] of the County of Pasquotank in North Carolina, Planter of the one part and Samuel ETHERIDGE of the County of Norfolk in the Colony of Virginia Planter of the other part ... John Earl of GRANVILLE by ... John Lord CARTERET of the one part and Jarvis JONES of the other ... give and grant ... 230 acres by one conditional Deed the 20th day of last December and signed ... by Col. Edwd. MOSELY & Col. Robt. HALTON Power of Attorney for the sd. Earl ... for 10 pounds Virginia Currency to the sd. Jarvis JONES in hand paid by the Said Samuel ETHERIDGE ... sold ... 125 acres being part of the above mentioned 230 Acres ... MCCOYS and JOY'S Corners ... ETHERIDGE'S Line ... Cypress Branch ... except MCCOY'S and JOY'S Patent taking part of the Land and likewise Richd. OVERTON'S Patent taking part ... which it is to be the sd. ETHERIDGE'S Loss ...
[B:100] ... *Signed*: Jarvis JONES. *Wit*: Henry U HOLLOWEL his mark, John CHAMBERLIN, Alexr. SPENCE. *Ack*: July Court 1750. *Regt*: 25 Sept. 1750.

Samuel WILLIAMS of Pasquotank County and Province of North Carolina for ... 20 pounds Virginia Currency ... paid by Thomas HOLLIDAY of the same place, Province & County afsd. Planter ... sold ... West Side of Arenuse Creek Swamp formerly belonging to John WINN and known by the name of [blank] Neck ... 120 acres ... according to the will of the said John WINN decd. ... 3 May in the 22d year of the Reign of our most gracious Sovereign King George the Second ... 1749. *Signed*: Saml. WILLIAMS. *Wit*: Wm. BURGES, Jno BROWN, Margaret BROWN. *Ack*: July Court 1750. *Regt*: 25 Sept. 1750.

[B:101] Austin SCARBOROUGH of Pasquotank County in the Province of North Carolina Planter for ... 20 pounds Current Money of Virginia ... paid by

Peter BROWN of Pasquotank County ... sold ... N. E. Side of Pasquotank River Contg 50 Acres ... joining to the Land of the afsd. Peter BROWN & Willm BURGES & Cornelius JONES Jr. ... Austin SCARBOROUGH do hereby declare myself to be the proper Owner by a hereditary Right of Inheritance ... 17 March 1750. *Signed*: Augustin X SCARBOROUGH his mark. *Wit*: John BURGES, Edwd FAIRCLOTH, Chas SCARBOROUGH. *Ack*: July Court 1750. *Regt*: 25 Sept. 1750.

Josiah HART of Tyrrell County in North Carolina for ... 15 pounds Current Money ... paid by William BURGES of Pasquotank County ... sold ... N. E. Side of Pasquotank River & on the N. W. Side of RAYMONS Creek being bounded on the Land of Thomas TOLKSEY and the Land of Cornelius JONES being conveyed out of Willm BURGES'S Patent & commonly known by the name of CLERKS? Reeds ... 100 Acres ... [B:102] ... 2 April 1750. *Signed*: Josiah HART. *Wit*: Saml. WILLIAMS, Jno SCARBOROUGH, Sarah X BURGESS her mark. *Proved*: July Court 1750 by the Oath of Jno. SCARBOROUGH. *Regt*: 25 Sept. 1750.

5 Aug. 1749 Betwixt John MCBRIDE of the County of Pasquotank, in the Province of North Carolina Planter of the one part, and John DUGGAN of Tyrrel County in the Province afsd. of the other part ... for 40 pounds Current Money ... sold ... 100 acres ... in the fork of the head of Pasquotank River it being part of a Tract belonging to a relapsed Patent bearing date 2 April 1724 and granted to Truman MCBRIDE ... Corner Tree of Jno KELLYS ... Line that was formerly James GARRIOTS? ... *Signed*: John X DUGGAN his mark, Mary D DUGGAN her mark. *Wit*: Gabl. TAYLOR, Jas MCBRIDE, Thomas SUTTON. *Proved*: July Court 1750 by the Oath of Gabl. TAYLOR. *Regt*: 25 Sept. 1750.

[B:103] 9 July 1750 Between William TAYLOR of the County of Pasquotank and Province of North Carolina Planter of the one part and John MCBRIDE of the said County of the other part ... for 10 pounds Virginia Money ... sold ... 100 Acres ... at the head of Pasquotank River in JOY'S Fork being part of a Tract of 480 Acres patented by Jno MCBRIDE ... 1749 ... Poplar Swamp ... to John KELLEY'S Corner Oak ... *Signed*: John MCBRIDE. *Wit*: Gabl. TAYLOR, James MCBRIDE. *Ack*: July Court 1750. *Regt*: 25 Sept. 1750.

9 July 1750 between William TAYLOR of the County of Pasquotank in the Province of North Carolina of the one part and John MCBRIDE of the said County Planter on the other part ... for 18 pounds Virginia Money ... sold ... 100 Acres ... head of Pasquotank River in JOY'S Fork being part of a Tract of 640 Acres patented by Truman MCBRIDE bearing date 1724 Beginning at a Pine in Caleb ABBOT'S Line ... [B:104] to Benjamin BURNHAMS Line ... Cowpen pond ... *Signed*: John MCBRIDE. *Wit*: Gabl. TAYLOR, James I MCBRIDE'S mark. *Ack*: July Court 1750. *Regt*: 25 Sept. 1750.

North Carolina) Pasquotank County) Dinah WEST of the County and Province Widow and Relict of Charles WEST late of this County decd. for ... my deceased Husband by his last Will did give and bequeath to his youngest Son Hezekiah WEST Three Negroes named as follows Cato, Mustapher and Sarah and the sd. Sarah being disposed to Thomas MEADS by my Husband in his Life time I therefore do by these presents give to my Son Hezekiah WEST in lieu of that Negro, a Negro Girl that I purchased of Benjamin PALMER named Rose, her and her Increase ... I likewise give to my Said Son Hezekiah WEST a new Bed and Furniture, one dozen of new Plates and all my Cattle and Hogs, likewise a new Chest of Drawers, also one new Pewter Dish ... 21 April 1750 ... *Signed*: Dinah WEST. *Wit*: The Mark of M. Mary WEST, Jno. MCKEEL. *Ack*: July Court 1750. *Regt*: 25 Sept. 1750.

[B:105] 24 May 1749 Between Benjamin SAWYER of the one party of the County of Pasquotank and Province of North Carolina and James SAWYER of the same place and Province afsd. of the other party ... for 50 pounds ... sold ... N. E. Side of Pasquotank River ... 100 acres of Land ... transferred from Richard to me ... *Signed*: Benjamin SAWYER. *Wit*: Jos. WILLIAMS, Caleb X SAWYER his mark. *Proved*: July Court 1750 by the Oath of Caleb SAWYER. *Regt*: 25 Sept. 1750.

Benjamin SAWYER of the County of Pasquotank in the Province of North Carolina do for the love good will and natural affection that I bear unto my Son Caleb SAWYER voluntarily and freely of my own good will

... give ... part of the plantation and land whereon I now live, it being that part that he the said Caleb now lives on called the lower side of the plantation ... North River Swamp ... 9 July 1750. *Signed*: Benjamin SAWYER. *Wit*: Tho. REDING, Jos: WILLIAMS, Saml. PHILLIPS. *Proved*: July Court 1750 by the Oath of Saml. PHILLIPS. *Regt*: 25 Sept. 1750.

[B:106] North Carolina) Pasquotank County) 25 Dec. 1748 and in the 21st year of the Reign of our Sovn Lord the King &c. Between Richd SAWYER of the one party and Thomas SAWYER of the other party ... for 150 pounds in Province Bills ... sold ... N. E. Side of Pasquotank River ... Caleb SAWYER'S Line ... Tract of Land formerly surveyed by Thomas COOPER ... 50 Acres ... *Signed*: Richard SAWYER. *Wit*: Jacob ALBERTSON, Caleb SAWYER. *Proved*: July Court 1750 by the Oath of Caleb SAWYER. *Regt*: 25 Sept. 1750.

[B:107] 8 Sept. 1749 ... on or about the year 1730 one James ROBERTSON, then a young Man and a Dancing Master or at least well skilled in dancing came before me then one of his Majesty's Justices of the Peace, and complained against one Thomas CROSBY for biting off a piece of his right Ear &c. whereupon a Warrant issued against sd. CROSBY and came to Trial &c. The plaintiff proved the fact by one Saml. TYLOR, and Sarah TYLOR Wife of the sd. Saml. TYLOR &c. the said CROSBY did then and there say and prove before me that the sd. ROBERTSON did in the Combat, between them bite off a piece of the sd. CROSBY'S finger; I then judged as the Ear being partly gone might be for greater Ignominy and Discredit, than the Loss of a Finger could be therefore ordered the said CROSBY to pay the Costs and so the Plff & Deft. made up the affair, but no Certificate of ROBERTSON'S Damage being then demanded now is given. Certified by me one of his Majesty's Justices of the Peace for the County of Tyrrel &c. *Signed*: Edmund SMITHWICK. And further the sd. ROBERTSON was in them Times held in good Esteem with all in our parts and not at all wanting, in his Behaviour or Credit amongst us. *Signed*: Edmd SMITHWICK. *Wit*: John STANSELL. Tyrrel County. I the Subscriber in my own Knowledge say that James ROBERTSON, a young Man and of very good credit and good Behaviour to all people ... *Signed*: Wm GARDNER T. Z.?
Johnston County. St. Patrick Parish. These are to

certify all persons whom it may concern on November 1730 or thereabouts Thomas CROSBY comes before me & makes Oath on the Holy Evangelist, that I the sd. CROSBY and James ROBERTSON had a quarrel and in the fight I the sd. CROSBY did bite a piece of the said ROBERTSON'S Ear off, and the sd. ROBERTSON did bite off a piece of finger which did plainly appear before me and this may certify all persons that all the damage that was done, in losing the sd. ROBERTSON'S right Ear & the sd. CROSBY'S finger and this the sd. CROSBY makes Oath before me one of his Majesty's Justices of the peace for the sd County, 31 Aug. 1749. *Signed*: Simon BRIGHT. Justice Peace. *Wit*: William COWARD. July Court 1750. These may certify that the afsd. Deposition and the within Certificates was exhibited into open Court by James ROBERTSON and prayed they might be recorded. *Regt*: 25 Sept. 1750.

29 Dec. 1749 Between Robert MURDEN of the County and Province afsd. Yeoman, and John MURDEN of the abovesaid County Planter ... for 10 pounds Stg Money of Gt. Britain ... sold ... Land whereon the sd. MURDEN now dwelleth being part of a large Tract that was surveyed for Jeremiah MURDEN and now is come in the possession of him the sd. Robert MURDEN being on the South Side of Pasquotank River ...
[B:108] ... line between William SEXTON and the sd. MURDEN ... River Swamp ... 100 acres ... *Signed*: Robert MURDEN. *Wit*: Obadiah SEXTON, William SEXTON. *Ack*: Oct. Court 1750. *Regt*: 16 Oct. 1750.

29 Dec. 1749 Between Robert MURDEN of Pasquotank County in the Province of North Carolina Yeoman & William SEXTON of the said County Planter ... for 10 pounds Stg Money of Gt Britain ... sold ... part of a larger Tract which was Surveyed and laid out for the said MURDEN ... whereon the said SEXTON now dwelleth, being on the South Side of Pasquotank River ... Branch between John MURDEN and the said SEXTON ... dividing line between the said William SEXTON and Obadiah SEXTON, his Brother ... 50 acres
[B:109] ... *Signed*: Robt. MURDEN. *Wit*: Obadiah SEXTON, John MURDEN. *Ack*: Oct. Court 1750. *Regt*: 16 Oct. 1750.

29 Dec. 1749 Between Robert MURDEN of the County of Pasquotank in the Province of North Carolina Yeoman

and Obadiah SEXTON of the abovesd. County Planter ... for 7 pounds Stg. Money of Gt Britain ... sold ... part of a larger Tract that was surveyed and laid out for the afsd. MURDEN, being the upper part of the Tract and in the same Land whereon the said SEXTON now dwelleth, being on the Westerly Side of the head of Pasquotank River ... River Swamp ... 30 Acres ... *Signed*: Robert MURDEN. *Wit*: William SEXTON, John MURDEN. *Proved*: Oct. Court 1750 by the Oath of Jno. MURDEN. *Regt*: 16 Oct. 1750.

21 July 1750 Between Esau ALBERTSON of the County of Pasquotank & Province of North Carolina Planter of the one part & Elias and Isaac ALBERTSON, Sons of the sd. Esau ALBERTSON both of the County and Province afsd. of the other party ... for the natural Love & affection ... and for the better maintenance ... give ... Tenement of Land ...
[B:110] ... 300 Acres ... on the Creek Swamp ... Cornelius JONES'S Line ... Griffith JONES'S Line ... being all my Land and plantation whereon I now dwell and give my Water Mill and all her appurtenances belonging to the said Mill that is across Arenuse Creek joining unto my Said plantation ... 26 July 1750. *Signed*: Esau ALBERTSON. *Wit*: Richard R GREGORY his mark, Thomas HOLLIDAY, Thomas T GREGORY. *Proved*: Oct. Court 1750 by the Oath of Thomas HOLLIDAY. *Regt*: 25 Oct. 1750.

6 Oct. 1750 and in the 24th year of our Sovn King George the Second ... Between Zachariah NIXON and Elisabeth his Wife of the County of Perquimons & Province afsd. Planter and Spinster of the one party, and William SIMPSON Merchant in Nixonton in the Province afsd and County of Pasquotank of the other party ... for 15 pounds 10 Shillings lawful Bills ... sold ...
[B:111] ... one half acre Lot in Nixonton, it being the Lot that numbers 85 in the plan of the said Town ... on the South End on the main Street adjacent to the Shipyard and on the West Side on the Lot that numbers 88 in the plan ... and the North End on the Lot that numbers 86 & on the E. Side on the Lot that numbers 15 ...
[B:112] ... *Signed*: Zacha. NIXON. *Wit*: Jos: ROBINSON, Thomas PEIRCE, Jos: PRITCHARD. *Proved*: Oct. Court 1750 by the Affirmation of Joseph ROBINSON. *Regt*: 16 Oct. 1750.

North Carolina 27 Sept. 1750 Between Zachariah NIXON & Elisabeth his Wife of the County of Perquimons & Province afsd. of the one party Farmer & Spinster and William LANE of Nixonton in the County of Pasquotank and Province afsd. Tavernkeeper of the other party ... Willm LANE proving the highest Bidder upon that Lot that numbers 2 in the plan of sd. Town at the Sum of 38 pounds Bills old Tenor ... sold ... Number 2 ... binding on number 3 on the E. Side and on the Lot that numbers 1 on the W. Side and on the Water Street on the S. End and on the Main Street on the No. End ...
[B:113] *Signed*: Zacha. NIXON. *Wit*: Jos: ROBINSON, Thomas PEIRCE, Jos: PRITCHARD. *Proved*: Oct. Court 1750 by the Oath of Joseph ROBINSON. *Regt*: 16 Oct. 1750.

North Carolina 8th of the 8th month commonly called October 1750 Between Zachariah NIXON of the County of Perquimons Farmer of the one part & John ANDERSON of the County and Province afsd. Farmer of the other part ... John ANDERSON proving to be the highest Bidder on that Lot that which numbers 9 in the plan of the said Town ... the Sum of 33 pounds 10 Shillings ... sold ...
[B:114] ... *Signed*: Zacha. NIXON. *Wit*: Jos: ROBINSON, Thomas PEIRCE, Jos: PRITCHARD. *Proved*: Oct. Court 1750 by the Affirmation of Joseph ROBINSON. *Regt*: 16 Oct. 1750.

North Carolina. Richard BRIGHT of the County of Pasquotank & Province afsd. for the love, good will, and affection which I have and bear towards my loving Grandson Solomon COOPER of the County and Province afsd. Planter have given ... 52½ acres of land, only excepting and giving my Son in law John COOPER and Sarah his Wife the use of the said Land during their Lives ... being part of a Patent granted to Owen REESE?, bearing date 1 April 1743 ... S. W. Side of Pasquotank River ... on the dismal
[B:115] ... 20 Sept. 1750. *Signed*: Richard BRIGHT. *Wit*: Joshua GAMBLING, James SMITH, James JONES. *Proved*: Oct. Court 1750 by the Oath of Joshua GAMBLING. *Regt*: 16 Oct. 1750.

North Carolina) Pasquotank County) 24 Aug. 1750 Between William TAYLOR of the sd County of the one part & Solomon TAYLOR of the sd County of the other

part ... for 50 pounds Virginia Currency ... sold ... commonly called the Quarter back of the fork of Pasquotank River and adjoining on John UPTON'S Land ... 280 acres ...
[B:116] ... *Signed*: William X TAYLOR his mark. *Wit*: Hezh. LINTON, Gabl. TAYLOR. *Proved*: Oct. Court 1750 by the Oath of Gabl. TAYLOR. *Regt*: 16 Oct. 1750.

North Carolina) Pasquotank County) Susannah PLATO single Woman of the Province & County afsd. for ... 31 pounds, 5 Shillings Current Money of Virginia Colony, or to the Value thereof in Province Commodities ... paid by Thomas HAMBLIN of the County and Province afsd. Carpenter ... sold ... all my third part of the land and plantation, that my father gave by his last Will and Testament to me contg 66 acres ... 2 Dec. 1749. *Signed*: Susannah E PLATO her mark. *Wit*: Thos. MEADS, Robt. HOSEA, Jno. MCKEEL. *Proved*: Oct. Court 1750 by the Oath of Robt. HOSEA. *Regt*: 16 Oct. 1750.

[B:117] 8 Oct. 1750 Between Jarvis JONES of the County of Pasquotank in North Carolina Planter of the one part and David DUNKIN of the same place Planter of the other part ... for 30 pounds Virginia Currency ... sold ... old JOYS fork joining on Joshua GAMBLINGS Land ... 100 acres ... part of a Tract of land from the Earl of GRANVILLE to the said Jarvis JONES contg 725 acres by one deed of Grant bearing date the 20th Dec. 1748 ... binding on Jacob BURNHAM'S Land ... AMES Line ... TOMBLINS Island Bridge ... *Signed*: Jarvis JONES. *Wit*: Joshua GAMBLING, Solomon TAYLOR, John TAYLOR. *Proved*: Oct. Court 1750 by the Oath of Joshua GAMBLING. *Regt*: 16 Oct. 1750.

[B:118] North Carolina) Pasquotank County) This Indenture Tripartie made the 5 Oct. 1750 Between William SIMPSON late of the Province afsd. Gentleman and Rebecca SWANN Daughter of Thomas SWANN OF Pasquotank County in the Province afsd. Gentn. decd. of the Second part Rebecca HUNTER Widow of Col Thomas HUNTER decd of the third part Whereas the afsd. Thomas SWANN in and by his last Will and Testament bearing date 7 April 1733 did amongst other Legacies and Bequeaths therein mentioned give all his Lands and Plantations in Moyock? and in the

Precinct of Currituck to his two Daughters viz. Rebecca & Elisabeth and that they be sold for Money and the money be equally divided between his said Daughters as also a Share of what Negroes that is raised out of his Stock of Negroes with a Bed, and Furniture & Several other things &c. And whereas a Marriage is intended shortly to be had and Solemnized between the sd. William SIMSON and the Said Rebecca SWANN and it is agreed ... William SIMSON ... shall not intermeddle with ... any part of the Estate given ... Rebecca SWANN ... but the same shall be and remain to and for the sole and separate use & Benefit of the sd. Rebecca SWANN ... [B:119] ... *Signed*: William SIMSON. *Wit*: C. HALL, Thos. TAYLOR, William DAVIS. *Ack*: Oct. Court 1750 from William SIMSON to Rebecca HUNTER and Rebecca SWANN. *Regt*: 16 Oct. 1750.

28 Dec. 1749 Between Joseph WILLIAMS of the County of Pasquotank of the one part and Joseph BELL of the same place and Province afsd. of the other part ... for 180 pounds ... sold ... 130 acres ... on the N. E. Side of Pasquotank
[B:120] River, it being the Tract or Parcel of Land I bought of Evan LURRY & Barbary his Wife ... *Signed*: Joseph WILLIAMS. *Wit*: R. MORGAN, John SAWYER. *Ack*: Oct. Court 1750. *Regt*: 16 Oct. 1750.

1 May 1750 Between John HASTINGS of the County of Pasquotank & the Province of North Carolina of the one part and Joseph WILLIAMS of the Same place ... of the other party ... for 20 pounds Proclamation ... sold ... Land [blank] of Joseph MORGAN ... N. E. side of Pasquotank Contg. 60 Acres ... *Signed*: John HASTINGS his mark. *Wit*: Dorothy X MORGAN her mark, Bett MORGAN. *Ack*: Oct. Court 1750. *Regt*: 16 Oct. 1750.

[B:121] 12 Jan. in the 32nd [sic] year of the Reign of our Sovn Lord George ... 1749/50 Between John HASTANES of Albemarle Cy and the Precinct of Pasquotank of the one part and Joseph SAWYER of the said County and Precinct of the other part ... for 30 pounds Current Money of North Carolina ... sold ... 10 acres of Land ... part of a Tract of Land surveyed for Thomas SAWYER ... N. E. Side of Pasquotank River ... Joseph MORGAN'S Line ... Alexander SAWYER'S Line ... 12 Jan. 1749/50.

Signed: John X HASTANES his mark. *Wit*: Richard SAWYER, Alexander A SAWYER his mark. *Ack*: Oct. Court 1750. *Regt*: 16 Oct. 1750.

[B:122] 8 Oct. 1750 & in the 33d [sic] year of the Reign of our Sovn Lord George ... Between Thos. SAWYER & Alexr. SAWYER of the County of Pasquotank in the Province of No. Carolina of the one part and Joseph SAWYER of the Same place ... for 30 pounds Virginia Money ... sold ... 35 Acres ... N. E. Side of Pasquotank River commonly called & known by the name of Broad Ridge & the Clover Pasture Ridge being part of a Patent granted to James MCDANIEL and a part of Jno SPENCES Patent & a part of Thos SAWYERS Patent ... Thos COOPER'S Line ... *Signed*: Thomas SAWYER, Alexander A SAWYER his mark. *Wit*: Joseph WILLIAMS, John HASTINS. *Proved*: Oct. Court 1750 by the Oath of Joseph WILLIAMS. *Regt*: 16 Oct. 1750.

[B:123] 25 Oct. 1749 Between John DIALL of Pasquotank County & Province of North Carolina Planter of the one part & Henry PENDLETON of the County & Province afsd of the other part ... for 37 pounds 10 Shillings Current Money of the Colony of Virginia ... sold ... 300 Acres ... a Patent bearing date 9 June 1714 Commonly known by the name of Sound Neck ... by the Sound Side called Albemarle DUCKINGFIELDS Corner Tree ... *Signed*: John DIALL. *Wit*: Saml HEIGHE, Timothy MEADS. *Proved*: Oct. Court 1750 by the Oath of Saml. HEIGHE. *Regt*: 16 Oct. 1750.

[B:124] Whereas a Marriage is intended to be had and shortly solemnized Between Joseph PRITCHARD Farmer of the County of Pasquotank and Elizabeth NEWBY of the County of Perquimons both of North Carolina, it is this day agreed ... by mutual Consent between the sd. Parties ... that the said Joseph PRITCHARD ... shall not ... lay any Claim or have it in their power to dispose of or detain from the said Elisabeth ... any of the following Articles of the sd. Elisabeth's Estate ... viz. One Negro Woman named Hagar, and the one half of her Increase ... one Negro Boy named Jacob, one Negro Girl named Sarah, one good Feather Bed & Furniture, one good Chest of Drawers, one Pine Oval Table, one good Seal Skin Trunk, one gilded Trunk, two english leather bottom Chairs, three flag'd? bottom ones, Six pewter plates, two middling Sized ones & one small pewter Dishes, three Silver Spoons, Ten middling likely head of Cattle, one cold Stitt?, one Middling Iron pot and hooks ... 11th day of the 2nd Month 1749. *Signed*: Joseph PRITCHARD, Elizabeth X NEWBY her mark. *Wit*: Caleb C ELLIOT his mark, Benja. PRITCHARD. *Ack*: Oct. Court 1750. *Regt*: 16 Oct. 1750.

15 May 1749 Between Thomas PENDLETON of the County of Pasquotank & Province of North Carolina Gentn. of the one party & Saml. WILLIAMS of the County and Province afsd. Planter of the other part ... for 50 pounds Current Money of Virginia ... sold ... [B:125] ... North Side of Pasquotank River being part of the Manor Land that was sold to the said Thos. PENDLETON by Henry WINSLOW [sic] the whole Manor Land Contg 3650 acres ... Beginning at ... plantation where one Benjn. BELL did live and the place called the Cotton Patch ... Saml. WILLIAMS now lives ... to the River ... 200 acres ... *Signed*: Thos. PENDLETON. *Wit*: Edwd. PHELPS, John CARTWRIGHT, Timothy T PENDLETON his mark. *Proved*: Oct. Court 1750 by the Oath of Jno. CARTWRIGHT. *Regt*: 16 Oct. 1750.

[B:126] North Carolina) Pasquotank County) John HOSEA of the County and Province afsd Planter for ... Love and Good Will & Affection which I have and do bear towards my Son John HOSEA of the County and Province afsd. ... give ... viz. One Negro Woman named Thank? she and her Increase, he dying without Heir I give the said Negro Woman with her Increase to Joseph PENDLETON'S two Daughters viz Mary & Deborah PENDLETON & likewise one Negro Boy named Jupiter & likewise he dying without Heir I give the Negroes Jupiter, Jos HOSEA'S Son Jos HOSEA as his or their own proper negroes ... 8 Jan. 1750/51. *Signed*: John HOSEA. *Wit*: Job. WINSLOW, Joseph X PENDLETON his mark. *Ack*: Oct. Court 1750. *Regt*: 16 Feby 1750.

Isaac STOKELY of the County of Pasquotank and Province of North Carolina, Planter for ... 50 pounds Current Money of Virginia ... paid by John HOSEA of the County and Province afsd ... sold ... 157 acres or the one half of a Patent of Land surveyed by Richard POPE, & bearing date the 21 Feby 1696 ... on the S. W. Side of Pasquotank River commonly called ... Rich Neck, it being part of a Deed that John MCKEEL sold to Stephen DELAMAR ... [B:127] ... 2 Dec. 1750. *Signed*: Isaac STOKELY. *Wit*: Stephen SCOTT, Saml. SCOTT. *Ack*: Jan. Court 1750. *Regt*: 16 Jany 1750.

North Carolina) Pasquotank County) Isaac FORBUSH of Pasquotank County in the Province of North Carolina Planter for ... 8 pounds Virginia Money ... paid by James FORBES Jr. ... sold ... on Pasquotank River Contg ... 12½ acres ... Beaver Dam Swamp ... 10 Feb. 1750. *Signed*: Isaac FORBES. *Wit*: James FORBES, Edward E FORBES his mark. *Ack*: Jan. Court 1750 from Isaac FORBES to James FORBES. *Regt*: 16 Jany 1750.

[B:128] John WHITE Senr of Pasquotank County and Province of North Carolina for 10 pounds Current Money of Virginia ... paid by Henry BRAY of the same County and Province afsd. ... sold ... N. E. Side of Pasquotank River Contg 50 Acres ... it being part of a Tract of Land which I bought of Thomas FORBES joining on John FORBES Line and GRIFFINS Line ... 7 Feb. 1748. *Signed*: John I WHITE his mark. *Wit*: James FORBES, William BRAY, Joel BRACKETT. *Ack*: Jan. Court 1750. *Regt*: 16 Jany 1750.

Henry HAYMAN of Pasquotank County and in the Province of North Carolina Planter for ... 40 pounds current Money of Virginia ... paid by Benjamin TORKSEY of the County & Province afsd ... [B:129] ... sold ... N. E. Side of Pasquotank River and at the head of Portahonk Creek ... CLERKS Reeds ... HAWKINS Line ... Creek Branch ... 100 Acres ... the old Plantation ... 10 Dec. 1750. *Signed*: Henry HAMAN. *Wit*: Wm BURGES, John BURGES, Mary M BEELS her mark. *Ack*: Jan. Court 1750 from Henry HAMAN to Benjn TORKSEY. *Regt*: 16 Jany 1750.

[B:130] North Carolina) Pasquotank County) 12 Dec. 1749 Between Stephen HALL of the one part Planter and Patrick POOL Planter of the other part ... for 2,100 pounds Weight of merchantable fresh pork ... ... sold ... between Little River and Pasquotank River contg 100 acres ... that Francis late of the County afsd by a Deed of Gift gave to his Son Francis HENDRICK ... part of that Tract ... commonly known by the name of the "Half way Tree Land" ...

[B:131] ... to be laid off at the Cost and Charges of the said Patrick POOL by agreement ... *Signed*: Stephen HALL. *Wit*: Joseph MORRIS, Joseph ROBINSON. *Proved*: Jan. Court 1750 by the Affirmation of Joseph ROBINSON. *Regt*: 16 Jany 1750.

19 March 1749/50 Between Samuel HEIGHE and Ann his Wife of Pasquotank County in the Province of North Carolina of the one part and Robert TODD of the Borough of Norfolk in Virginia Merchant of the other part ... for 258 pounds Current Money of the Colony of Virginia ... sold ... Newbegun Creek ... purchased by the sd. Samuel & Ann of William BROTHERS Junr. and where the sd. HEIGHE now lives Contg 150 acres ... together with a Negro Man named David & a Negro Woman named Betty with her future Increase and 40 head of Cattle ... in case the said Saml or Ann his Wife should on or before the 1 March 1752/3 pay ... unto the sd. Robert TODD ... 258 pounds Current money of Virginia together with the lawful Interest of North Carolina ... then this Instrument of Writing to be absolutely void ... *Signed*: Saml. HEIGHE, Ann A HEIGHE her mark. [B:132] *Wit*: Willm. GREGORY, Saml. SCOLLAY, James HEIGHE. *Proved*: Jan. Court 1750 Deed of Mortgage from Saml. HEIGHE & Ann his Wife to Robert TODD by the Oath of William GREGORY. *Regt*: 16 Jany 1750.

North Carolina) Pasquotank County) 10 Sept. 1750 Between Robert MURDEN & Catherine his wife of the County & Province afsd. of the one part and Isaac STOKELY of the same County of the other part ... for the Exchange of Two plantations and a piece of Woodland Ground ... sold ... S. W. Side of Pasquotank River ... 250 acres ... Creek Swamp ... Nathanl GRAY'S Line to David PRITCHARDS, then on John MURDENS to the River Pocoson, MURDEN'S new Survey ...
[B:133] ... *Signed*: Robert MURDEN. *Wit*: David PRITCHARD, Tho: TAYLOR. *Ack*: Jan. Court 1750. *Regt*: 16 Jany 1750.

North Carolina) Pasquotank County) Hannah STAFFORD of the County of Pasquotank and in the Province of North Carolina ... for 25 pounds Current Money of Virginia ... paid by Isaac STOKELY of the same County & Province afsd. ... sold ... 125 Acres ... S. W. Side of Pasquotank River lying between

David PRITCHARD and the afsd. Isaac STOKELY Land and the property of Wm CARTWRIGHT decd. & given by the sd. decd. to Hannah STAFFORD ... Wm CARTWRIGHT Senr Corner Tree ...
[B:134] ... 14 Dec. 1749. *Signed*: Hannah H STAFFORD her mark. *Wit*: David PRITCHARD, Jacob ALBERTSON. *Proved*: Jany Court 1750 by the Oath of David PRITCHARD. *Regt*: 16 Jany 1750.

North Carolina) Pasquotank County) John DAVIS of the County of Pasquotank in the Province of North Carolina ... for 20 pounds ... paid by Isaac STOKELY of the same County and Province afsd. ... sold ... 10 Acres ... S. W. Side of Pasquotank River lying between Sarah TRUEBLOODS and the afd. STOKELY'S Land ... River Swamp ... DAVIS'S Branch ... the piece of Land is known as Long point ... 12 July 1750. *Signed*: John DAVIS. *Wit*: Joseph X SANDERLIN mark, Thomas SAWYER. *Ack*: Jany Court 1750. *Regt*: 16 Jany.

[B:135] North Carolina) Pasquotank County) George WARD of the County of Onslow and in the Province of North Carolina ... for 10 pounds ... paid by John DAVIS of the County of Pasquotank & Province afsd. ... sold ... 50 Acres ... S. W. Side of Pasquotank River ... Creek Swamp ... 8 Nov. 1748. *Signed*: George X WARD his mark. *Wit*: Isaac STOKELY, Joshua J DAVIS his mark. *Proved*: Jany Court 1750 by the Oath of Isaac STOKELY. *Regt*: 16 Jany 1750.

North Carolina) Pasquotank County) 7 July 1750 Between Christopher CARTWRIGHT of the County and Province afsd. of the one part Joiner, and Edward SCOTT planter of the County and Province afsd. of the other part ... Christopher CARTWRIGHT for and in Consideration of the Exchange of a parcel of Woodland adjoining to Thomas CASEY'S Line, SMITHSON'S Land ... for the Exchange of the Woodland delivered by me the said Edward SCOTT
[B:136] ... sold ... S. W. Side of Pasquotank River ... 100 acres ... being the uppermost part of the said Land belonging to William COLE a GRAYS old field ... E. side of Knobs crook Creek Swamp ... Cypress Branch ... SMITHSON'S Line ... *Signed*: Edward SCOTT, Mary M SCOTT her mark. *Wit*: Thos. TRUEBLOOD, Josiah TRUEBLOOD. *Ack*: April Court 1751. *Regt*: 18 April 1751.

[B:137] 26 Sept. 1750 Between Mr. Francis CLARKE of Princess Ann County of the one part and Captn James KEMP, Major Thomas WALK and Arthur SAWYER of the same County of the other part ... for 100 pounds Current Money of Virginia ... sold ... 1,218 acres as by plan and Survey thereof made by Mr Richd MCCLURE the 10 Sept. 1745 and is the same Land which the said Francis CLERK purchased of John DURRANS? King of the Yeopim Indians & James BARKER? as by Deed dated the 10th day of Nov. 1749 ... It is hereby declared to be the true Intent ... if the said Francis CLERK ... on or before the 6 May 1752 satisfy and pay ... 100 pounds & lawful Interest ... be utterly Void and of no effect ...
[B:138] ... *Signed*: Francis CLERKE, James KEMP, Thomas WALK. *Wit*: Saml. HOLLOWELL, Willm MALBON, John ACKISS. *Proved*: April Court 1751 Deed of Sale of Mortgage from Francis CLERK to James KEMP, Thomas WALK & Arthur SAWYER by the Oath of Saml. HOLLOWELL. *Regt*: 18 April 1751.

North Carolina) Pasquotank County) Christopher CARTWRIGHT of the Province and County afsd. for ... the Exchange of a certain piece of Land to me in hand delivered by Edwd. SCOTT ... sold ... one part of a registered Tract of Land whereon Joseph CARTWRIGHT formerly lived ... 100 acres ... S. W. Side of Pasquotank River ... Knobs Crook Creek ... TULLEY'S Corner ...
[B:139] 28 Nov. 1750. *Signed*: Christopher CARTWRIGHT. *Wit*: Thomas TRUEBLOOD, Josiah TRUEBLOOD. *Proved*: April Court 1751. *Regt*: 18 April 1751.

North Carolina) Pasquotank County) Job CARTWRIGHT of the County and Province afsd. for ... 14 pounds, 14 Shillings & 4 pence ... paid by Edwd. SCOT ... sold ... one part of a registered Tract of Land it being a Conveyance out of Job. CARTWRIGHTS now granted patent ... 100 acres ... S. W. Side of Pasquotank River ... Abel TRUEBLOODS Line ... Josiah TRUEBLOODS Line ... 26 Sept. 1750. *Signed*: Job. CARTWRIGHT. *Wit*: Thos. TRUEBLOOD, John CASSE. *Ack*: April Court 1751. *Regt*: 18 April 1751.

[B:140] North Carolina. 9th day of the Second Month commonly called april 1751 Between Thomas NICHOLSON in Perquimons County Merchant of the Province afsd of the one part & Stephen SCOT of

Pasquotank County and Province afsd. Merchant of the other part. Whereas Joseph GLASTER by his last Will & Testament in writing bearing date the 27th day of the tenth Month commonly called January 1718 gave ... to Ruth his Daughter Wife of the sd. Stephen SCOTT as also to one Sarah another of his Daughters the Wife of Wike HUNNICUTT in Virginia all his Lands as well in Carolina as Virginia ... to be equally divided between them ... whereas the Said Ruth ... 150 acres ... adjoining to Land belonging to David GEORGE ... the said Stephen SCOTT and Ruth his wife ... for the conveying ... of the above recited Tract ... as is expressed in a deed of Sale bearing date the 10th day of 8th month commonly called Oct. 1744 ... for 5 pounds lawful Money of Gt. Britain ... and to the Intent that the Said Thomas NICHOLSON shall and will reconvey the said Tract of Land ... unto Stephen SCOT ... or to the Said Ruth ... on the S. Side of Newbegun Creek ...
[B:141] ... unto said Stephen SCOTT ... in discharge of the Trust reposed in me the sd. Thomas NICHOLSON ... and at the special Instance and immediate Request of him the sd. Stephen SCOTT and according to the special Trust ... of the above recited Deed from Stephen SCOTT and Ruth his wife unto me the said Thomas NICHOLOSN ... *Signed*: Thomas NICHOLSON. *Wit*: Joseph ROBINSON, Thos SYMONS, Zach: NIXON. *Ack*: April Court 1751. *Regt*: 18 April 1751.

North Carolina) Pasquotank County) Job CARTWRIGHT of the Province and County afsd. for ... 14 pounds, 14 Shillings and 4 pence ... paid by Josiah TRUEBLOOD ... sold ... part of a registered Tract of Land it being a Conveyance out of Job CARTWRIGHT'S now granted patent ... 100 acres ... S. W. Side of Pasquotank River ...
[B:142] ... MABSON'S Corner ... CARTWRIGHT'S Line ... 9 Sept. 1750. *Signed*: Job CARTWRIGHT. *Wit*: Thos. TRUEBLOOD, Joshua TRUEBLOOD. *Ack*: April Court 1751. *Regt*: 18 April 1751.

Joseph MORRIS of Pasquotank County in the Province of North Carolina ... whereas his Excelly Gabl. JOHNSTON and the rest of his Council did grant unto me the sd. Joseph MORRIS of the County afsd. Planter a Tract of Land contg 168 Acres ... for 50 pounds ... paid by my Brother John MORRIS of the County

afsd. ... sold ... one half part of the above mentioned 168 acres of Land ...
[B:143] ... Spring Branch ... division between Joseph and John's plantation ... Great Branch ... 8 April 1751. *Signed*: Joseph MORRIS. *Wit*: Richard R T JAMES his mark, Ann A OVERMAN her mark. *Ack*: April Court 1751. *Regt*: 18 April 1751.

North Carolina) Pasquotank County) 27 Oct. 1750 By and Between David DUNKIN of the said County of the one part & Henry EVANS of the said County of the other part ... for 35 pounds Current Money of Virginia ... sold ... known by the name of the middle Island and Landing Island on the N. E. Side of Pasquotank River ... patented by Thomas BETTOS?
[B:144] and the said patent assigned to John JONES and left by the last Will and Testament John JONES to Jarvis JONES Son of said John JONES ... John BISHOP'S Corner Tree ... 200 acres of Land ... *Signed*: David DUNKIN. *Wit*: Hezekiah LINTON, James SMITH, Joshua GAMBLING. *Ack*: April Court 1751. *Regt*: 18 April 1751.

26 March 1751 and in the 24th year of the Reign of our Sovn Lord George the Second ... Between Jarvis JONES of the County of Pasquotank in North Carolina Planter of the one part & Richard NICKINS of the County of Currituck & Province afsd. Tailor of the other part ... for 12 pounds 10 Shillings Virginia Currency ...
[B:145] ... sold ... S. Side of the Great Swamp ... by the Road Side ... flat Swamp ... to the Great Swamp Bridge ... 70 acres of Land & Swamp being part of a larger Tract contg 615 acres & by one deed of Grant of the Earl of GRANVILLLE to the said JONES ... 20 Dec. 1748 ... *Signed*: Jarvis JONES. *Wit*: Joseph JONES, Henry LAWLY, Henry X HOLLOWELL his mark. *Ack*: April Court 1747. *Regt*: 18 April 1751.

9 April and in the 24th year of the Reign of our Sovereign Lord George the Second ... Between William WILLIAMS of North Carolina, Pasquotank County of the one part & Jarvis JONES of the same place of the other part ... for
[B:146] 25 pounds Virginia Currency ... sold ... 300 acres as by Patent granted to William PHILLIPS bearing date 13 march 1746 ... Easternmost Branch of the fork of Pasquotank River ... in the Desart ...

Signed: William WILLIAMS. *Wit*: Tho: WEEKS, Josiah CARTWRIGHT, John REDING. *Ack*: April Court 1751. *Regt*: 18 April 1751.

North Carolina. 4 April 1751 Between Daniel JACKSON of the County of Pasquotank in the Province of North Carolina Planter of the one part and David JACKSON of the same County & Province afsd of the other part ... for 5 pounds lawful Money of Gt. Britain ... sold ... S. W. Side of Pasquotank River contg 126 acres ... part of a new Survey lately taken and patented by the afsd. Danl. JACKSON ... Saml. JACKSON decd. his Line ... Thomas CASE'S Corner ... William SIMSON'S ... Job JACKSON'S Corner ... [B:147] ... *Signed*: Danl. JACKSON. *Wit*: Moses JACKSON, William W SIMSON his mark. *Ack*: April Court 1751. *Regt*: 18 April 1751.

William BURGES of Pasquotank County & Province of North Carolina for ... 40 pounds current Money of Virginia ... paid by John SQUIRES of the same County & Province afsd. ... sold ... part of a Tract of Land which was conveyed to me from Ann JONES bearing date the 14 July 1730 ... given to the said Ann JONES in the last Will and Testament of her deceased Father Cornelius JONES ... 75 Acres ... [B:148] ... 19 Feb. 1750/51. *Signed*: Wm. BURGES. *Wit*: Stephen BRANT, Roger SQUIRES, Bevley? B BRANT her mark. *Ack*: April Court 1751. *Regt*: 18 April 1751.

Cornelius FOREHAND for the Sum of 10 pounds ... paid by Caleb BURNHAM ... sold ... 50 acres ... being part of JOY'S patent ... fork of Pasquotank being the Land that was Cornelius FOREHANDS ... 30 Oct. 1750. *Signed*: Cornelius X FOREHAND his mark. *Wit*: Joshua GAMBLING, Benjamin BURNHAM. *Ack*: April Court 1751. *Regt*: 18 April 1751.

[B:149] John BURGES of Pasquotank County and Province of North Carolina Planter for ... 2 pounds Current Money of Great Britain ... paid by Jno BROWN of Pasquotank afsd. ... sold ... North River Swamp ... an Island in the Swamp ... 310 acres ... by patent under the Hands of Edward MOSELY and Robert HATTON, Agents for John Lord CARTERET Earl of GRANVILLE and bearing date 20 Dec. 1748 ... sell one Moiety or half part of said Island ... 25 Dec. 1748.

Signed: John BURGES. *Wit*: Sarah X BROWN her mark, Peter P BROWN his mark, Josiah HARTX? *Ack*: April Court 1751. *Regt*: 18 April 1751.

3 April 1751 & in the 24th year of the Reign of our Sovereign Lord George the Second ... Between Jarvis JONES of the County of Pasquotank in North Carolina of the one part & Isaac BRIGHT of the same place Planter of the other part ... for 6 pounds Virginia Currency ...
[B:150] ... also for ... the Rents ... sold ... North Side of Pasquotank River Contg 50 acres of Land & Swamp being part of a larger Tract of 725 acres by one deed of Grant from the Earl of GRANVILLE to the said JONES dated 20 Dec. 1748 ... to the Road ... James JONES Land called TOMLIN Island ... Cypress Run ... Moses MCFARSON'S Land ... *Signed*: Jarvis JONES. *Wit*: Joseph MACKFARSON, Alexander SPENCE, Moses M MACKFARSON his mark. *Ack*: April Court 1751. *Regt*: 18 April 1751.

Thomas BURGES Junr. of Pasquotank County & Province of North Carolina for ... 50 pounds current Money of Virginia ... paid by Thomas TORKSEY of the same County and Province afsd. ... sold ... N. E. Side of Pasquotank River Binding on Raymon's Creek being part of a Tract of Land granted by patent to Stephen BURGES bearing date 1721 and given to his Son Stephen BURGES in his last Will and Testament then given from him to his Son
[B:151] Thomas BURGES in his last Will and Testament ... 100 acres ... head of Targinton Gut ... between Thomas CARTWRIGHT and Thomas BURGES ... between Thomas BURGES & Stephen BURGES so binding on Charles WRIGHTS Line to the Creek ... 19 Jan. 1748/9. *Signed*: Thomas BURGES. *Wit*: John SQUIRES, John CARTRITE, Isaac CARTWRIGHT. *Proved*: April Court 1751 by the Oath of John SQUIRES. *Regt*: 18 April 1751.

18 Feb. 1750/1 ... Edmund JACKSON of Pasquotank & Province of North Carolina Planter for ... 3 pounds, 10 Shillings Virginia Currency ... paid by Hezekiah CARTWRIGHT of the County and Province afsd. Planter ... sold ... 5 Acres ... fork of Knobs crook ... head of the land which was patented by Henry
[B:152] NICHOLS, the Patent bearing date 1715 ... Between Thomas PRITCHARD and the Land formerly

called COOPERS ... *Signed*: Edmund JACKSON. *Wit*: Thomas WEEKS, Josiah CARTWRIGHT, Danl. WILLIAMS. *Ack*: April Court 1751. *Regt*: 18 April 1751.

John COATS of Pasquotank County & Province of North Carolina Planter for ... 2 pounds Current Money of Gt. Britain ... paid by John SIKES of Pasquotank afsd. ... sold ... being in North River Swamp [B:153] ... 450 Acres ... John COATS took up as by a patent under the hand of Edward MOSELY and Robert HALTON agent for John Lord CARTWRIGHT Earl of GRANVILLE and bearing date the 20th day of Dec. 1748 ... one Moiety or 200 acres of said Tract of Land being divided by a Line agreed upon ... FORBES'S Corner ... 3 Feb. 1749. *Signed*: John COATS. *Wit*: Jas FORBES, Elizabeth FORBES, John SIKES. *Proved*: April Court 1751 by the Affirmation of James FORBES. *Regt*: 18 April 1751.

North Carolina) Pasquotank County) Robert BAILY of the Province and County aforesaid ... for 50 pounds Current Money of Virginia ... paid by John HOSEA of the County and Province afsd. ... sold ... [B:154] ... 55½ acres with plantation ... North Side of Little River ... Joseph WHITES Line ... Robert LOWRYS side Line ... 19 March 1751. *Signed*: Robert BAILY, Elisabeth X BAILY her mark. *Wit*: Job WINSLOW, John ARMOUR, Saml SCOTT. *Ack*: April Court 1751. *Regt*: 18 April 1751.

6 April 1751 and in the 24th year of the Reign of our Sovn Lord George the Second ... Between Jarvis JONES of the County of Pasquotank in North Carolina of the one part & Moses MACKFARSON of the same place Planter of the other part ... for 25 Shillings Virginia Currency ... also for the Rents ... [B:155] ... sold ... North Side of the River ... 125 acres ... part of a larger Tract of 725 acres by one deed of Grant from the Earl of GRANVILLE to the said JONES dated 20 Dec. 1748 ... Bounded ... James JONES and the said Moses MACFARSON ... up the Road near the Mill Run Bridge ... 50 acres of Land already marked by a Line of Trees for Isaac BRIGHT ... *Signed*: Jarvis JONES. *Wit*: Joseph MACKFARSON, Isaac BRIGHT, Alexander SPENCE. *Ack*: April Court 1751. *Regt*: 18 April 1751.

6 Nov. 1750 in the 23rd year of the Reign of our

Sovereign Lord George the Second ... Between Jarvis JONES of the County of Pasquotank in North Carolina Planter of the one part & Joseph MACKFARSON of the same place Planter of the other part ... for 3 pounds Virginia Currency ... also for ... the Rents ... sold ... N. E. Side of Pasquotank River [B:156] being part of a larger Tract of Land, from the Earl of GRANVILLE to the said Jarvis JONES Contg 615 acres by one deed of Grant bearing date the 20 Dec. 1748 ... Bounded ... Great Swamp Bridge ... William SIKES Bridge ... Great Swamp Desart ... Contg 128 acres ... *Signed*: Jarvis JONES. *Wit*: James JONES, James SPENCE, Mary M JONES her mark. *Ack*: April Court 1751. *Regt*: 18 April 1751.

John WALLIS of the County of Pasquotank and in the Province of North Carolina ... for 20 pounds in pork and Corn ... paid by Samuel CORLING of the same place and County and province afsd. ... sold ... [B:157] ... parcel of Land ... joining one Benjamin HARRISON'S Corner ... Joseph GILFORDS Line to the said GILFORD'S Cart Road ... COSAN Branch to John HAWKINS Line ... Isaac HARRISON'S Corner ... 50 Acres ... 1 Jan. 1750. *Signed*: John X WALLIS his mark, Sarah X WALLIS her mark. *Wit*: Saml. WILLIAMS, Jacob C CORELLEN? his mark, Ruth R WALLIS her mark. *Proved*: April Court 1751 by the Oath of Jacob CORLING. [sic] *Regt*: 18 April 1751.

North Carolina) Pasquotank County) Robert BAILY of the place afsd. Farmer for ... the Swap or Exchange of a certain plantation of Zephaniah WHITE'S lying on the N. E. Side of Little River, lying between Robert LOWRY'S Land and Nehemiah WHITE'S Land ... sold ... 200 acres ... to be laid off by the said Robert BAILY & Zephaniah WHITE as they have agreed ... part of a Tract contg 308 acres according to the Patent ... on the JOY Thicket on one Side & John WHITE'S & Robert DAVIS'S on the other Side ... [B:158] ... 13 Sept. 1749. *Signed*: Robert BAILEY. *Wit*: Joseph ROBINSON, John OVERMAN. *Proved*: April Court 1751 by the Affirmation of Joseph ROBERTSON. [sic] *Regt*: 18 April 1751.

Edmund CHANCEY Senr of North Carolina & County of Pasquotank ... sell all my Right ... 100 acres ... S. W. Side of the main Swamp of Newbegun Creek between the two Lines of John BROTHERS &

Francis HENDRICK decd. which Land was lawfully surveyed ... patent granted to me for 449 acres bearing date 5 Jan. 1714 ... Mouth of a Great Branch that runs through Lawrence KEATONS Patent ... unto John BROTHERS Senr. ... for 18
[B:159] pounds Current Money of Virginia ... 5 April 1751. *Signed*: Edmund CHANCEY. *Wit*: Robert HALL, Oliver SALTER, Rachel CHANCEY. *Ack*: April Court 1751. *Regt*: 18 April 1751.

North Carolina. 4 April 1751 Between Danl. JACKSON of the County of Pasquotank in the Province of North Carolina of the one part & William SIMPSON of the County & Province afsd. of the other part ... for 500 pounds lawful Money of Great Britain ... sold ... 126 acres ... Thomas CASE'S Line ... East End of the Savannah ... the narrow passage ... David JACKSON'S Line, which said Land the afsd. Danl. JACKSON hath lately taken up surveyed and patented ... S. W. Side of Pasquotank River ...
[B:160] ... *Signed*: Daniel JACKSON. *Wit*: Moses JACKSON, David D JACKSON his mark. *Ack*: April Court 1751. *Regt*: 18 April 1751.

North Carolina. 4 April 1751 Between Danl. JACKSON of the County of Pasquotank in the Province of North Carolina Planter of the one part & Thomas CASE of the same County & Province of the other part ... for 5 pounds lawful Money of Great Britain ... sold ... 126 acres of Land ... being part of a new Survey taken up and surveyed by the afsd. Danl. JACKSON ... S. W. Side of Pasquotank River ... David JACKSON'S Corner, then down Job CARTWRIGHTS Line to the End of the thick patch ... known by the name of Edwd. JACKSON'S Body plantation ...
[B:161] ... *Signed*: Danl. JACKSON. *Wit*: Moses JACKSON, William W SIMSON his mark. *Ack*: April Court 1751. *Regt*: 18 April 1751.

North Carolina) Pasquotank County) 13 Nov. 1750 Between Robert BAILY of the one part Farmer and Robert WHITE of the other part Farmer both of the County and Province afsd. ... for 13 pounds 10 Shillings Current Money of Virginia ... sold ... part of a Tract of Land contg 108 Acres ... that Zephaniah WHITE now dwells on ... on Robert DAVIS'S Line & then on Robert LOWRY'S & William TURNER'S Land known by the name of David BAILY'S Glade ...

[B:162] ... *Signed*: Robert BAILEY. *Wit*: Jas: GREGORIE, Joseph ROBINSON. *Proved*: April Court 1751 by the affirmation of Joseph ROBINSON. *Regt*: 18 April 1751.

Ephraim OVERMAN of the Province of Pasquotank & Precinct of North Carolina have assigned all my Right ... of the within mentioned Patent ... unto Ephraim BRIGHT ... *Signed*: Ephraim OVERMAN. *Wit*: John SMITHSON, Christopher CARTWRIGHT. *Proved*: April Court 1751 by the Oath of John SMITHSON. *Regt*: 18 April 1751.

John COOPER & Sarah his Wife of Pasquotank ... for 100 pounds Sterling Money of Gt. Britain ... paid by Isaac SAWYER of the afsd Precinct ... sold ... 52½ acres ... South of Pasquotank River ... in the Dismal ...
[B:163] ... 5 Jan. 1750. *Signed*: X Sarah COOPER her mark and I John COOPER his mark. *Wit*: James A MACKDANIEL his mark, T Thomas TEMPLE his mark. *Proved*: April Court 1751 by the Oath of Thomas TEMPLE. *Regt*: 18 April 1751.

Thomas BURGES & my Wife Mary BURGES for ... 10 pounds Current Money of Virginia ... paid by William BRAY of the same County and Province afsd. ... sold ... Tract of Land which formerly belonged to John GILFORD known by the name of Dogwood Ridge and at his decease fell by Heirship to the Said Mary BURGES ... 12½ Acres ... 23 March 1750/51. *Signed*: Thomas BURGES, Mary X BURGES her mark. *Wit*: John SQUIRES, Roger SQUIRES, Elisabeth X SQUIRES her mark. *Ack*: open Court in due form of Law. *Regt*: 15 July 1751.

[B:164] North Carolina. Abazanner PERKINS of the County of Pasquotank in the Province afsd ... for 50 pounds Cash ... paid by Thomas BURGES ... sold ... 112 acres ... N. E. Side of Pasquotank River called RAYMAN'S Creek ... John HARDIN'S Land ... 18 Aug. 1750. *Signed*: Abazzaner X PERKINS his mark. *Wit*: John CARTRITT, John SQUIRES, Wm BRAY. *Ack*: July Court 1751. *Regt*: 15 July 1751.

[B:165] 7 Jan. 1750 Between Joseph REED of Perquimons County in the Province of North Carolina Farmer of the one part and Timothy MEADS of Pasquotank County in the Province afsd. Planter of the other part ... for 100 pounds lawful Money of Gt. Britain ... sold ... two certain Tracts ... N. E. Side of Little River both contg ... 80 Acres ... one which contains 55 acres ... Oliver SALTERS Line ... Main Road ... Timothy MEADS Line ... the other which contains about 25 acres ... Branch which formerly belonged to Oliver SALTER ... (except the Liberty John PEGGS hath of Oliver SALTER of Cutting of Trees in the last mentioned parcel) ... *Signed*: Joseph REED. *Wit*: Henry DELON, Saml. SUTTON. *Ack*: April Court 1751. *Regt*: 18 April 1751.

[B:166] North Carolina) Pasquotank County) William DAVIS for ... 104 pounds Current Money of this Province ... paid by William ARMOUR of the Province & County afsd. ... sold ... Tract of Land lying on or near the plantation or Land of Thomas ARMOUR & Joseph REED ... plantation of George WINBERRY ... being yet unsurveyed, Contg by Estimation 50 acres ... 17 Feby 1750/51. *Signed*: William X DAVIS his mark. *Wit*: Thomas ARMOUR, Robert ARMOUR. *Proved*: April Court 1751 by the Oath of Thomas ARMOUR. *Regt*: 18 April 1751.

[B:167] North Carolina. John HOSEA of the County of Pasquotank in Province afsd. ... for 120 pounds Current Money of the Colony of Virginia ... paid by Joseph HOSEA ... sold ... Land that the afsd. John HOSEA bought of Isaac STOKELY contg 157 acres lying and binding on the Land or plantation Thomas PENDLETON bought of Joseph ARMOUR it being the West End of 314 acres that is in Richd POPE'S Patent ... 8 April 1751. *Signed*: John HOSEA. *Wit*: Hen: PENDLETON, Thomas ARMOUR, William HIXON. *Ack*: April Court 1751. *Regt*: 18 April 1751.

Peter BROWN of Pasquotank County in North Carolina for ... the affection Love and Good will I bear to my Son John BROWN ... give ... five Negroes viz¢ One Negro Woman named Tamr?, one Negro Woman named Cye, one Negro Boy named Will, one negro Boy named Sam? and one Negro Boy named Dunk ...
[B:168] 27 March 1750. *Signed*: Peter P BROWN his mark. *Wit*: William WRIGHT, James I CREECH his mark. *Ack*: April Court 1751. *Regt*: 18 April 1751.

North Carolina) Pasquotank County) Abraham HOSEA of the County and Province afsd. for ... 310 acres of

Land and 5 pounds proclamation Money ... paid by William DAVIS of the County & Province afsd ... sold ... part of a Tract ... on the head of Thomas ARMOUR'S Line on the S. W. Side of Pasquotank River Contg. ... 300 acres, a plantation that Benjamin PALMER formerly tended commonly called by the name of PALMER'S Quarter ... to Thomas GASKINS Line ... [B:169] ... 2 March 1750/51. *Signed*: Abraham HOSEA. *Wit*: Thomas T JAMES his mark, Jonathan HOWELL. *Ack*: April Court 1751. *Regt*: 18 April 1751.

North Carolina) Pasquotank County) William DAVIS for ... a plantation Contg 300 acres of Land together with 5 pounds proclamation Money ... paid by Abraham HOSEA ... sold ... Two certain plantations ... 310 acres ... on the head of Great Flatty Creek ... BRATCHERS? plantation ... Mr Edmund GALES Line ... the other plantation called Neats ... Benjamin GILES Corner Tree by a Branch of Flatty Creek ...
[B:170] ... 2 March 1750/51. *Signed*: William X DAVIS his mark. *Wit*: Thomas T JAMES his mark, Jonathan HOWELL. *Ack*: April Court 1751. *Regt*: 18 April 1751.

18 Sept. 1749. This Indenture or Lease made and indented Between Elisabeth WILLIAMS of the one part & Lodwick WILLIAMS of the other part ... lett a part of the plantation she lives now upon ... Gumberry Swamp ... all the Woodland Land and the Land he the sd Lodwick WILLIAMS has cleared ... Excepting Rail Timber & Fire Wood for her own use & Liberty to feed and raise Hogs upon it ... Elisabeth & Wm LODWICK [sic] do here both consent together in the Sum of 500 pounds Stg. money neither of them to give lease to nobody to cut any Wood or Timber without they are both agreed ... he to pay one half bushel of Wheat yearly during the term of her natural life ... 18 Sept. 1749. *Signed*: Eliza. E WILLIAMS her mark. *Wit*: Josiah WILLIAMS, Tully SAWYER. And furthermore he the said Lodwick WILLIAMS is to keep a good Cross Fence and She the said Elisabeth WILLIAMS is not to break in upon his cleared Ground, nor he ... to break in upon her cleared Ground as her fence now stands without his leave and furthermore she letts ... one half the Benefit of an Orchard & the Cider, he the said Lodwick to help to trim the Trees and to help to find a Trough and to fence the Orchard in

she to find a good hand to help him ... 18 Sept. 1749. *Signed*: Elisabeth E WILLIAMS her mark. *Wit*: Josiah WILLIAMS, Tully SAWYER. ... April Court [B:171] *Proved*: by the Oath of Tully SAWYER. *Regt*: 18 April 1751.

10 April 1751 Between Jacob CARON of the County of Currituck in the Province of North Carolina of the one part and Nathanl WILSON of Pasquotank County in the Province afsd. of the other part ... for 25 pounds current Money of the Colony of Virginia ... sold ... 100 acres ... part of a Tract of Land contained in a Deed bearing date the [blank] Nov. 1741 ... North River Swamp joining on Malachi WILSON'S Line ... Jacob's Swamp ... *Signed*: Jacob CARON. *Wit*: John BURGES, S PLOMER. *Ack*: April Court 1751. *Regt*: 18 April 1751.

[B:172] 11 April 1751 & in the 24th year of the Reign of our Sovereign Lord George the Second ... Between Jarvis JONES of the County Pasquotank in North Carolina Planter of the one part & Joshua GAMBLING of the Same Planter of the other part ... for 30 pounds Proclamation ... sold ... unto the said Moses MACKFARSON [sic] ... N. E. Side of Pasquotank & Contg 100 acres ... part of a larger Tract of Land of 725 acres by one deed of Grant from the Earl of GRANVILLE to the said Jarvis JONES dated 20 Dec. 1748 ... old William JONES Corner ... Cypress Swamp ... *Signed*: Jarvis JONES. *Wit*: Tho: TAYLOR, Robert MURDEN. *Ack*: April Court 1751. *Regt*: 18 April 1751.

[B:173] North Carolina) Pasquotank County) 7 May 1748 Between Samuel JACKSON the Younger of the one party Farmer of the place afsd. & Willis WILLIAMS of the other party and place afsd. Farmer ... for 80 pounds Current Money of Virginia ... sold ... 100 acres ... N. E. Side of Pasquotank River Known by the name of School House Neck, 50 Acres ... part of that Land that Benjamin PHILLIPS bought of Jno SCARBORO and the other 50 the said Benjamin PHILLIPS had by Exchange of Jno COOK Weaver, and the Said Benjamin PHILLIPS sold and conveyed the said 100 acres of Land to the abovesd. Saml. JACKSON by a Deed of Sale bearing date the 30 April 1746 ... and registered the 20 May 1747 in Book D, folio 84 ... marked Line between the said Benjamin PHILLIPS and the said John COOK when they changed Land ... William JONES'S Line ... Captn. Cornelius RELF'S Corner Tree standing in White Oak Neck ... John PUGH'S head line ... Christopher WILLIAMS Back Line [B:174] ... *Signed*: Saml. JACKSON. *Wit*: Joseph ROBINSON, Mary ROBINSON. *Ack*: April Court 1751. *Regt*: 18 April 1751.

North Carolina. 21 Feb. 1746/7 and in the 19th year of the Reign of our Sovn Lord George the Second ... David DUNKIN of Pasquotank County Planter of the one part & Jarvis JONES of the other part ... for 30 pounds Current Money of the Colony of Virginia ... sold ... Pasquotank River and joining to Joseph MACKFARSONS Land and contg 70 acres taken out of a patent Contg 400 Acres ... Bear Spring ...
[B:175] ... Great Swamp ... *Signed*: DAVID D DUNKIN his mark. *Wit*: Joseph MACKFARSON, John CHAMBALIN. *Ack*: April Court 1751. *Regt*: 18 April 1751.

Thomas CHARTWRIGHT of the County of Pasquotank in the Province of North Carolina Planter for ... 60 pounds Virginia Currency ... paid by Alexander JACK of the afsd. County & Province Merchant ... sold ... S. W. Side of Pasquotank River ... Danl. ROADS'S Line ... William SAWYERS Line ... Mouth of broad Gut at the River ... 60 acres ... being a Tract of Land by Two Deeds of Sale, the one from William RELFE the other from Danl. ROADS both bearing date the 2 March 1737 assigned over from John SMITH to Jonathan HIBBS [B:176] ... 12 June 1750. *Signed*: Thos. CHARTWRIGHT. *Wit*: Abel TRUEBLOOD, Edwd. SCOTT, Thos. CHARTWRIGHT his C Mark. *Proved*: July Court 1751 by the Oath of Thos. CHARTWRIGHT. *Regt*: 6 Aug. 1751.

North Carolina) Pasquotank County) 10 Sept. 1750 Between Isaac STOKELY & Mary his Wife of the County & Province afsd. of the one part & Robert MURDEN of the said County & Province of the other part ... for the Exchange of Two plantations and a piece of Woodland ... sold ... S. W. Side of Pasquotank River contg 250 acres formerly surveyed and patented for Relf GARNETT & also all that plantation ... patented by William CHARTWRIGHT and likewise a parcel of Woodland contg 10 acres which the said Isaac STOKELY bought of John ODANIEL to him the sd. Isaac MURDEN [sic] ... William WAYMANS Line ...
[B:177] ... River Swamp ... *Signed*: Isaac STOKELY.

Wit: David PRITCHARD, Tho: TAYLOR. *Ack*: April Court 1751. *Regt*: 18 April 1751.

Macrora SCARBROUGH of the County of Perquimons in the Province of North Carolina for 17 pounds Current Money of Virginia ... paid by Benjamin PHILLIPS of the County of Pasquotank in the Province afsd. ... sold ... N. E. Side of Pasquotank River ... River Swamp ... John RELF'S Corner ...
[B:178] ... 100 acres ... 1751. *Signed*: Mac. SCARBOROUGH. *Wit*: John SOLLEY, Saml. PRITCHARD. *Ack*: April Court 1751. *Regt*: 18 April 1751.

North Carolina) Pasquotank County) 9 May 1749 Between Gabl. BURNHAM of the one party Farmer & James WARD Farmer of the other party ... for 55 pounds Current Money of the Province afsd. ... sold ... 50 acres ... South Side of Pasquotank River ... Turkey Ridge ...
[B:179] ... *Signed*: Gabriel B BURNHAM his mark. *Wit*: James Poolman DUFFEY, Mary M DUFFEY. *Proved*: April Court 1751 by the Oath of James DUFFEY. *Regt*: 18 April 1751.

North Carolina) Pasquotank County) Miriam RITIGA for ... 5 pounds 12 Shillings and 6 pence Current Money of the Province of Virginia ... paid by Benjamin MEADS of the same County & Province ... sold ... 62 Acres being the one half of 124 acres formerly granted by Patent to Col. John PAILINS, and the sd. Patent being assigned over to my father by the said PAILINS ...
[B:180] ... 30 Nov. 1749. *Signed*: Miriam X RITIGA her mark. *Wit*: Joshua U DAVIS his mark, David N DAVIS his mark. *Proved*: Jany Court 1751 by the Oath of Joshua DAVIS. *Regt*: 18 Jany 1751.

North Carolina. Nathan SMITH of Craven County in the Province afsd. Gentleman & Elisabeth my Wife ... for 75 pounds current Money of the Colony of Virginia ... paid by Thomas TAYLOR of Pasquotank County in the Province afsd. ... sold ... 172 acres ... Richard MADRAN'S Corner ... George HARRIS'S Line ... granted by patent bearing date 27 Sept. 1715 unto Levi CREASY & ... conveyed by Deed bearing date 19 July 1721 unto Mary GIBBLE Widow & by the said Mary and Arthur MABSON her Husband to their Daughter Elisabeth MABSON now Wife of the afsd. Nathan SMITH

... being the plantation whereon Edwd SCOTT now dwells ...

[B:181] ... 25 March 1749 & in the 22d year of His Majesty's Reign. *Signed*: Nathan SMITH, Elizabeth SMITH. *Wit*: Danl. GRANDIN, Rt. LOVICKE?. *Ack*: 25 March 1748 Nathan SMITH & Elizabeth his Wife came before me Enoch HALL Esqr. Chief Justice of the said Province. *Regt*: 18 Jany 1751.

INDEX

Proper names and place names, except Pasquotank, Albemarle and North Carolina, are included in this index. Variant spellings are grouped together with cross-references. In many cases, more than one entry for the same name can be found on the page indicated. All subject entries are underlined. Indians, Mulattoes and Negroes who have only first names are indexed under those headings.

www.ingramcontent.com/pod-product-compliance
Lightning Source LLC
Chambersburg PA
CBHW071823270326
41929CB00013B/1892
9781556133084